AF394524

ABANDONED
INDUSTRIAL PLACES

ABANDONED
INDUSTRIAL PLACES

Factories, laboratories, mills and mines that the world left behind

DAVID ROSS

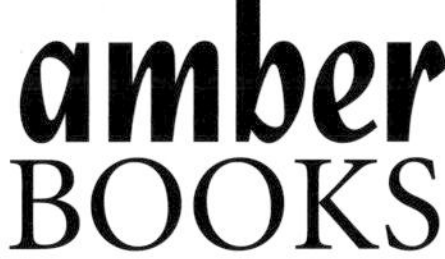

This Amber edition first published in 2020

Published by
Amber Books Ltd
United House
North Road
London N7 9DP
United Kingdom
www.amberbooks.co.uk
Instagram: amberbooksltd
Facebook: amberbooks
Pinterest: amberbooksltd
Twitter: @amberbooks

ISBN: 978-1-78274-984-4

Project Editor: Michael Spilling
Design: Keren Harragan
Picture Research: Terry Forshaw

Printed in China

Contents

Introduction 6

North America 8

Central and South America 68

Europe 98

Africa and the Middle East 166

Asia and the Pacific 186

Picture Credits 224

Introduction

The pleasure of viewing a ruin is an old human trait. Ancient writers liked to muse on the idea of a city or castle reduced to a haunt of owls, with nettles and brambles growing out of broken paving and crumbling walls. In modern, post-industrial times, this notion has taken a sharper edge. The lives of industrial installations are measured in decades rather than centuries. In many places, still-recent installations stand redundant and silent.

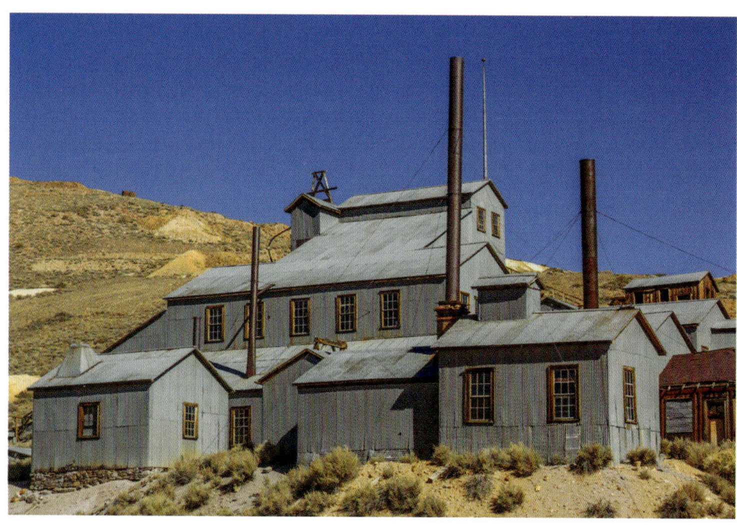

Surprisingly often, these buildings, factories, mills or hospitals still have their machinery or furnishings left intact, with everyday articles lying about, as though the people who worked there had been suddenly spirited away.

This collection of images takes us right round the world. For those who look for it, from Alaska to Patagonia, from Norway to Japan and Nigeria, remains of the industrial past are all around us.

ABOVE:
Bodie, Abandoned Gold Rush Town, California, USA
Gold was discovered here in 1876 and led to the growth of a sizeable town, but with the seam worked out, there was nothing to sustain a community at its altitude of 2554m (8379ft) and the population drifted away. By 1933 it was unpopulated, and its state of 'arrested decay' makes it a visitor attraction today.

OPPOSITE:
Australia Mill, Dinorwic Slate Quarry Works, Wales
With 36 slate-cutting saws, this workshop was set up in 1924 when the quarry employed around 3000 men. After 200 years of operation, it was closed abruptly in 1969. By that time it employed only a tenth of the old number, and much of the site was already disused.

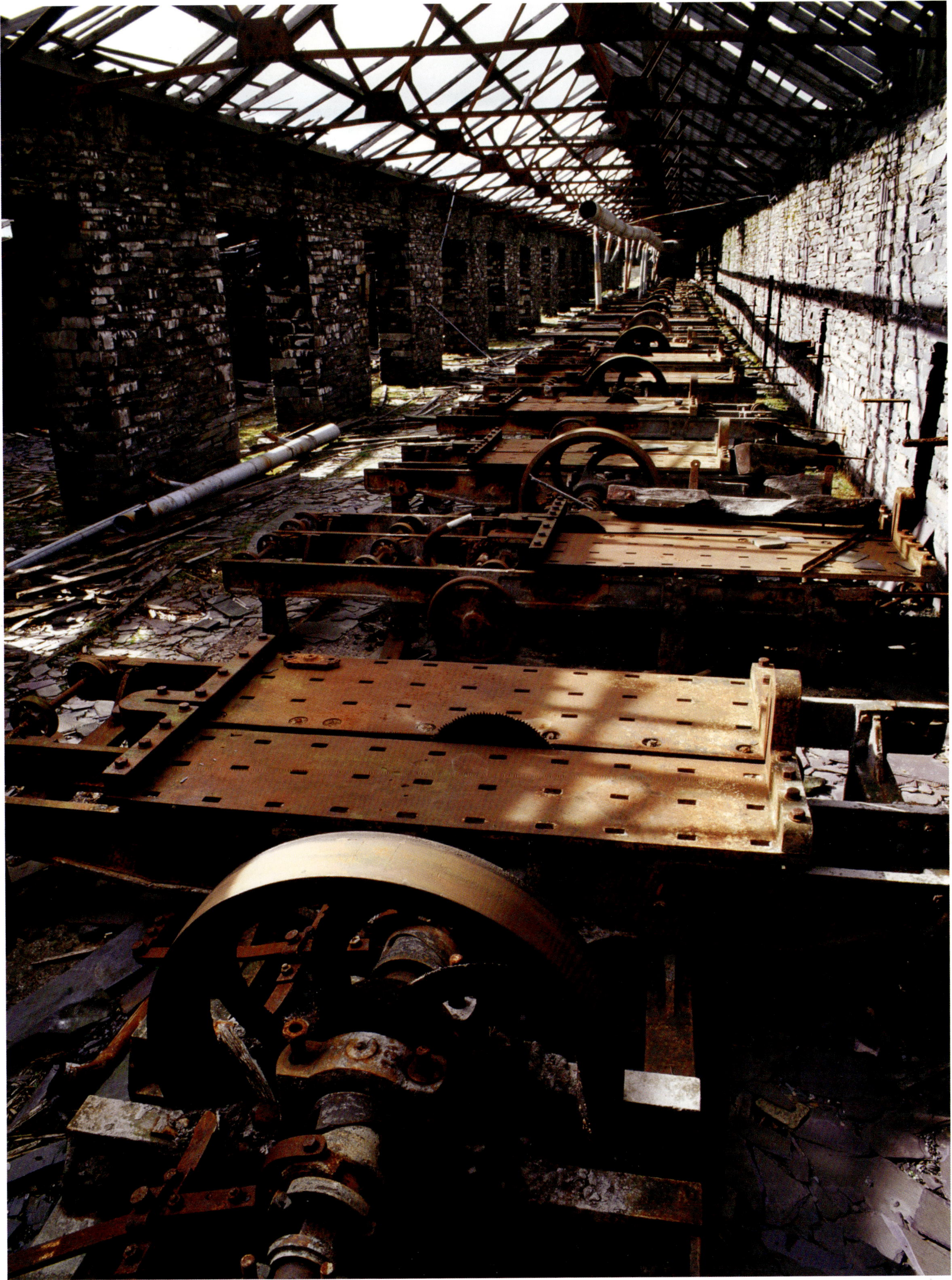

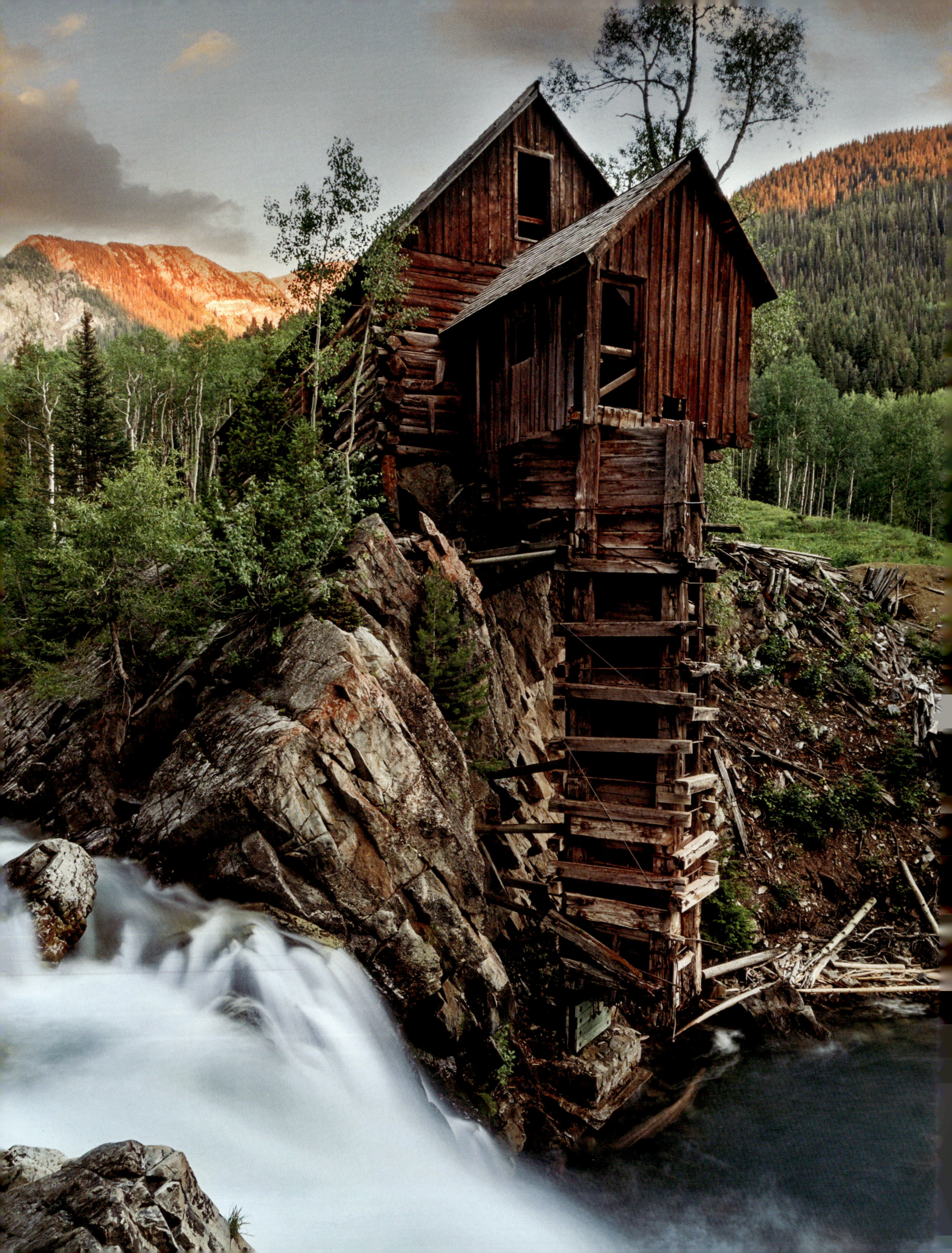

North America

All over North America, physical evidence can be found of past industry – gold rushes, coal mines, shipyards, distilleries. The resultant ghost towns, their streets lined with empty houses, still hold memories of a departed population. Some are wide open, left to decay and crumble, many have been preserved as 'heritage sites' in towns or districts which once earned their living from mine or factory; others are fenced off and forbidden, possibly for good reason. Floors may be holed and stairways unstable, and toxic pollution is common. None of that deters the new breed of 'urban explorers' who seek out abandoned sites, find a way in, and revel in the eerie atmosphere of silence and decay. In the perspectives of long lines of dead machines, the sudden changes of height, the mazes of workrooms where no-one has worked for decades, the explorers finds adventure, akin to caving, and accept the hazards as part of the game. Some are graffitists, others are photographers, some just enjoy the combination of discovery and exclusivity – for the moment, the place is theirs alone. The keenest will travel great distances if they learn of a special site, knowing it may soon be demolished, or rescued and re-tenanted.

Crystal Mill, New Mexico, USA
Water from the Crystal River was diverted down the wooden tower to drive an air compressor, which in turn powered drilling machinery in the adjacent mine shafts. The structure was built in 1892 and operations ceased in 1917. Its remoteness has helped to preserve it.

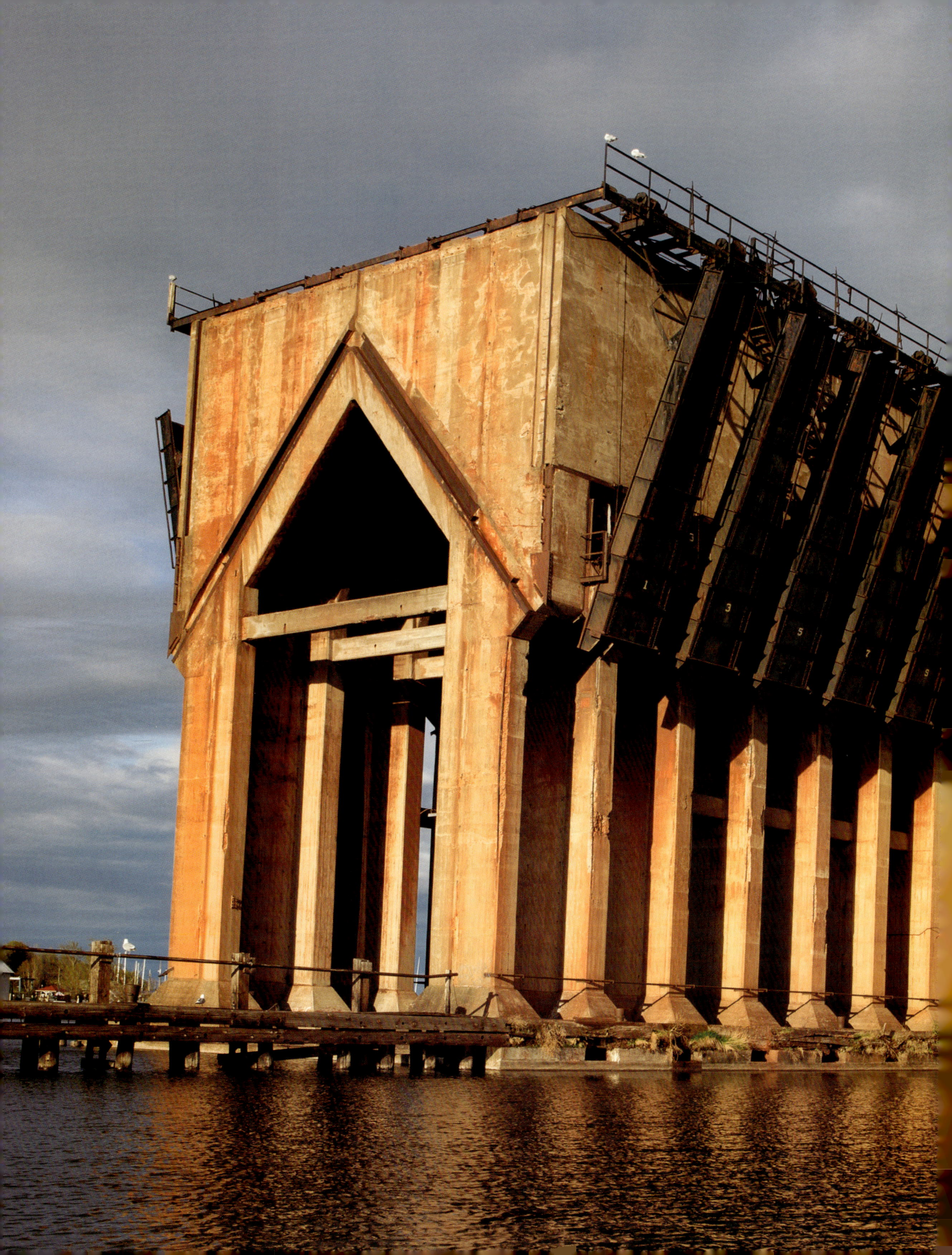

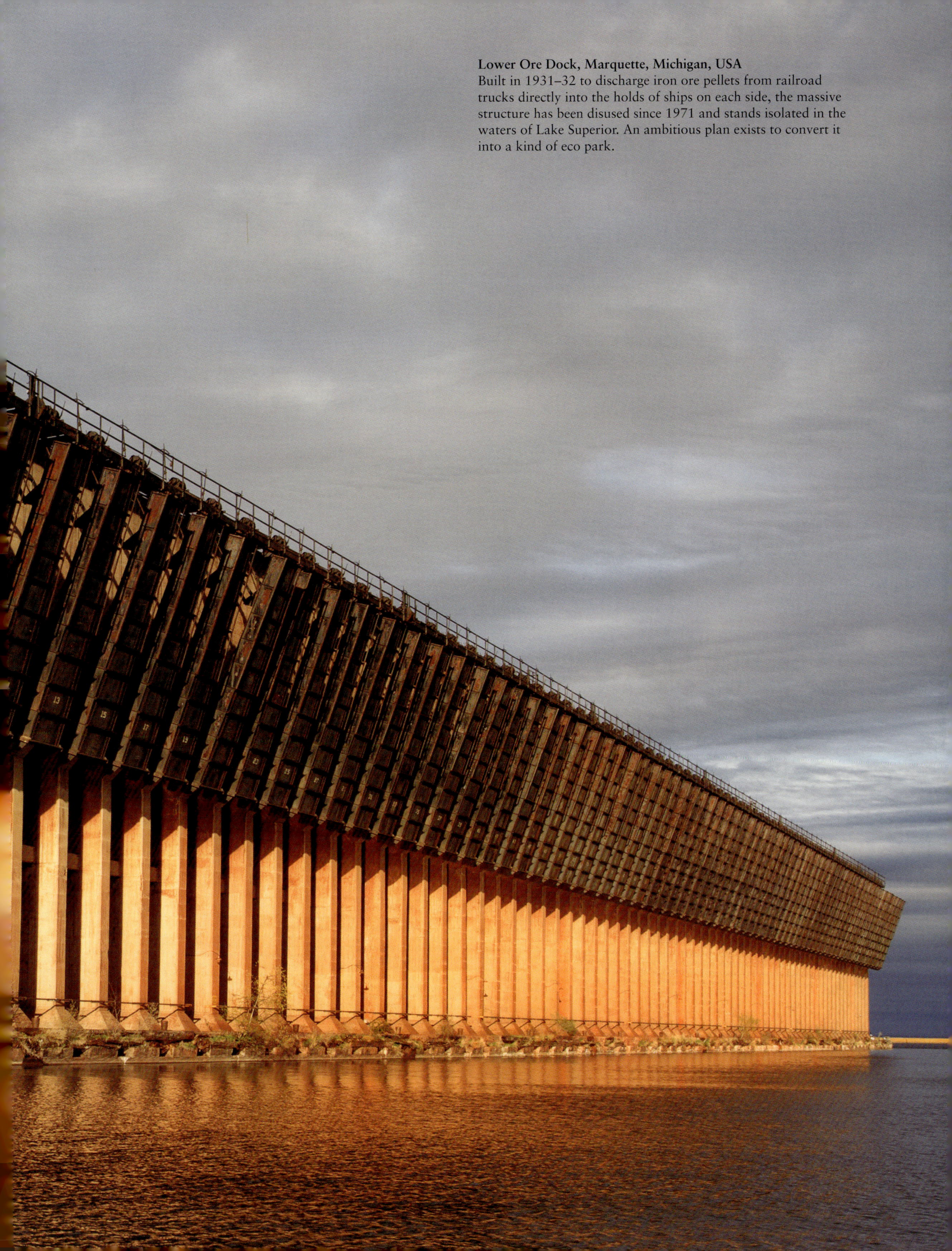

Lower Ore Dock, Marquette, Michigan, USA
Built in 1931–32 to discharge iron ore pellets from railroad trucks directly into the holds of ships on each side, the massive structure has been disused since 1971 and stands isolated in the waters of Lake Superior. An ambitious plan exists to convert it into a kind of eco park.

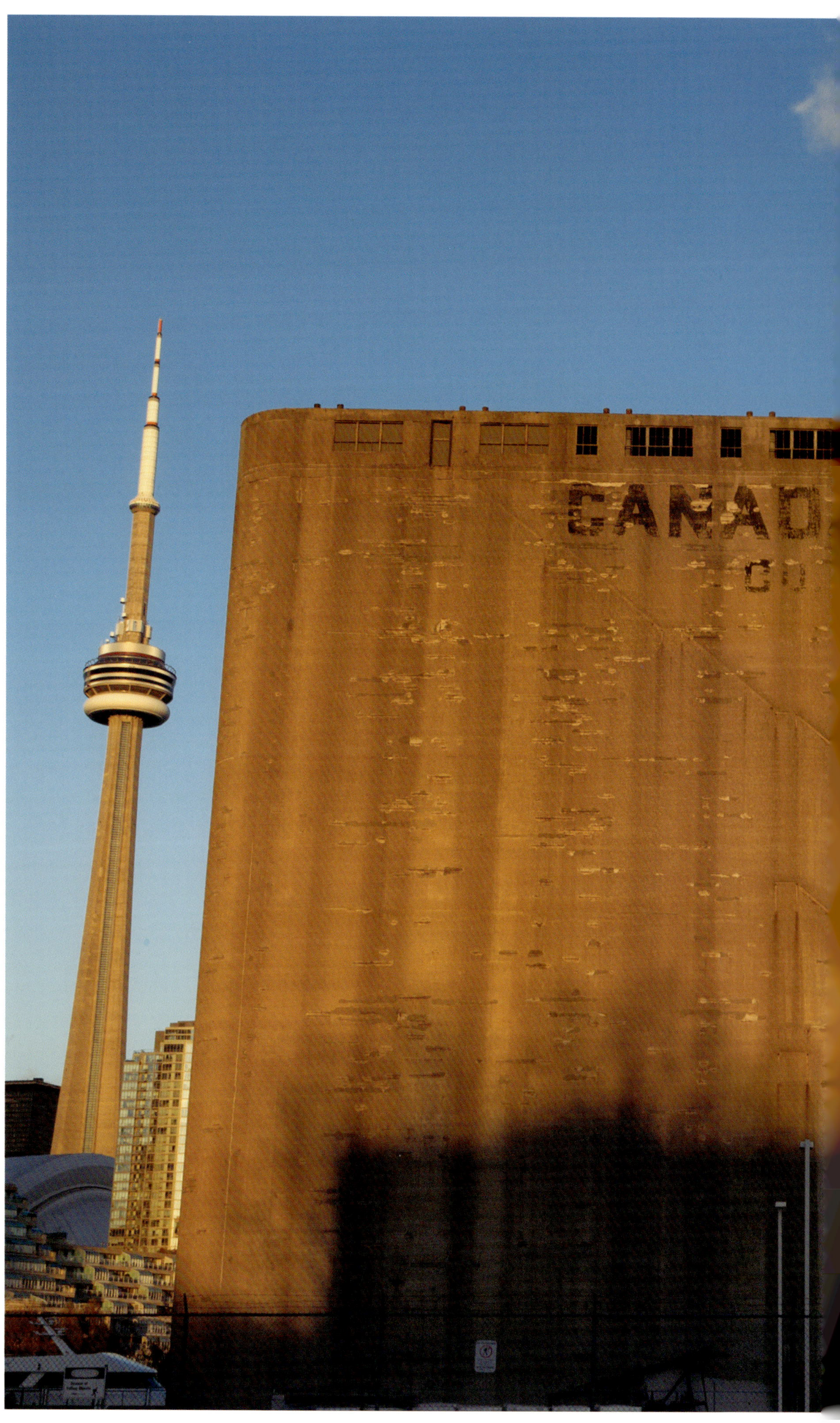

Canada Maltings Silo, Toronto, Ontario, Canada
Standing 37m (120ft) high, this grain store was innovative in its use of concrete in 1928. Its starkly modernist design also contributes to making it a landmark in architectural history and, once scheduled for demolition, it is now intended to become a centrepiece on Toronto's harbourfront.

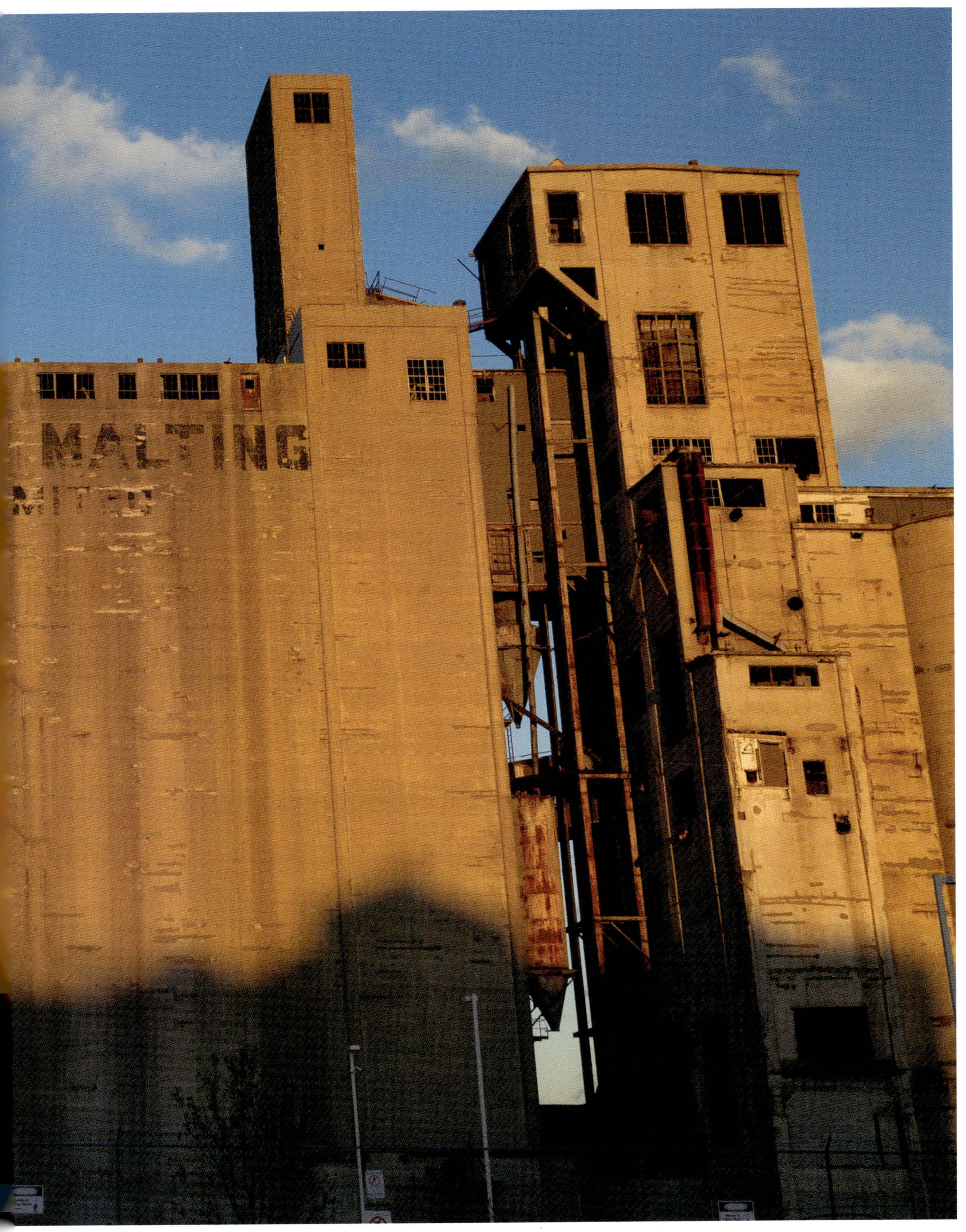
MALTING
NITED

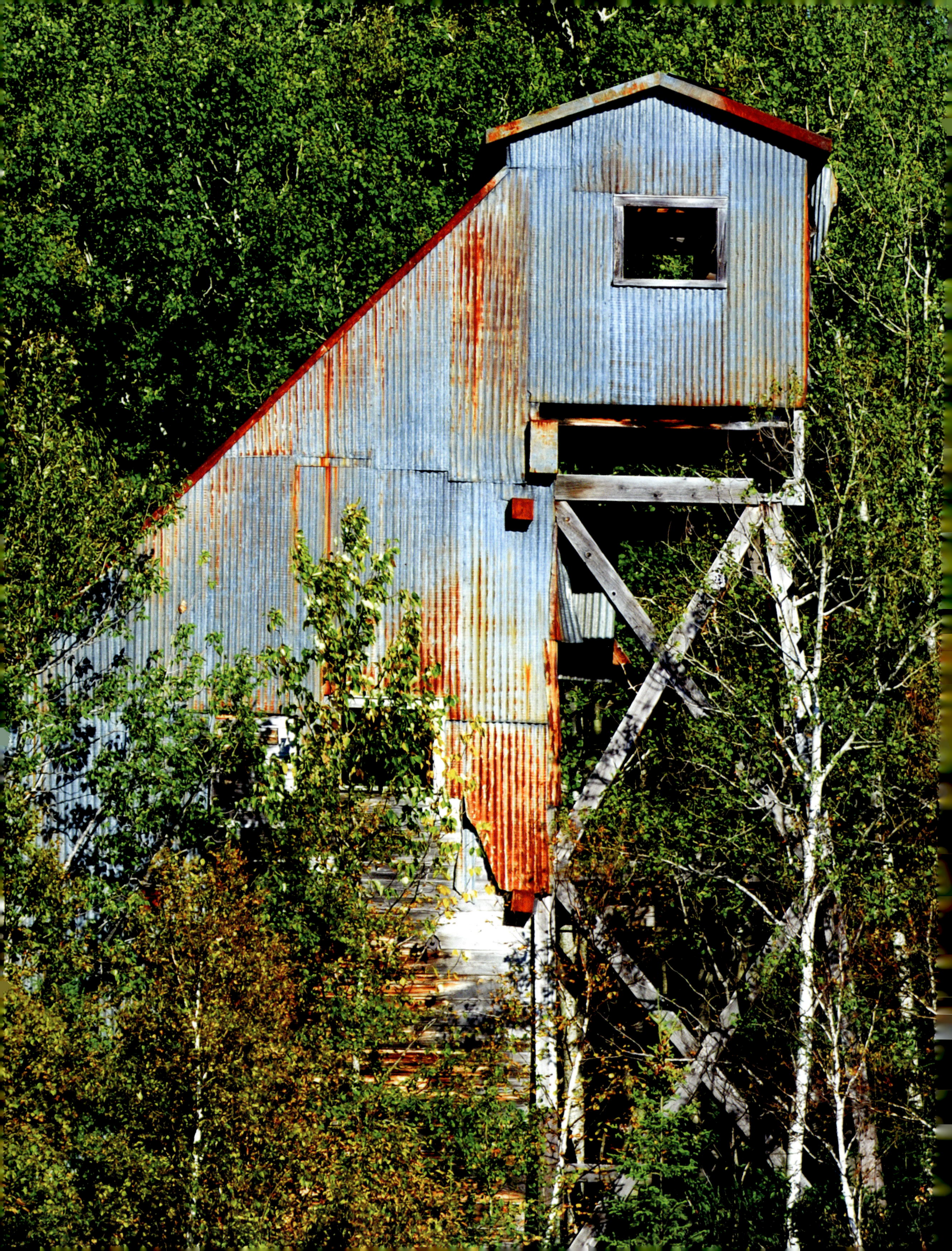

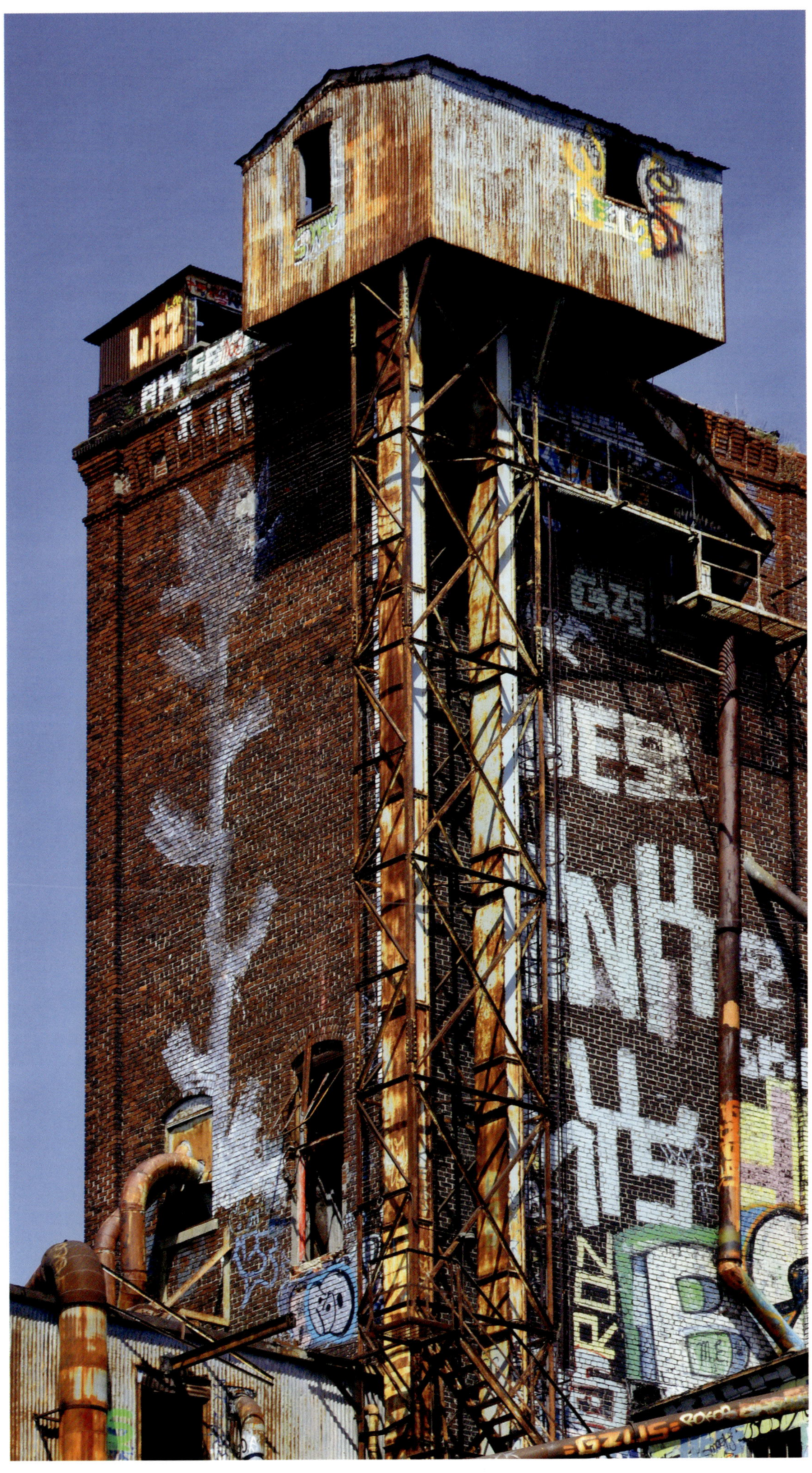

Smith Thorne Mine, Tionaga, Ontario, Canada
The headframe of a gold mine in densely wooded country. Started in 1935, the shaft continues down at the same angle for 174m (570ft). Gold and other precious minerals were sought, but despite some hopeful finds, the mine never went into commercial production.

LEFT:

Former Malting Silo, Montréal, Québec, Canada
Graffiti writers have risen to the challenge of this abandoned Canada Maltings silo tower by the Lachine Canal in Montréal. Brick-built in 1904, it was the largest malt-house of its time in North America. Closure of the canal in the 1970s and outdated technology led to its abandonment. By the late 1980s it was left to urban explorers and graffitists.

OVERLEAF:

Atlas Coal Mine, East Coulee, Alberta, Canada
Now a national historic site, the mine was active from 1917 to 1979, one of over 130 in the Drumheller Valley. Visitors can explore some of its underground tunnels as well as the original buildings. The large structure is Canada's last wooden coal tipple, for loading coal into railroad cars.

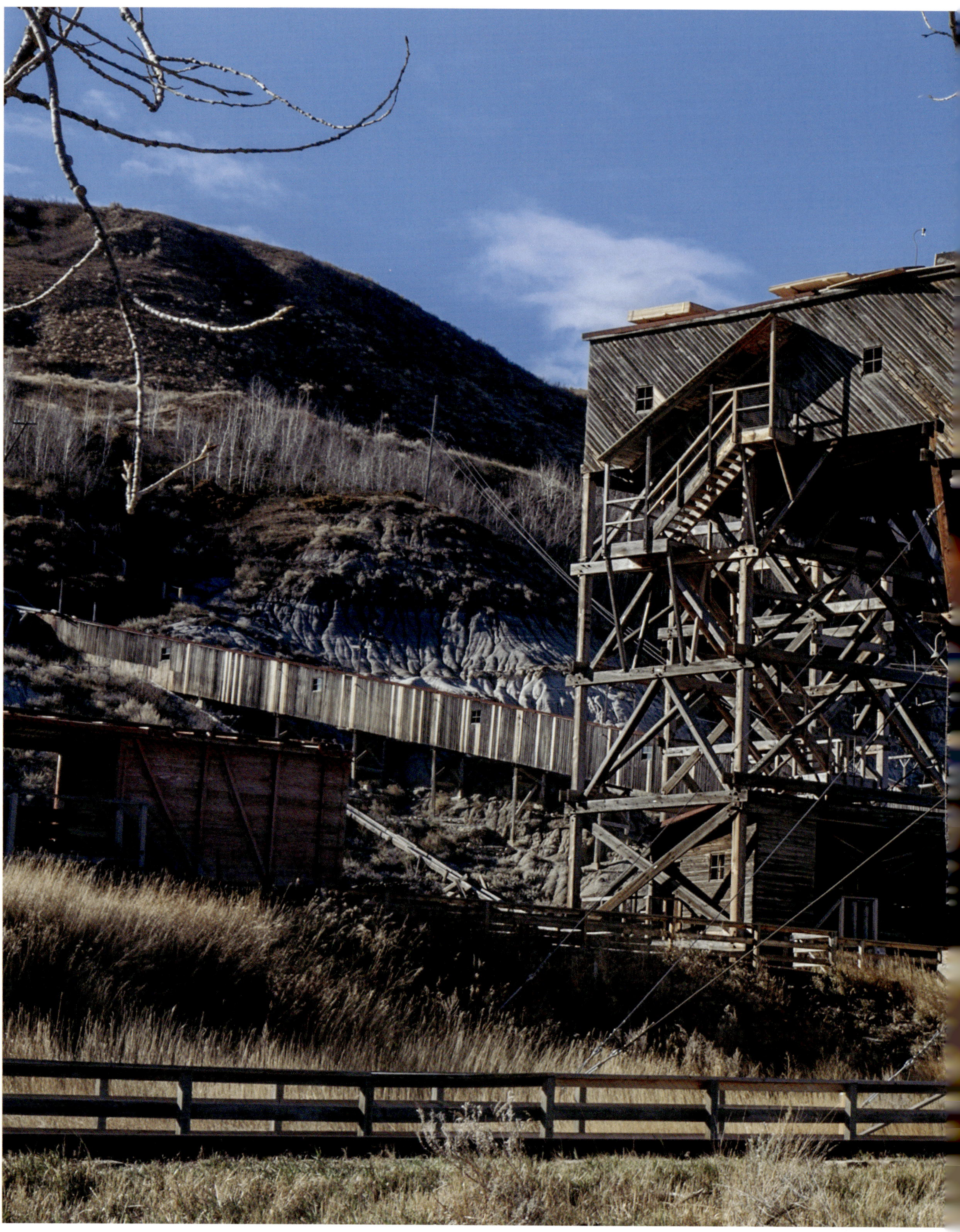

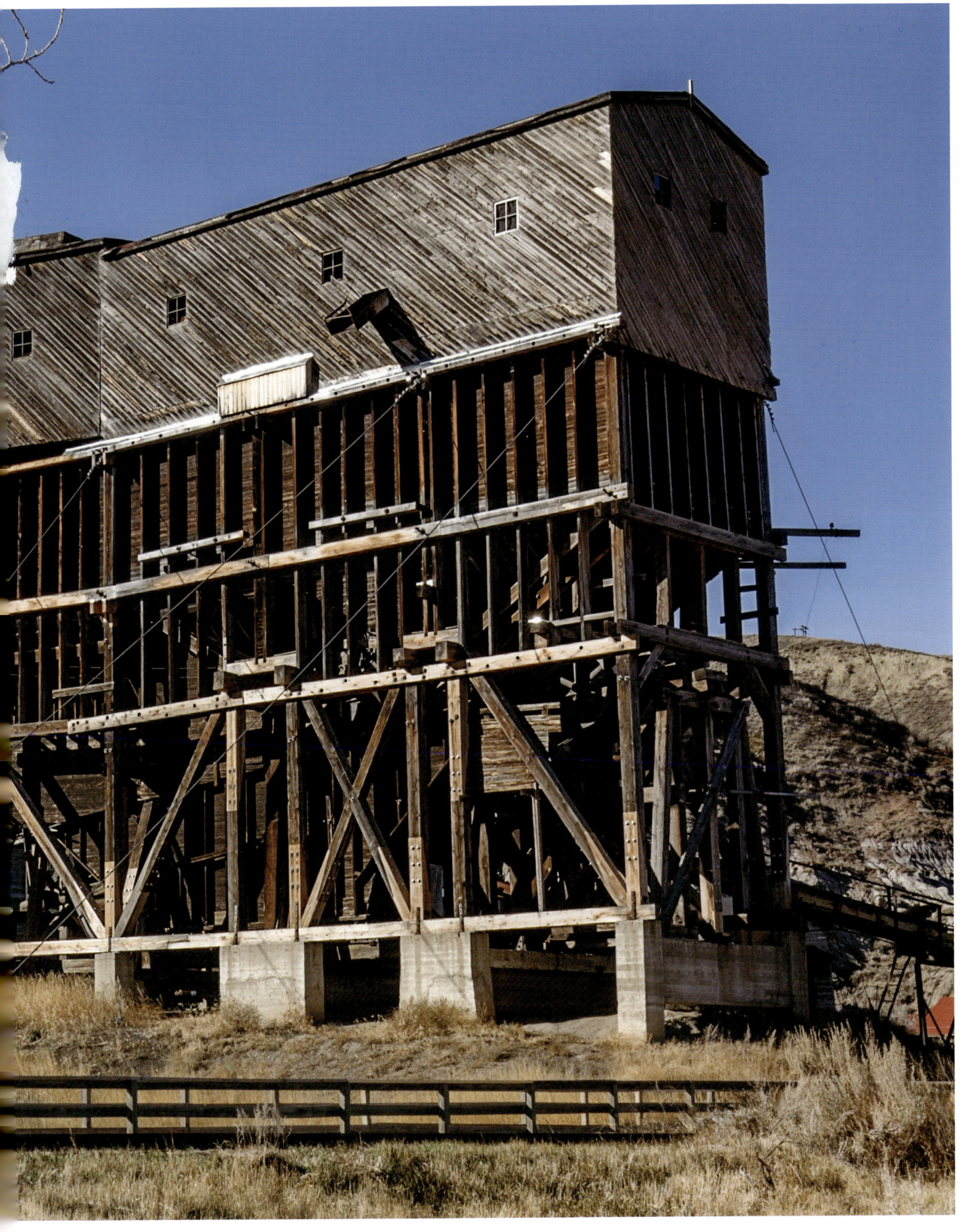

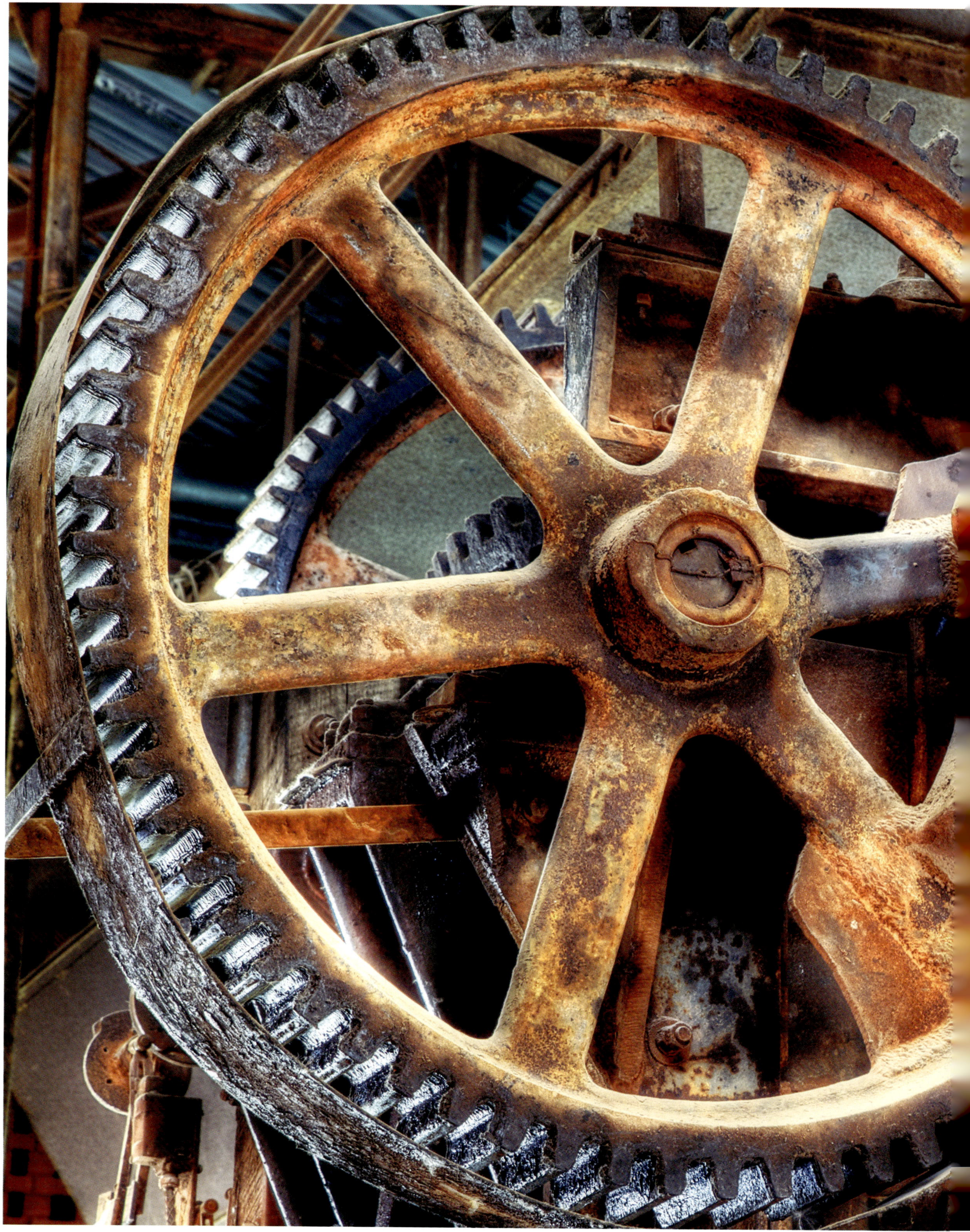

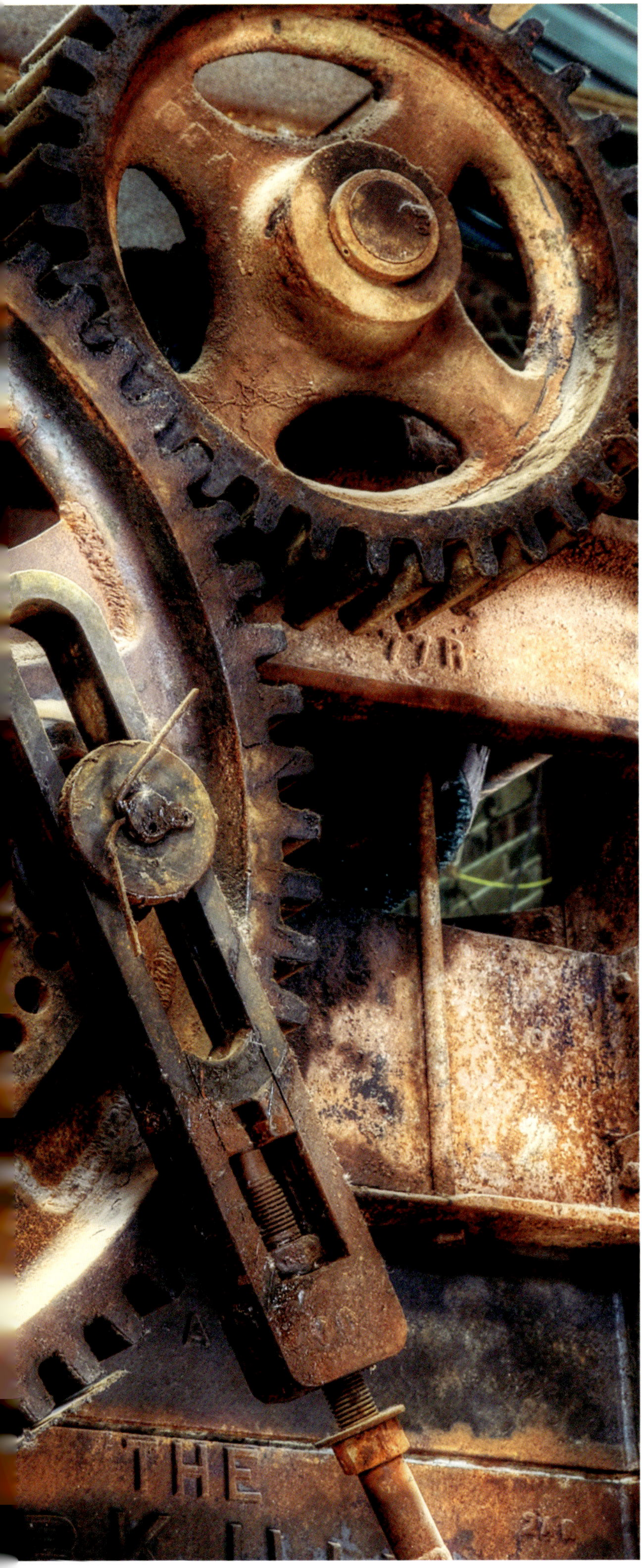

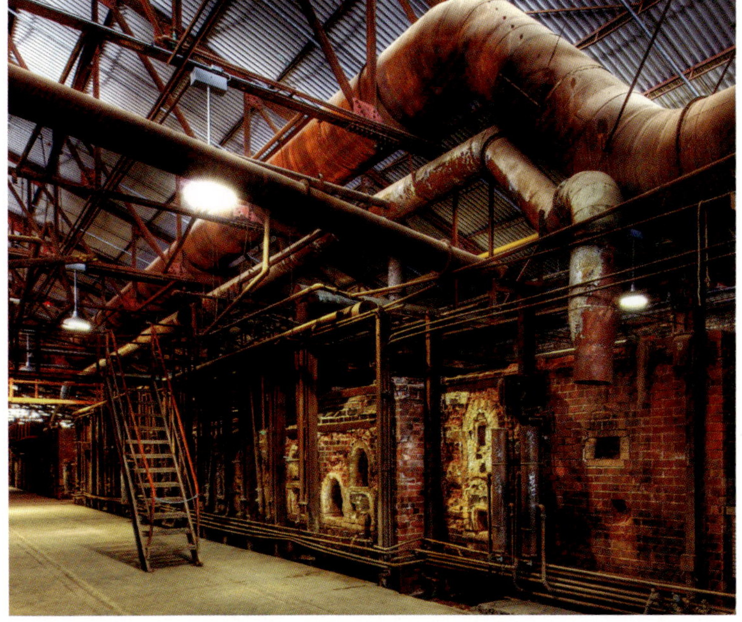

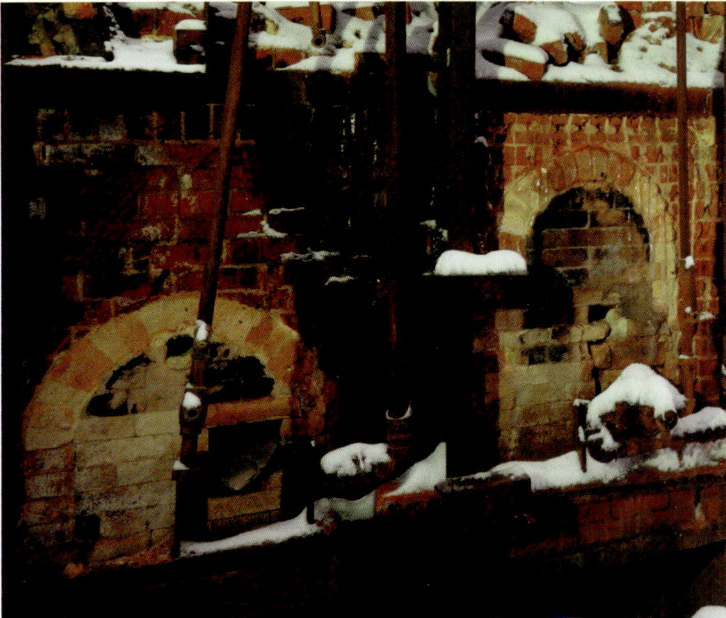

Don Valley Brickworks, Toronto, Canada
Situated by a quarry, right on top of its raw materials, the works produced up to 114,000 bricks a day from 1889 to 1997, by which time the clay, shale and sand deposits were exhausted. Nowadays it is part parkland, part industrial museum, with much of the heavy processing equpment still in situ, while wildlife reclaims the ponds and hollows.

Lille Coal Mines, Crowsnest Pass, Alberta, Canada
The derelict coke ovens have an antique look that belies their 20th century construction. The Lille mine was active from 1902 to 1913, producing good coking coal. The name comes from the French home town of the original mine owner. A small company town grew, flourished and died along with the colliery.

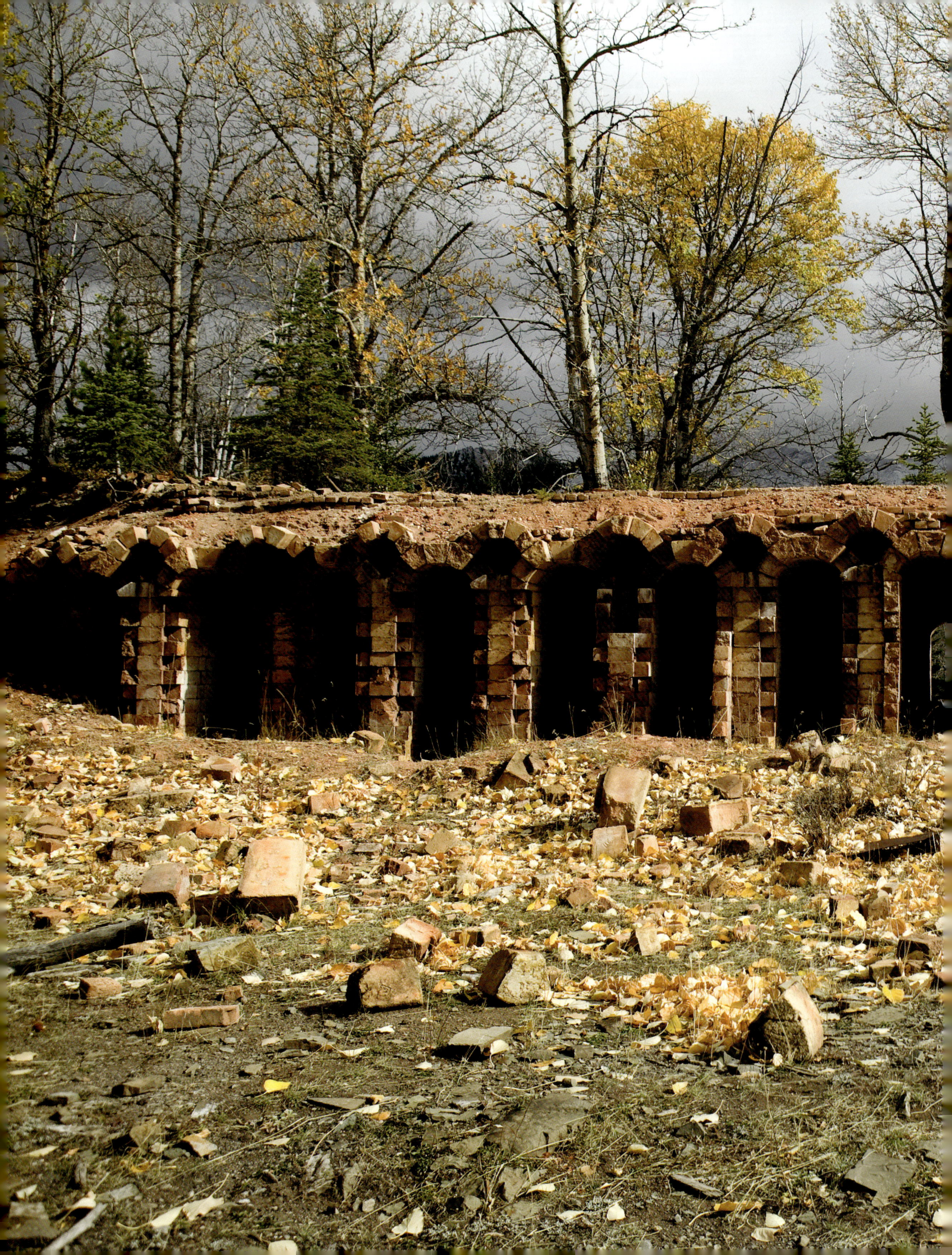

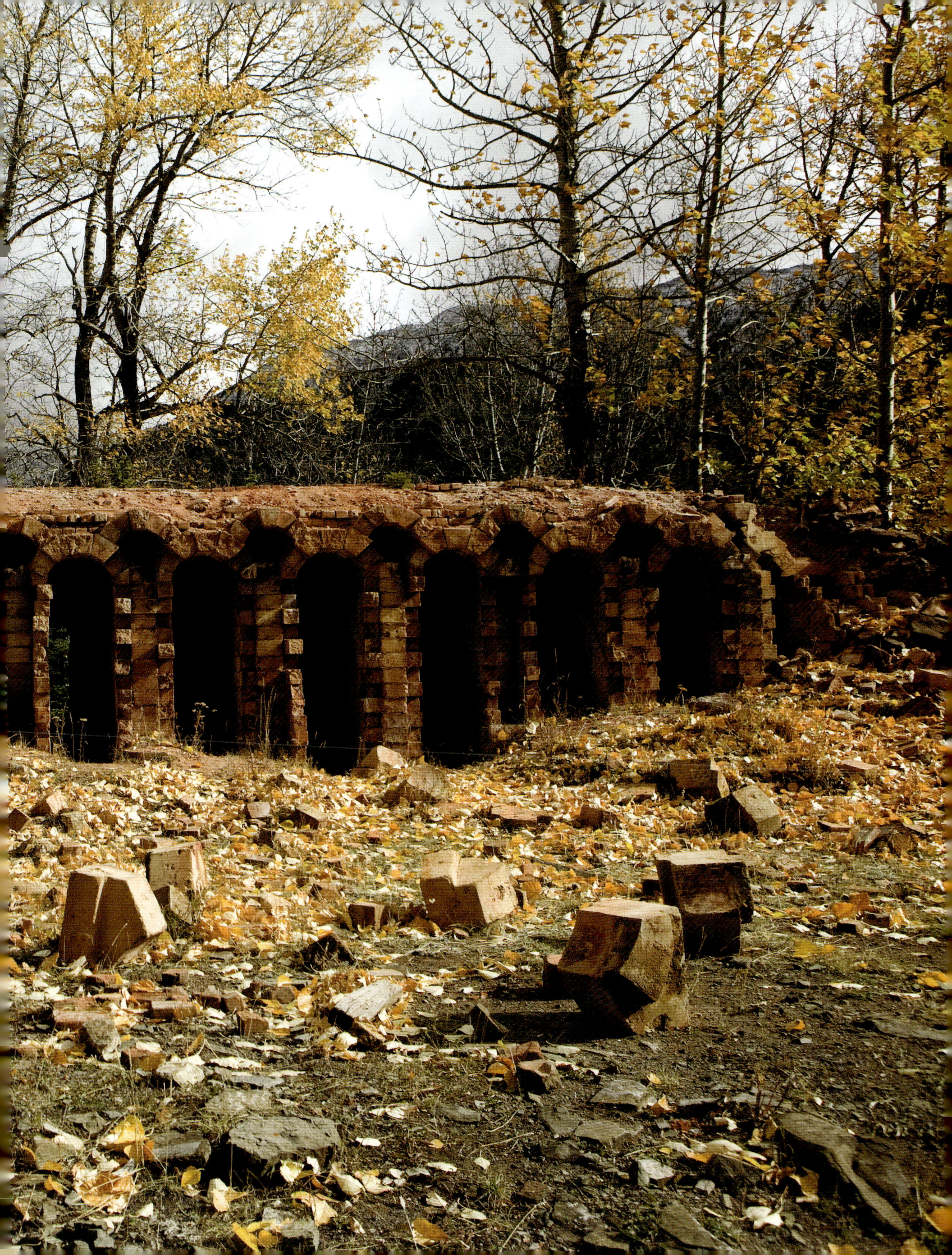

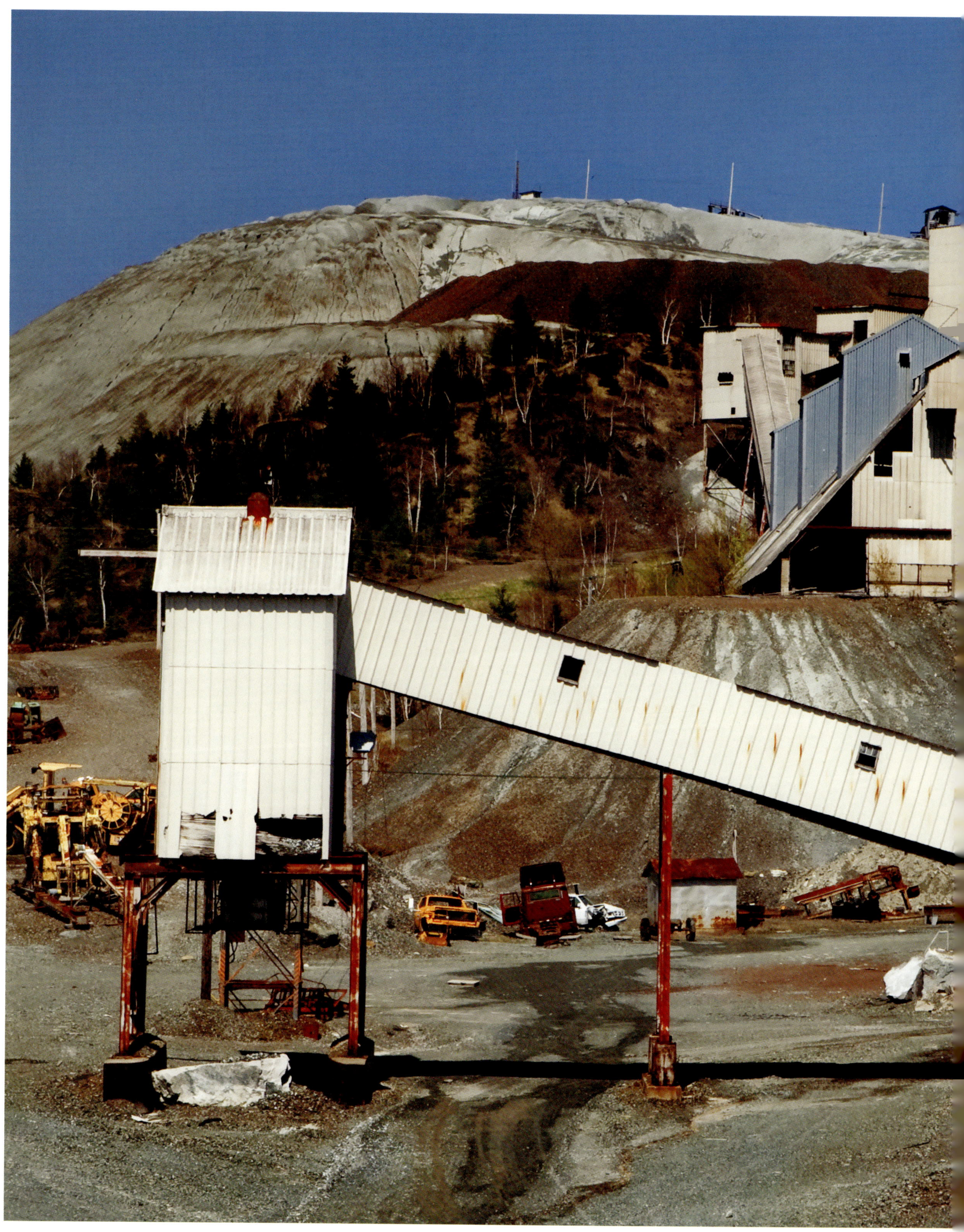

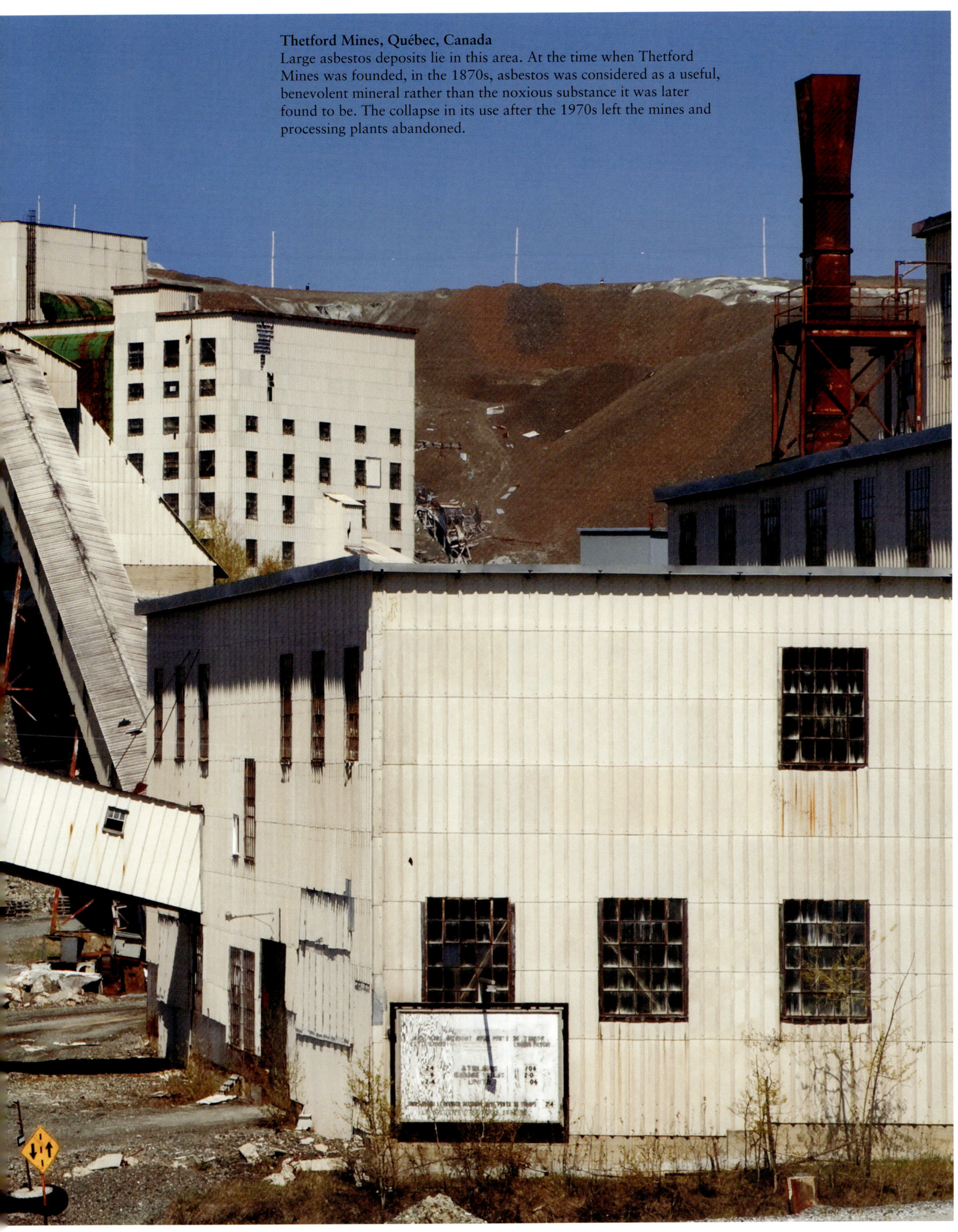

Thetford Mines, Québec, Canada
Large asbestos deposits lie in this area. At the time when Thetford Mines was founded, in the 1870s, asbestos was considered as a useful, benevolent mineral rather than the noxious substance it was later found to be. The collapse in its use after the 1970s left the mines and processing plants abandoned.

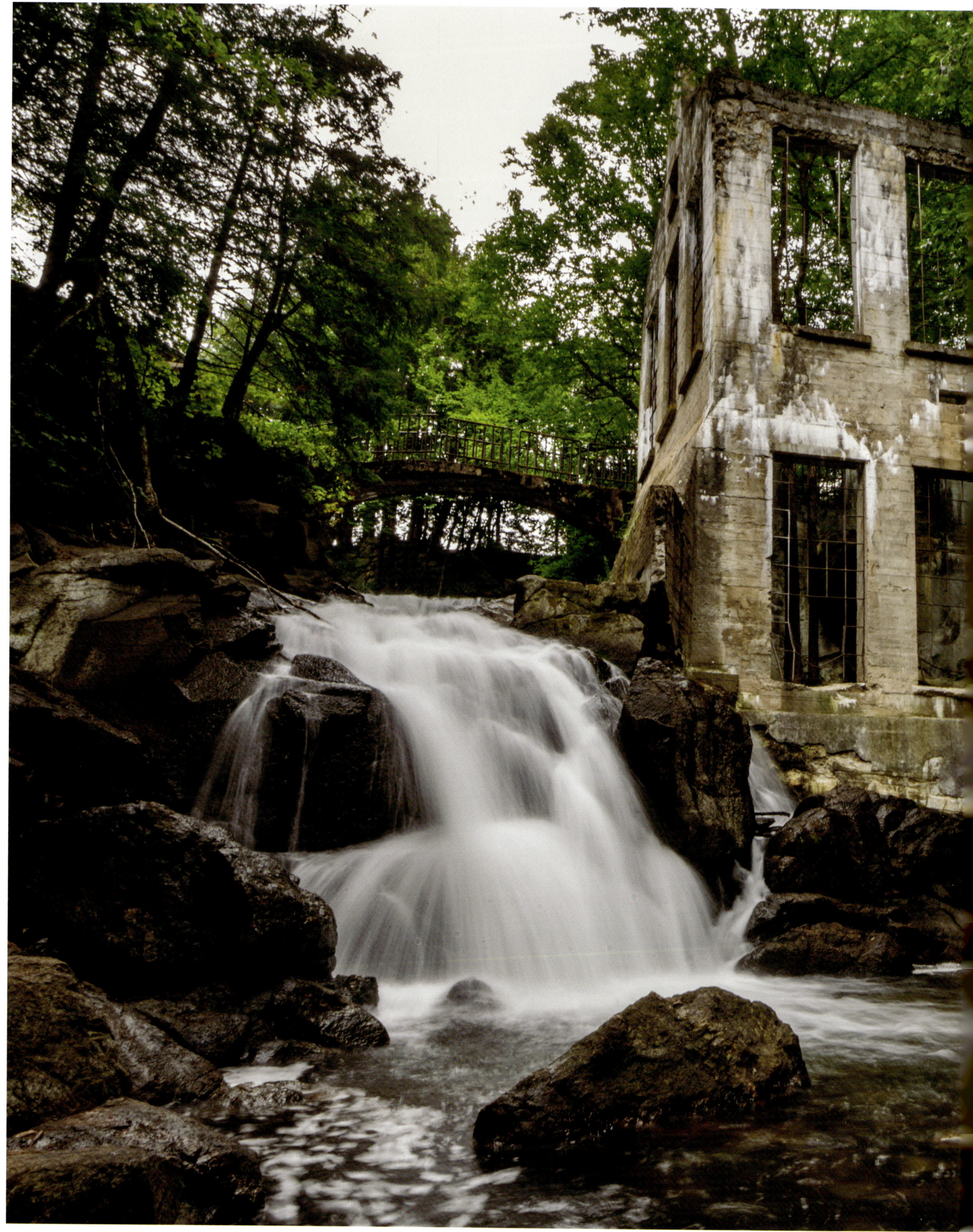

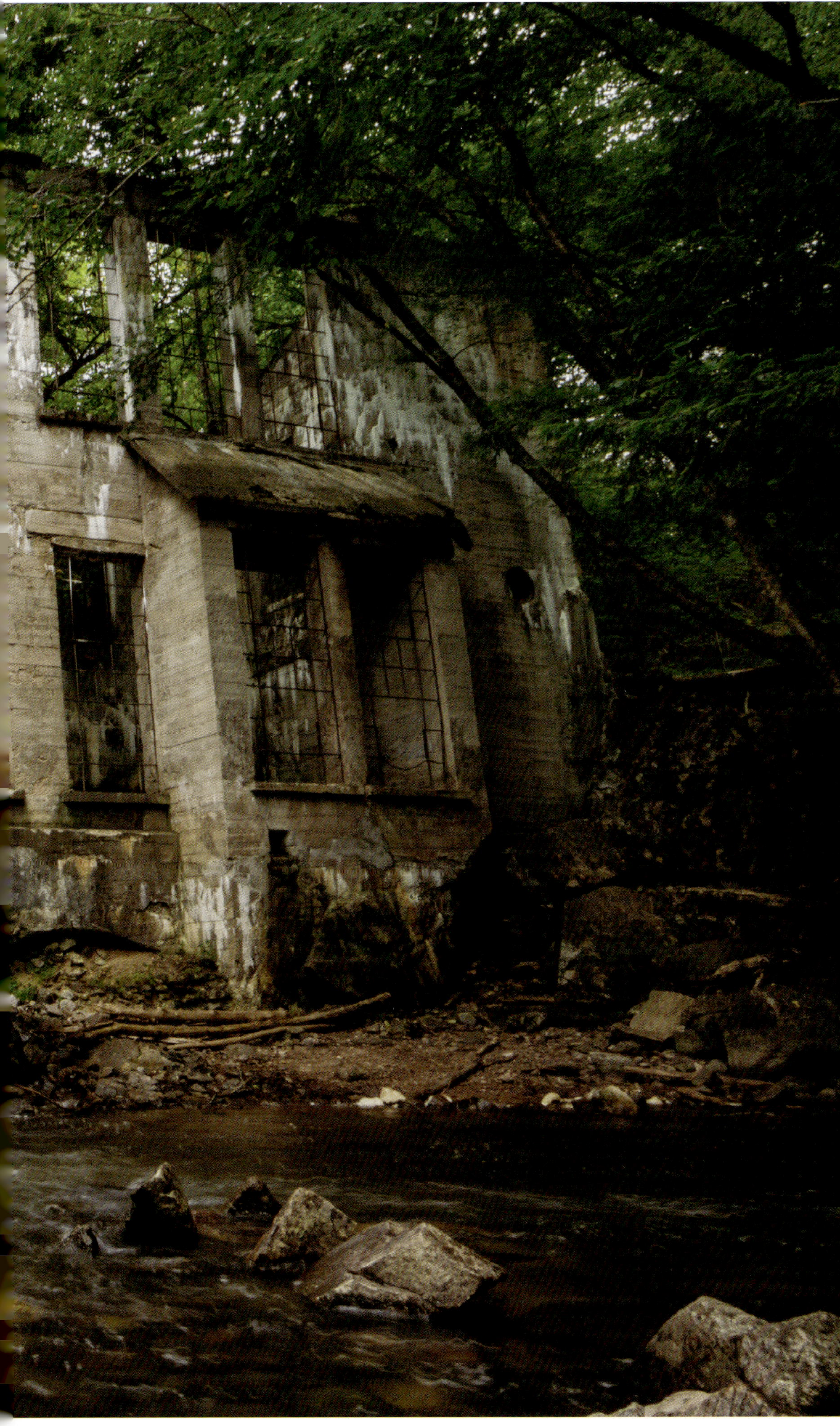

Wilson Carbide Mill, Gatineau, Ottawa, Canada
Thomas 'Carbide' Wilson (1860–1915) discovered the process of making calcium carbide, a valuable chemical compound. He built a factory here, using water power to generate the necessary electricity: the world's first phosphorus acid condensation plant.
The technology was right but the finances went wrong. The ruins remain as a memorial to the venture.

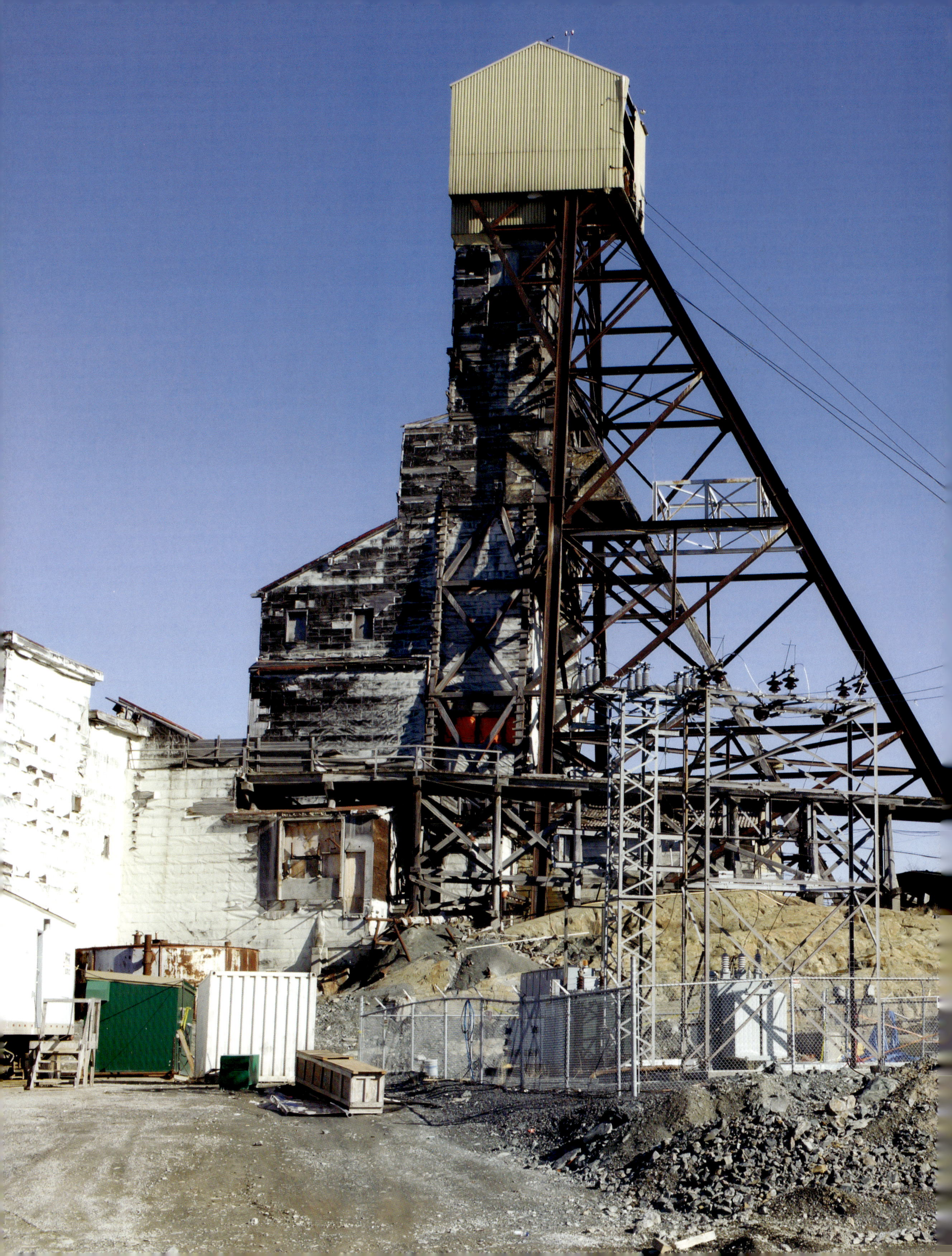

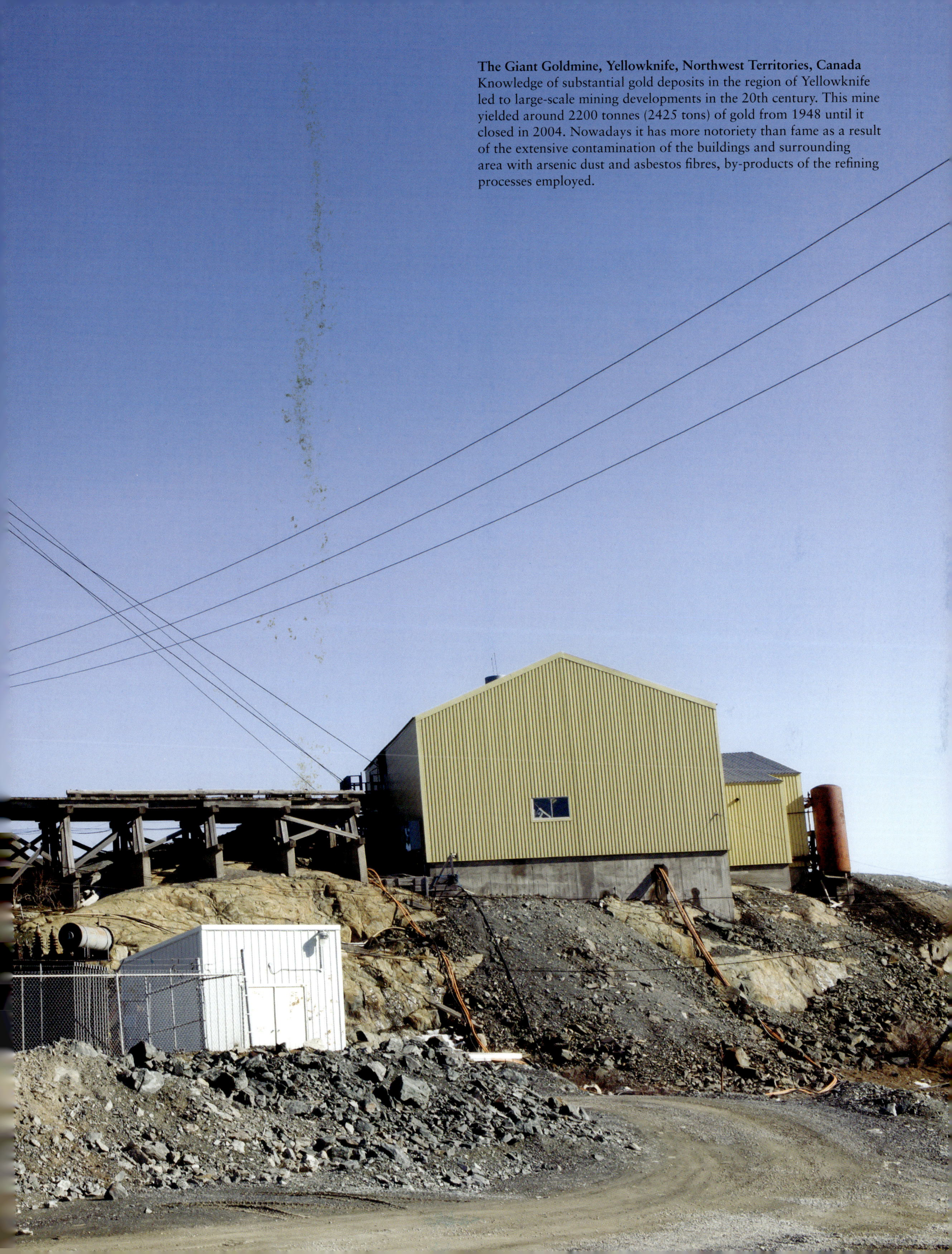

The Giant Goldmine, Yellowknife, Northwest Territories, Canada
Knowledge of substantial gold deposits in the region of Yellowknife led to large-scale mining developments in the 20th century. This mine yielded around 2200 tonnes (2425 tons) of gold from 1948 until it closed in 2004. Nowadays it has more notoriety than fame as a result of the extensive contamination of the buildings and surrounding area with arsenic dust and asbestos fibres, by-products of the refining processes employed.

Sawmill, Balaclava, Ontario, Canada

In 1855 a sawmill was built, using water power from Constant Creek, and the community which developed was called Balaclava after the Crimean War battle of 1854. The last water-powered mill in Ontario, finally closing down in 1967, it still contains pieces of machinery from its early days, and its sawdust-burner tower. Already in severe decline, Balaclava became a ghost town of increasingly ramshackle wooden buildings.

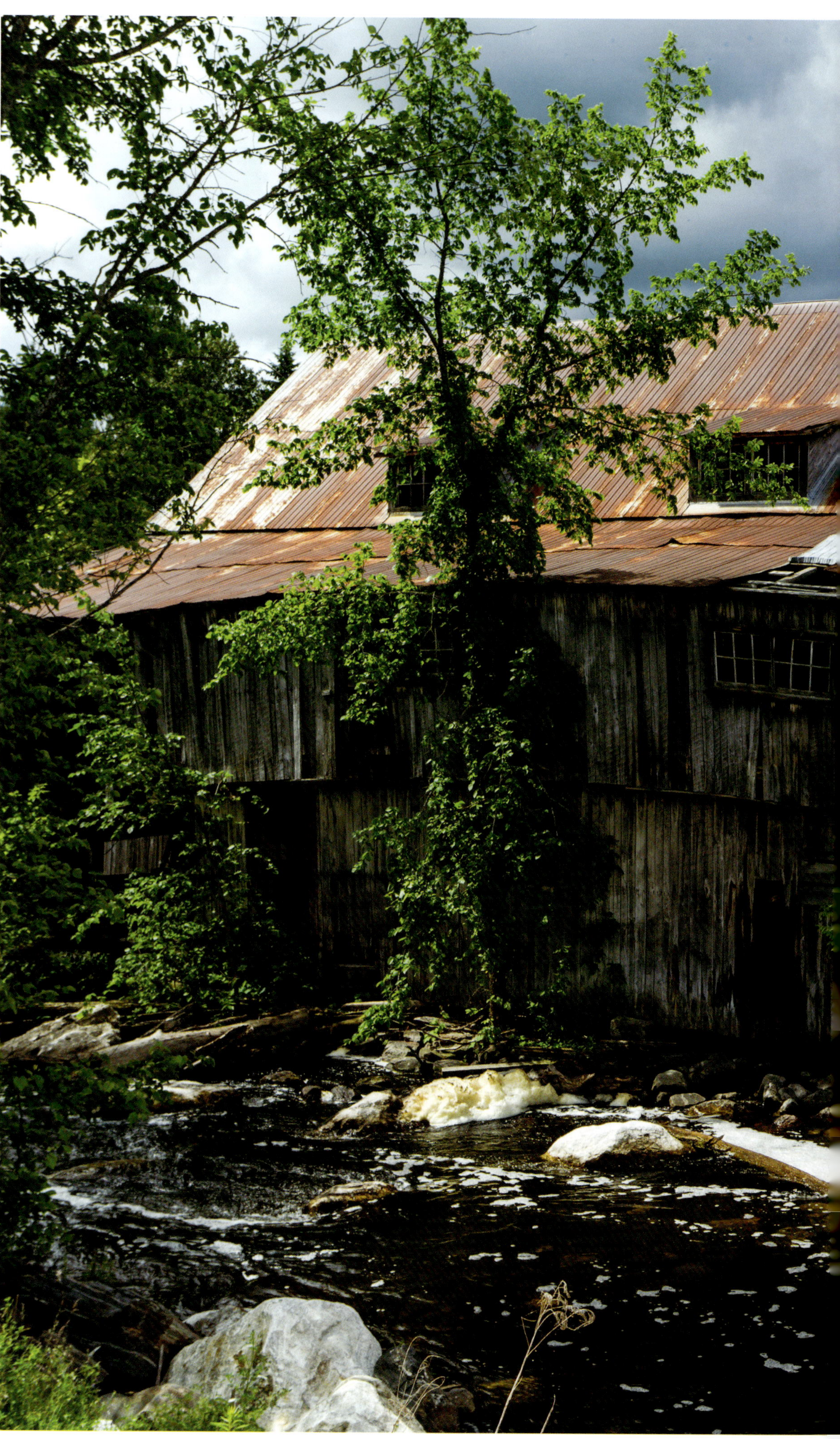

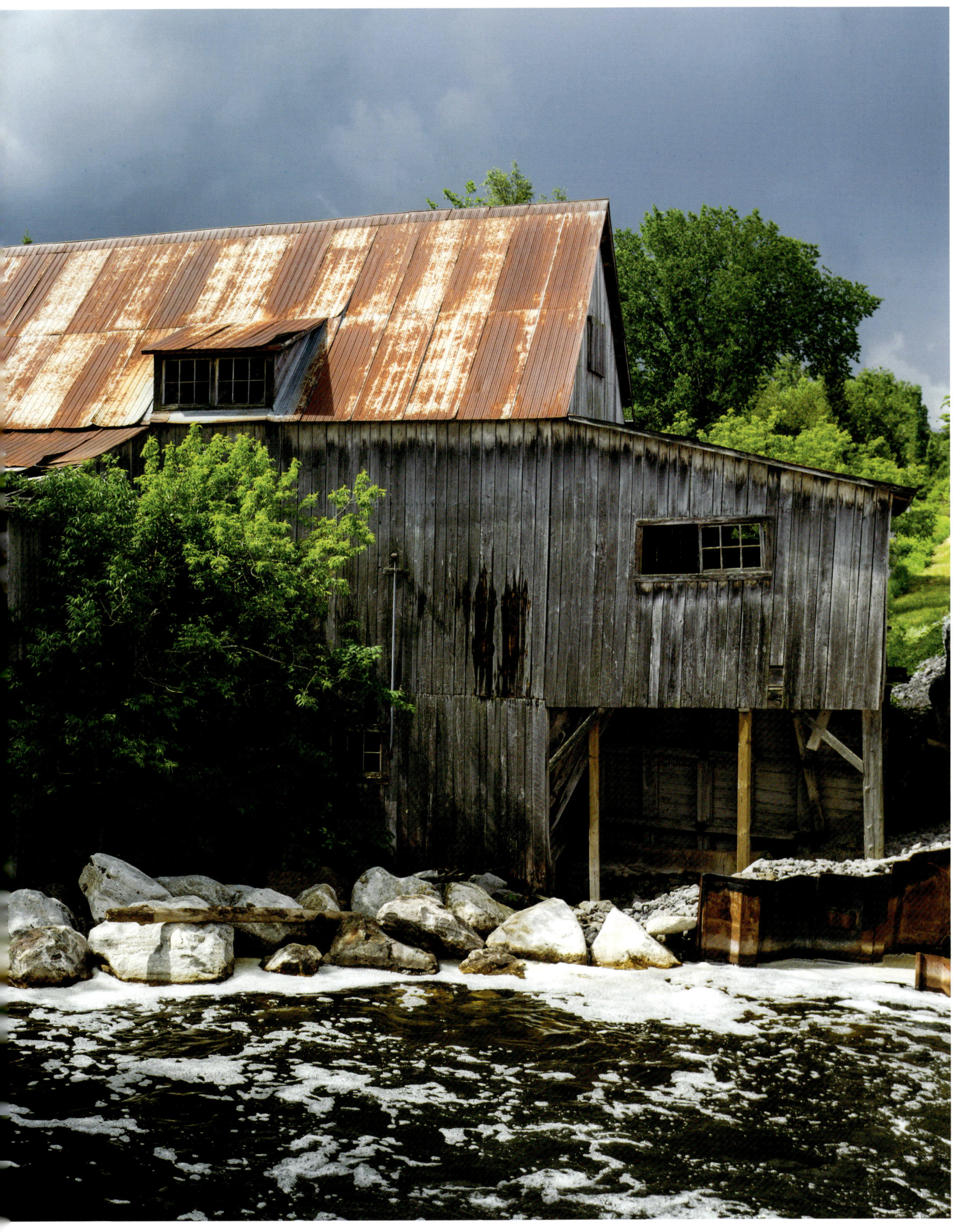

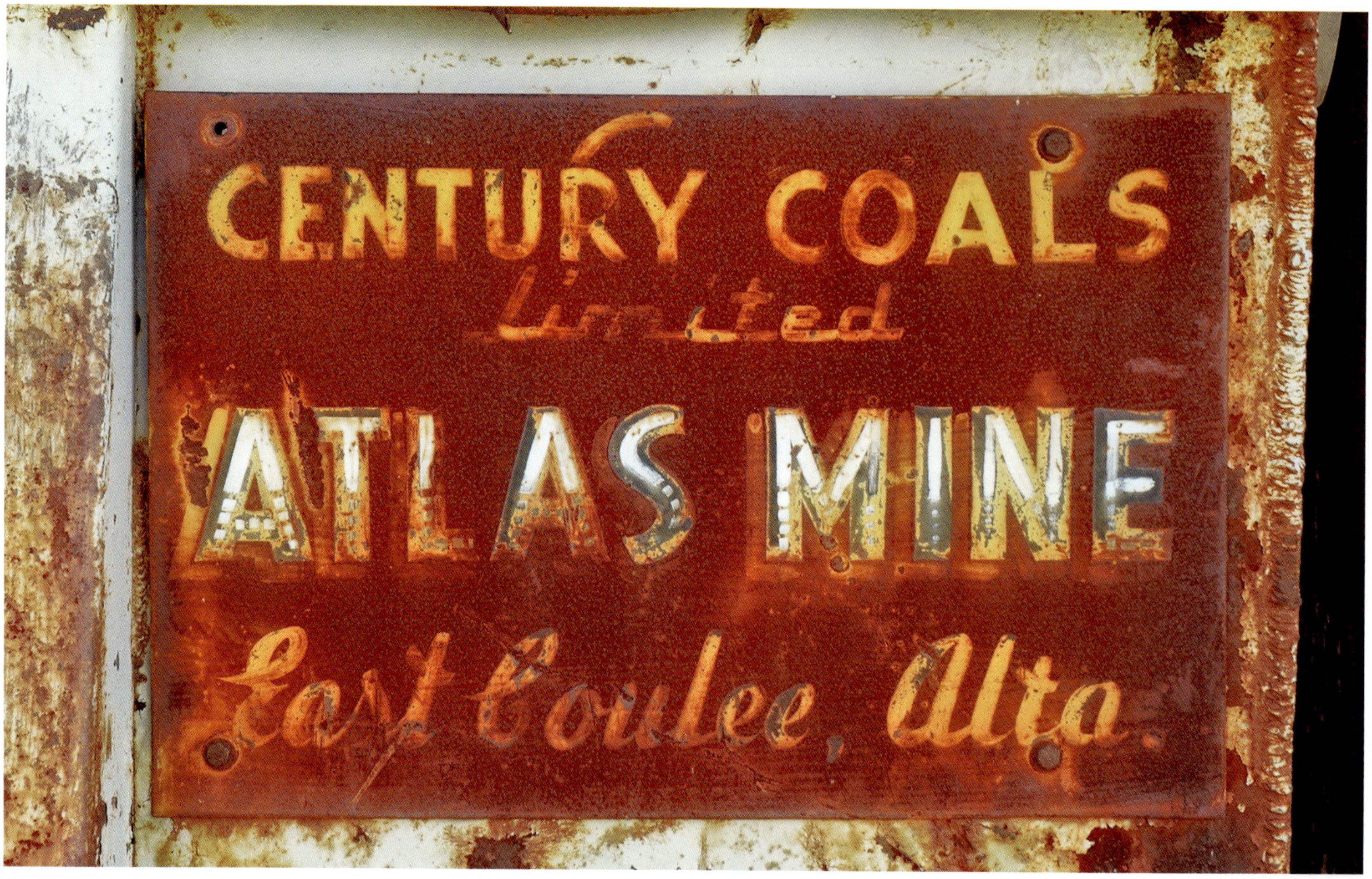

CENTURY COALS
limited
ATLAS MINE
East Coulee, Alta.

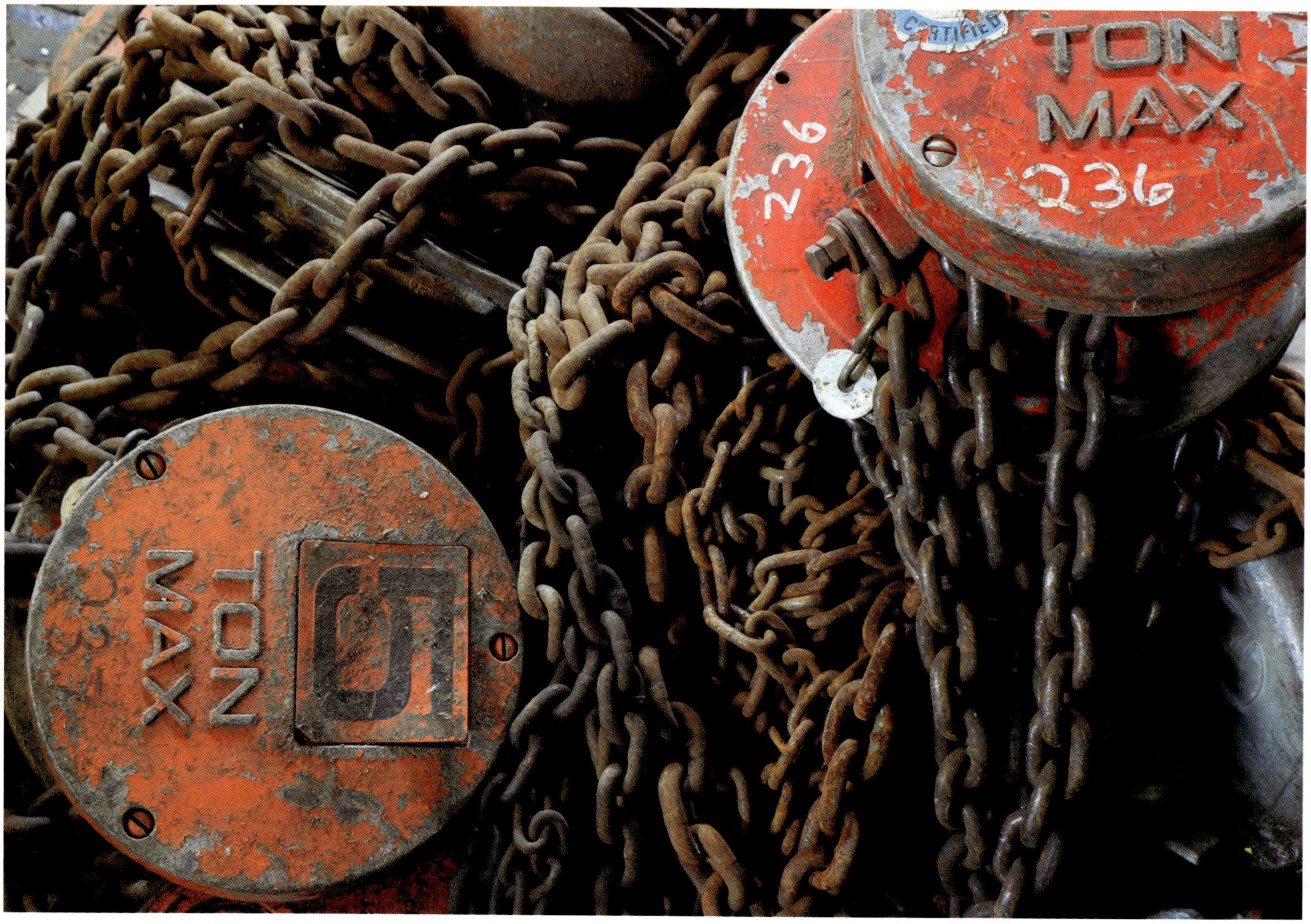

CERTIFIED
TON
MAX
236
236
TON
MAX
0

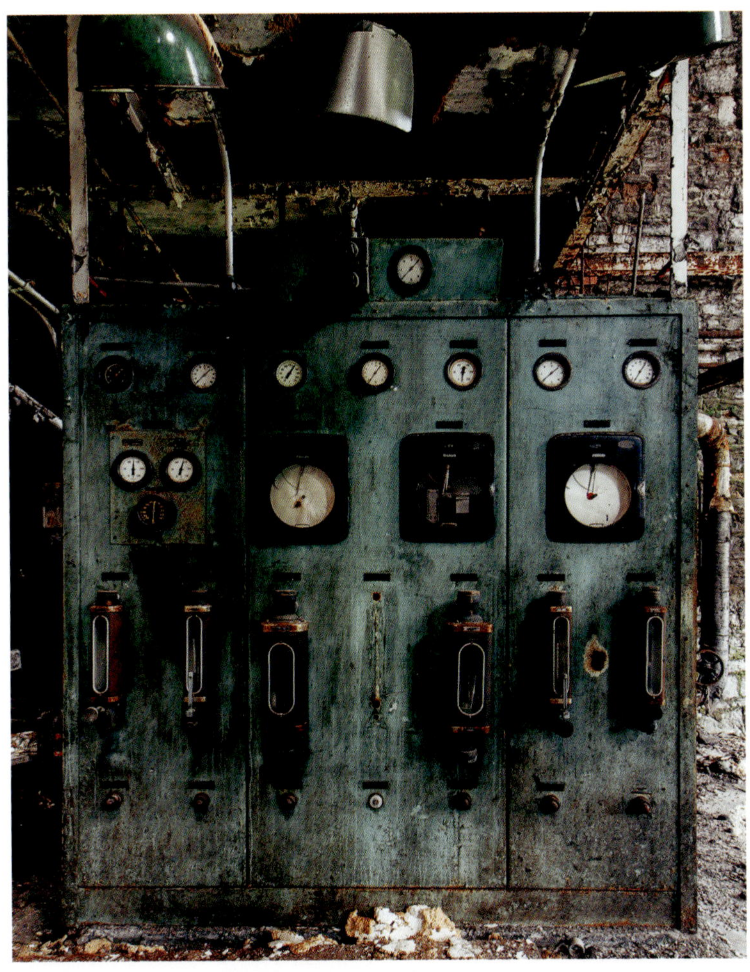

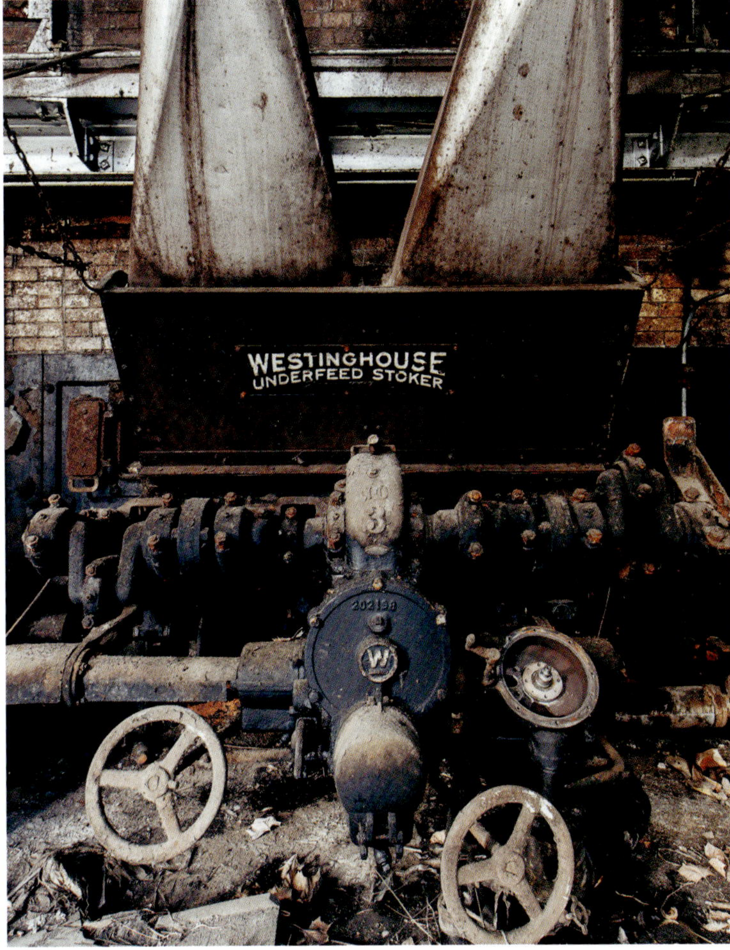

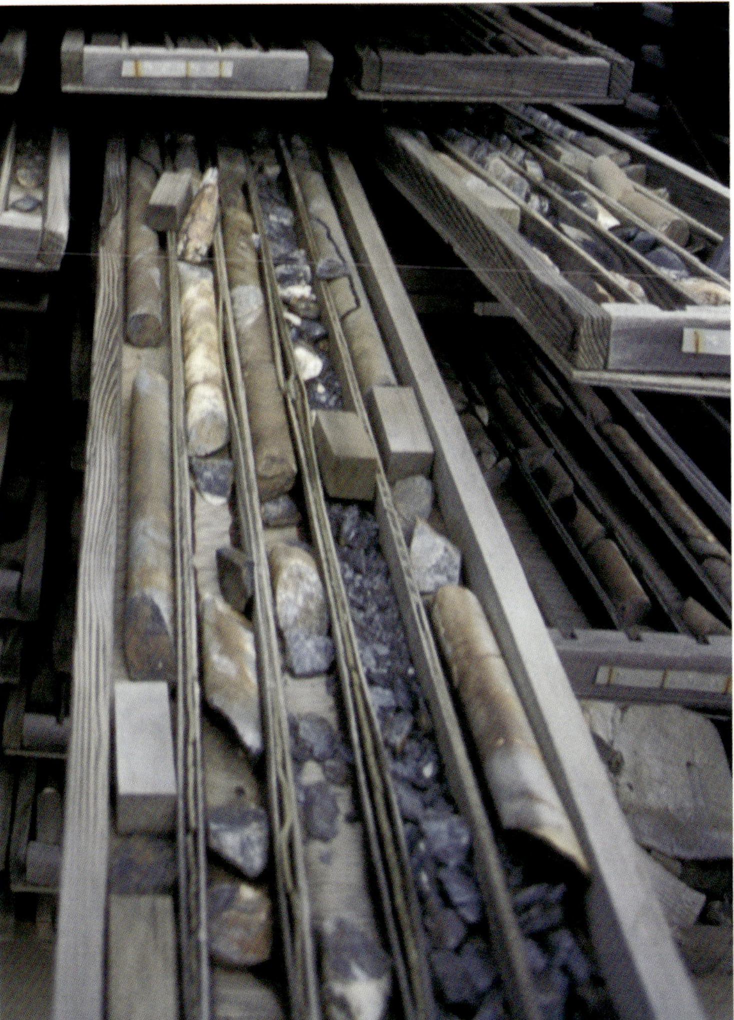

OPPOSITE TOP:

Signboard from Atlas Mine, East Coulee, Alberta, Canada

Century Coals were the operators of the Atlas mine from 1932 to 1984. In 1979 when the mine ceased production, the company handed the site over to the local historical society and it has since become the Atlas Coal Mine National Historic Site, giving visitors interpretive tours of the miners' work and way of life.

OPPOSITE BOTTOM:

E.B. Eddy Paper Mill, Hull, Ottawa, Canada

Chains and lifting gear were only part of the industrial remnants at this riverside papermill, built in the 1880s and closed in 2007. Once the district was a prime papermaking one. Now the factory is under redevelopment as a waterside residential, retail and recreation area, though local activists had hoped to restore it as an industrial museum.

TOP LEFT AND ABOVE:

Old Crow Distillery, Kentucky, USA

Named for the Scottish chemist and pioneer US distiller James Crow (1779–1856), the distillery was built in 1882 and closed down 105 years later. New technology introduced at various times, such as these electric heating controls, and automatic stoking, were not enough to sustain its profitability.

LEFT:

United Keno Hill Mine, Elsa, Yukon, Canada

Trays of geological samples show silver, lead and zinc-bearing ores from the once-productive mine, closed in 1989. Elsa, the company-owned mining town, has been largely dismantled, and what remains is largely converted to storage space for mining and environmental clearing equipment.

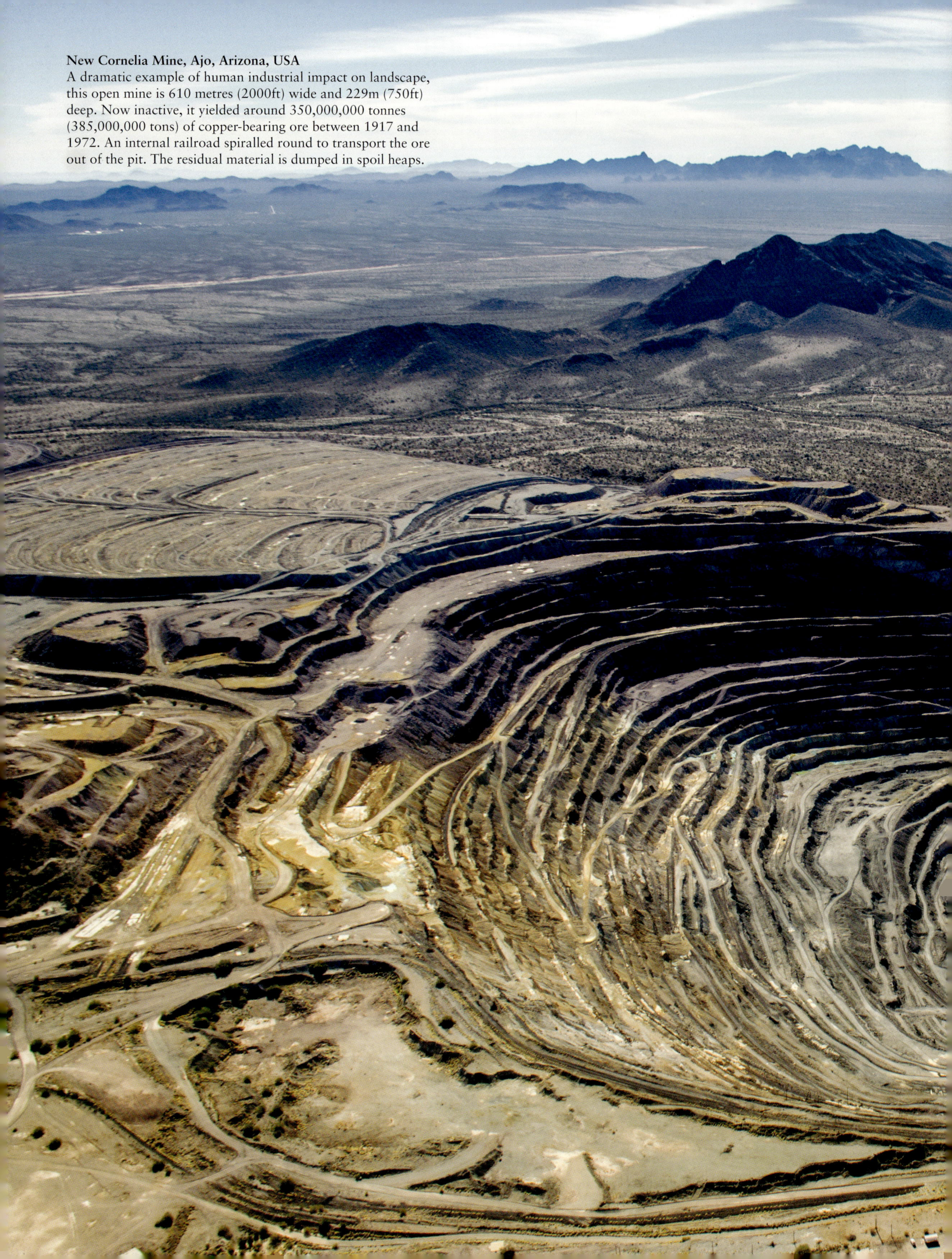

New Cornelia Mine, Ajo, Arizona, USA
A dramatic example of human industrial impact on landscape, this open mine is 610 metres (2000ft) wide and 229m (750ft) deep. Now inactive, it yielded around 350,000,000 tonnes (385,000,000 tons) of copper-bearing ore between 1917 and 1972. An internal railroad spiralled round to transport the ore out of the pit. The residual material is dumped in spoil heaps.

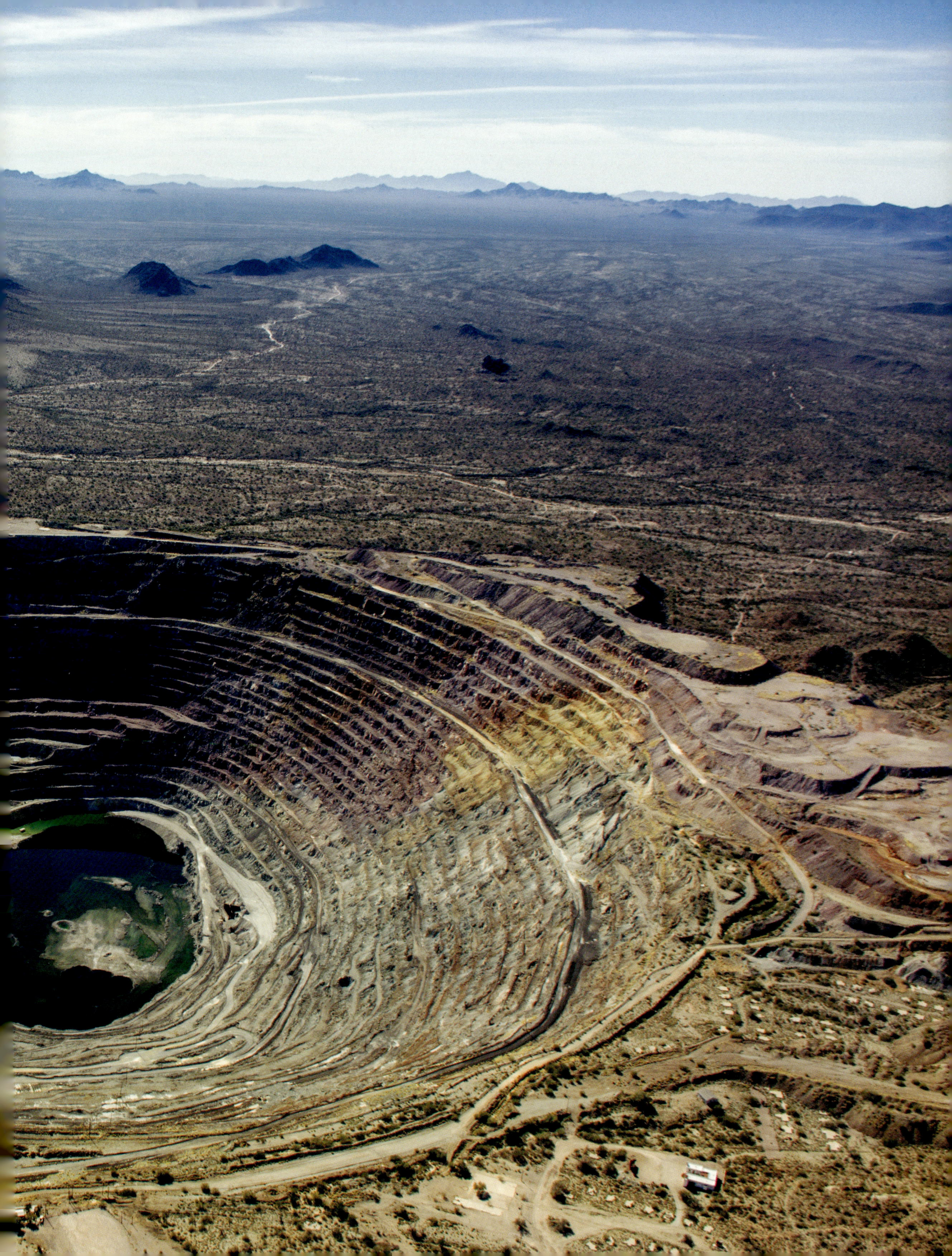

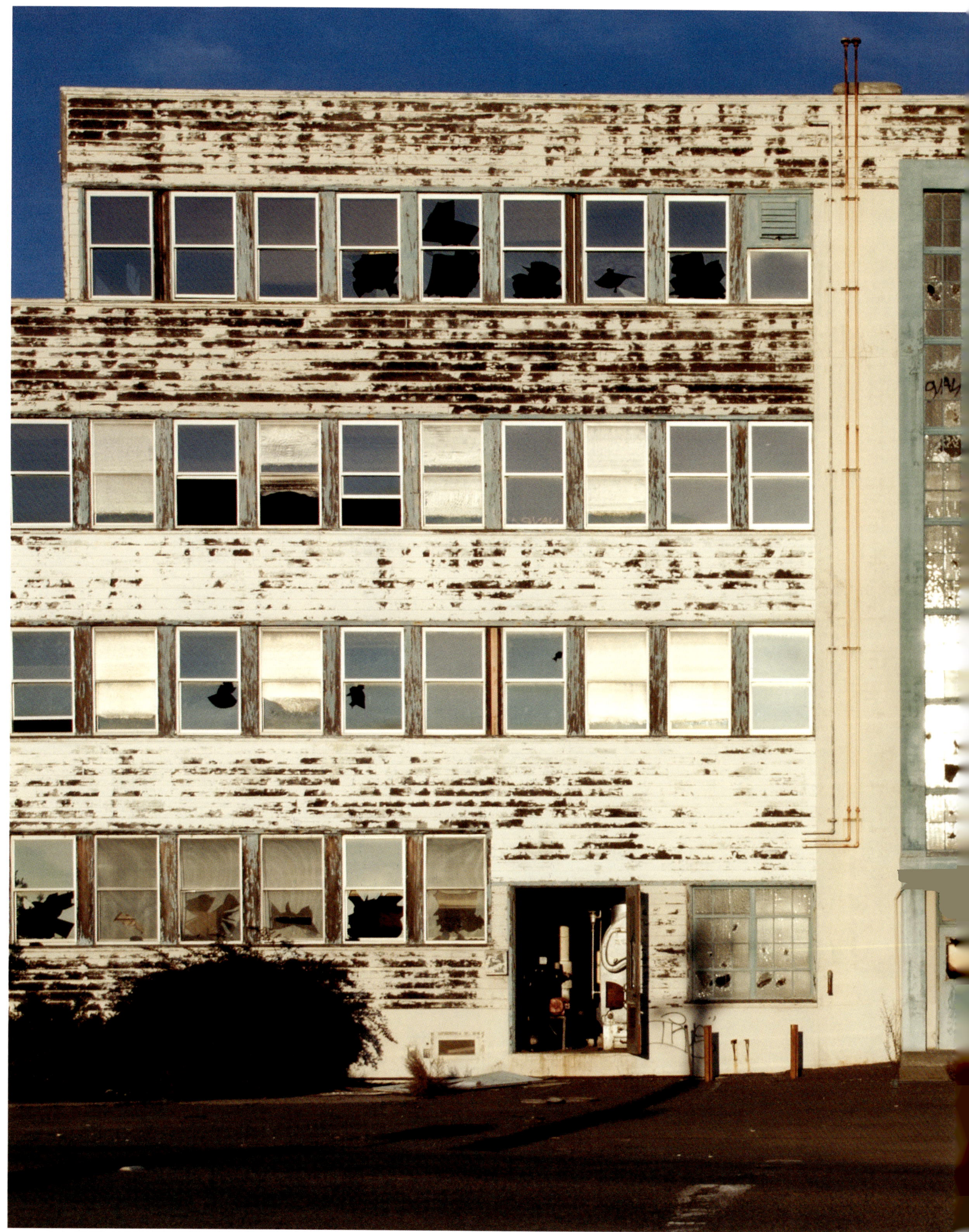

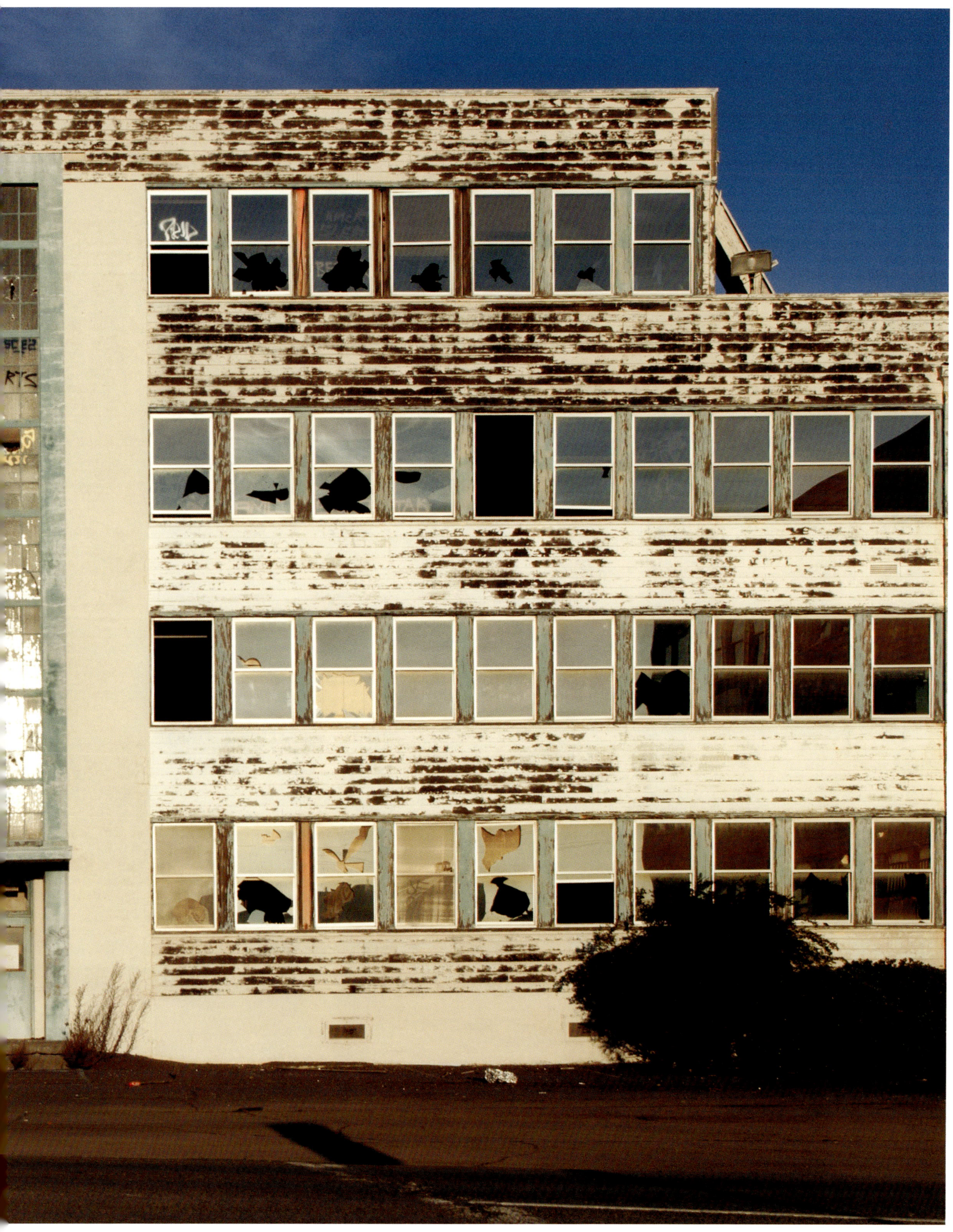

PREVIOUS PAGES:
Former US Naval Base, Mare Island, Vallejo, California, USA
Mare Island is actually a peninsula. A naval base was first established here in 1853. During World War II up to 50,000 workers were engaged in the repair of warships and construction of submarines. The base was decommissioned in 1996. Though some parts are in use for industrial, commercial and academic purposes, much, like this administrative block, stands empty.

RIGHT:
Former US Naval Base, Mare Island, Vallejo, California, USA
A rank of oil-fired boilers was installed in 1945 at the peak of wartime activity to supply steam power to the naval works at Mare Island. The Titusville Ironworks company was founded in Pennsylvania in 1860 and produced a wide range of equipment, including pumps and petrol engines as well as boilers. Dismantling of these massive artefacts is problematic because of the asbestos lagging.

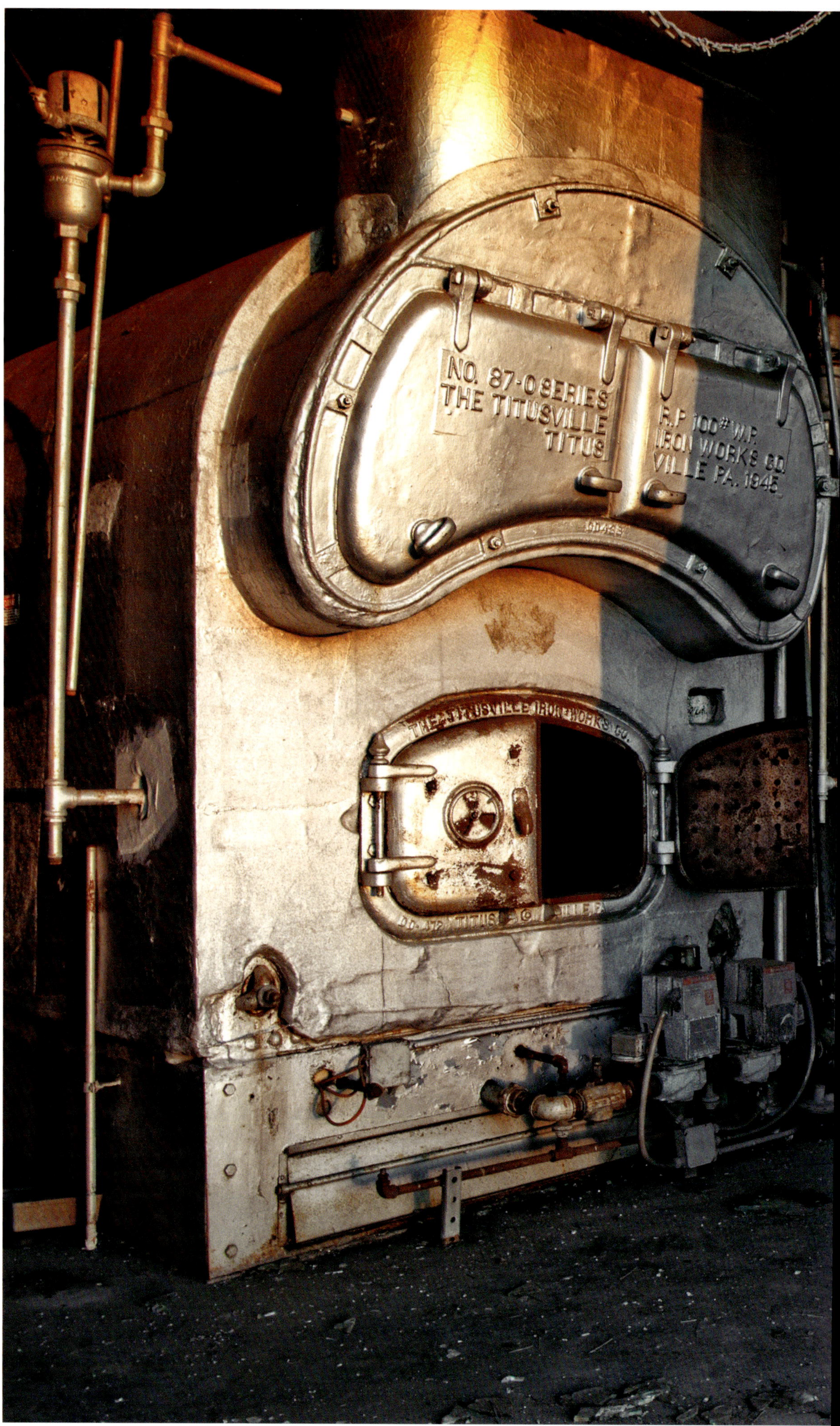

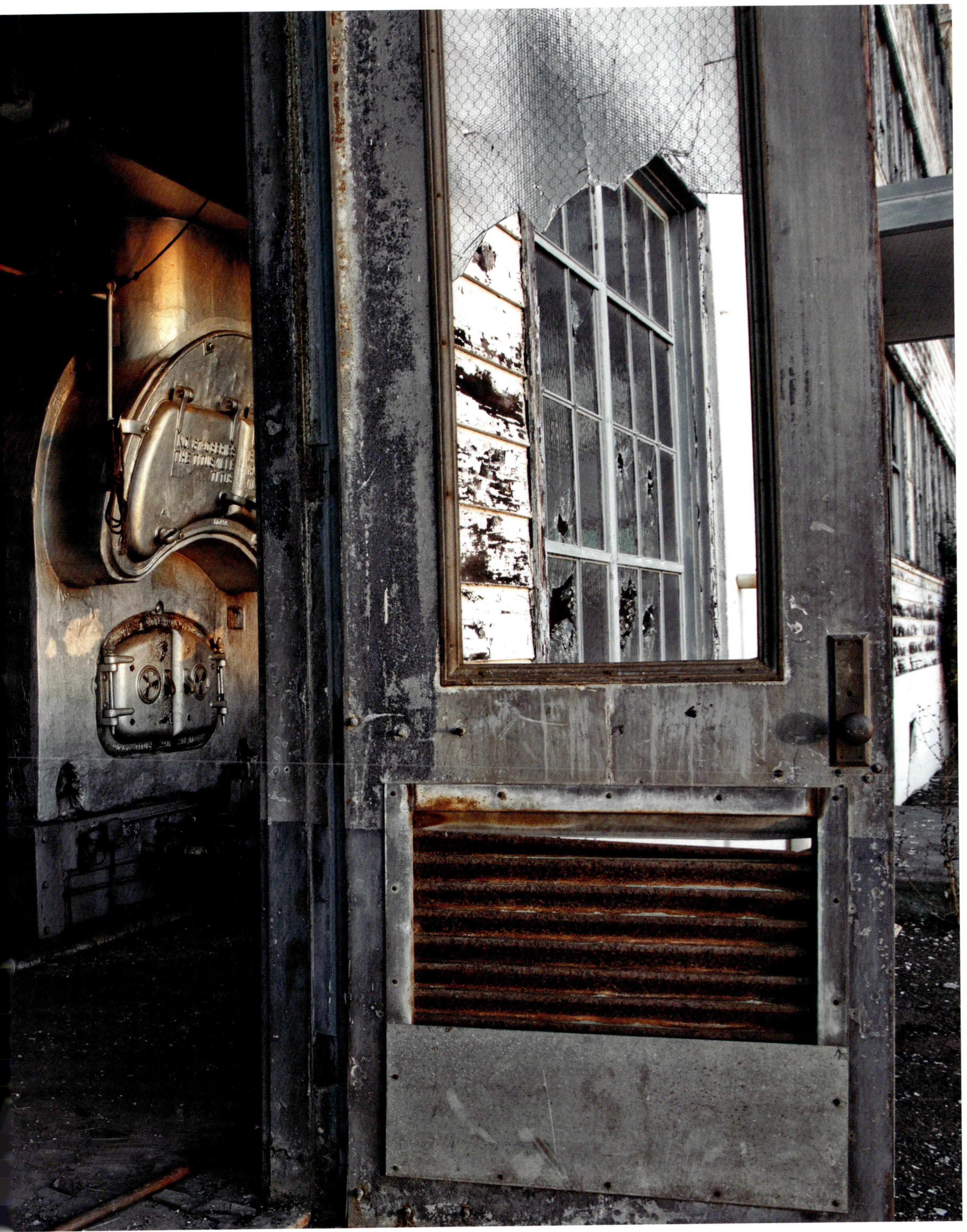

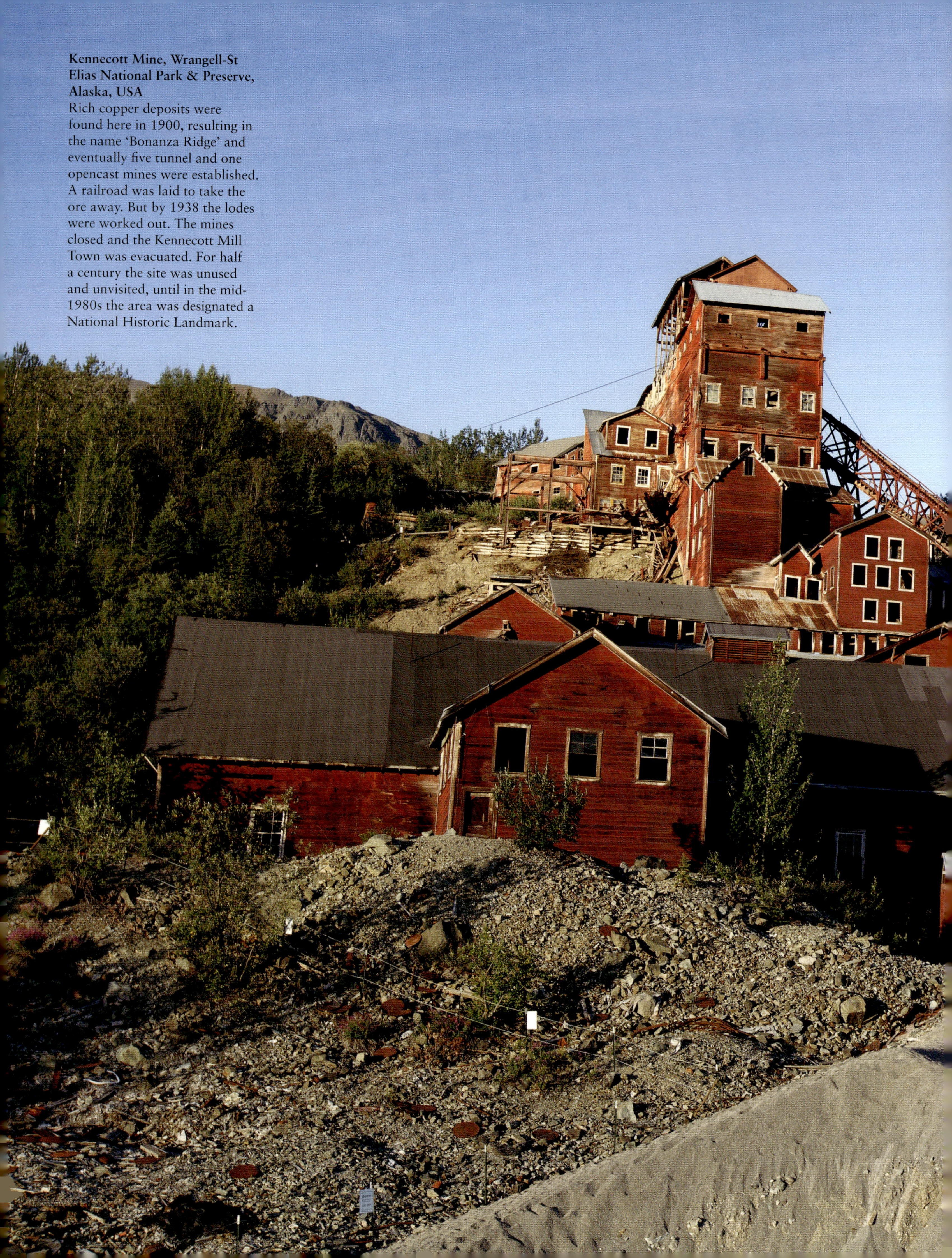

Kennecott Mine, Wrangell-St
Elias National Park & Preserve,
Alaska, USA
Rich copper deposits were
found here in 1900, resulting in
the name 'Bonanza Ridge' and
eventually five tunnel and one
opencast mines were established.
A railroad was laid to take the
ore away. But by 1938 the lodes
were worked out. The mines
closed and the Kennecott Mill
Town was evacuated. For half
a century the site was unused
and unvisited, until in the mid-
1980s the area was designated a
National Historic Landmark.

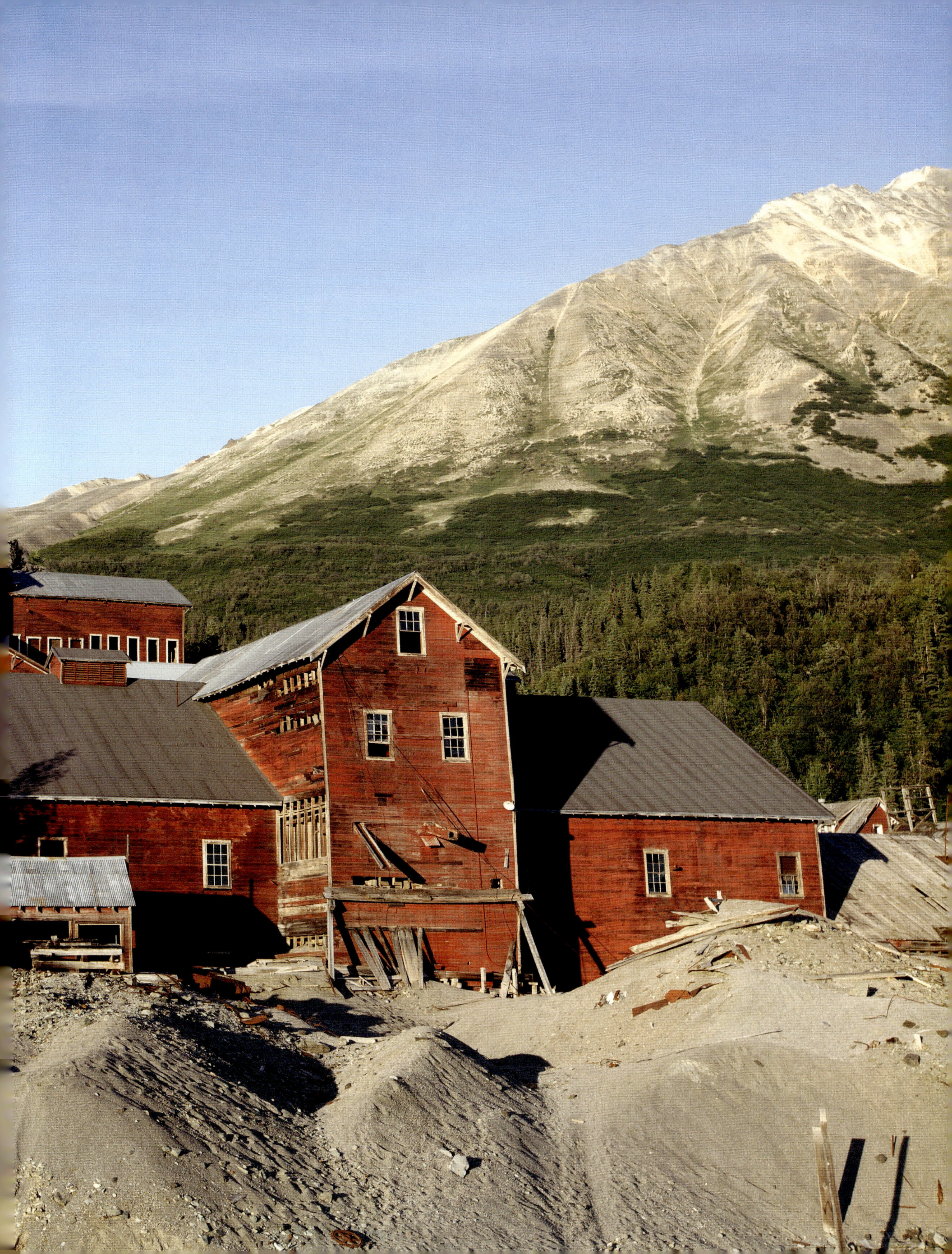

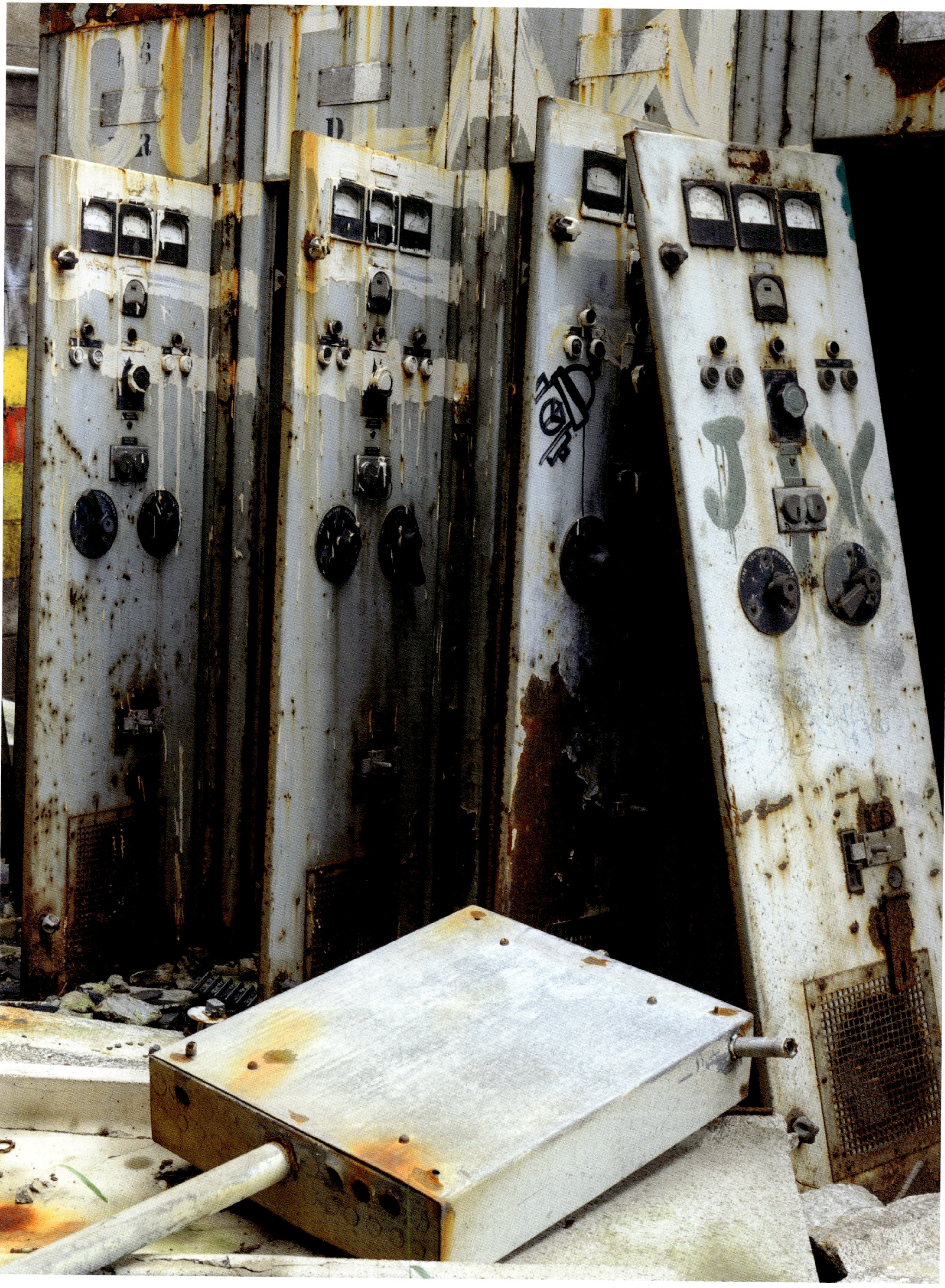

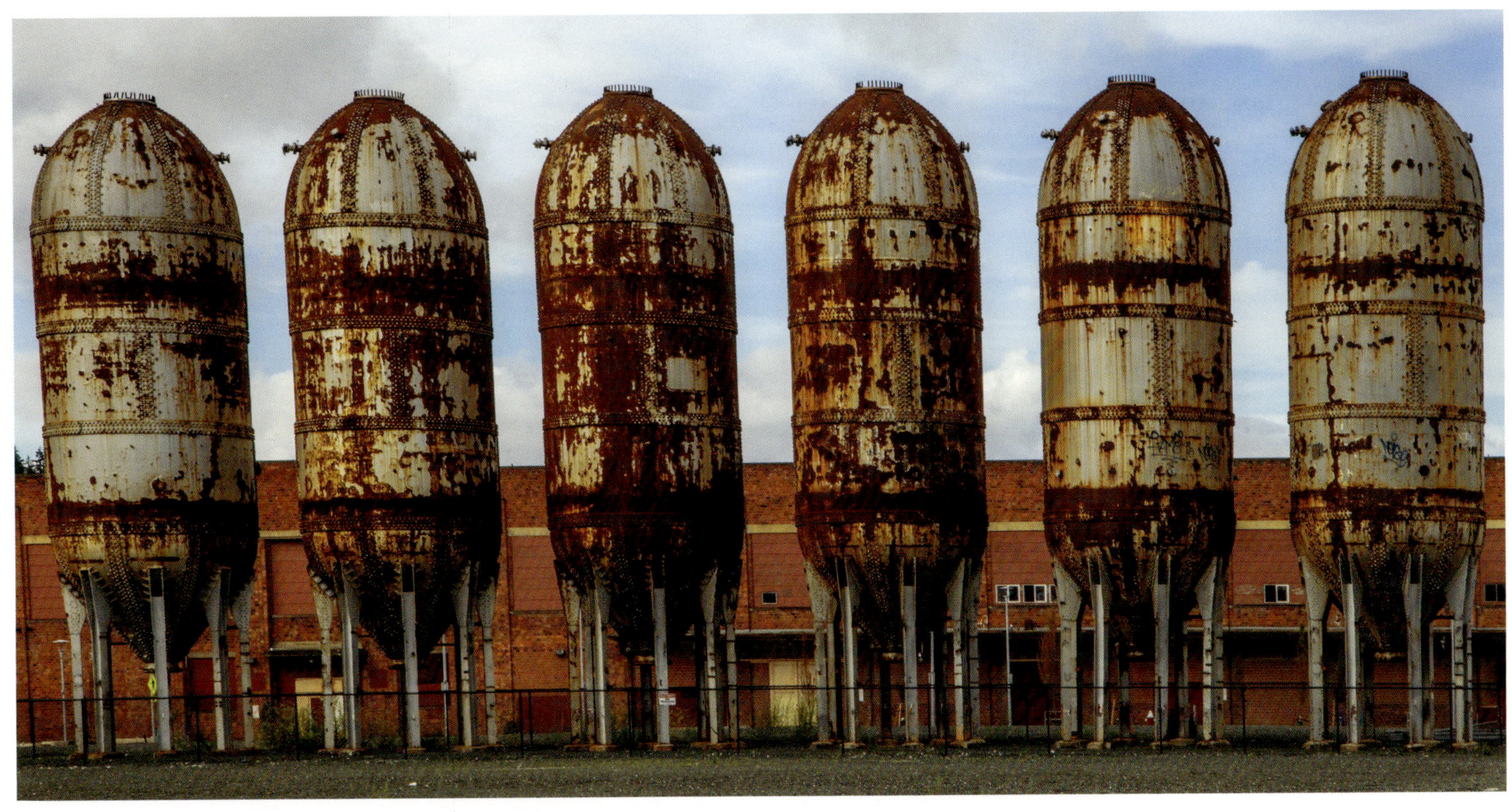

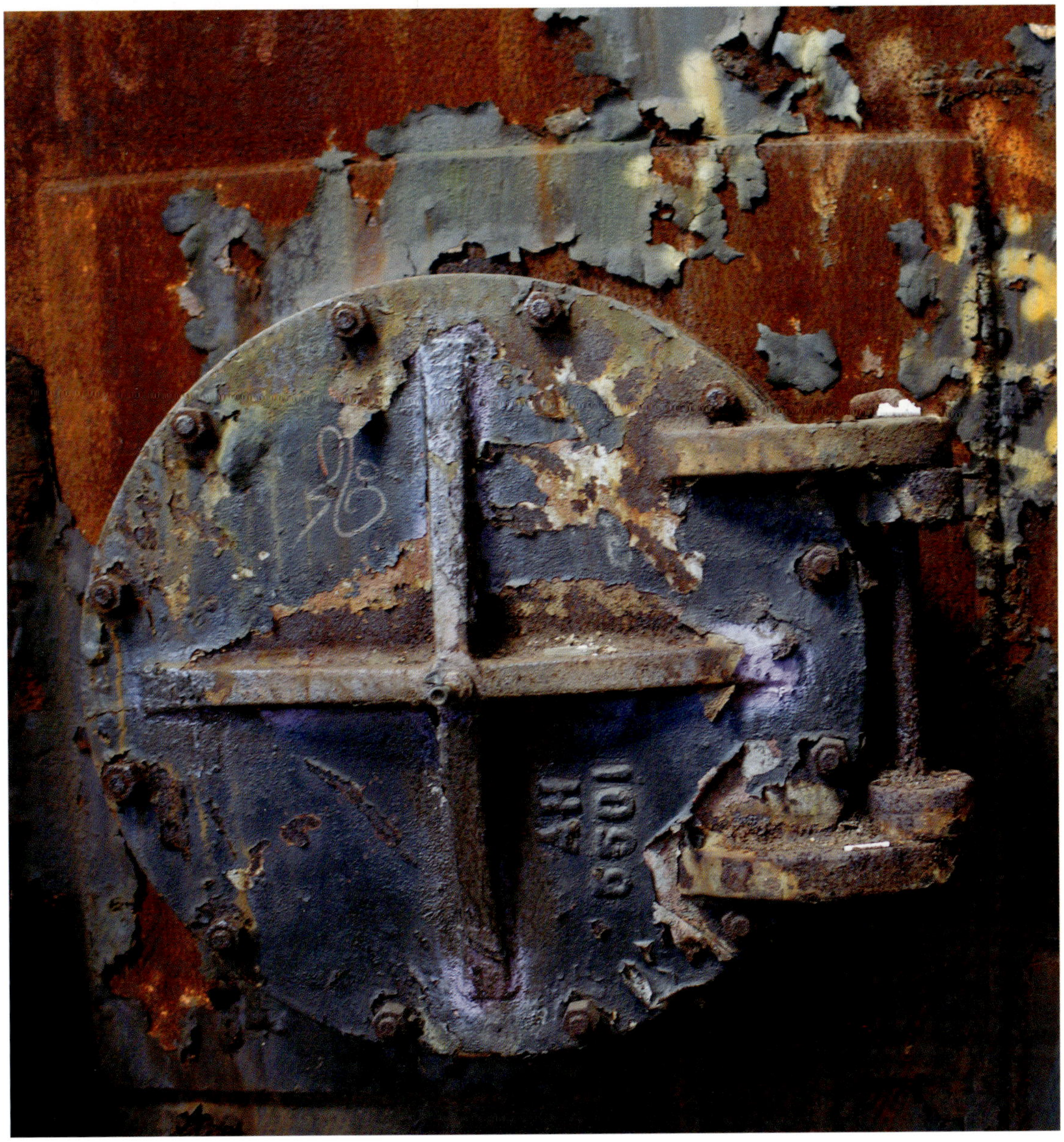

Carrie Blast Furnace, Braddock, Pennsylvania, USA
Not for easy opening: twelve bolts secure this access port to a pressurised boiler or tank holding steam to work the machinery. The ports could be opened to allow for periodic washing out of the inside, to remove build-ups of chemicals or impurities.

ABOVE:

Georgia Pacific Paper Mill, Bellingham, Washington, USA
Wood chip digesters stand in a row at this disused pulp mill which once dominated the town's waterfront. In these towers wood chips were converted into pulp by saturation with sulphuric acid. Now the entire site has been cleared as Bellingham reinvents itself as a post-industrial tourist centre.

LEFT:

Carrie Blast Furnace, Braddock, Pennsylvania, USA
Disconnected remnants of once-functional and expensive equipment, like these electrical control panels, have a pathos of their own. They are in the derelict complex of Blast Furnaces 6 and 7, all that remains of the huge Homestead Steelworks – a metal jungle of pipework, gantries, girders and crucibles, where rivers of molten steel once ran to the accompaniment of ferocious noise, and which now seem eerily silent.

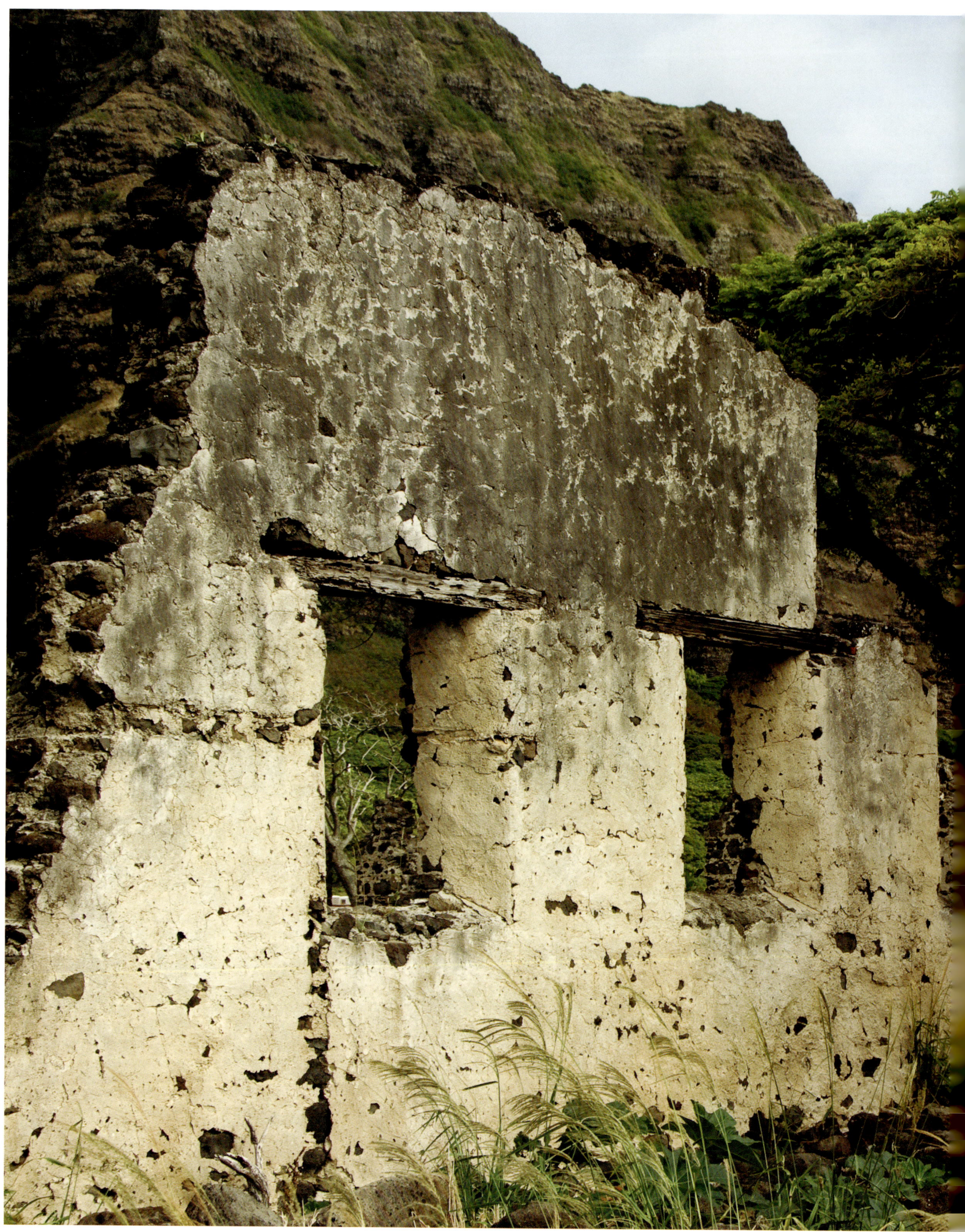

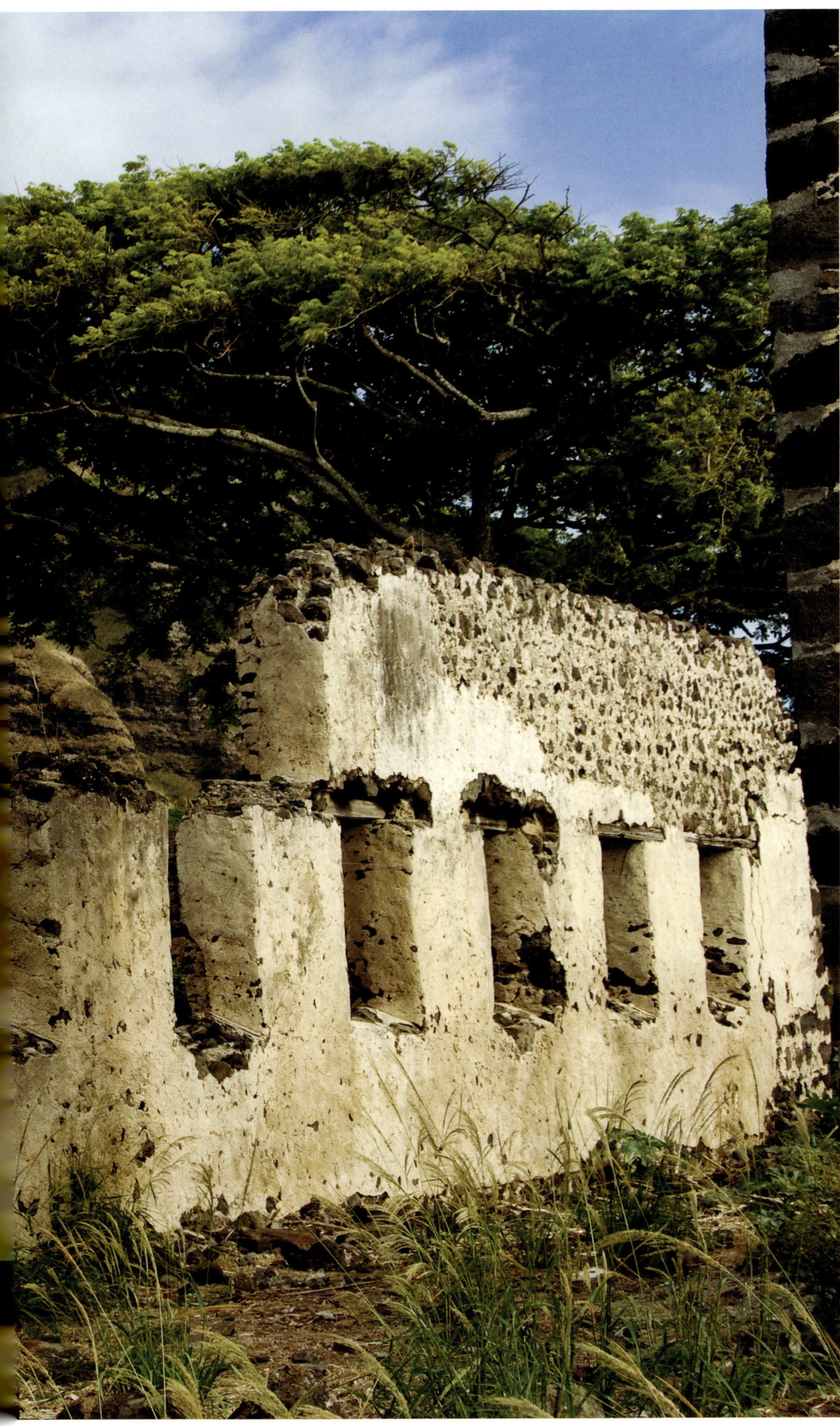

Sugar Cane Mill, Maui, Hawaii, USA
In 1858 this was among the first sugar-processing works in Hawaii, harbinger of an industry that flourished until the late 20th century. Cast-iron machinery powered by steam crunched and squeezed the canes to extract the juice. Abandoned in 1879, the building deteriorated into a picturesque ruin covered in creepers and vines. Now partially restored as a resort venue, it still conveys a hint of the vigour of primitive industry.

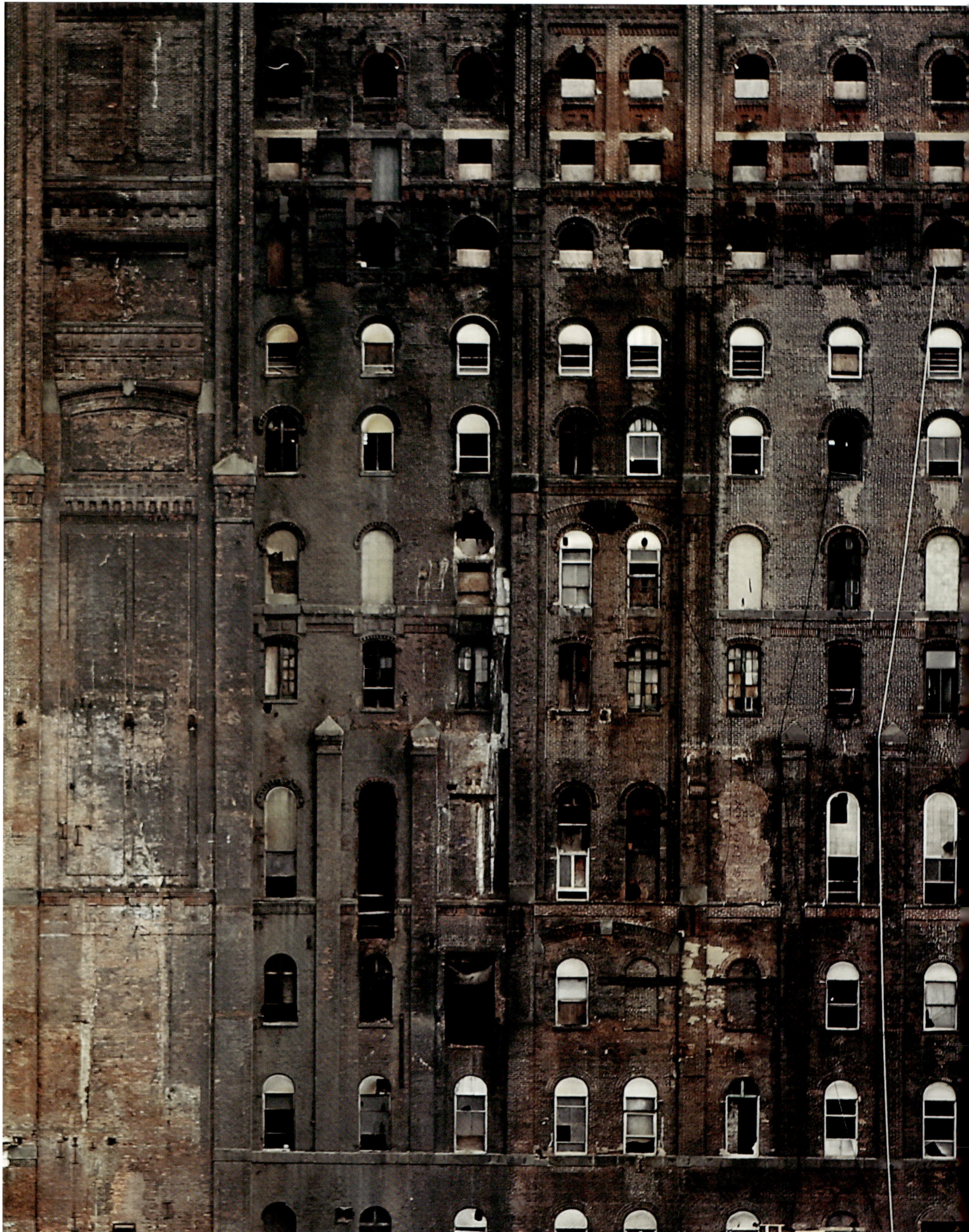

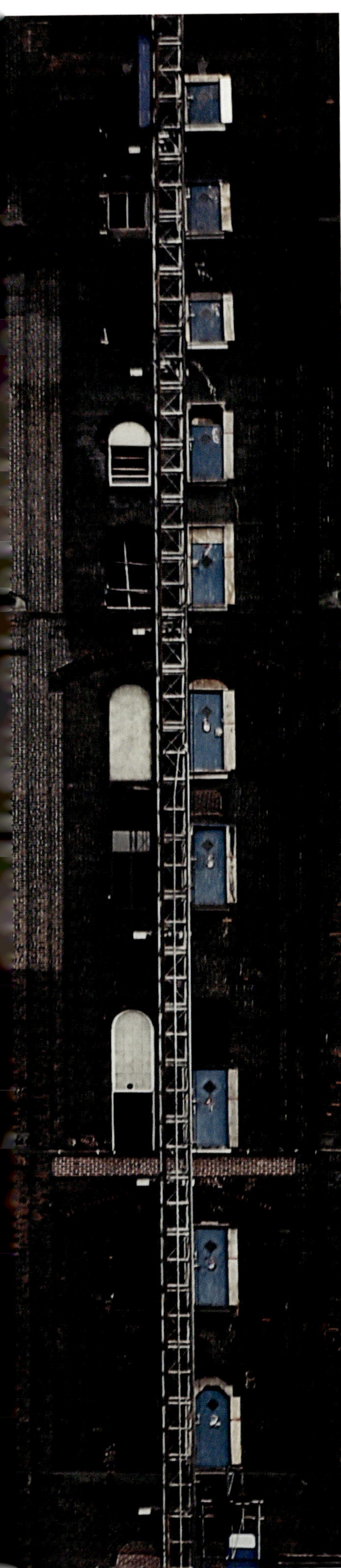

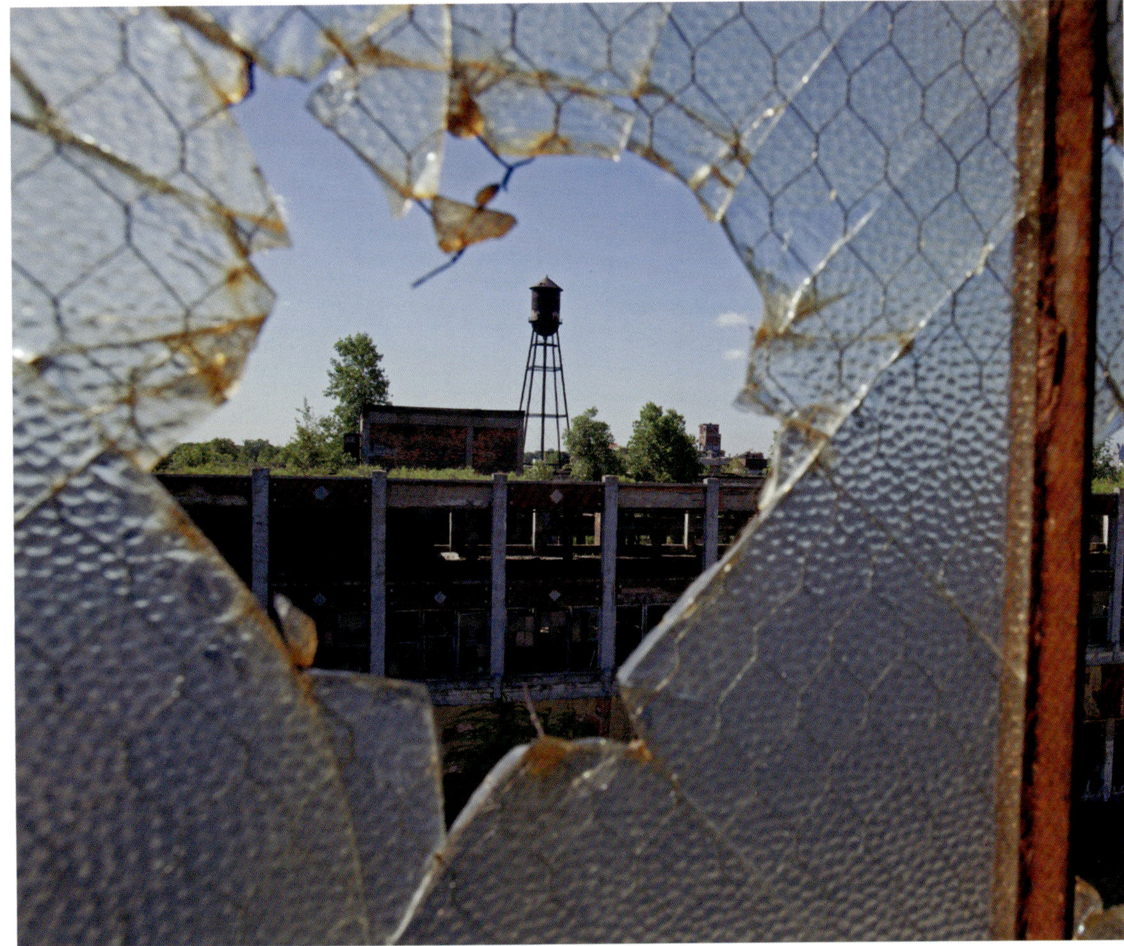

LEFT:

Domino Sugar Refinery, Williamsburg, Brooklyn, New York, USA

This massive building, with many classical touches to its architecture, was the world's largest sugar refinery when built in 1882. It ceased production in 2004, and is now undergoing conversion into a residential block. The former wharf area is a public park, where salvaged pieces of the sugar-processing machinery are on exhibit in 'Artifacts Walk'.

ABOVE:

The Packard Plant, Detroit, Michigan, USA

The water tower of the Packard motor factory was a familiar landmark on Detroit's East Grand Boulevard. Opened in 1903, it was the first factory site in the USA to use reinforced concrete. Car production ended in 1958, since when the site has had a variety of owners but remains a scene of dereliction.

Guano Mine, Grand Canyon, Arizona, USA
Sitting close to the edge of the Grand Canyon, the mine dates from 1957 when the U.S. Guano Corporation purchased the mining rights to extract guano, or bat droppings, from a local cave. The existing structure was designed to fix a steel cable 2300m (7500ft) across the canyon in order to haul a cable cart up from the mine below. The mine was closed in 1960 after it had been drained of guano.

Willow Steam Plant, Philadelphia, Pennsylvania, USA
This large building was part of the city centre's steam system after it was built by the Philadelphia Electric Company in 1927. Full of pipes, gauges and other industrial refuse, the building's prominent smokestack is 50 metres (163ft) high. The plant was closed in the 1970s and has been sealed by the city's fire department because it contains dangerous materials such as asbestos.

Michigan Central Station, Detroit, Michigan, USA
Built in the grand style when Detroit was becoming a hub of the automative industry, the station resembled classical Roman baths, backed by a massive office block. The last train ran from here in January 1988, since when curious visitors have run the risk of falling plaster or stonework, until 2018 when the Ford Motor Company acquired it for conversion into a high-tech campus site.

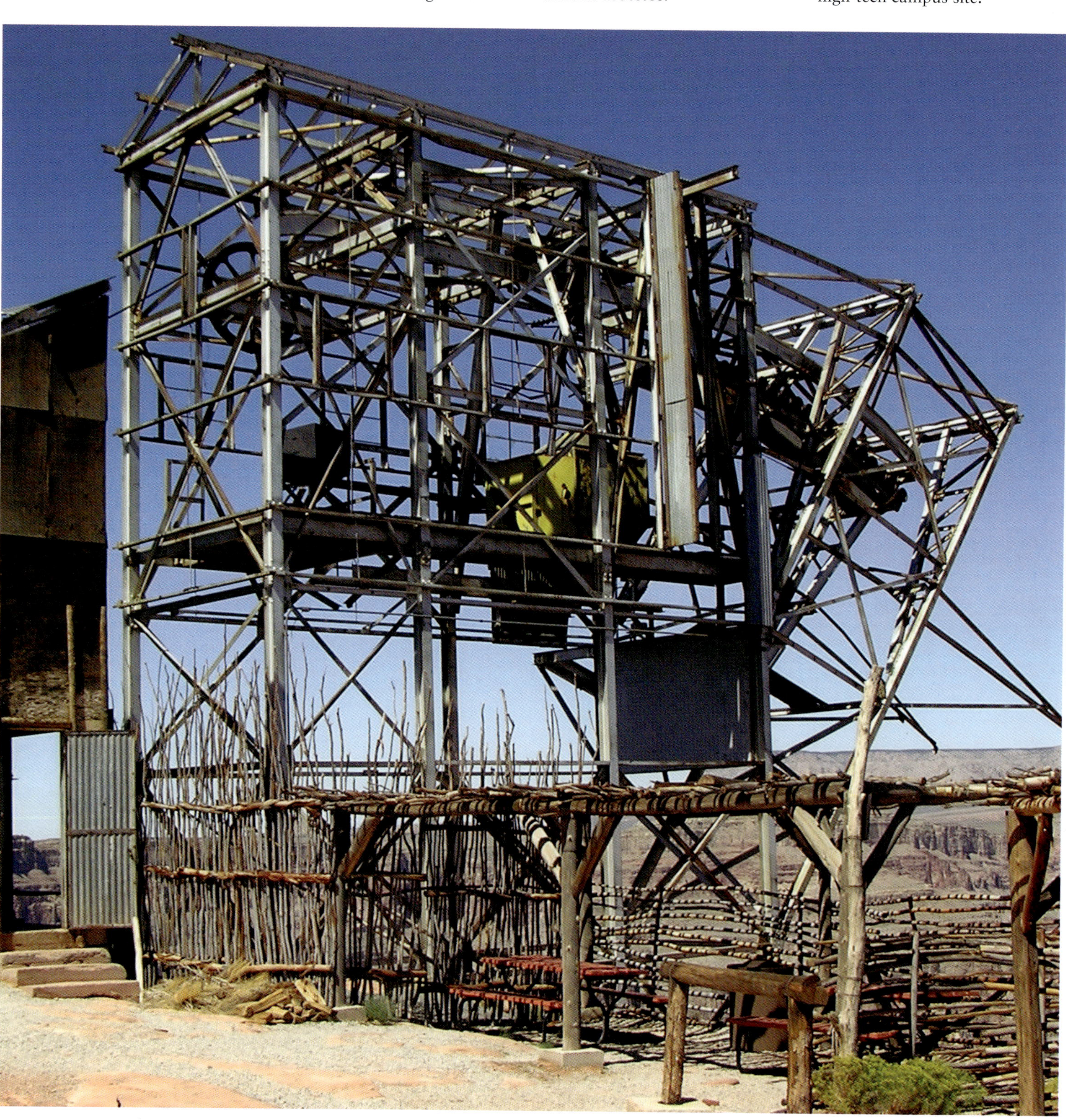

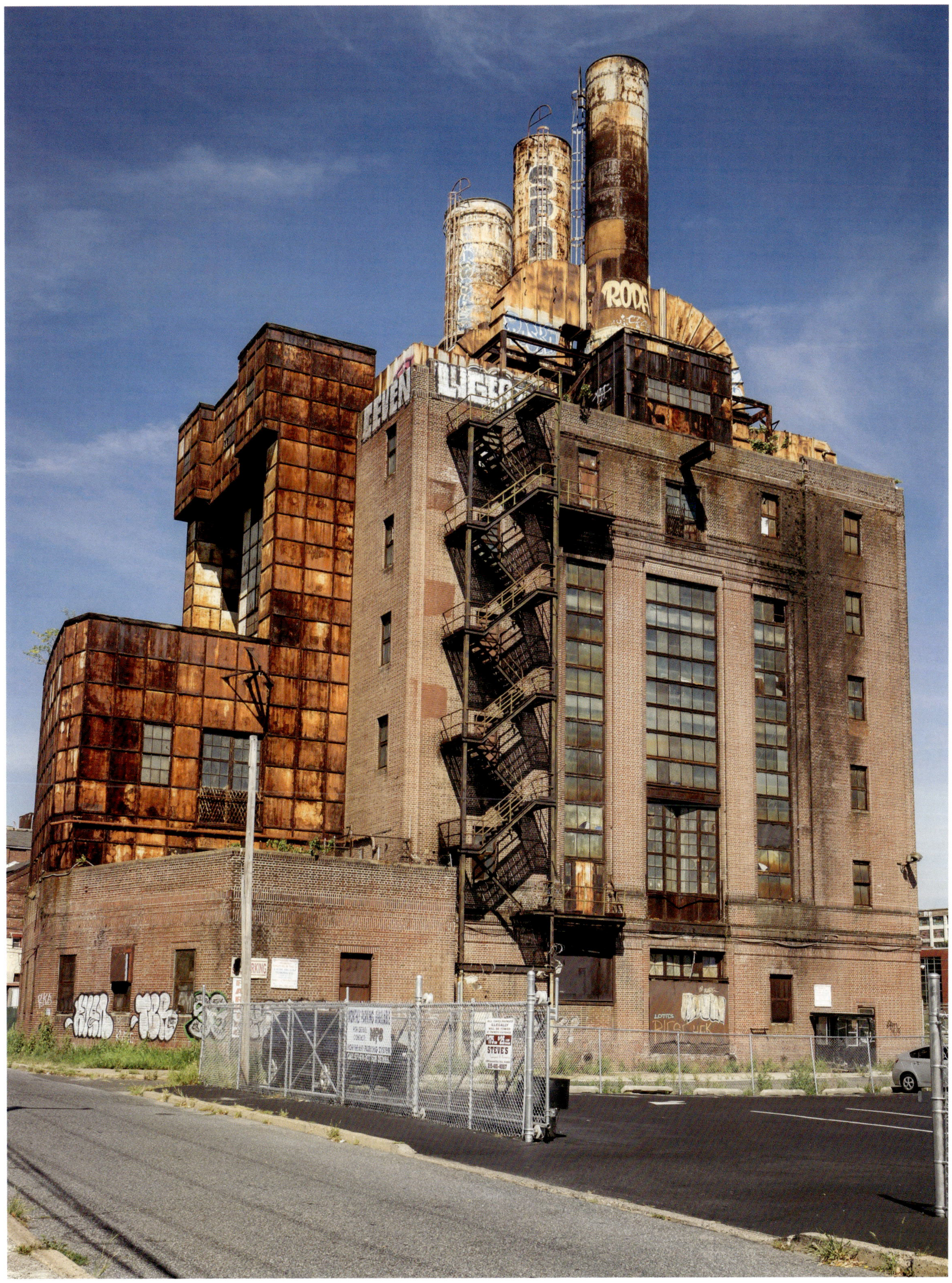

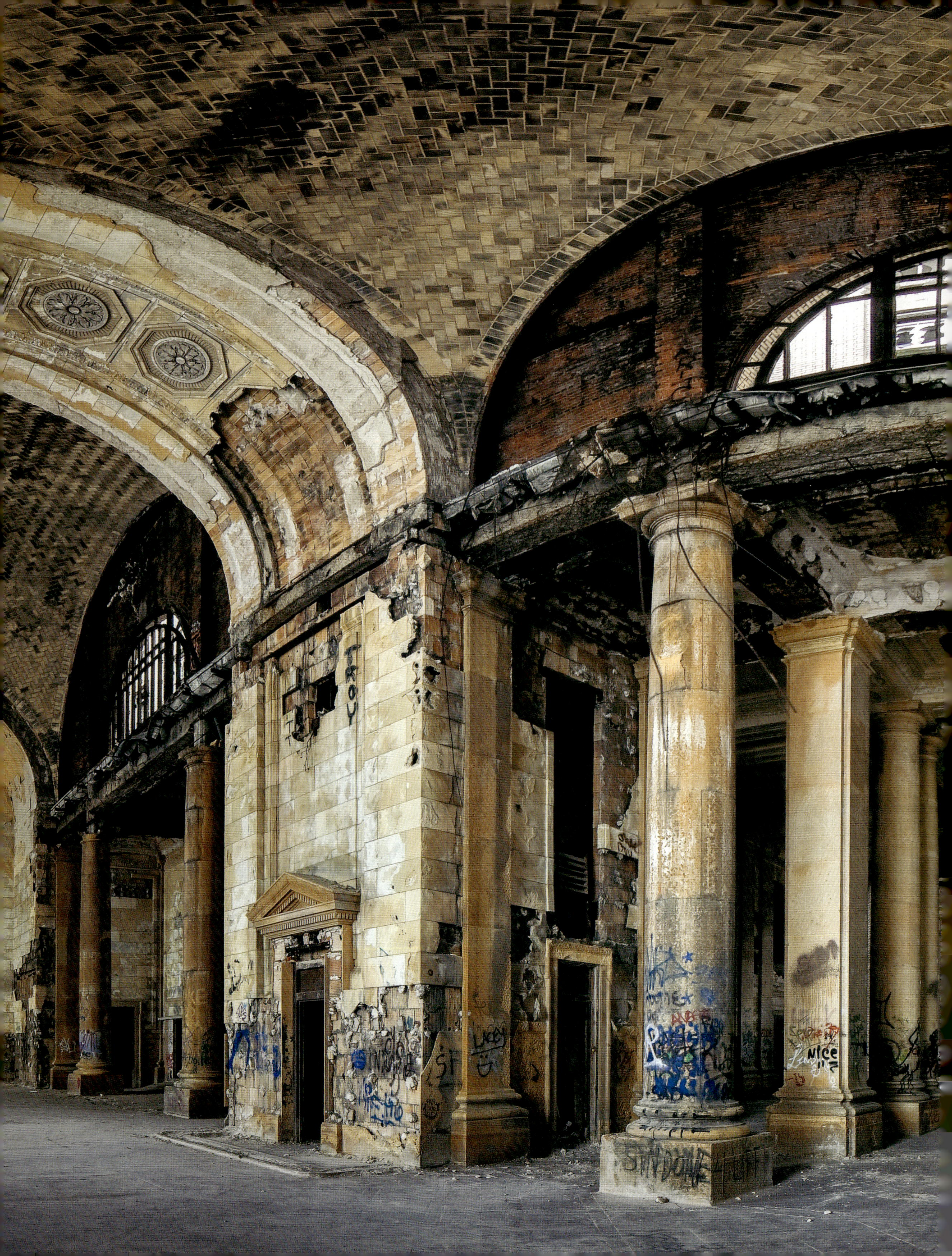

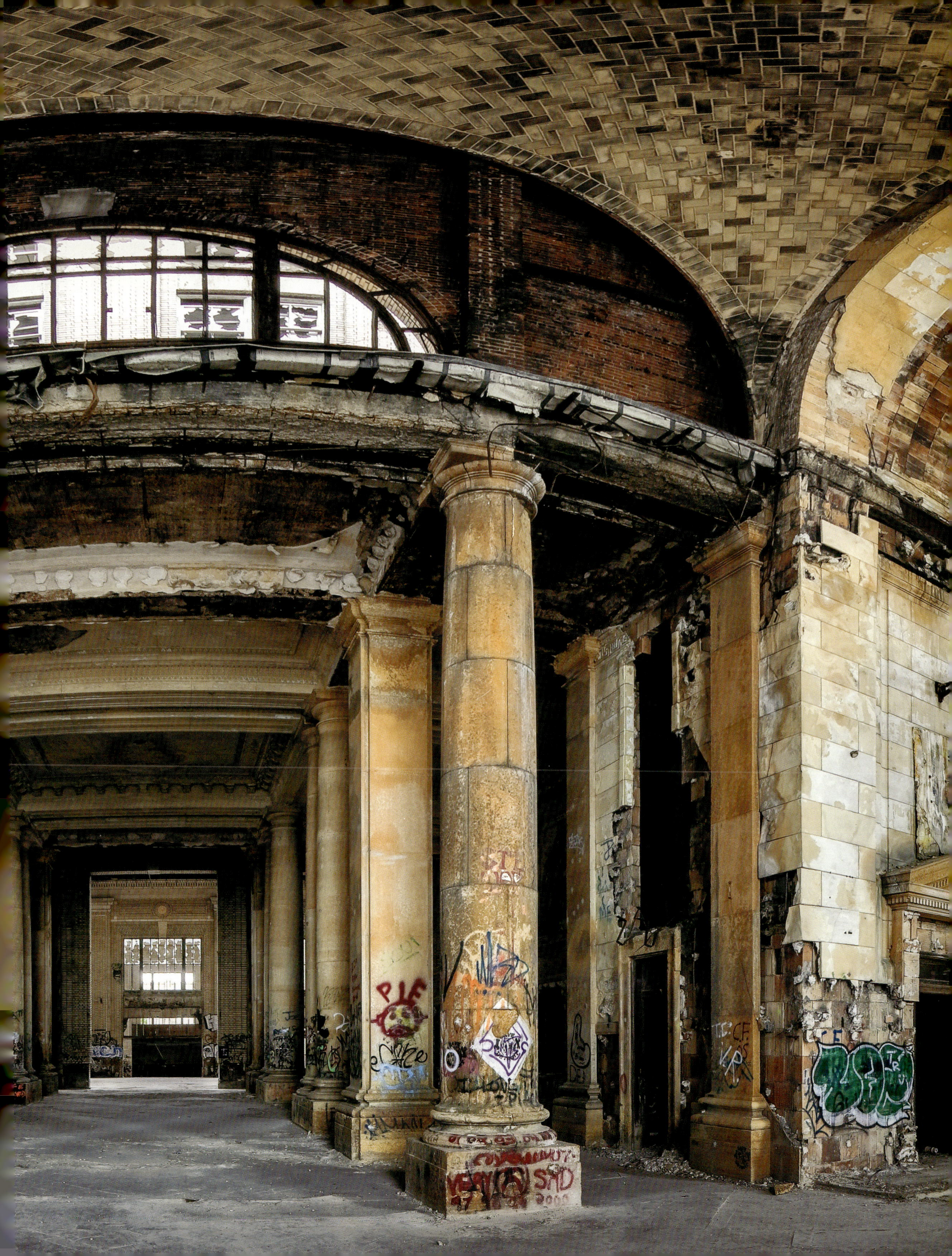

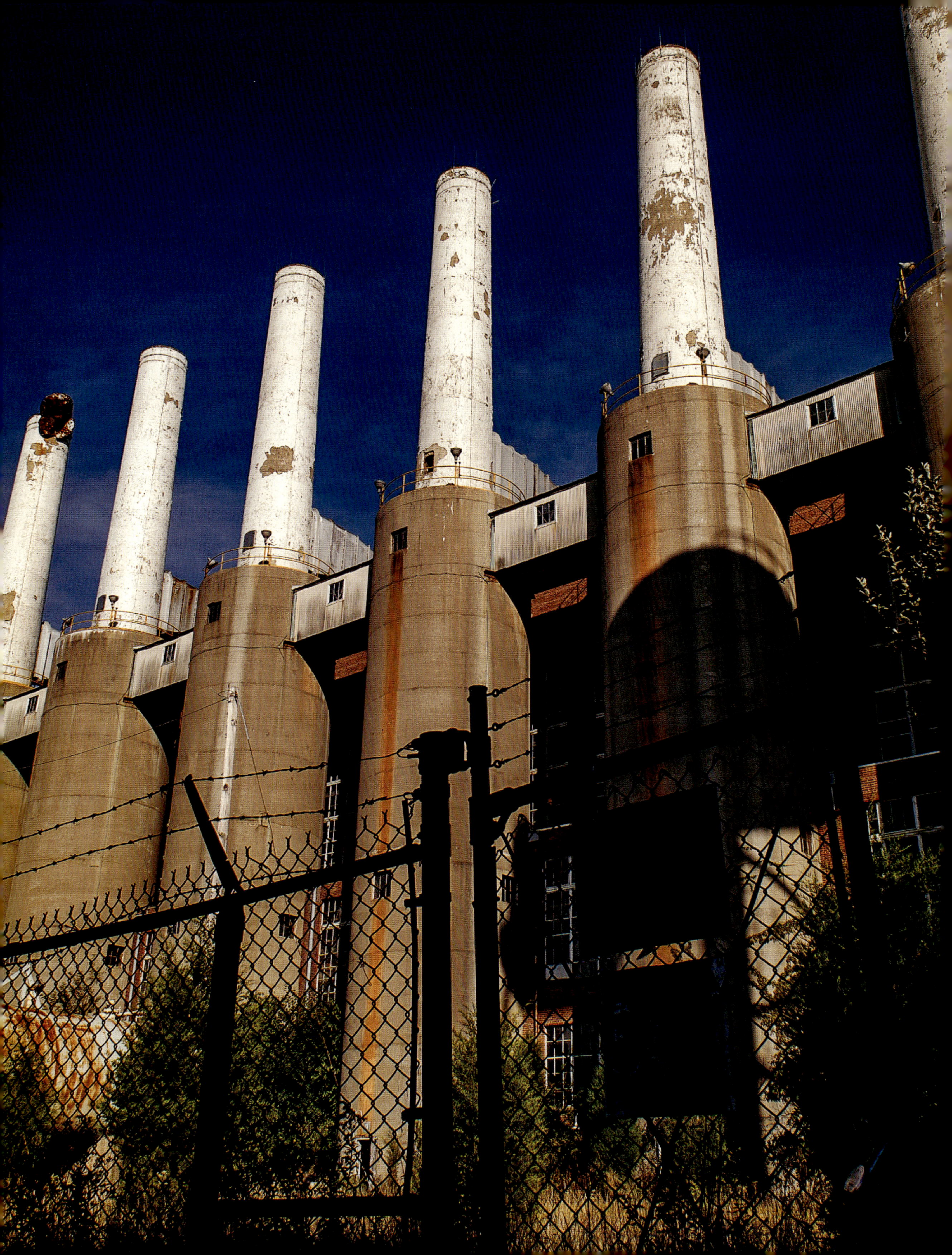

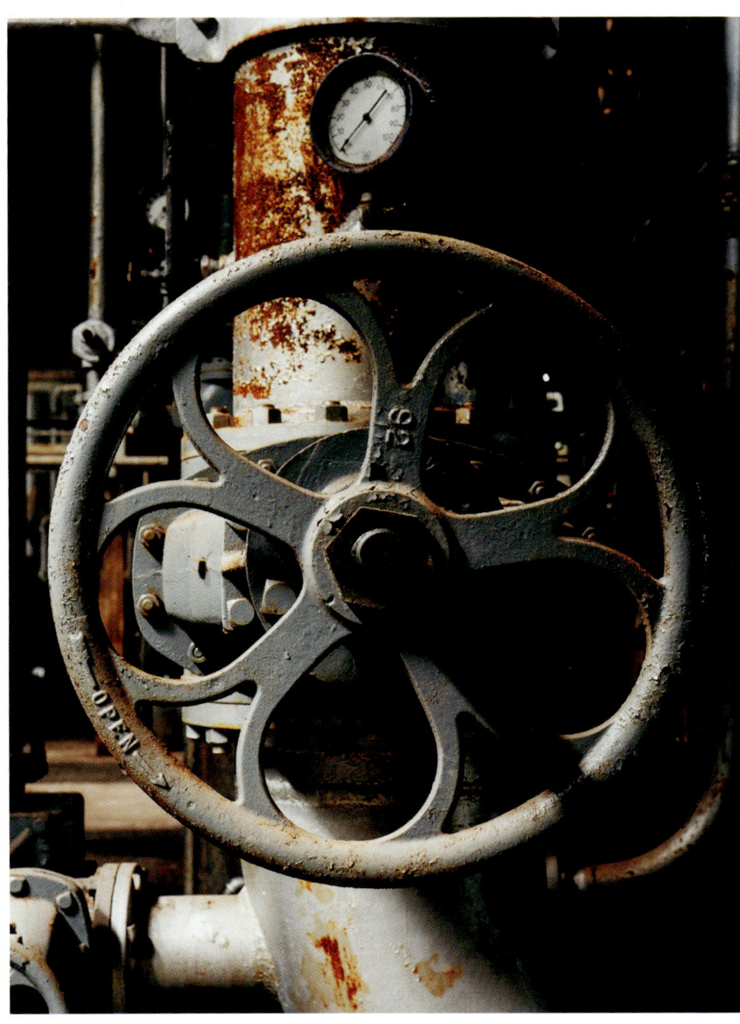

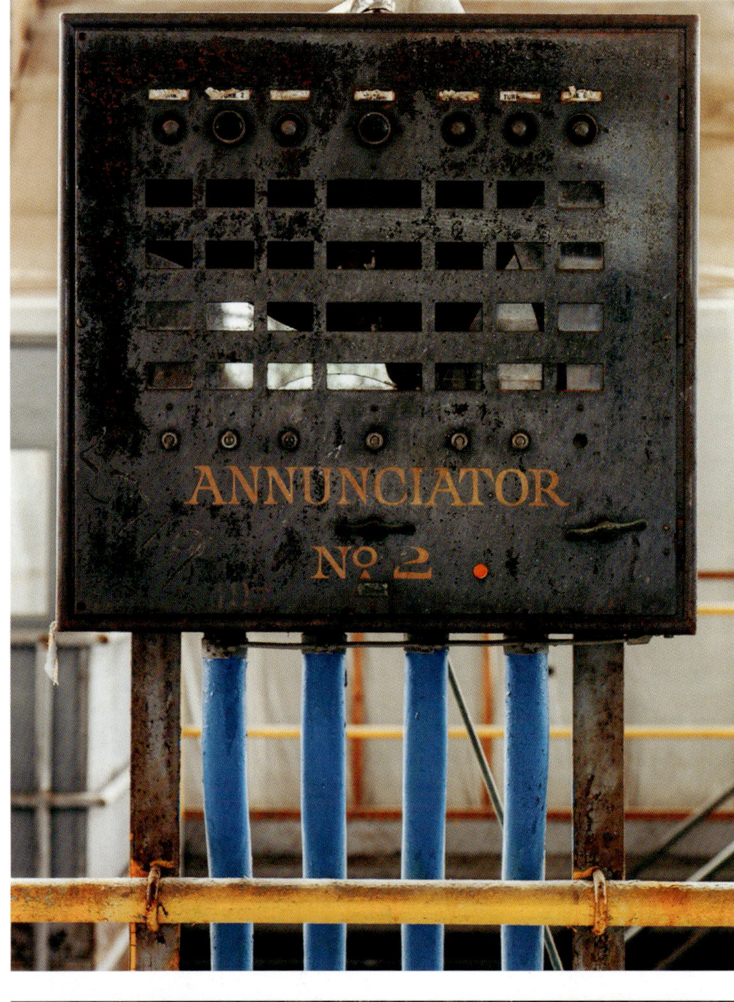

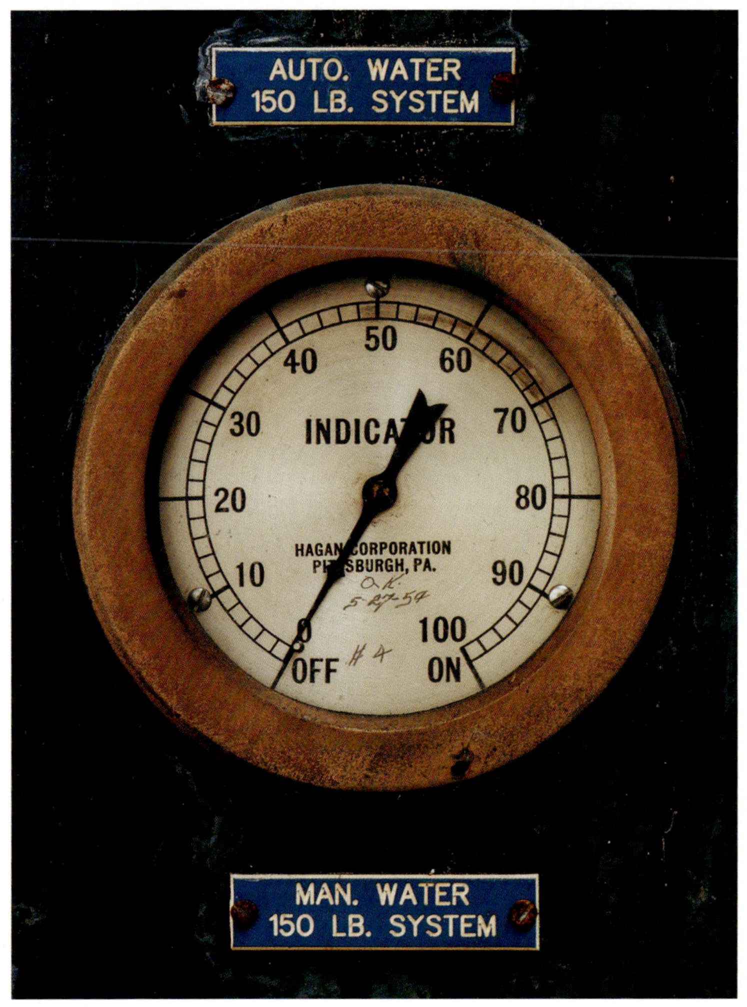

OPPOSITE:

Indiana Army Ammunitions Plant, Charlestown, Indiana, USA

From 1941 to 2012 the five stacks of INAAP marked the site of the world's largest smokeless powder factory. By the time of its closure in 1992, employee numbers had dwindled from 17,585 in 1945, to 750. It was said to be the largest abandoned industrial site in the USA, its buildings and grounds heavily contaminated by toxic chemicals. A long-term demolition and clearance project began in 2004.

ALL PHOTOGRAPHS ON THIS PAGE:

Indiana Army Ammunitions Plant, Charlestown, Indiana, USA

In a huge explosives complex, safety was a permanent issue. Water sprinkler systems were installed to deal with fires, with manual and automatic controls. Annunciators were electric monitor panels which flashed warning lights in the event of any failure in the circuits. In the fifty-year working history of the plant the only serious explosion was one which destroyed two storage 'igloos', killing three workers, in April 1966.

Fisher Body Plant 21, Detroit, Michigan, USA
Fisher Body, part of General Motors since 1926, constructed car bodies for various GM marques. This six-storey plant on Piquette Street was built in 1919 to the design of Albert Kahn on similar lines to his earlier Packard plant. It closed on 1 April 1984 and has been disused since 1993. The interior is stripped but is still contaminated by toxic residues.

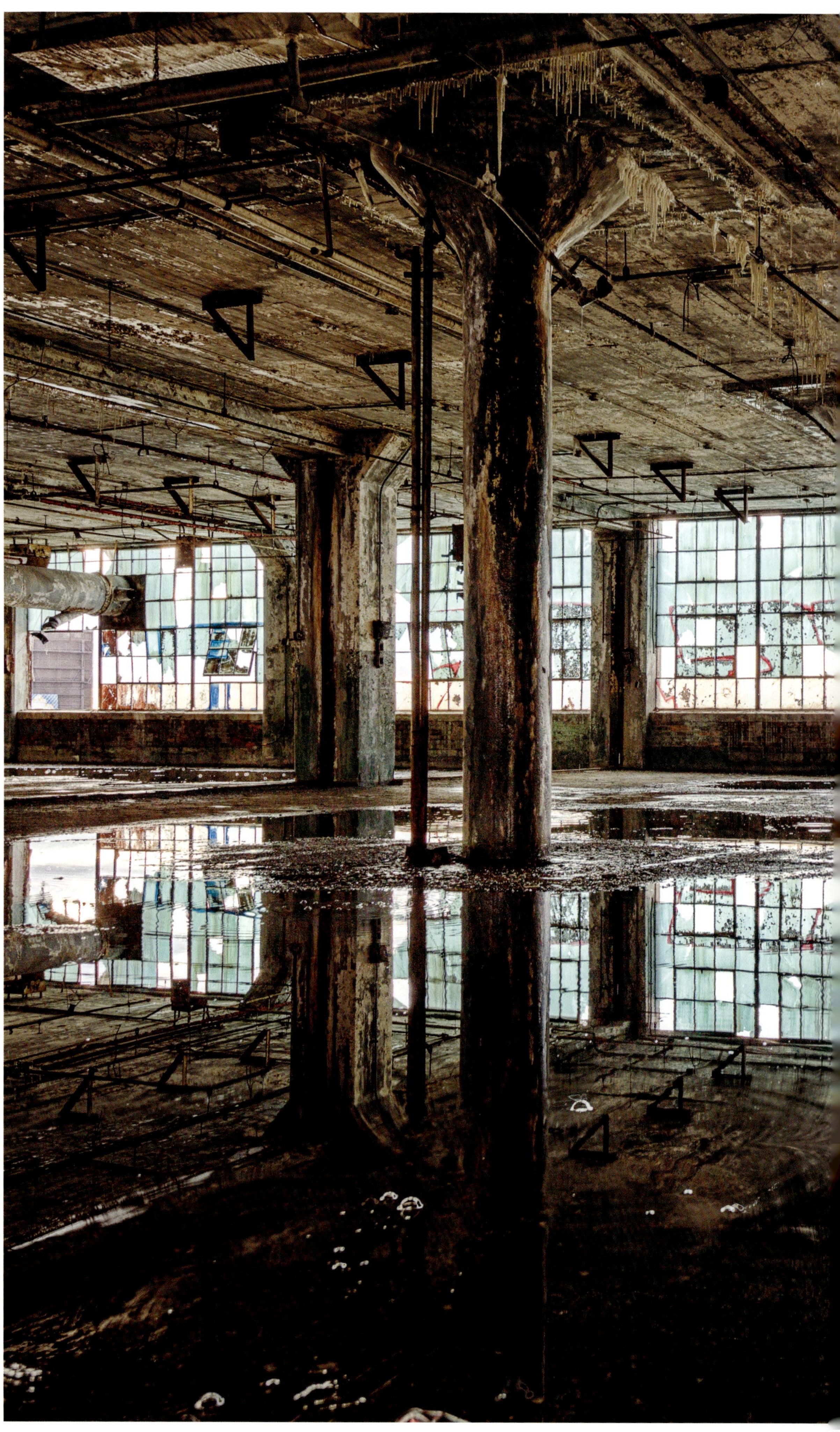

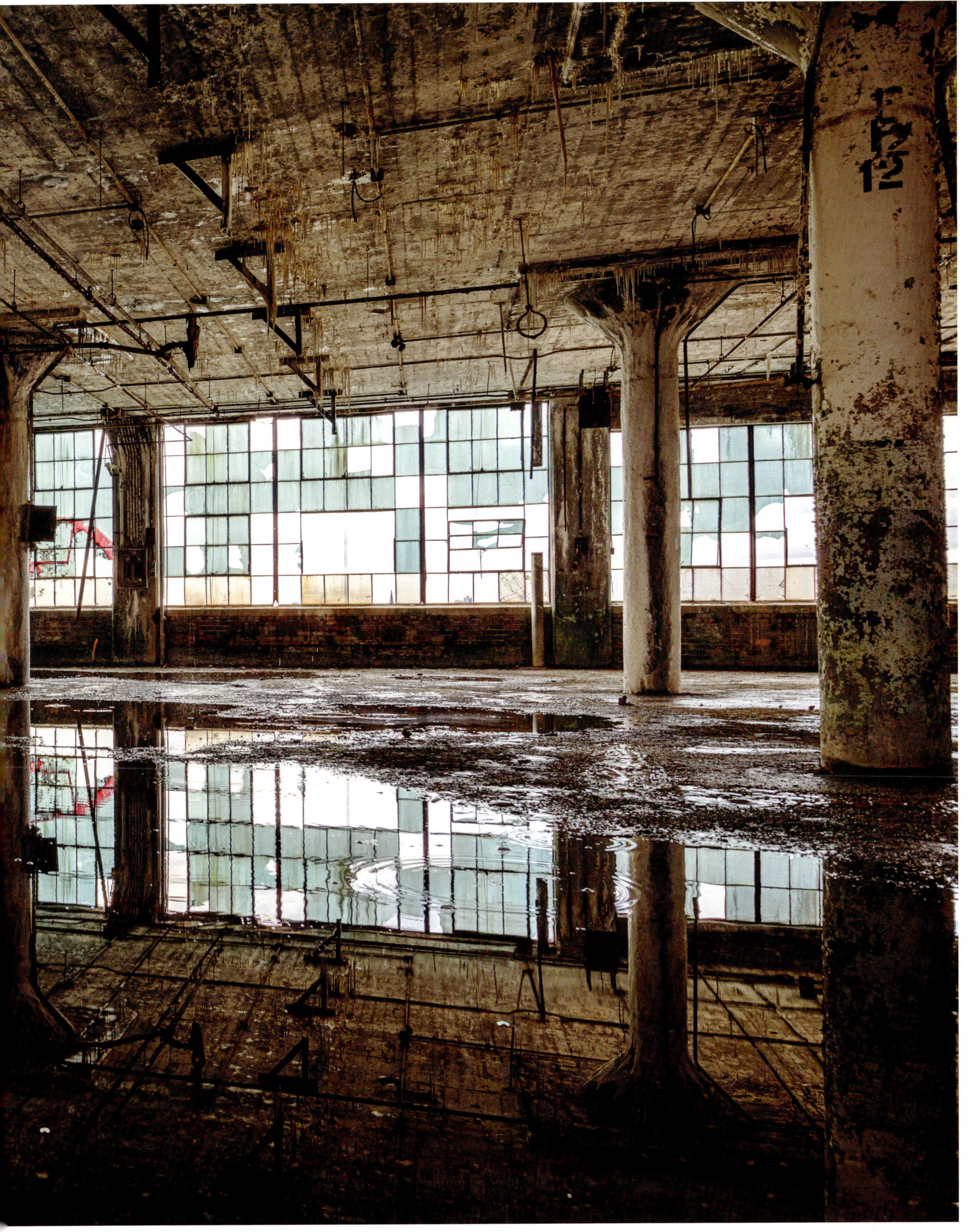

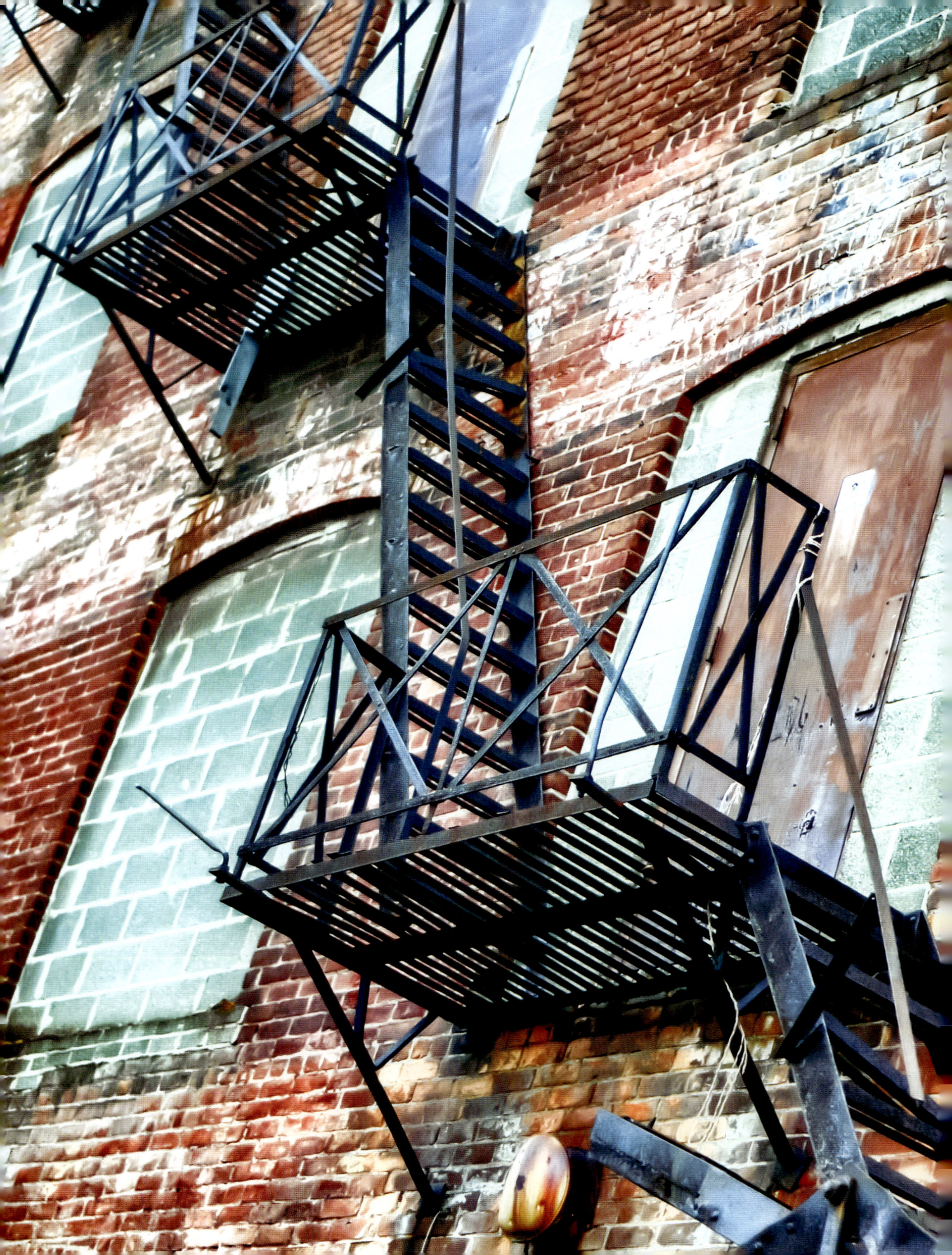

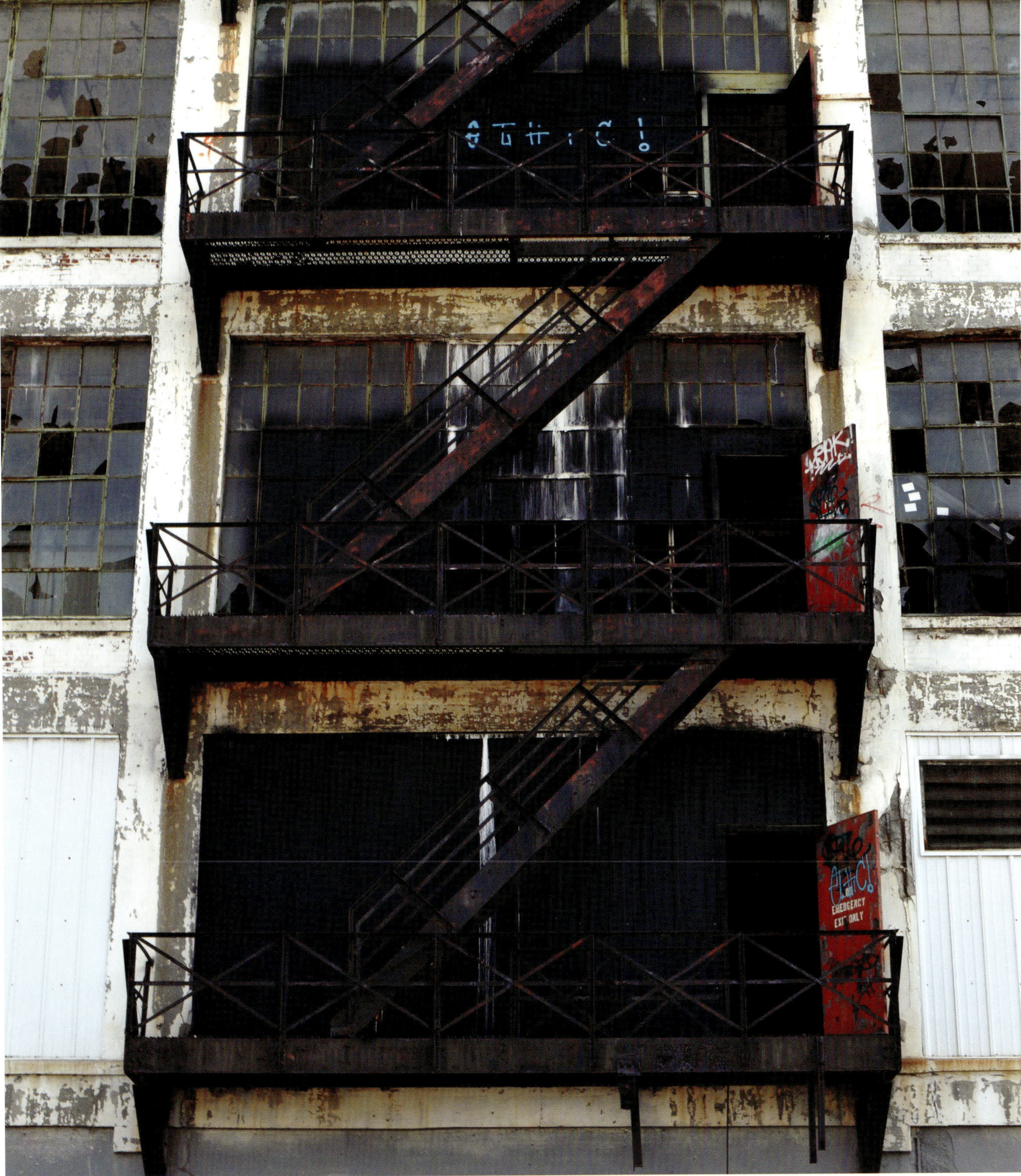

OPPOSITE:

Cartercar Factory, First Street, Pontiac, Michigan, USA

The Cartercar was a now largely forgotten American marque from 1905 to 1915. Its factory in Pontiac was built in 1907, and like others at the time was a multi-storey construction, though of brick on an iron frame rather than of concrete. Fire precautions were normally insisted on by insurance companies and external fire escape stairs were fitted. The ladder type here contrasts with the stair-type in the above image.

ABOVE:

Fisher Body Plant 21, Detroit, Michigan, USA

An external view showing how the large windows incorporate fire escape doors. These stairs are of use to urban explorers, though often the lowest set of steps has been removed or hinged up to prevent illicit access.

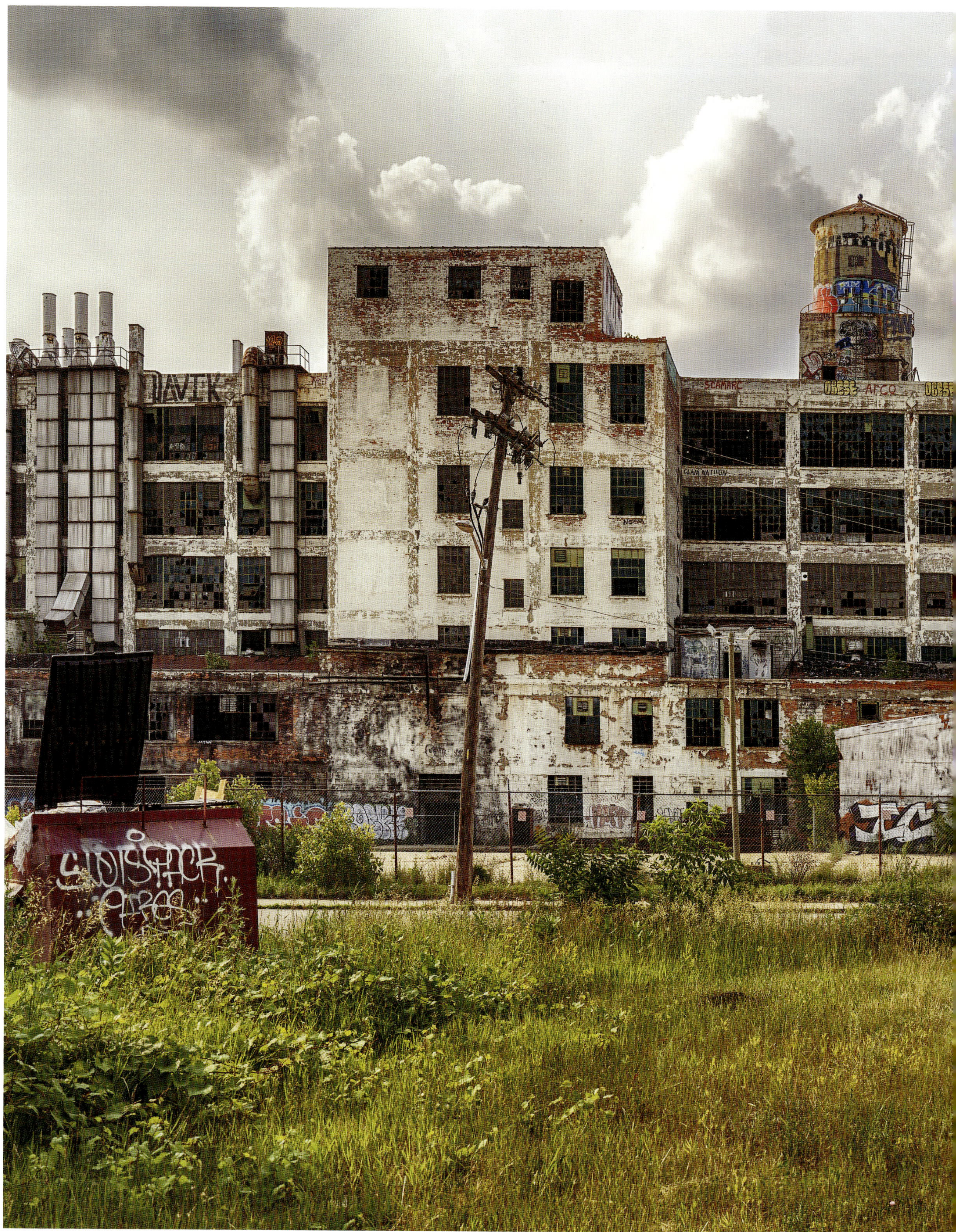

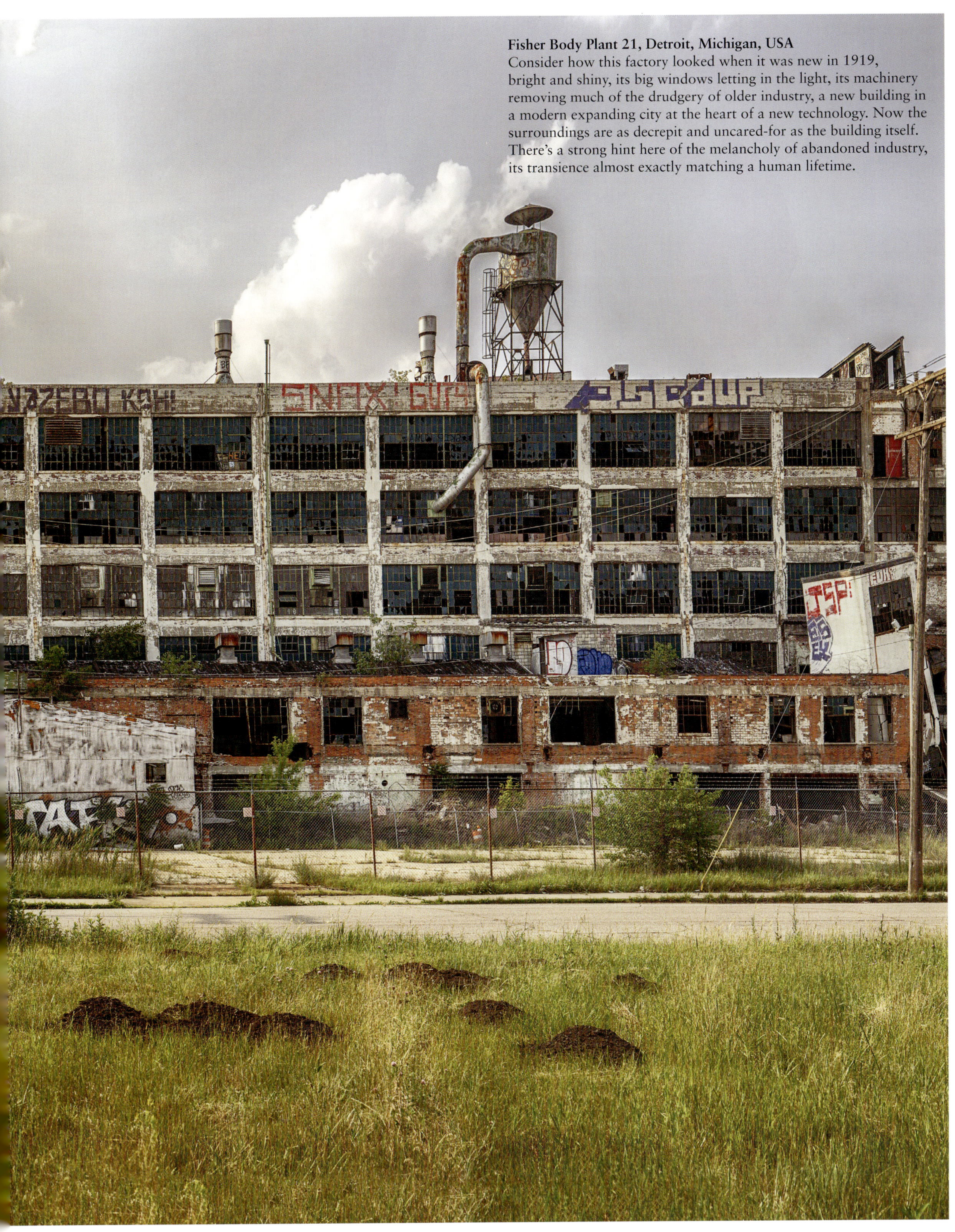

Fisher Body Plant 21, Detroit, Michigan, USA
Consider how this factory looked when it was new in 1919, bright and shiny, its big windows letting in the light, its machinery removing much of the drudgery of older industry, a new building in a modern expanding city at the heart of a new technology. Now the surroundings are as decrepit and uncared-for as the building itself. There's a strong hint here of the melancholy of abandoned industry, its transience almost exactly matching a human lifetime.

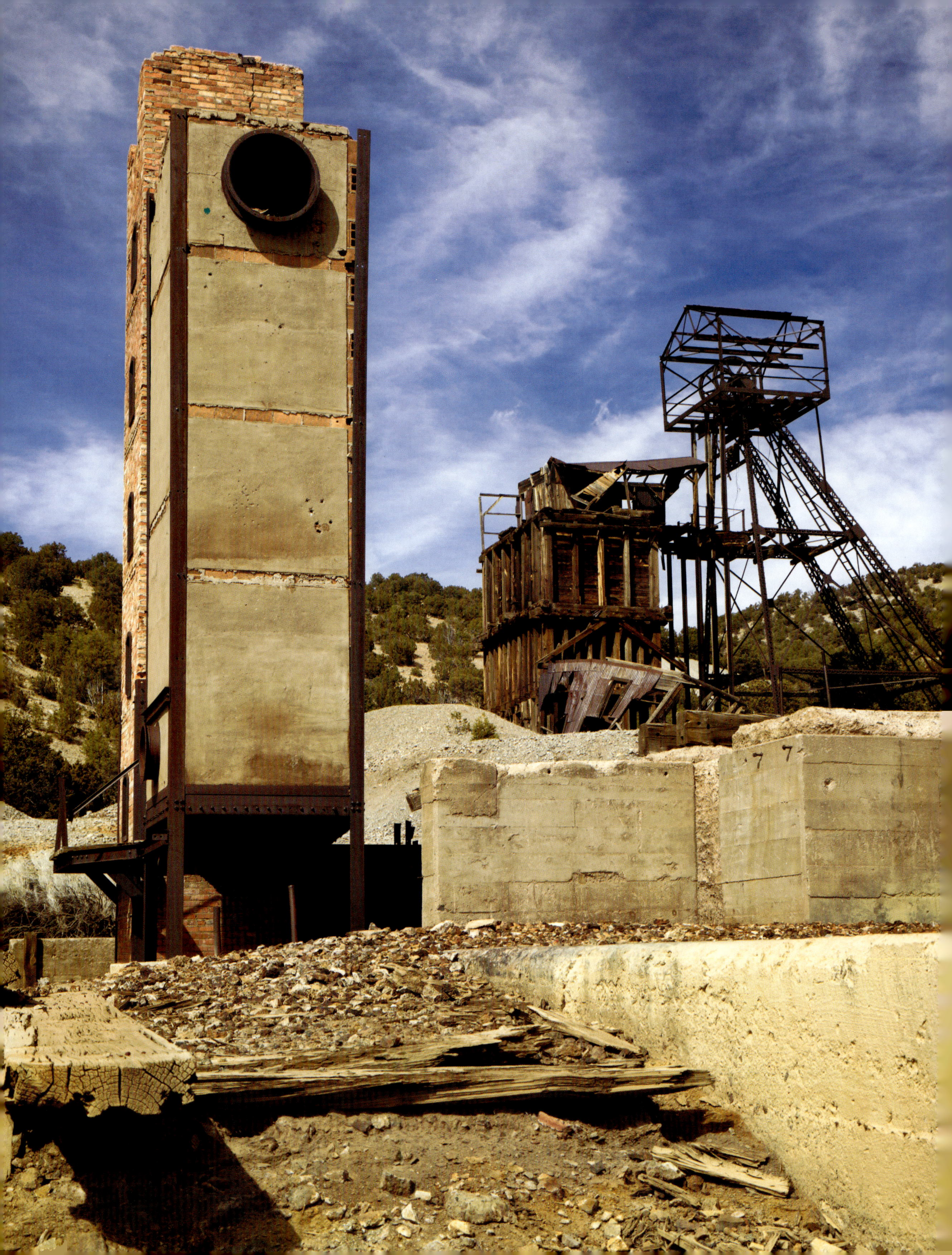

Kelly Mine, Socorro, New Mexico, USA
This was a multi-mineral mine bringing up zinc, lead, copper, gold and silver from 1878 to 1957. Once the mine was closed there was nothing to sustain the local community and Kelly became a ghost town. Still standing are two smelting towers, one of brick and a more recent one of iron and concrete; and the headframe with its winding wheels.

Mariscal Mine, Big Bend National Park, Texas, USA
Cinnabar ore was dug out here, to be refined as mercury. Seen from below its remains might resemble temples of some strange cult, but they housed condensing chambers, a furnace room, storage space and workers' accommodation. At one time it produced almost a quarter of the USA's mercury supplies, but it has been abandoned since 1943.

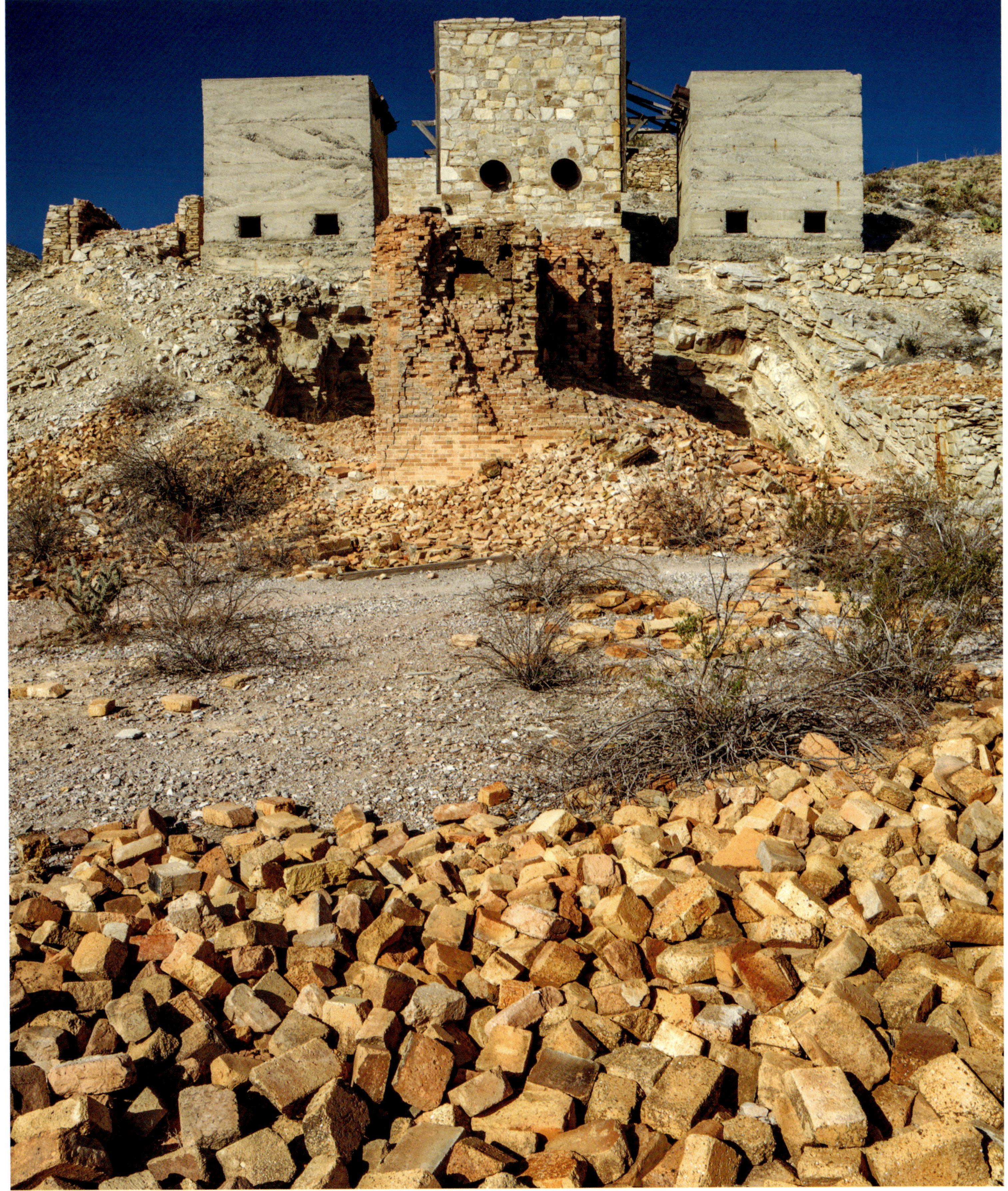

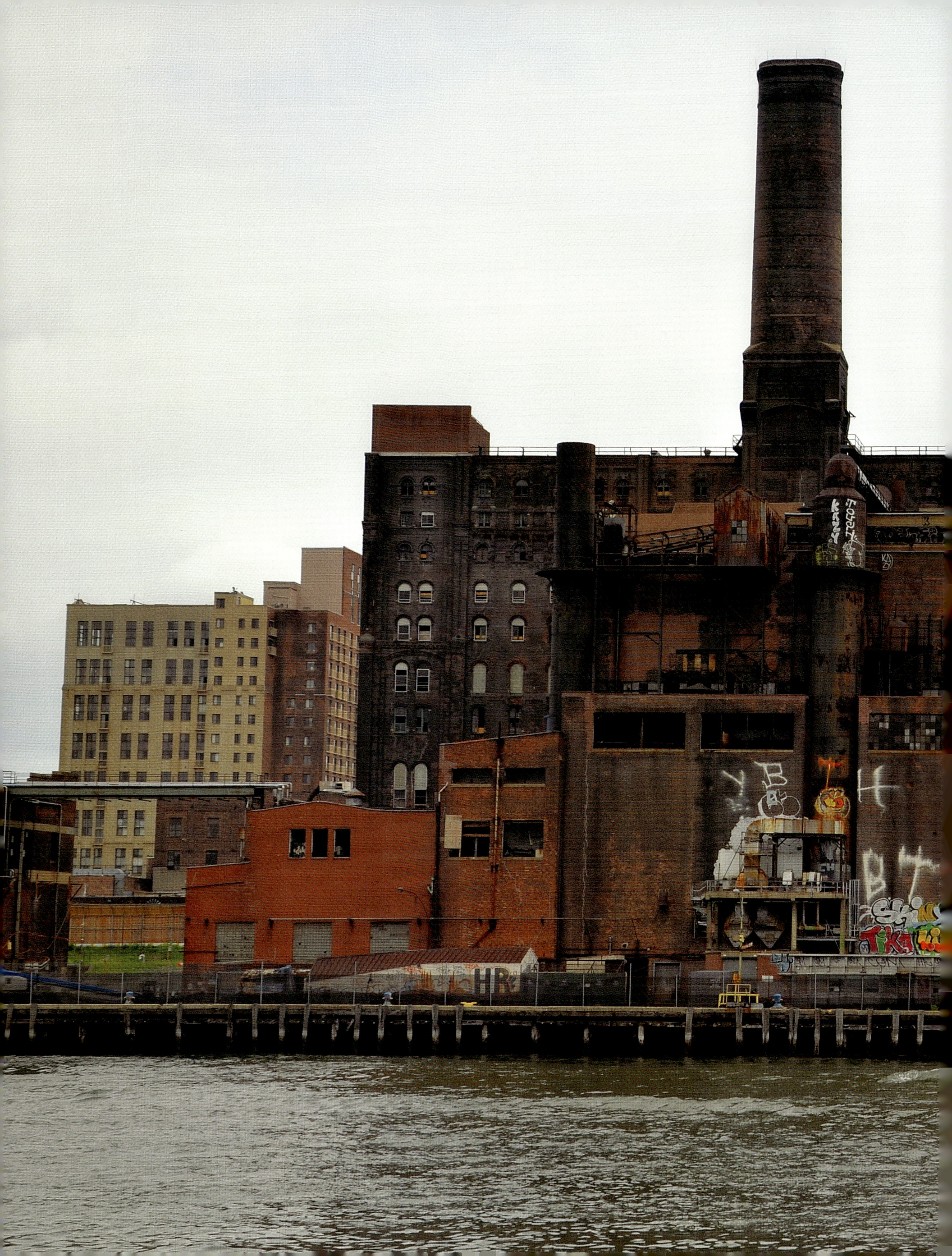

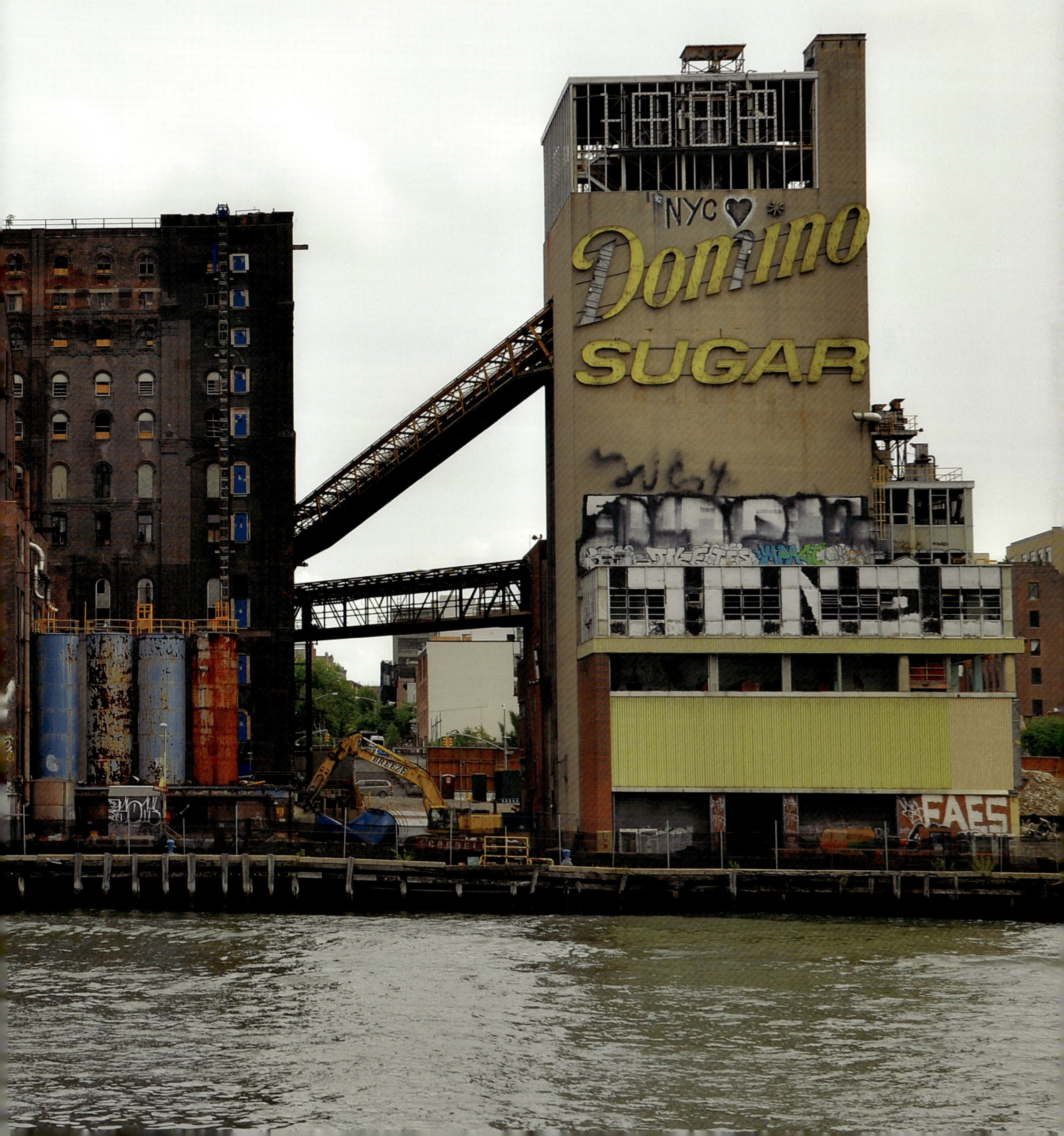

Domino Sugar Factory, Brooklyn, New York, USA
Time-worn and redundant, the Domino factory still shows an architectural care and finish that contrasts with the more modern, featureless buildings behind and its own ugly companion. This and the wharfside buildings have been demolished but the main block, with its elegant double smokestack, is due for restoration in a grand revamp of the waterfront area.

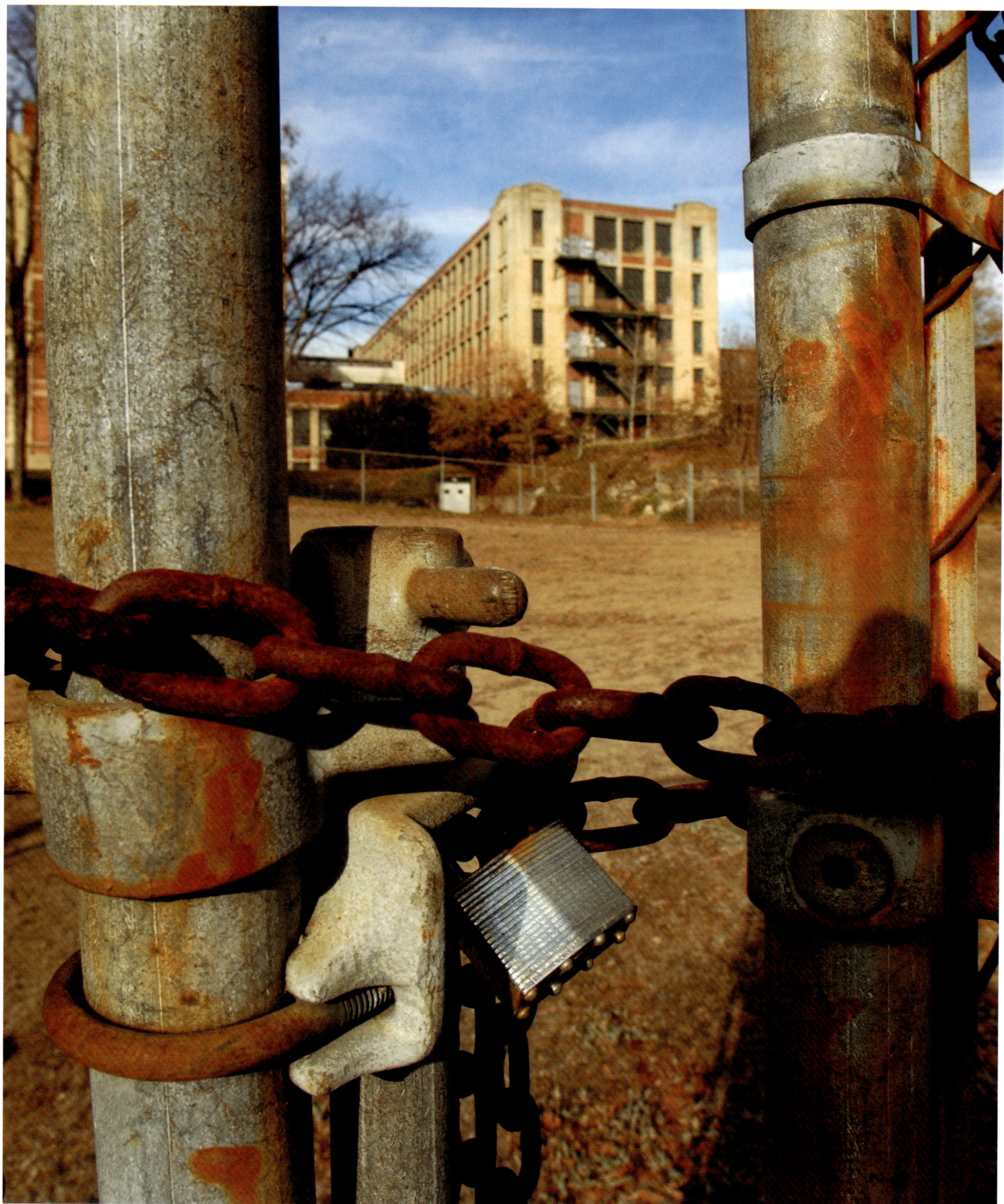

Stenton Trust Mills, Sanford, Maine, USA
Behind these locked gates stood part of a once-vast complex of textile mills dating back to 1867. These buildings were erected in the 1920s. Unused since 1955, one block was ravaged by fire in 2017 and finally demolished in 2019.

Bethlehem Steel Plant, Pennsylvania, USA
It looks as though a lithe intruder could slip easily into the locked complex. Actually informative tours are available, taking visitors round the blast furnaces, moulding troughs, chemical retorts, catwalks and gantries of the industrial colossus which ceased the white-hot business of steel production in 1995.

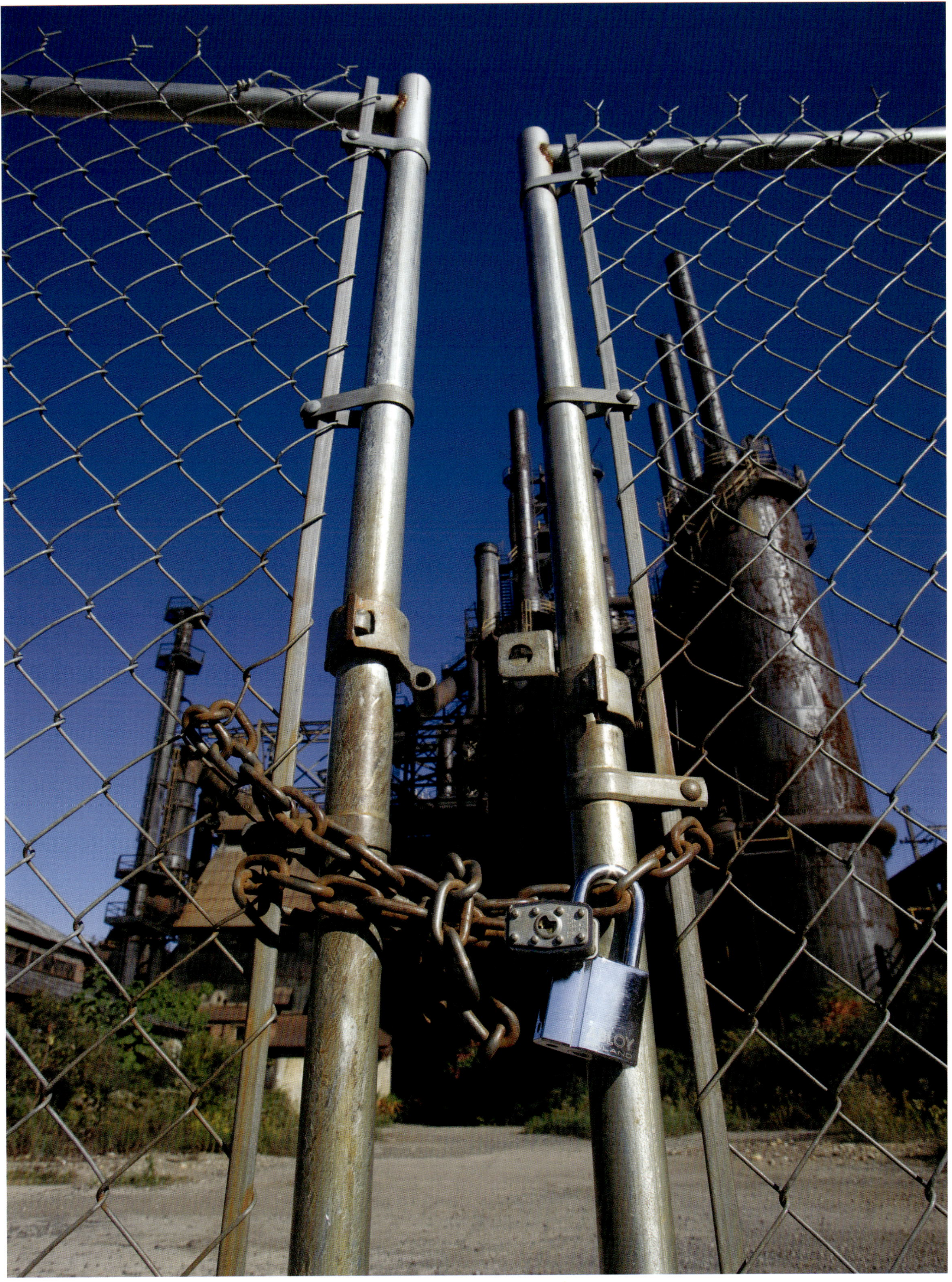

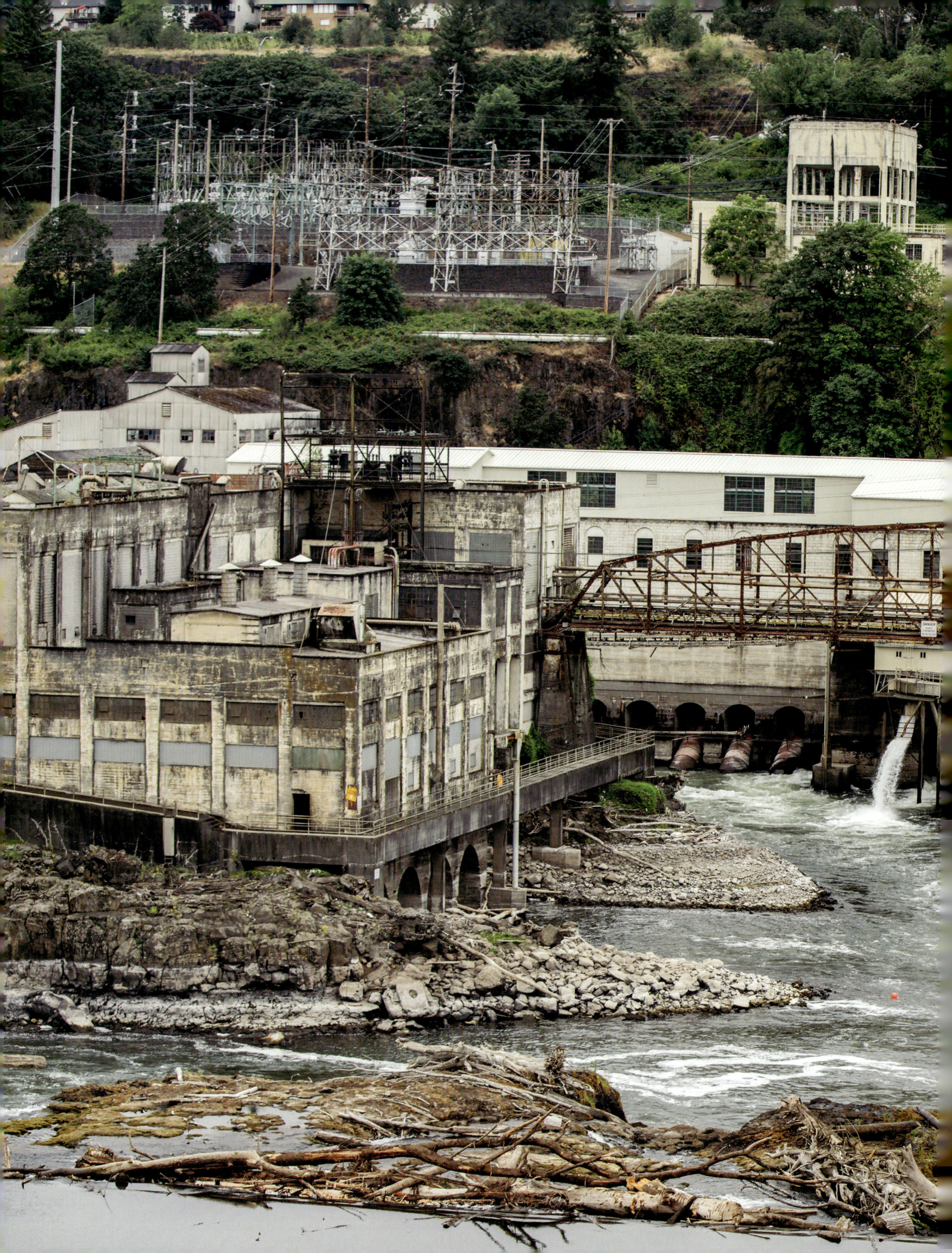

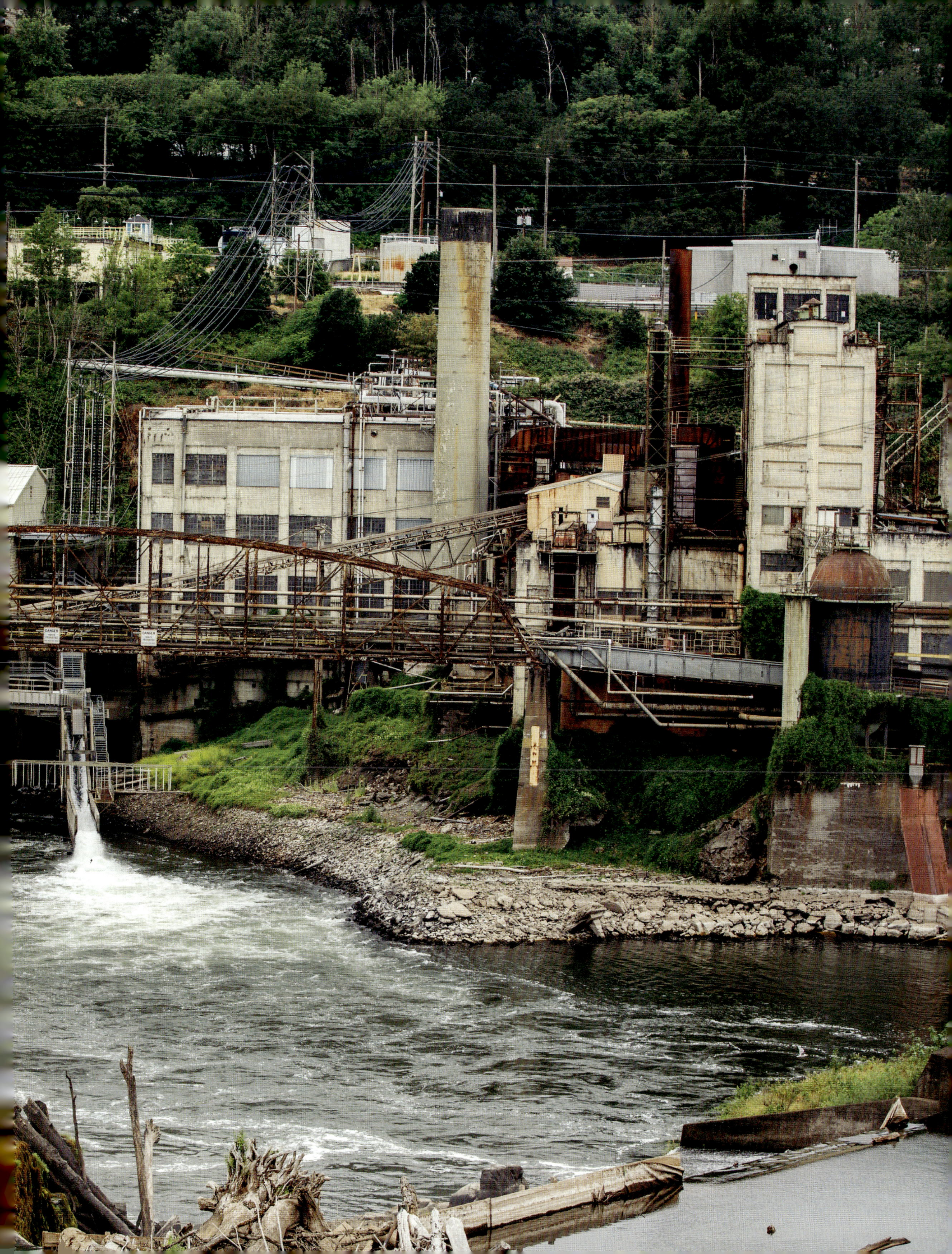

Blue Heron Paper Mill, Willamette Falls, Oregon, USA

Wood, electric power, water … the dense array of poles, wires, piping, spillways, conveyors and ventilators display graphically what a paper mill needed to function. Power generation from the falls prompted the establishment of a mill in the 1880s. Most of the buildings on the 23-acre site are 20th century. Local First Nation groups were displaced when sawmilling began here in the 1850s: now the Confederated Tribes of Grand Ronde are repurchasing their old home ground.

BELOW:

Oil Derrick, Maricopa, San Joaquin Valley, California, USA

Rich oil reserves here were exploited from the early 20th century. The remains of many pumpjacks like this can be seen, and others are still at work. They operate on the principle of a suction pump: a rod is lowered into the well from a weighted beam, then lifted, raising the pressure in the well-shaft and drawing up oil behind it. Pumpjacks are used when oil lies near the surface, at low pressure.

RIGHT:

Harmony Borax Works, Furnace Creek, Death Valley, California, USA

Borax is a mineral which, when reduced to powder, is used in bleaching and cleaning and various chemical processes. The Harmony Works flourished briefly between 1883 and 1889, digging out local deposits, boiling the ore to powder, and using wagon teams of 20 mules to haul the milled powder to the nearest railhead.

BELOW RIGHT:

Inyo Mine, Echo Canyon, Death Valley National Park, California, USA

The mining equipment surviving here represents the victory of reality over expectations. Including a 50-ton (45.3-tonne) ore bin, an ore crusher and ball mill, it was installed by different owners over several decades, following the discovery of high-grade ores which always turned out to be in small deposits. Since 1941 it has been unworked.

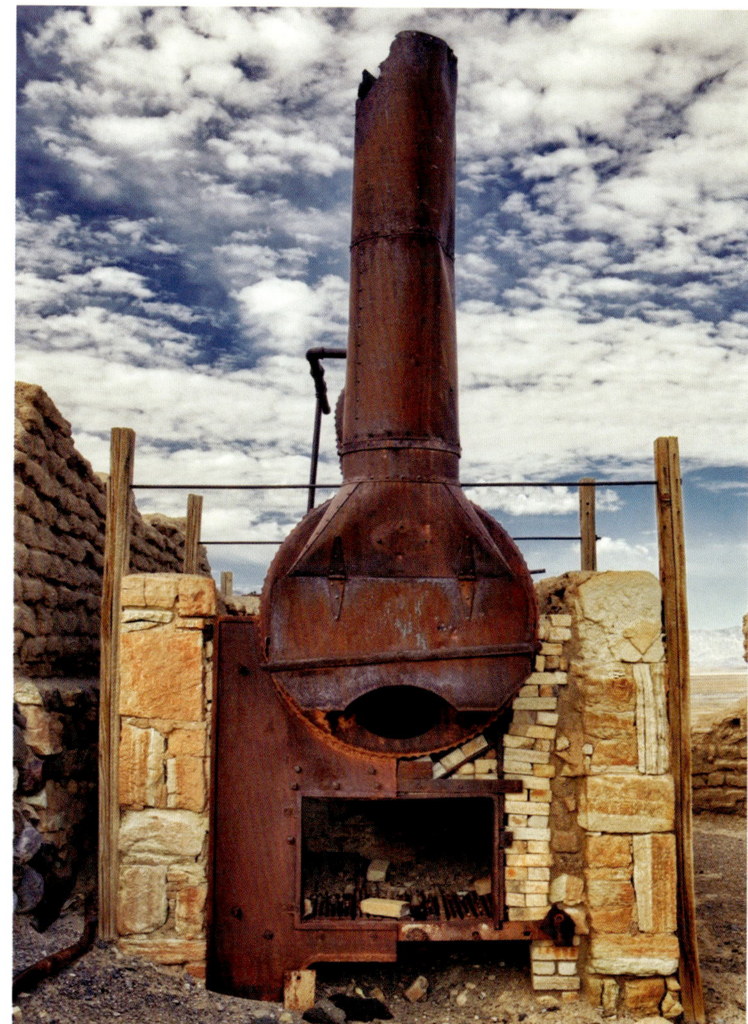

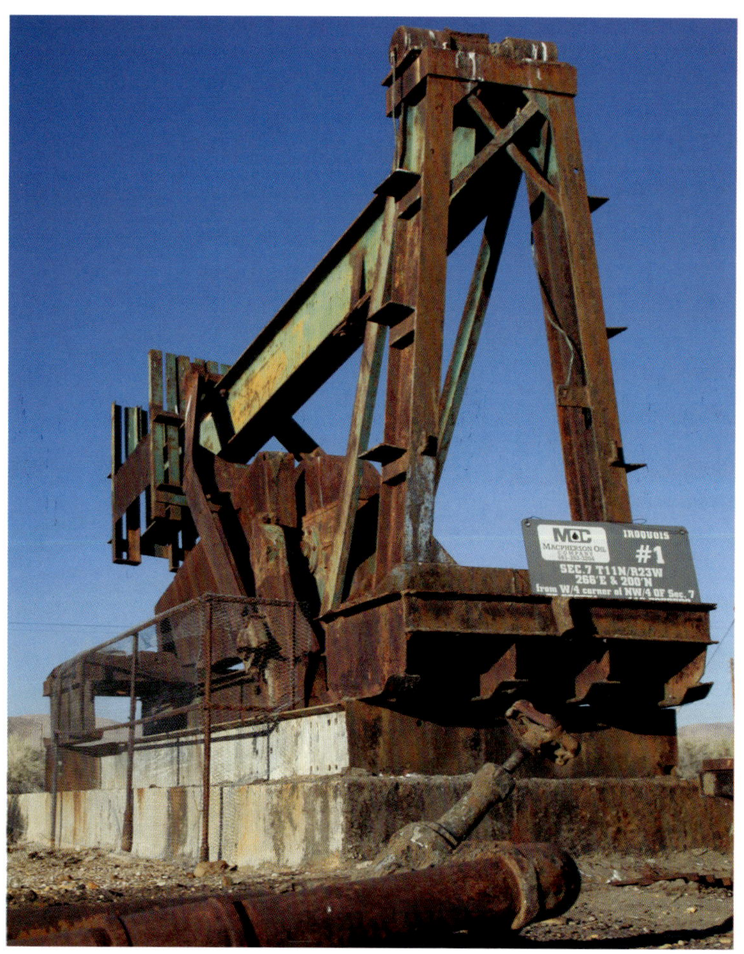

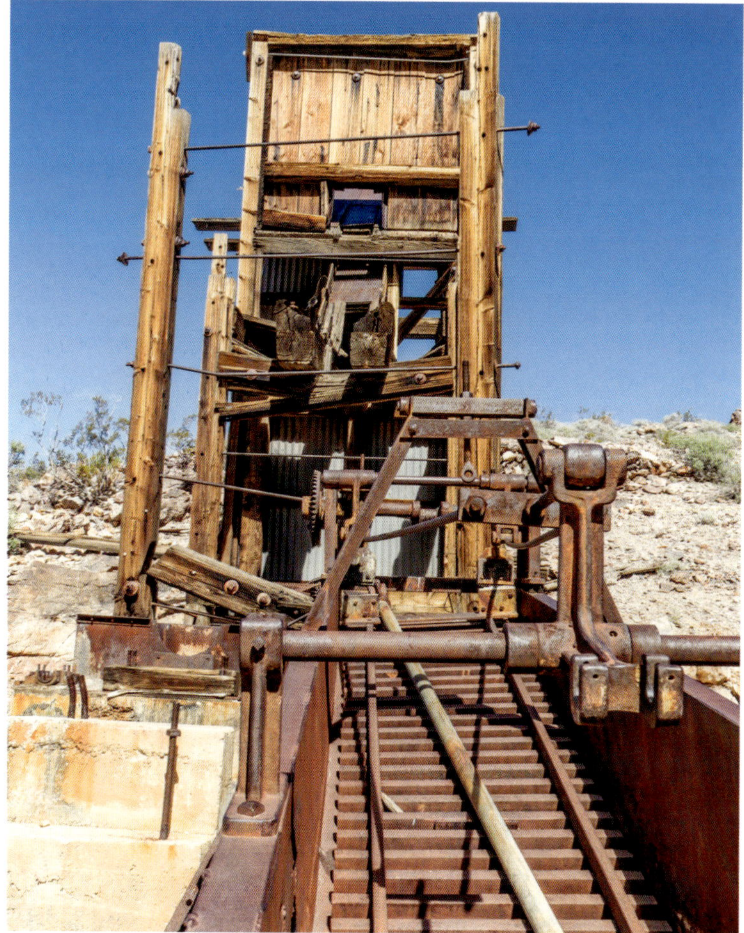

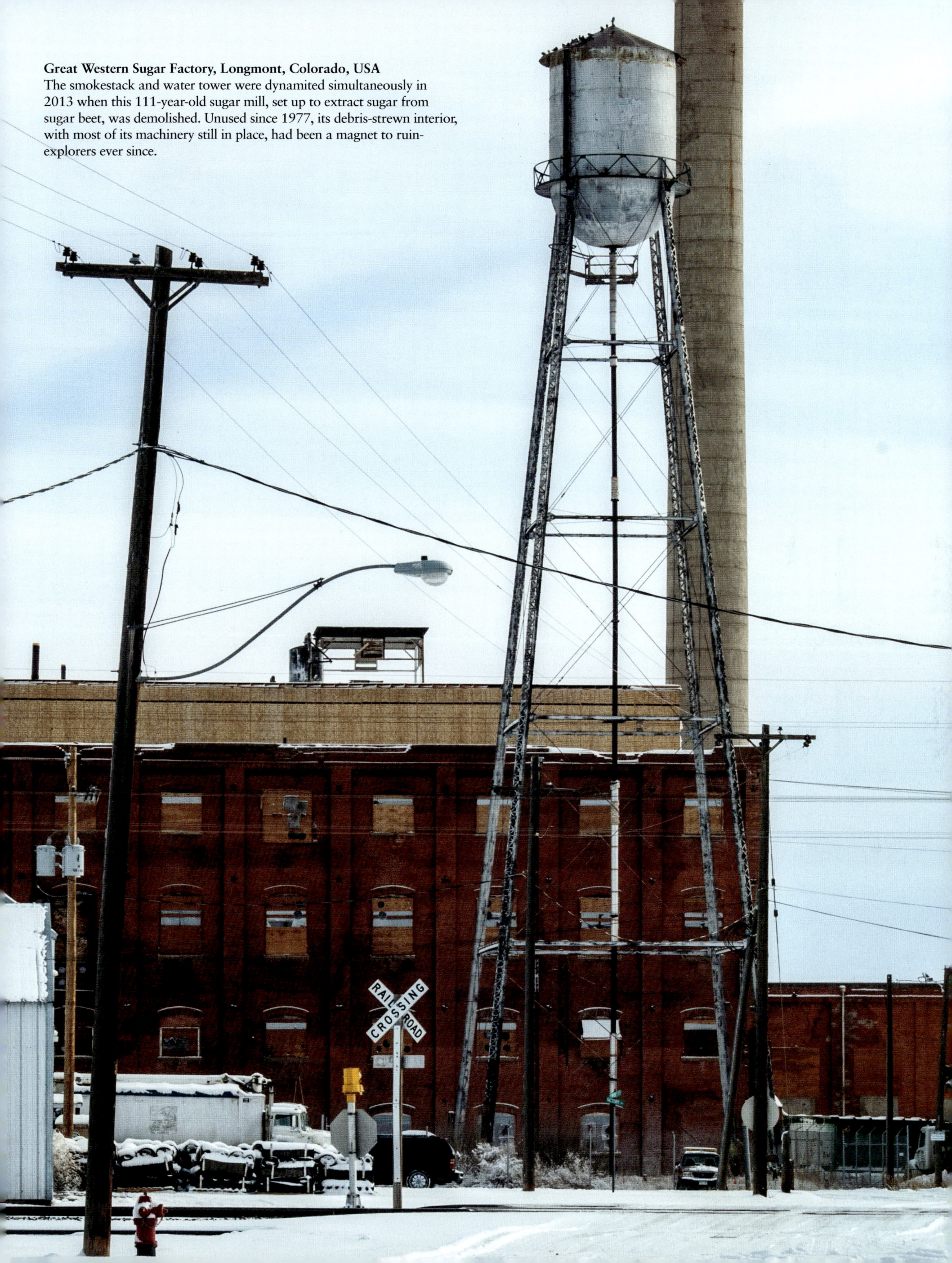

Great Western Sugar Factory, Longmont, Colorado, USA
The smokestack and water tower were dynamited simultaneously in 2013 when this 111-year-old sugar mill, set up to extract sugar from sugar beet, was demolished. Unused since 1977, its debris-strewn interior, with most of its machinery still in place, had been a magnet to ruin-explorers ever since.

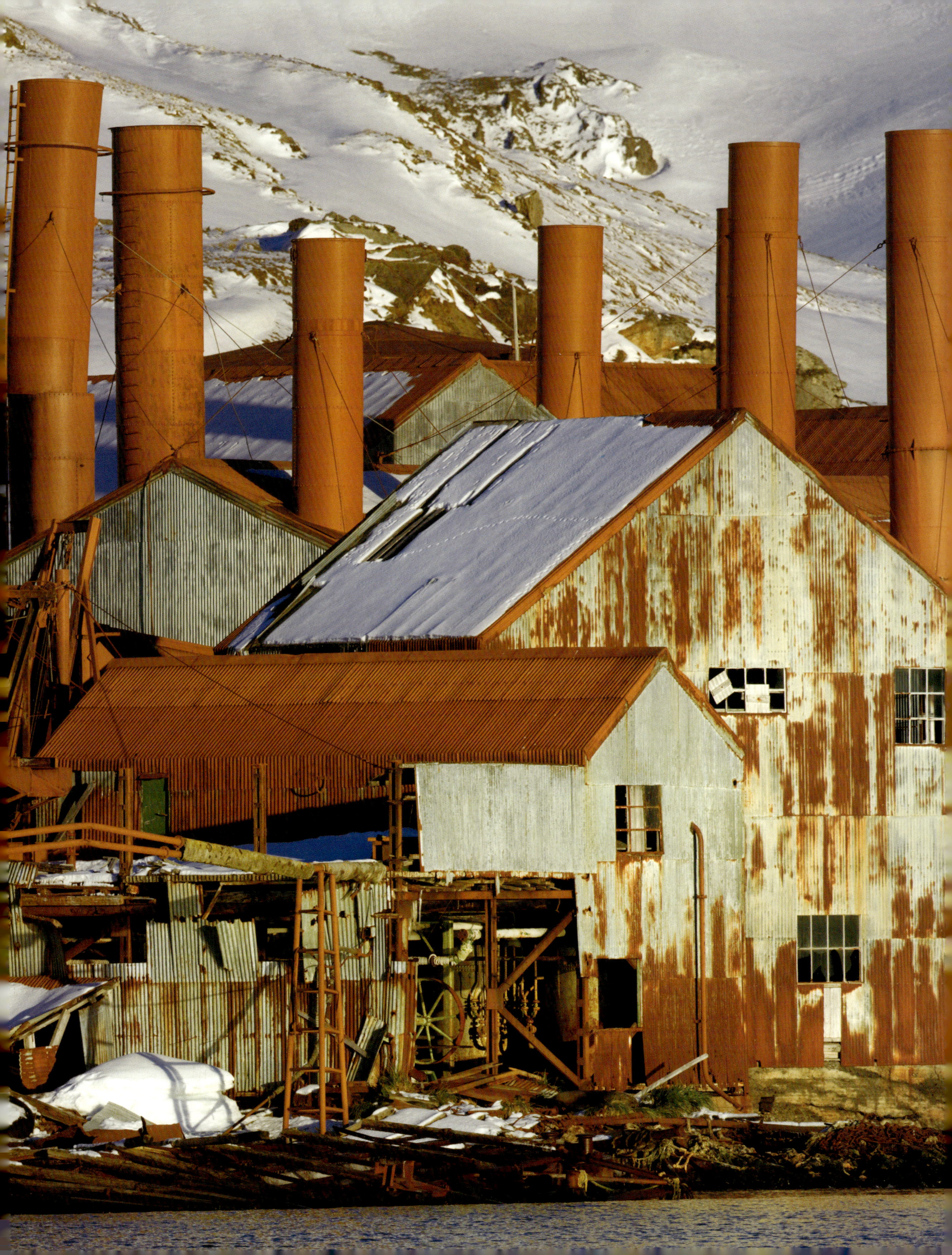

Central and South America

The exploitation of natural resources lies behind much of the industrial relics of South America: minerals were dug out using tools and machinery brought in from Europe. Often the gold and silver mines enlarged smaller ones from earlier times. The demand for precious metals led to the establishment of towns in extremely inhospitable locations, high in the Andes or on the windswept sub-Arctic islands when the whaling industry's shift from the whale-depleted northern hemisphere to the South Atlantic brought a transient rough lifestyle. Motor magnate Henry Ford attempted to create his own rubber-growing kingdom in the Amazon jungle. Large-scale cattle farming led to the need for huge slaughterhouses, with canning plants alongside. Establishments like these could be closed at a day's notice depending on the movement of capital and commodity markets in London or New York.

'Heritage' preserved sites are found here, though not as frequently as in Europe and North America. These industries were introduced, owned and largely manned by strangers. For centuries, slave or semi-slave labour was enforced when large numbers of manual workers were needed. What many of these sites offer is raw history, not curated, tidied up and explained, but exposing a past that can be touched and felt in a different way from a museum visit.

OPPOSITE:
**Stromness Whaling Station,
South Georgia**
An eerie feature of the tumbledown buildings here is the clashing and creaking of corrugated iron caused by the almost incessant wind. Today South Georgia is unpopulated by humans and access to the site is forbidden for safety reasons.

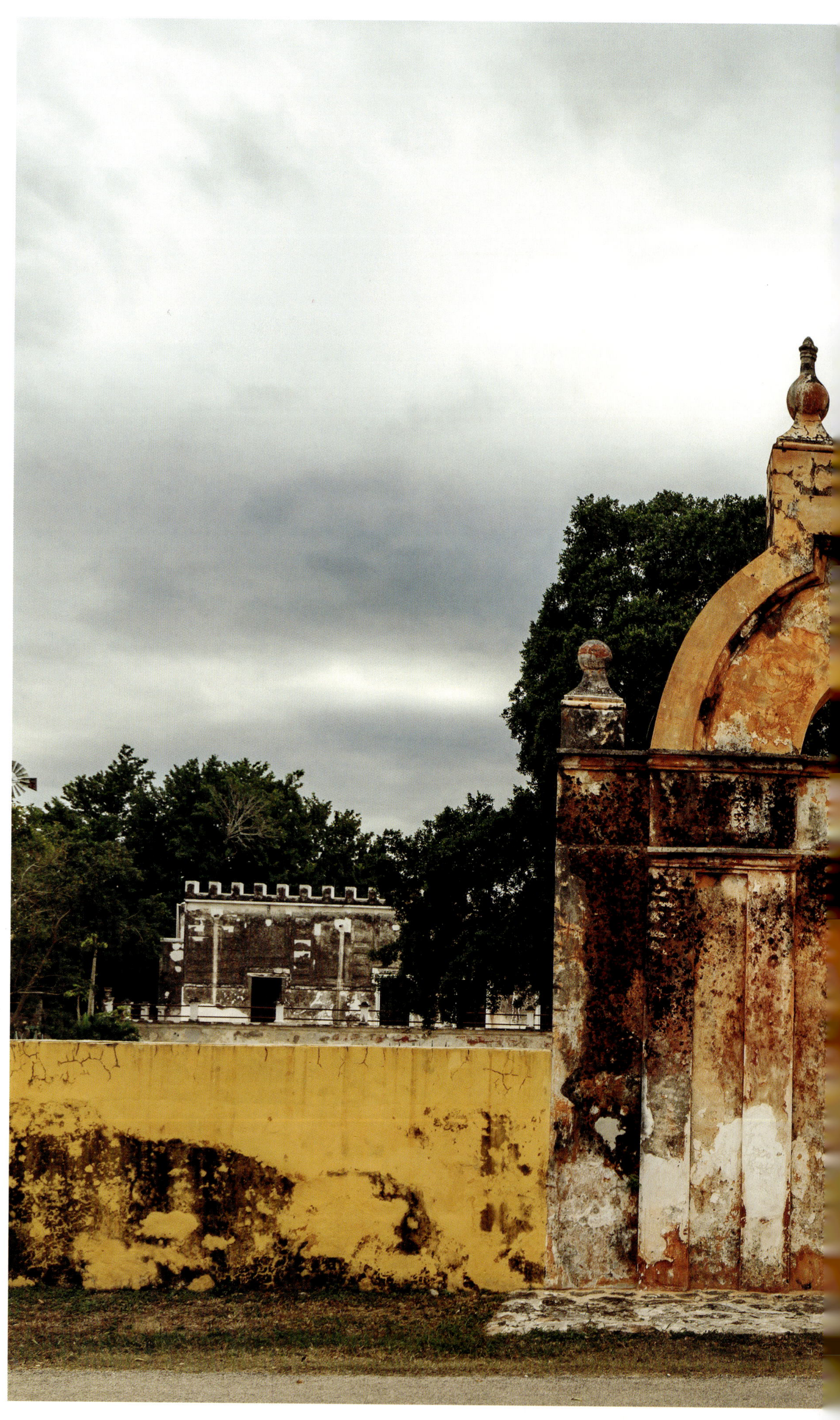

Hacienda Yaxcopoil, Yucatán, Mexico
Ornamental entrance gate of a vast estate founded in the 17th century. Its wealth, based on the culture and processing of sisal hemp, the main source of ropes and netting until the advent of artificial fibres, reached a peak in the 19th century. The cutting and shredding sheds, with their machinery, remain intact as an example of colonial industry.

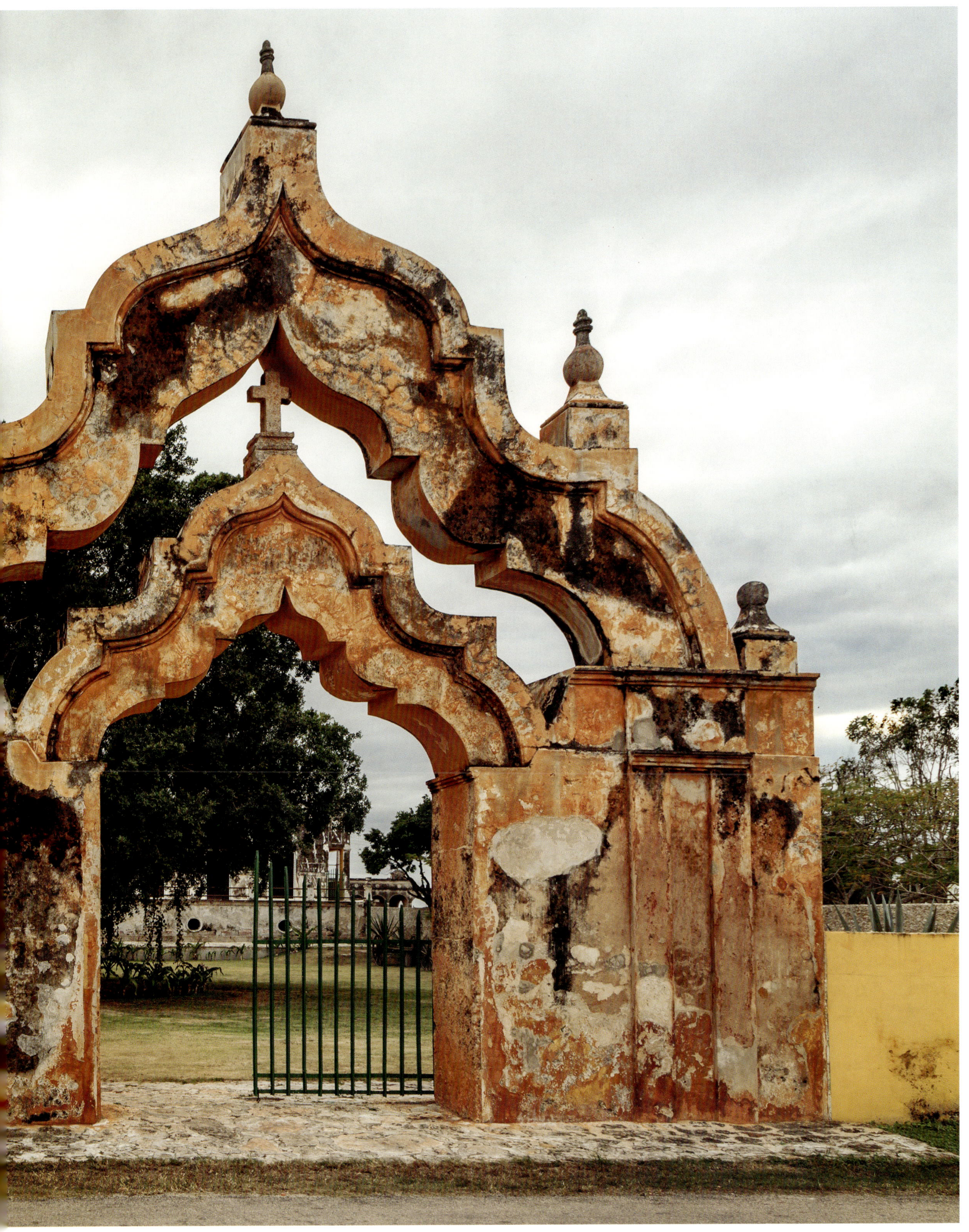

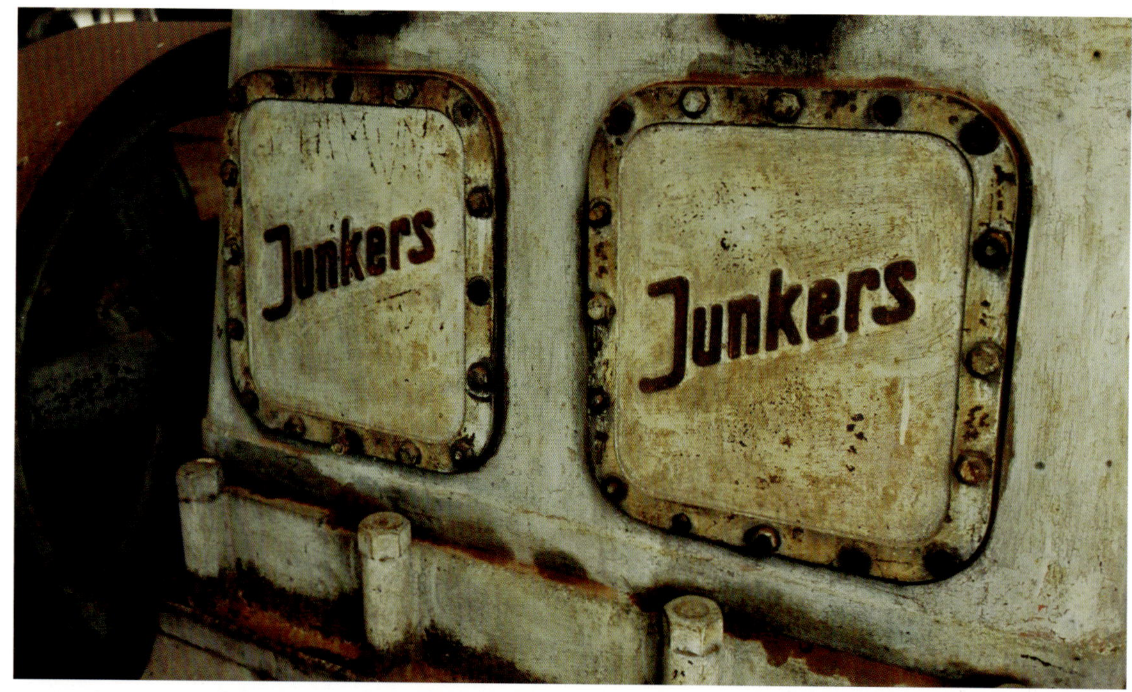

TOP RIGHT:

Rubber Works, Fordlandia, Pará State, Brazil

In 1928 motor magnate Henry Ford established a vast rubber plantation and factory in jungle country by the Amazon River, hoping to provide tyres for all his new cars. It was a disastrous failure, with nothing to show for an investment of over $20 million. Boilers and other machinery imported from Germany remain in the derelict factory.

BOTTOM RIGHT:

Coffee Processing Works, Pepperpot Plantation, Paramaribo, Suriname

The old coffee and cacao plantation is now a nature park. Production ended in 1996 but the grinding machines, roasting ovens (seen here) and other apparatus for large-scale coffee production can still be seen in the dilapidated wooden buildings.

OPPOSITE TOP LEFT AND BOTTOM:

Santa Laura Saltpetre Plant, Atacama Desert, Chile

Standing isolated in one of Earth's driest places, this plant leached, purified and recrystallised saltpetre (potassium nitrate) from local deposits for export to Europe. Its activity lasted from 1872 to 1960, since when the arid climate has helped to keep its machinery rust-free. With its adjacent ghost town it is a UNESCO World Heritage Site, restored after earthquake damage in 2014.

OPPOSITE TOP RIGHT:

Liebig Extract of Meat Factory, Fray Bentos, Uruguay

From 1859 to 1979 an increasingly large meat processing works turned live cattle into corned beef, tinned and exported to world markets. The town's name became a brand. Now the huge complex has been preserved as the 'Museum of the Industrial Revolution', displaying the process of industrial meat production.

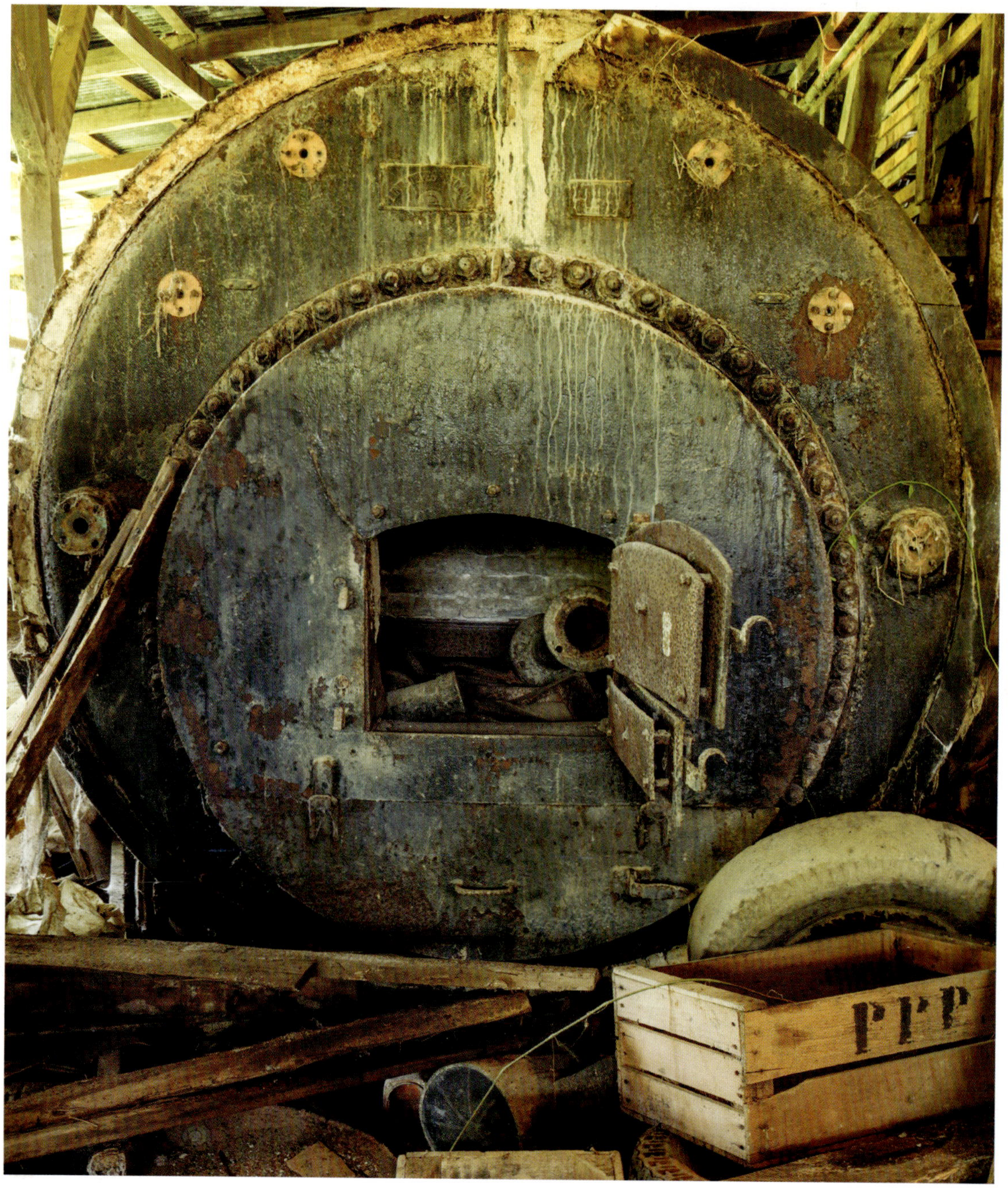

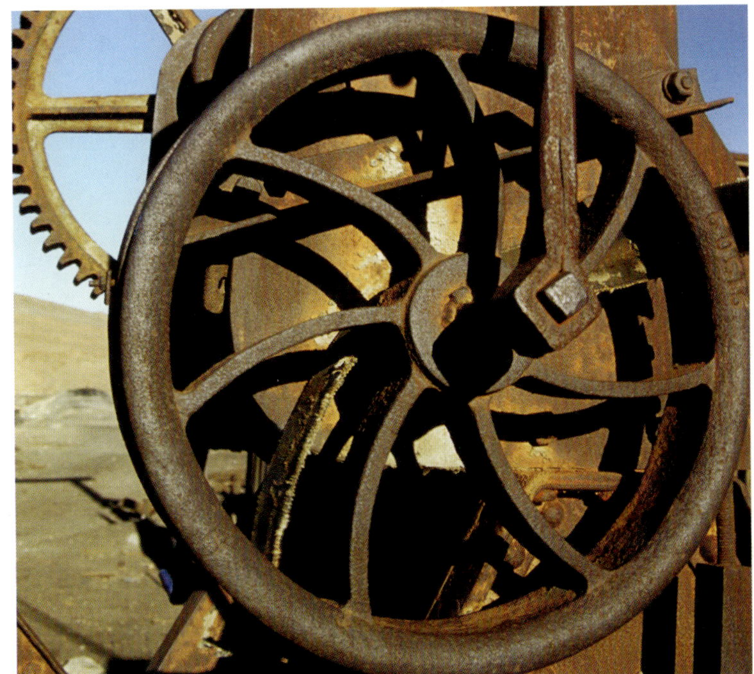
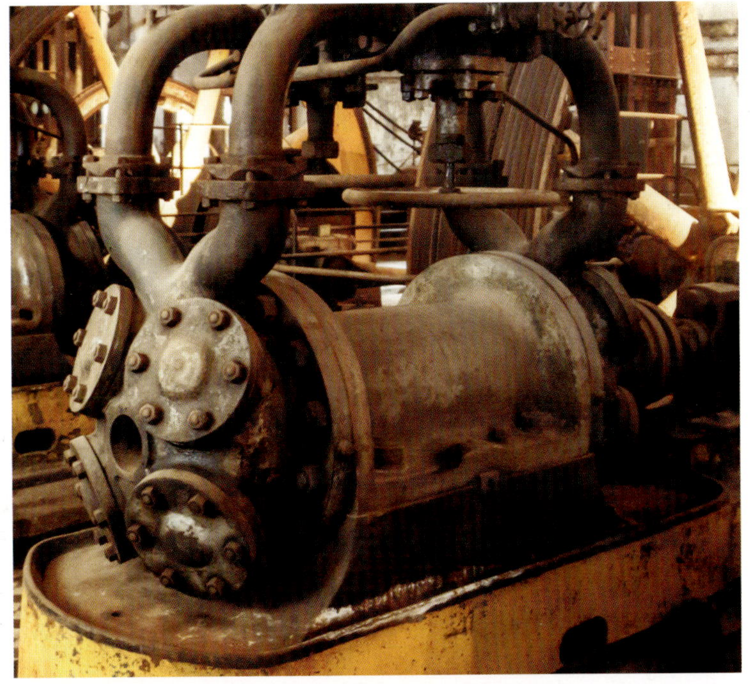

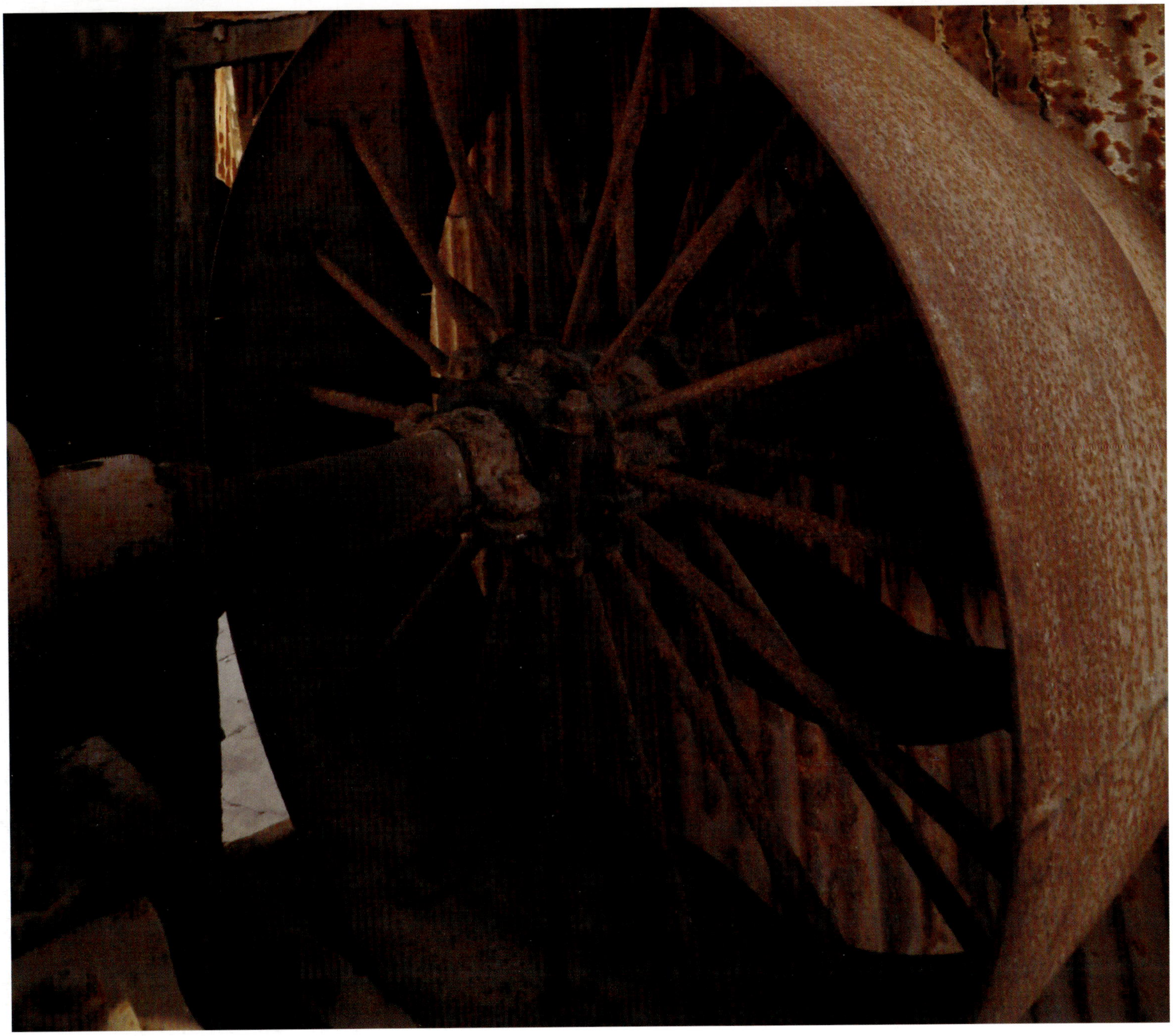

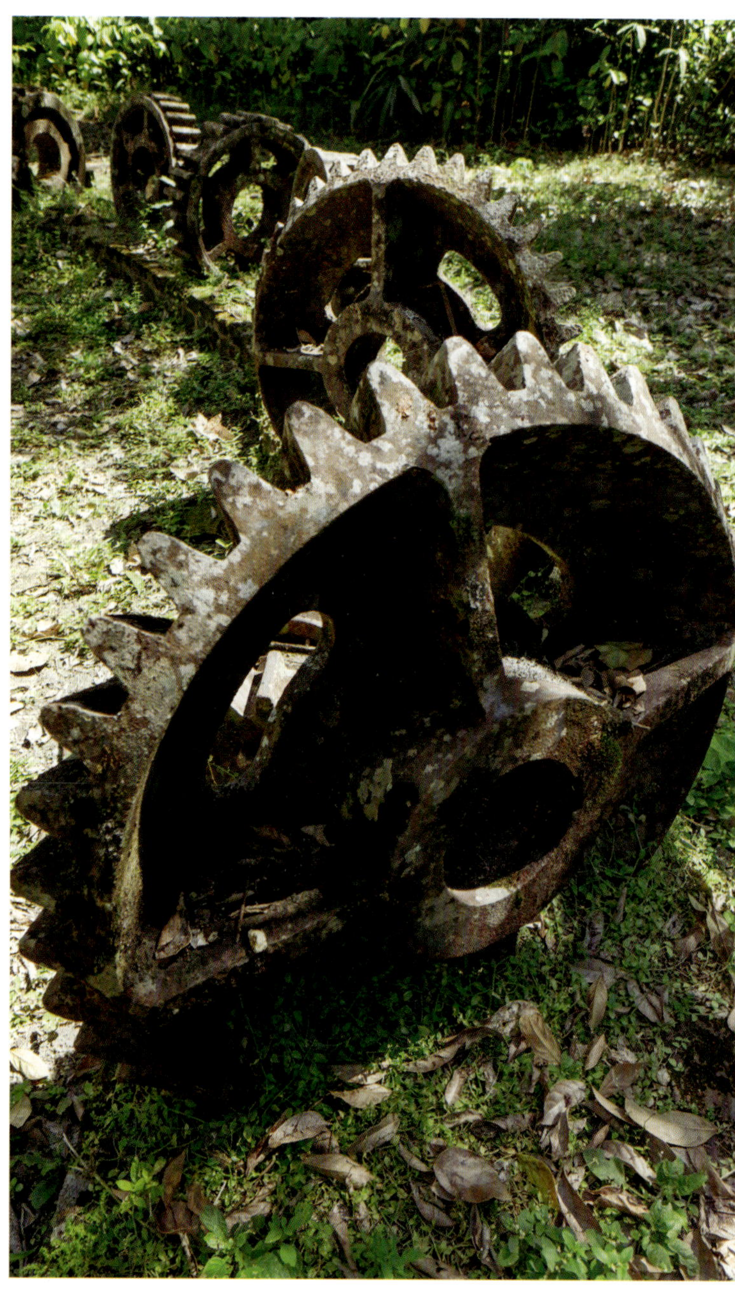

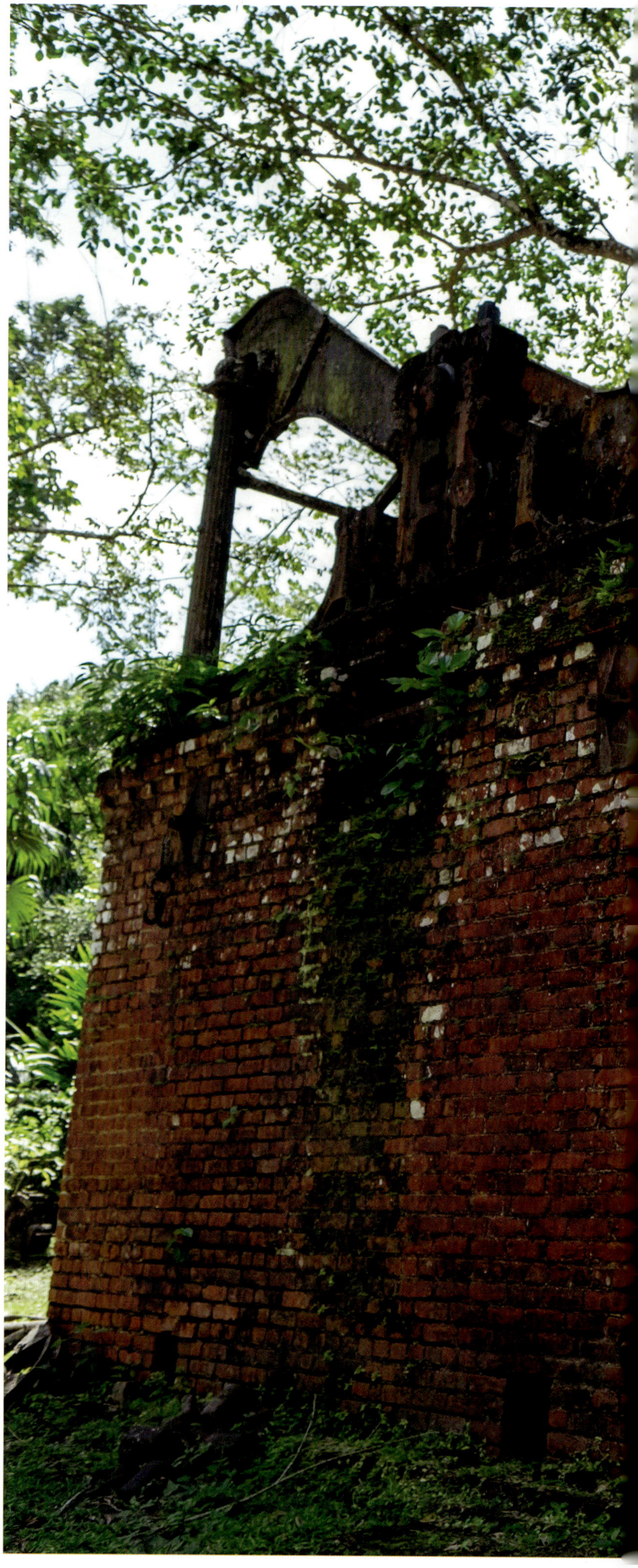

Lamanai Sugar Mill, Belize
Strangler figs and other tropical
plants have established their grip
on the Lamanai ('submerged
crocodile') sugar works, first
established in 1860 with capital
from British investors. It lasted
only 15 years. The imported
machinery was left to rust as
there were no facilities for
dealing with scrap iron. It
is unlikely that the investors
saw any return on their funds.
Tourists visit the ruins, though
the far more ancient Mayan
temple site close by is in a better
state of preservation than the
gradually crumbling sugar works.

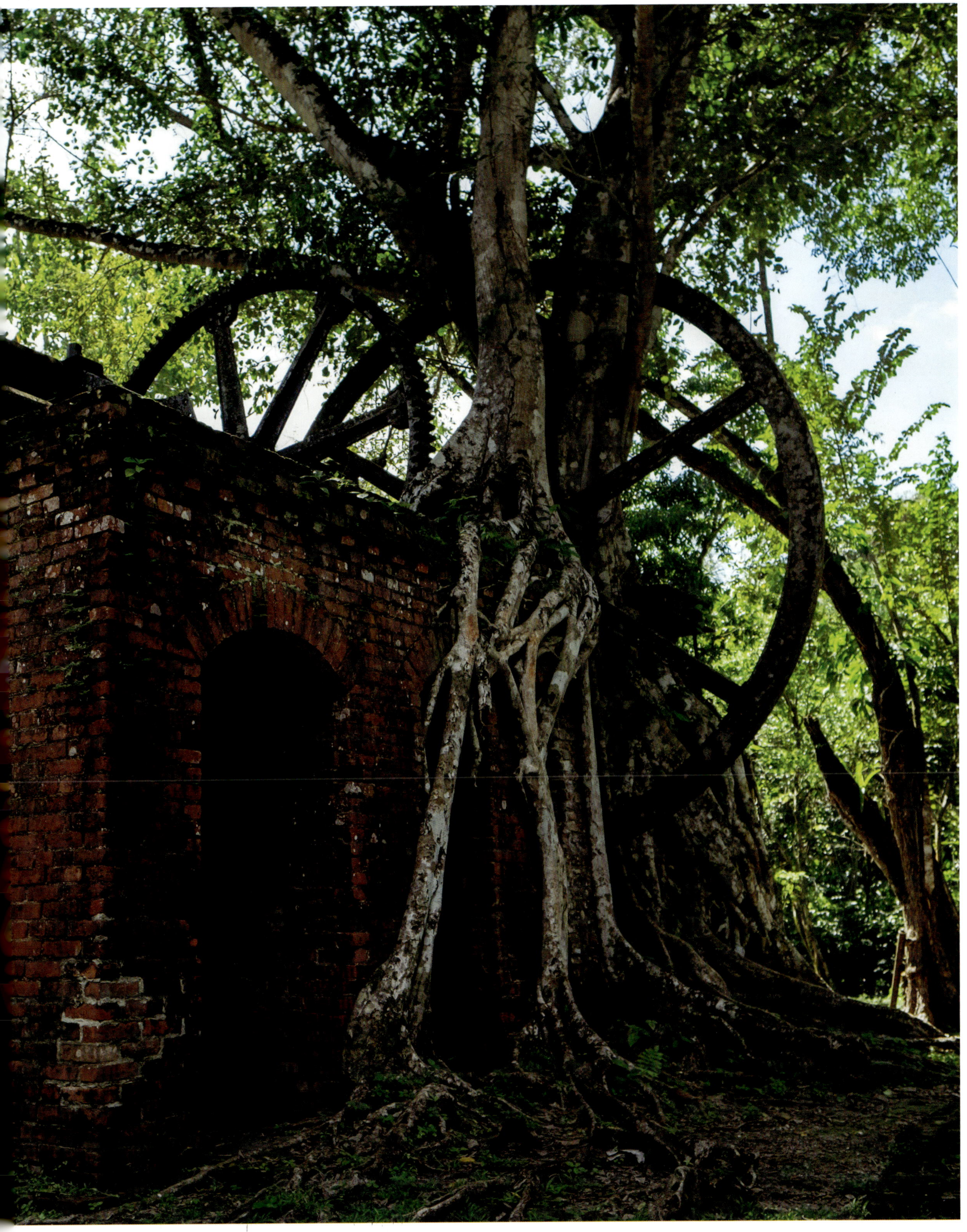

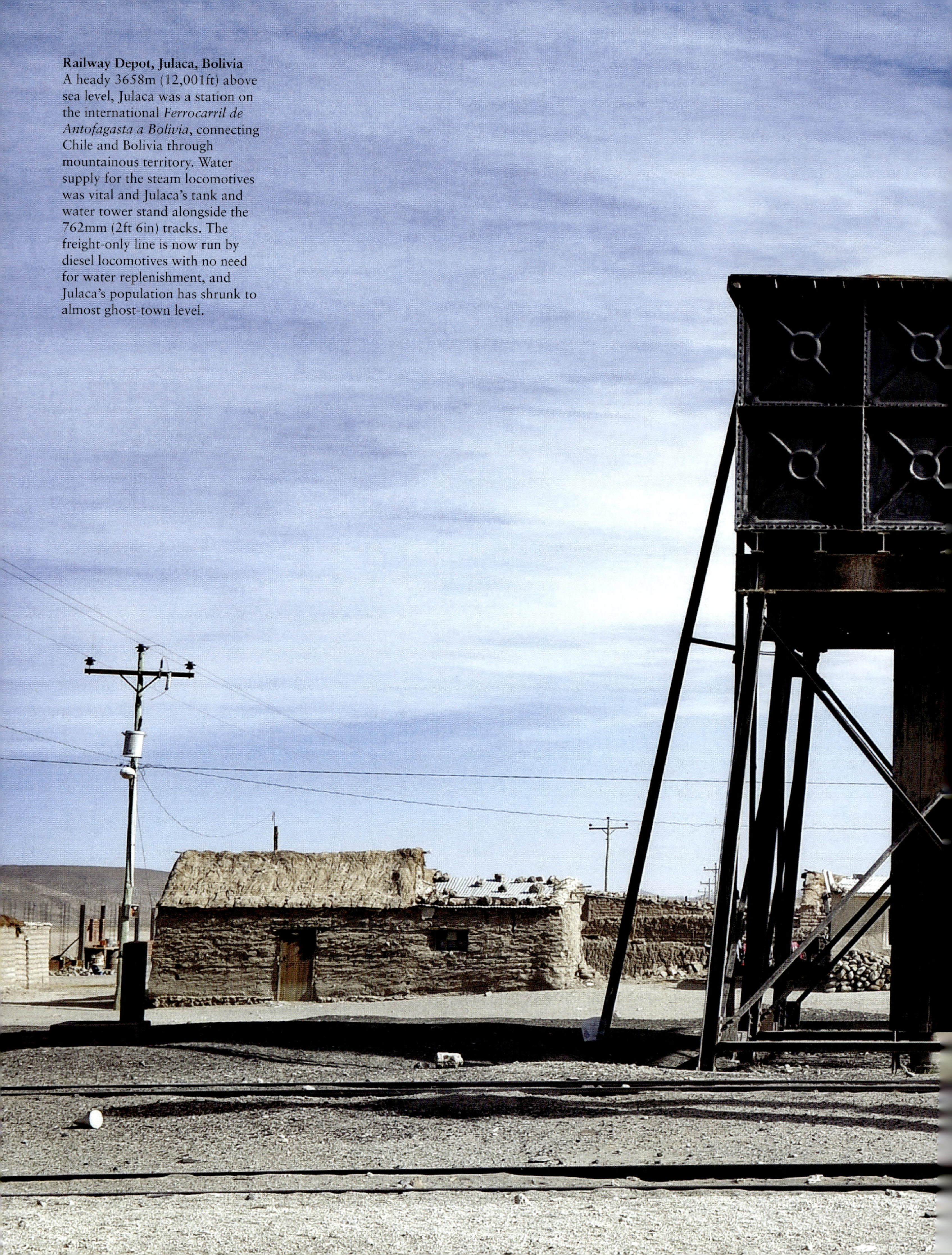

Railway Depot, Julaca, Bolivia
A heady 3658m (12,001ft) above sea level, Julaca was a station on the international *Ferrocarril de Antofagasta a Bolivia*, connecting Chile and Bolivia through mountainous territory. Water supply for the steam locomotives was vital and Julaca's tank and water tower stand alongside the 762mm (2ft 6in) tracks. The freight-only line is now run by diesel locomotives with no need for water replenishment, and Julaca's population has shrunk to almost ghost-town level.

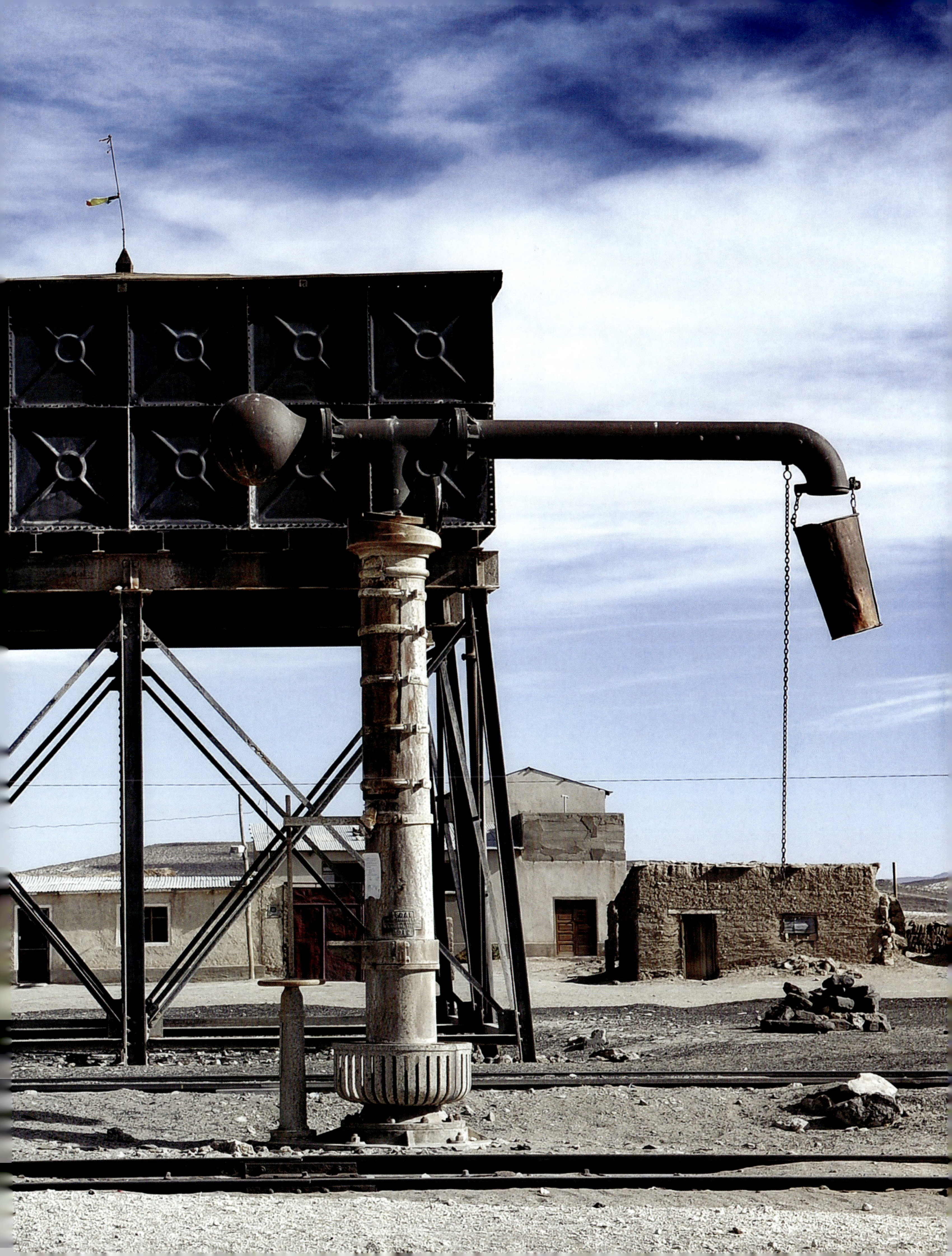

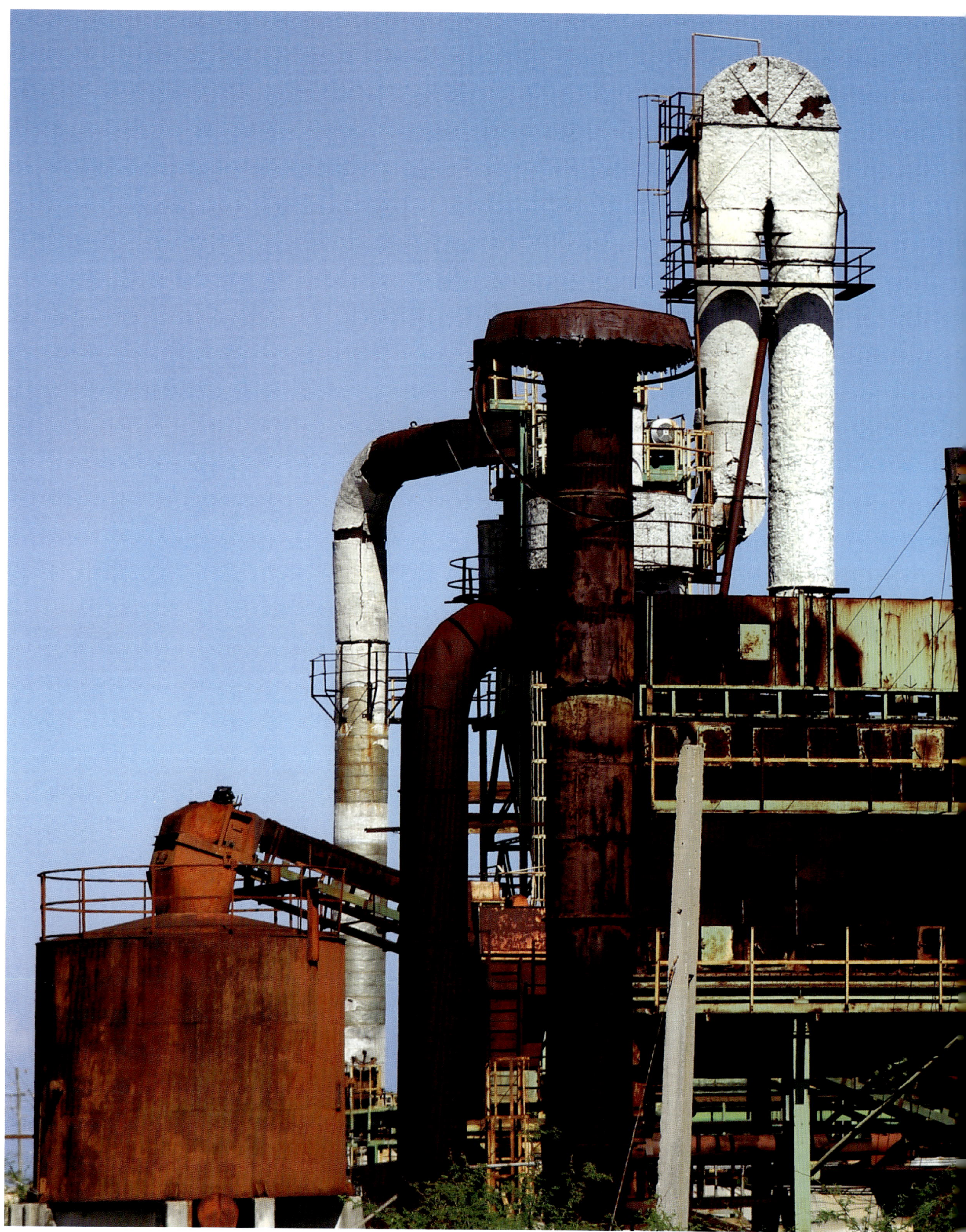

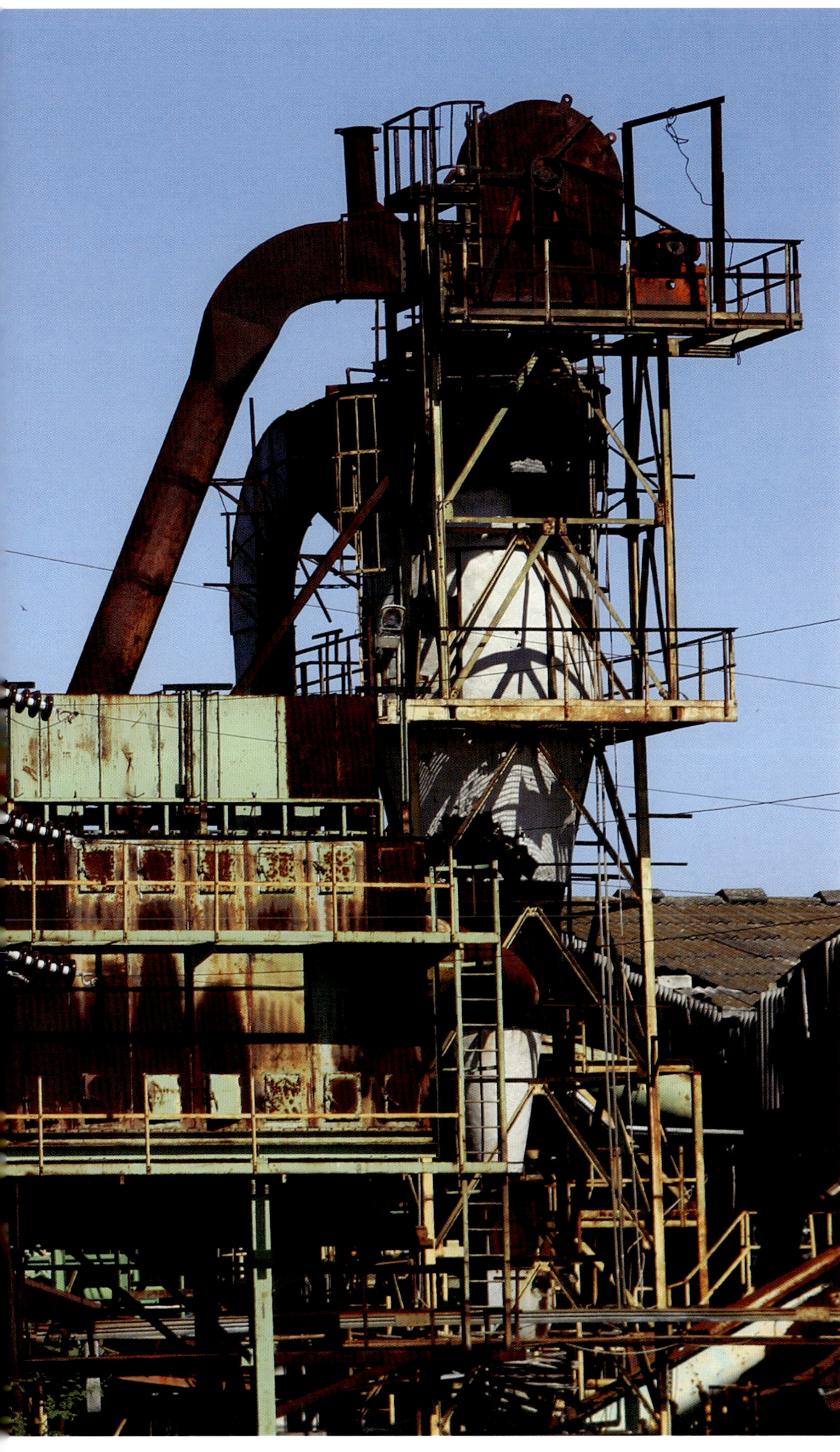

Camilo Cienfuegos (formerly Hershey) Sugar Works, Cuba
Businessman and chocolate magnate Milton Hershey first bought land in Cuba in 1916 to process cane sugar after the supply of sugar from Europe was disrupted by World War I. The Central Hershey factory was established in 1917, and a town of 180 homes was built to house the factory workers. A well-known philanthropist, Hershey also had constructed a medical centre, free school, movie theatre, baseball stadium and golf course. The mill was one of the most productive in the world, making sugar and molasses for both Hershey chocolate and Coca Cola. After Hershey's death in 1945 the factory was sold on, and later taken into public ownership by Fidel Castro's government in 1959.

RIGHT:

Camilo Cienfuegos (formerly Hershey) Sugar Works, Cuba
The sugar works and employees' village were founded in 1916 by Milton Hershey, American sugar magnate, and named after him. After the Cuban revolution of 1959 the town and refinery, now state-owned, were renamed after one of Fidel Castro's commanders. The fall of the Soviet Union in 1991 removed the refinery's largest customer and in 2002 it was shut down. Most of the buildings seen here were demolished in 2016.

OVERLEAF:

Stromness Whaling Station, South Georgia
The on-shore station, for boiling down whale blubber and bones into oil, was set up in 1912. With other South Georgia whaling depots it accounted for the lives of over 175,000 whales. In 1931 it was converted to a ship-repair yard, and in 1961 it was abandoned.

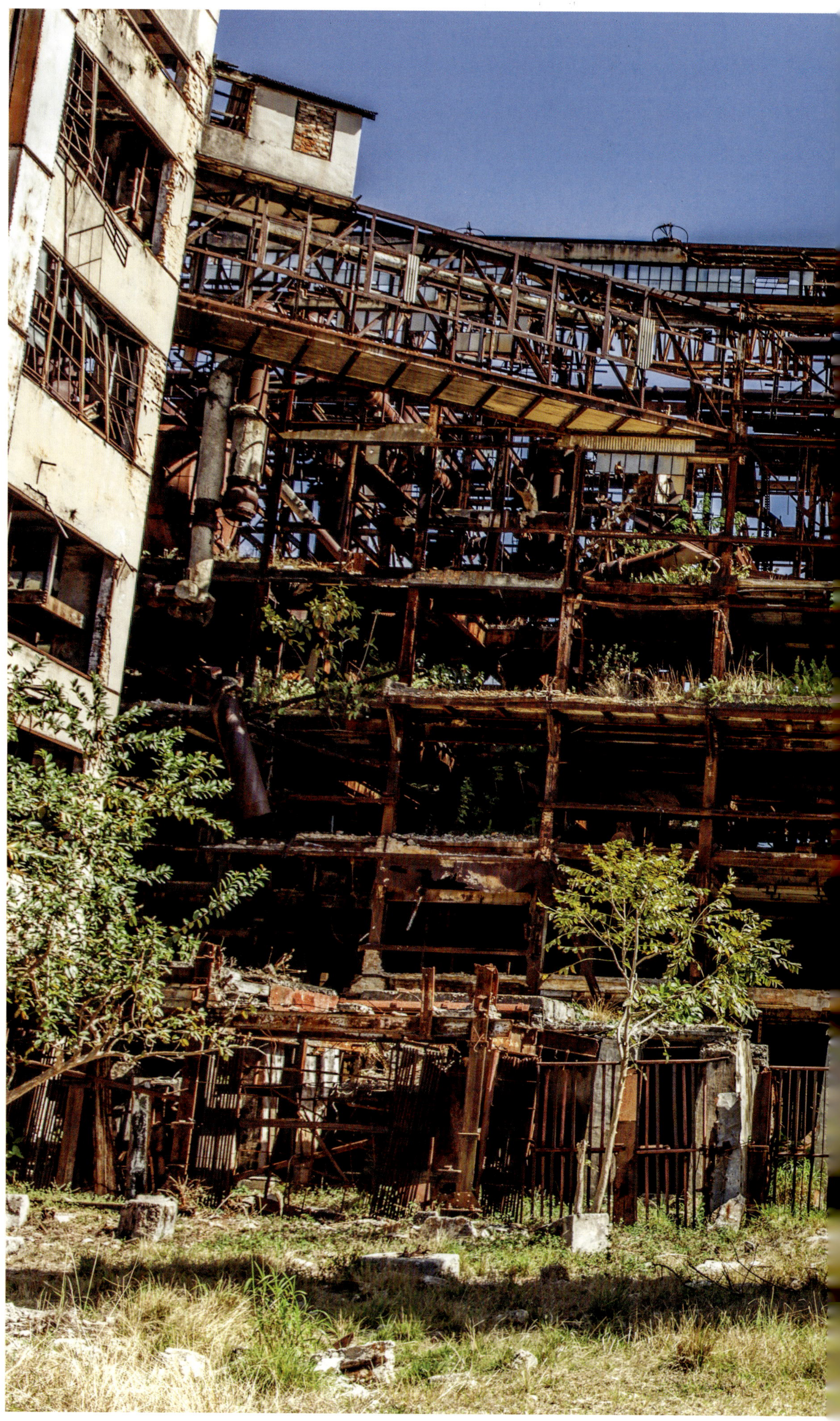

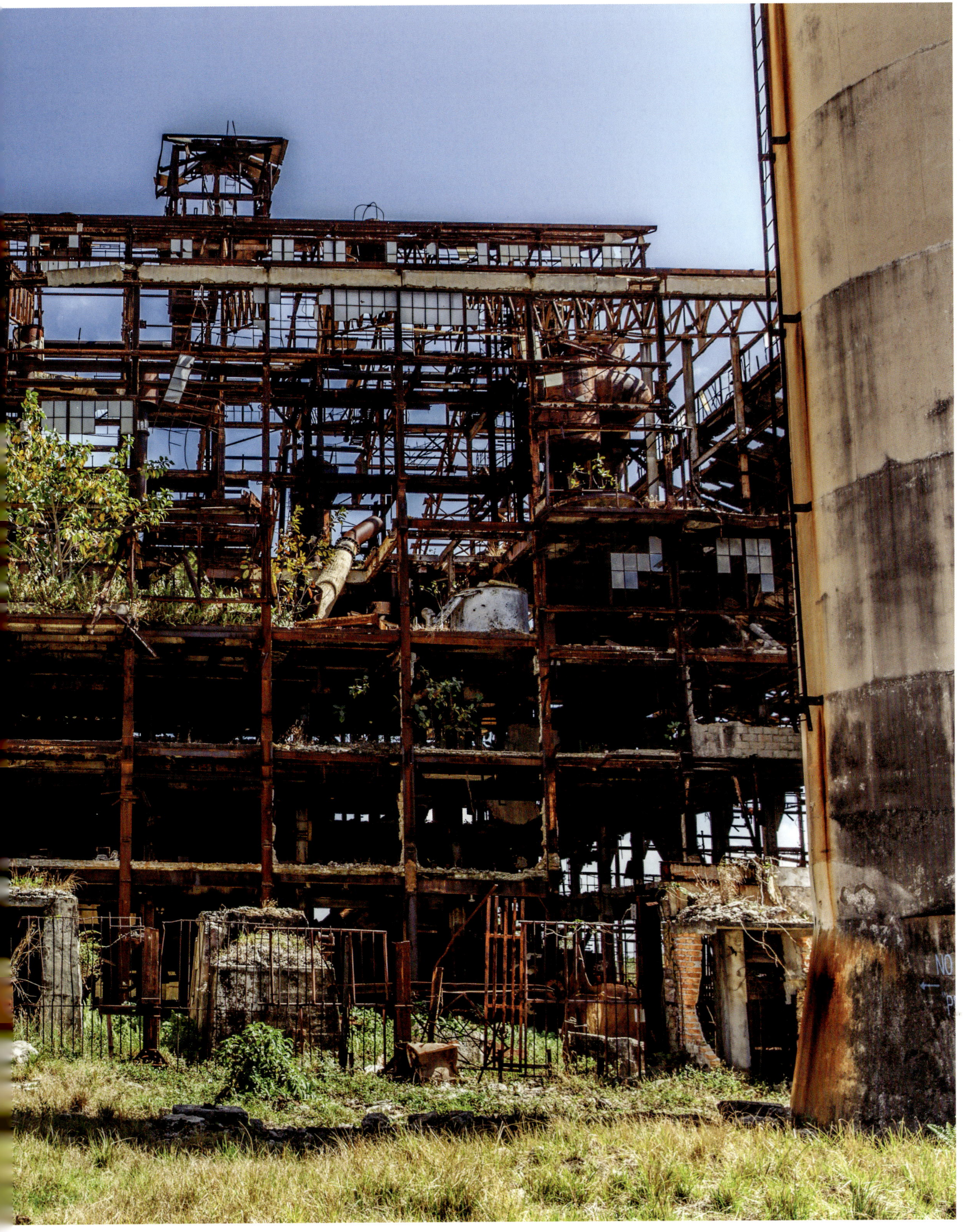
NO
P

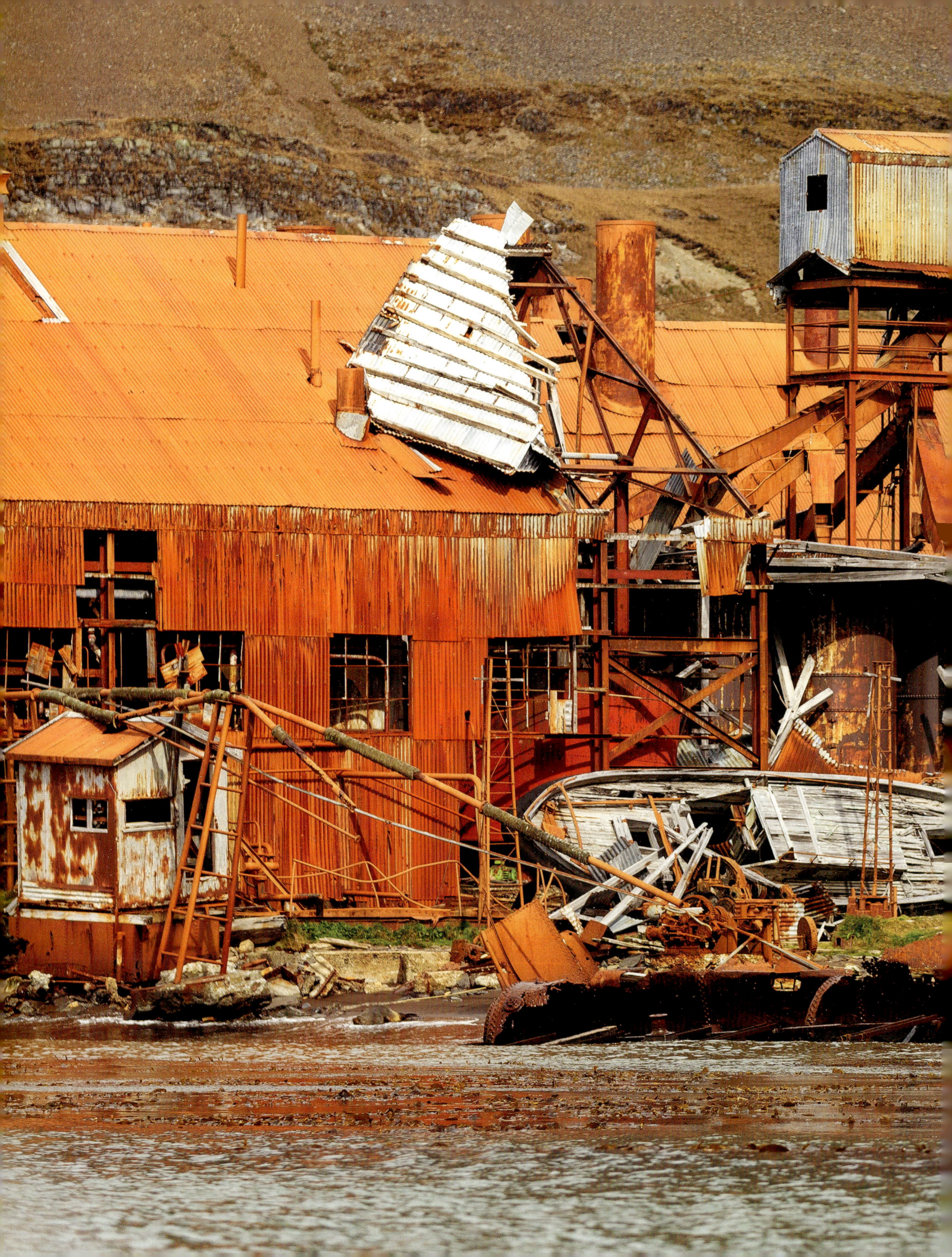

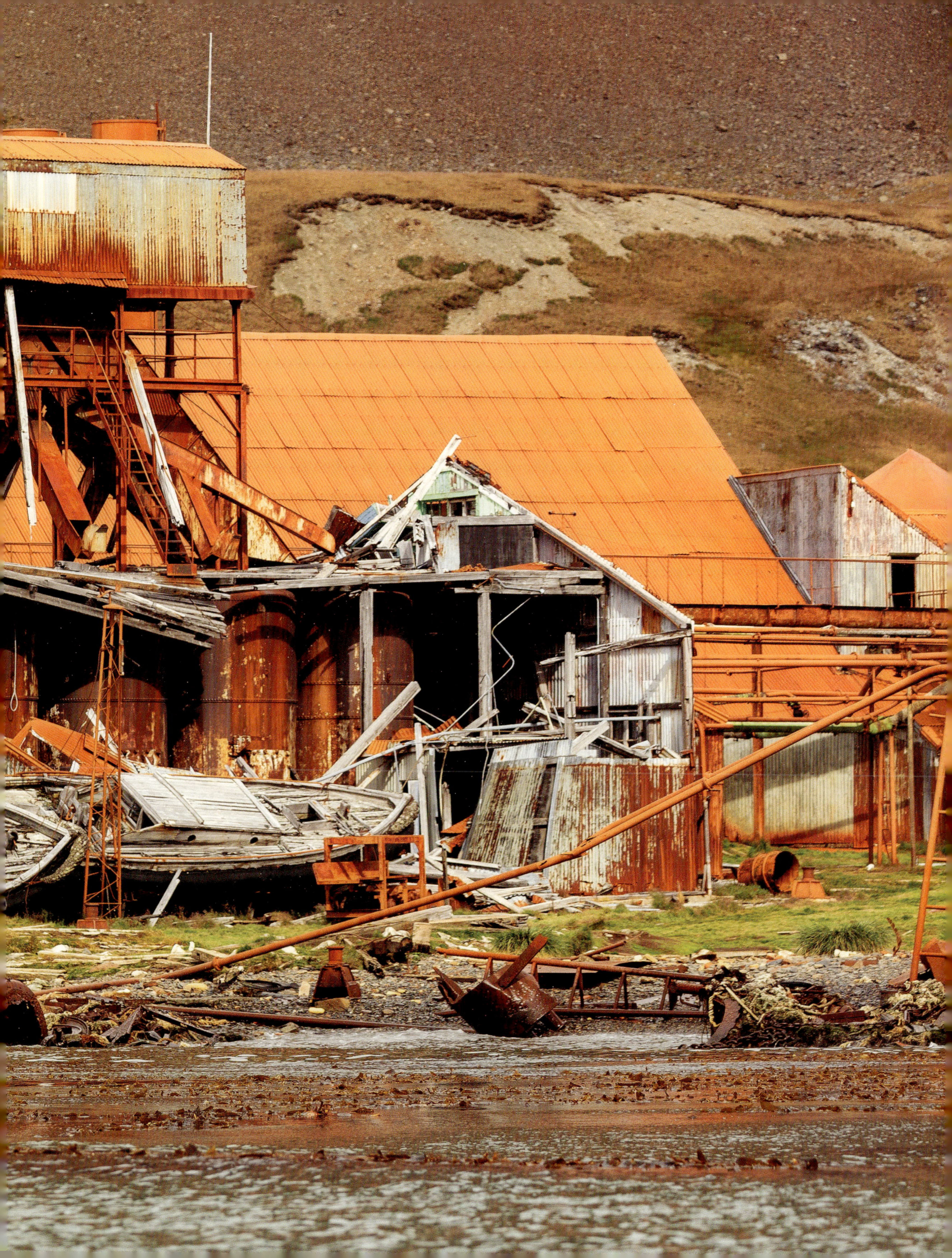

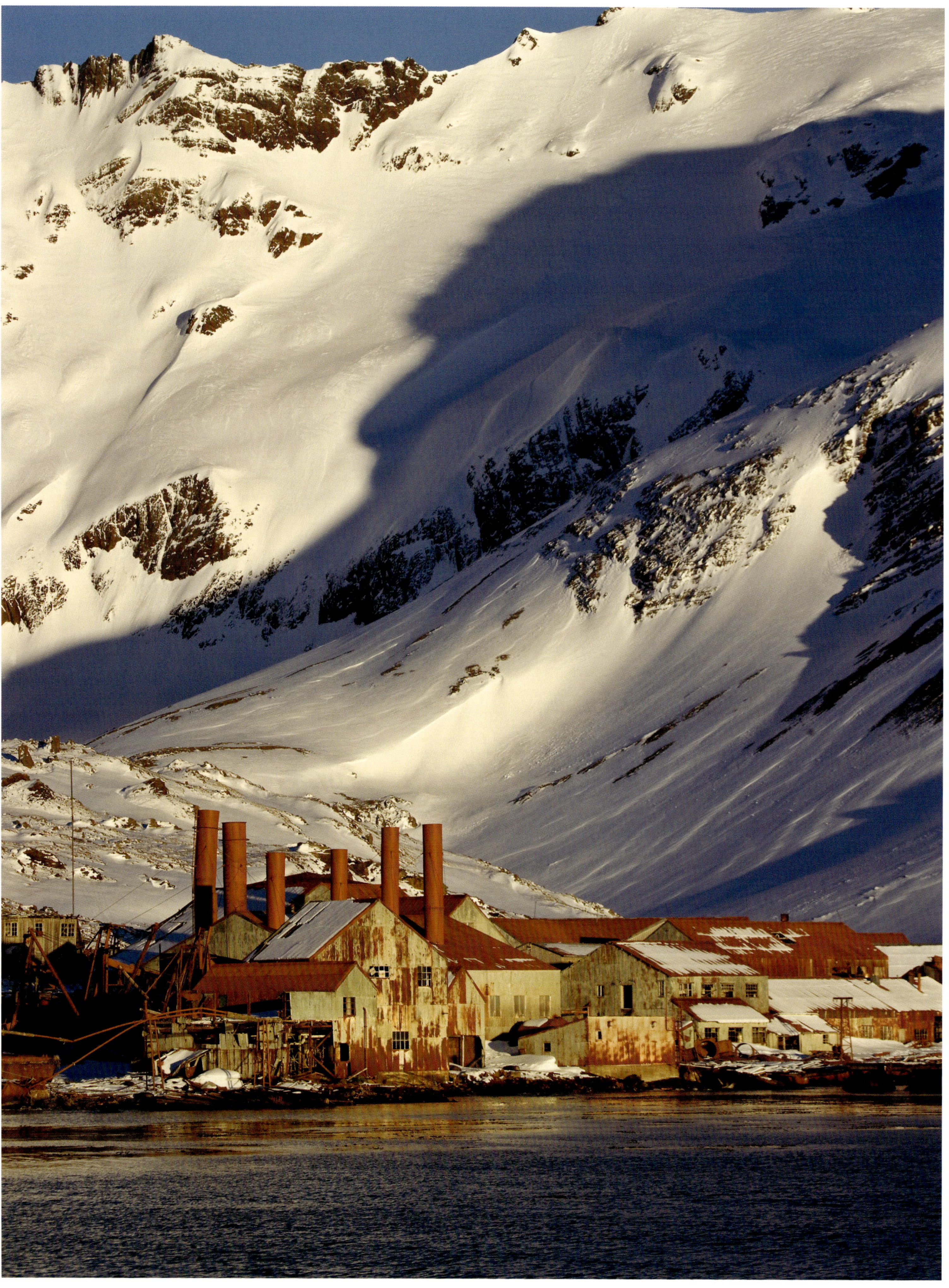

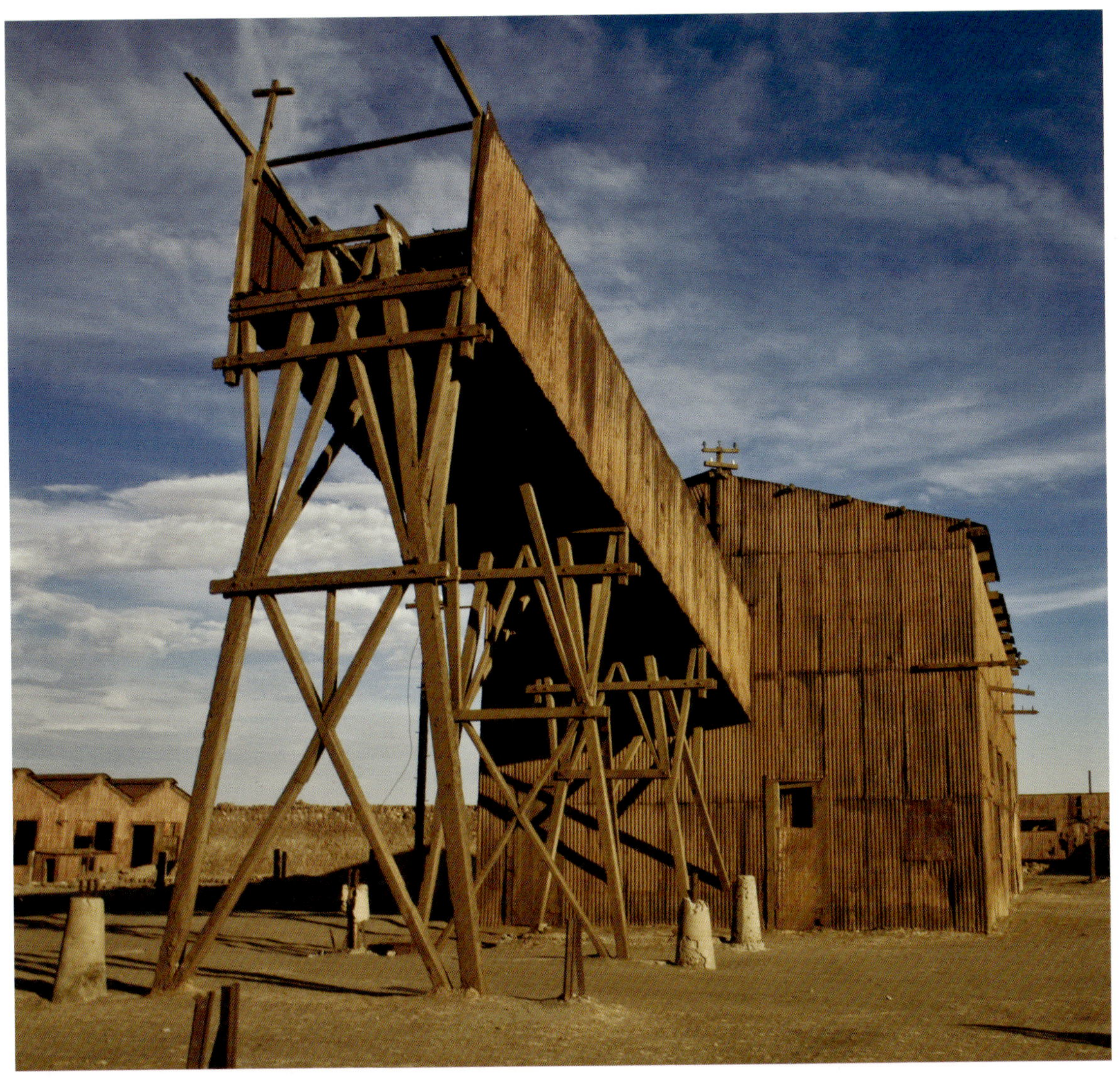

Whaling Station, Leith Harbour, South Georgia
A whaling company from the Scottish port of Leith set up this depot in 1909. Whale oil was stored in massive tanks and shipped to Europe. A temporary home to all-male crews working 12-hour shifts as the slaughtered whales were dragged ashore, it was finally abandoned in 1965, leaving industrial detritus.

LEFT:

Santa Laura Nitrate Works, Chile
Started in 1872 when demand for nitrates was high, and named in honour of the owner's wife, this saltpetre extraction works struggled after production of artificial nitrates began in the 1920s, and finally closed in 1958.

BELOW:

Illegal Mine Site, Tambopata, Peru
An ugly blotch of pollution marks one of many illegal gold-mines in this area of Peru – a problem shared with neighbouring countries, where organised criminal groups set up transient sites, often using forced labour. Deforestation, water pollution and land contamination are left, due to the use of mercury in the gold separation process.

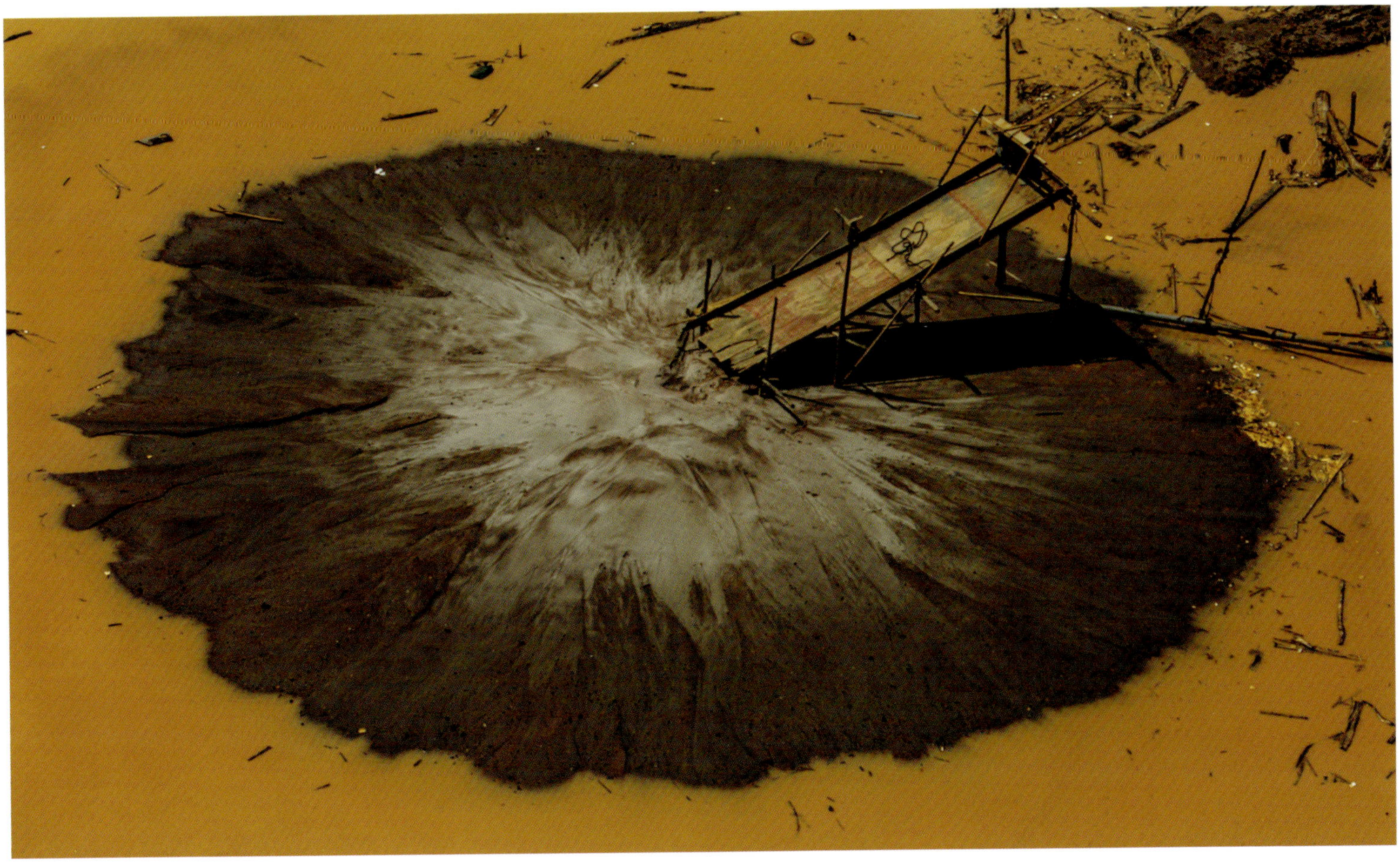

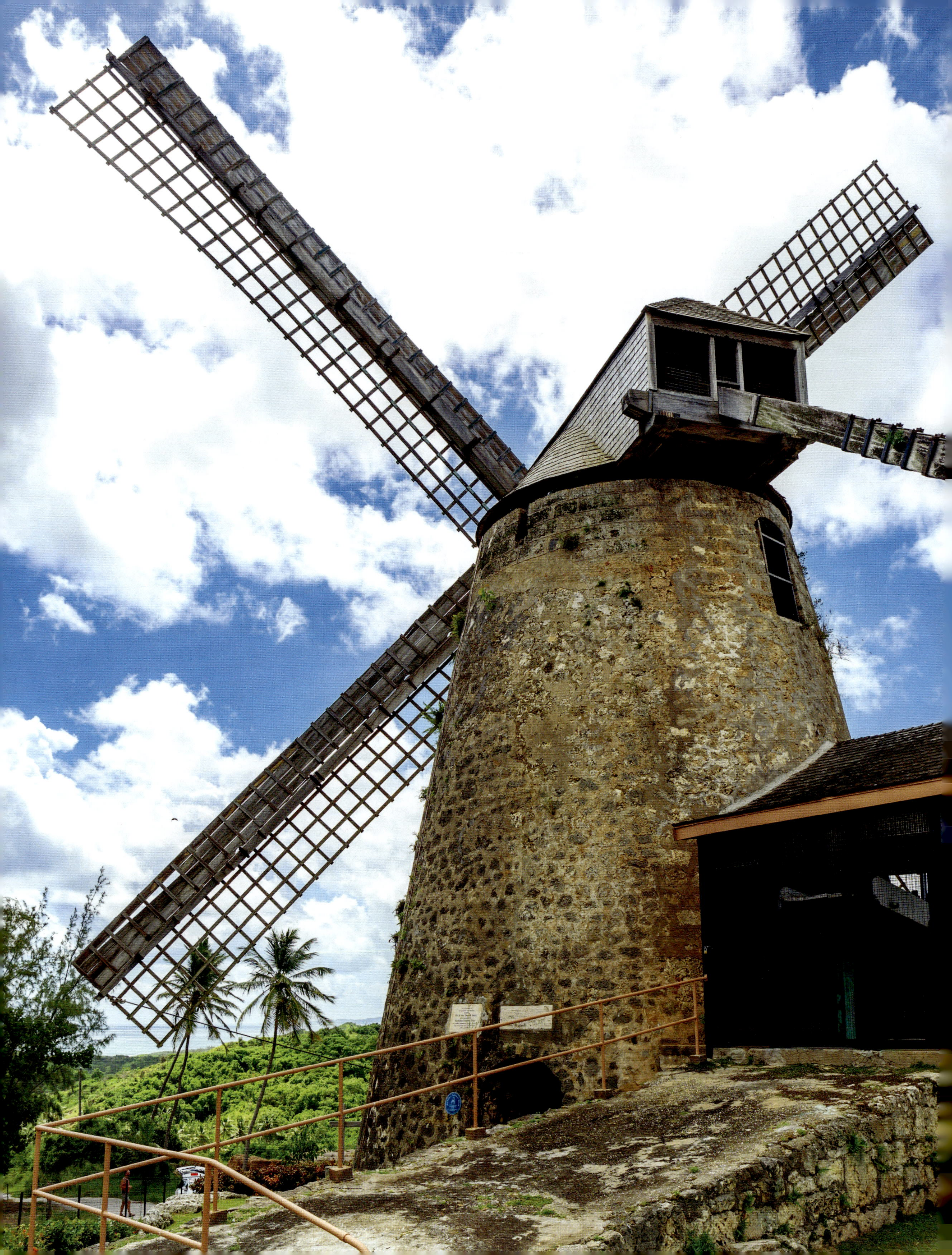

**Morgan Lewis Sugar Mill,
St Andrew, Barbados**
Slavery underpinned the colonial
economy of Barbados when this
mill, the only complete wind-
powered sugar-mill remaining in
the Caribbean, was established.
Out of commercial use since
1947, it was identified in 1996
as one of the world's 100 most
endangered historic sites. Since
then it has been restored, and still
grinds sugar cane on occasion,
using the original equipment.

**Oil Platform, Piura Province,
Peru**
Exploitation of undersea oil
fields off Peru's north coast has
left numerous platforms like
this one, stripped of machinery,
and now colonised by sea birds,
with its lower ledges forming
resting-places for sea lions.
The platforms are also popular
locations for scuba diving – a
unique aspect of abandoned
industrial structures.

**Rincon Nuclear Dome,
Puerto Rico, USA**
In 1960 this dome was built
to house a Boiling Nuclear
Superheater Reactor (BONUS),
an experimental type of nuclear-
powered electricity generator.
Completed in 1965, the plant
operated until 1968 when the
BONUS design was terminated for
cost, technical and safety reasons.
The reactor vessel, along with other
component parts and radioactive
material, is encased in a three-storey
high concrete monolith.

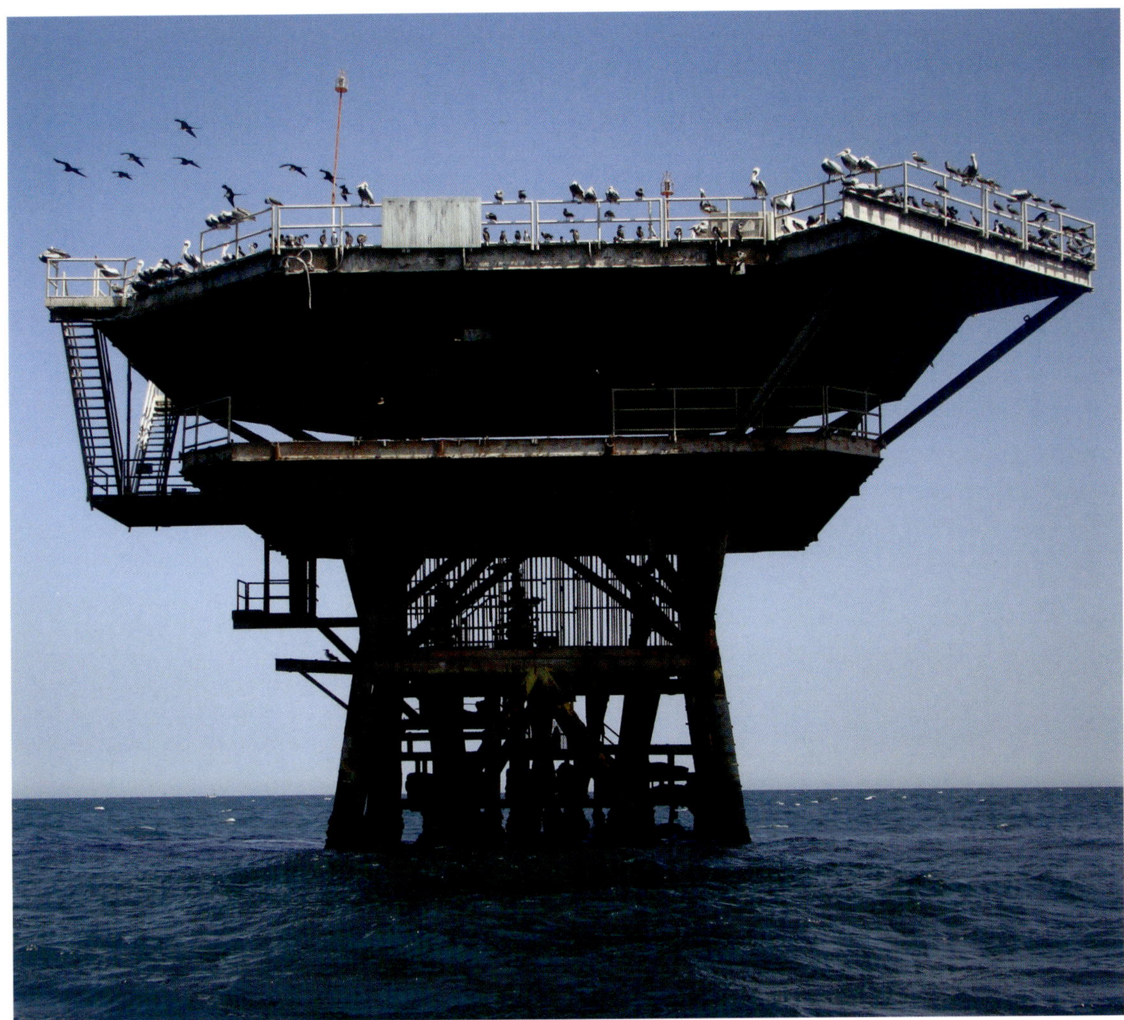

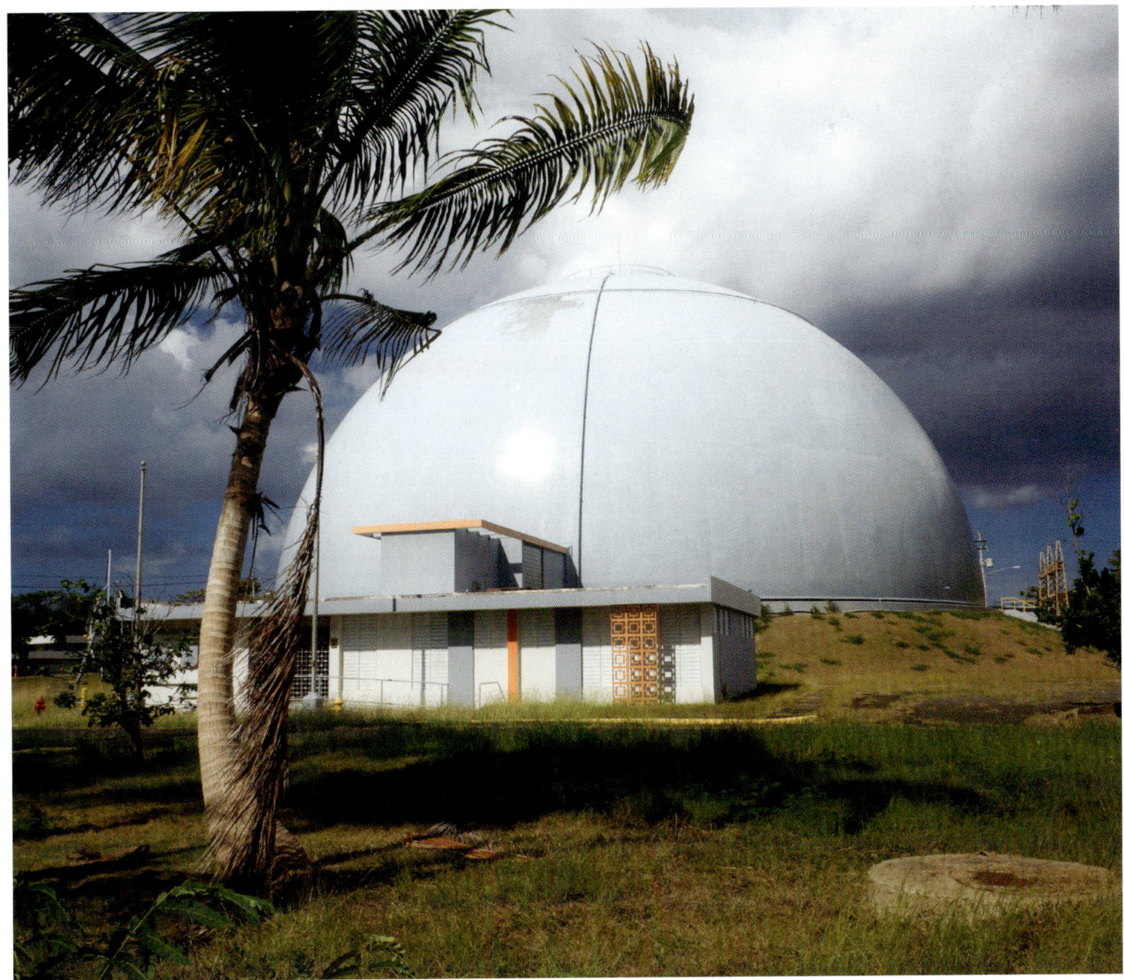

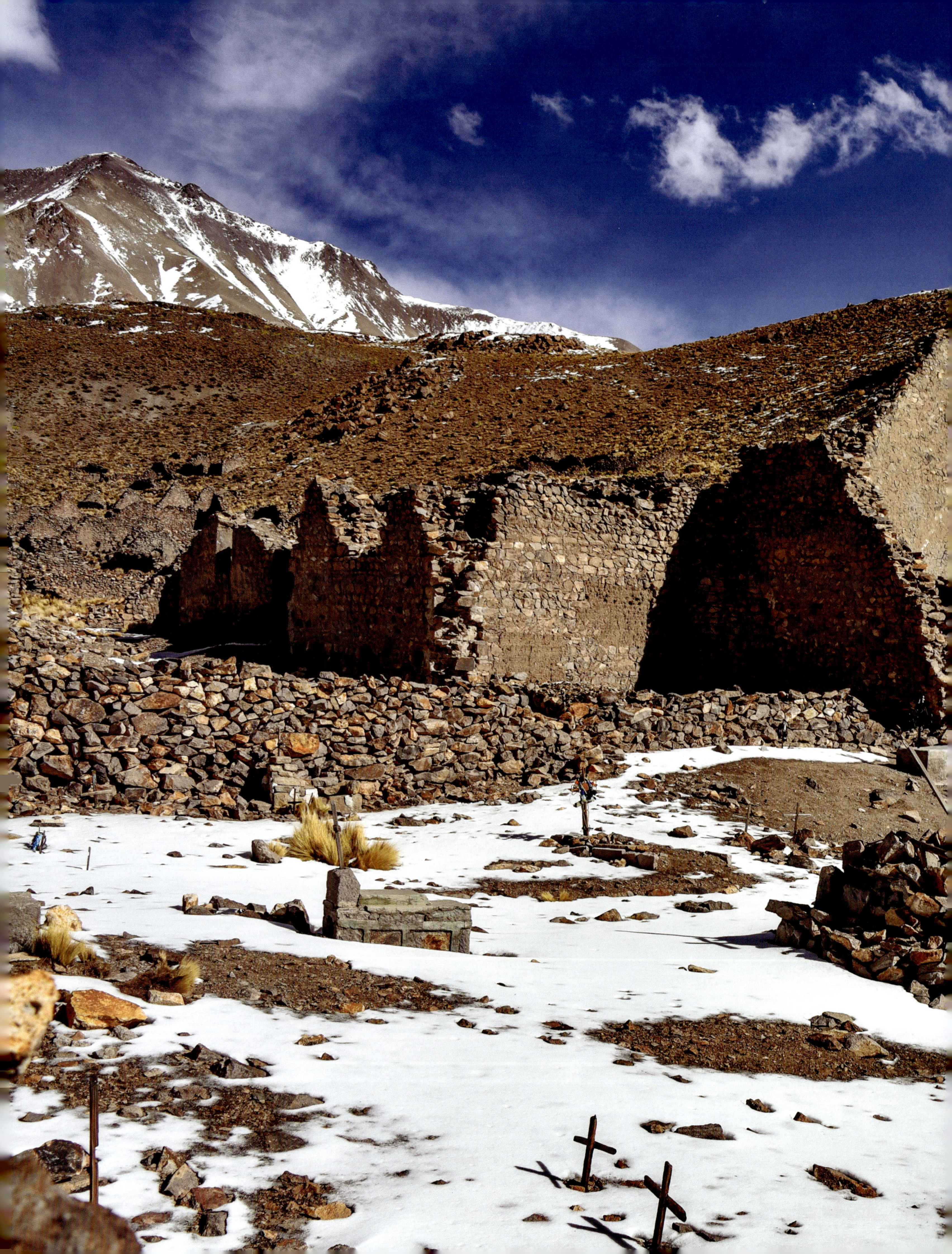

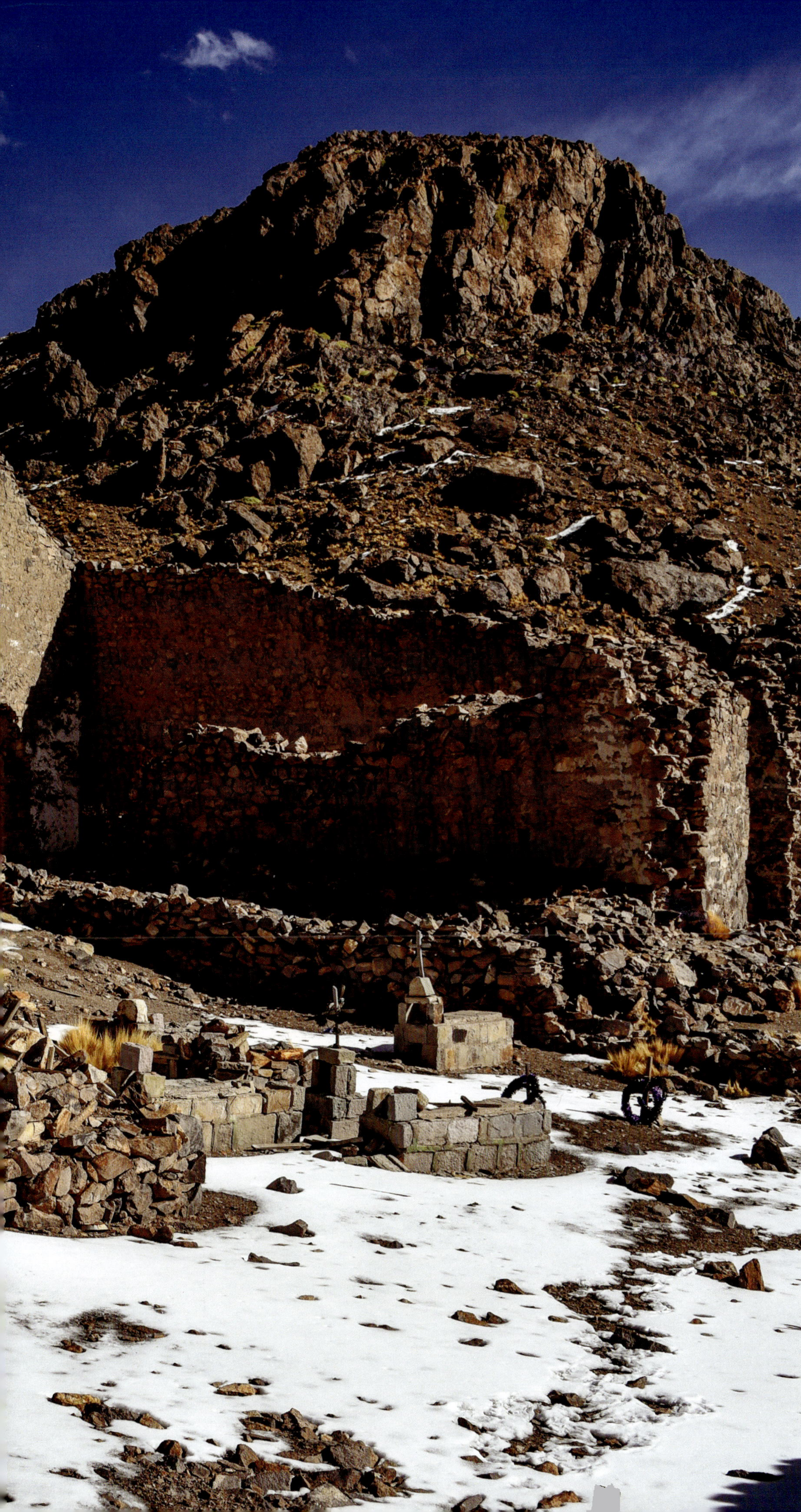

**San Antonio de Lipez,
Potosí Province, Bolivia**
Only the lure of high earnings
from a silver mine could have
got large numbers of people to
live in this inhospitable location
over 4550m (15,000ft) above
sea level, now a *pueblo fantasma*
(ghost town). Silver was mined
here since the early 16th century,
but with exhaustion of the high-
quality ore, decline set in and
little happened after the 1870s.
The area has much in the way of
mining relics from the Spanish
colonial period, with open (but
dangerous) shafts and adits.

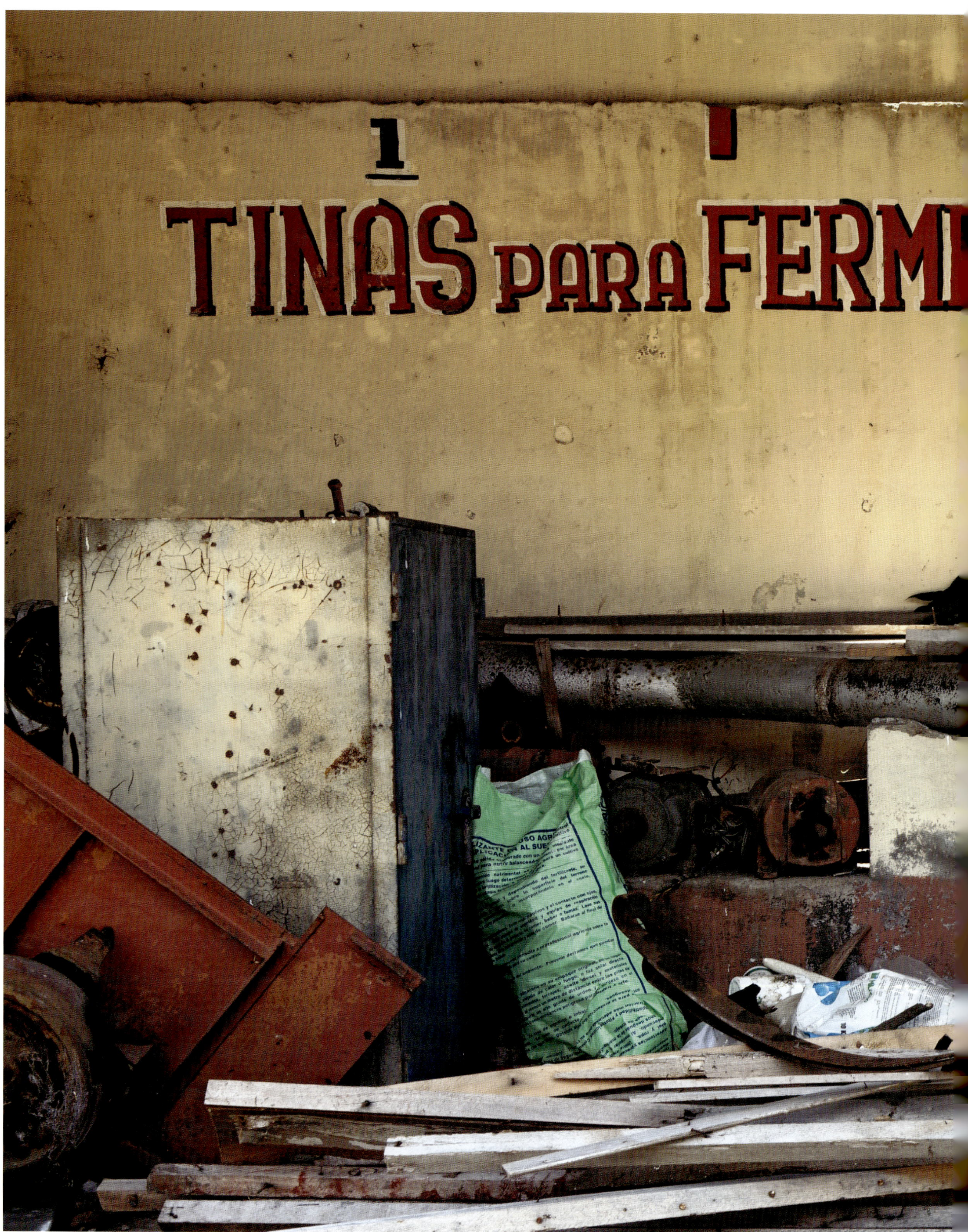

1
TINAS PARA FERME

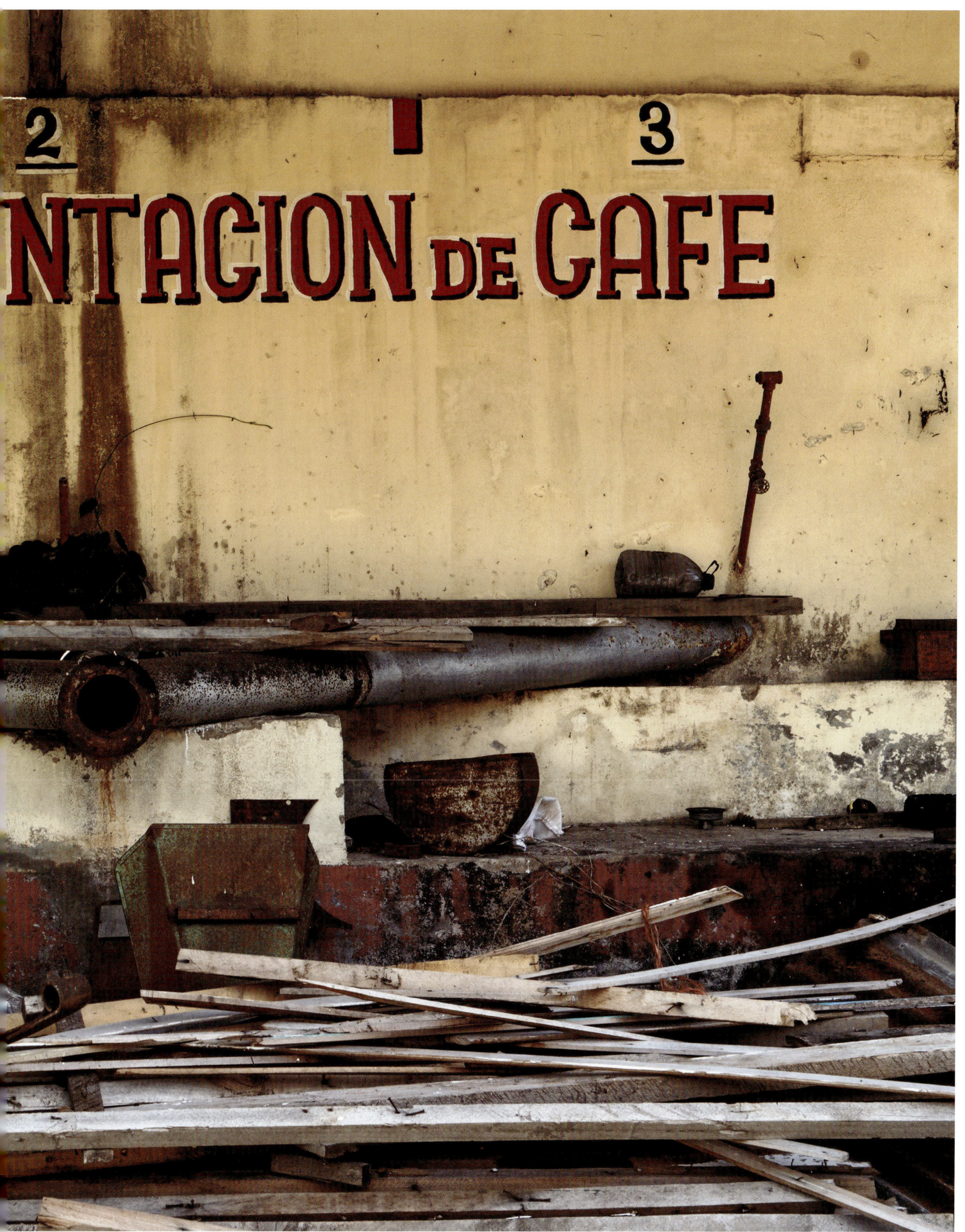

2
3
NTACION DE CAFE

Princesa Janca Coffee Factory, Boquete, Panama
Fermentation vats are among the disused equipment in the old buildings of the coffee company. Founded in 1951, the factory is close to the Finca Arco Iris plantation in the Panamian highlands.

Engenho Central, Piracicaba, São Paulo State, Brazil
A vast riverside sugar-mill designed in 'French style', it was established in 1881 and became Brazil's largest. In 1974 it closed and its sugar plantations were sold for residential building development. The building is being redeveloped as a cultural centre, including a theatre space and sugar museum.

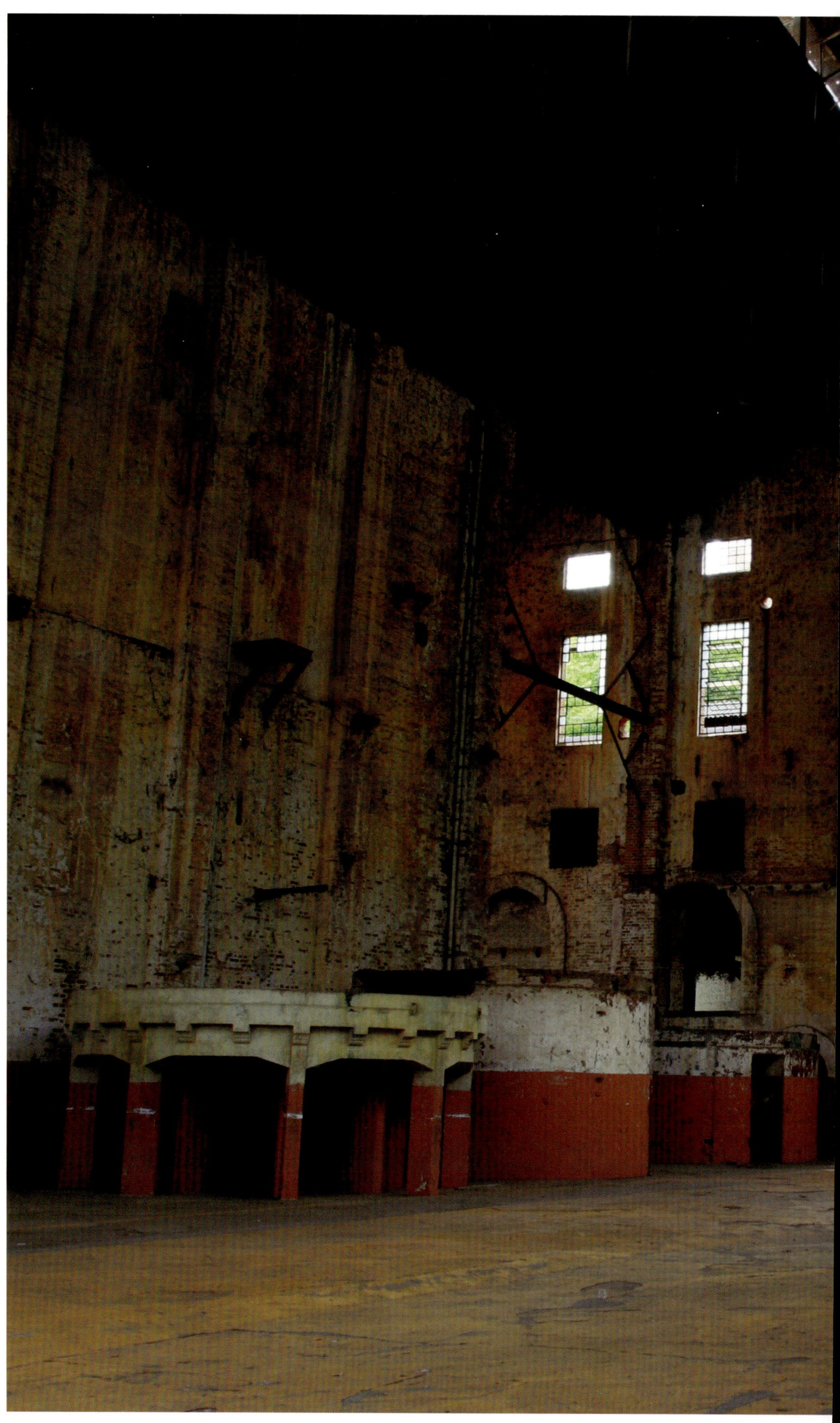

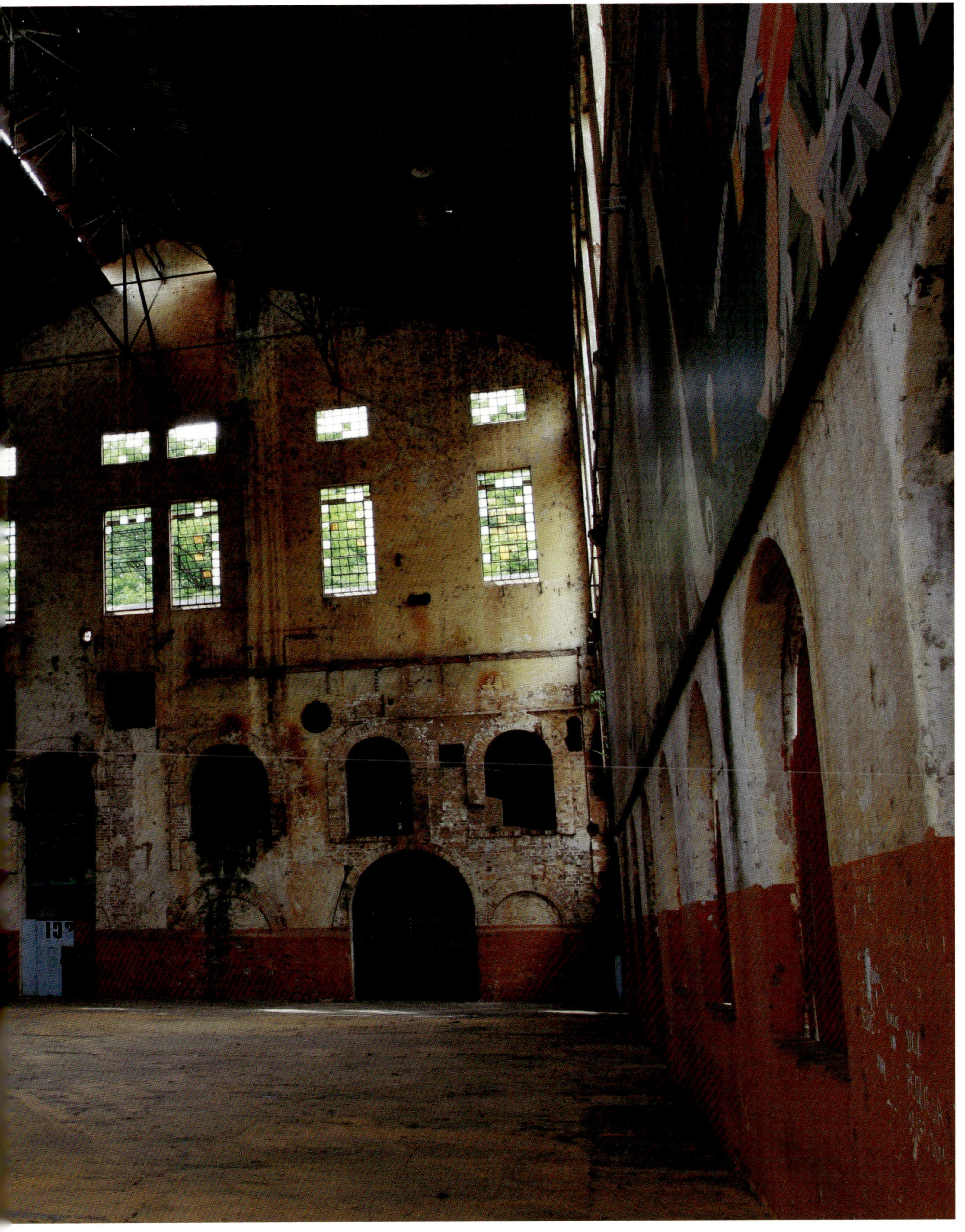

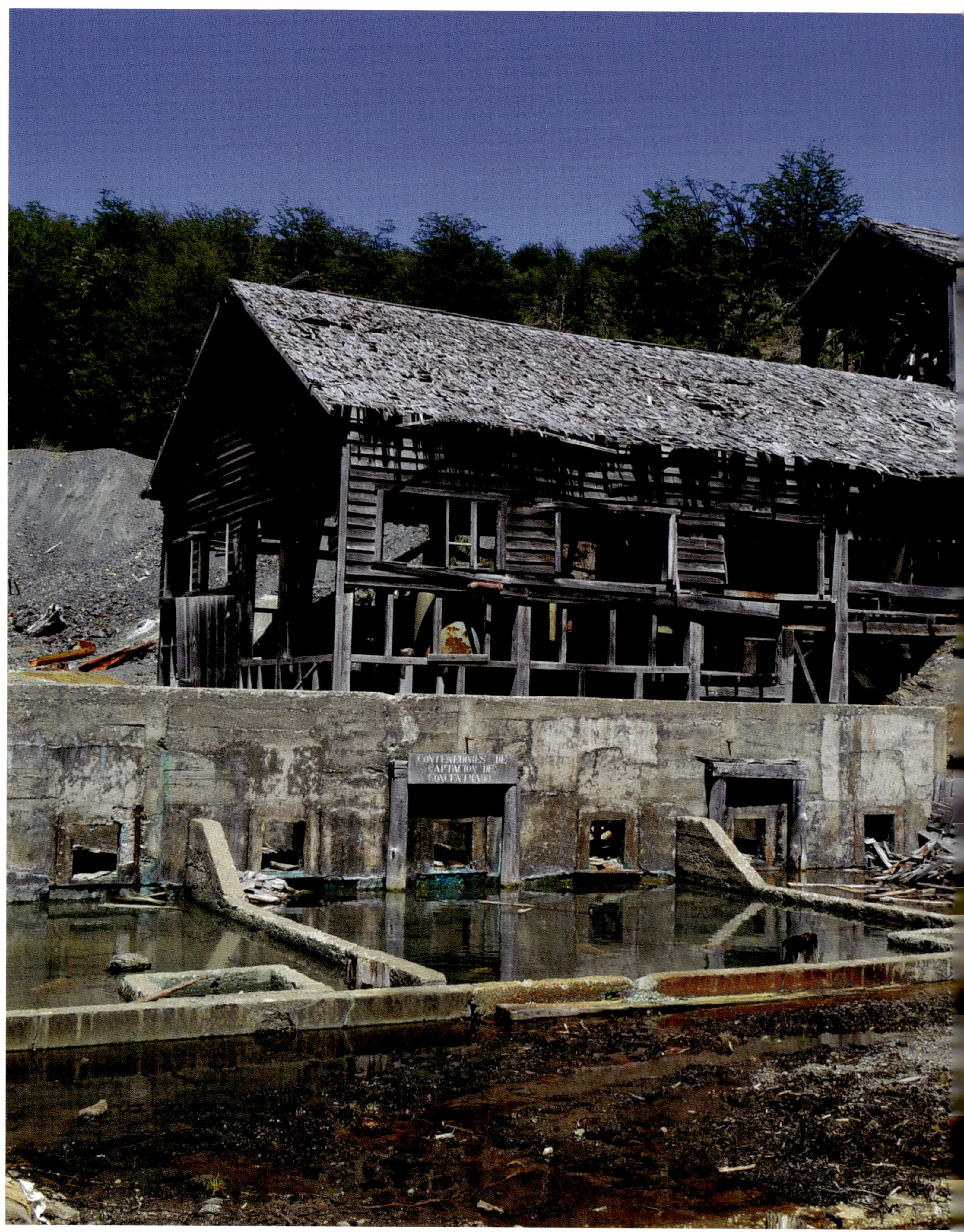

CONTENEDORES DE
CAPTACION DE
CONCENTRADO

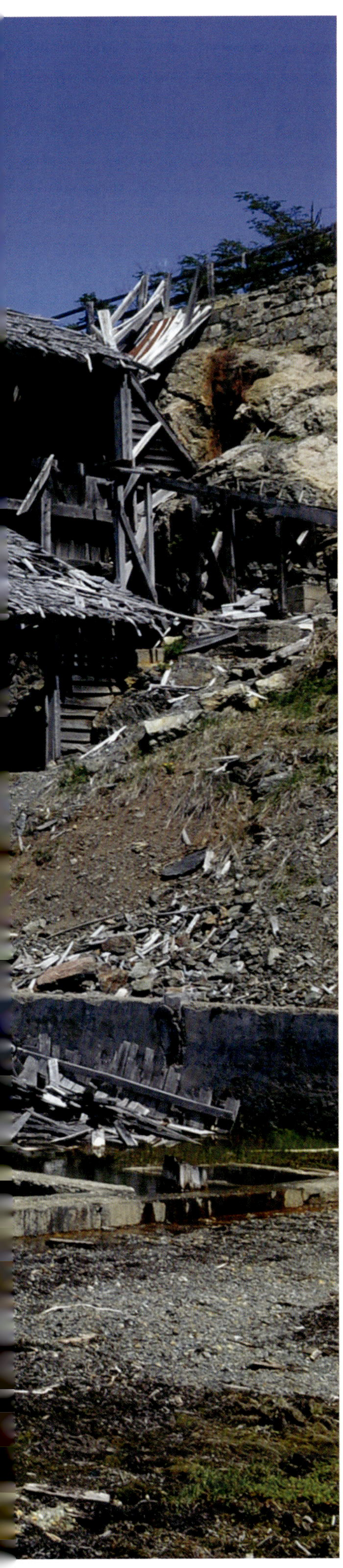

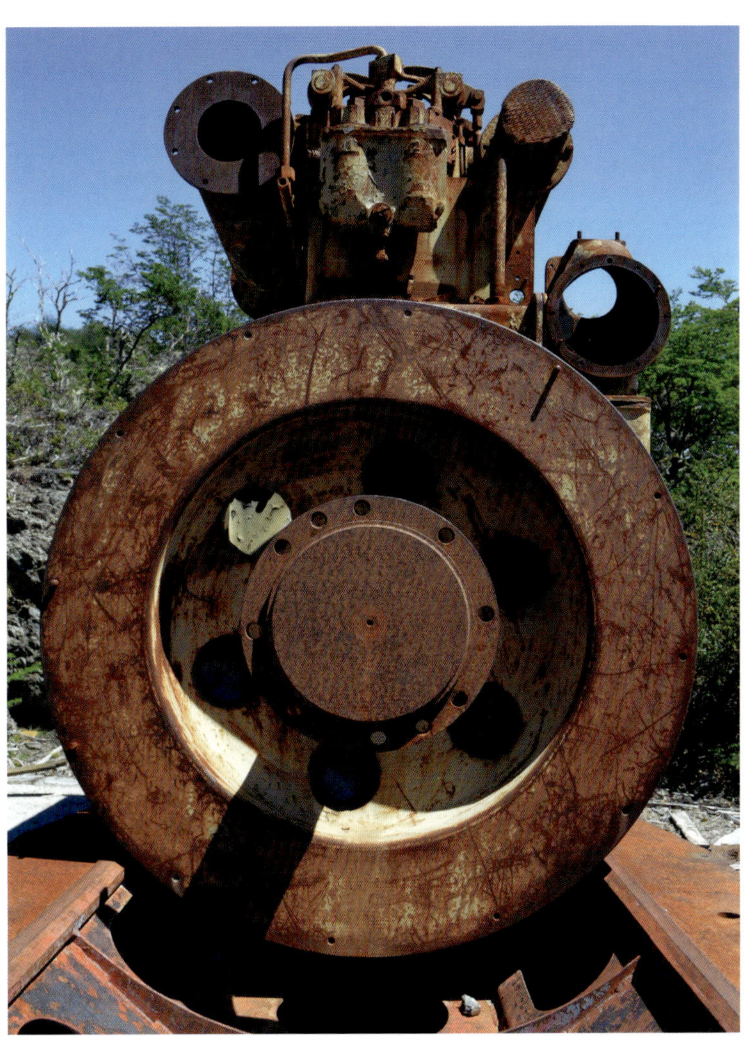

Mine Workings, Puerto Guadal, Patagonia, Chile
Known as the *mina escondido* or hidden mine because of its remote site, it was active for two decades from the 1960s to the 1980s, in the extraction of lead, zinc and copper. The site remains largely intact and still contains much in the way of processing machinery.

BELOW:

Disused Electrical Generating Plant, Oeiras, Piauí State, Brazil
The town's original electricity supply plant, built in Art-Deco style in the 1930s, with a diesel-powered generator, stands desolate, surrounded by industrial debris. Discussion goes on about how it can be restored and put to use.

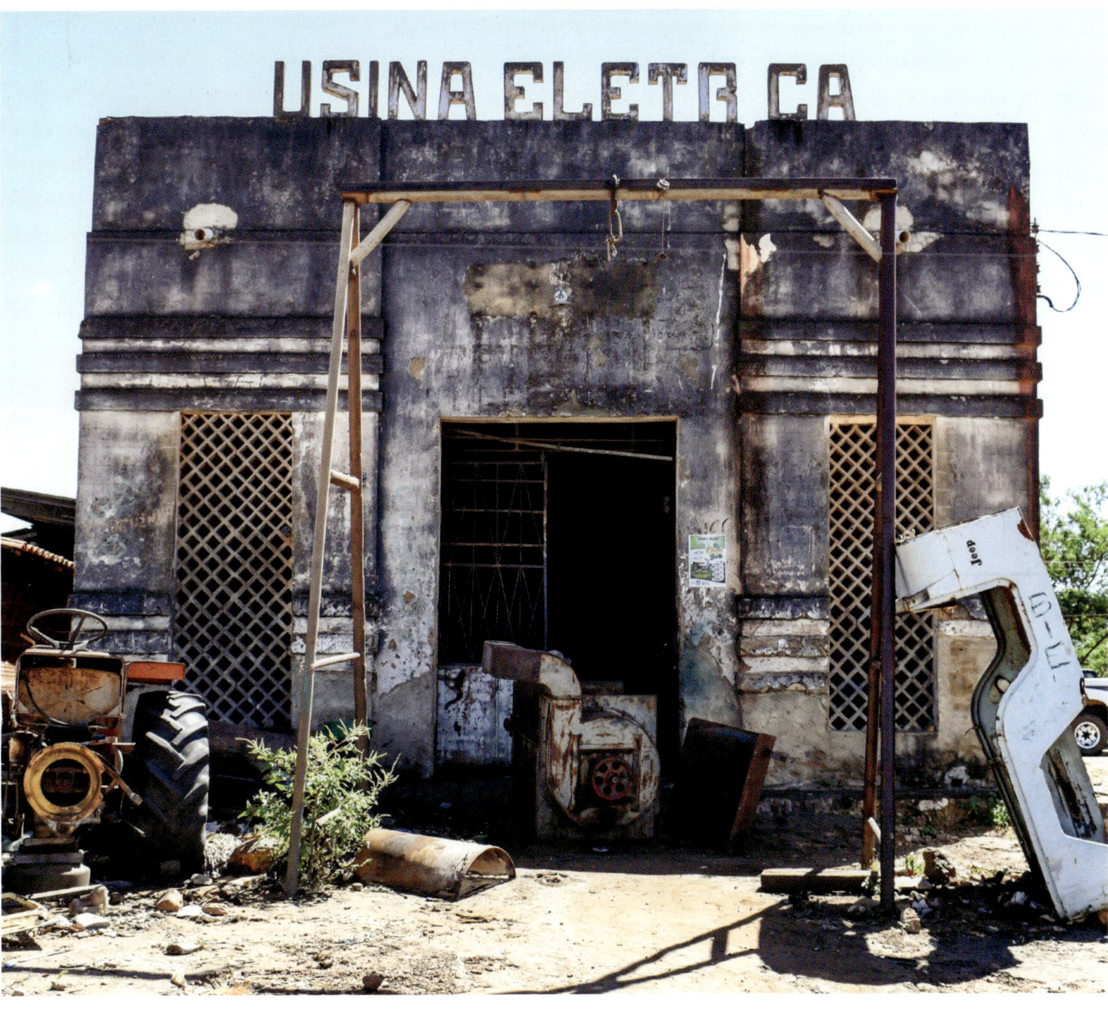

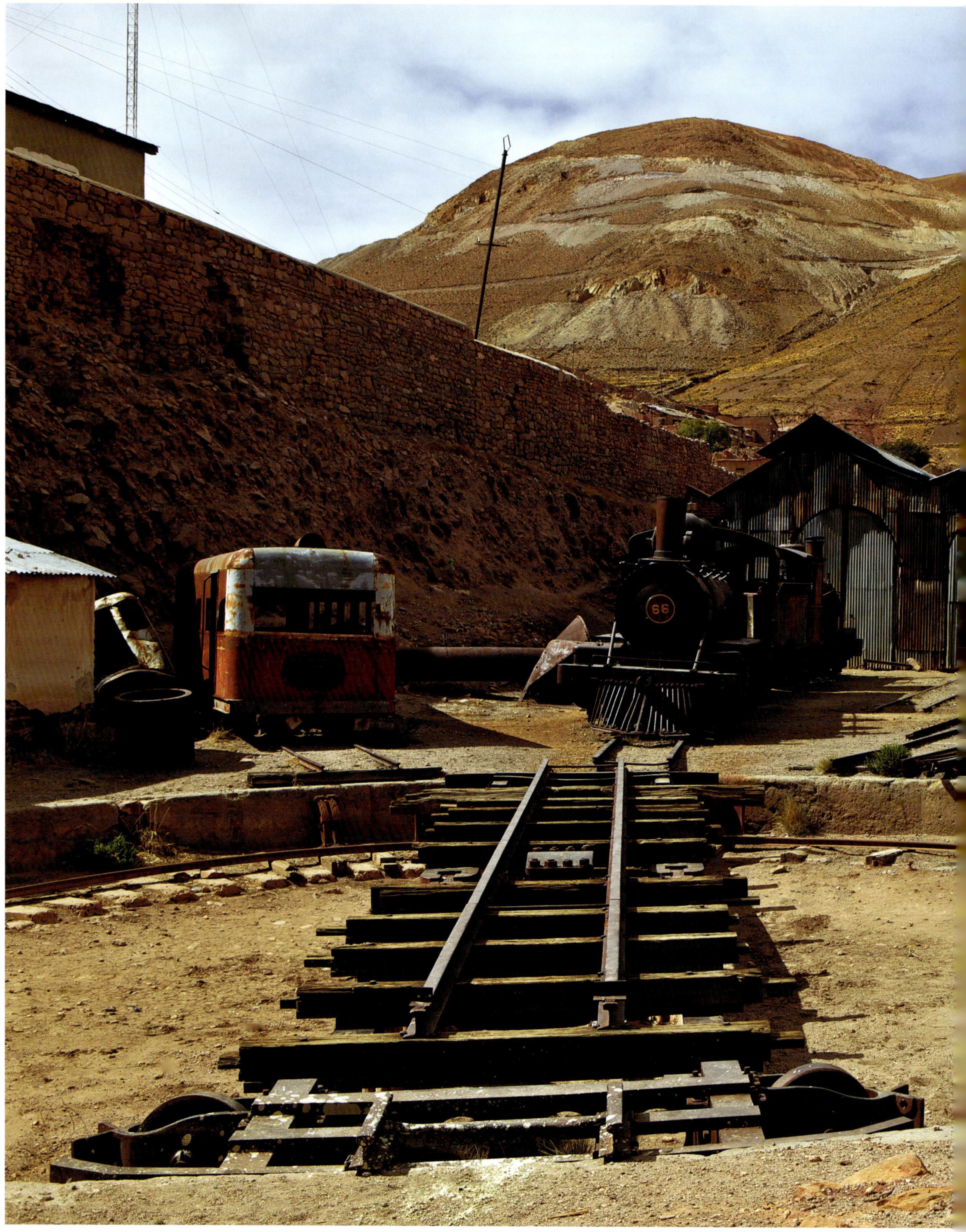

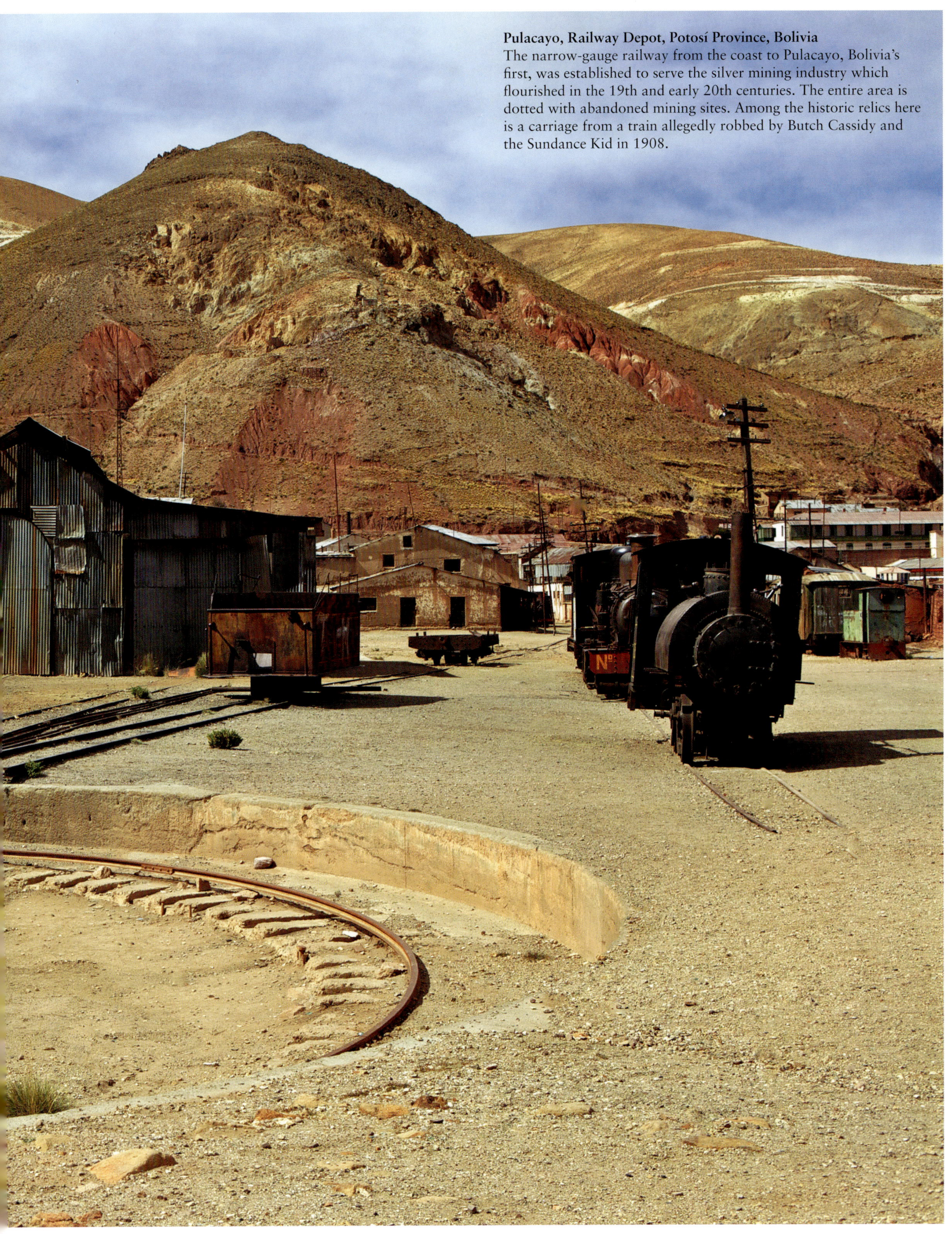

Pulacayo, Railway Depot, Potosí Province, Bolivia
The narrow-gauge railway from the coast to Pulacayo, Bolivia's first, was established to serve the silver mining industry which flourished in the 19th and early 20th centuries. The entire area is dotted with abandoned mining sites. Among the historic relics here is a carriage from a train allegedly robbed by Butch Cassidy and the Sundance Kid in 1908.

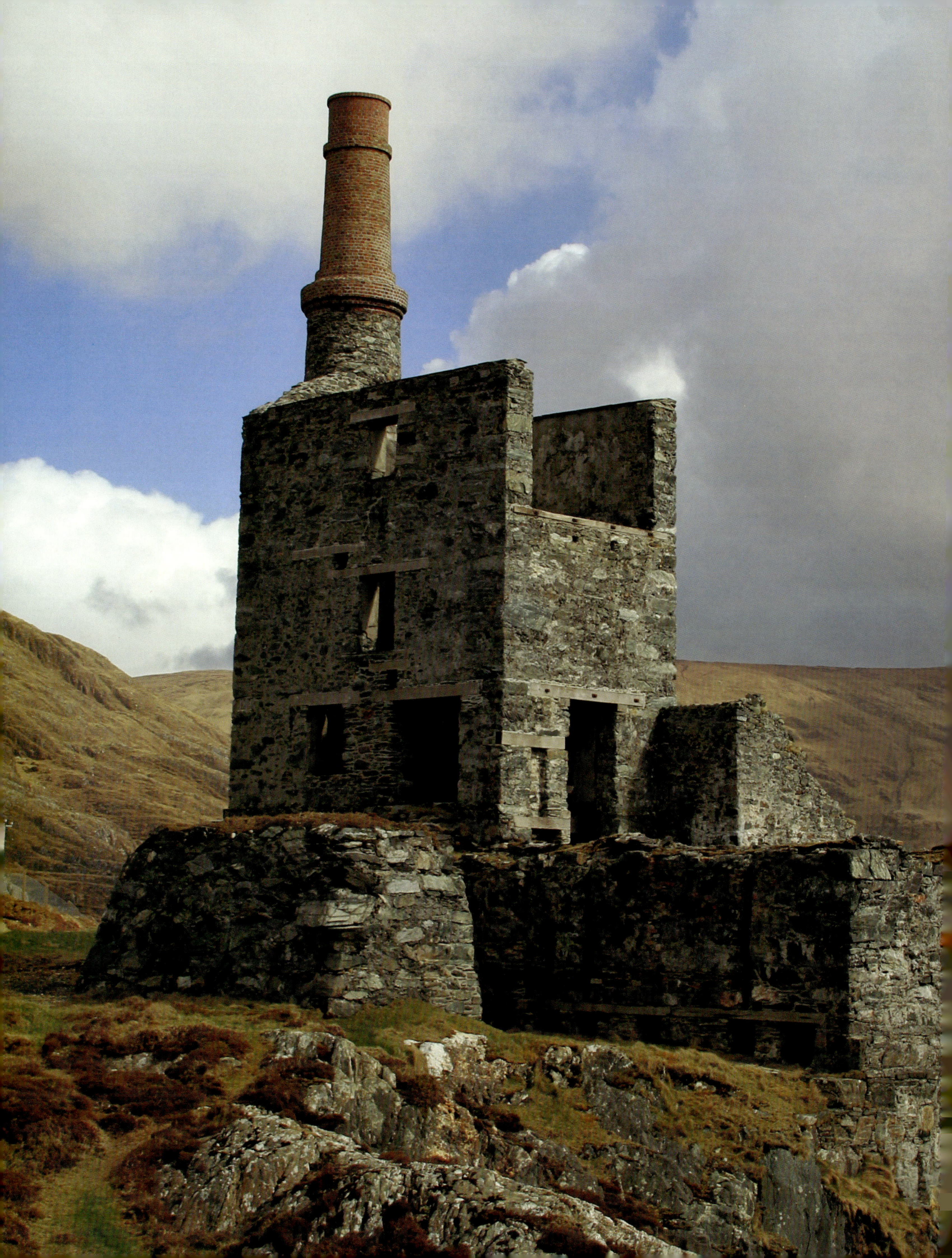

Europe

It was in Europe that the modern industrial era began, with the development of the steam engine and the large-scale use of iron. Before then, large factories had been rare, and the only power sources were wind and water. Every site was a greenfield one.

But transience was built in from the start. When a mine was worked out, it was left; sometimes its machinery was removed to another mine, but often it was easier and cheaper to equip the new place with more up-to-date gear.

Ironworks were set up close to ore deposits and closed when these were exhausted. Factories, built of stone or solid brick, were more durable, though conditions inside were increasingly unacceptable to the workers.

As technical improvements became more frequent, even relatively new industrial buildings often became outdated, and were left when the makers transferred to new premises. They are not relics of the age of steam but of the age of technology, and the sight of shiny valves and electrical apparatus permanently turned off has a poignancy of its own.

For some it induces a sense of anger at the sheer waste implied by modern machinery standing disused; for others they mark progress towards cleaner, less energy-intensive industry.

**Allihies Copper Mine,
West Cork, Ireland**
An isolated hillside engine house, massively built to withstand Atlantic storms and vibrating machinery, remains to mark the site of a remarkable mining operation which ran from 1812 to 1885, employing around 1500 people at its peak. A museum in the village and a 'coppermine trail' explain the mine's history.

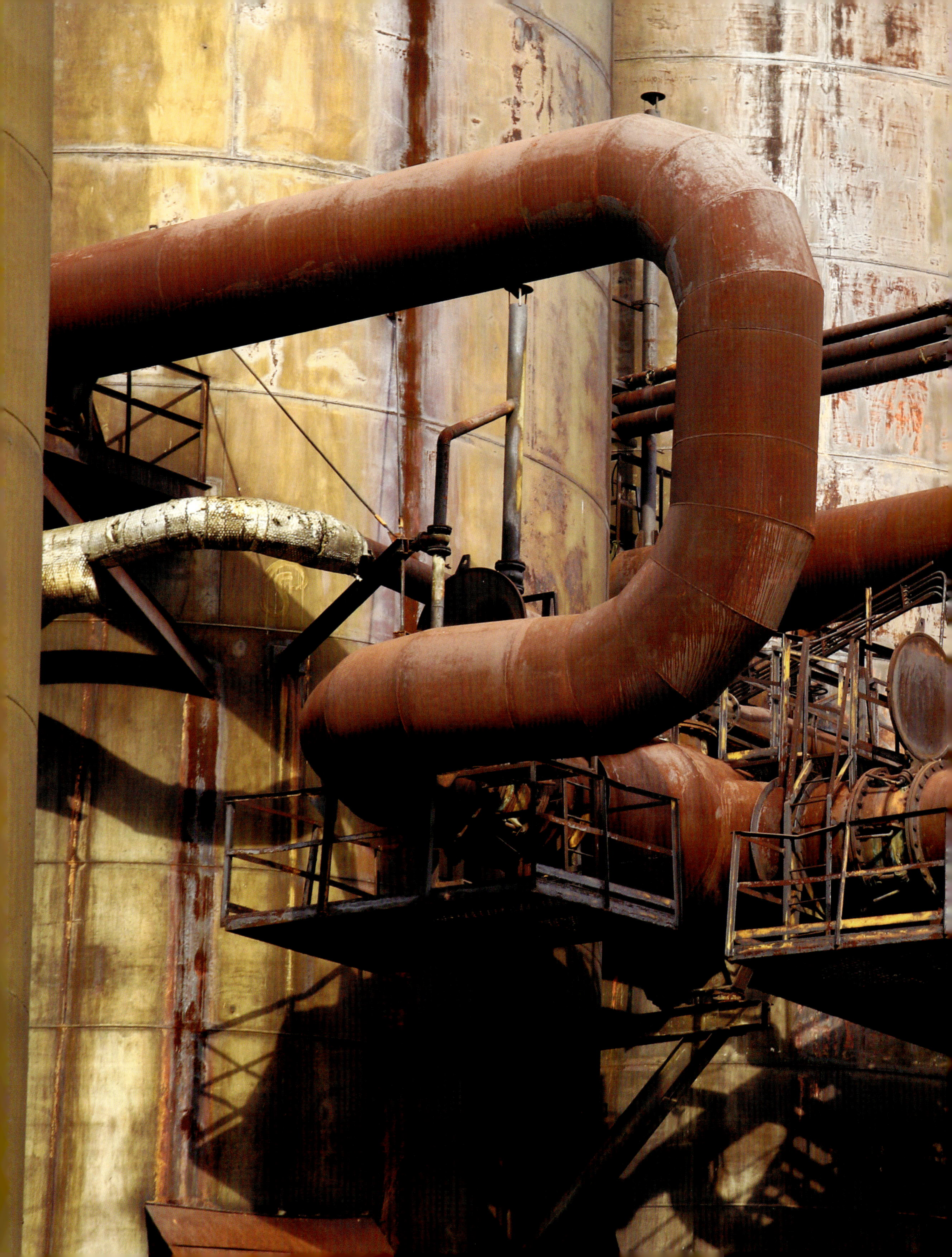

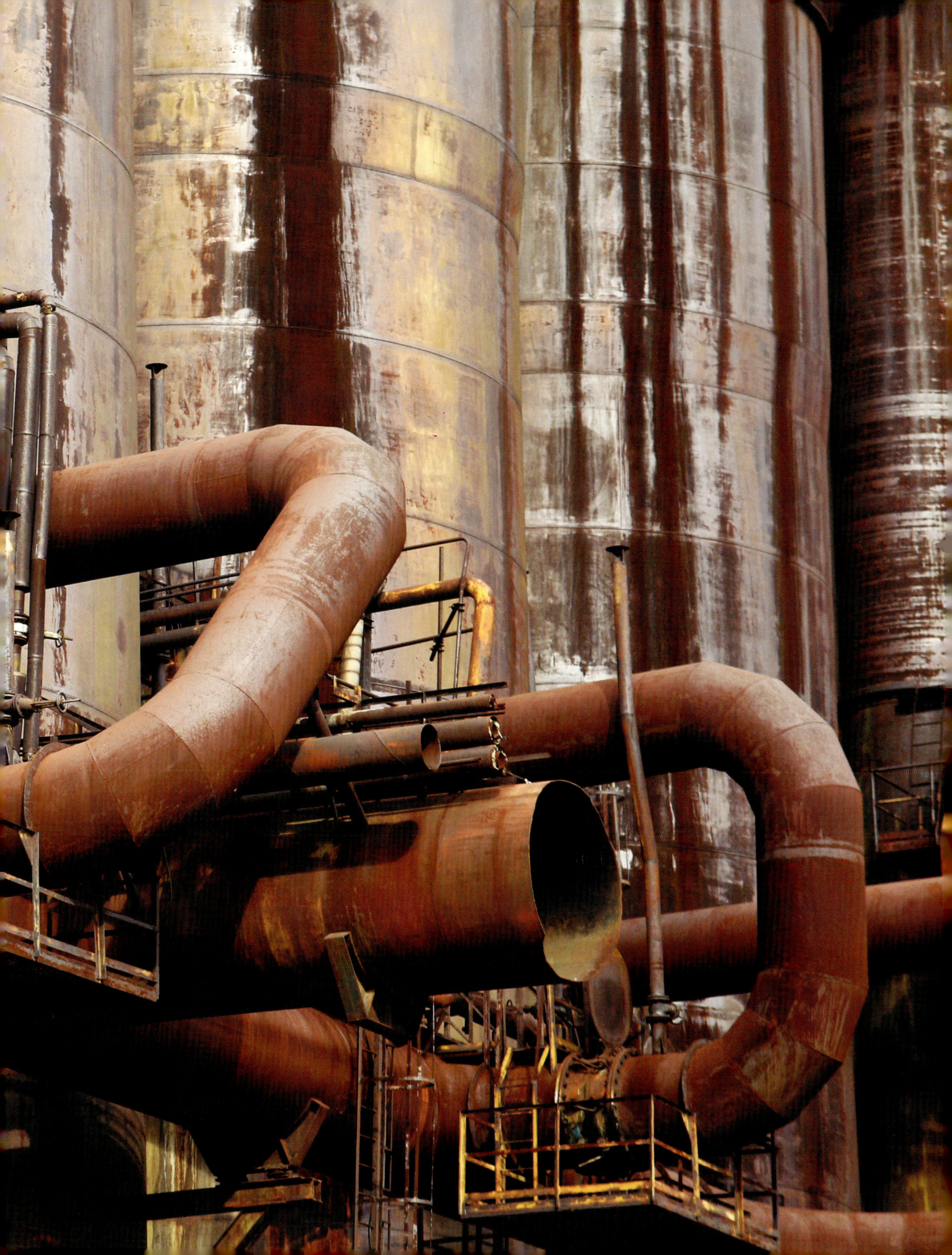

Ironworks Interior, Dolni Vitkovice, Czech Republic
Iron smelting was carried on in this district between 1830 and 1998, with a steadily expanding range of blast furnaces and coke ovens, burning locally-mined coal. The ironworks were saved from demolition to be maintained as an industrial museum. Its vast gas tank is now a concert hall.

Pottery Kilns, Stoke-on-Trent, England
Around 1900 there were some 4000 of these 'bottle ovens' in England's Potteries district, creating a highly distinctive (and very smoky) industrial landscape; now only 47 remain. Some were freestanding, others protruded from factory buildings. Furnaces below the brick structures distributed heat through the bottle-shaped structure where newly-moulded chinaware was hardened and glazed on trays made of clay.

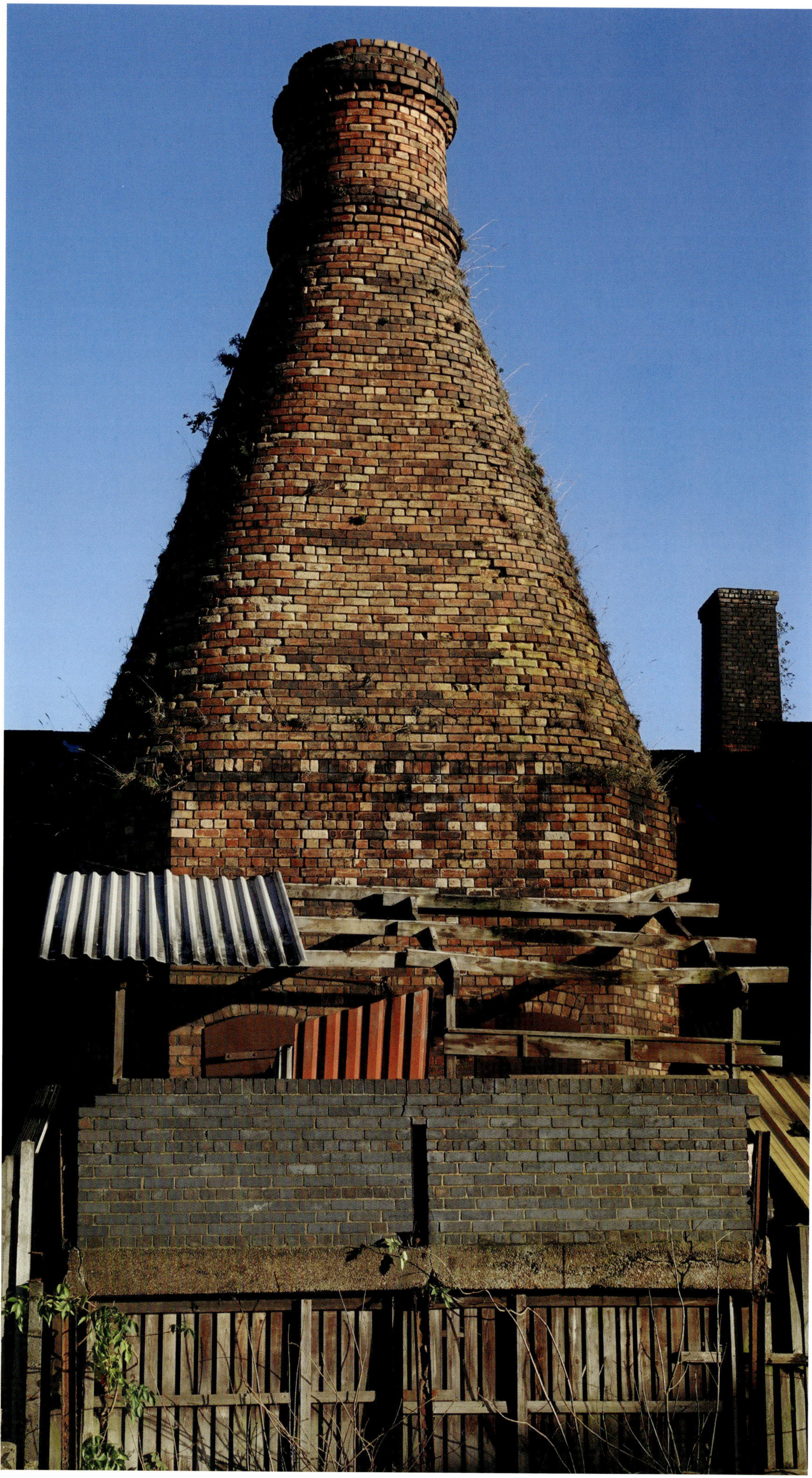

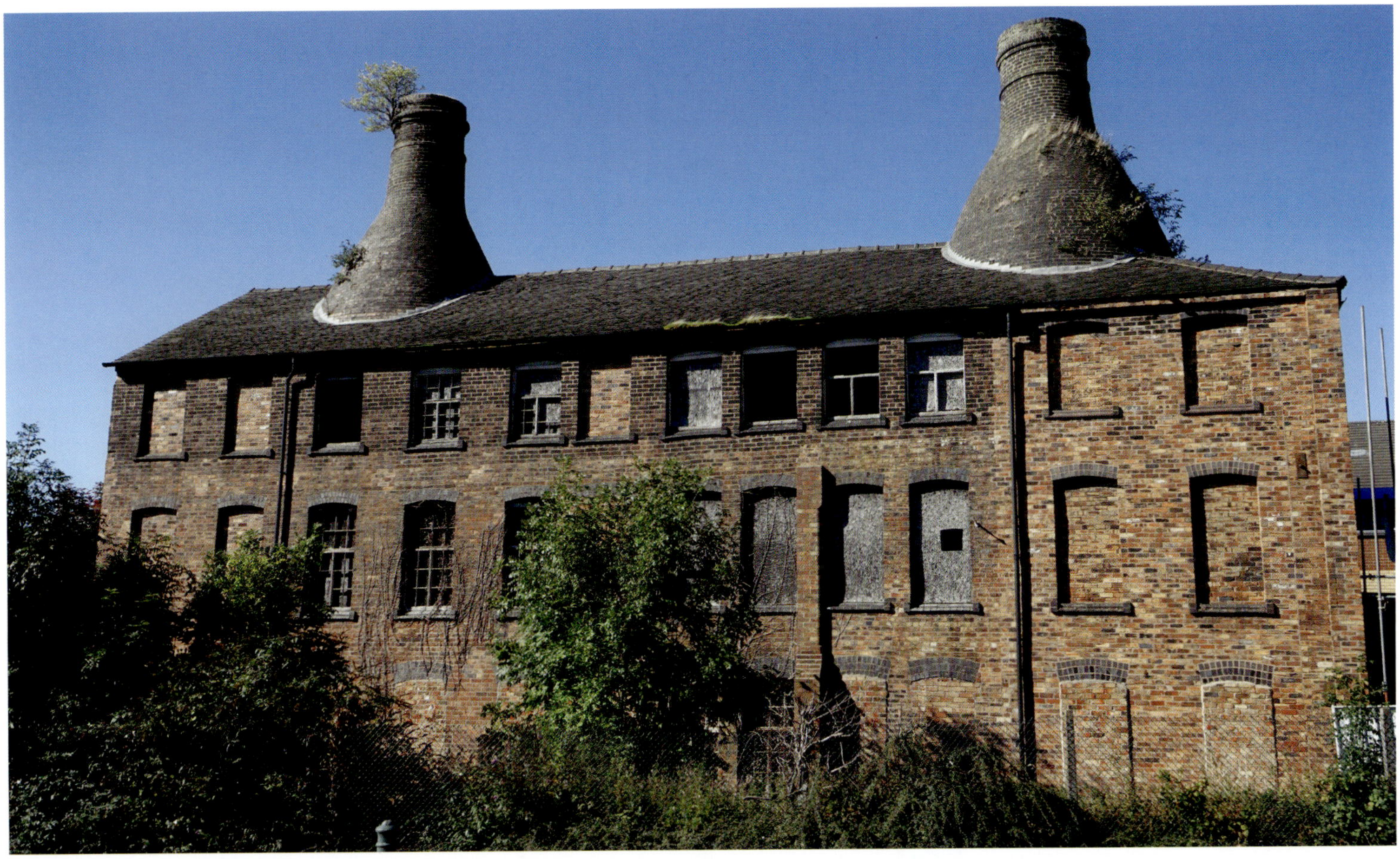

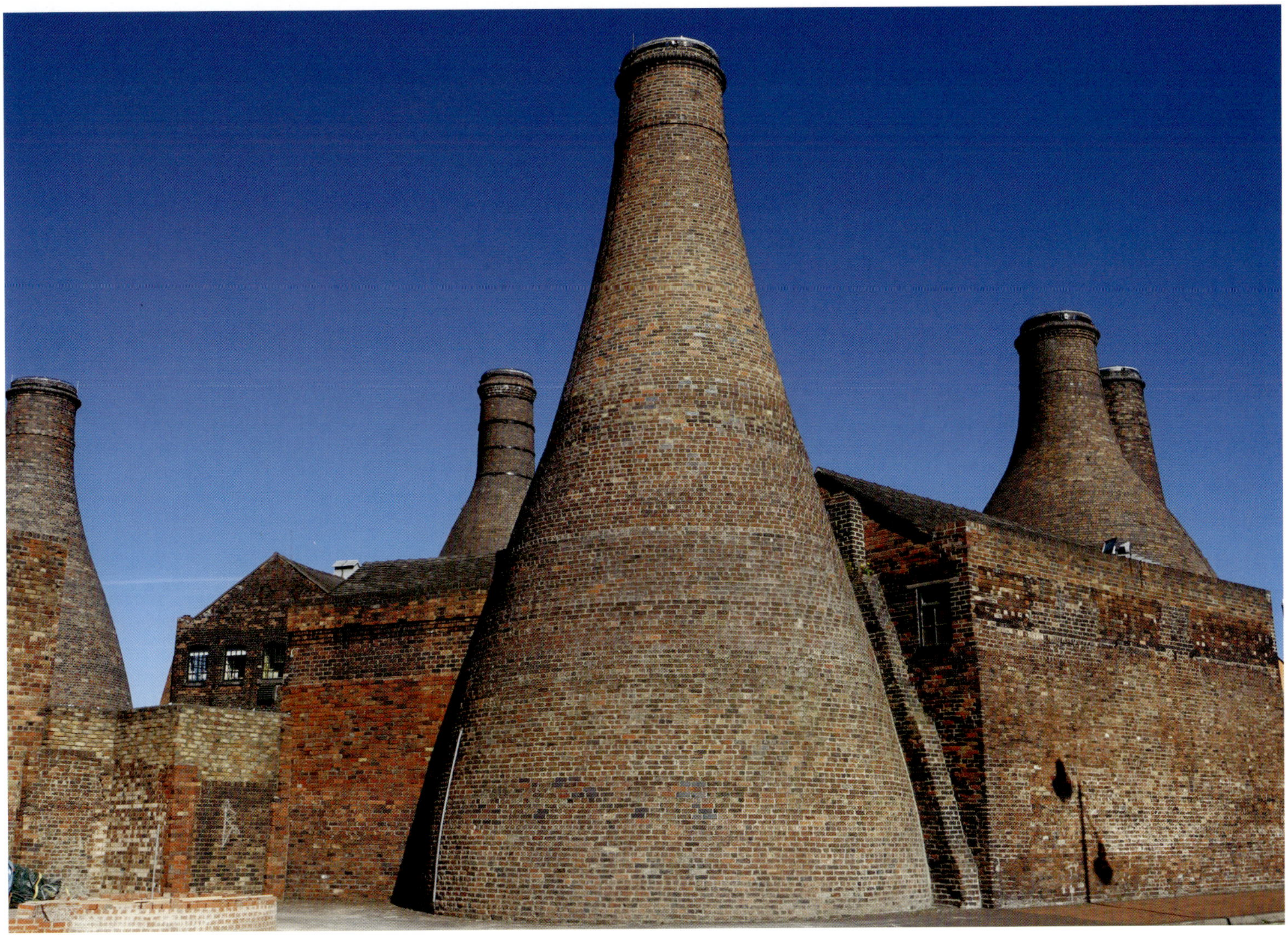

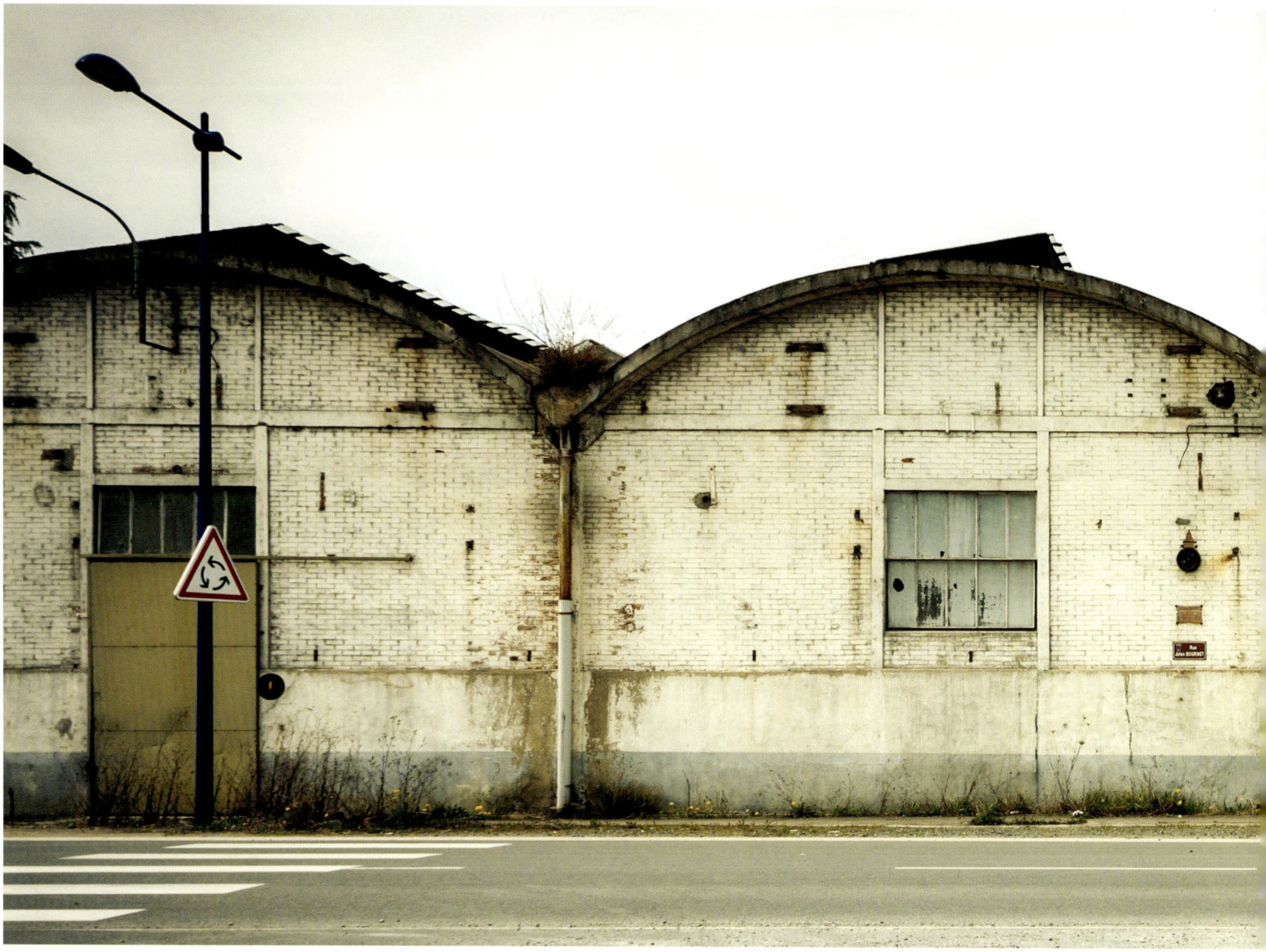

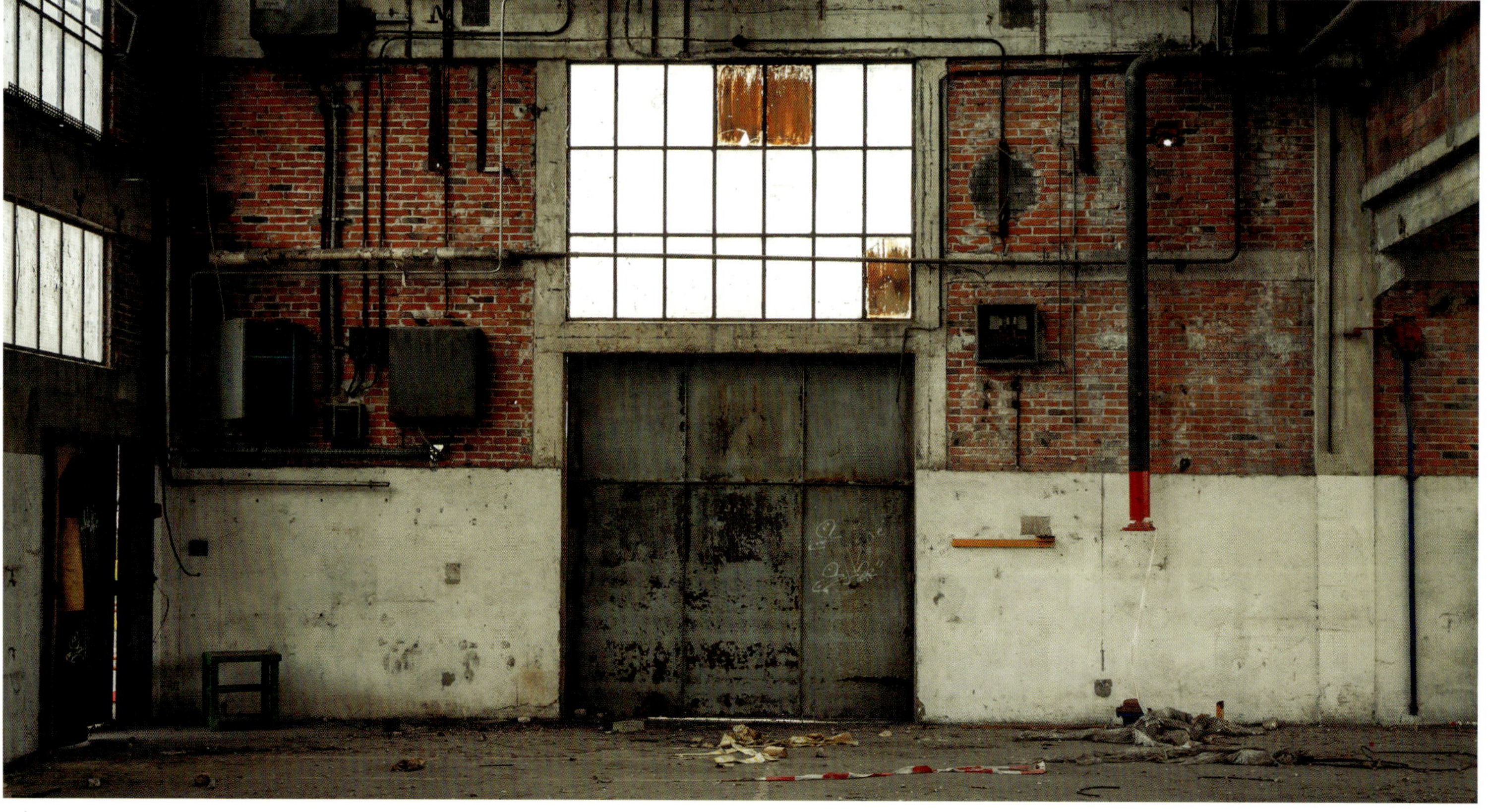

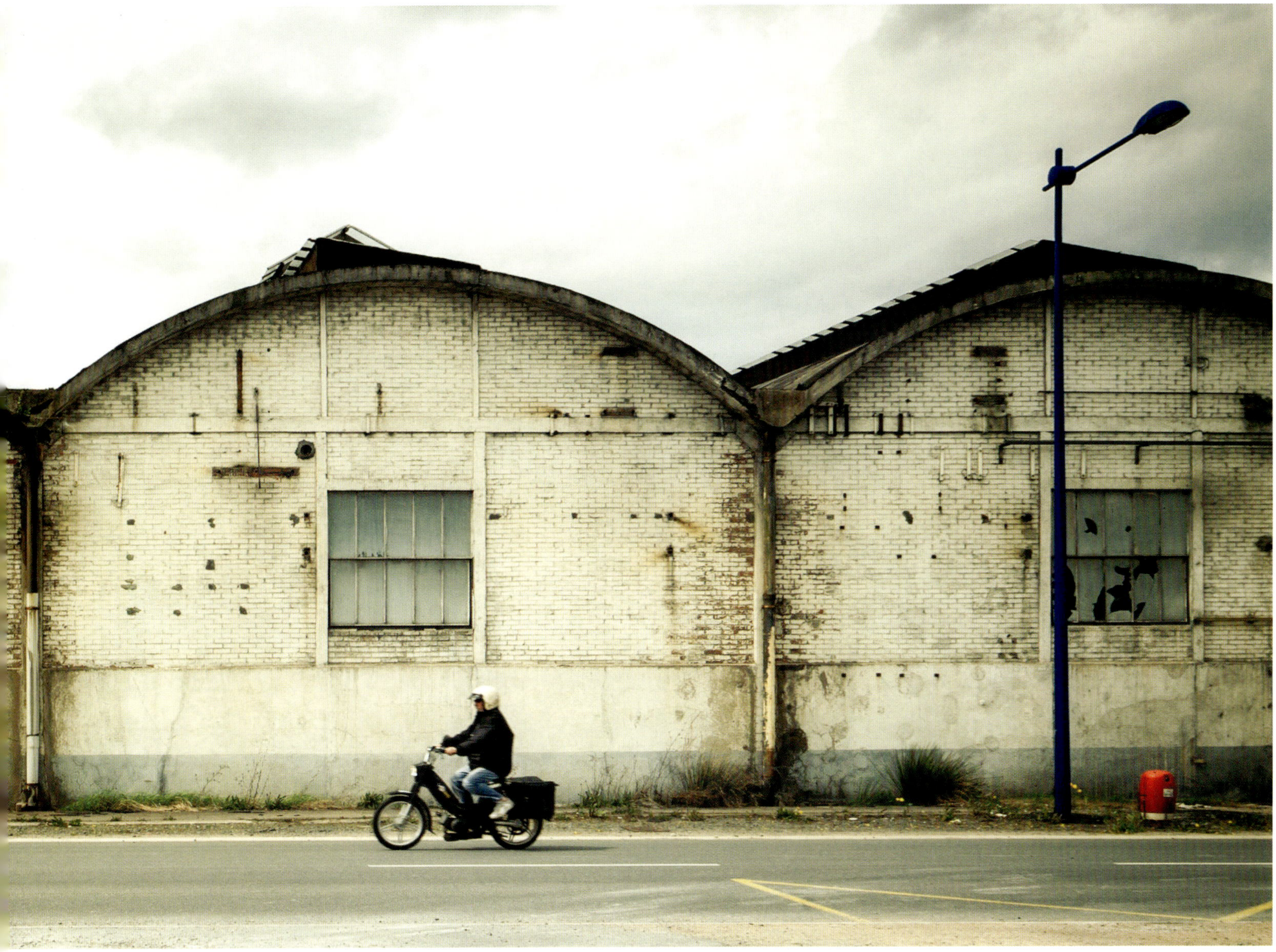

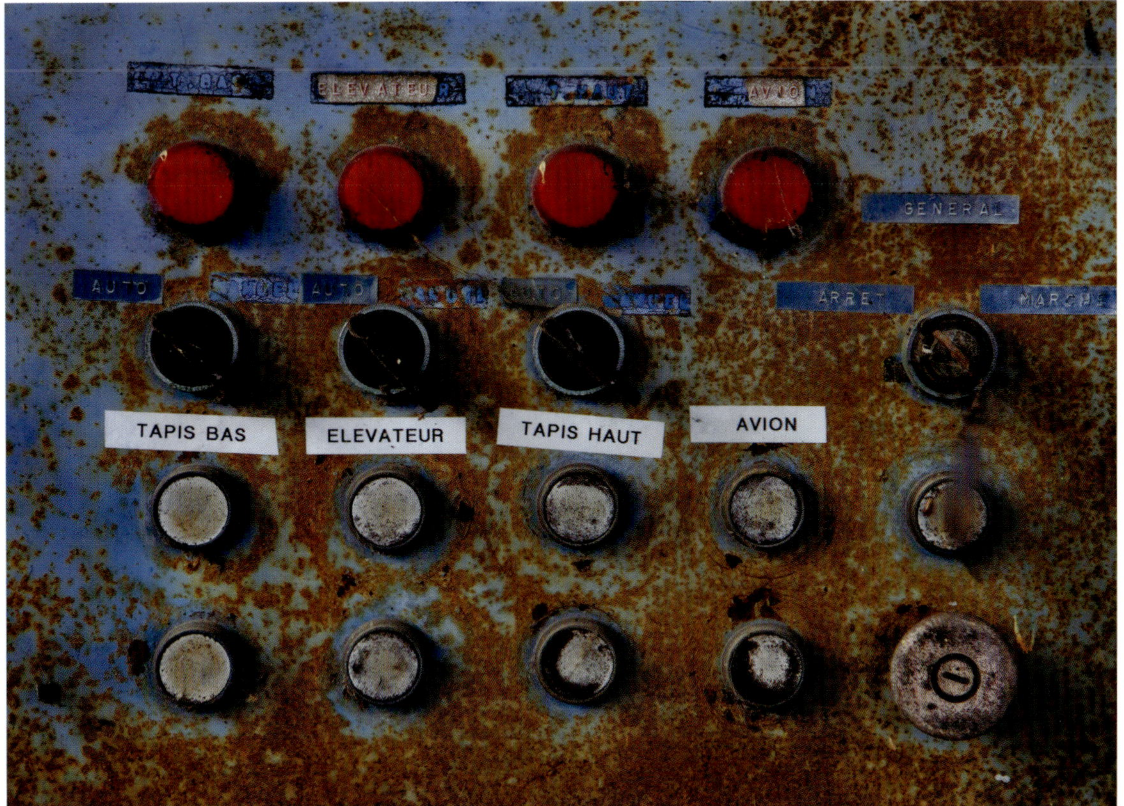

Tyre Factory Buildings, Montluçon, Allier, France
The Dunlop company began making tyres for European car makers here in 1919 and became the town's main employer, occupying an increasingly large site, with buildings and installations built over nine decades. These ventilated buildings, probably used for storing raw materials, became redundant around 2000, making a forlorn contrast to the rest of the site.

LEFT:

Derelict Distillery, Lézignan-Corbières, Aude, France
The switch panel from an industrial hoist at the Coopérative Audoise de Distillation's now-demolished brandy distillery, which ceased production in 2007. Most of the functional equipment has been reinstalled in other distilleries in the region.

Kelenföld Power Station, Budapest, Hungary
Hungary was at the forefront of early electric technology and this 1914 power station was one of the most advanced in the world. It supplied power until 2007, and remains intact with its turbines, generators and switchgear, as well as its splendid control room ceiling.

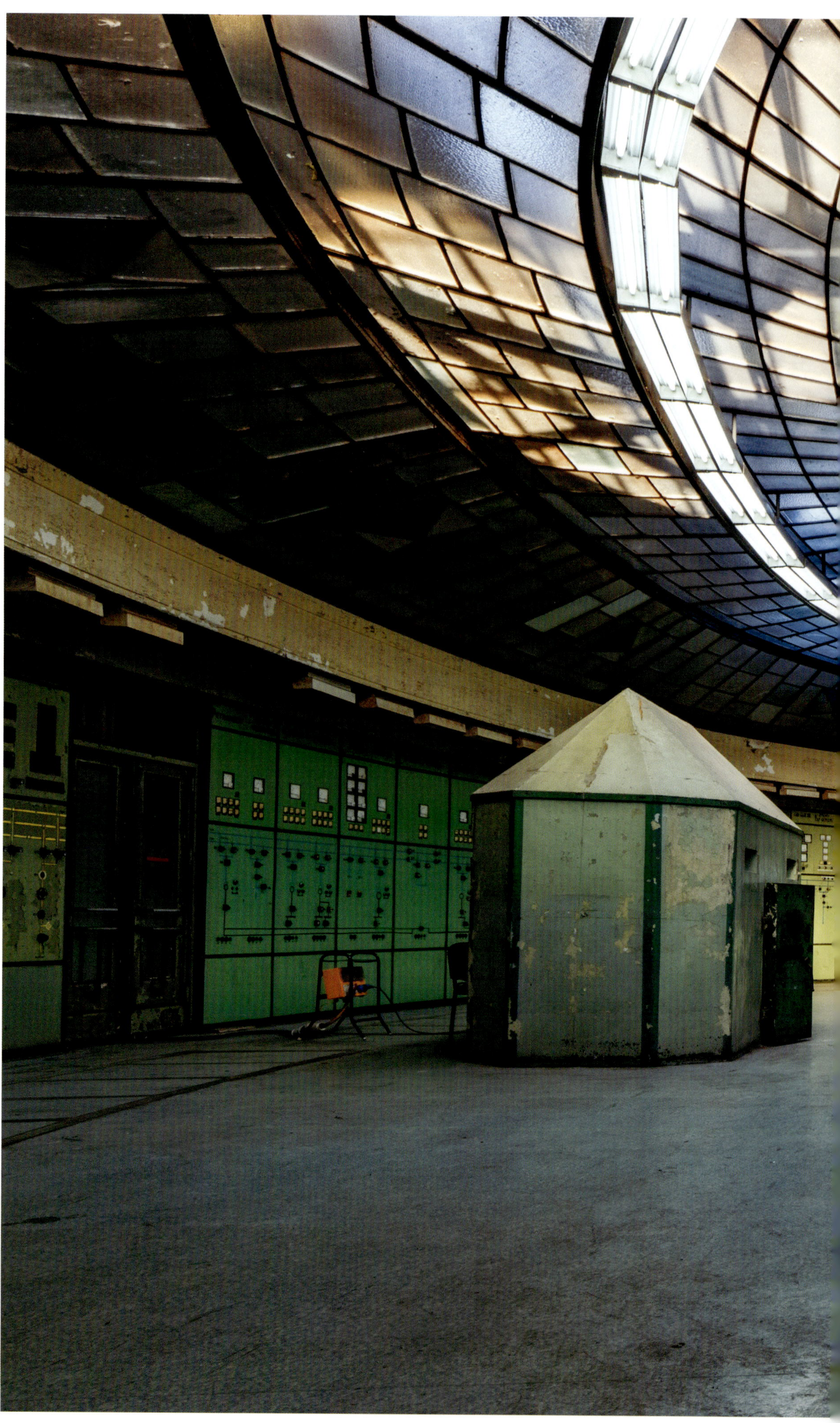

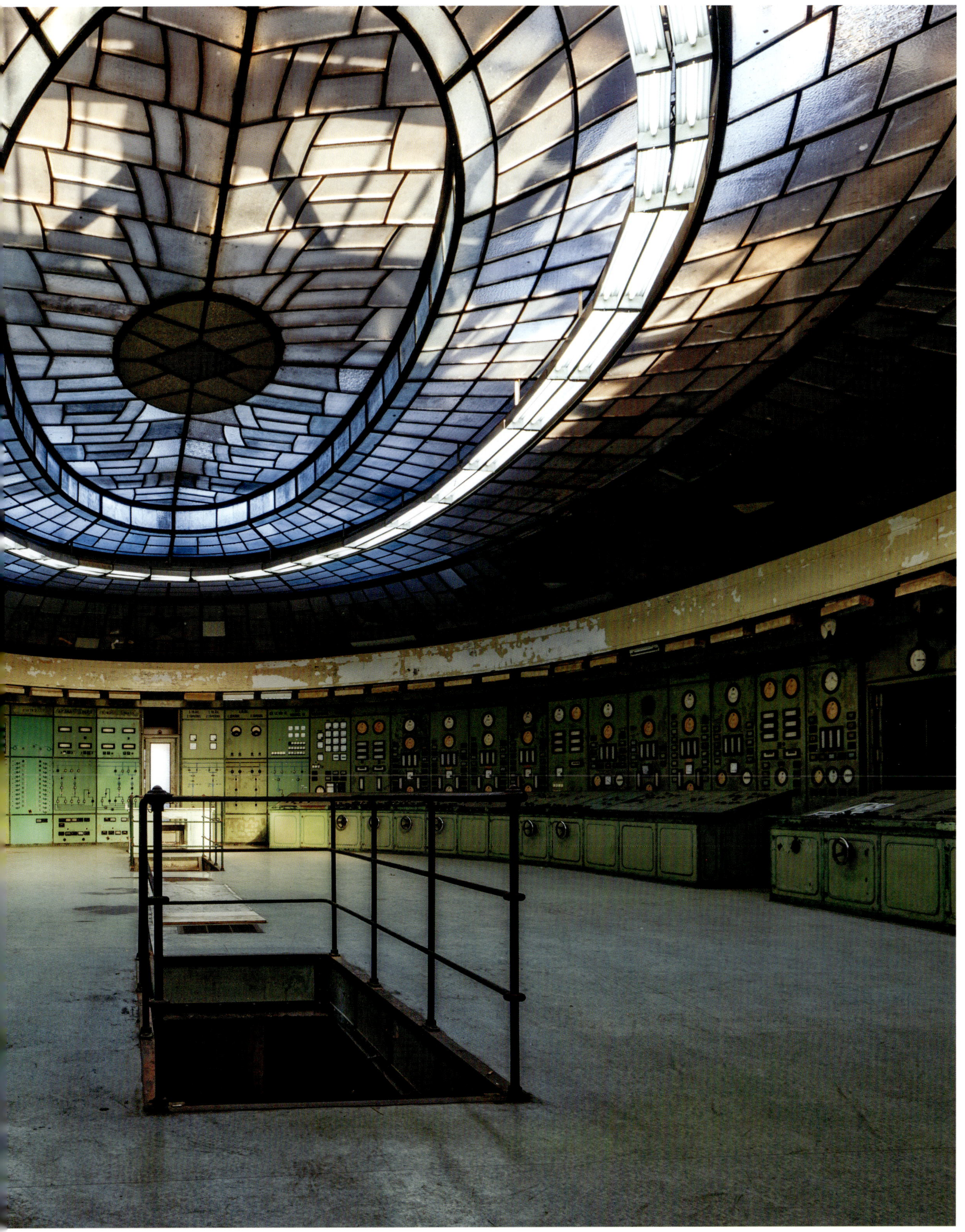

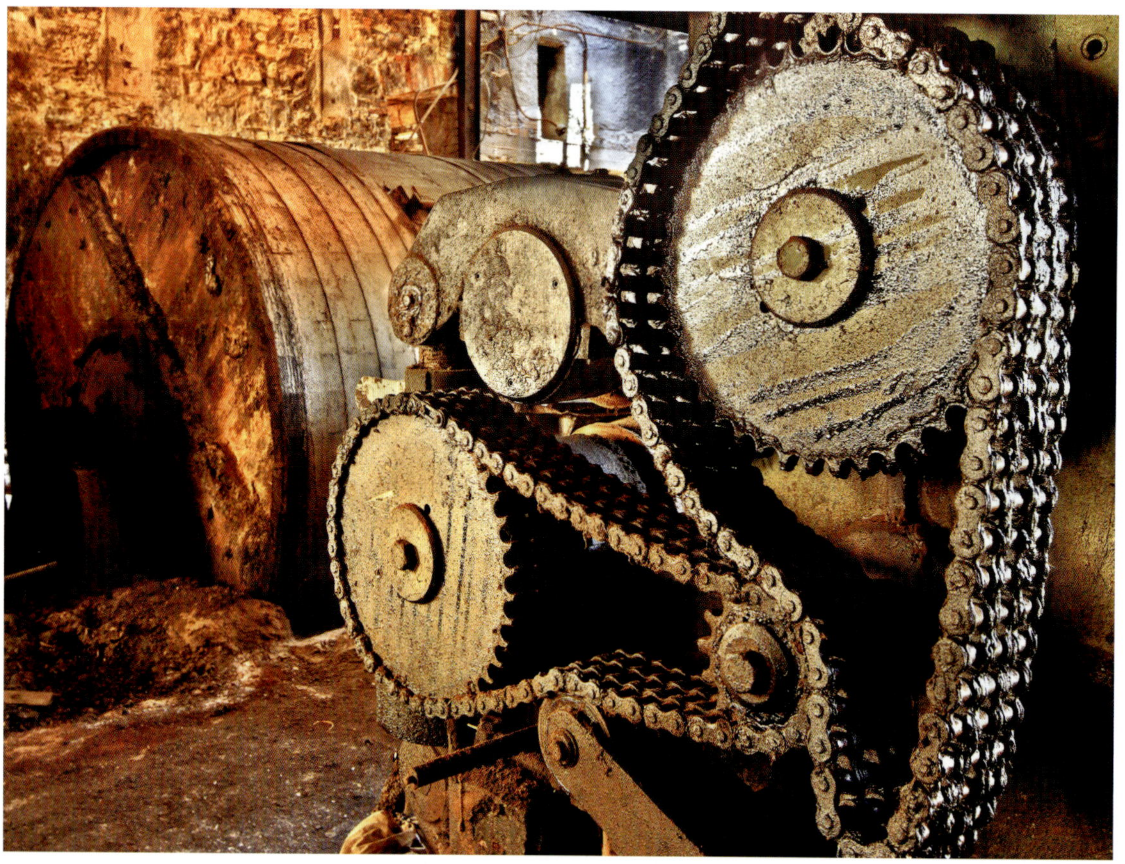

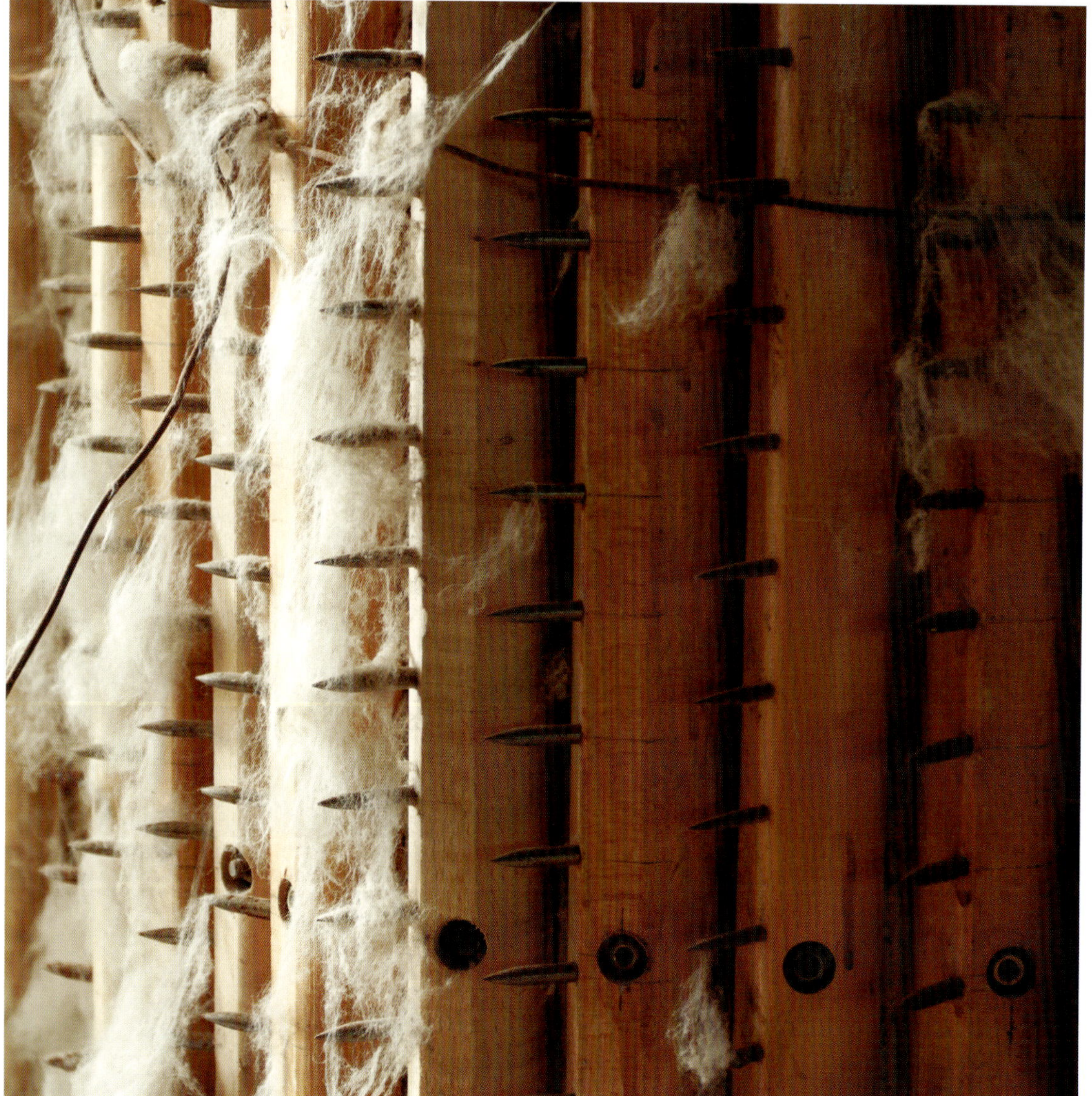

Tannery in Karlovasi, Samos, Greece

Processing animal hides for leather was the main industry here until the 1930s, and many derelict tanneries can be found. This one however has become a museum, where 19th and 20th century mechanised equipment can be seen, and the whole process of tannery can be followed.

Spinning Mill, Widzew, Łódž, Poland

Łódž was pre-eminently a textile making city and had many spinning mills. The full process from baled wool to fine threads began with carding machines like this, which formed long strands ready for spinning. The wooden frames were replaced by metal drums worked by steam.

St Aldegonde Brewery, Ricksteenweg, West Flanders, Belgium

Belgium had hundreds of small local breweries, most of which had disappeared before the vogue for craft beers arrived. This one went out of business sometime before 2000. It produced other drinks as well as beers, and these bottles, still sitting on the filling line in 2014, look more suitable for soft drinks.

Ore Processing Works, Erzgebirge, Czech Republic

The Erzgebirge (ore mountains) range near Karlovy Vary are rich in minerals. Metals like silver and tin have been mined here for centuries, and uranium was extracted between 1947 and 1958. This Piranesi-like plant with its staircases to nowhere was one of many now-derelict sorting and processing sites in the mountains.

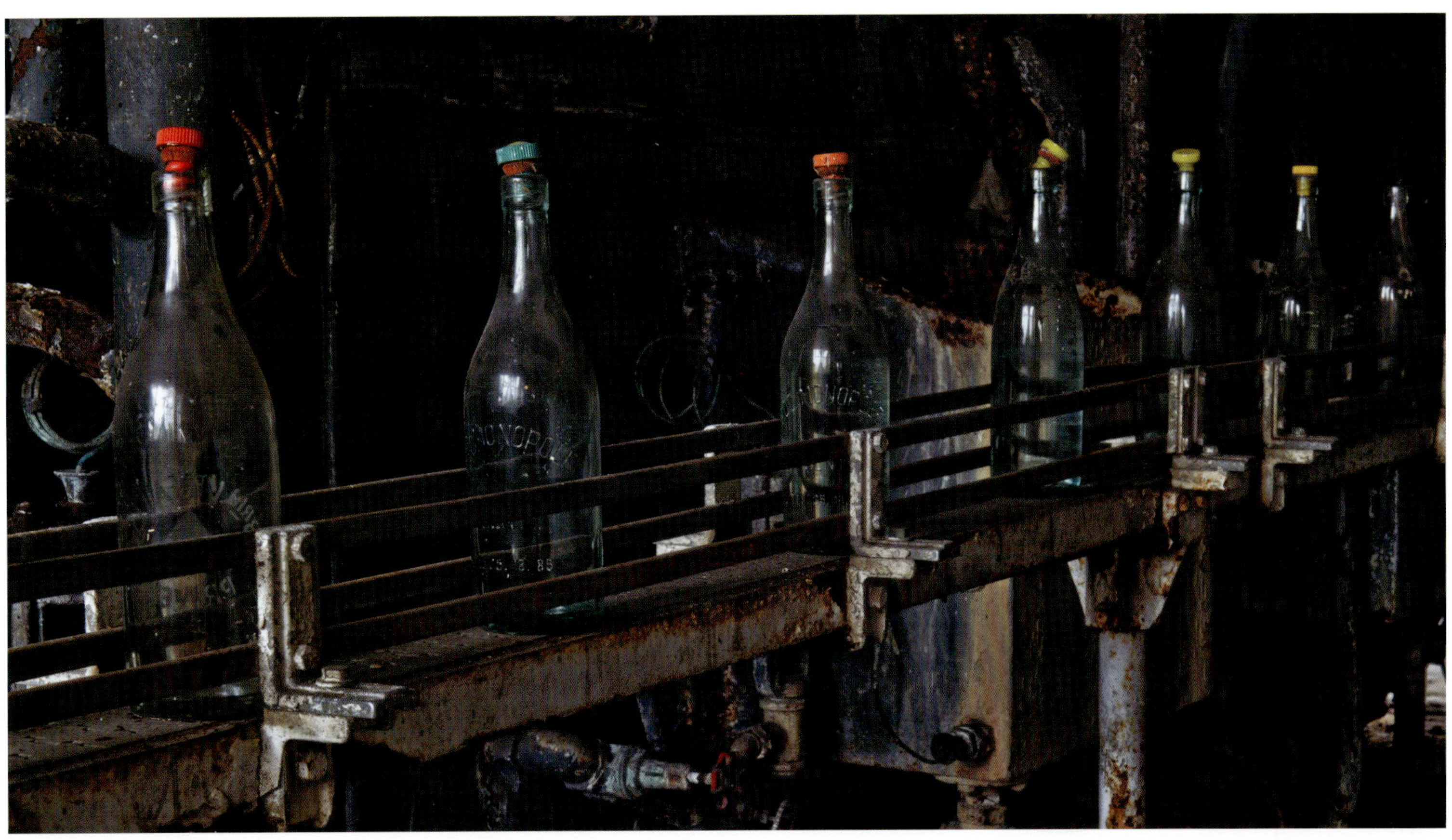

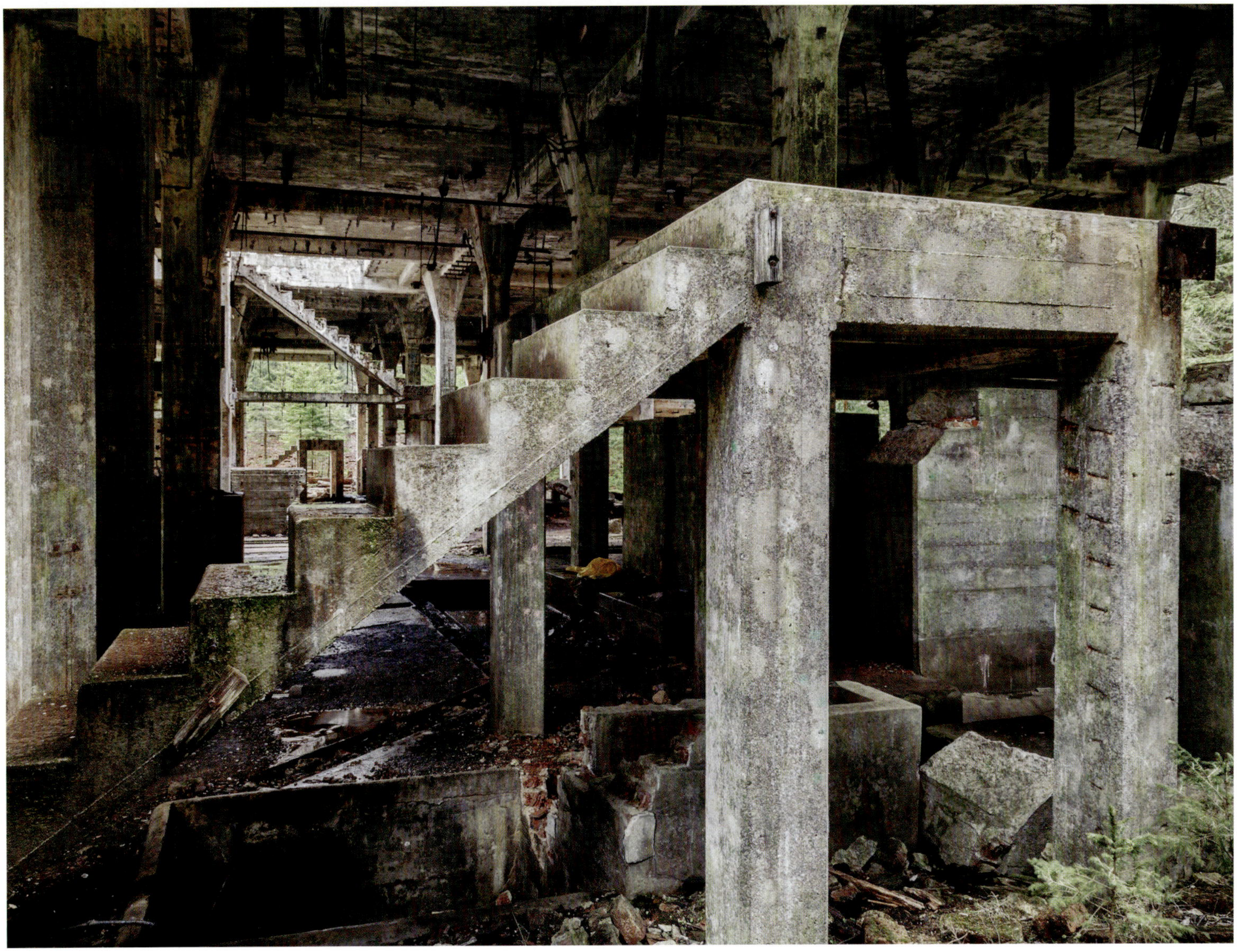

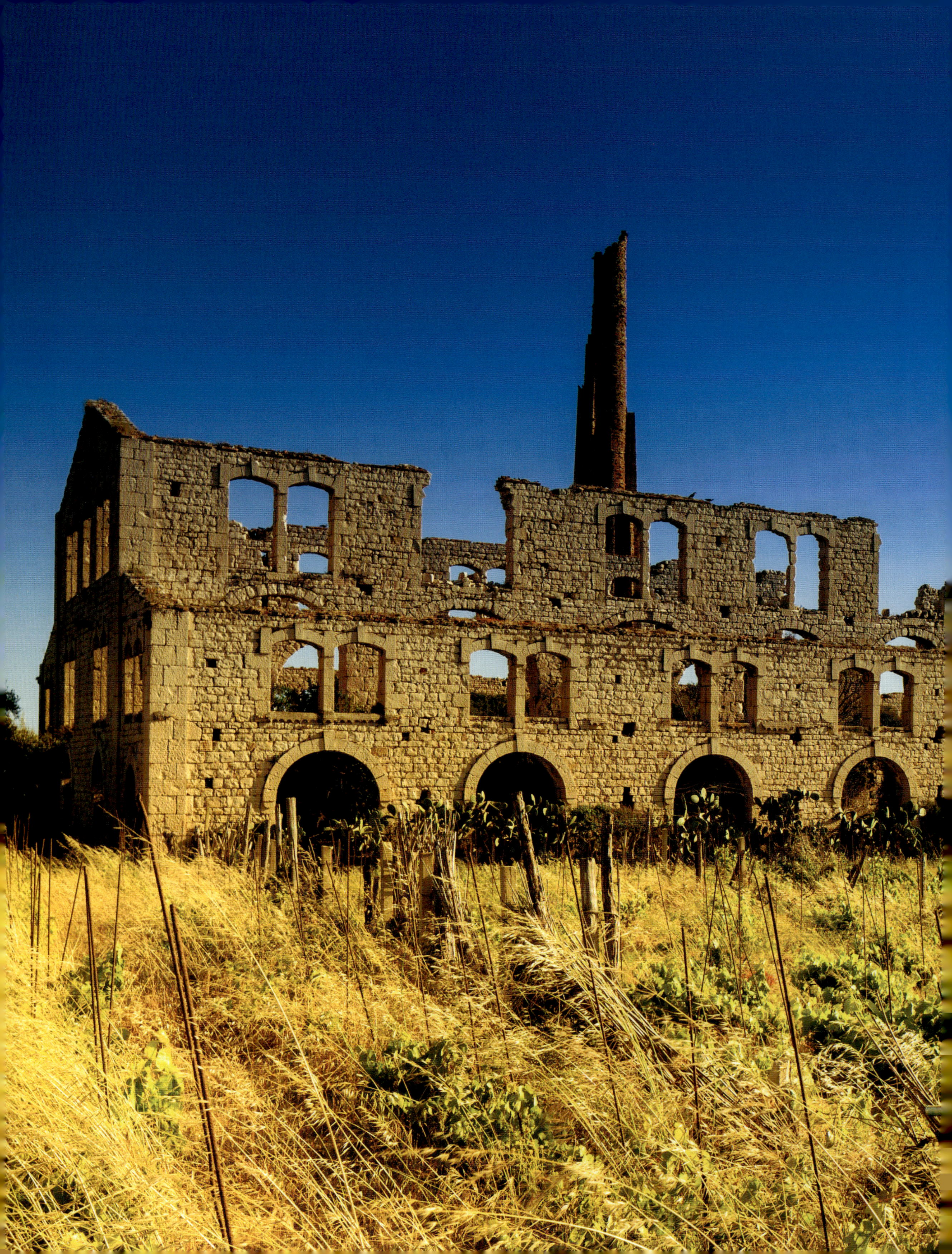

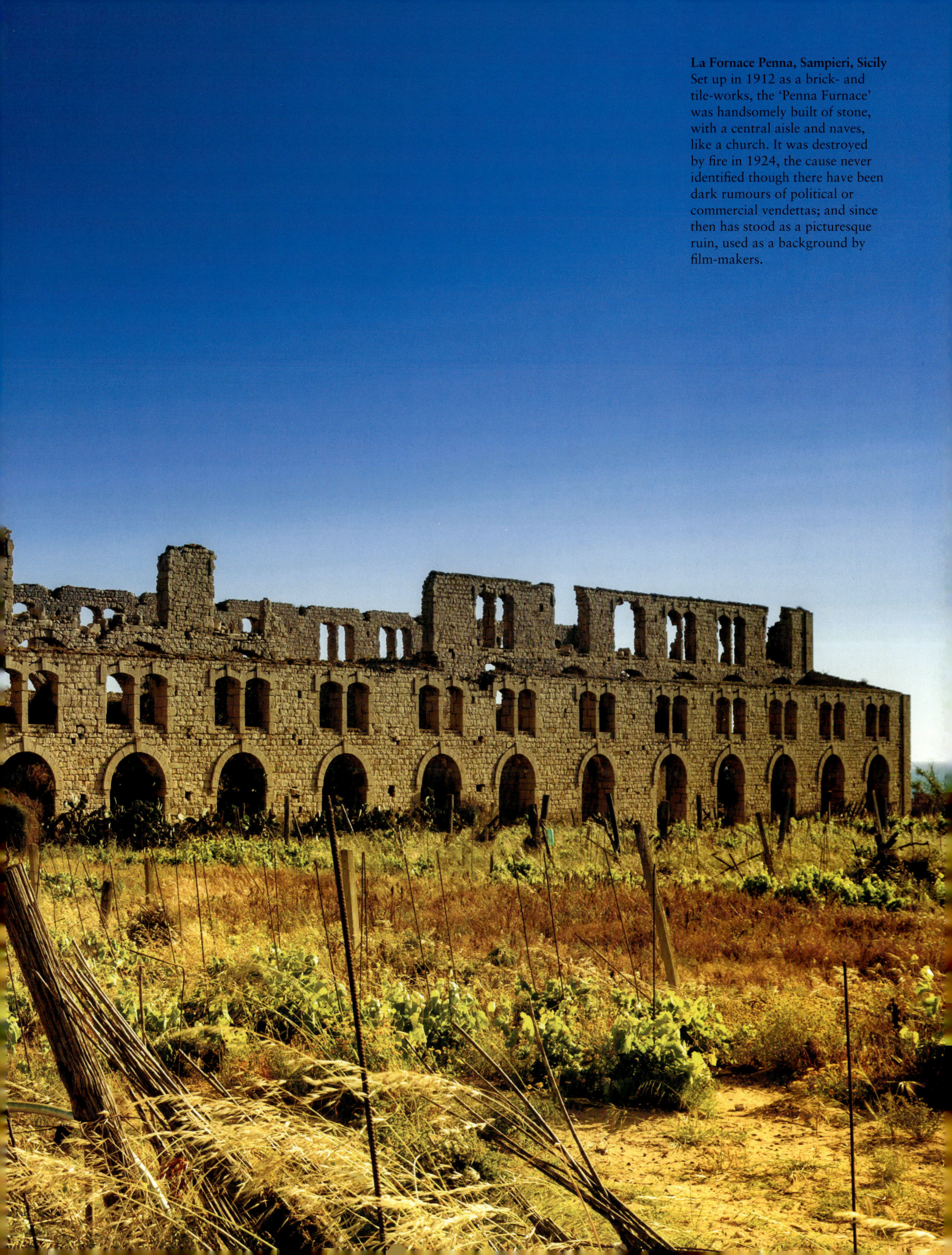

La Fornace Penna, Sampieri, Sicily
Set up in 1912 as a brick- and tile-works, the 'Penna Furnace' was handsomely built of stone, with a central aisle and naves, like a church. It was destroyed by fire in 1924, the cause never identified though there have been dark rumours of political or commercial vendettas; and since then has stood as a picturesque ruin, used as a background by film-makers.

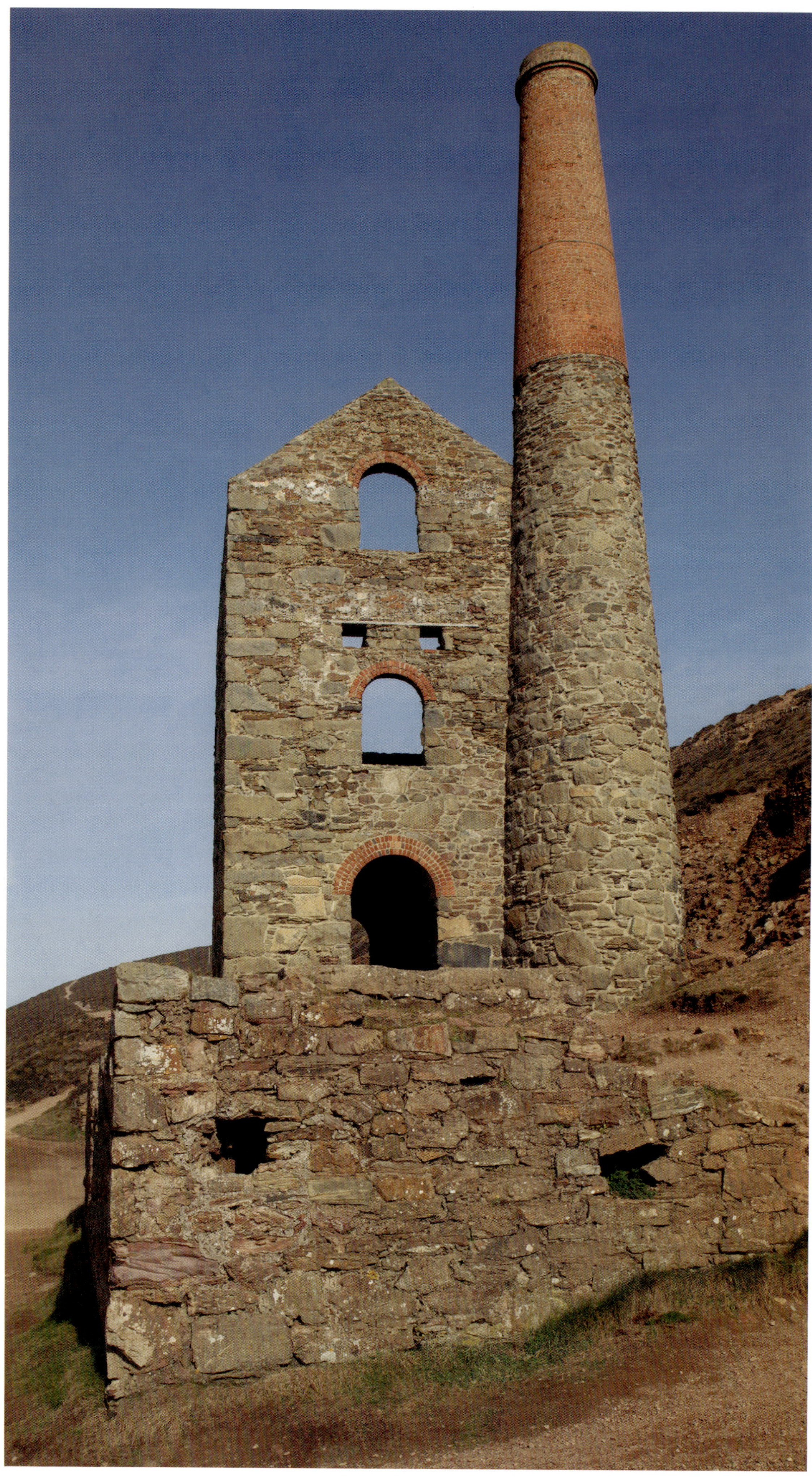

RIGHT:

**Engine House, Wheal Coates
Tin Mine, Cornwall, England**
Towanroath Engine House was
built on its cliff-top site in 1872
to pump water out of a deep
shaft which extended under
the sea. The brick extension to
its chimney and the brickwork
round the arches probably date
from 1911 when, after a twenty-
year closure, the mine briefly
reopened.

OPPOSITE TOP LEFT:

**Abandoned Warehouse,
Bulverhythe, East Sussex,
England**
A section of the façade of this
now demolished building,
shows a typical approach to the
construction of a large industrial
building, increasingly common in
the 1940s and 50s, of modular
sections: ribbed concrete panels
and large glazed spaces with
aluminium frames. They did not
weather well.

OPPOSITE TOP RIGHT:

**Disused Water Works,
Low Bradfield, South
Yorkshire, England**
Abandoned and fenced off since
1994, this water treatment works
was set up in 1913. A favourite
haunt of ruin explorers and
graffiti practitioners, it is stripped
of almost all its equipment
and increasingly invaded by
vegetation.

OPPOSITE BOTTOM:

**Waterfront Warehouses,
Liverpool, England**
In contrast to the building above
(left) these warehouses were
built to be permanent, and their
iron frames and brick walls have
outlived their function as storage
sheds. Seen here in neglect, they
have been restored and given new
purpose in the renaissance of
Liverpool's waterfront district.

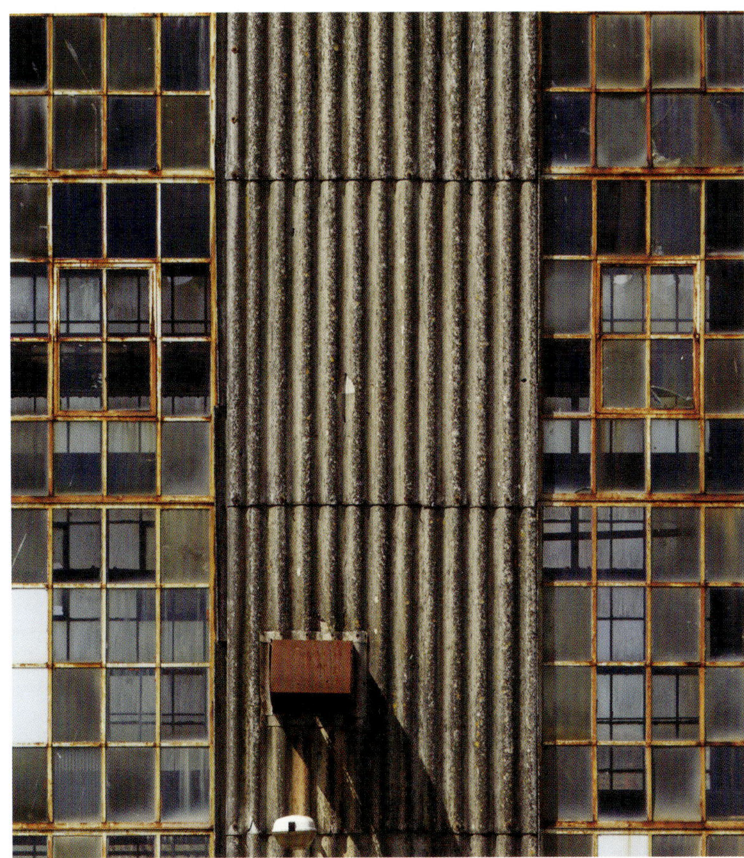

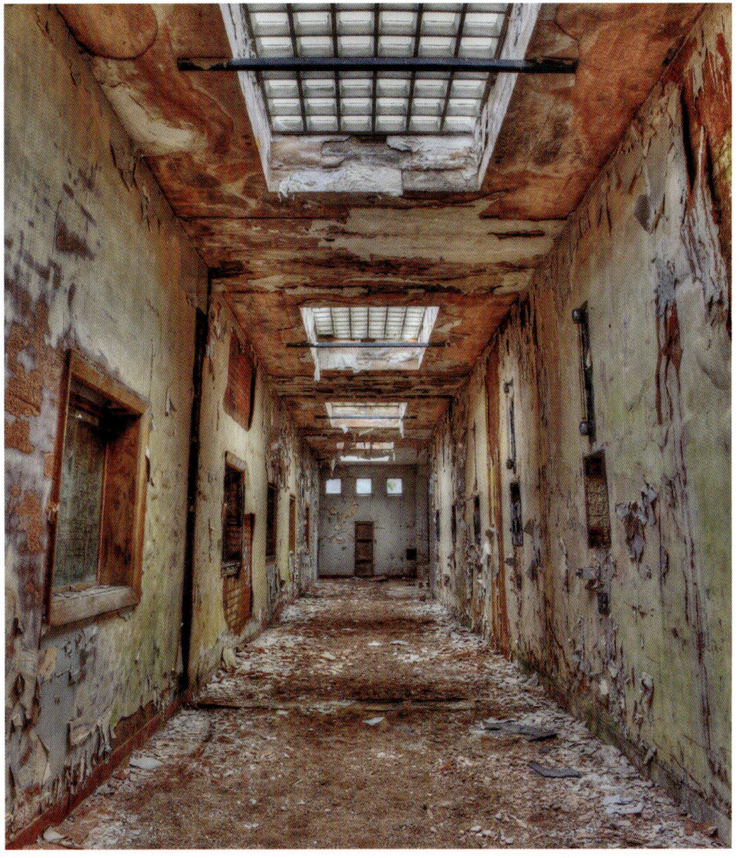

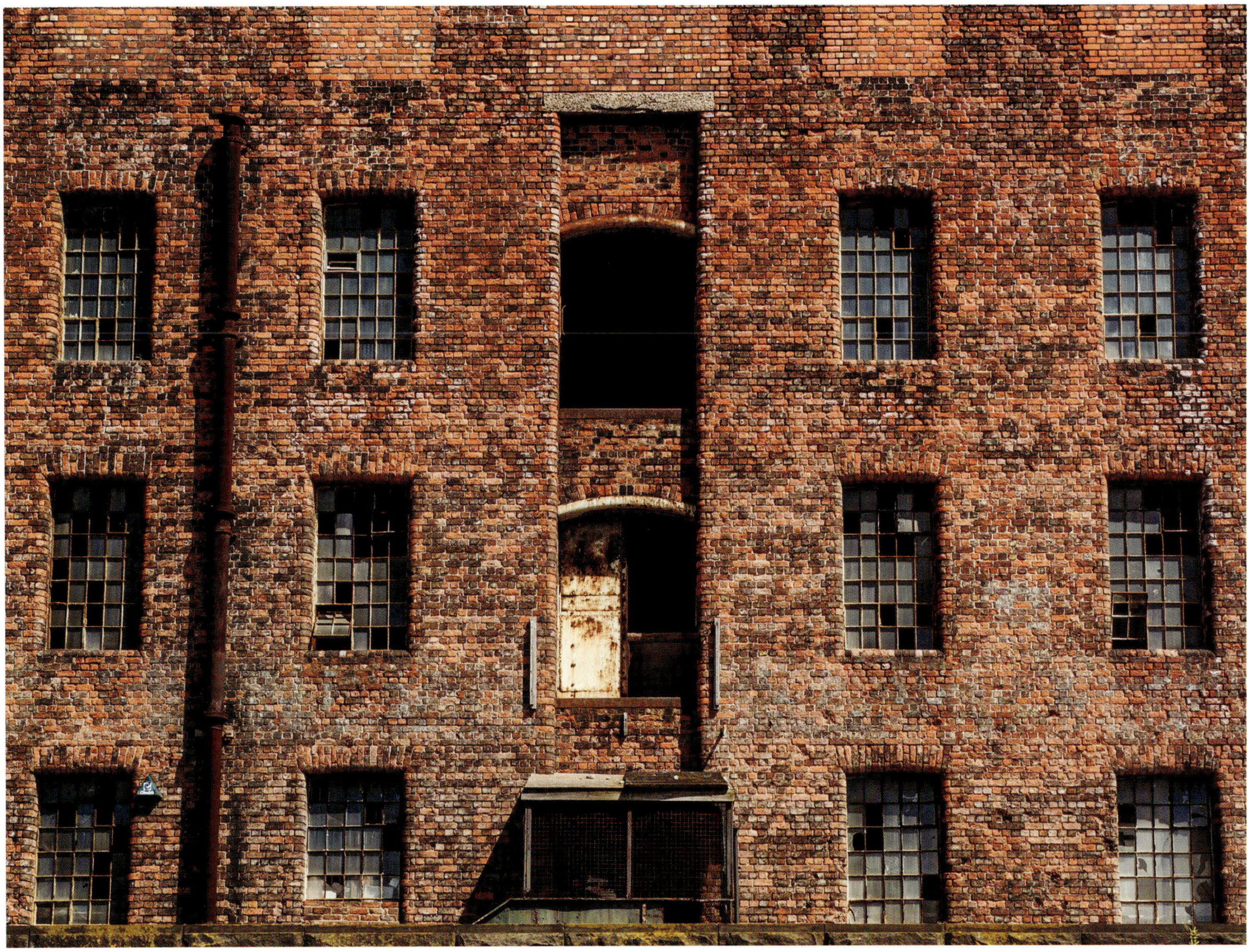

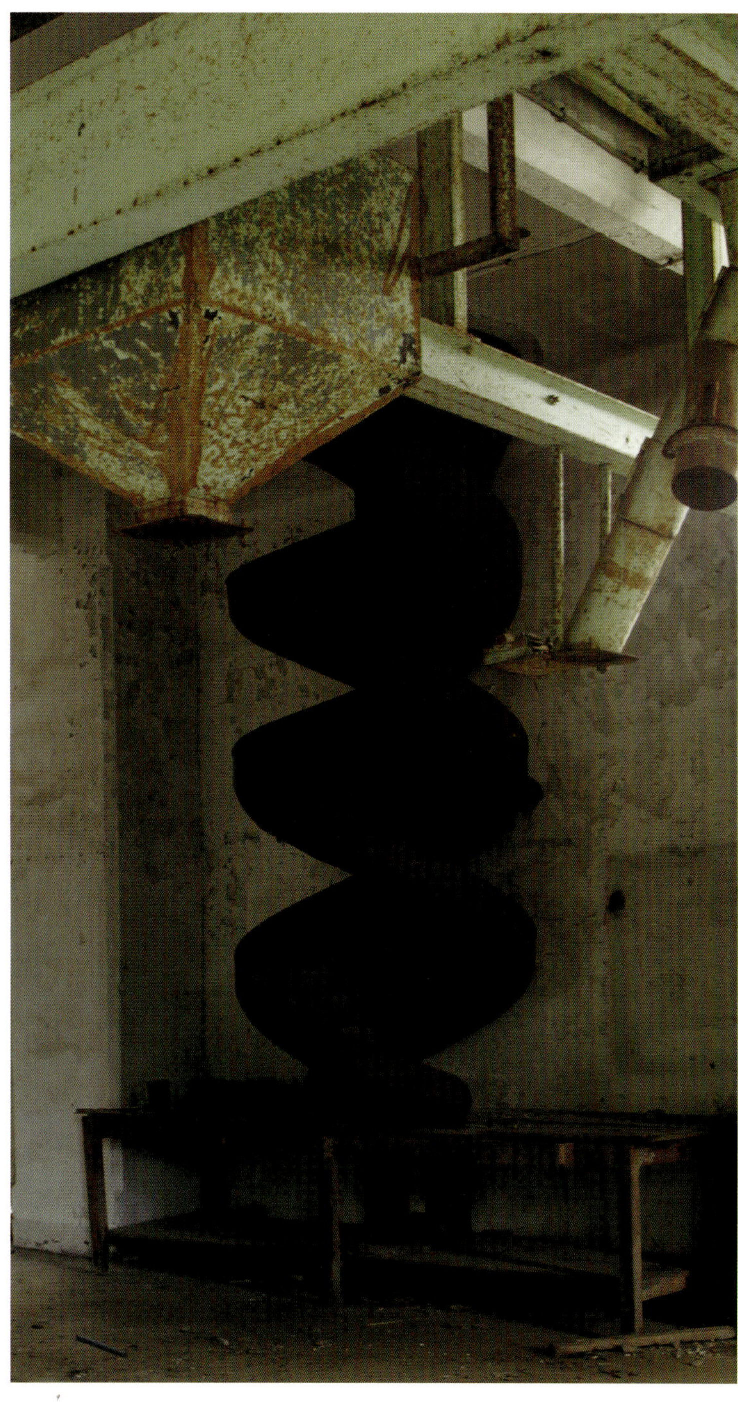

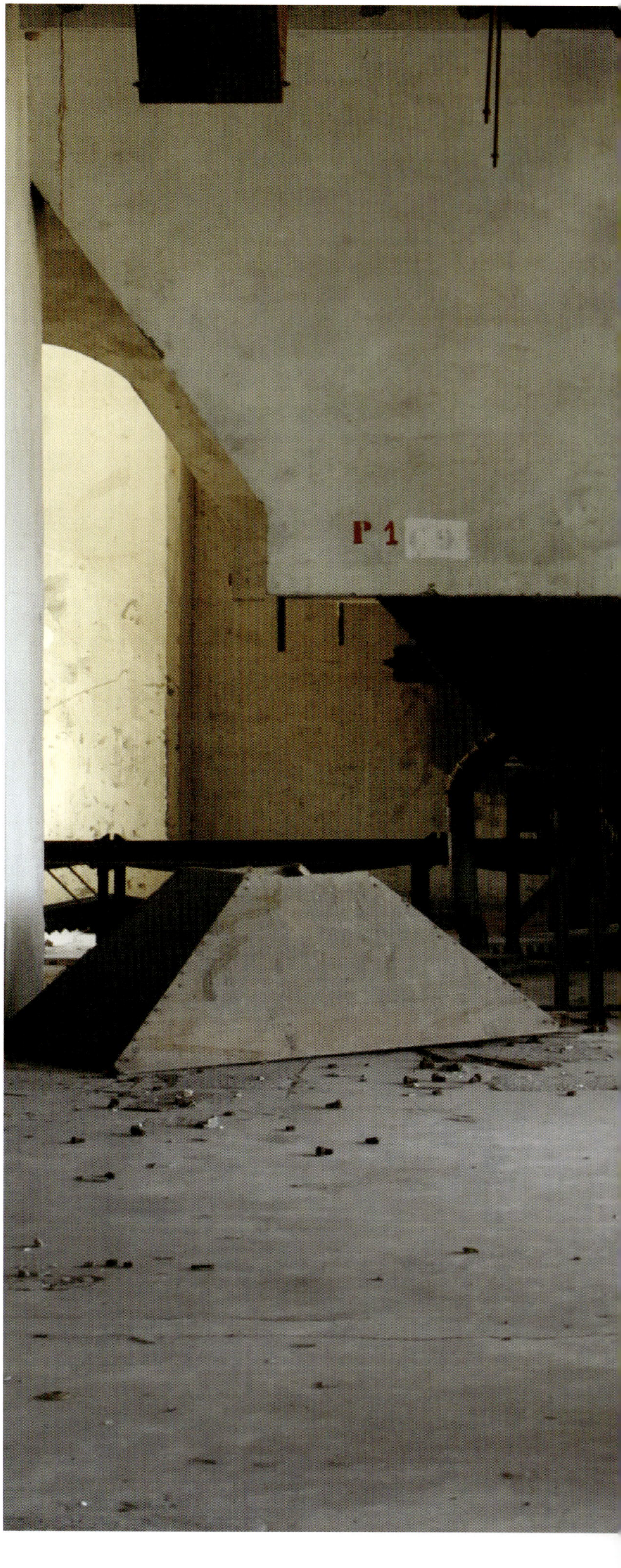

ABOVE AND RIGHT:
**La Rizerie, Port Saint-Louis
du Rhône, Bouches-du-Rhône,
France**
Built in the 1930s of concrete, to
store, mill and pack rice grown
in the adjacent Camargue area,
this factory's exterior and interior
details show the style of the
period. In World War II it was
used as a base by the German
army and its structure remains
inside a military area.

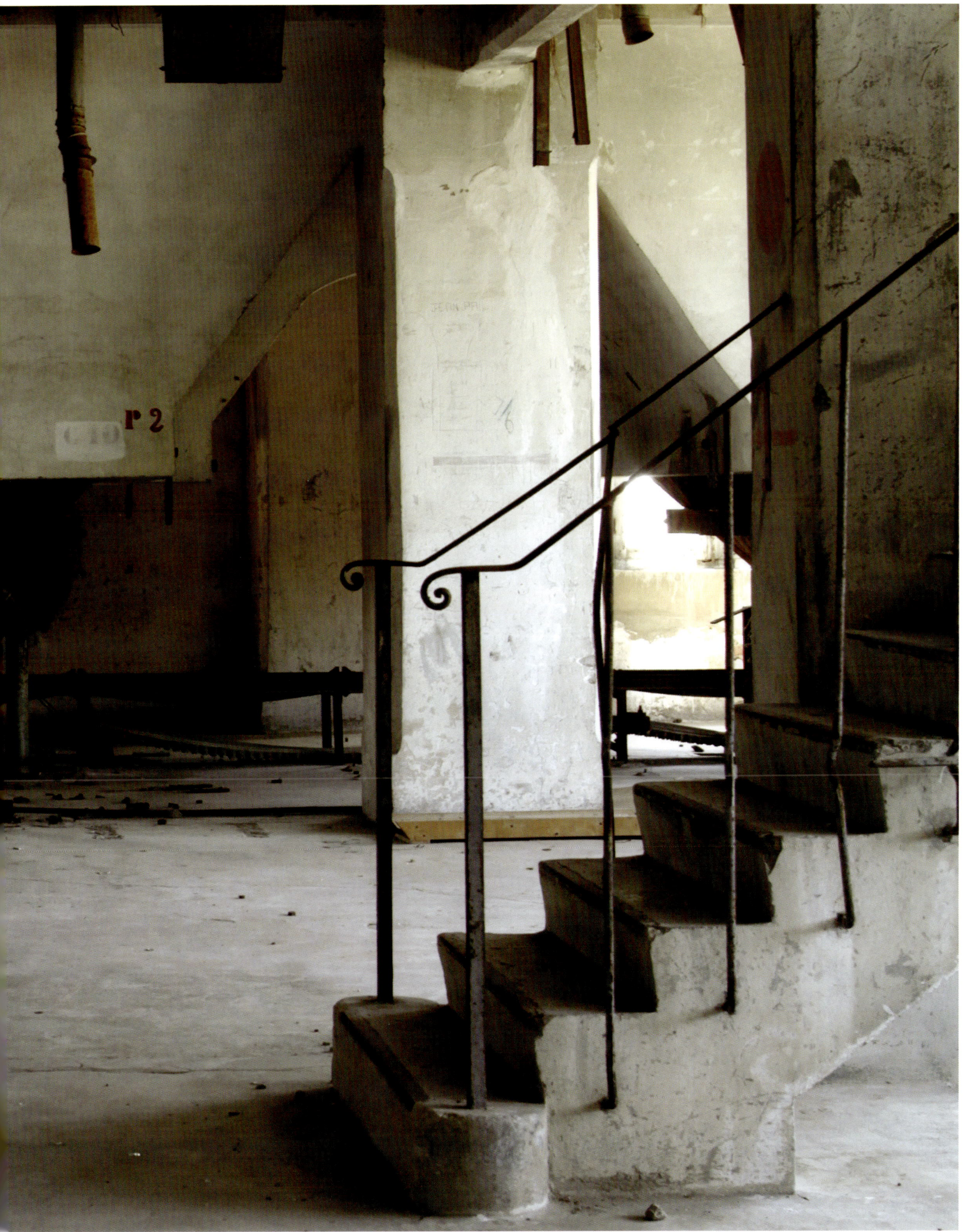

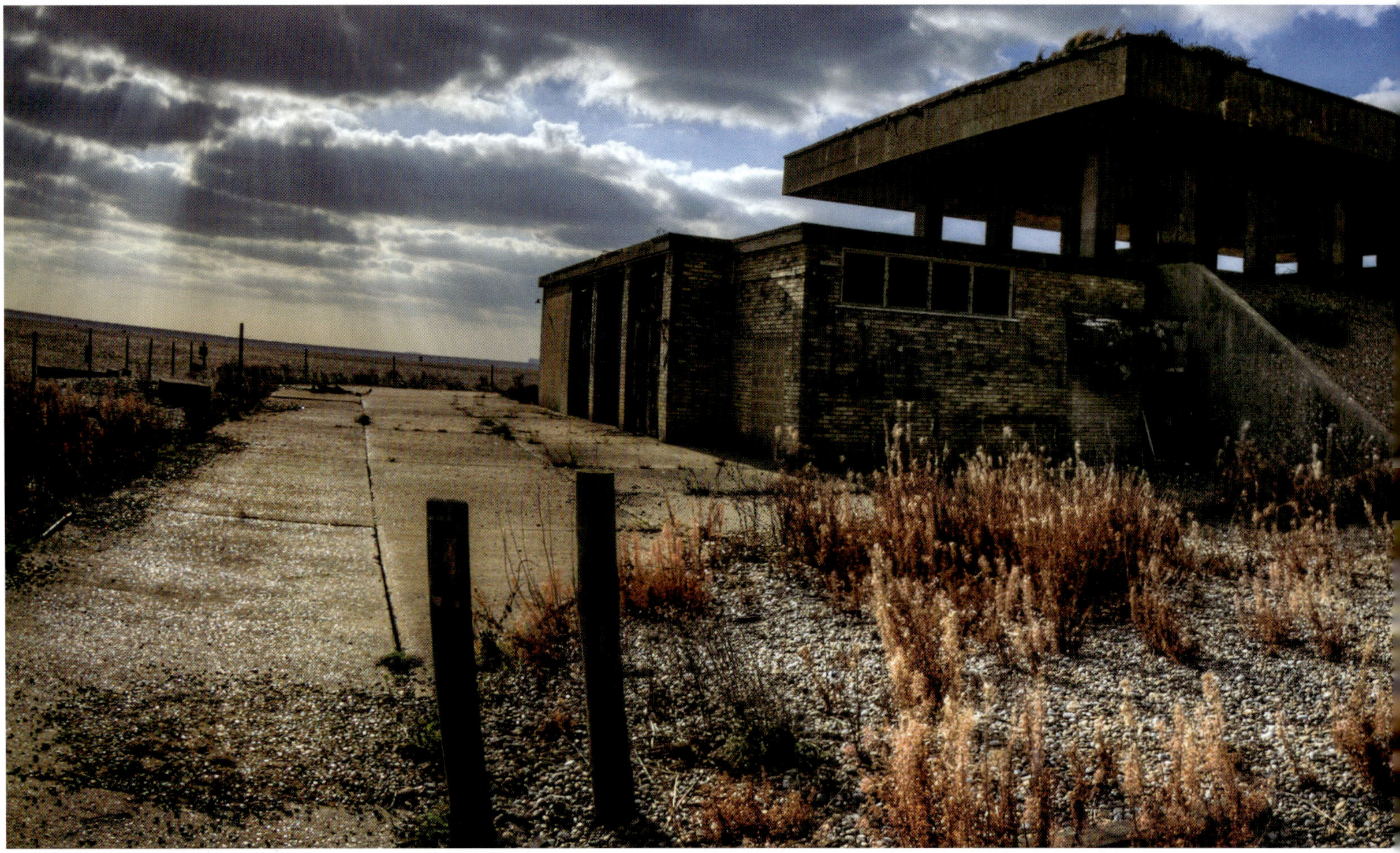

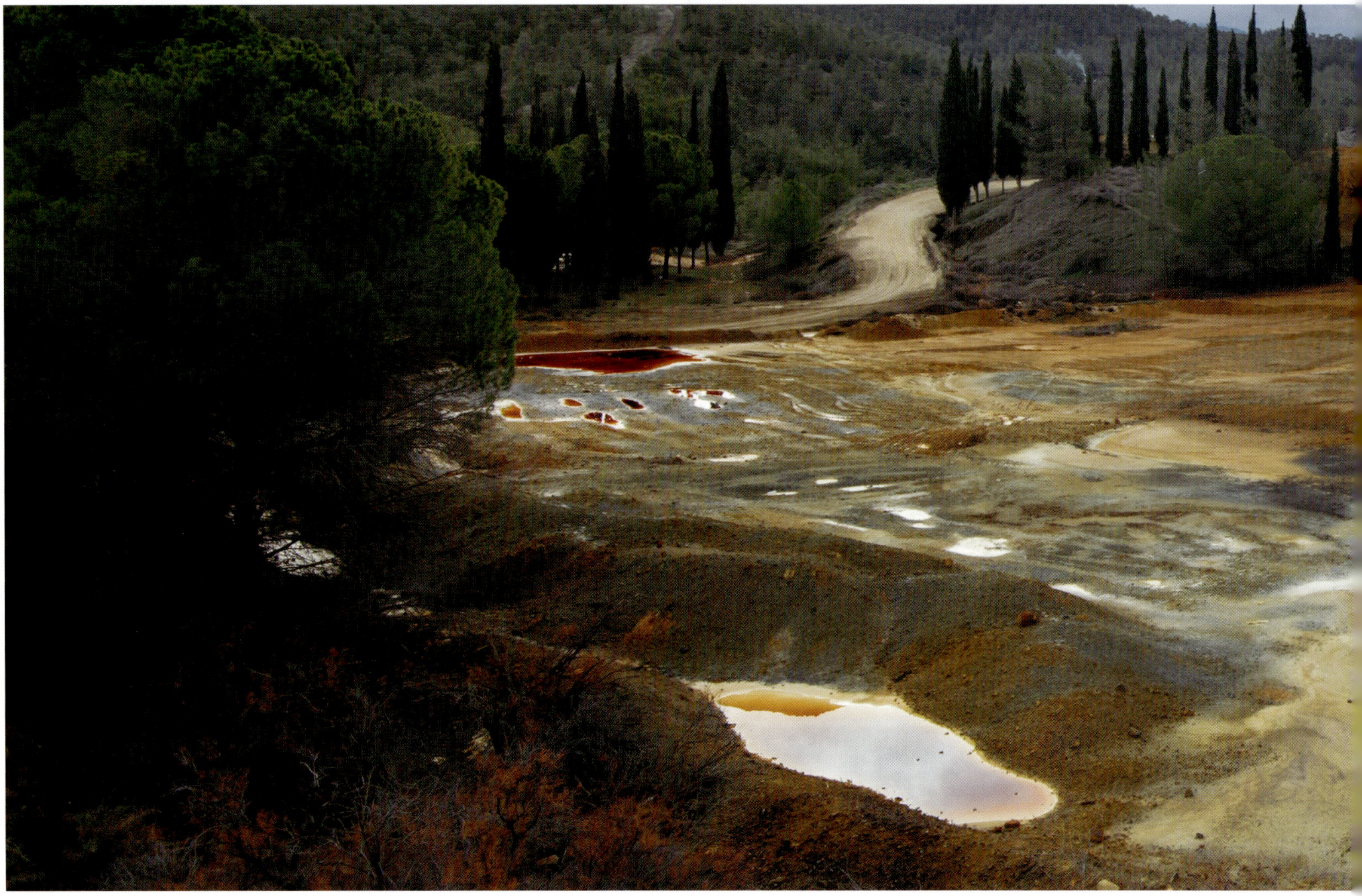

Atomic Weapons Research Establishment, Orford Ness, Suffolk, England
Secret military activity on this off-shore bank of shingle began in World War I. In the 1950s it was used for testing the components of nuclear weapons. Massively-walled concrete shells were built below ground with test laboratories above, known as 'the pagodas'. Work here ended in 1971 and the place remains evocative of the Cold War and its threats of mutual destruction.

The Red Lake, Mitsero, Cyprus
Residues from copper mining stain the ground and water, while rusting rail tracks and ore extraction equipment cover a wide area. Known since ancient times, the mines were at their busiest in the British colonial period, up to 1979, when they became unprofitable and production ceased.

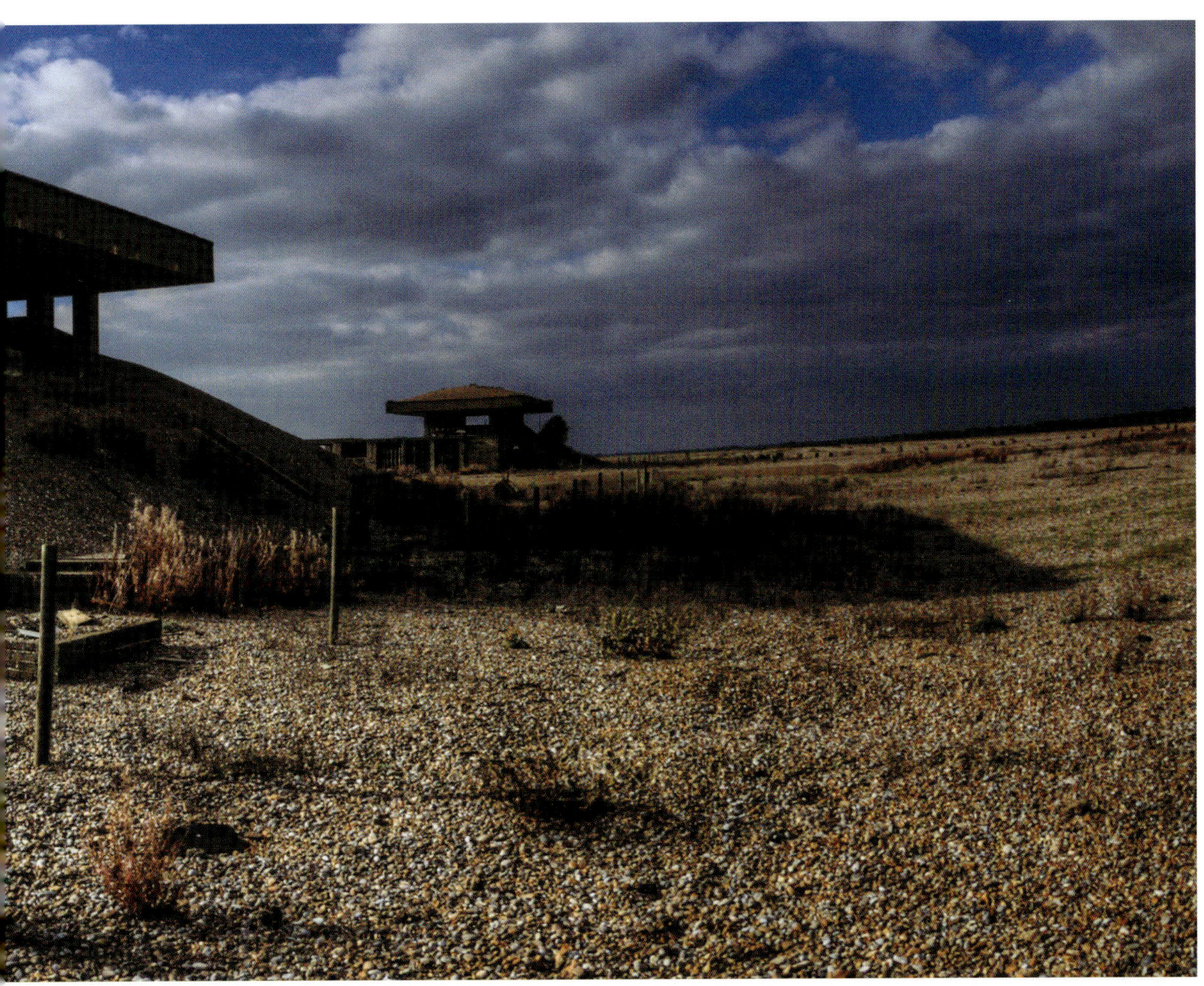

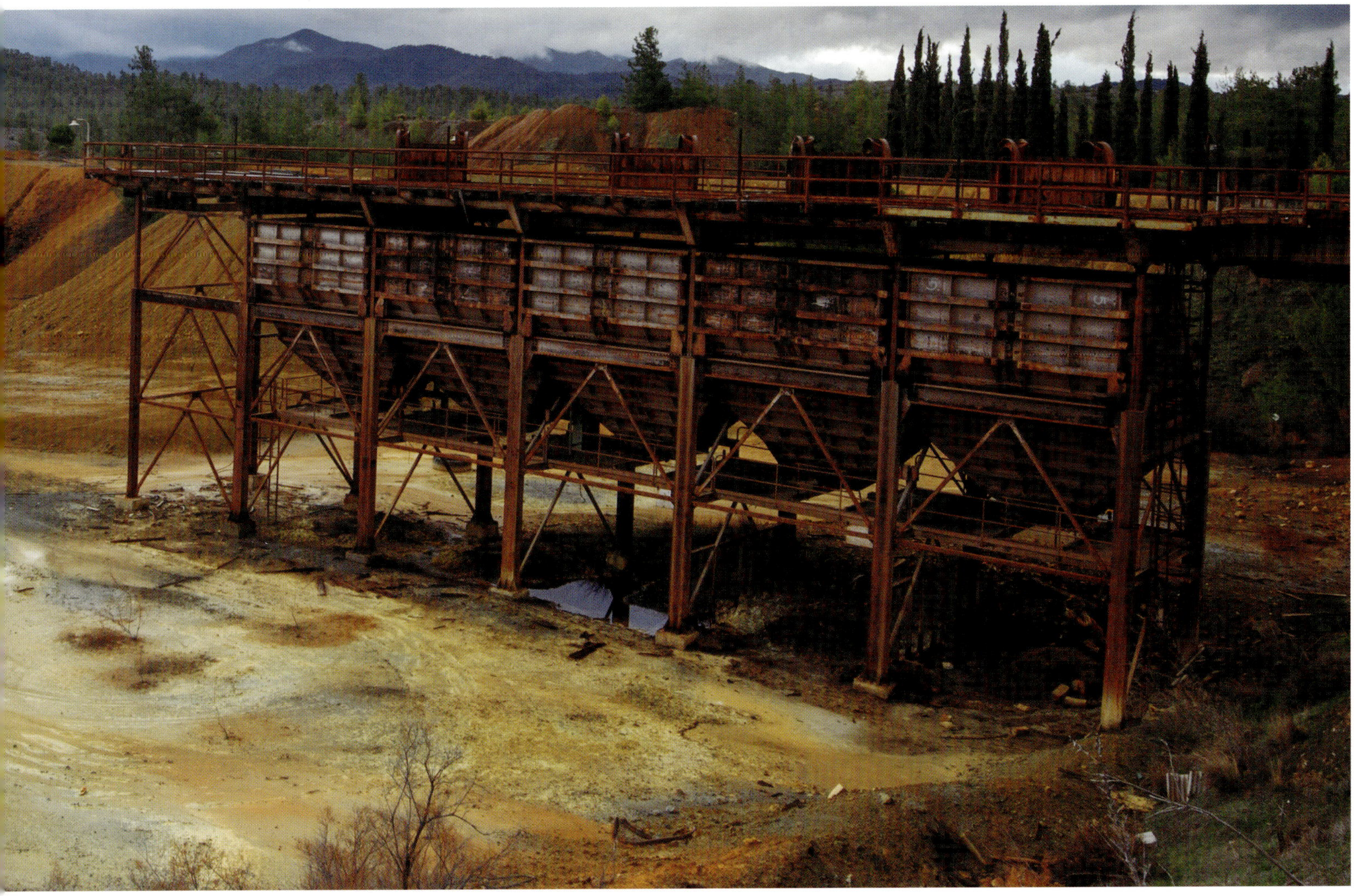

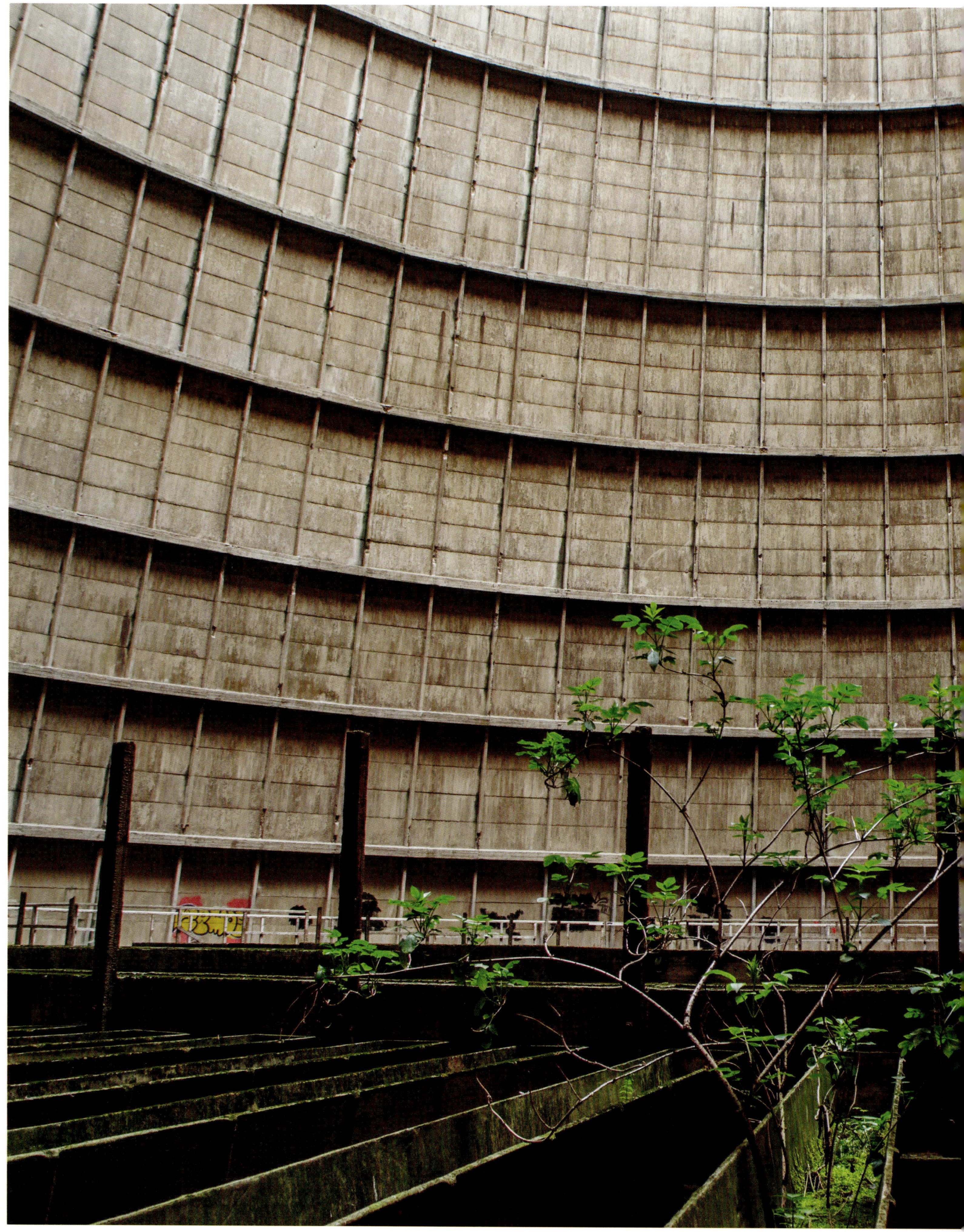

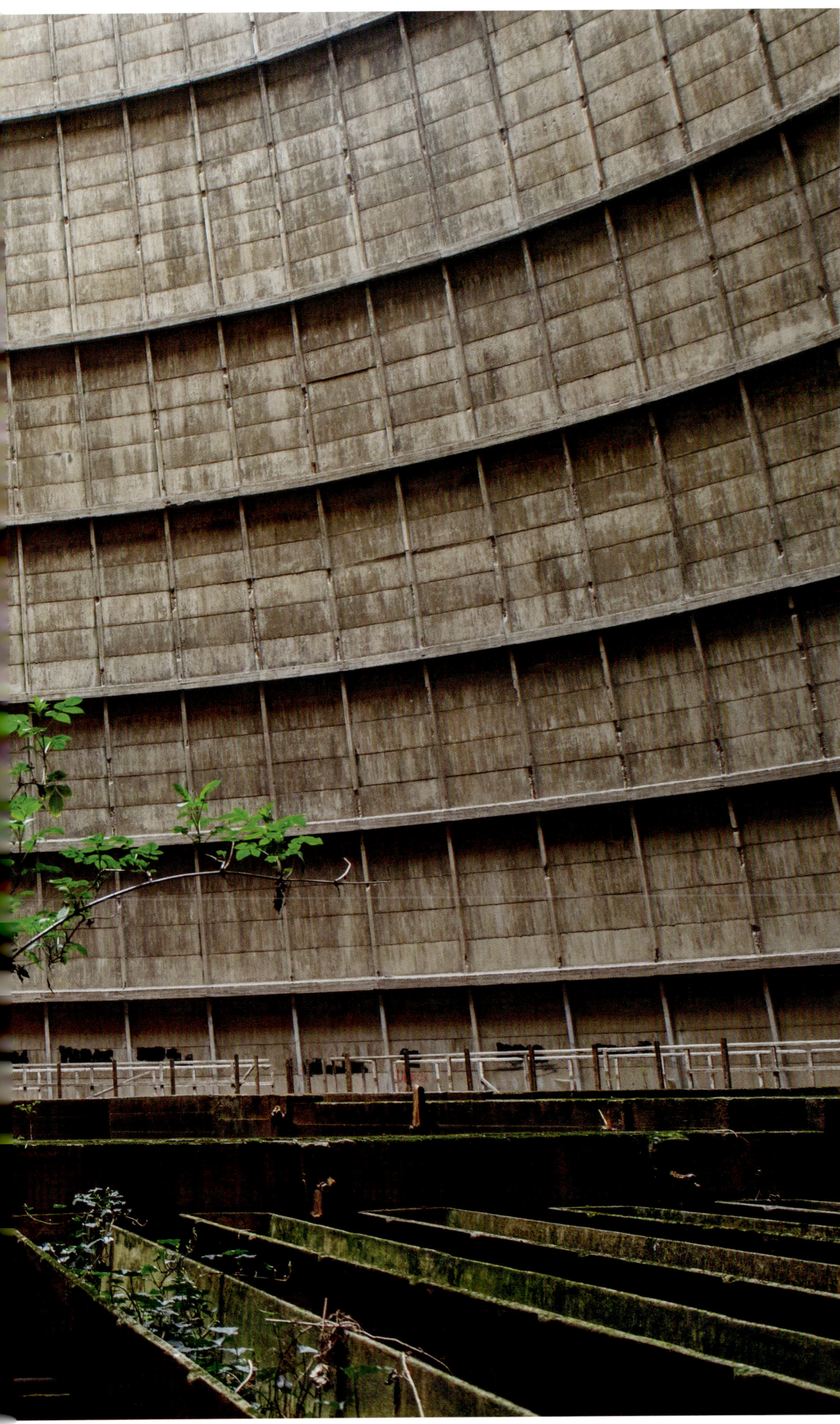

Disused Cooling Tower, Charleroi, Belgium
Part of coal-burning Power Plant IM, built in 1921, this vast cooling tower was said to be capable of cooling 2,182,000 litres (480,000 gallons) of almost-boiling water a minute. But the plant also produced 10 per cent of the country's CO2 emissions, and was shut down in 2007. The power station has been demolished but the tower remains intact.

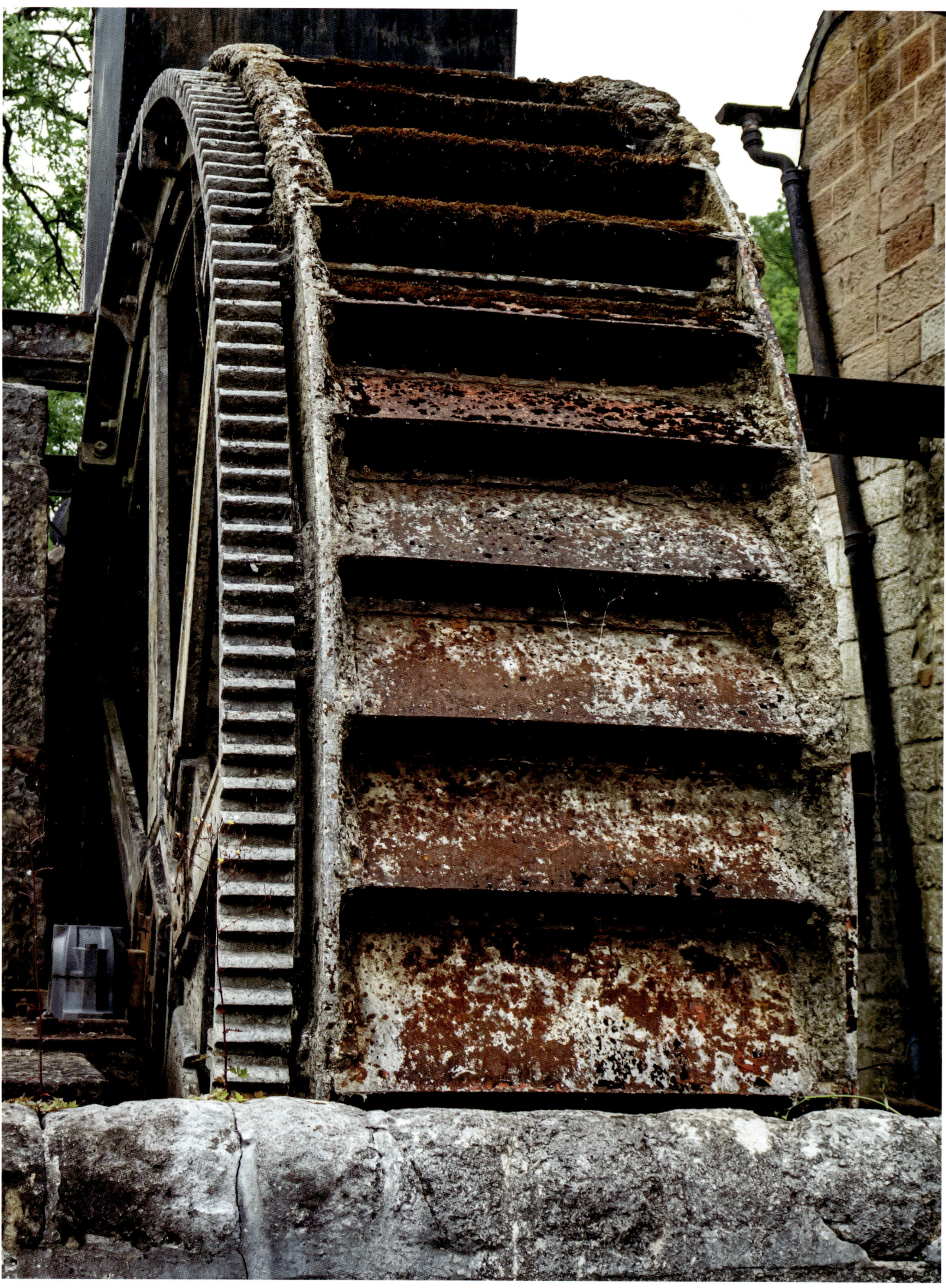

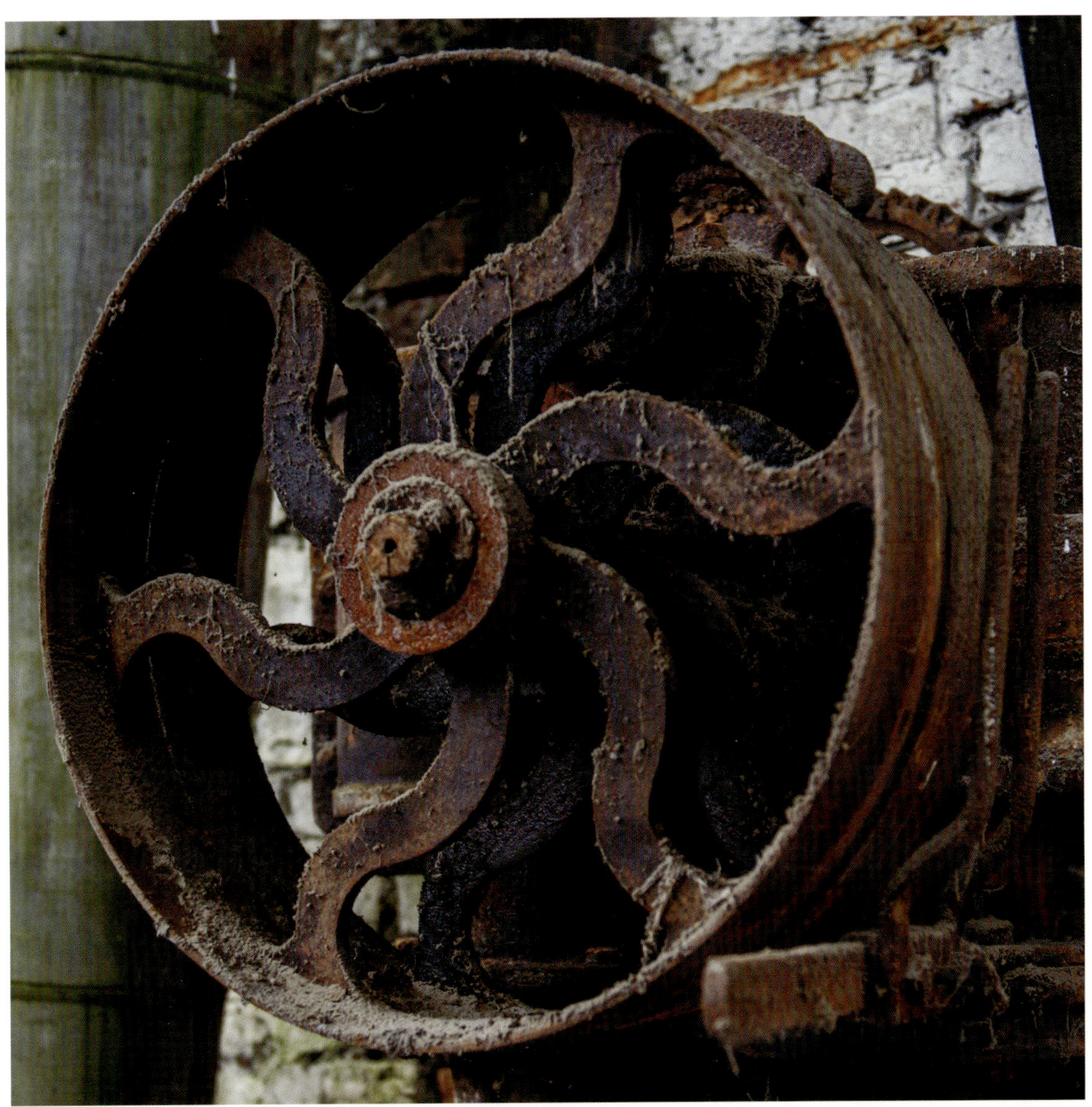

Cromford Corn Mill, Cromford, Derbyshire, England
Cromford is one of the cradle-places of the industrial revolution. The corn mill, powered by the breast-shot waterwheel seen here, ground corn for the industrial workers in the village's textile mill complex. It was built around 1780, and parts of the original mechanisms still survive.

LEFT:

Tone Dyeworks, Wellington, Somerset, England
Established around 1830, with most of its fittings installed by the 1920s, the works were abandoned in 2000. While visitors, official and otherwise, have left their mark, the interior is remarkably complete, as is the water management system.

BELOW:

Ditherington Flax Mill Maltings, Shrewsbury, Shropshire, England
Tank volume gauges from the former maltings, which closed in 1887 and were left derelict until a regeneration project began in 1905. The building, originally a flax mill, is the first iron-framed building in the world, erected in 1797.

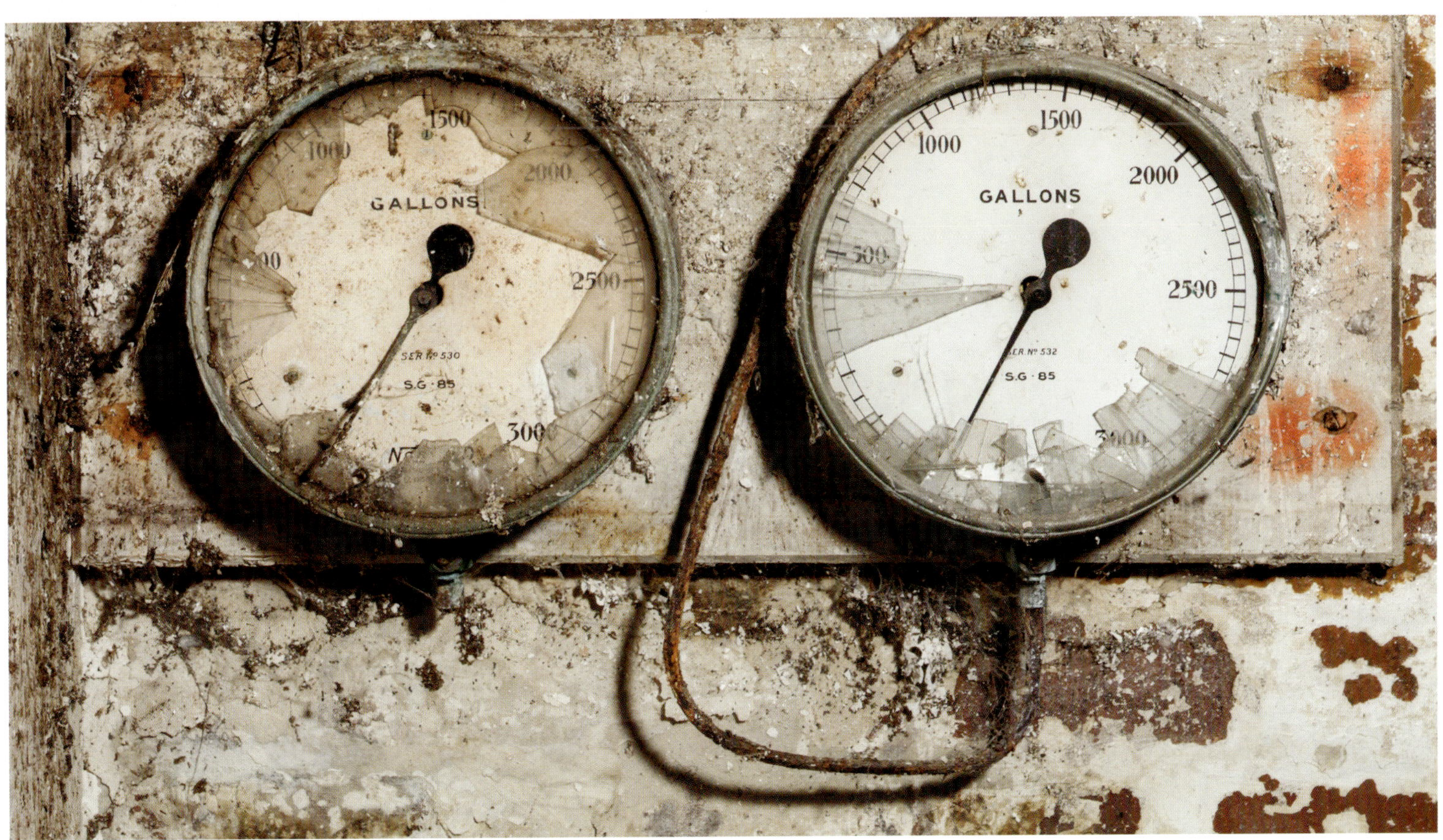

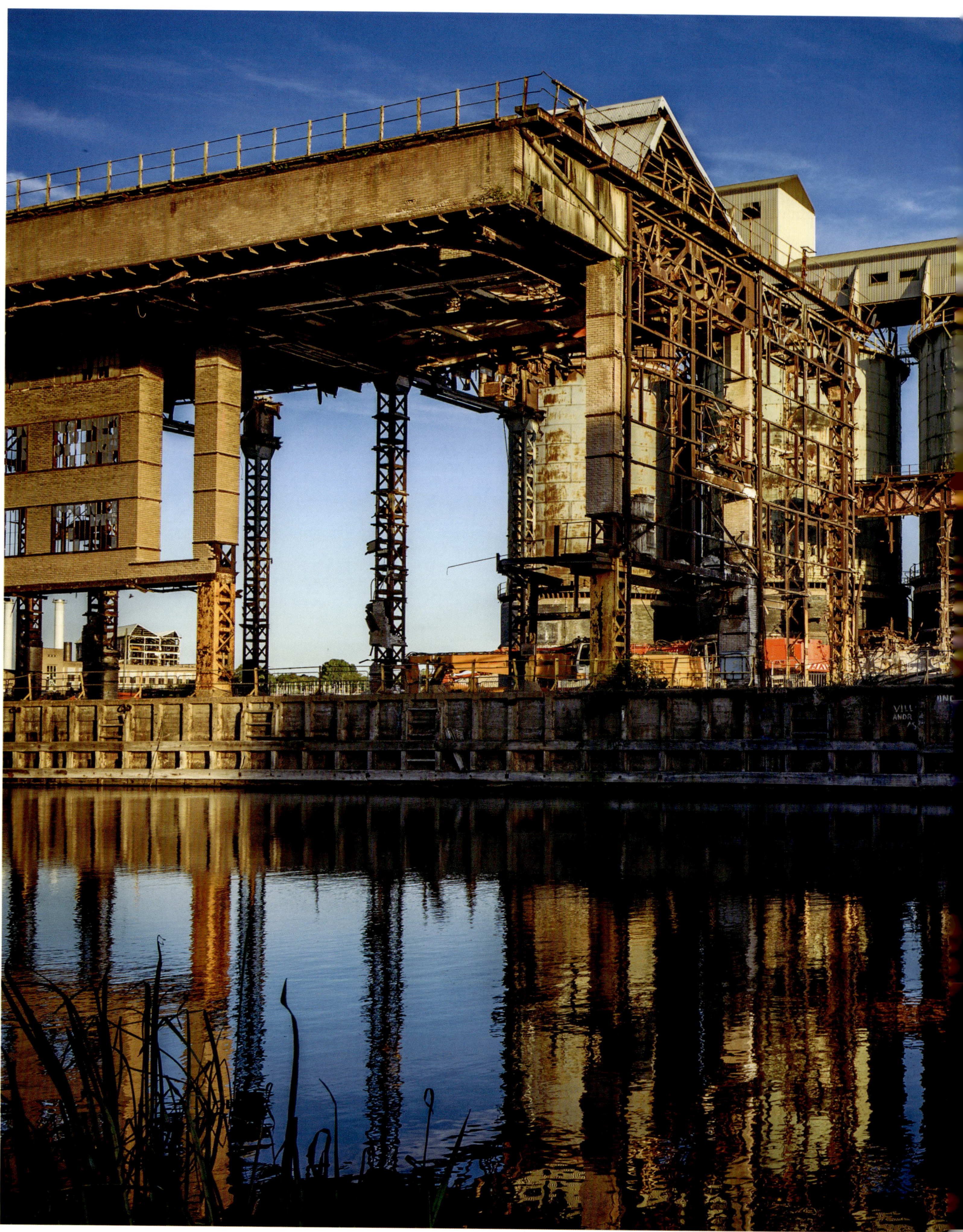

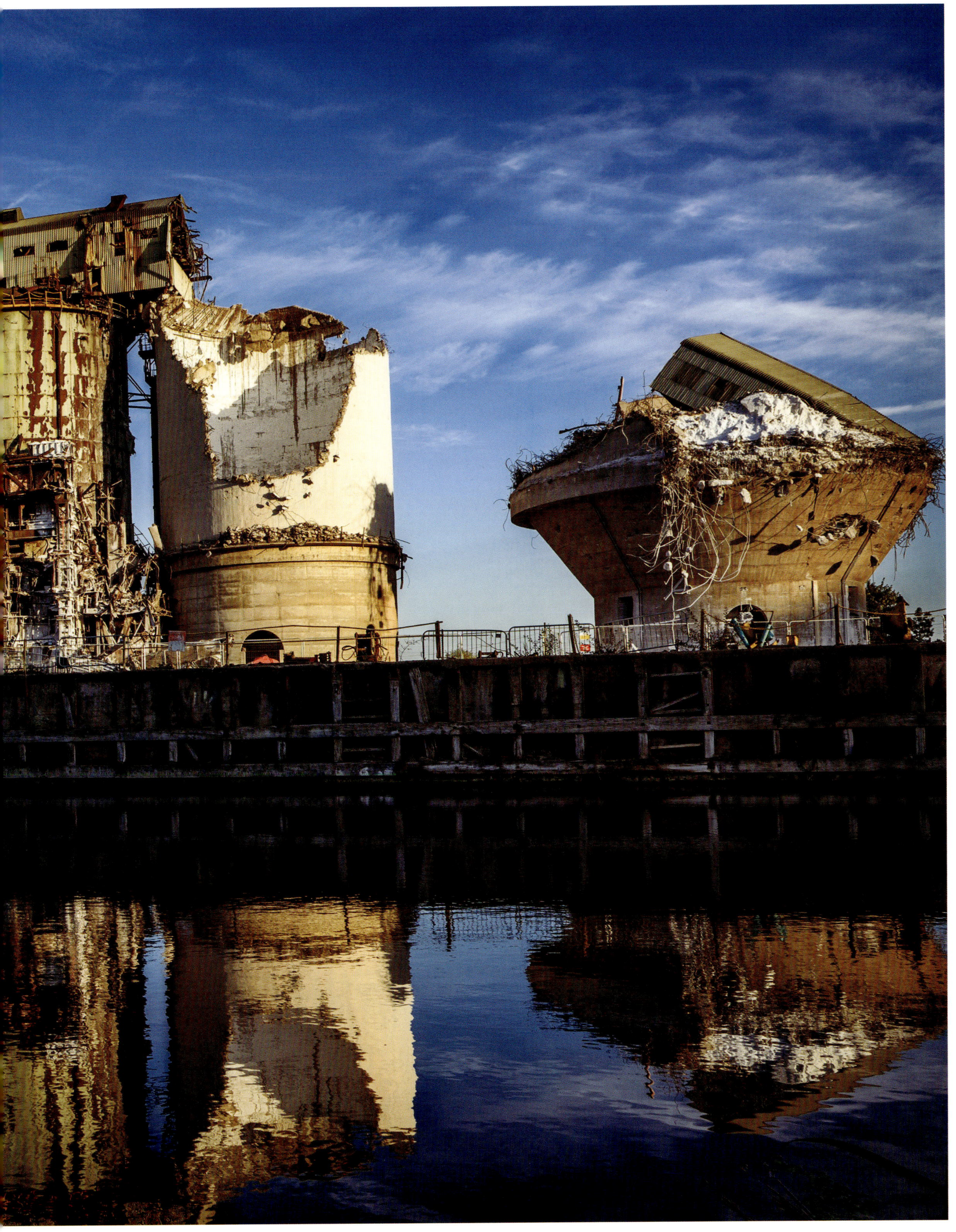

**Soda Ash Plant, Winnington,
Northwich, Cheshire, England**
Geological deposits of salt and
limestone led to the siting of a
massive sodium carbonate plant
here in 1926. Production of soda
ash and calcium chloride ended
in February 2014 and the giant
ash silos are seen here in process
of demolition in late 2016.

Shoe Factory, Catania, Sicily
Dating from the 1930s, in
contemporary Deco e Razionale
style, the building suffered in the
heavy bombardment of Catania
in 1943 and was restored in
1949. Shoe manufacture ceased
here in the 1950s, since when
when the building has had
occasional use as overflow
classroom space for a school but
still awaits a new purpose.

**Abandoned Factory, Łódž,
Poland**
The disused and dilapidated
factories remaining from Łódž's
once-vibrant textile industry are
favourite sites for film-makers,
providing ready-made, bleakly
atmospheric backgrounds
conveying the impression of a
run-down, post-industrial society.

**Former Silk Factory, Rhodes,
Greece**
Silk-making was always a
secretive industry, guarding its
techniques. This high-walled
structure, built round a central
courtyard, enabled seclusion
and a relatively cool working
environment. The origin of
the works is obscure. Silk was
produced and spun here, but
taken to Rhodes town for
weaving.

Mlyn Maria, Wroclaw, Poland
Old Wroclaw was built on
islands in the Oder River, joined
by fords, then bridges. The Maria
Mill, used for centuries to grind
corn, was one of two which
combined the function of bridge
and water mill. The disused
building is sandwiched between
adjacent houses on its branch of
the river.

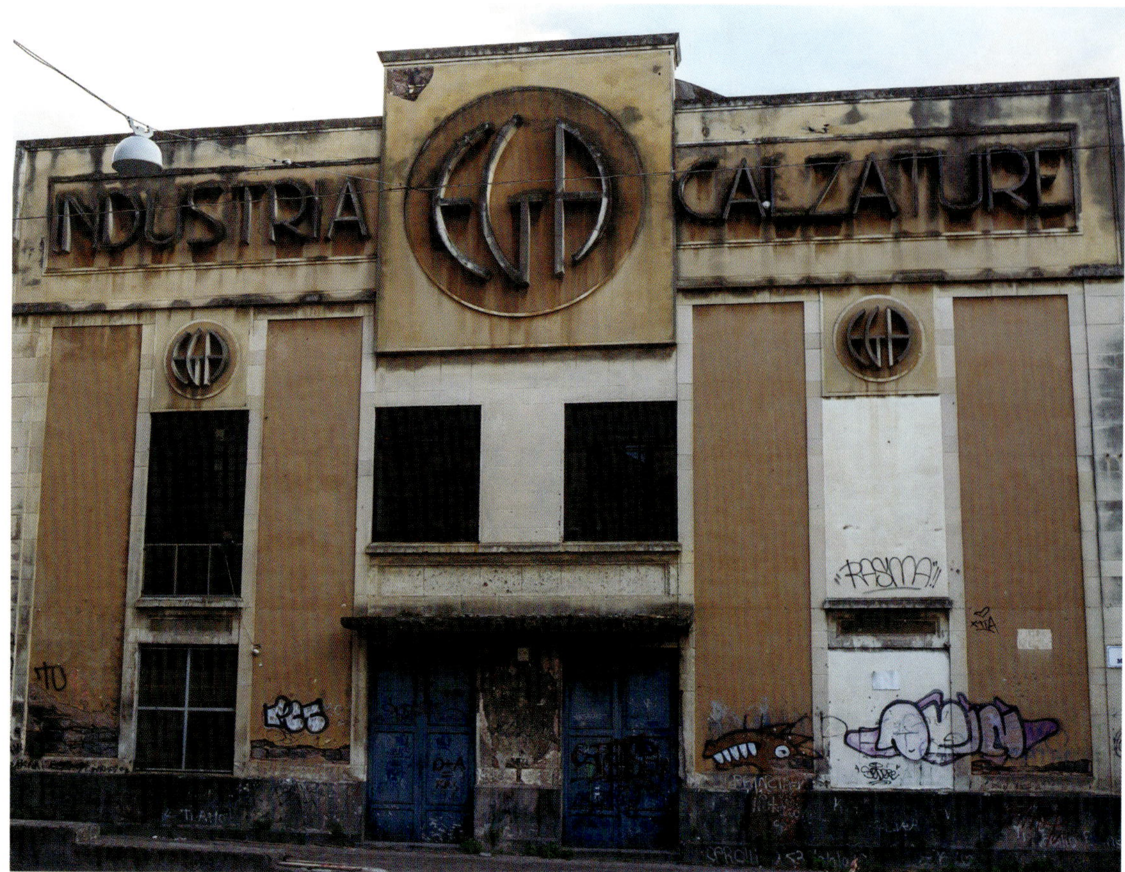

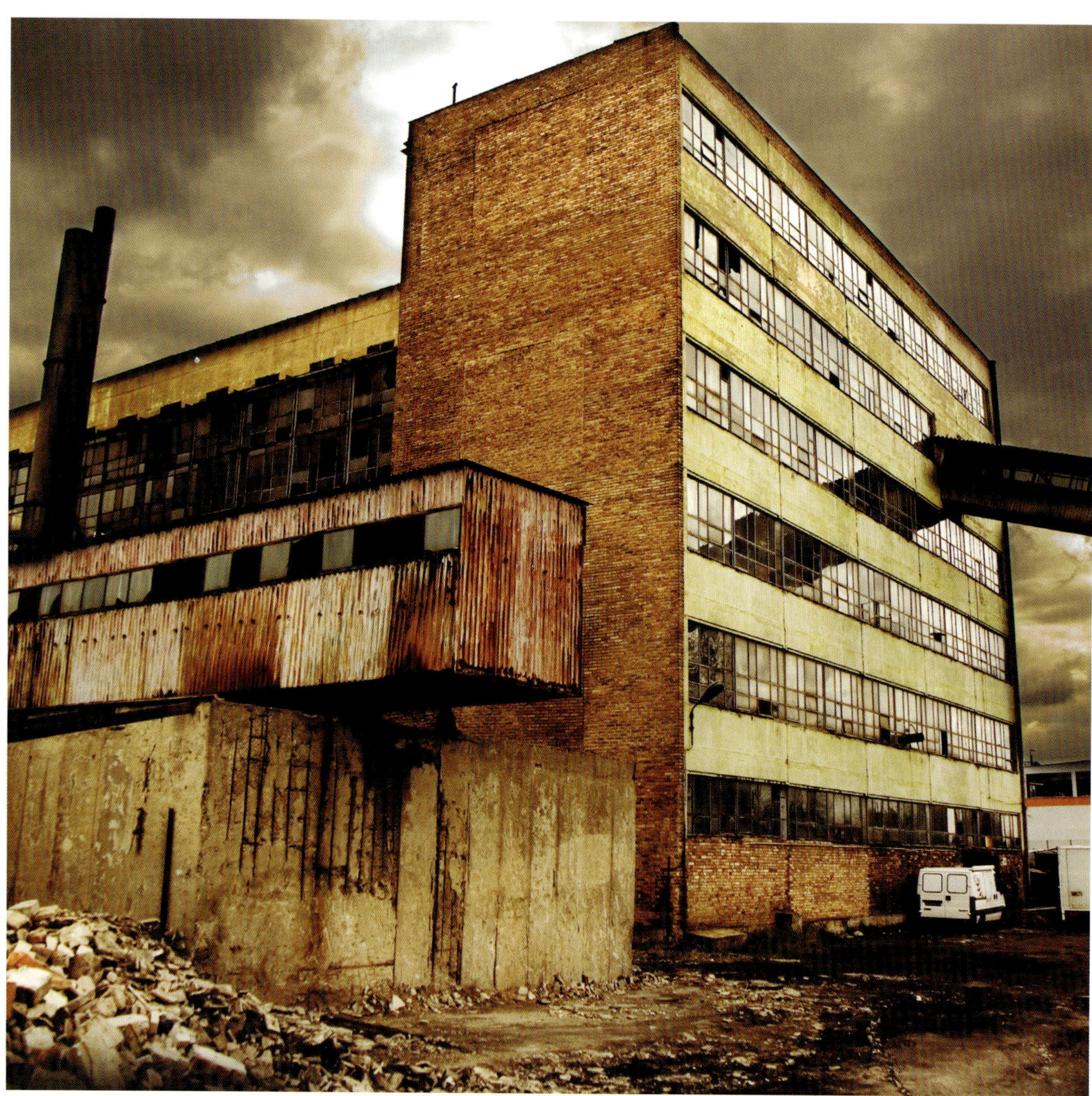

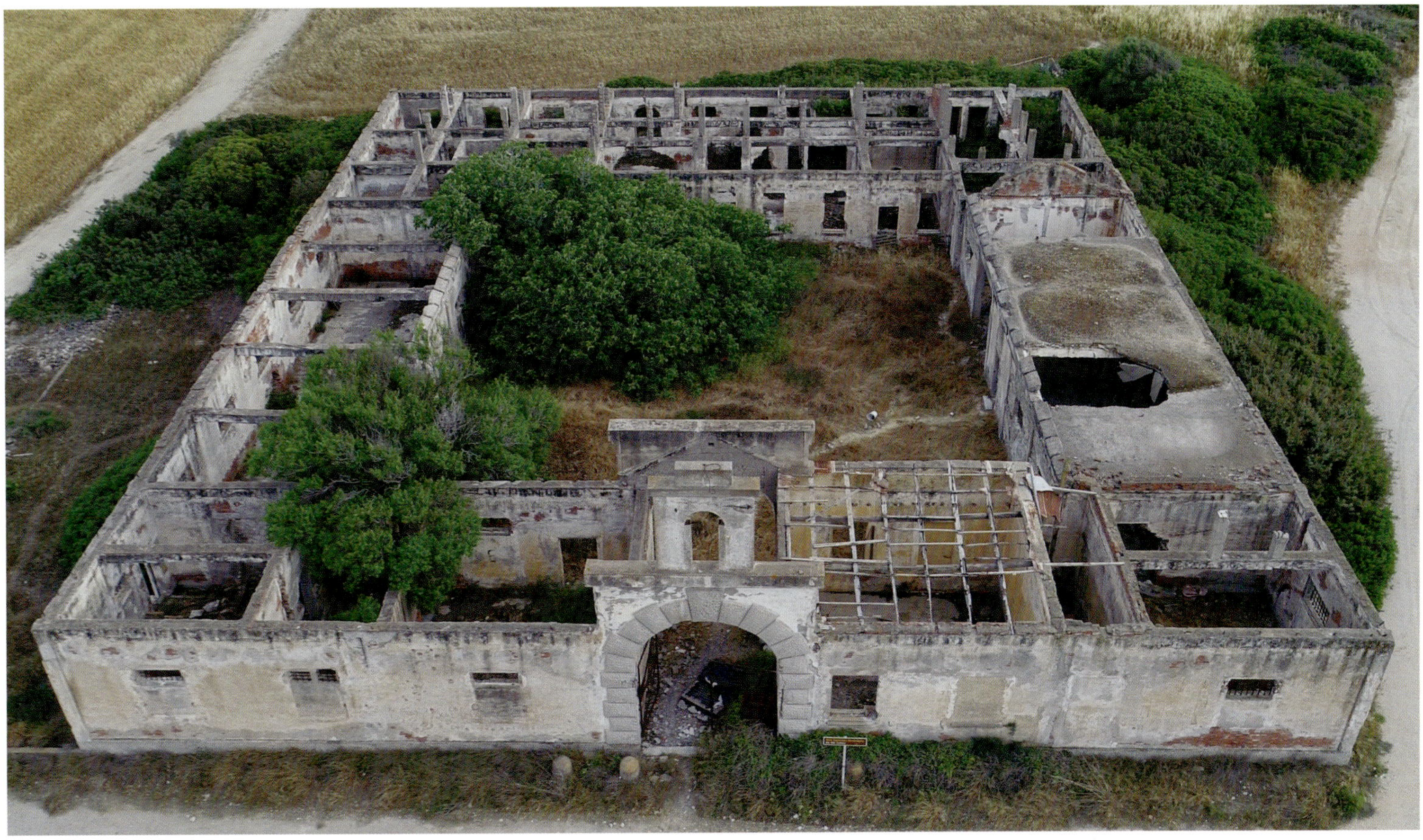

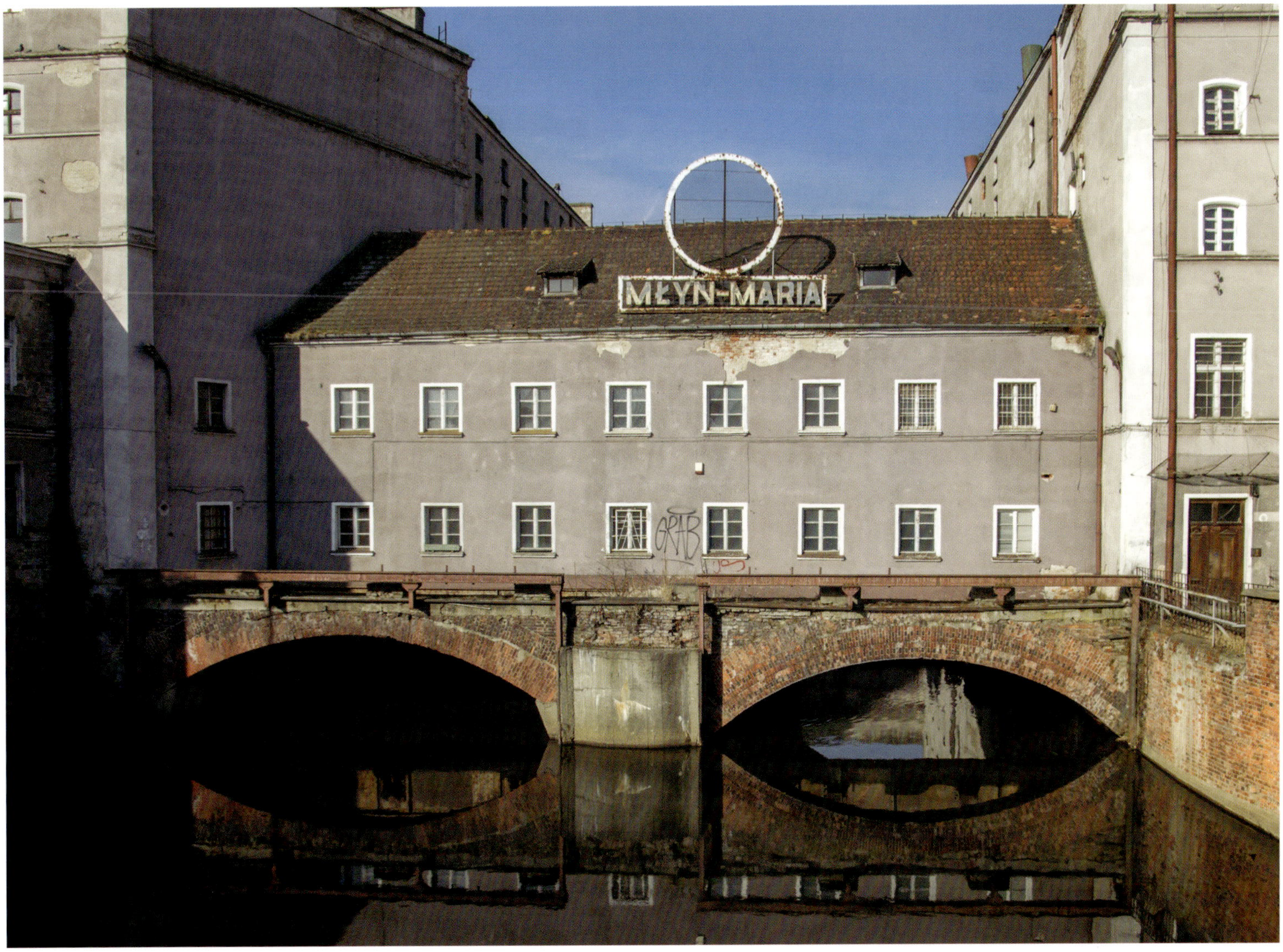

MŁYN-MARIA

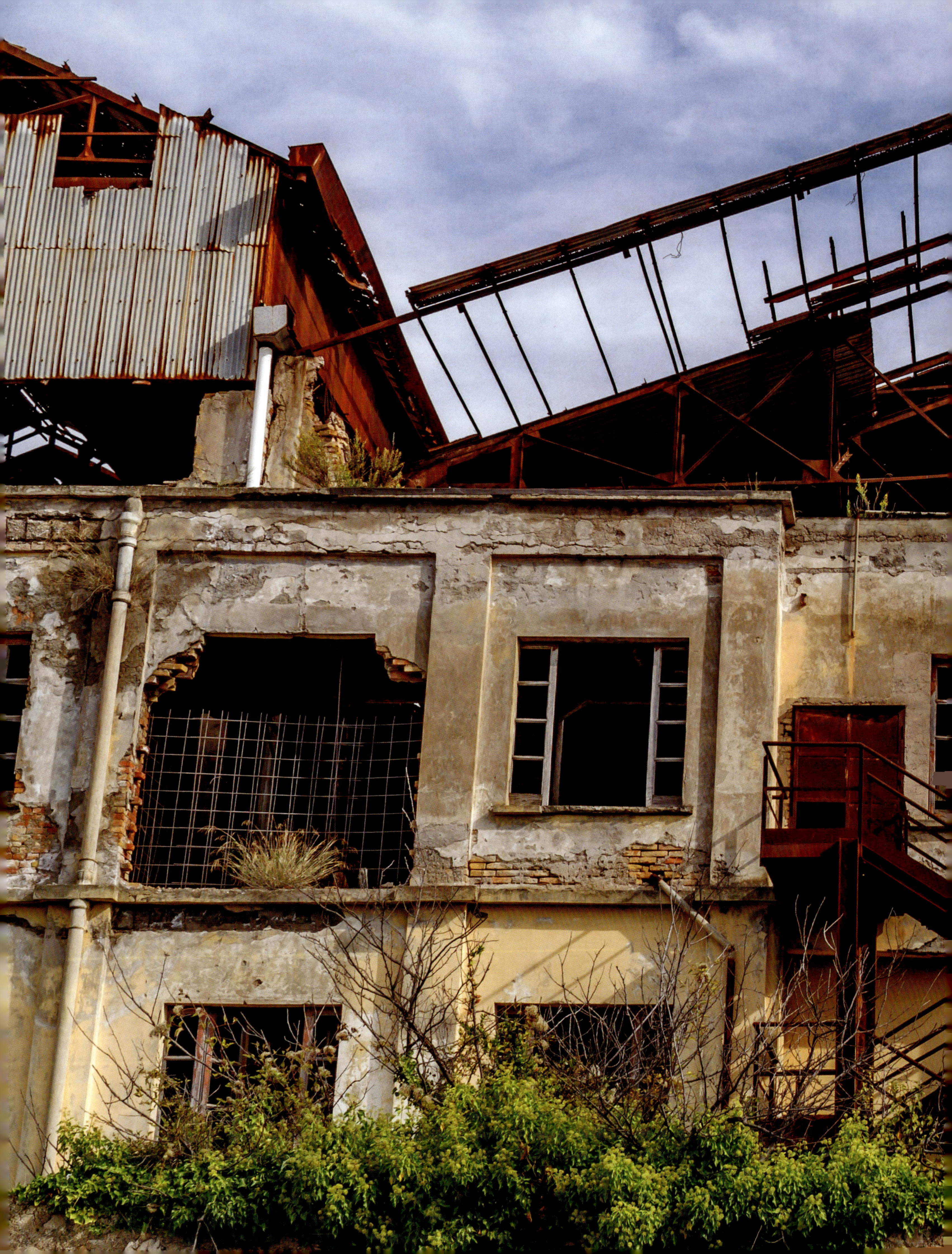

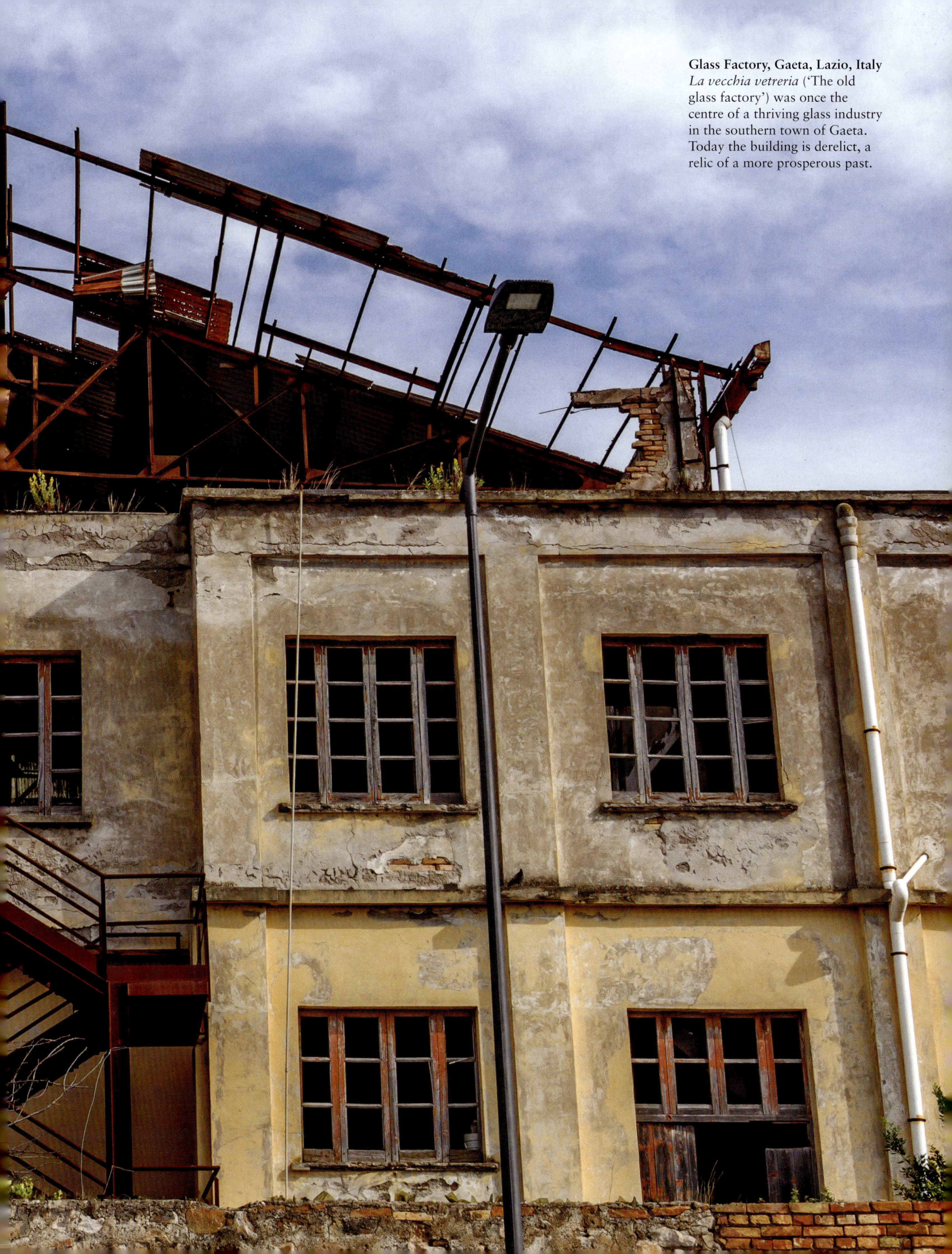

Glass Factory, Gaeta, Lazio, Italy
La vecchia vetreria ('The old glass factory') was once the centre of a thriving glass industry in the southern town of Gaeta. Today the building is derelict, a relic of a more prosperous past.

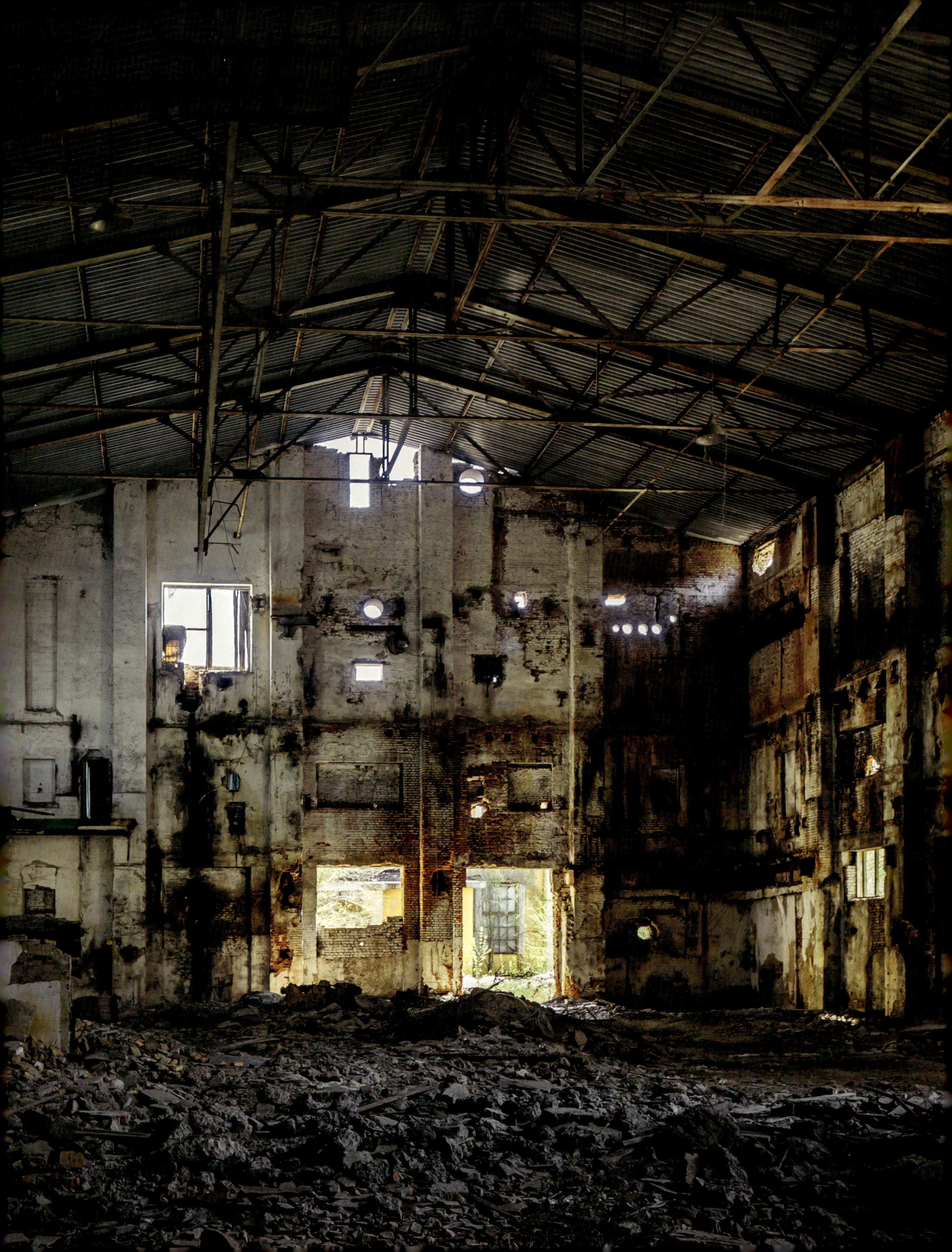

OPPOSITE:
Sugar Factory, Ramon, Voronezh, Russia
Russian philanthropist Eugenia Maksimilianovna inherited the
factory in the late 19th century, and quickly increased production
by switching from manual labour to using the latest machinery.
A refinery and steam-powered confectionery were added, the latter
being awarded a prize in the 1899 Paris Exhibition. The plant
survived the Russian Revolution and was only shut down in 2000.

BELOW:
Disused Lime Kilns at Ruskeala Marble Quarry, Karelia, Russia
Marble was quarried here since 1769 for building and decoration,
but spoil and reject marble was also ground and heated into lime at
these works. The entire vast quarry complex was abandoned in the
20th century and is now a popular visitor attraction.

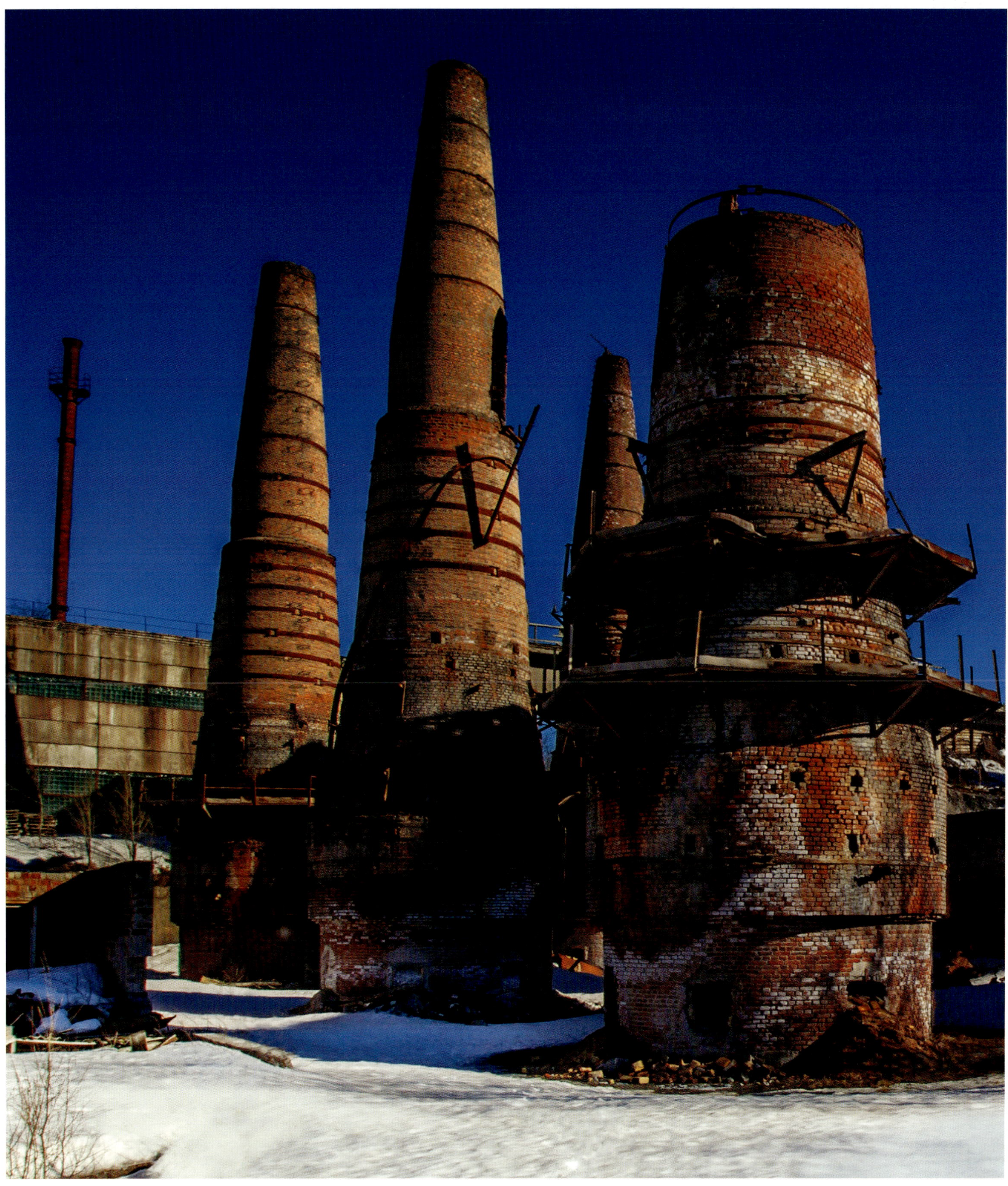

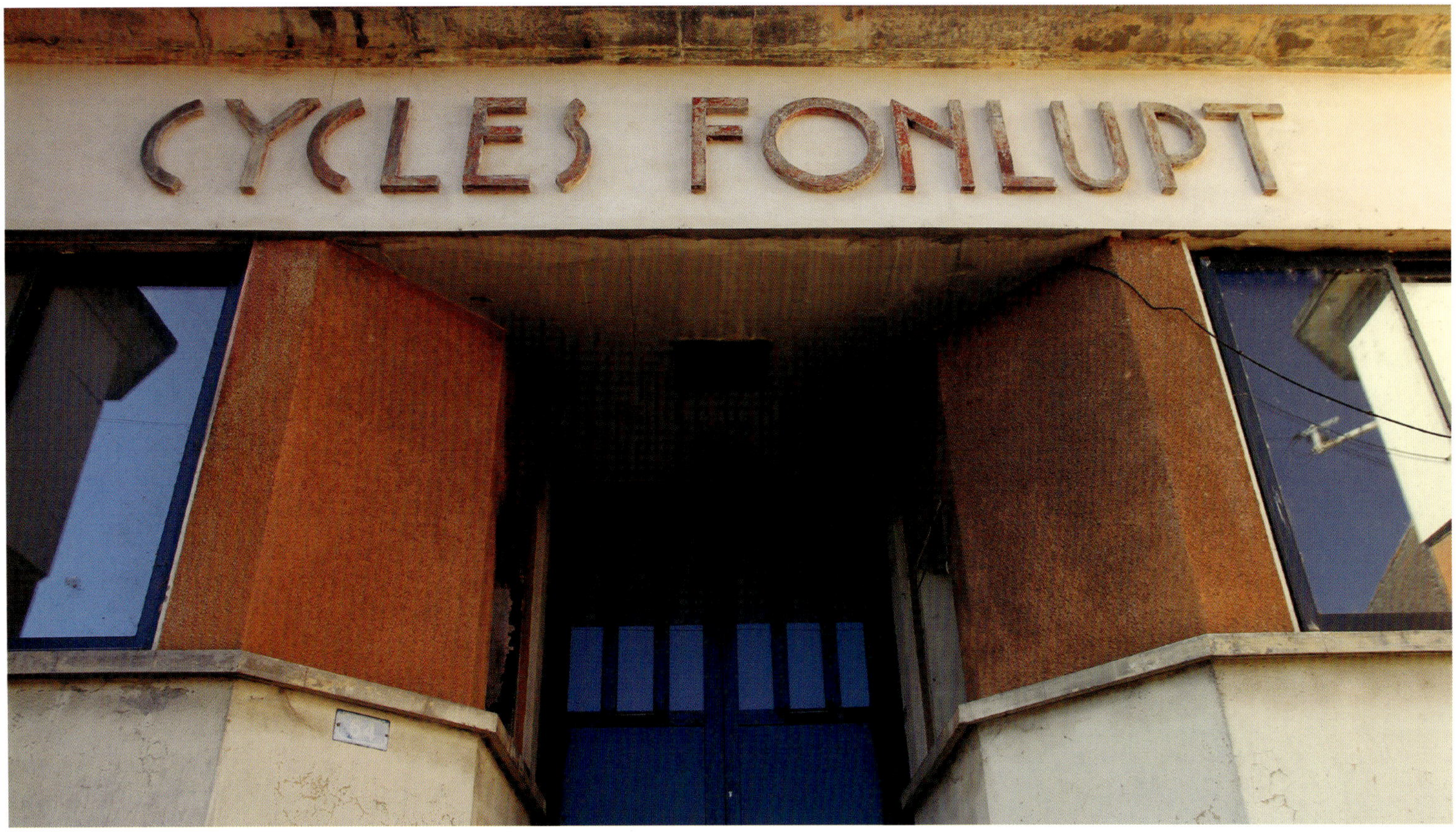

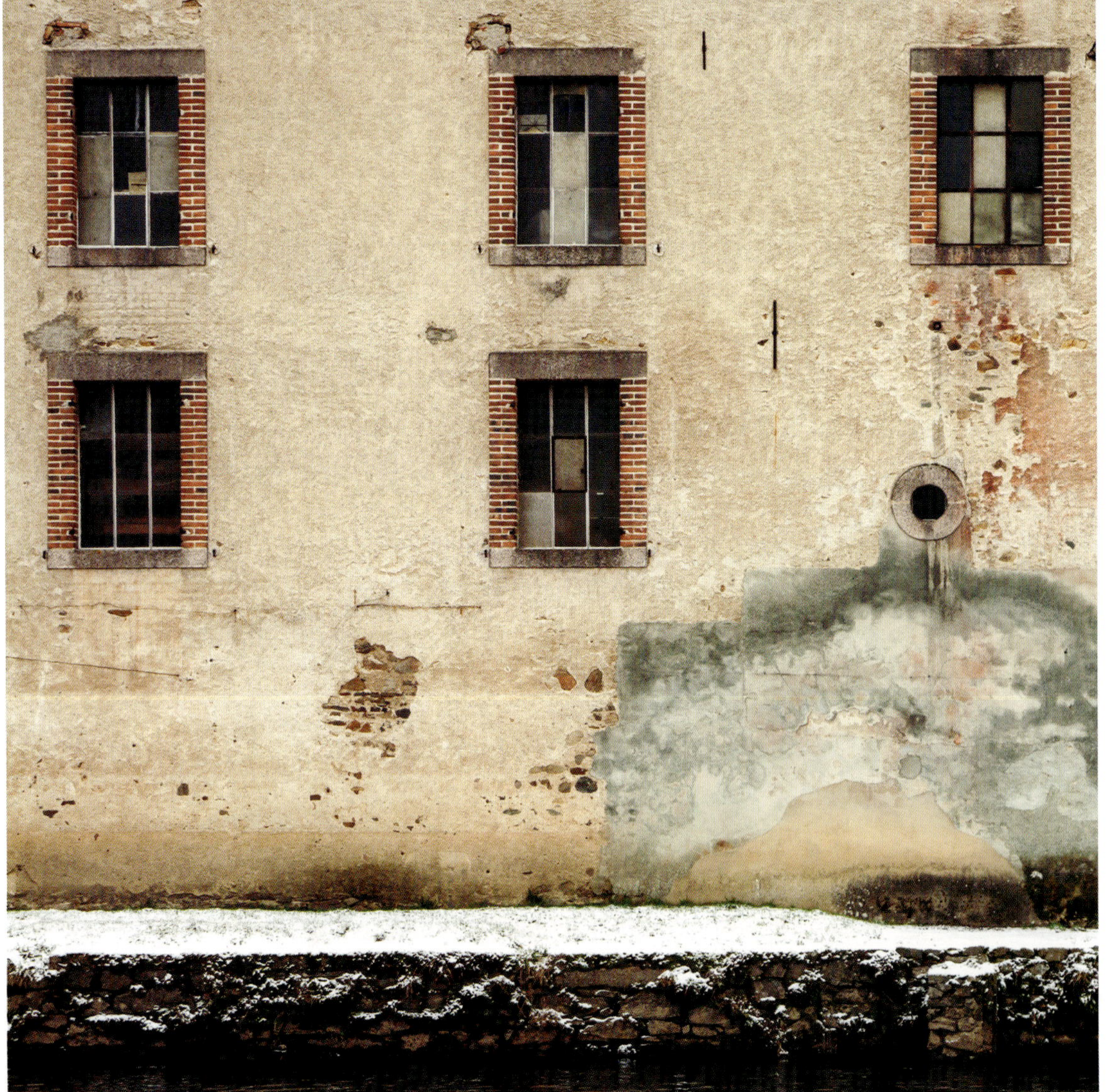

Cycle Depot and Offices, La Clayette, Saône et Loire, France
Set up in 1920, the Fonlupt company produced lightweight racing and touring bikes, also motorised bicycles after 1925. Its factory at La Clayette assembled all machines by hand until framebuilding was contracted out in 1971. The disused building was destroyed by fire in June 2016.

Old Paper Mill, La Celle-Dunoise, Creuse, France
A former paper mill stands alongside its feeder stream in the Creuse River valley. The valley was an important papermaking centre from the 17th to the 20th centuries. Many have been converted for other purposes, some are ruined, others like this one stand empty.

Former Du May Cutlery Factory, Thiers, Puy-de-Dôme, France
The 'Valley of Factories' by the Durolle River in Thiers, once a decrepit industrial zone, has undergone regeneration in recent years as an 'Industrial Adventure Park'. Thiers was France's principal cutlery producer, producing razors and industrial blades as well as domestic knives and forks. The Du May cutlery works, closed in 1985, is an integral part of the scheme.

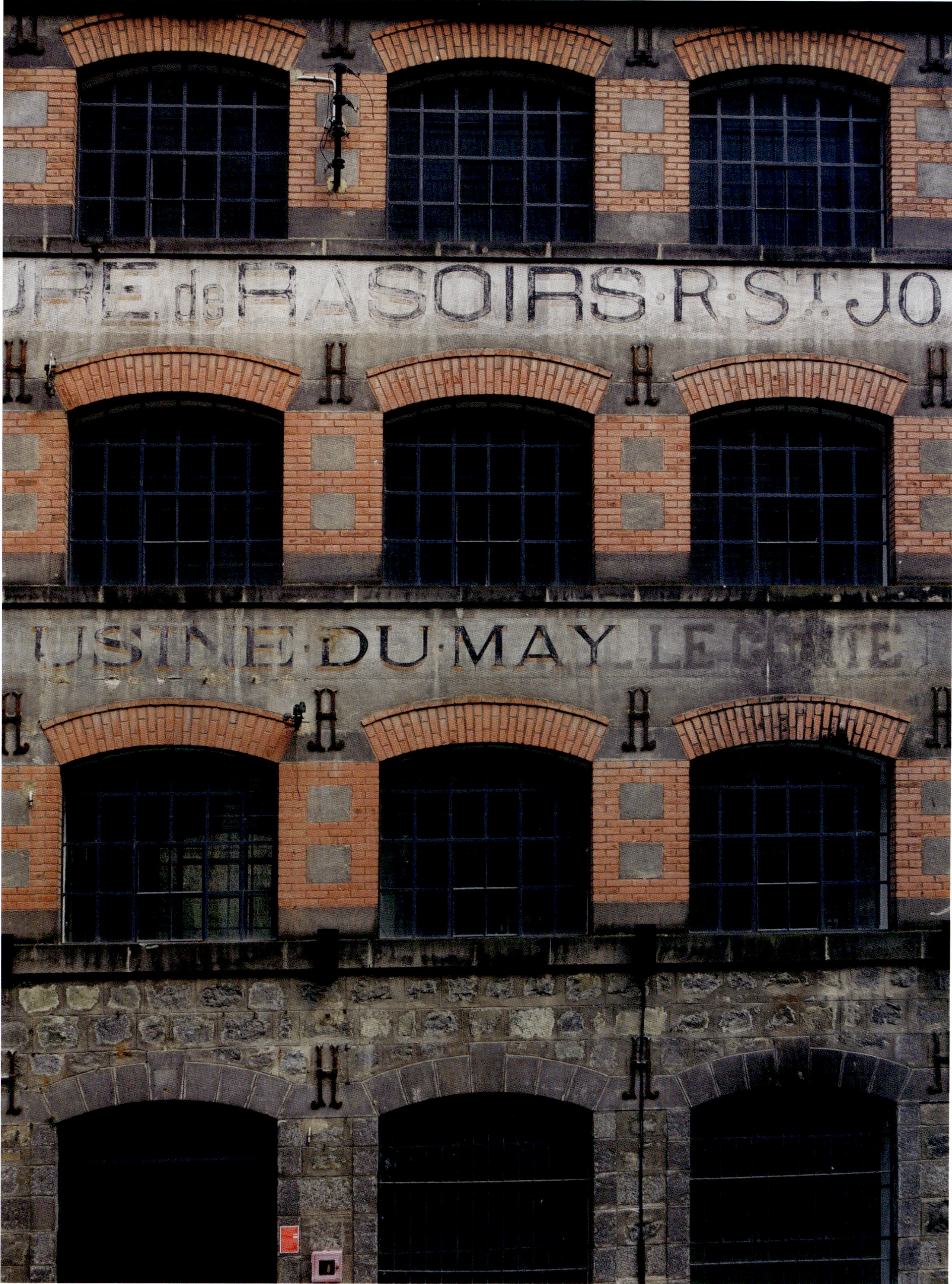
JRE de RASOIRS · R · St JO
USINE · DU MAY LE COTE

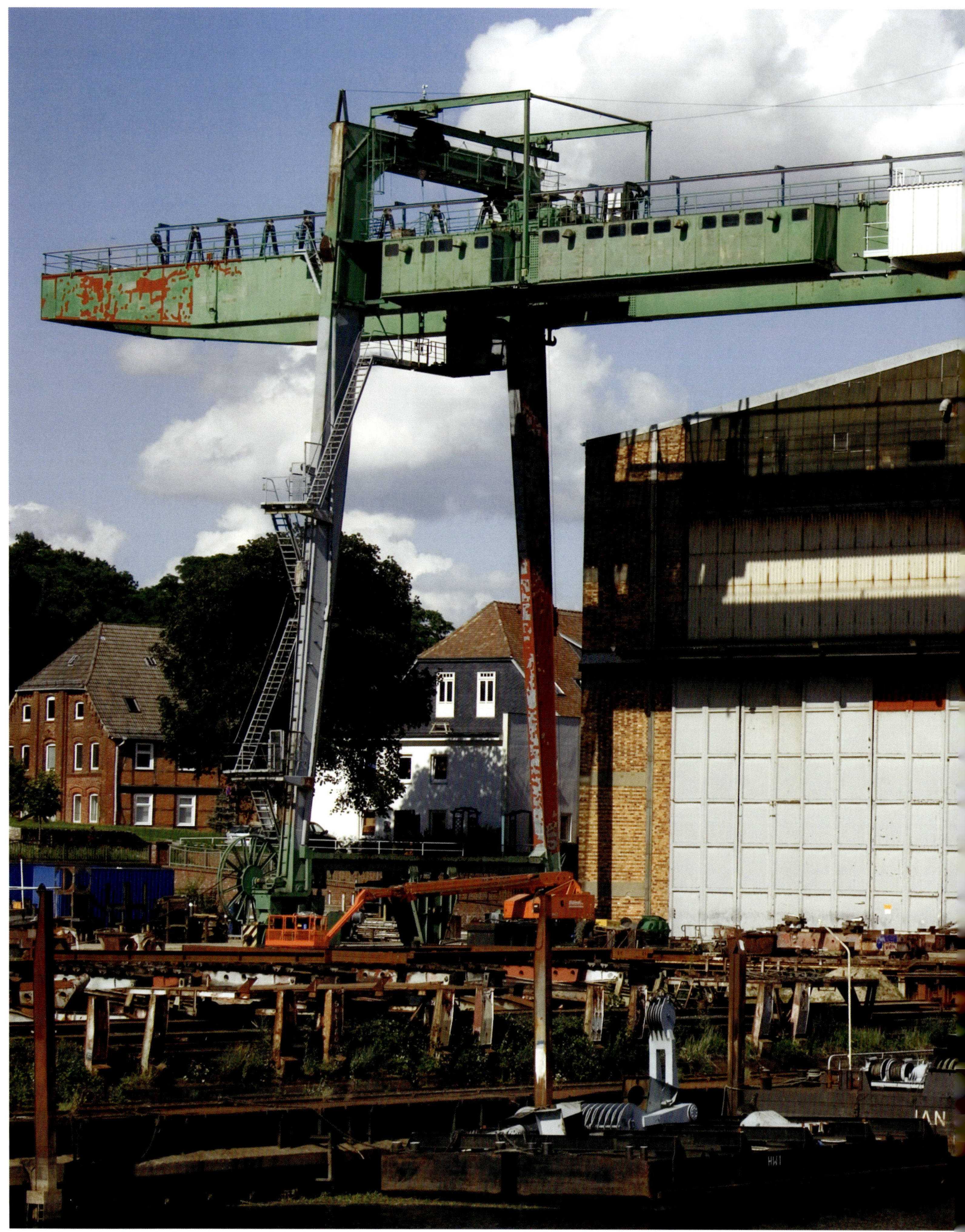

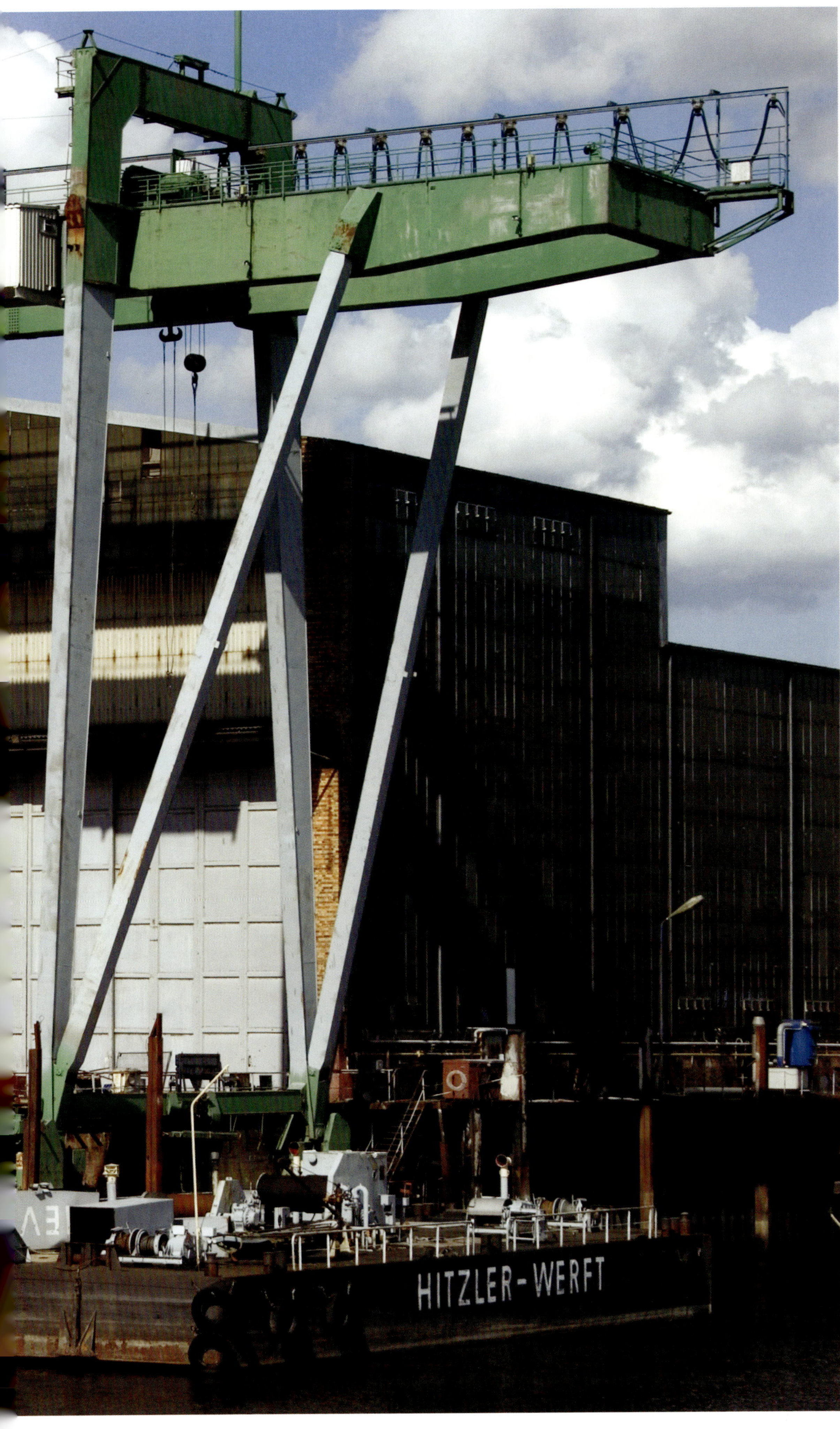

LEFT:

LEFT:
Disused Shipyard on the River Elbe, Boizenburg, Germany
The Elbewerft yard specialised in fishing vessels and river cruise ships. Ships have been built here since 1793. Despite modernising its facilities after the 1970s, since German reunification in 1990 it became part of a larger group, failed to attract new investment and was closed down by 2019.

OVERLEAF:
Naval Craft, Peenemünde, Vorpommern, Germany
Peenemünde is best known as the launch site of V2 rockets in World War II, but its harbour was a temporary home in 2013 to these ex-Swedish Navy Hugin-class patrol boats, stripped of their armament and fast-drive main engines and awaiting a buyer. The deck-rails indicate that they were intended for minelaying.

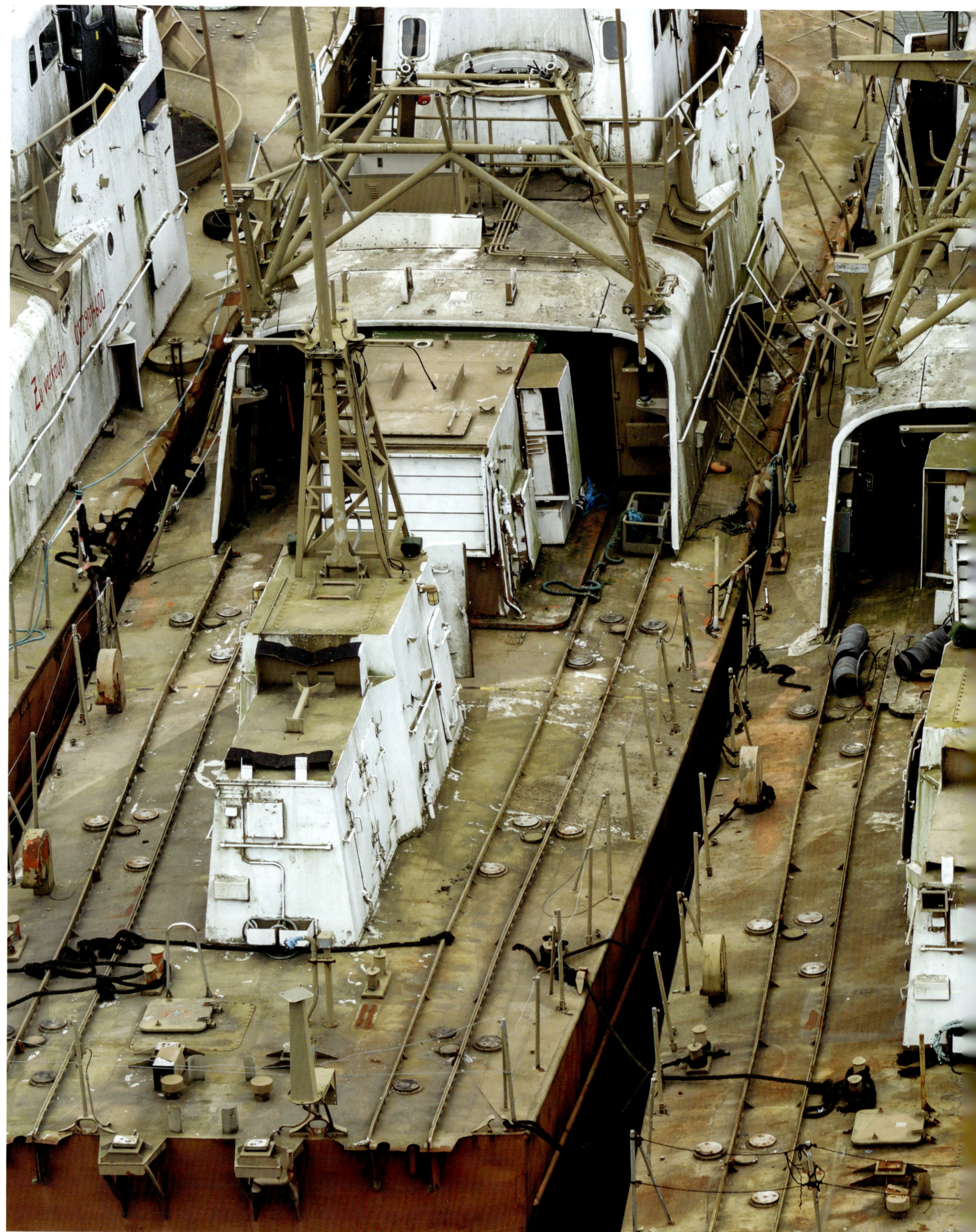

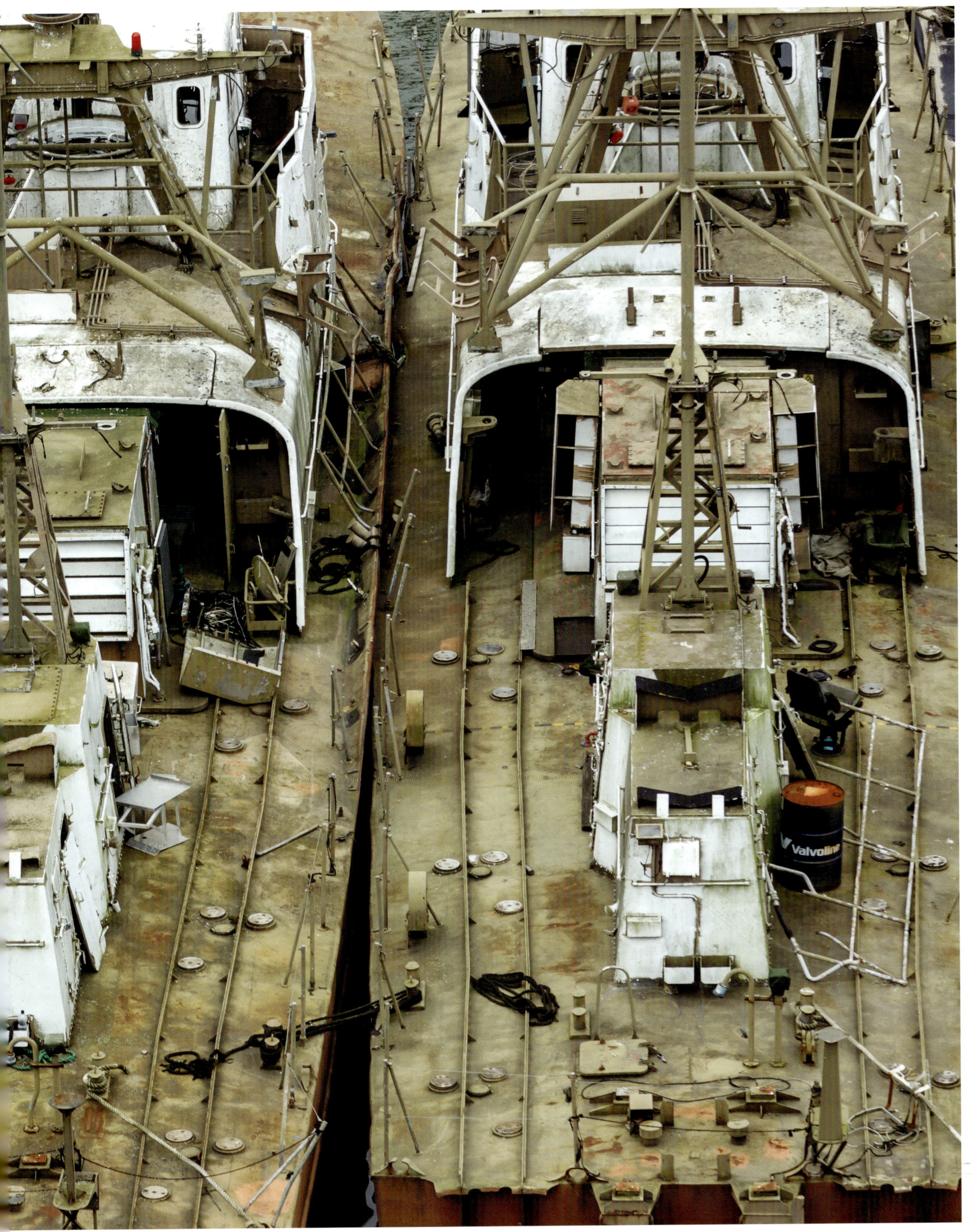

Valvoline

Beelitz Hospital, Beelitz-Heilstätten, Germany
Originally a tuberculosis sanatorium, this vast hospital complex functioned through both World Wars and finished as a Soviet Army institution in the 1990s. Today an overhead walkway allows visitors.

BELOW:

Cattle-stabling Shed at Rosenau Slaughterhouse, Kaliningrad, Russia
Opened in 1895 when the area was part of imperial Germany, this was part of a then ultra-modern industrial complex for mass meat production. Here animals were brought in and held before being slaughtered. Much of the site was destroyed in World War II.

OPPOSITE:

Ceramics Factory, Wächtersbach, Hesse, Germany
Using local white clay, ceramic ware was made here since 1832. Production ended in 2011, under pressure from Asian imports which, the German producers claimed, were cheaper because less concern was paid to ecological aspects of manufacture.

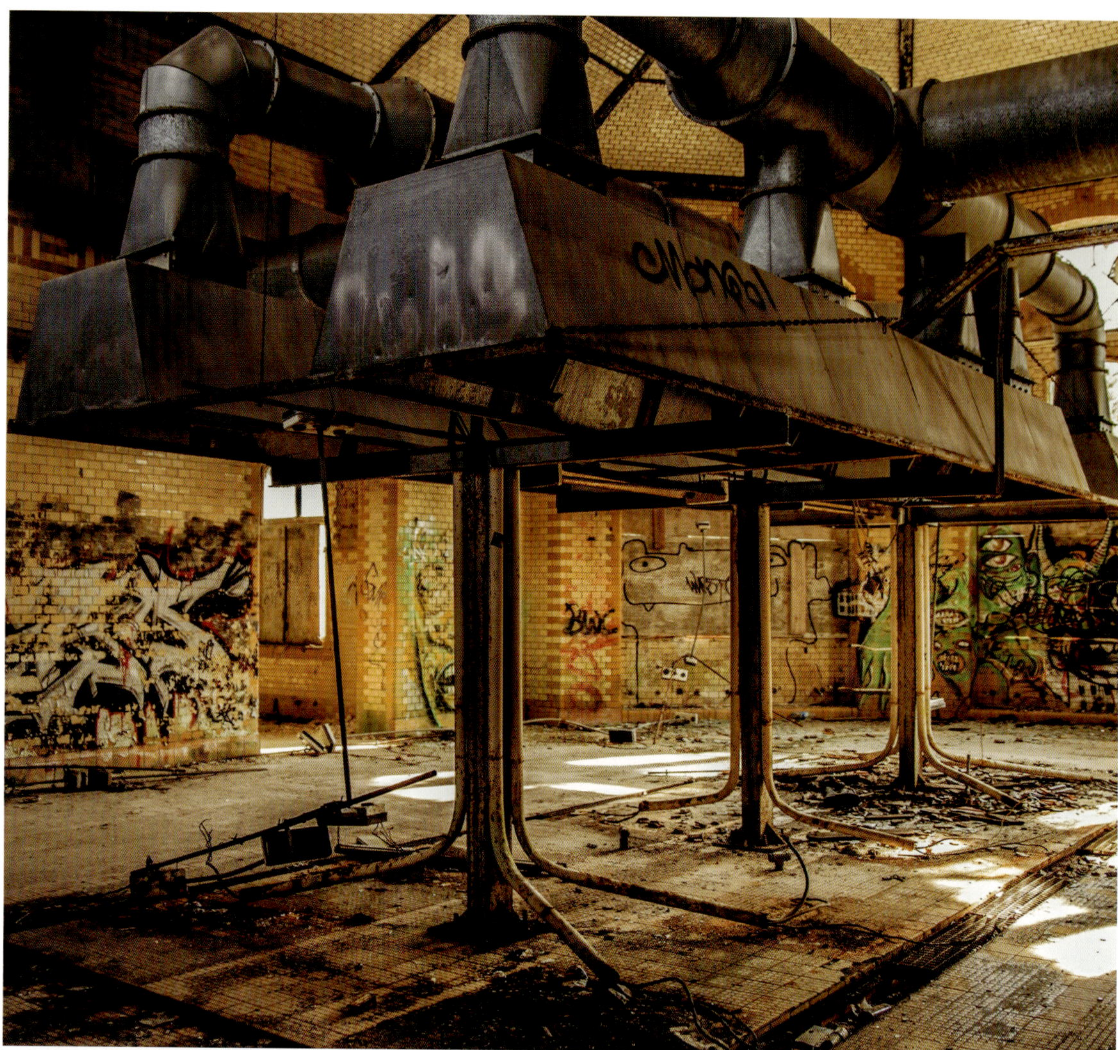

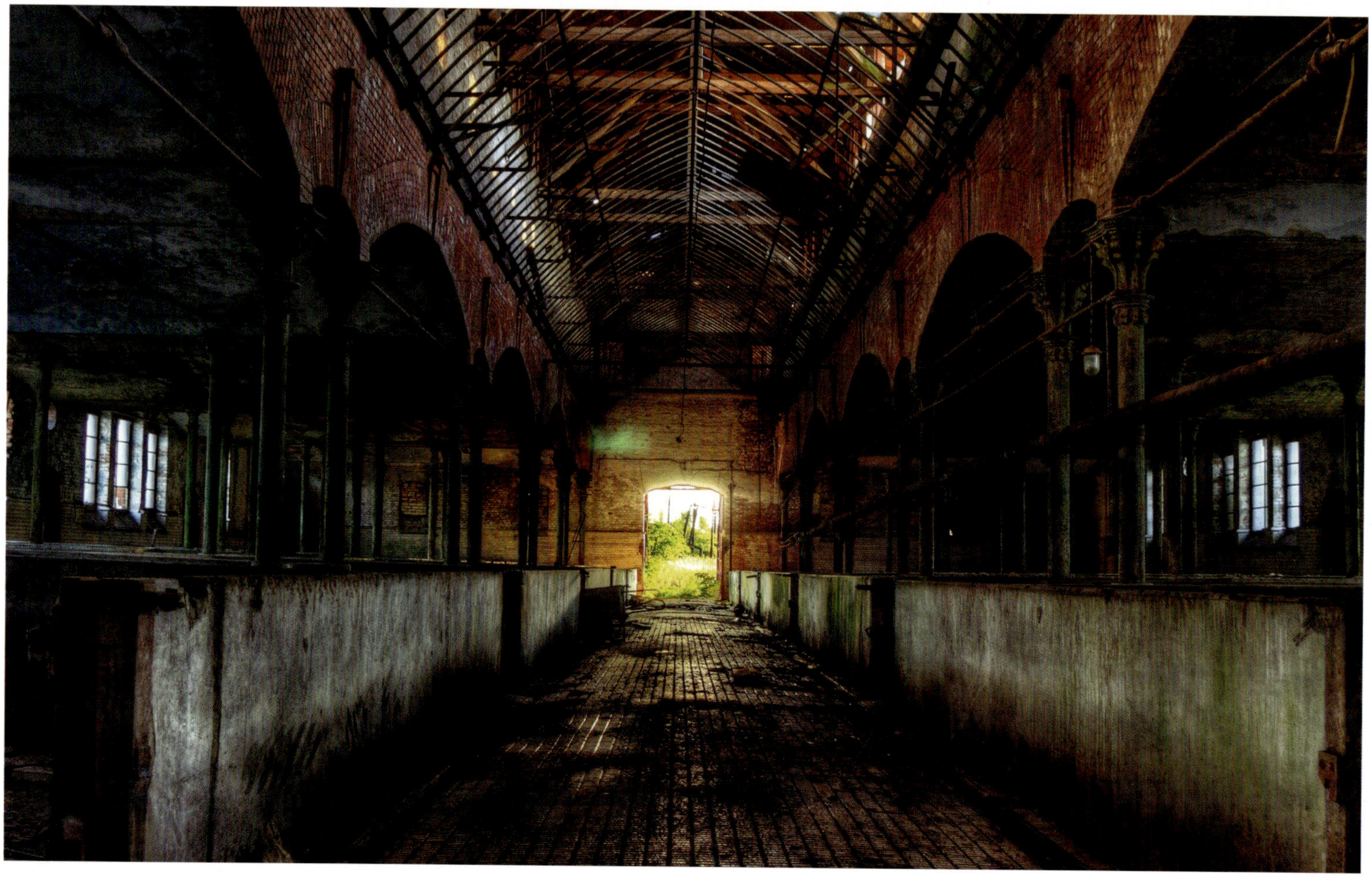

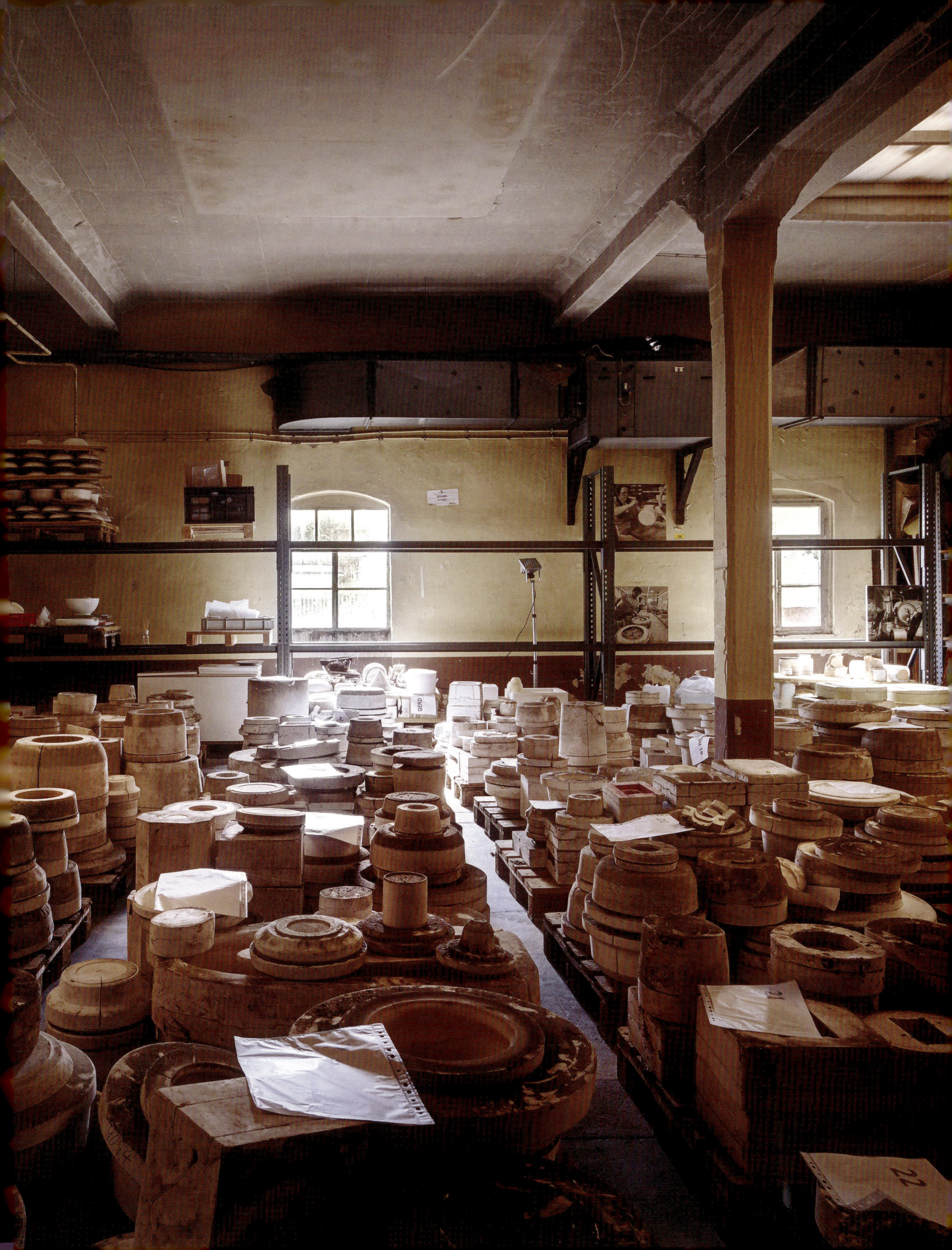

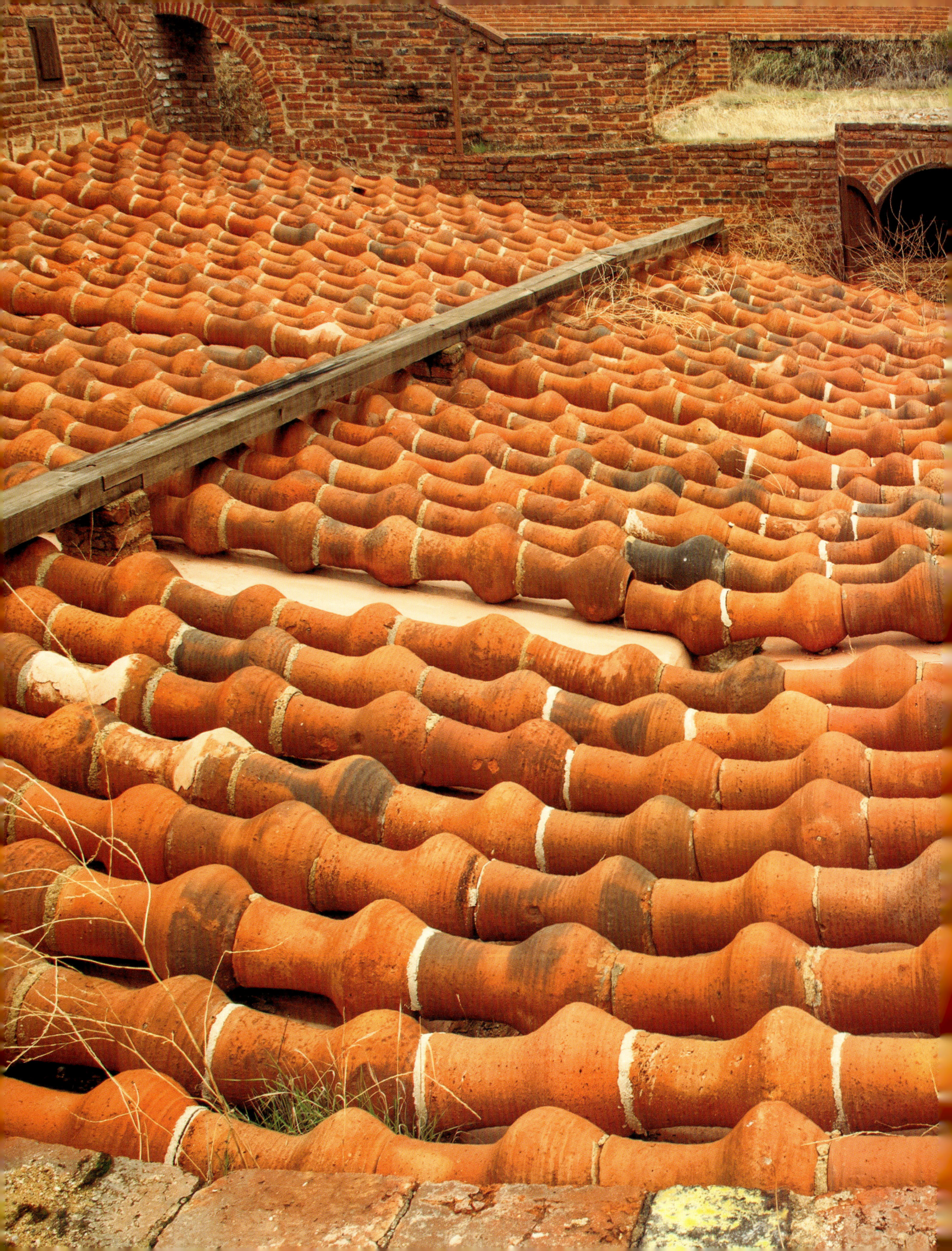

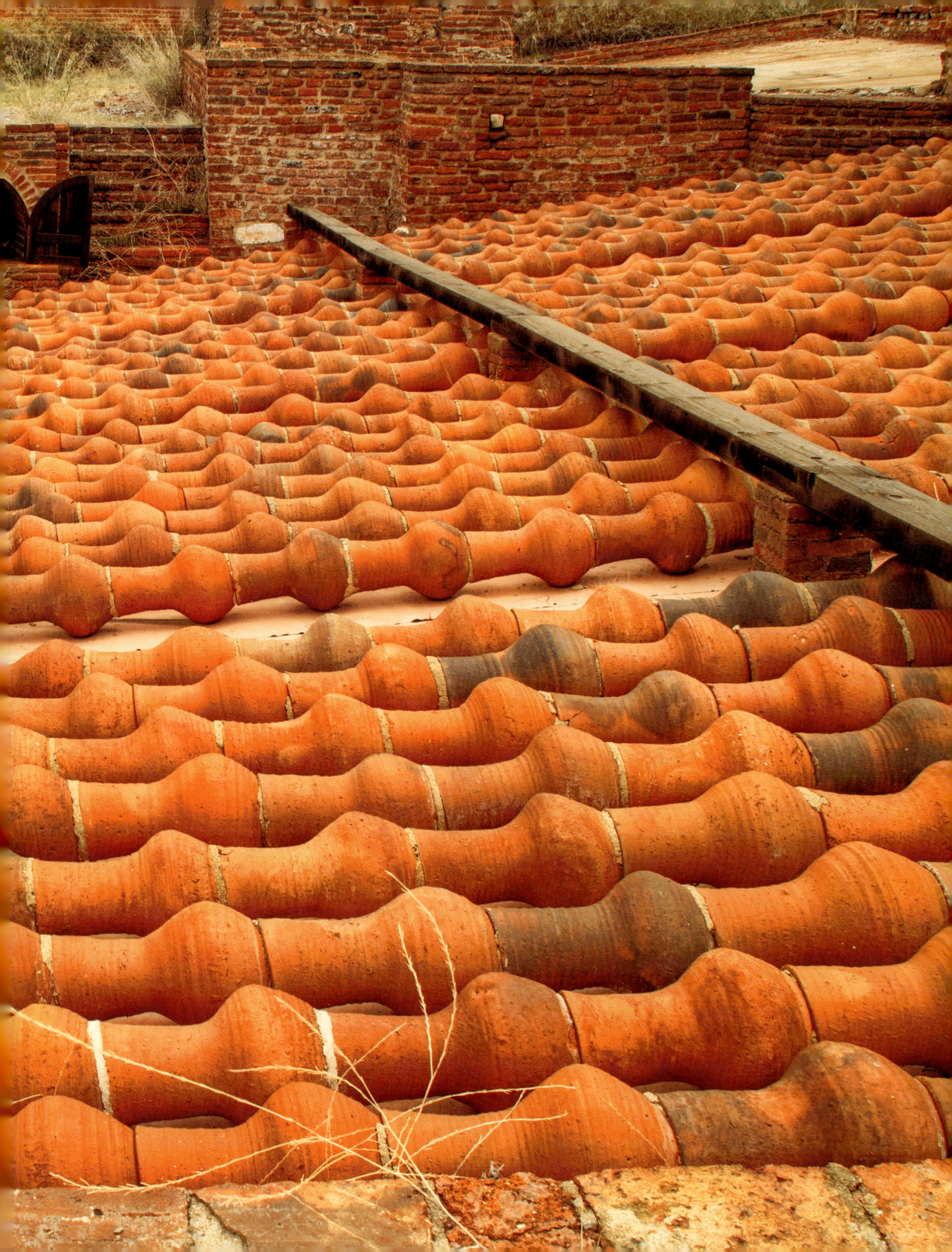

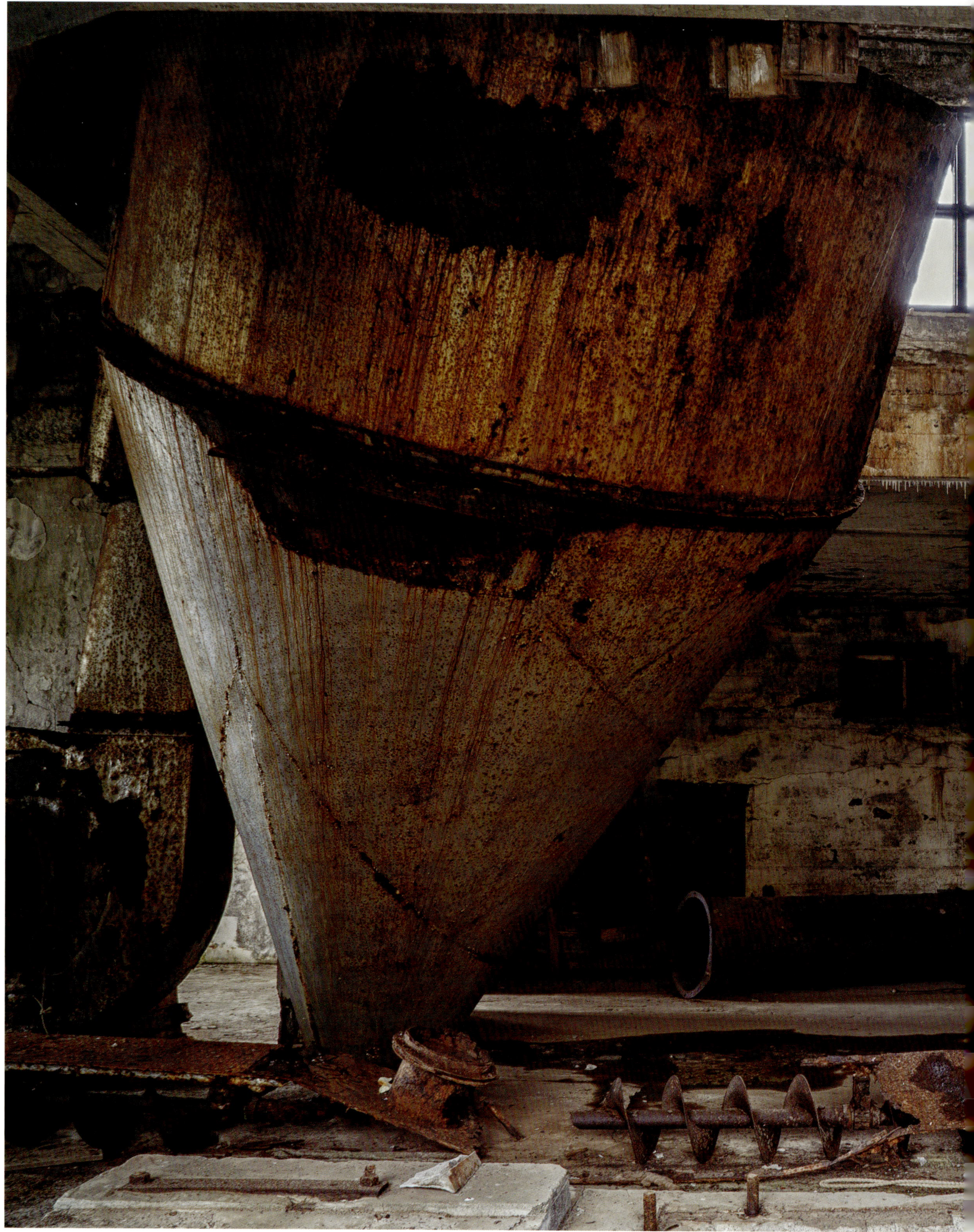

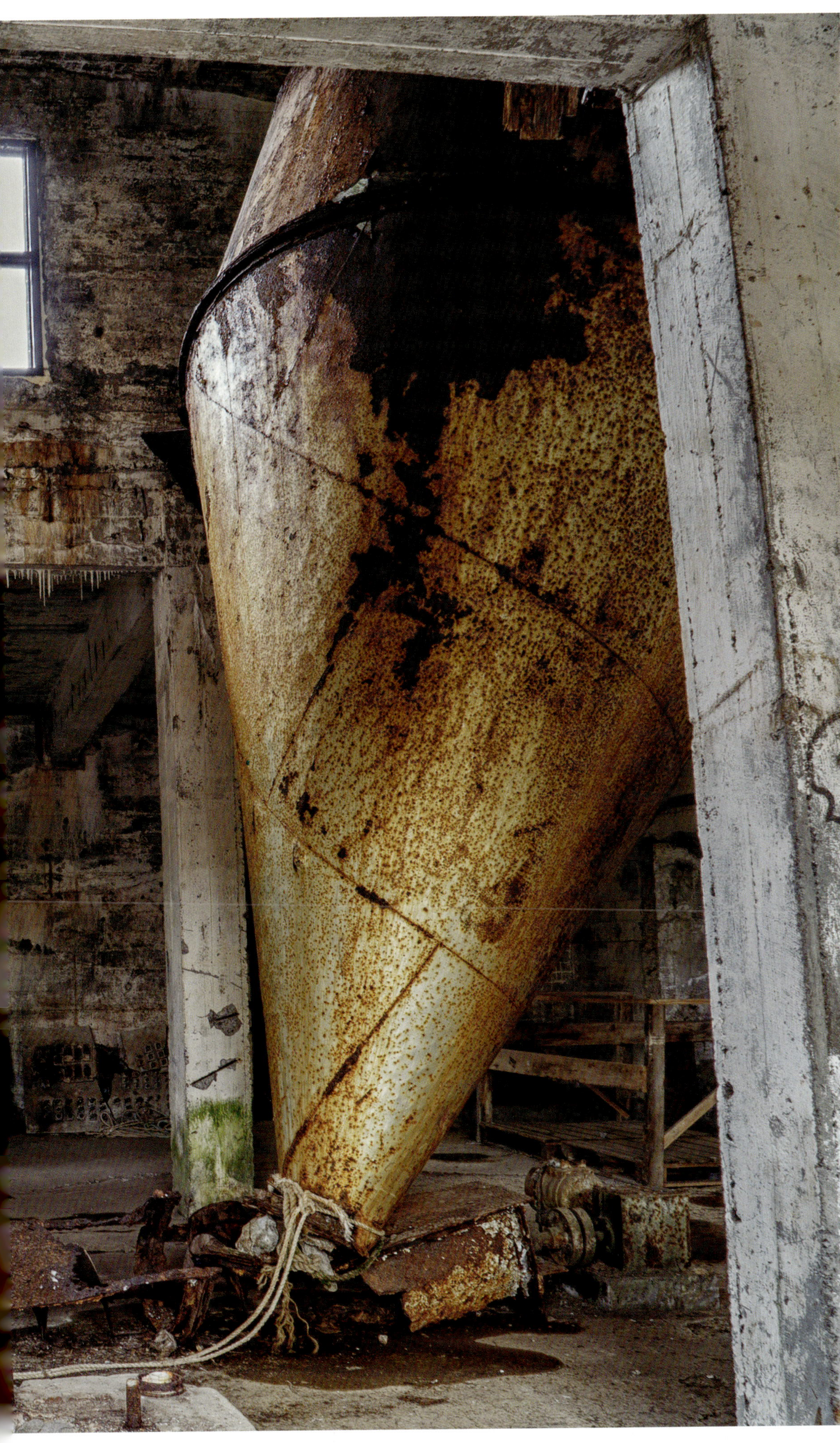

PREVIOUS PAGES:
**Mercury Distillation Flasks,
Almadén Mine, Ciudad Real,
Castile, Spain**
The world's largest known
mercury deposit is here, and
mining, which had gone on for
centuries, ended in 2000 due to
a fall in demand and low prices.
Collection of distilled mercury
in earthenware pots has gone
on since Roman times: here an
on-site kiln produced the flasks in
large numbers.

LEFT:
**Old Fish Processing Factory,
Djupavik, Iceland**
A fishy aroma still hangs in
the chill air of what was in
1935 Iceland's largest concrete
building, producing fish oil
and fish meal. By the 1950s the
herring had been fished out and
the factory was abandoned with
its equipment. Now it has been
partly cleared and developed
with performance and exhibition
spaces, even inside the huge oil
tank.

OVERLEAF:
**Duga Radar Installation,
Chernobyl, Ukraine**
In the radiation zone of
Chernobyl, amid bits of its own
fallen debris, stands a huge
Cold War memento, the 700m
(765 yd) high wall of latticed
steel towers set up in the early
1970s as a sophisticated missile
detection system, and remaining
a closely guarded secret until
the Chernobyl disaster made it
unusable.

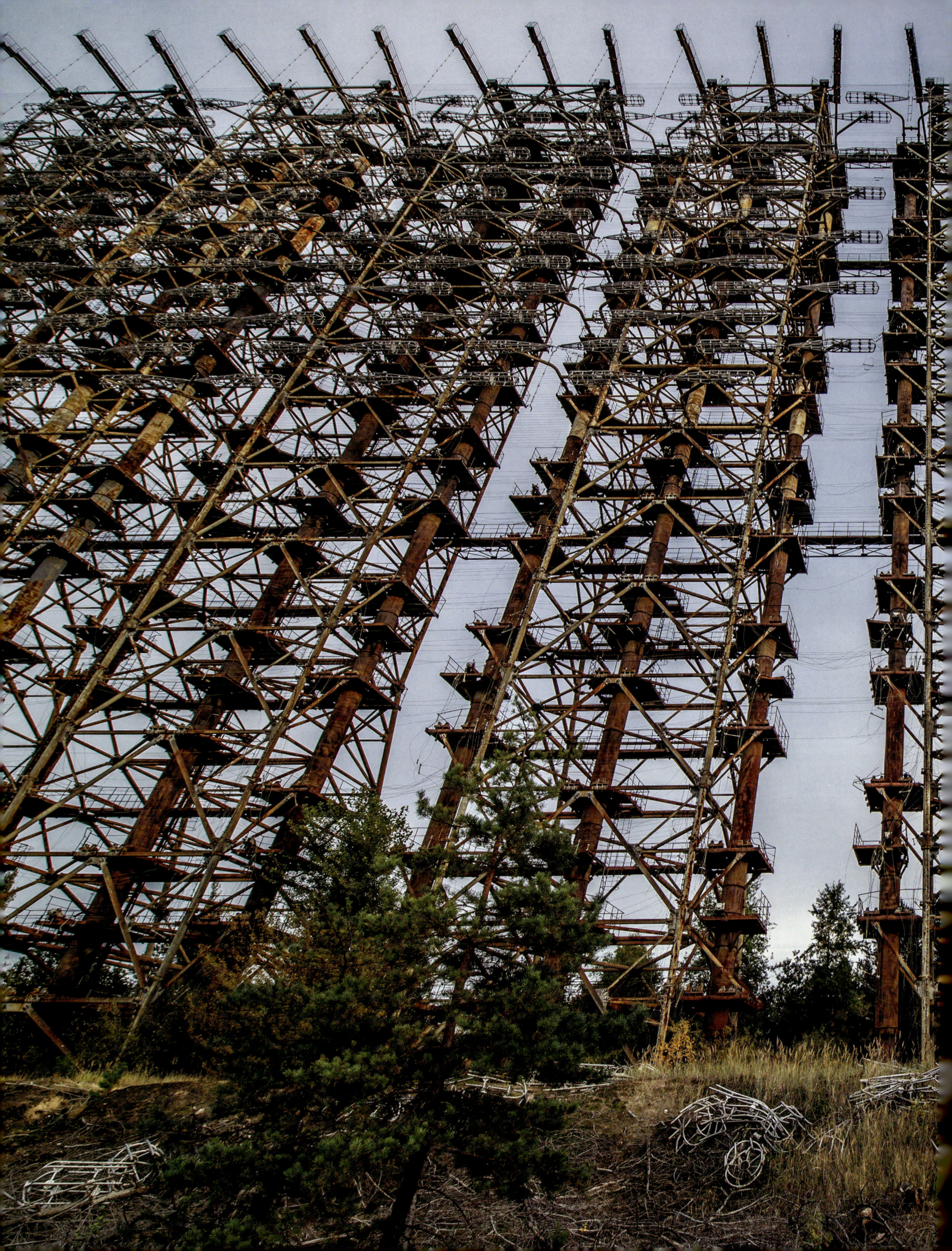

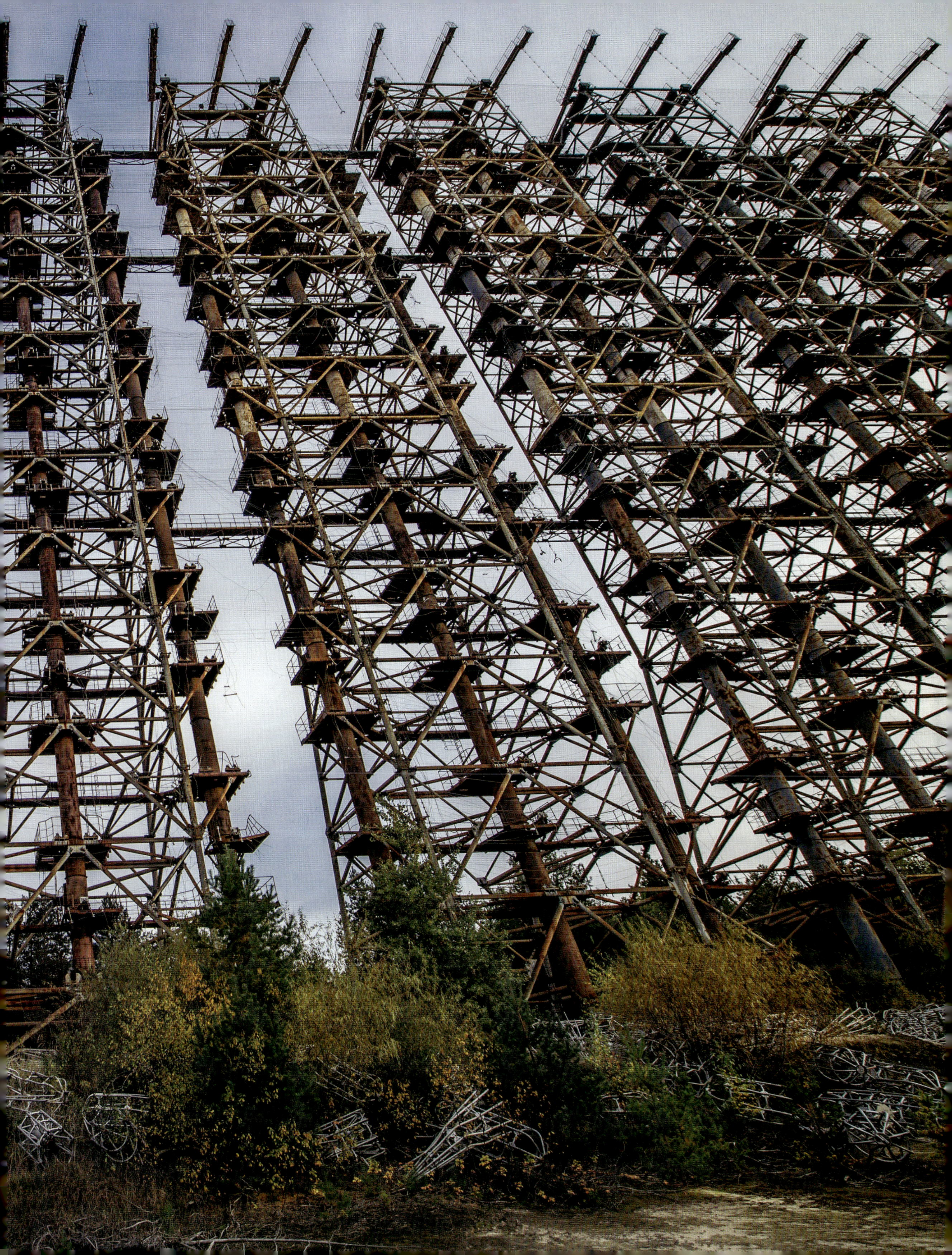

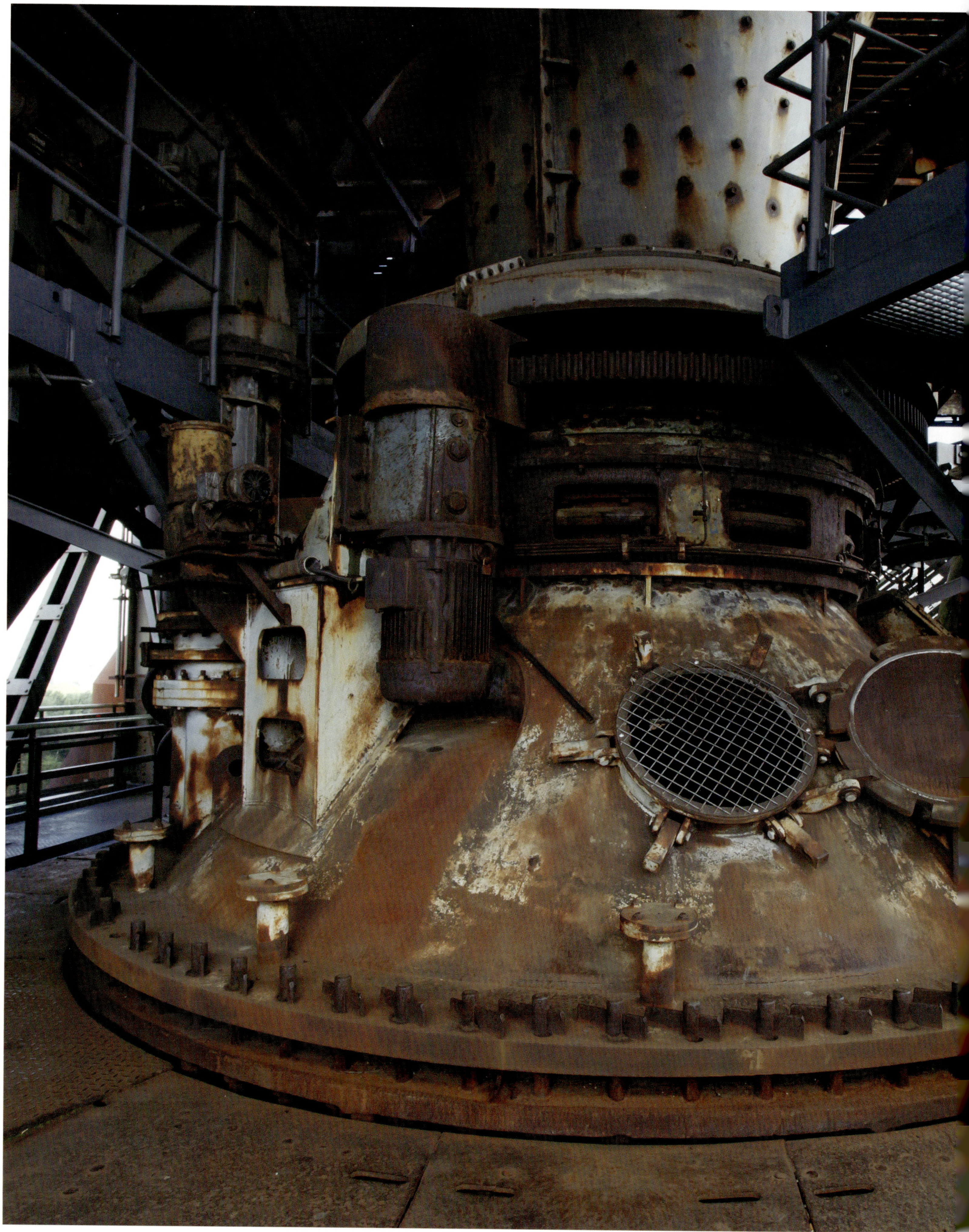

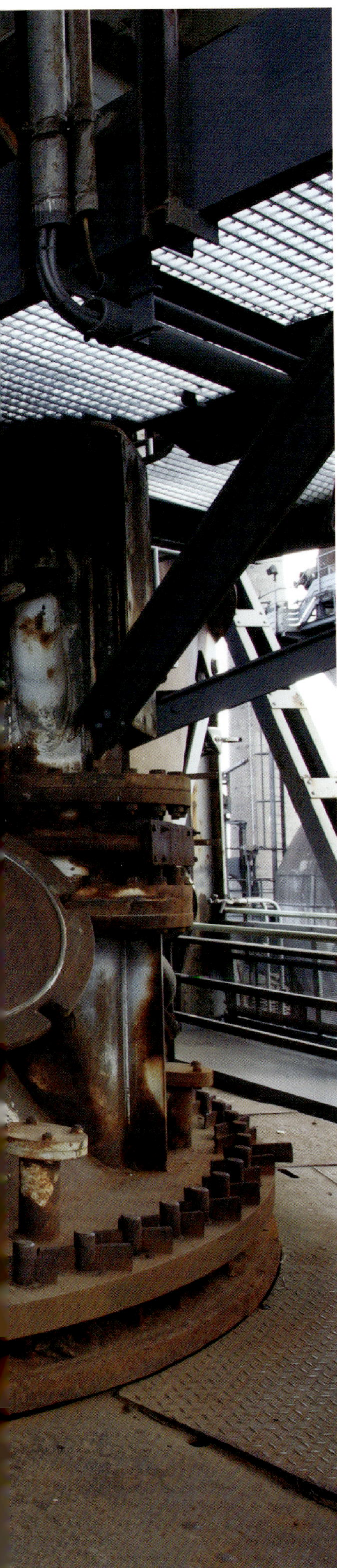

LEFT:

Landschaftspark Nord, Duisburg, North Rhine-Westphalia, Germany
Heavy industry brought both wealth and blight to Germany's Ruhr district and the closed-down Thyssen-Meiderich blast furnace complex is the centrepiece of an ambitious landscaping project intended to link past, present and future in a recreational area for locals and visitors.

BELOW:

Abandoned Factory, Laupheim, Baden-Württemberg, Germany
Laupheim is a centre of mechanical engineering and pharmaceuticals. These part-modernised control valves, photographed before a factory's demolition, with new automatic units inserted in older pipework, suggest that it was a chemicals plant.

OVERLEAF:

Bunabhainneader Whaling Station, Isle of Harris, Scotland
Between 1903 and 1920 this was a substantial whale processing works, until the North Atlantic whale population was almost wiped out. The works were briefly revived in the 1950s but since then demolition and erosion have left only a surviving chimney, though the foundations and lower parts of many of the buildings are still visible.

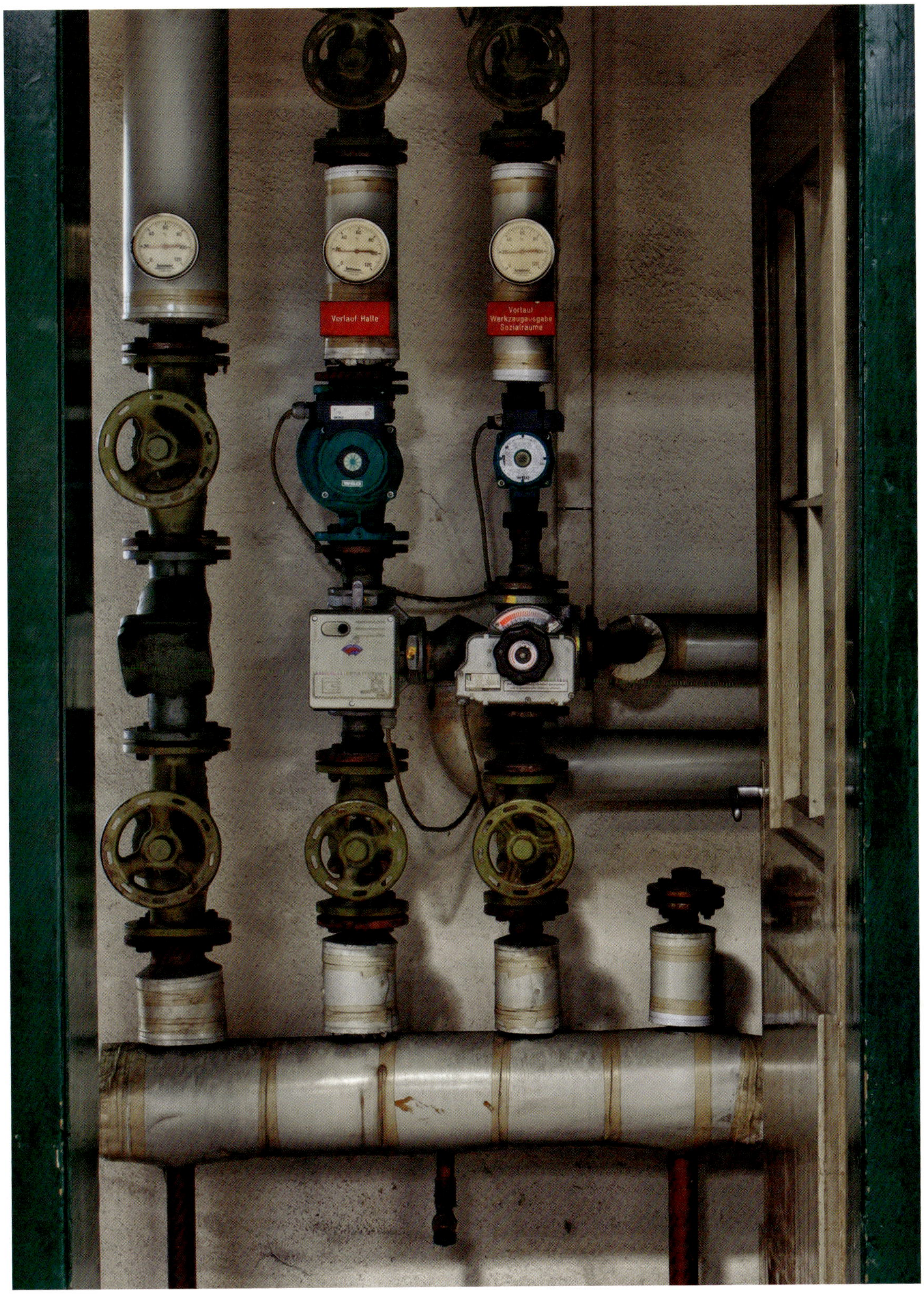

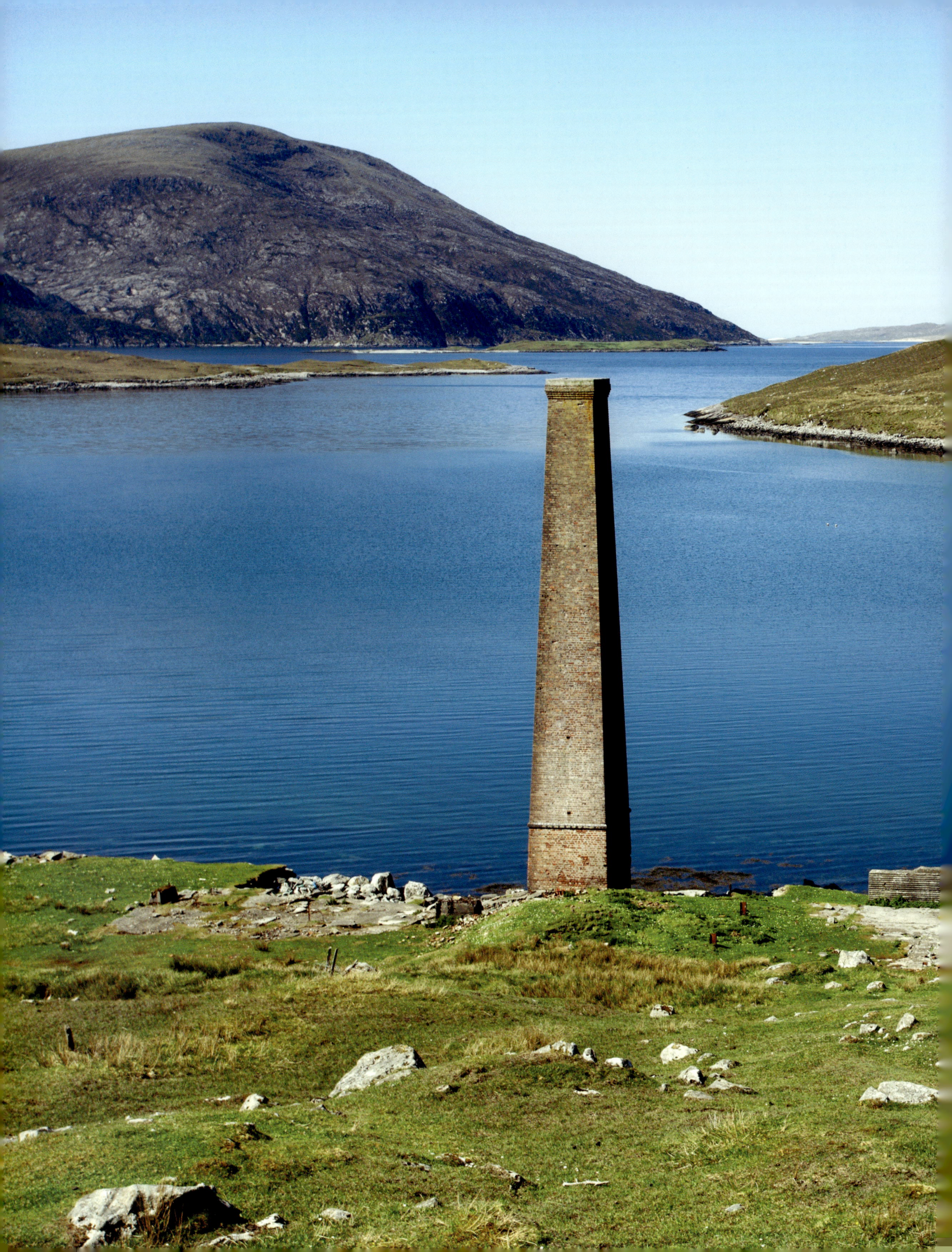

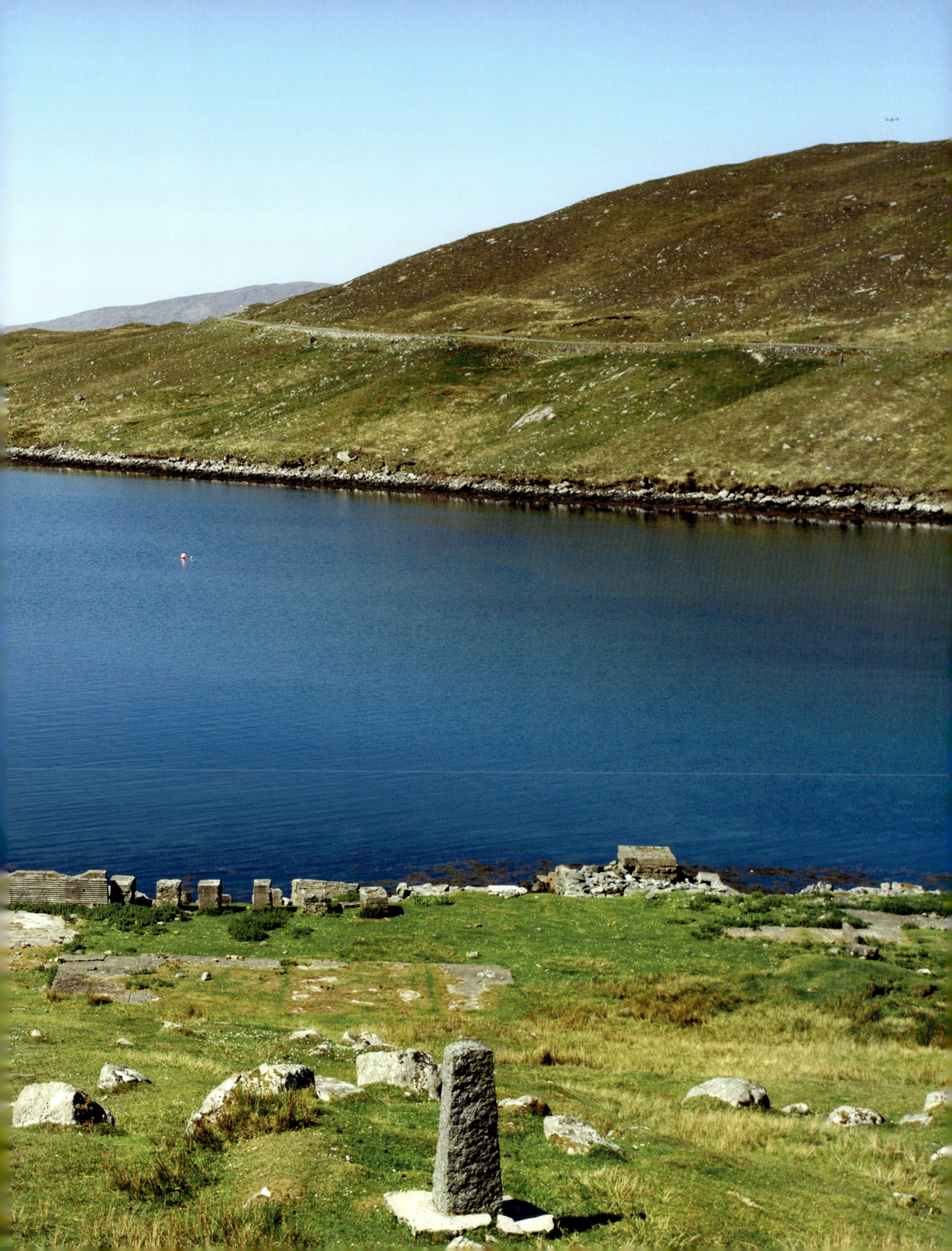

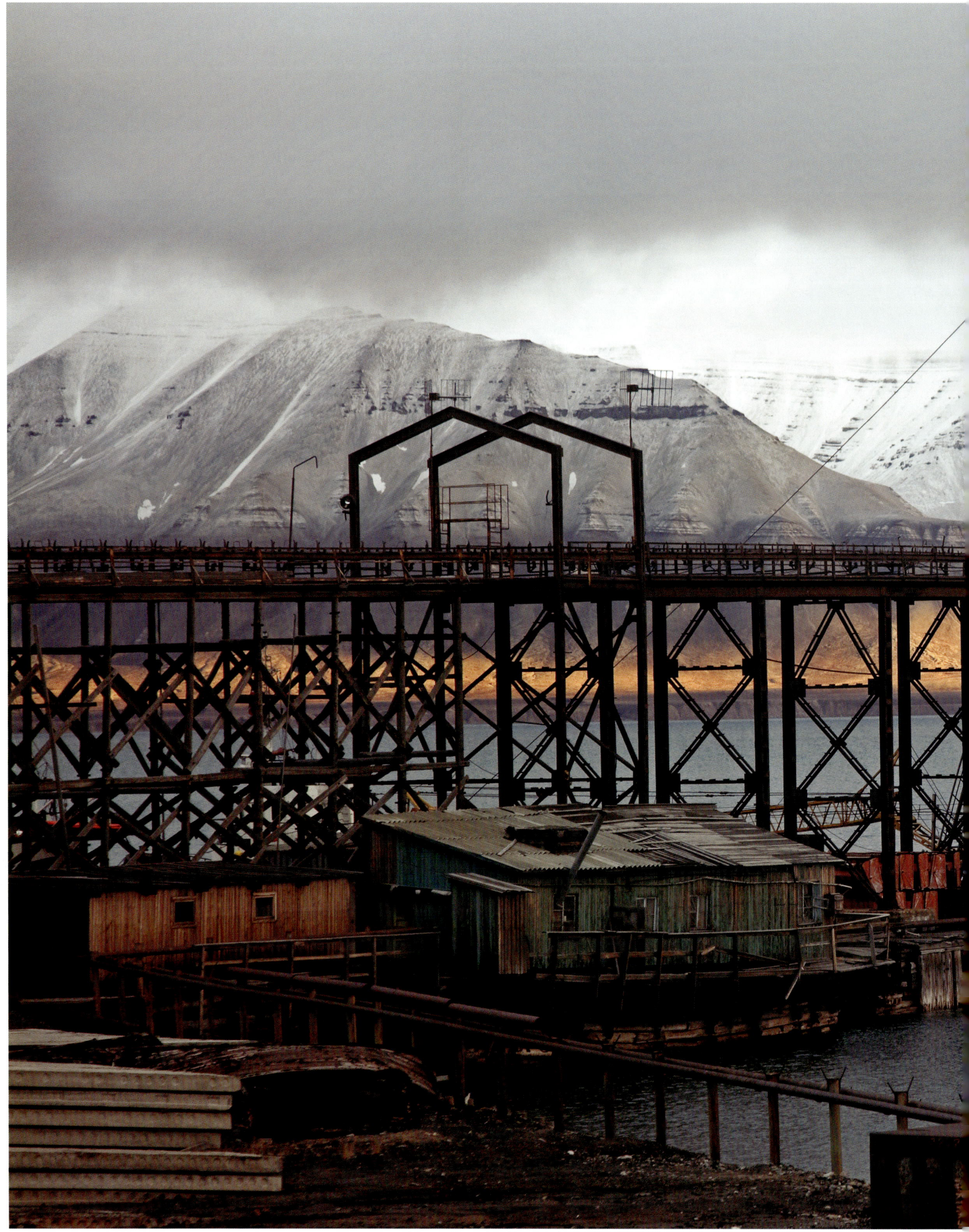

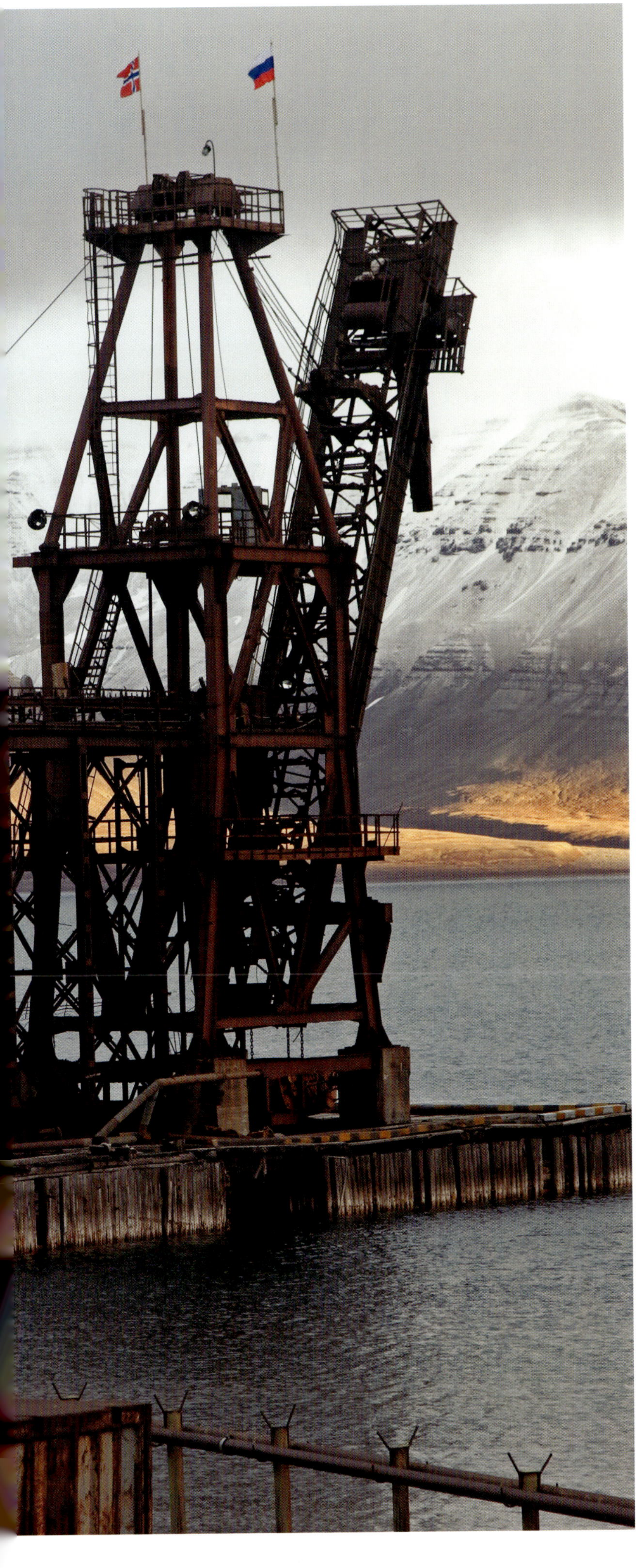

LEFT AND BELOW:
**Pyramiden Coal Mine,
Spitsbergen, Norway**
The remains of a large coal mine
and its working community,
abandoned since 1998, still stand
here. The mine was close to the
shore and coal was carried by
conveyor belt to the loading jetty.
The company was Russian, and
built a village with apartment
blocks and a community centre
for the workers.

OVERLEAF:
**Mirny Diamond Mine,
Sakha Republic, Russia**
This enormous pit has been dug
out since 1955 as the world's
most productive diamond mine.
At 525m (1700ft) deep and
1200m (3900ft) across, it is
claimed as the second-largest
man-made hole in the earth.
Subterranean mining continues.
A substantial new town extends
right to the lip of the pit.

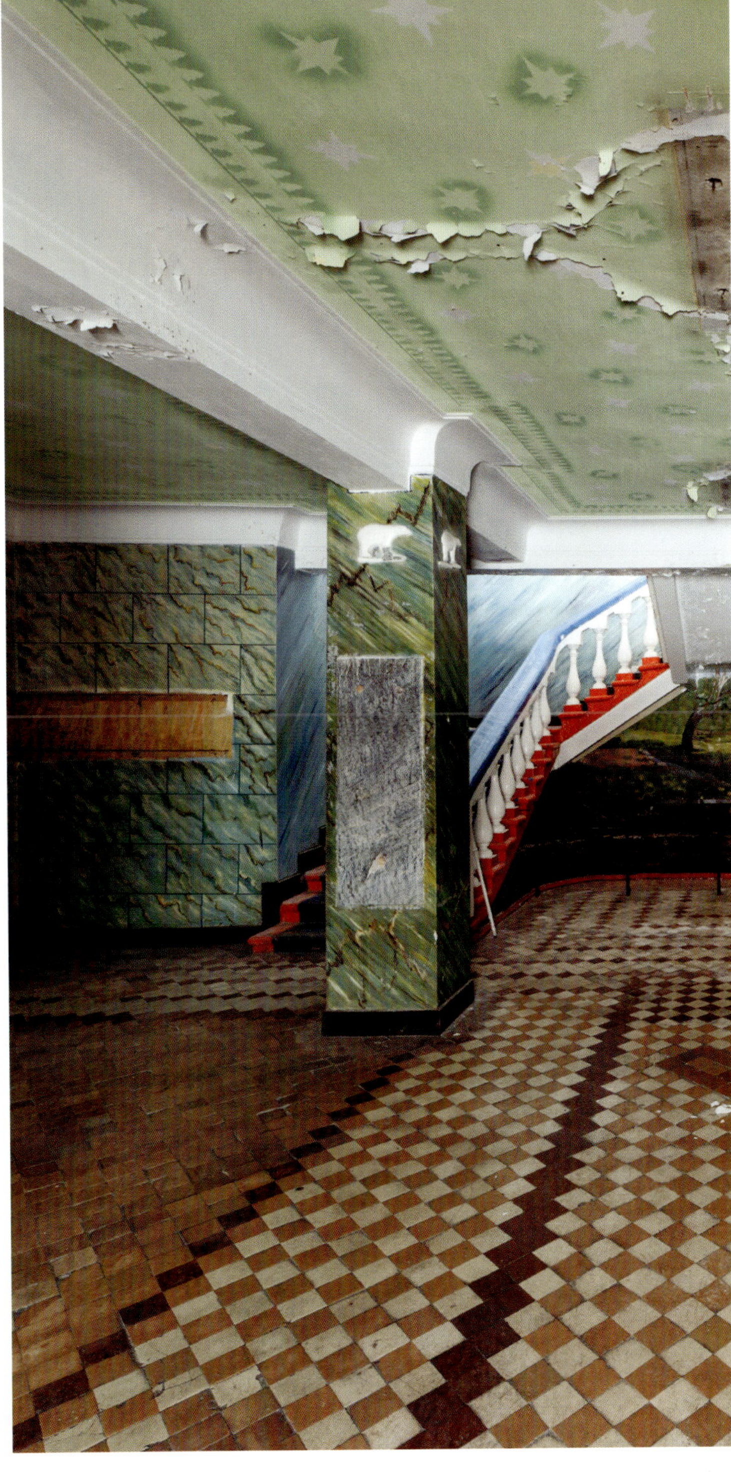

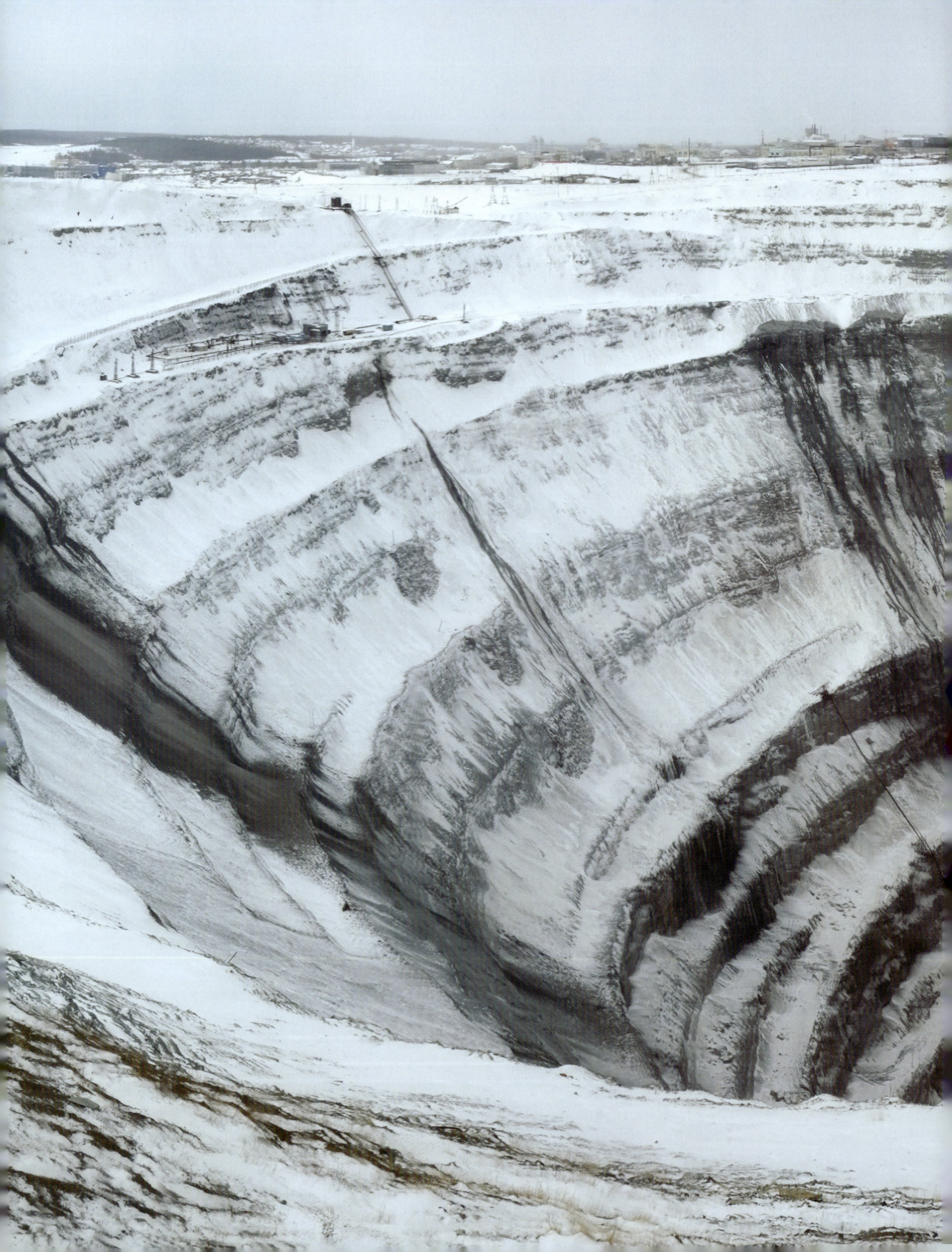

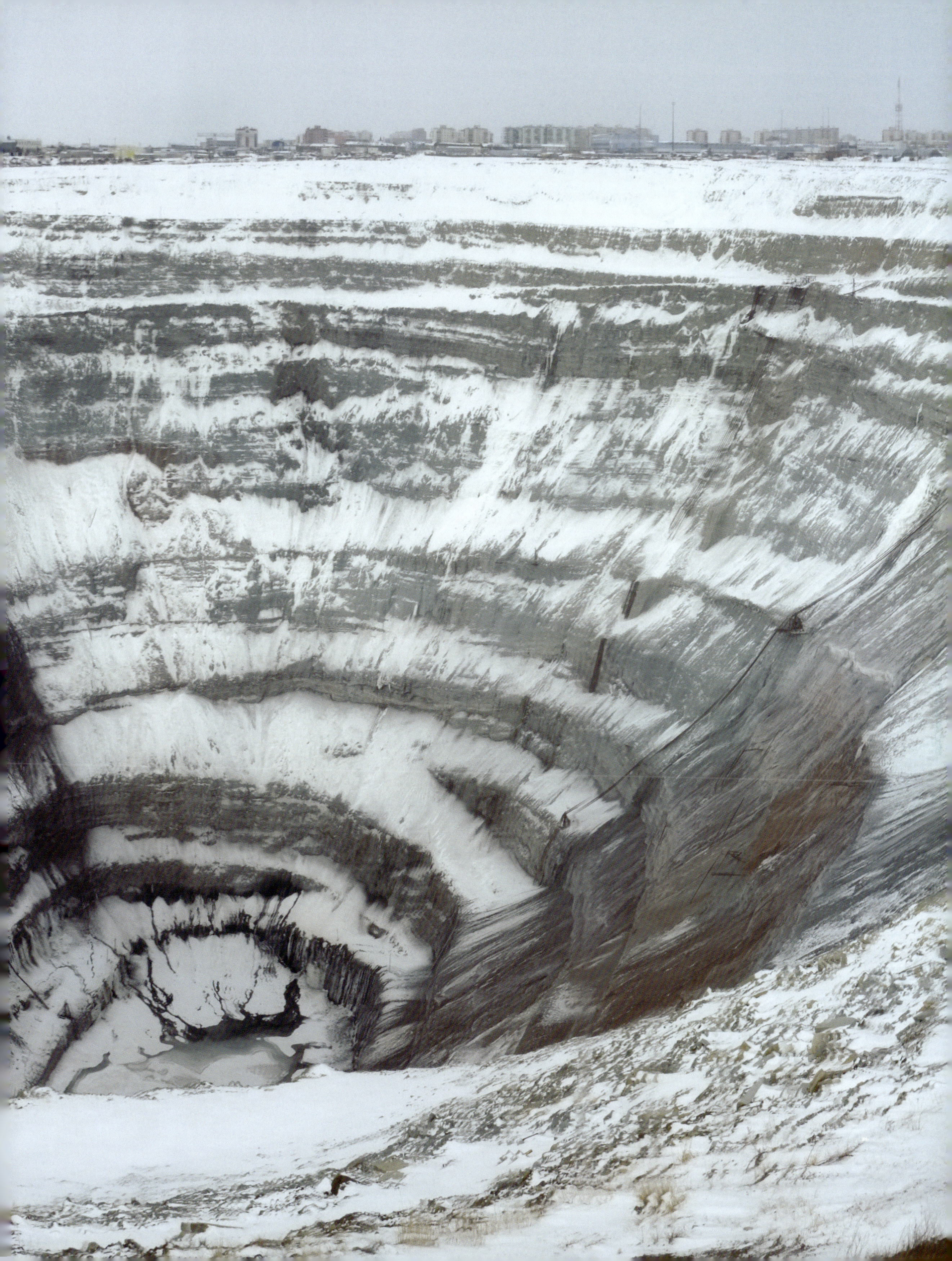

**Outer Walls of Gas-Holders,
Wola Gasworks, Warsaw, Poland**
The large Wola Gasworks are
now an industrial museum but
the two large gas-holders, rebuilt
in original style after 1945, and
functional until 1978, are not
part of it. The internal structures
have been removed but the brick
shells remain, their huge roofed
inner space a temptation to
urban explorers.

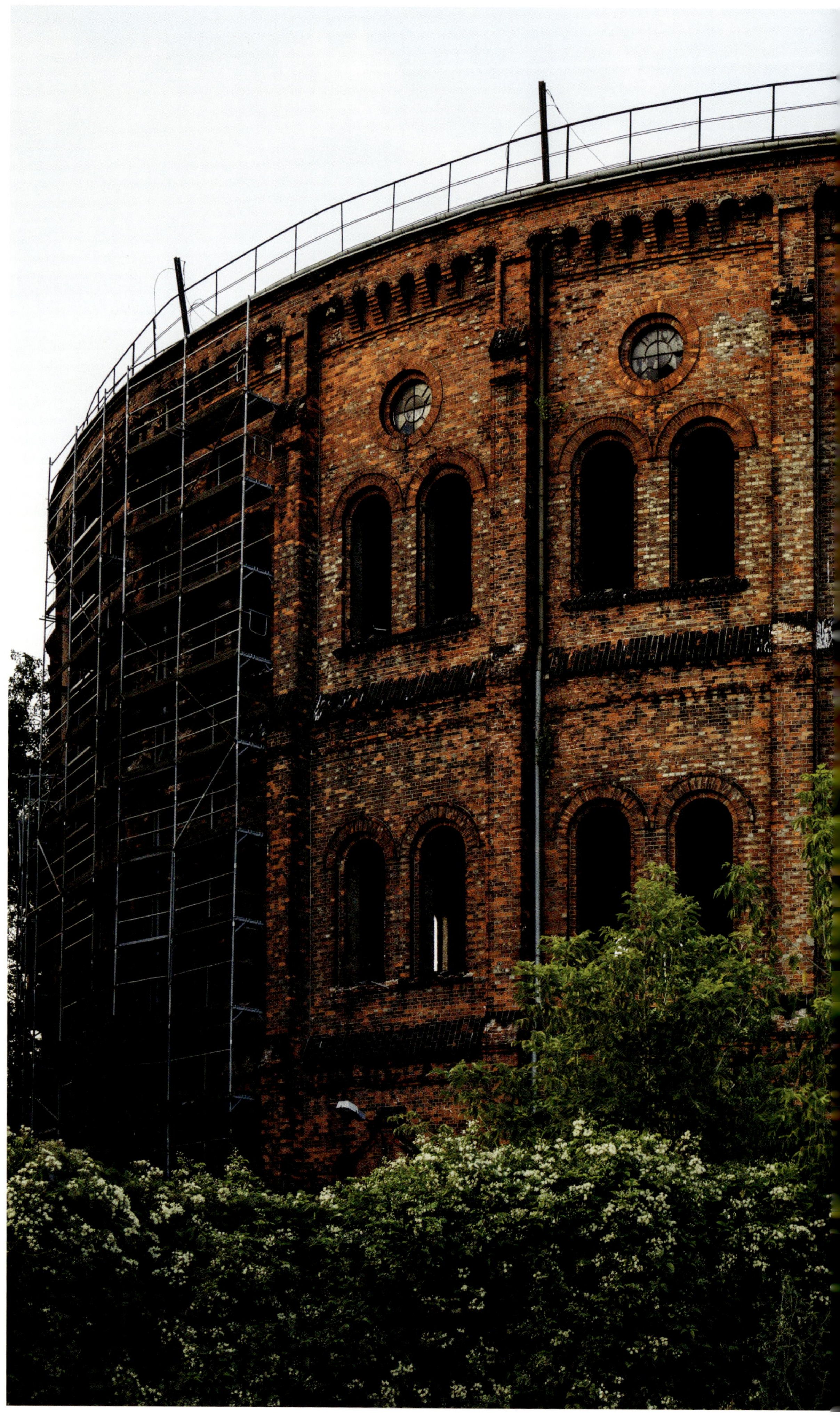

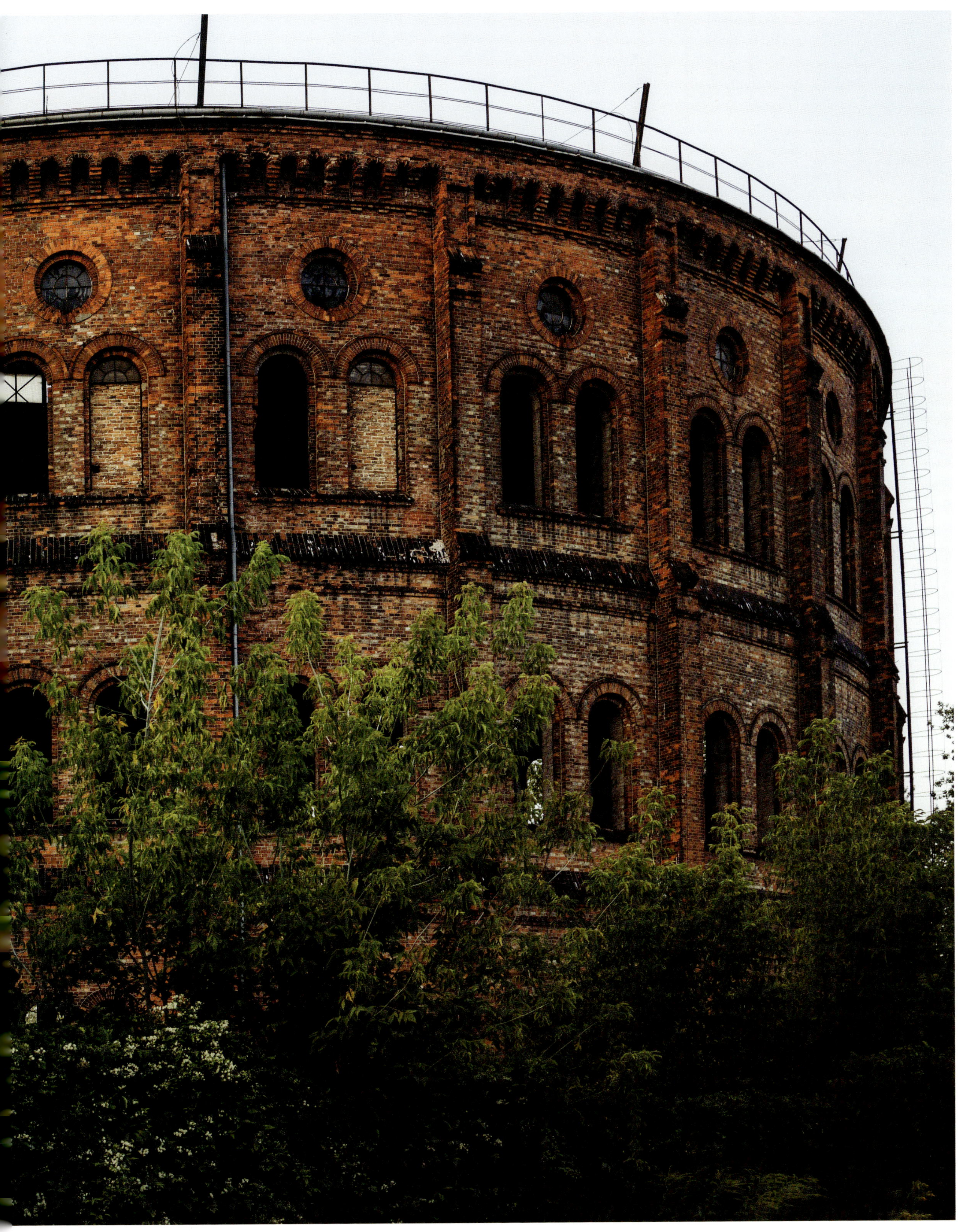

BELOW:
Dinorwic Slate Works, Llanberis, Wales
The slate mining region of North Wales is a treasure ground for the
industrial ruin hunter and archaeologist. There are museum sites but
also many locations on the open mountainsides. This is the remains
of a polishing machine at the Dinorwic Quarry.

OPPOSITE:
Cwmorthin Slate Mine, Blaenau Festiniog, Wales
Mining finally ended here only in 2000 but the ruins and spoil
heaps date from much earlier. The hillside is seamed with five levels
of underground workings, some still accessible to experienced
visitors and containing much in the way of artefacts in their tunnels
and chambers.

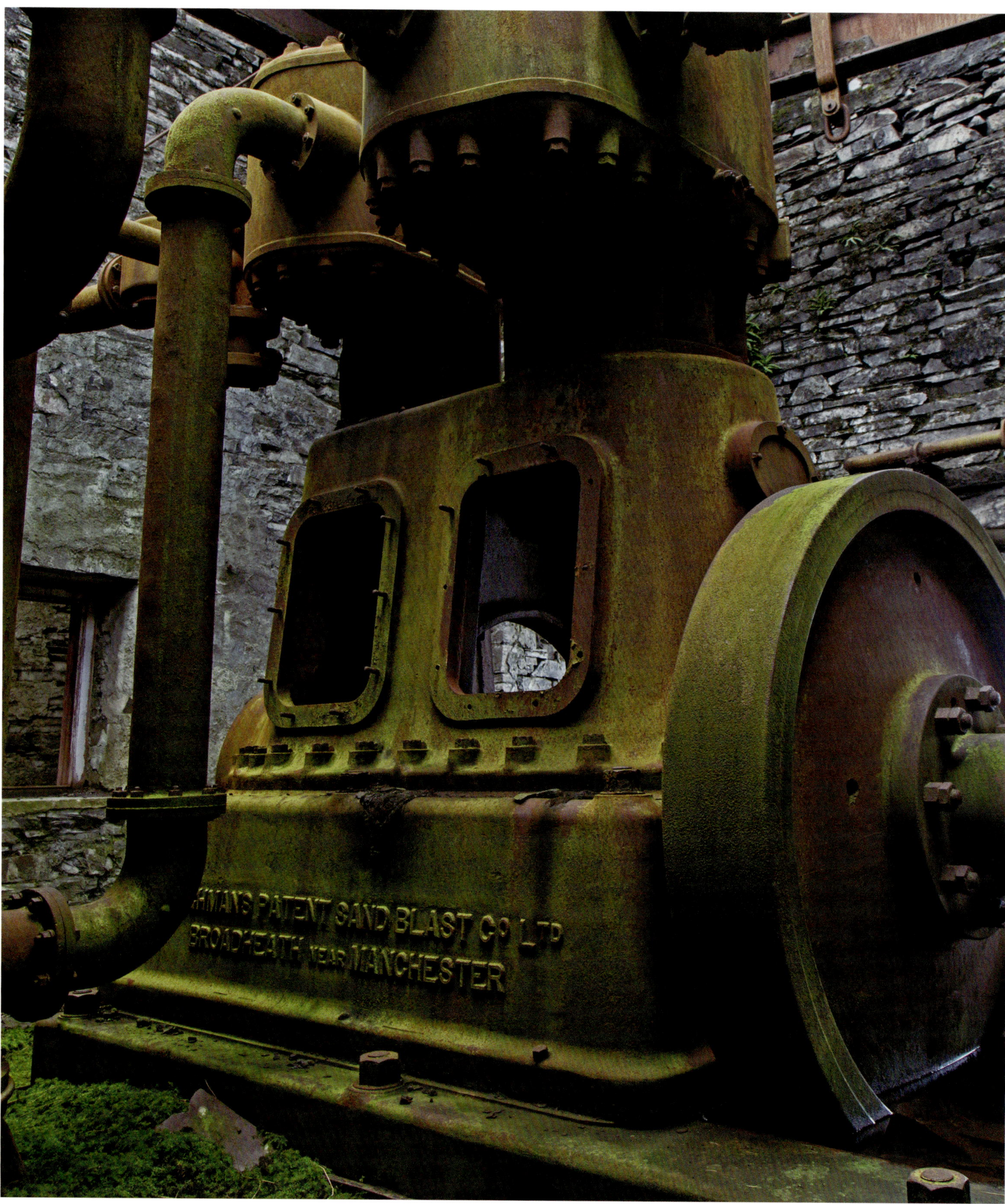
HMANS PATENT SAND BLAST Co LTD
BROADHEATH NEAR MANCHESTER

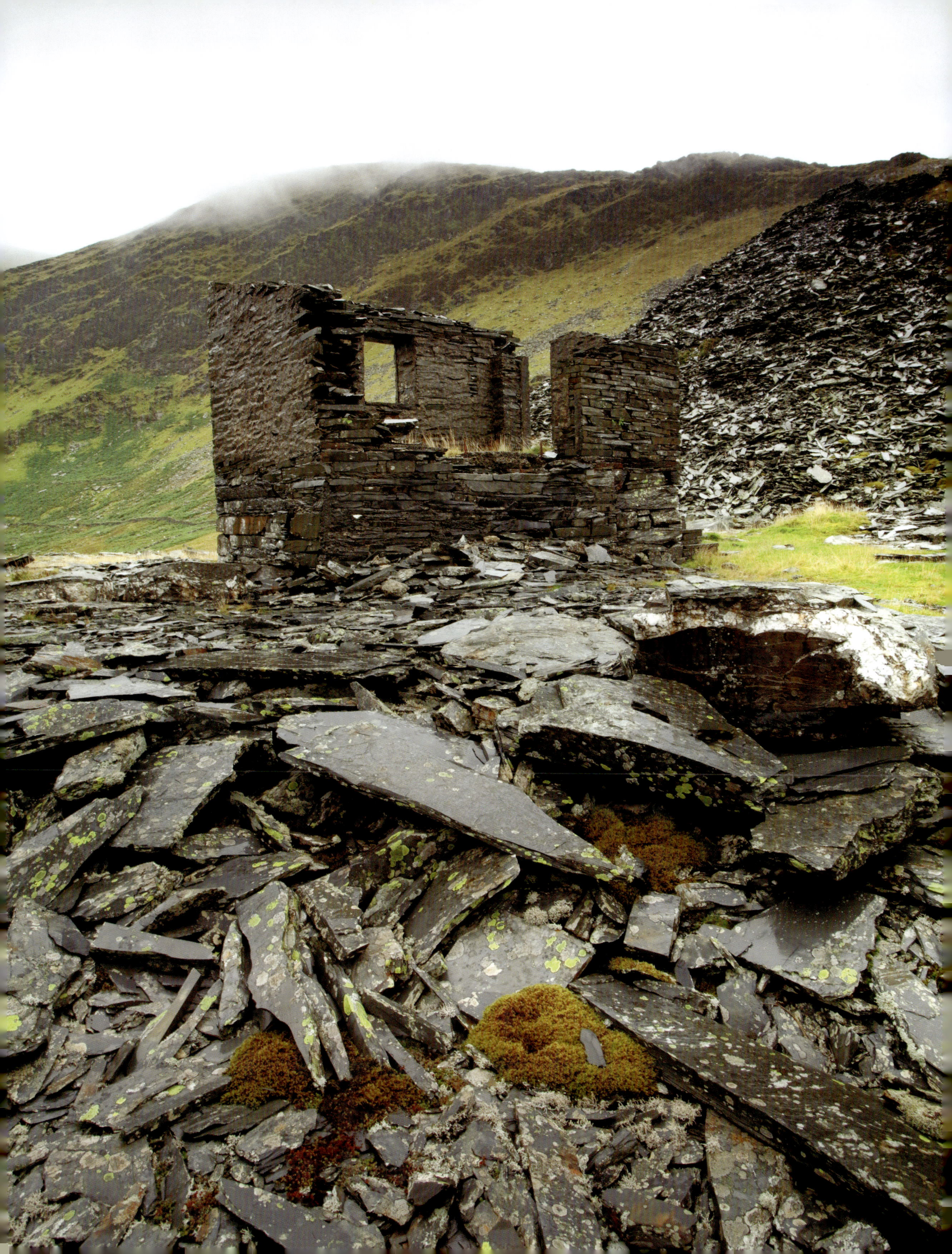

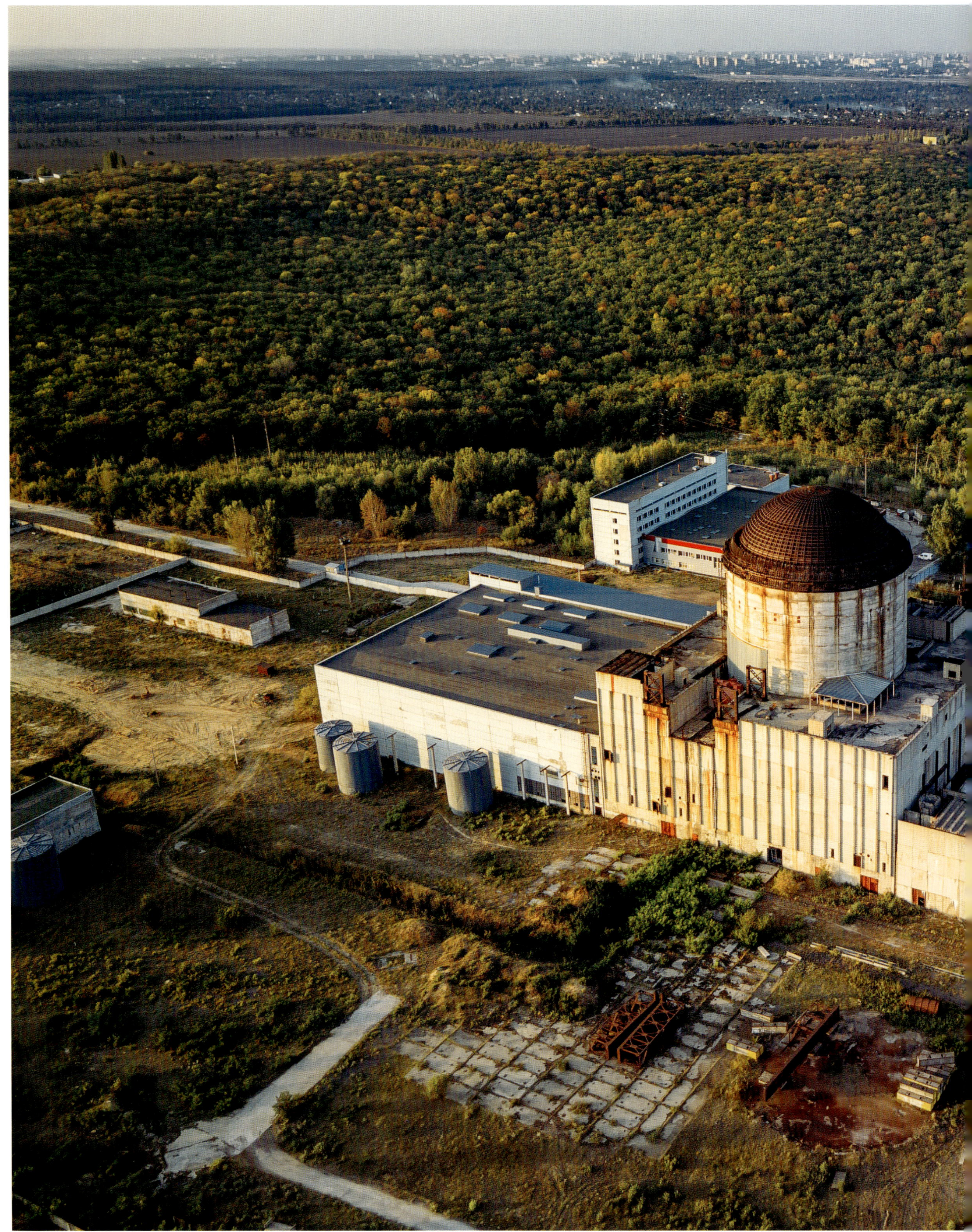

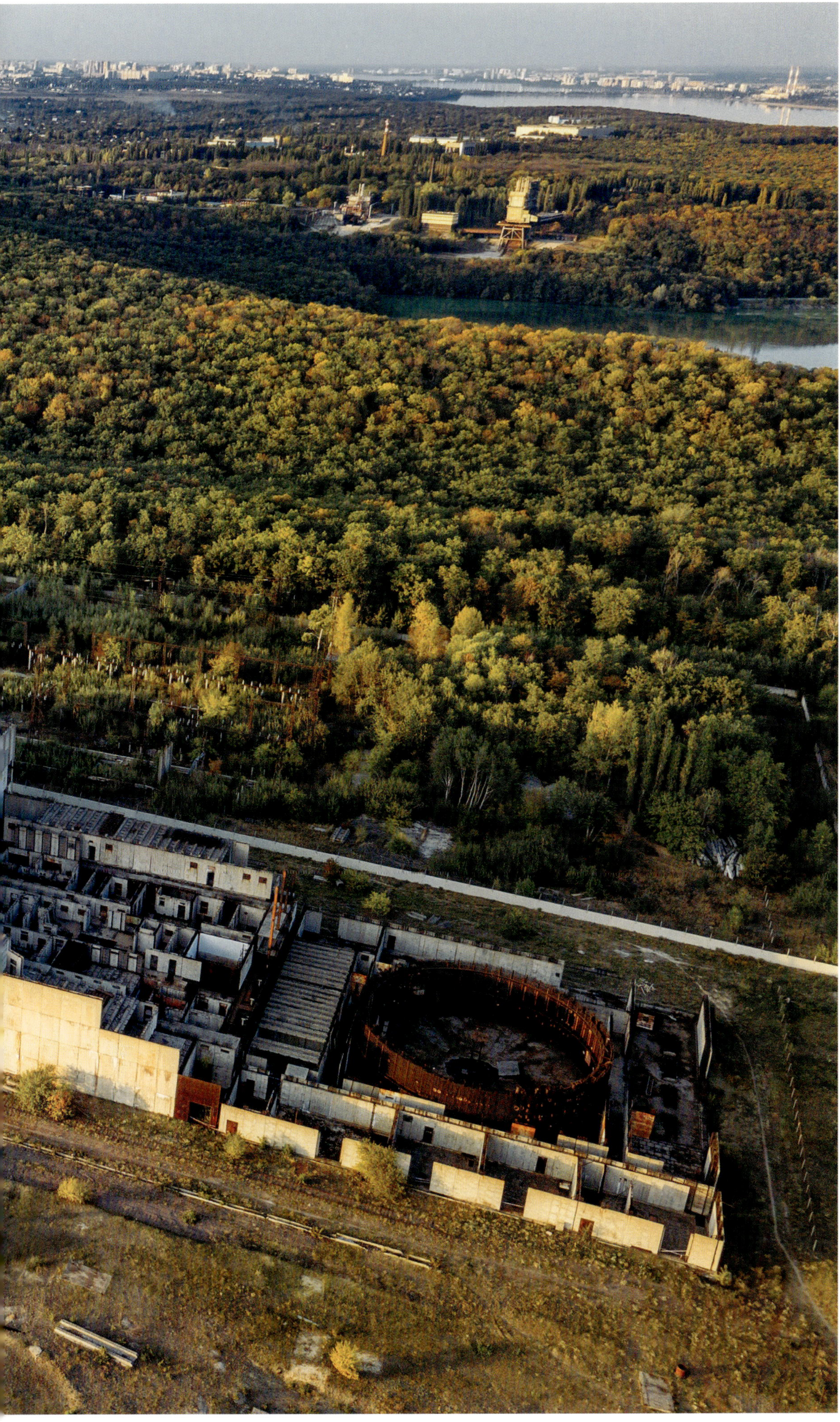

Nuclear Plant I, Voronezh, Russia
Intended to provide electric power and hot water to the city, this experimental plant was constructed between 1983 and 1990 but never completed due to concerns about its safety. After being 'frozen' for thirty years, dismantling and site clearance began in 2019. A new nuclear plant is under development alongside.

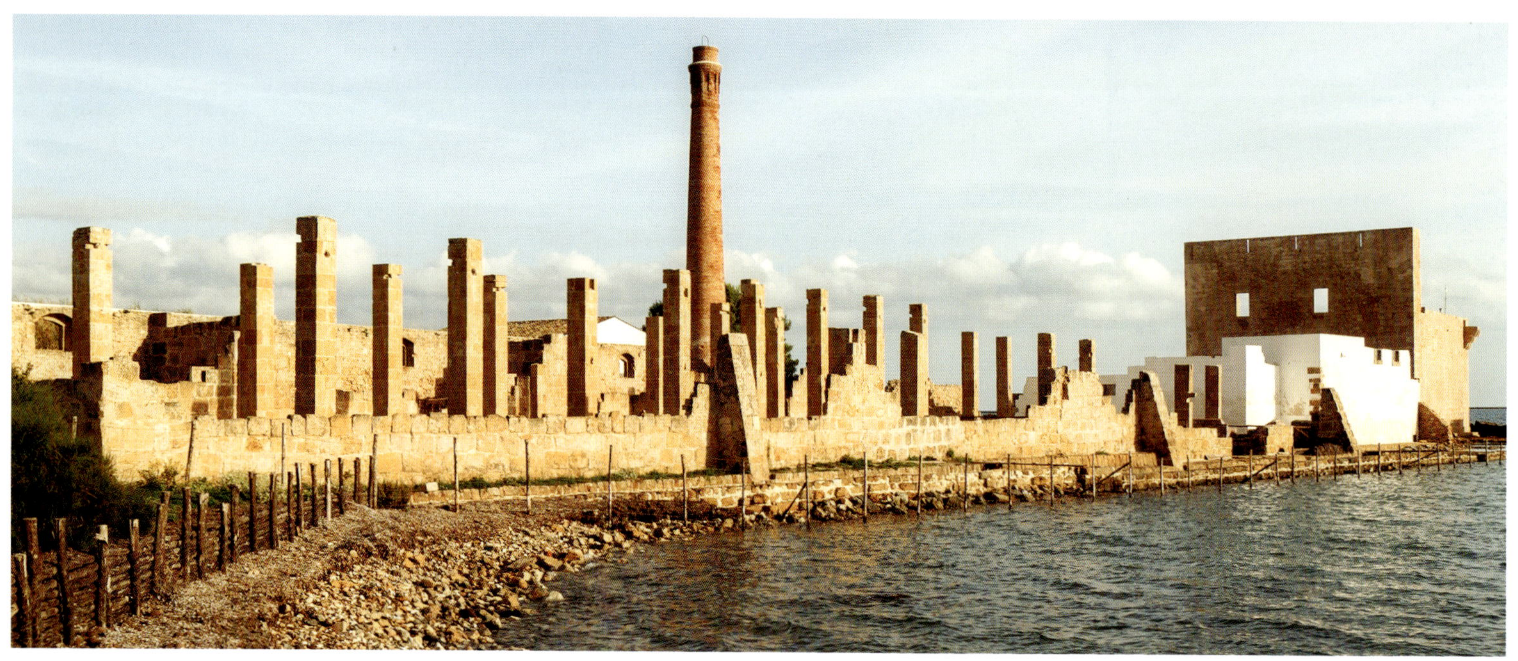

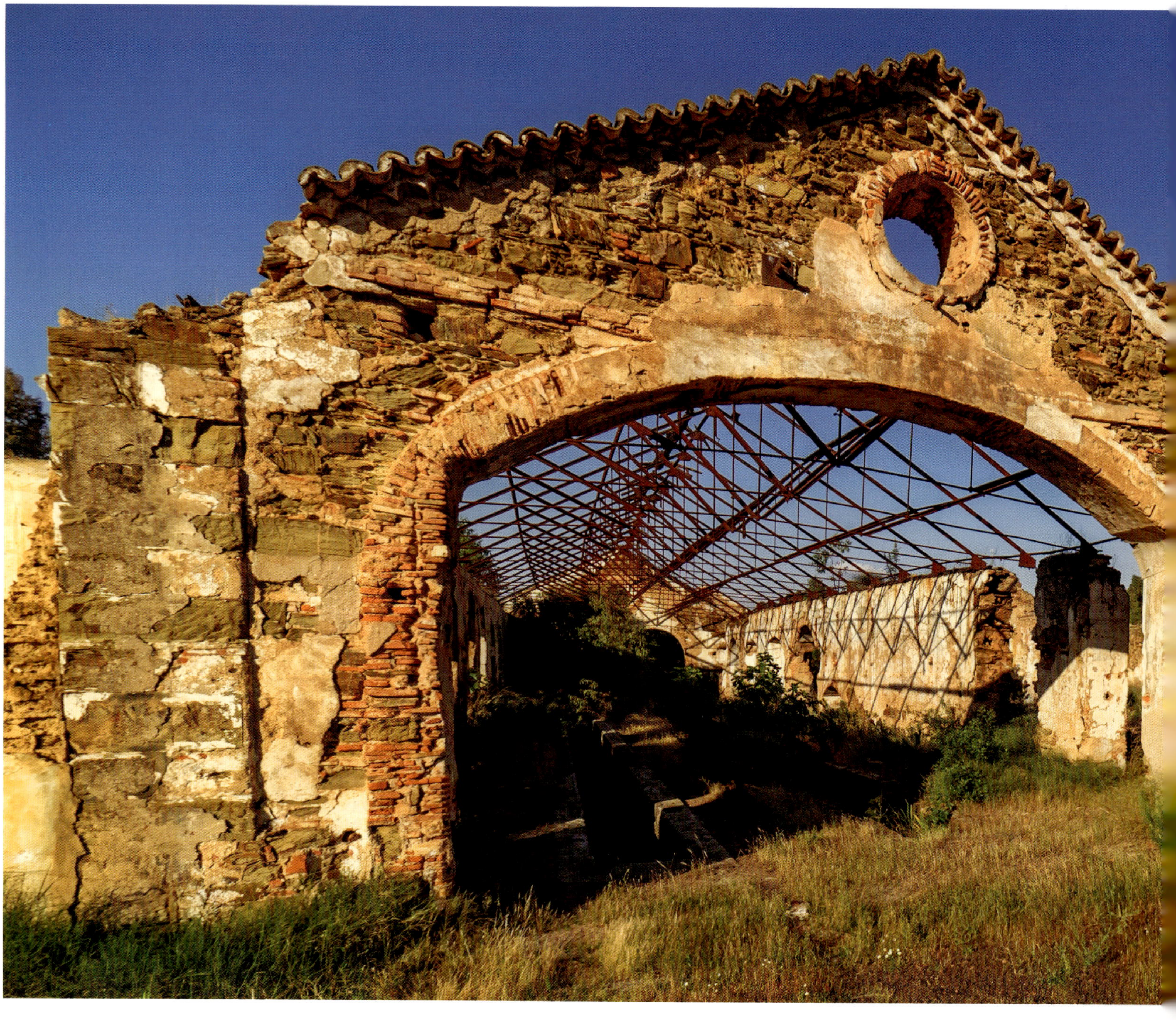

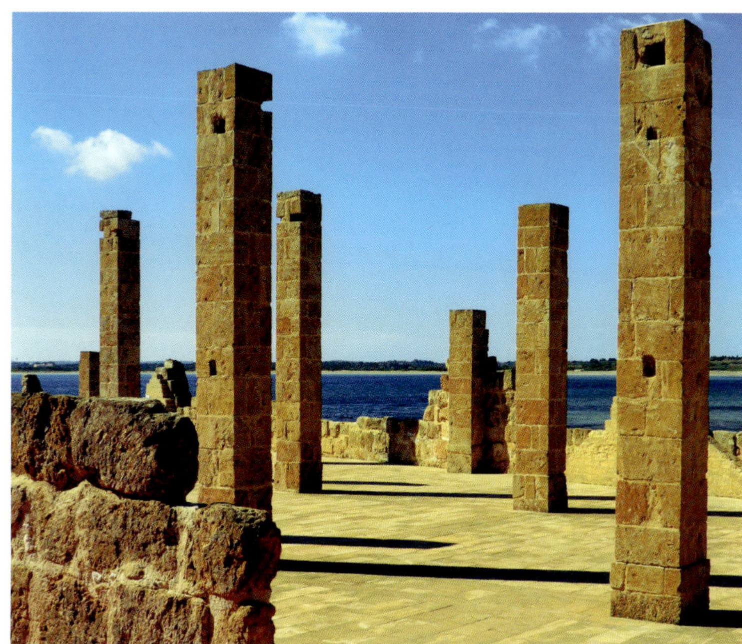

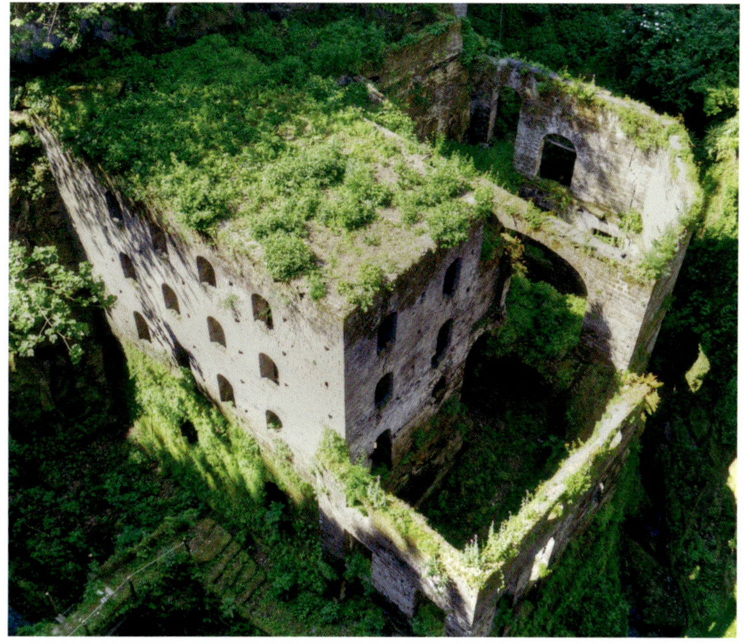

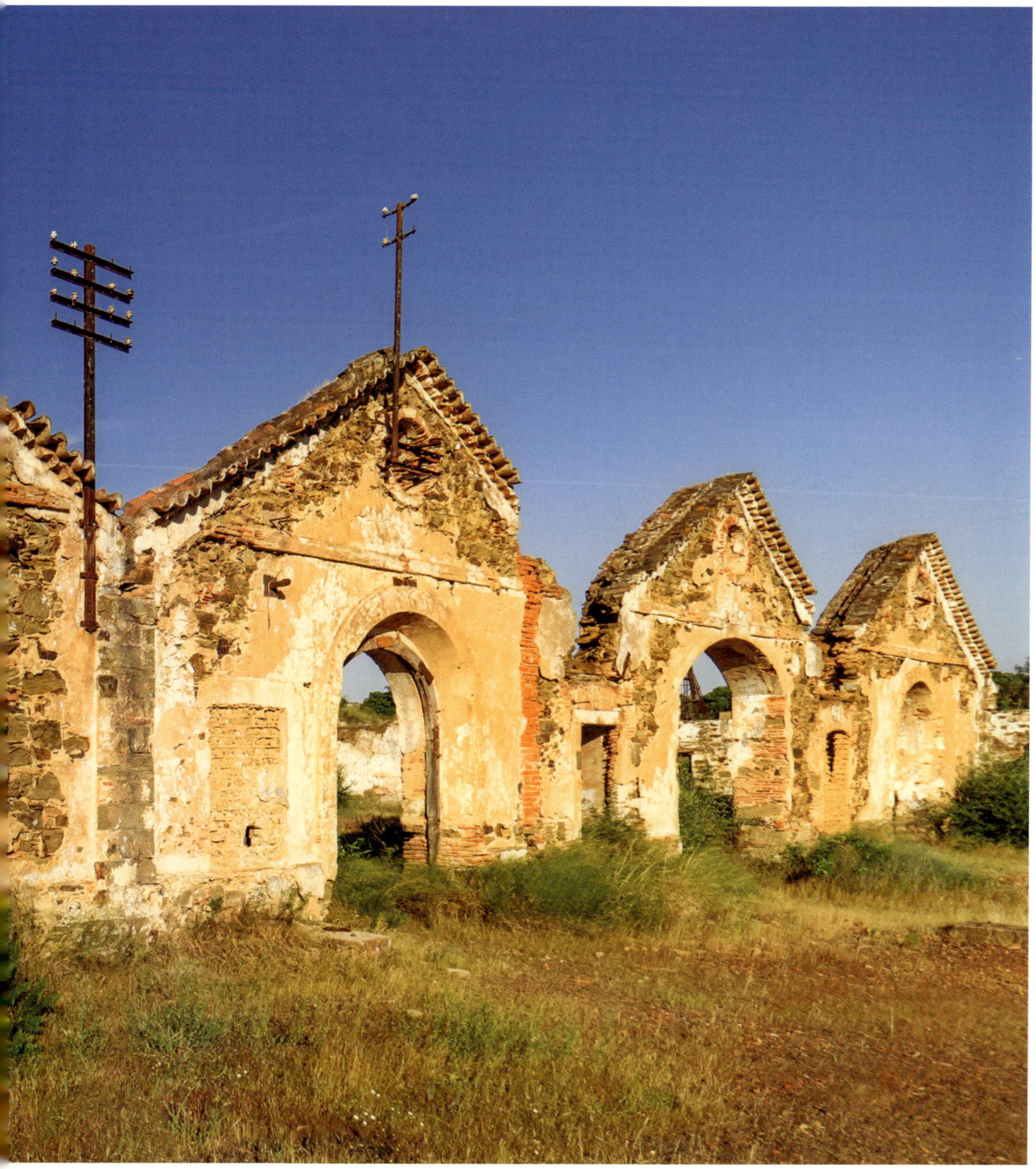

Tuna Processing Works, Vencicari, Sicily, Italy
Now set in a nature reserve, the *tonnara* or tuna works has a history going back to the Moorish rule in Sicily, though these ruins date from its 18th century heyday. It encompasses both a fishing site and processing chambers. It ceased activity in 1943. Recently some houses and other parts of the site have been renovated.

Former Wheat Mill, Vallone dei Mulini, Sorrento, Italy
Vegetation is reclaiming this tall mill building, picturesquely set on a ledge where steep valleys intersect. Water power was the original attraction, though a chimney indicates a steam engine was installed later. It fell into disuse in the mid-1860s.

Mina de São Domingos, Corte do Pinto, Alentejo, Portugal
Started up in 1855 as a copper mine, it switched in the 1920s to mining pyrites for the manufacture of sulphuric acid, when these sheds, with their processing troughs, were built near the open-cast pit. Acid contamination of the site and its effect on the workforce led to closure in 1966.

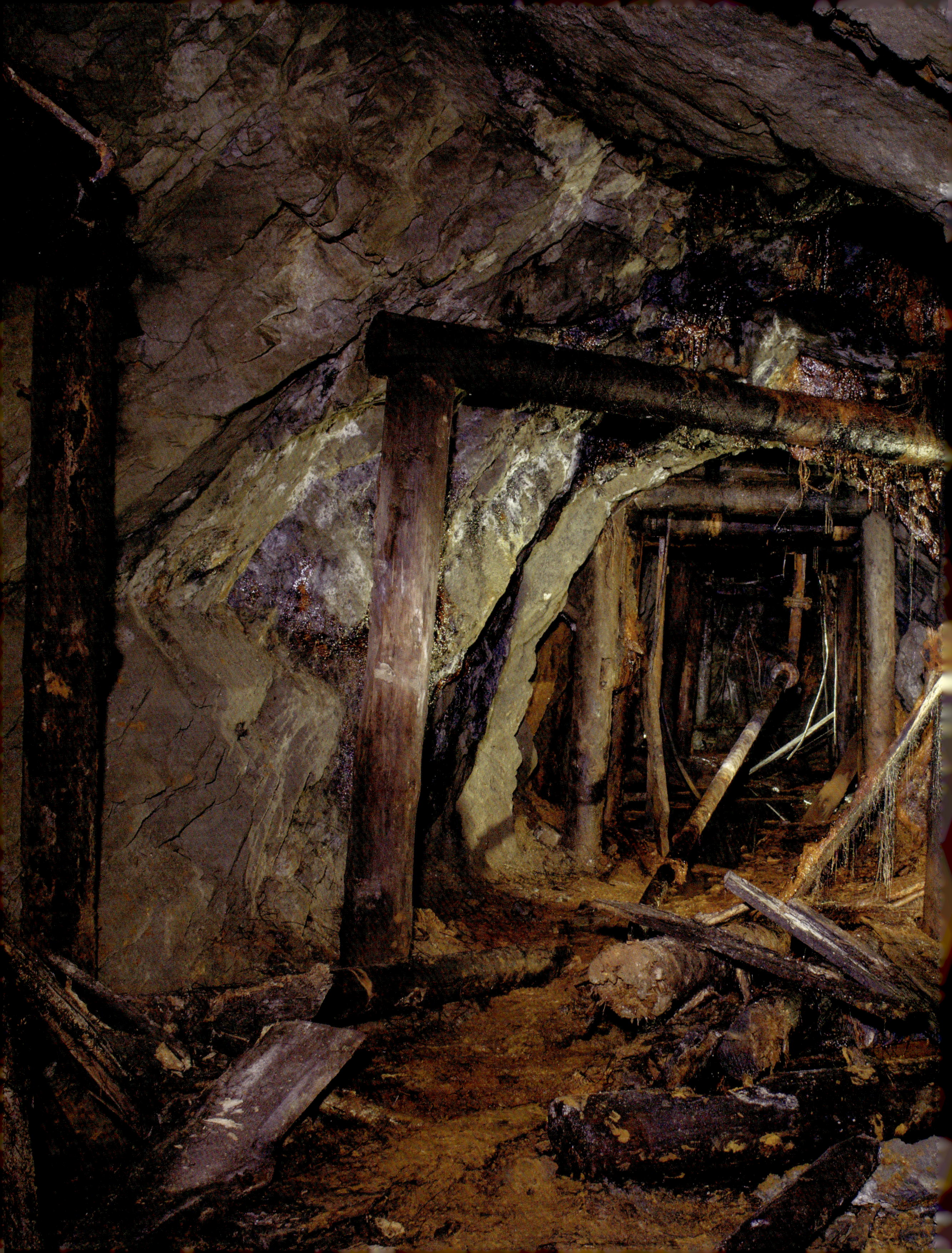

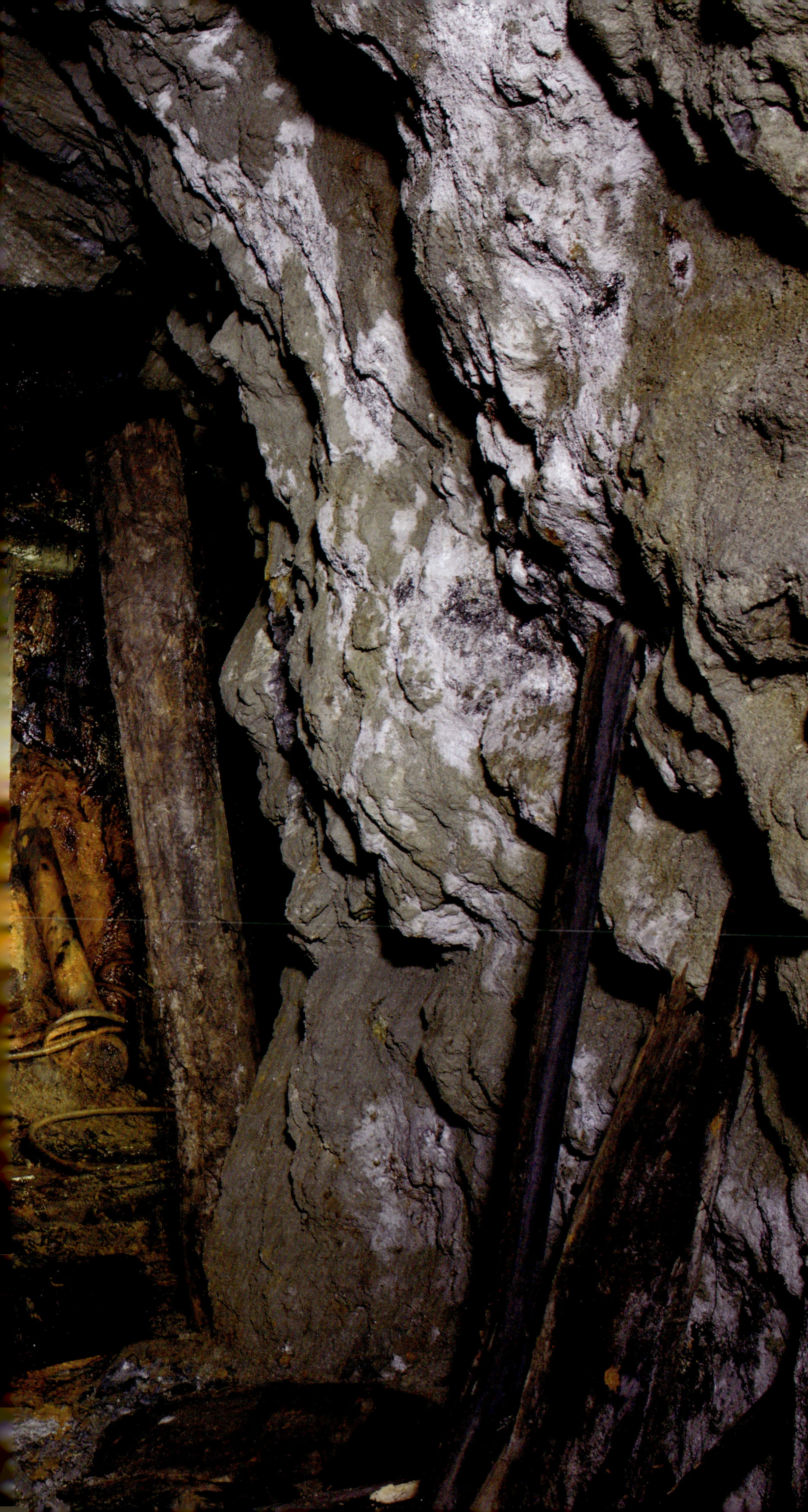

Antimony Mine, Pezinok, Slovakia
A geologist's dream site, this mining district is celebrated for its multiplicity of rare mineral specimens. There are many adits apart from this one, some in a dangerous state and others now lost, as well as open pits now partially filled in. Active mining ended around 1990.

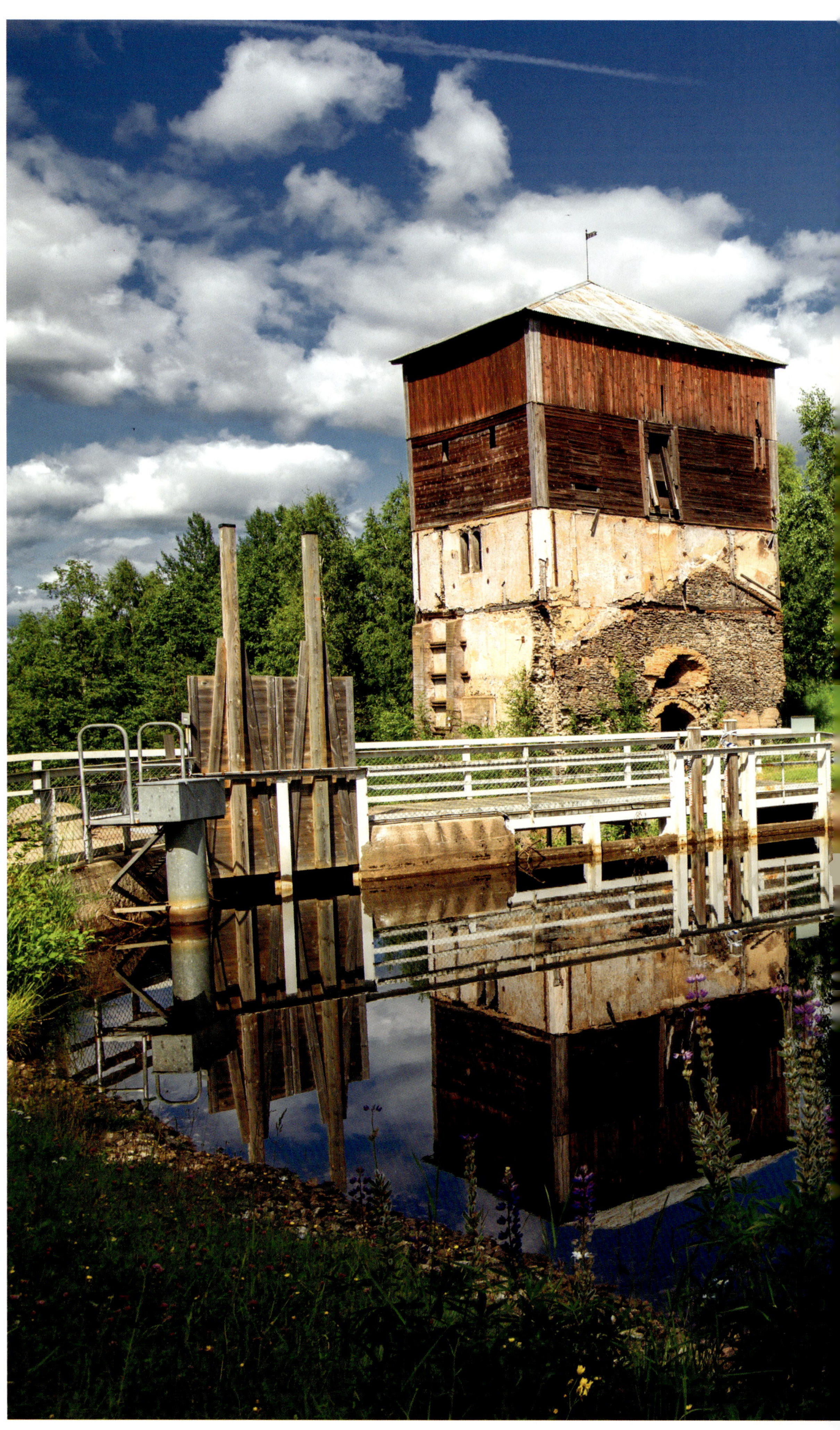

Old Ironworks at Ulvshyttan, Bergslagen, Sweden
Originally operated by water power, this remarkably well-preserved foundry dates its origins to 1500. Adjacent ore deposits helped to maintain it, but when these ran out in 1964 it was no longer viable. It remains a fine example of an early industrial complex.

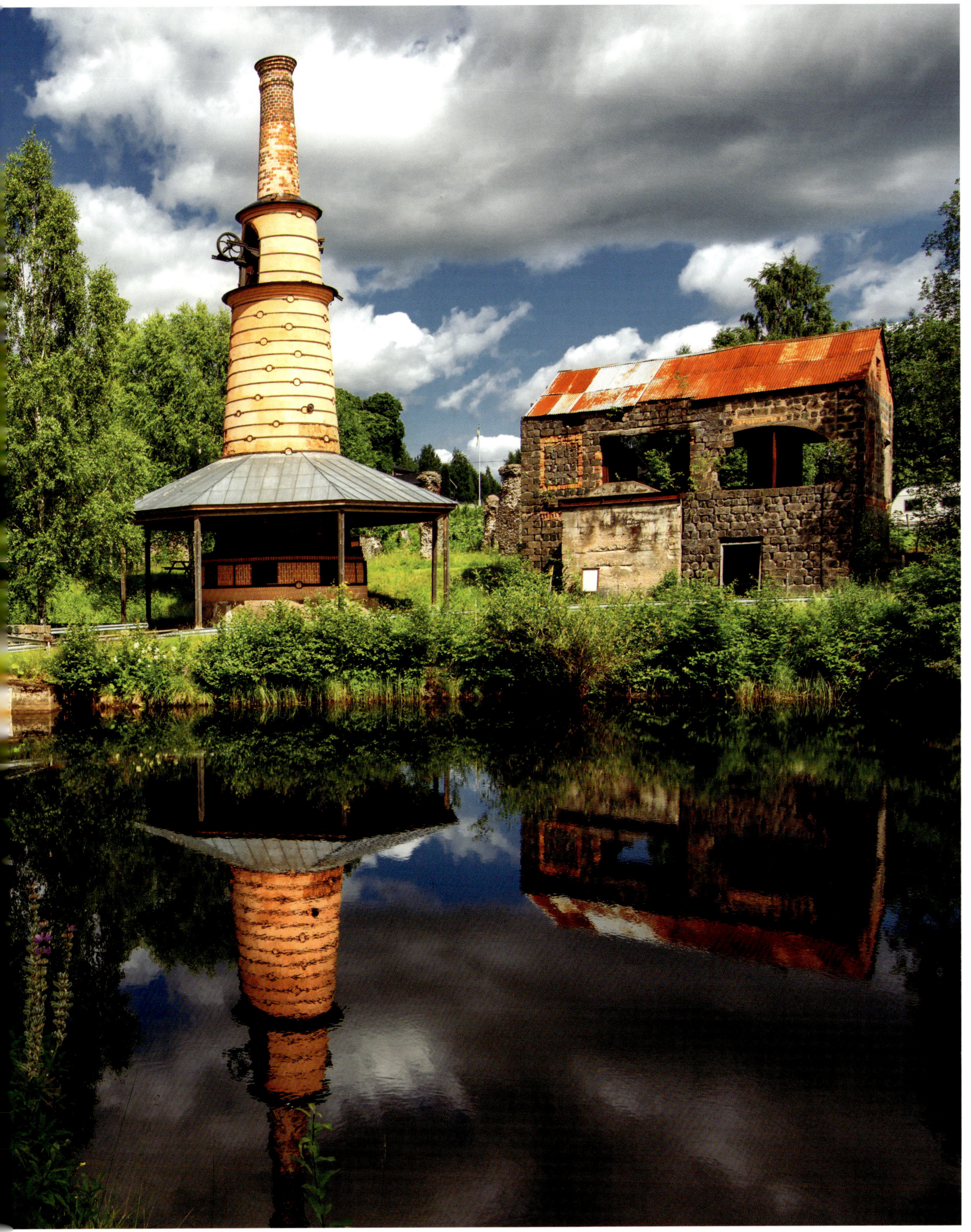

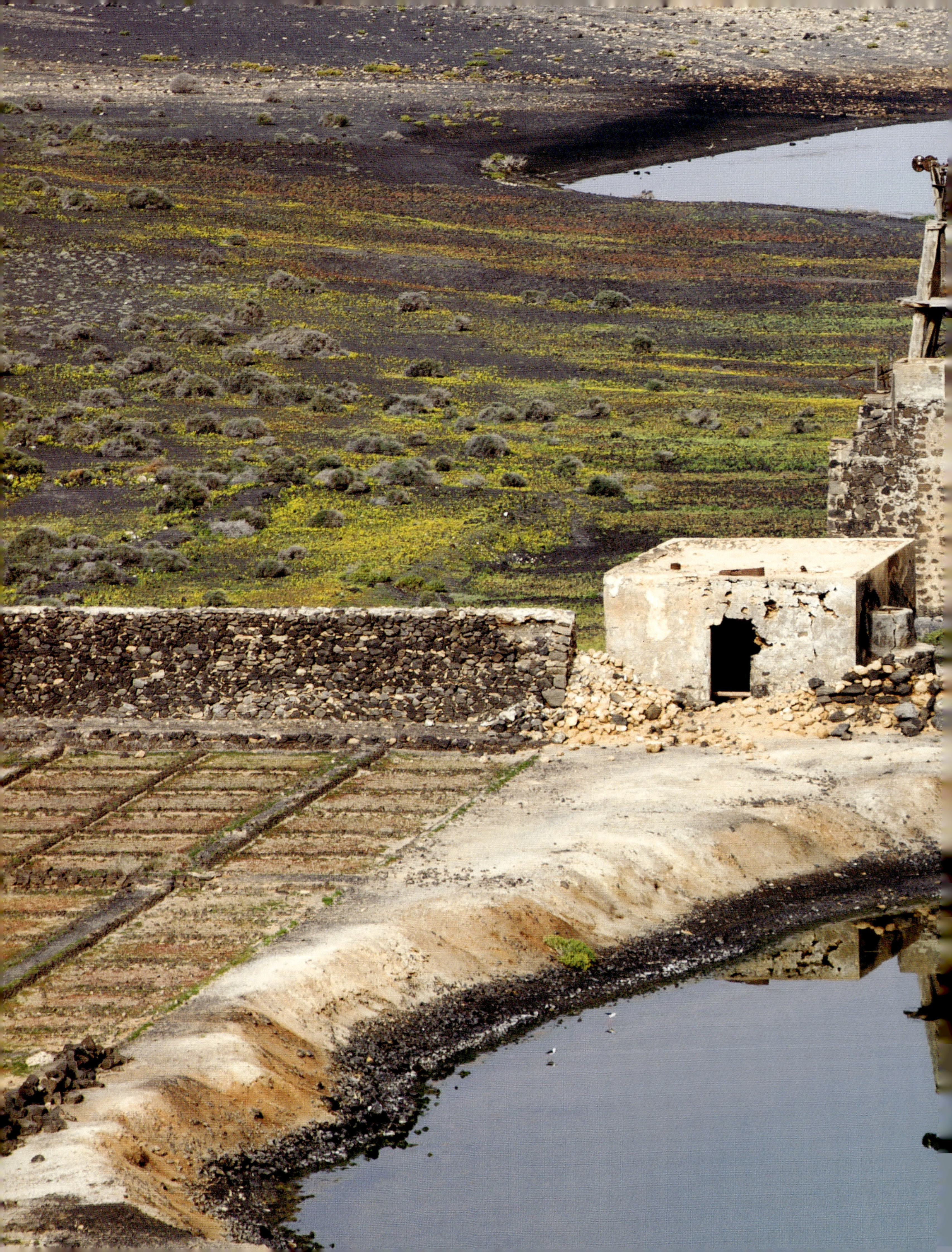

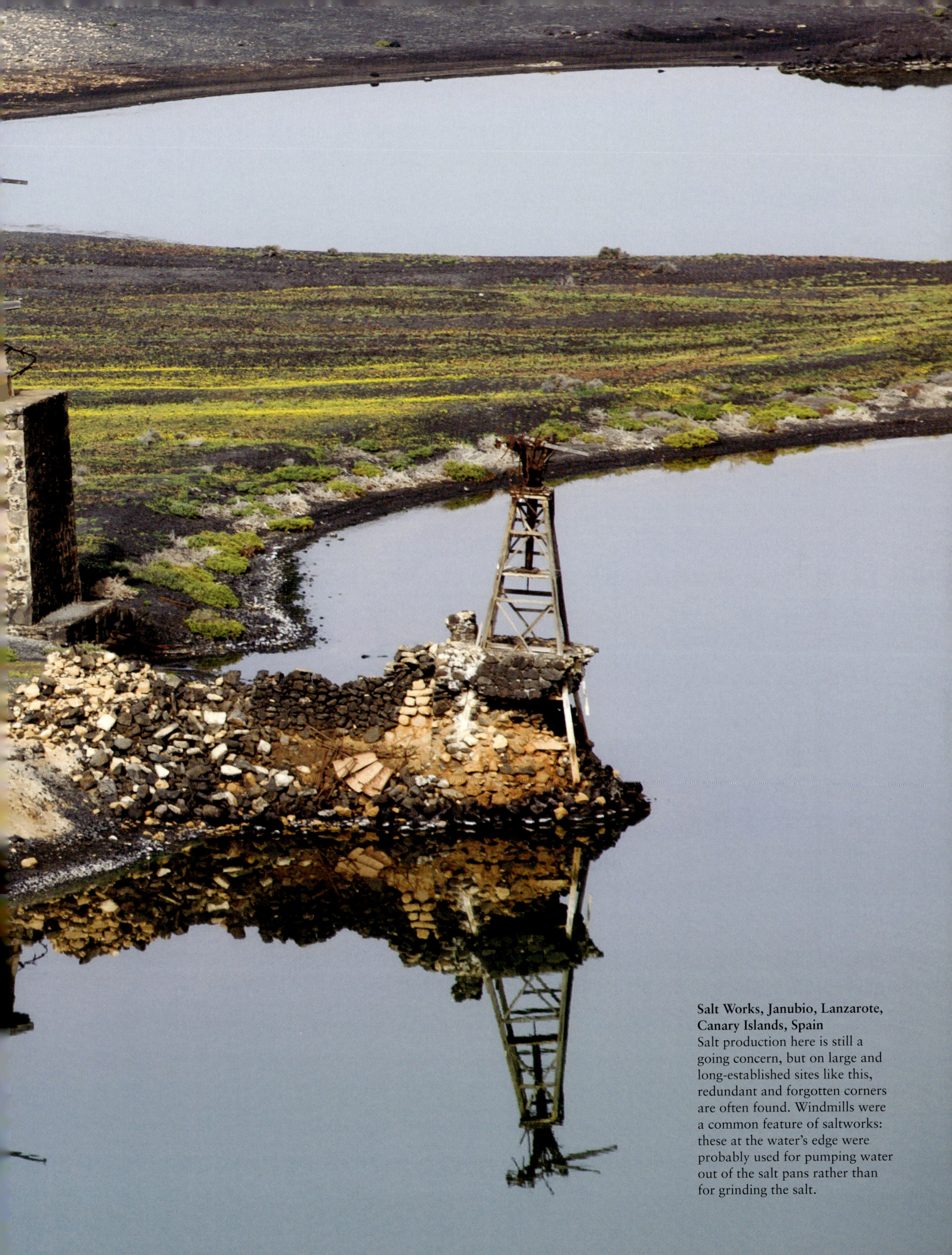

Salt Works, Janubio, Lanzarote, Canary Islands, Spain
Salt production here is still a going concern, but on large and long-established sites like this, redundant and forgotten corners are often found. Windmills were a common feature of saltworks: these at the water's edge were probably used for pumping water out of the salt pans rather than for grinding the salt.

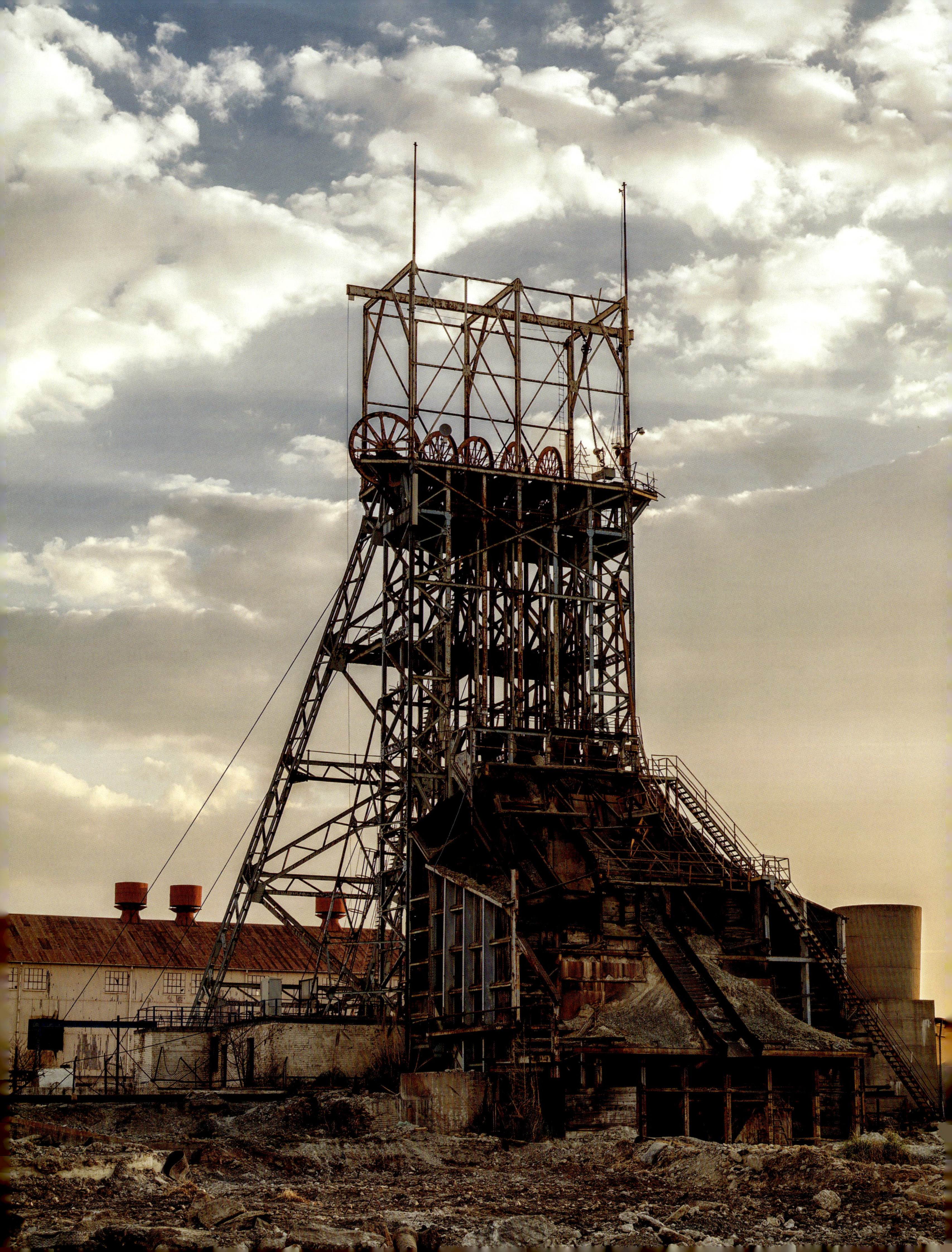

Africa and the Middle East

As in South America, the main reason for abandoned industry in this vast area is the exploitation of mineral resources. Gold mining of course features prominently, as does copper mining. In both cases separating and refining of the usable mineral content has created huge ongoing problems of toxic waste and polluted water. The same can be said of the oil industry which has ravaged large tracts of territory in West Africa, leaving them in need of, not yet receiving, long-term recovery treatment. Other sites are of the see-it-while-you-can sort, like the Star Wars film set in Tunisia that is threatened by the movement of huge sand dunes. Some show that abandoned industry even on a very localised scale, like a street workshop in Cairo, can still prompt a sense of kinship with whoever worked here, struggling and apparently failing to make a living, and leaving the rather pathetic remains behind.

What they all display is what a perceptive historian called 'the escape from order', a strong element in the appeal of abandoned sites. No longer in the system, they are excluded, left to decay in a limbo of their own. That pattern of decay, the non-functional equipment, the rubbish and debris strewn about, the rusting cog-wheels, peeling plaster or broken walls, speaks strongly to us, nudging us out of our safe zone, reminding us that everything we make can be reduced to this.

OPPOSITE:
Pithead Frame, Aurora Gold Mine, near Johannesburg, South Africa
Multiple winding wheels are mounted on the frame, which hauled up buckets of gold-bearing ores for processing in the sheds behind. The mine closed down in controversial circumstances in 2012, putting 5000 people out of work.

Okiep Copper Mine, Northern Cape, South Africa
Cornish-type architecture and machinery are a feature of this copper mine, first established in 1856. Two beam engines were acquired in the 1870s and 1880s to pump water from the lower levels of the 208m (682ft) shaft.

BELOW:

Aouli Lead Mine, Drâa-Tafafilet, Midelt Province, Morocco
A substantial community lived in this now deserted and remote locality during the life of the lead mine, set up in 1936 and active into the 1980s. Extensive parts of the mine's infrastructure remain, partly built into the hillside.

OPPOSITE:

Diamond Mine, Alexander Bay, Northern Cape, South Africa
This area was known as the Diamond Coast. Fossilised oyster beds at the mouth of the Orange River also holds diamonds washed downstream. This derelict building held crushers and separators.

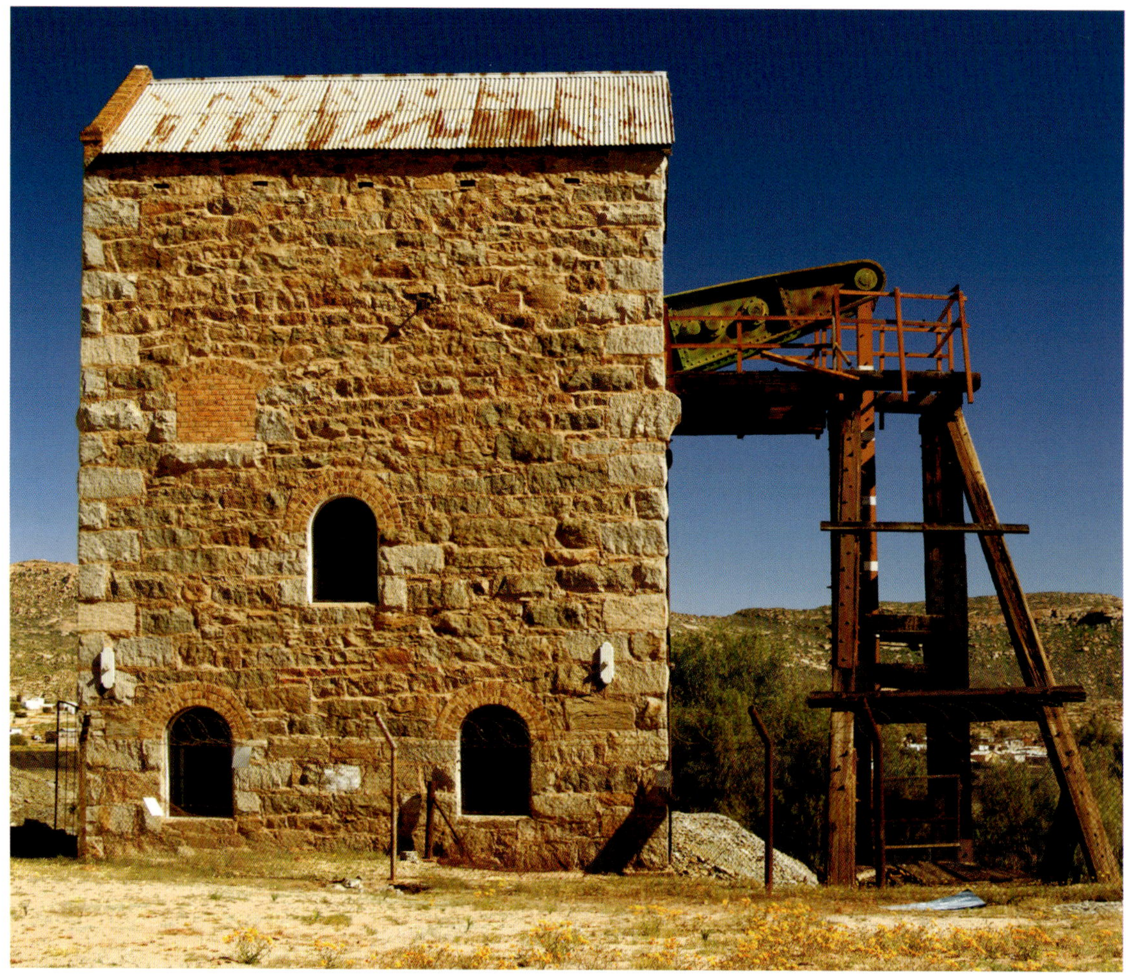

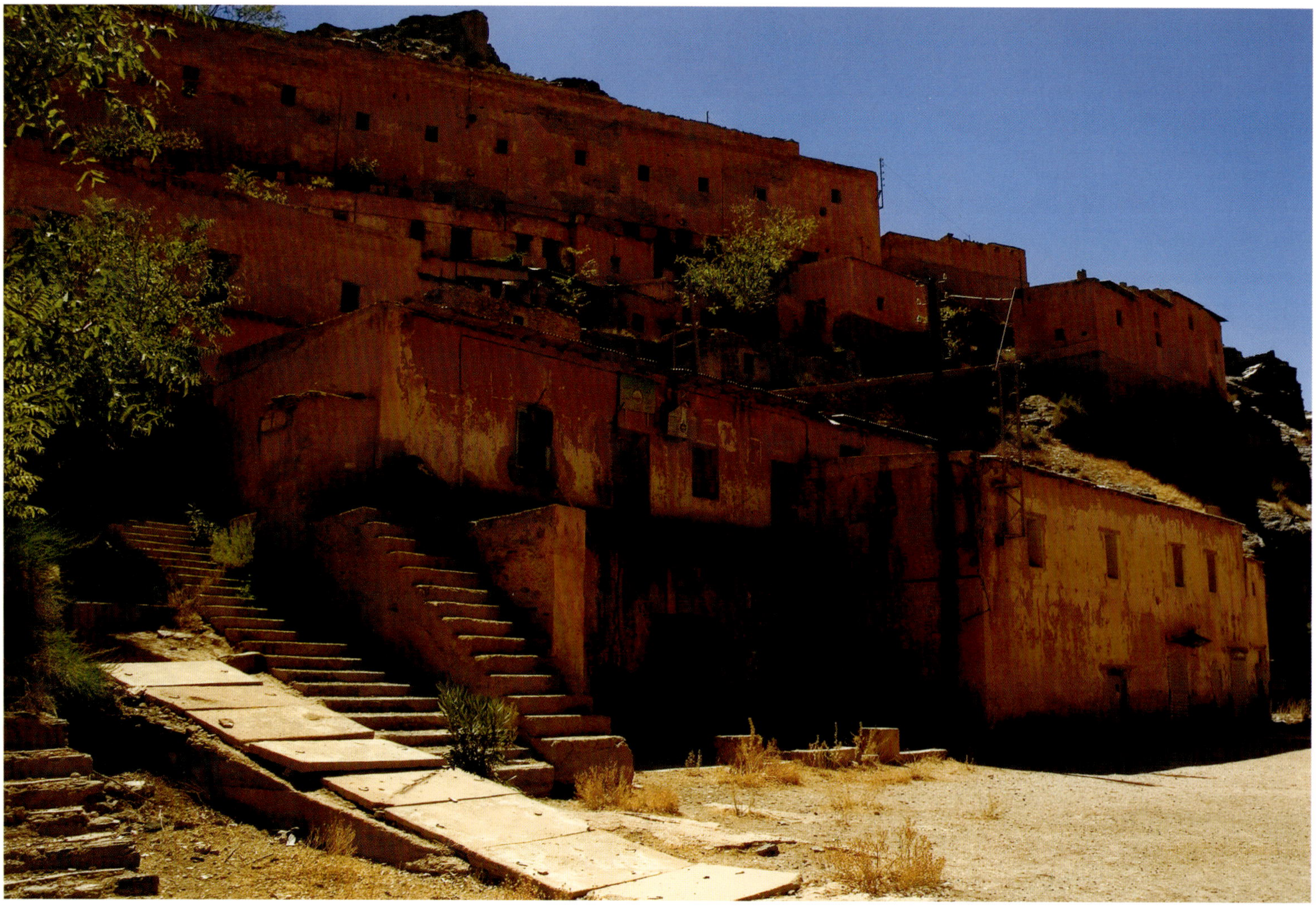

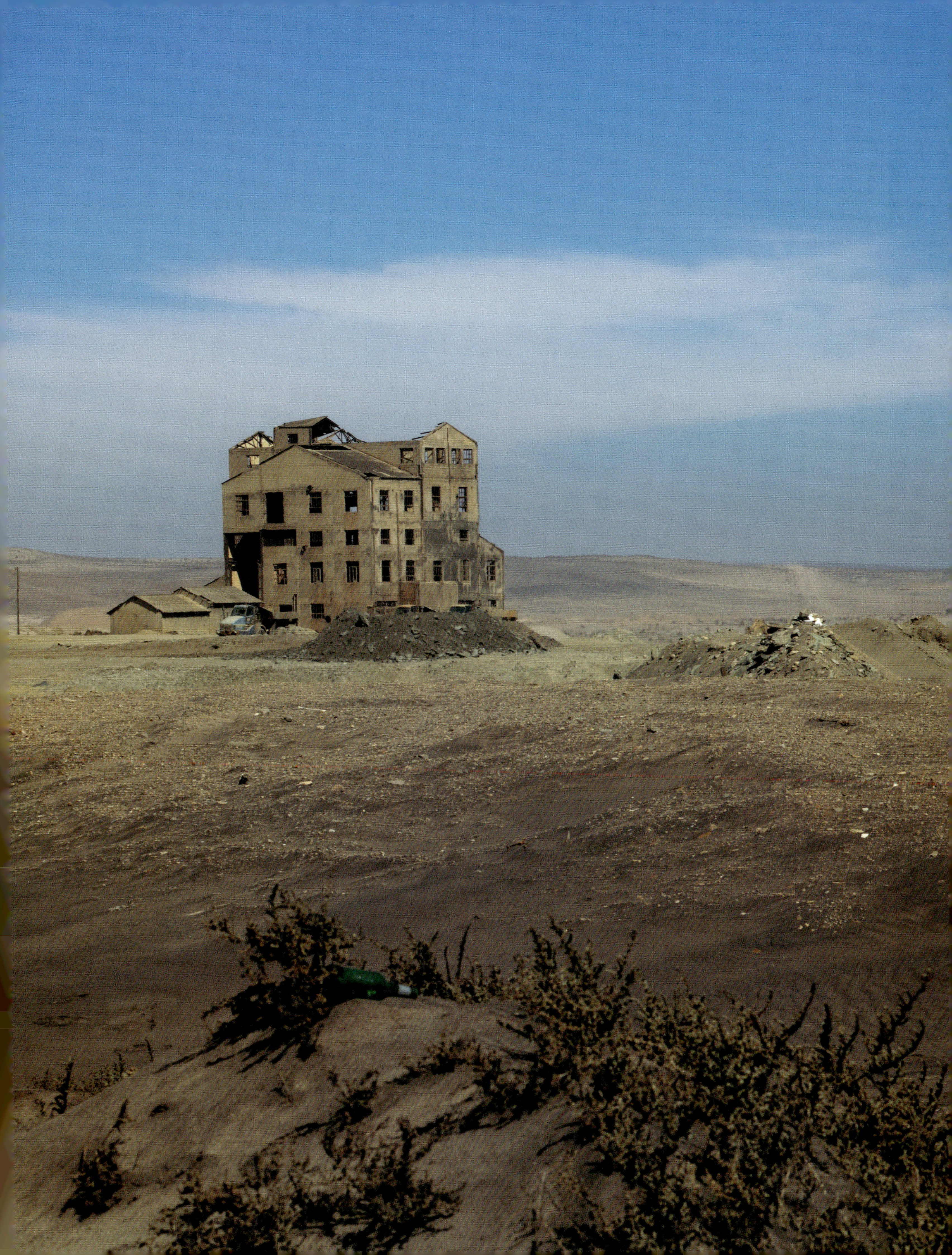

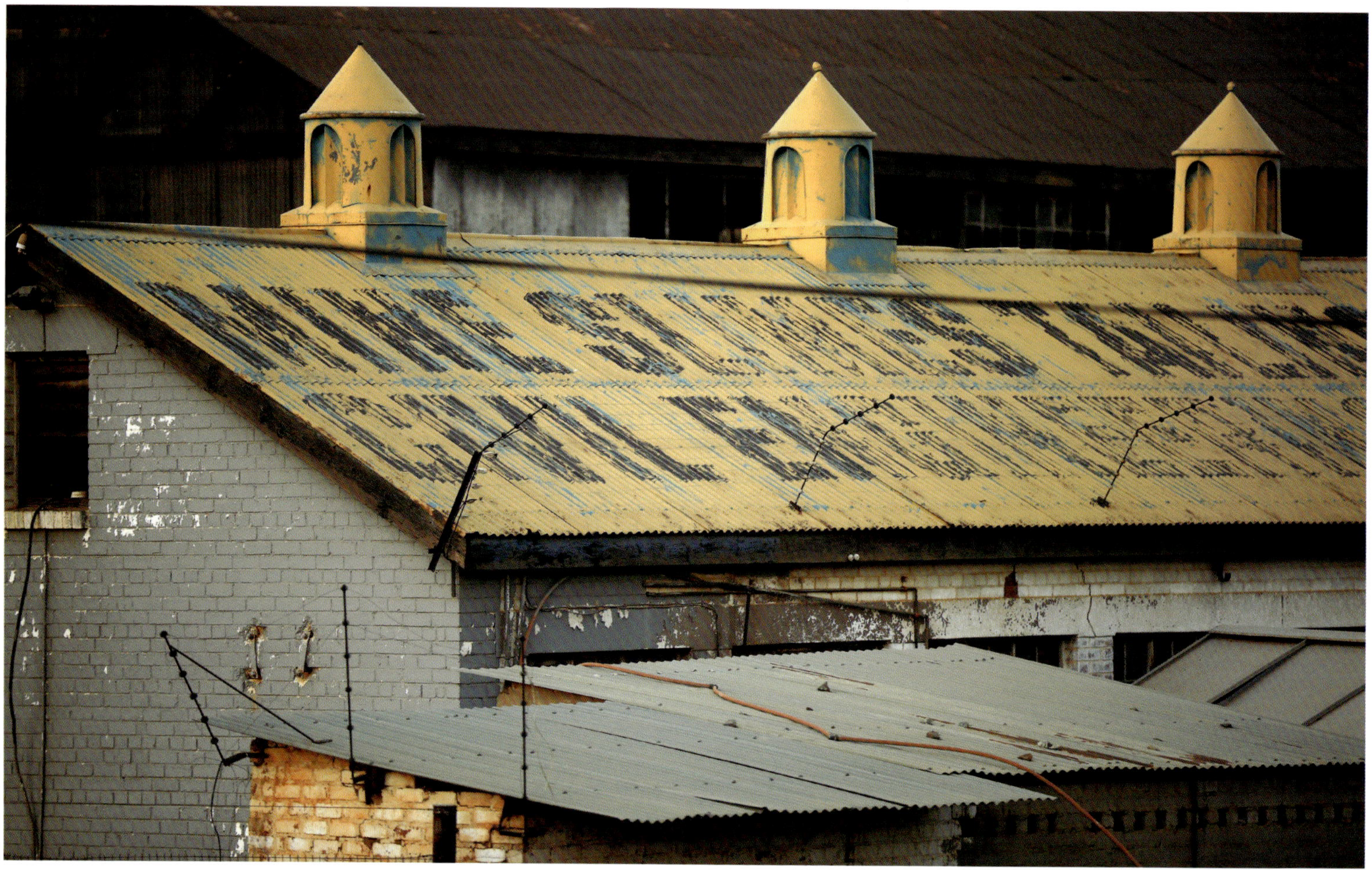

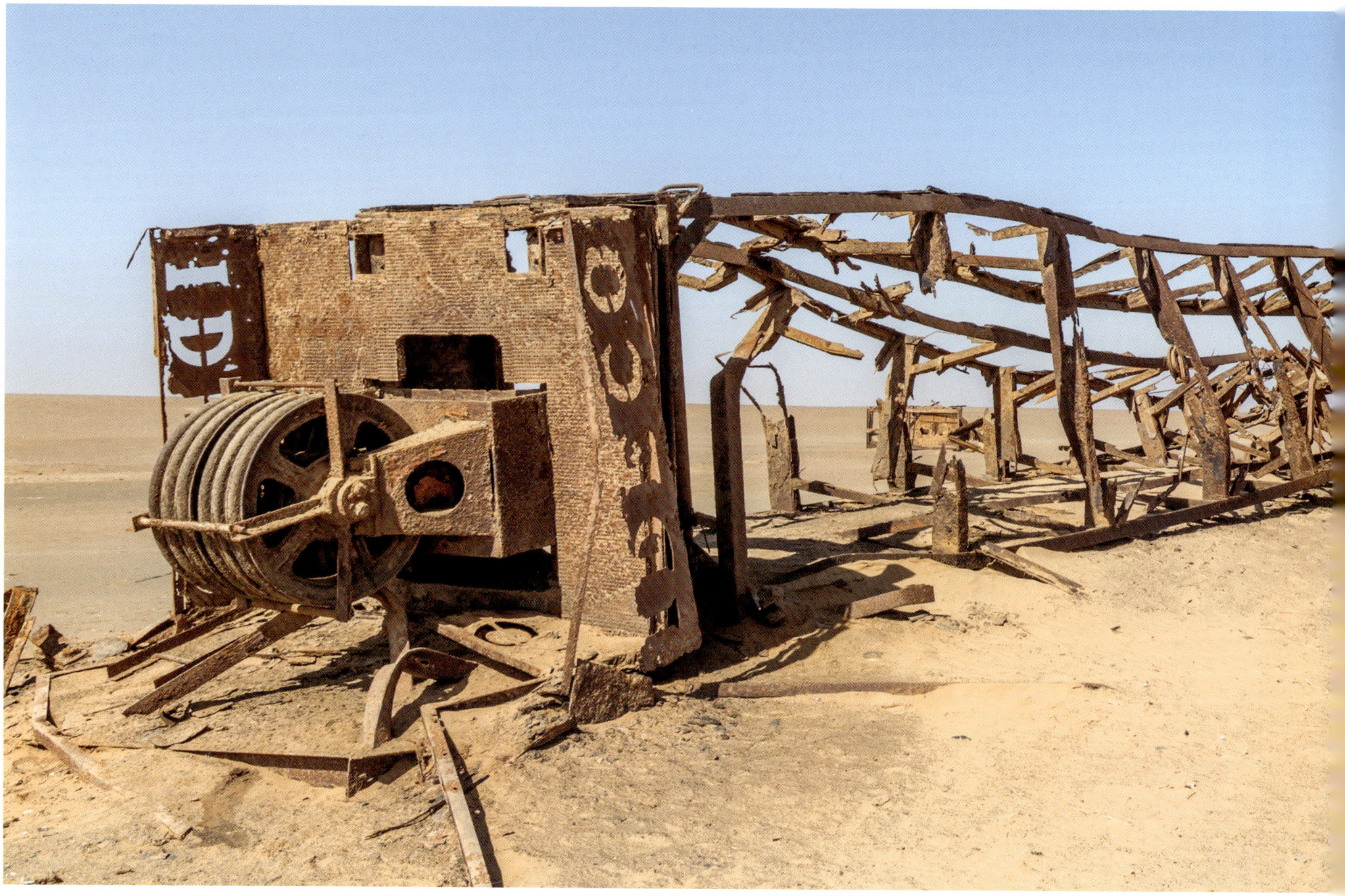

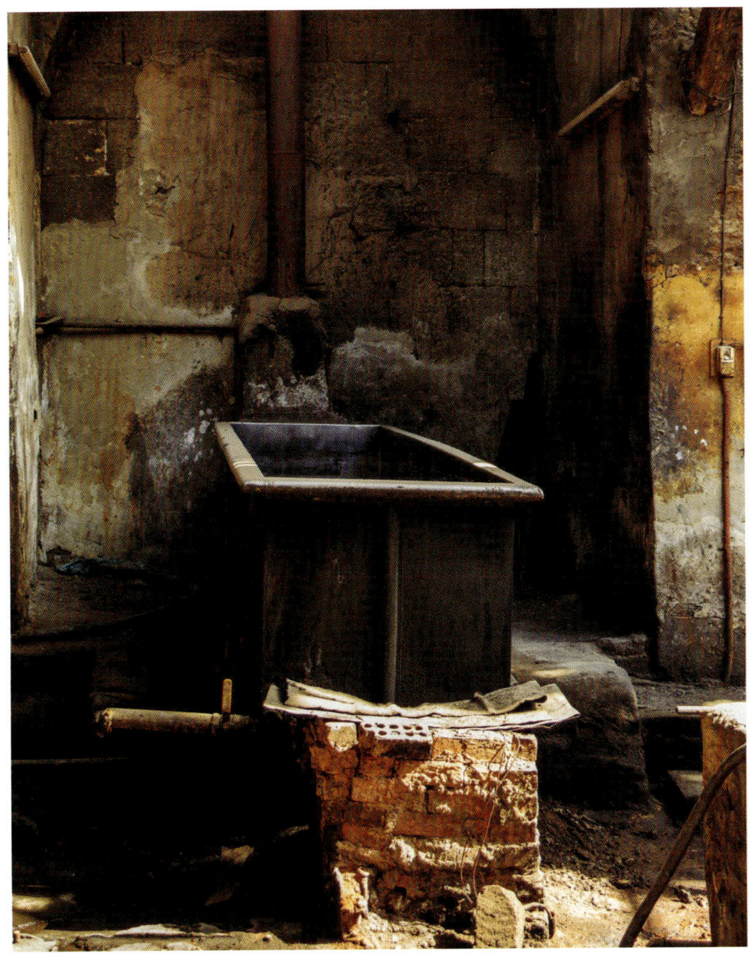

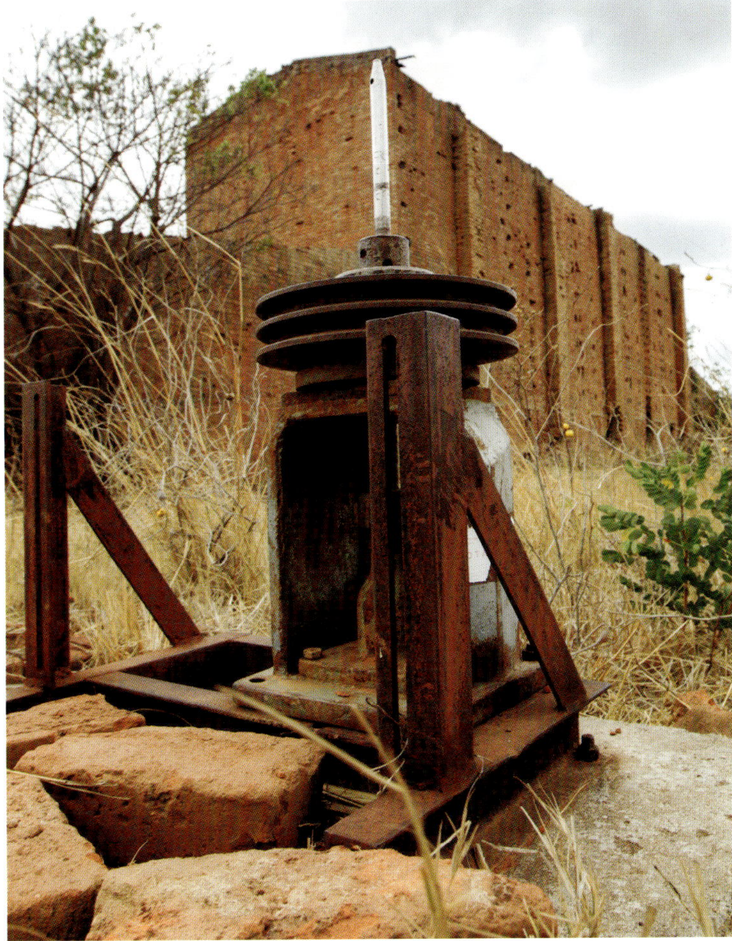

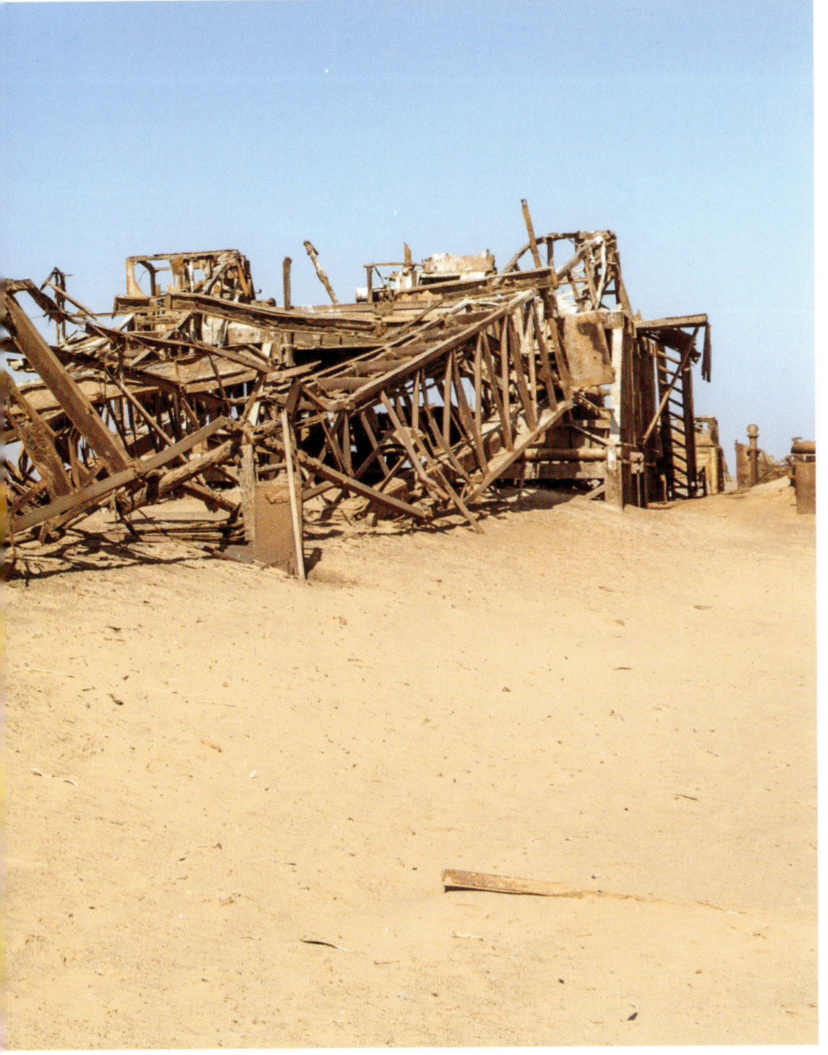

Crown Mines, Johannesburg, South Africa
Over 160 million tons of rock were dug out here in the quest for gold. Now a Johannesburg suburb, the mounds of gangue (spoil left after acid treatment of the ore) and some of the many brick and corrugated iron refining sheds still remain as a reminder of the days, less than a century ago, when it was a vast mining camp.

Abandoned Oil Well on the Skeleton Coast, Namibia
Remnants of oil and gas workings from a brief oil boom in the 1960s vie with animal bones and dead trees to give this desert coastline its by-name. For some observers, industrial relics in such a remote and inhospitable region have a poignancy of their own.

Disused Dyer's Shop, Cairo, Egypt
Not all abandoned industry need be on the grand scale. In the crowded streets of Old Cairo were many small artisanal workshops. Here a dyer's premises, with the trough for boiling and steeping cloth, and its stove, lie open and disused.

Disused Tobacco Barn, Zimbabwe
Zimbabwe has an ideal climate for tobacco growing and many international tobacco companies had estates and factories here. Decline in world demand and the country's economic problems have led to the run-down and closure of many facilities, including this decaying, brick-built barn or drying house.

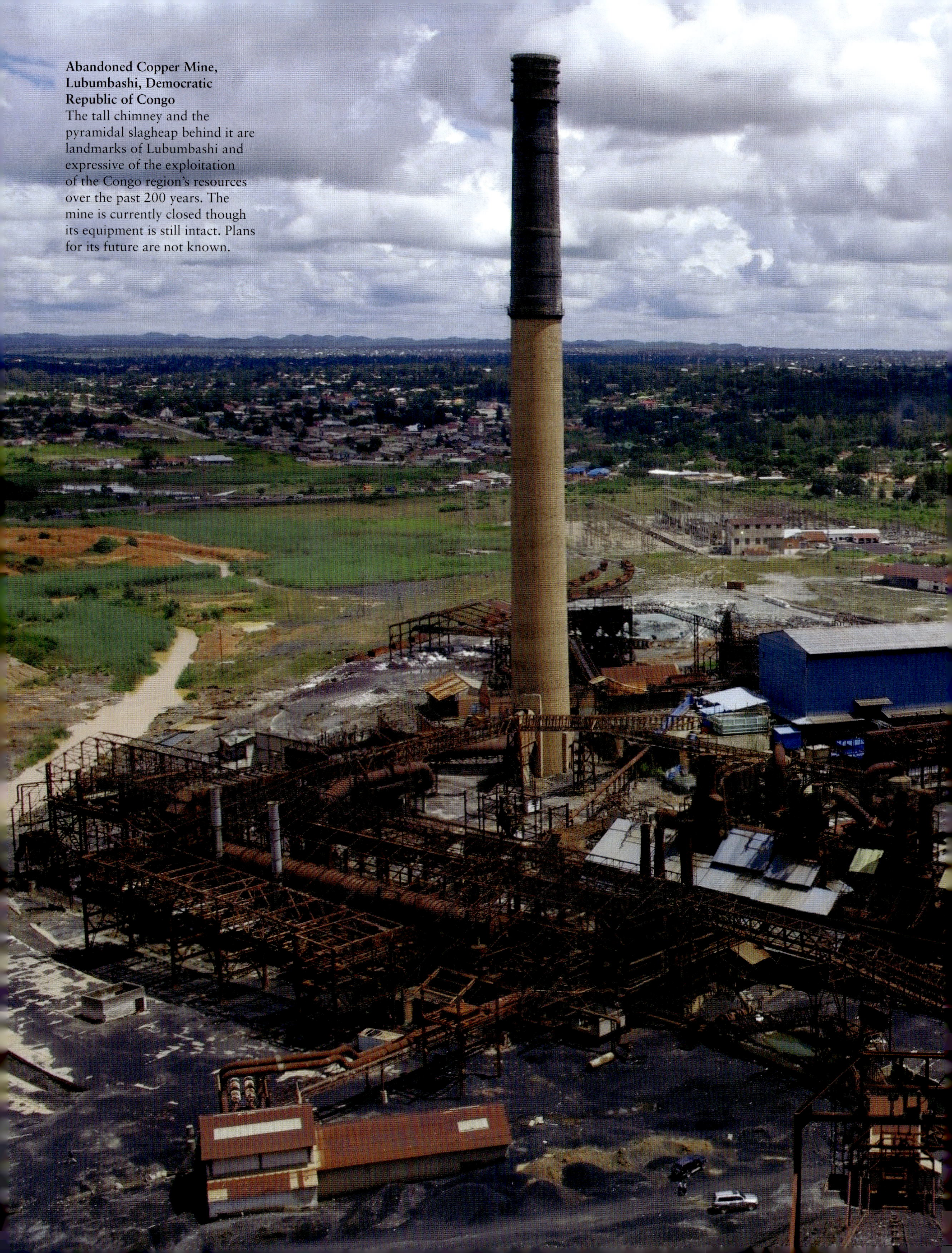

Abandoned Copper Mine, Lubumbashi, Democratic Republic of Congo
The tall chimney and the pyramidal slagheap behind it are landmarks of Lubumbashi and expressive of the exploitation of the Congo region's resources over the past 200 years. The mine is currently closed though its equipment is still intact. Plans for its future are not known.

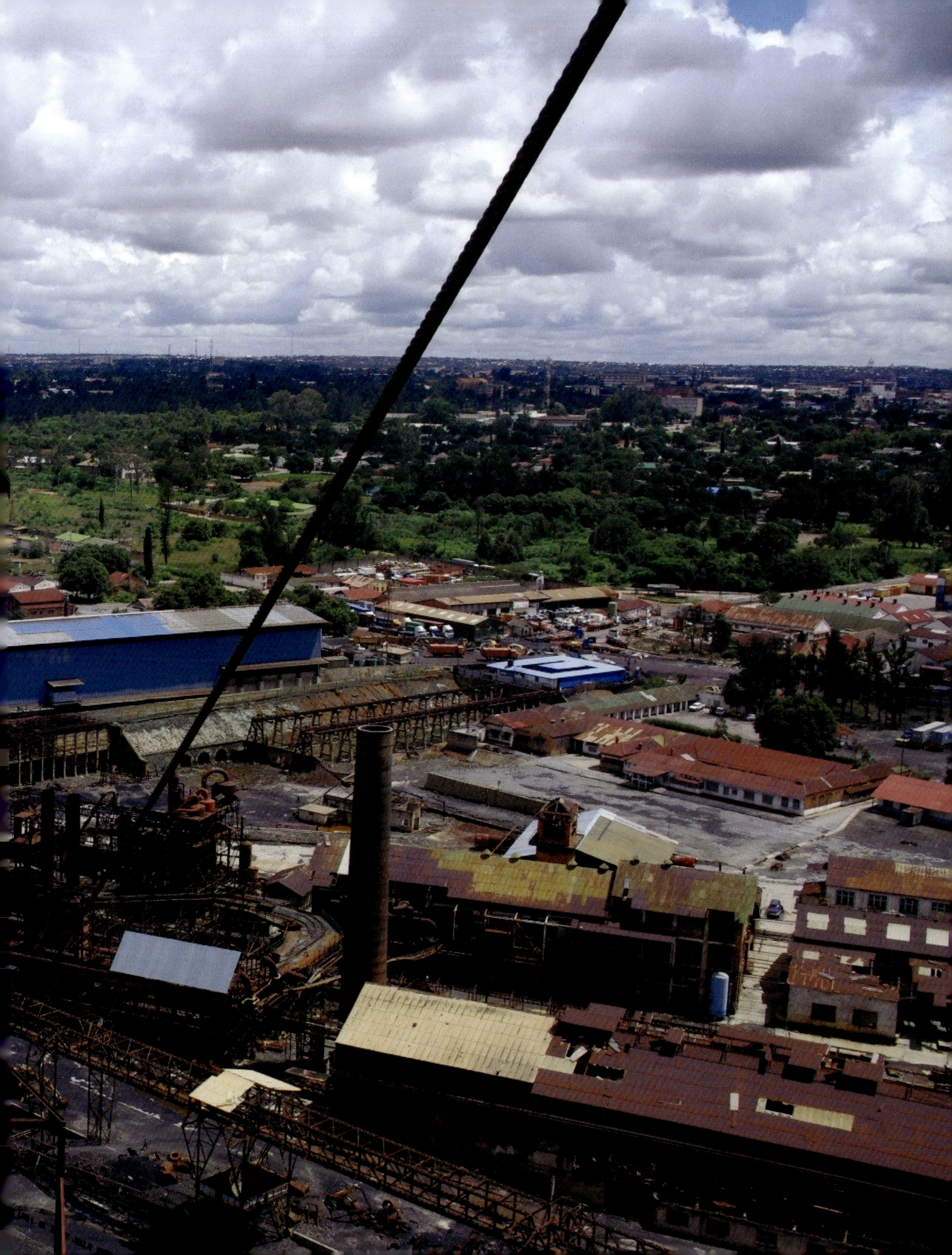

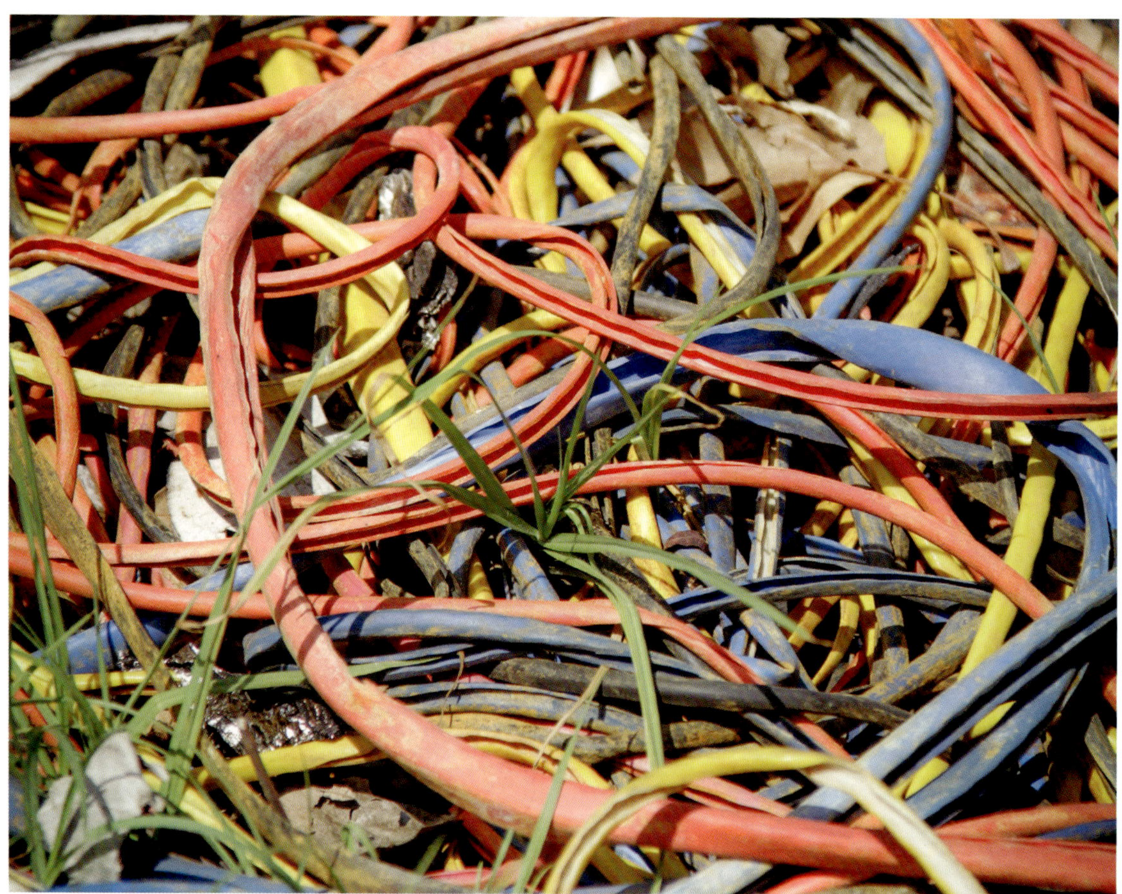

Gold Mine, Blyvooruitzicht, Gauteng, South Africa
For a time, between 1937 and 2013, this was the richest gold mine in South Africa. It stopped production in 2013 and like many other mines round the world, its equipment, some usable, some only fit for scrap like this tangled heap of electrical cables, remain on site, in the hope of a reopening one day.

BELOW:

Oil Pipes, K-Dare, Niger Delta, Nigeria
Much of the Niger delta landscape is an industrial wasteland initiated by the discovery and extraction of oil in the region. K-Dare was a large oil-flow station combining the supply of raw oil from numerous wells, and is at the centre of legal claims against international oil companies for causing and failing to manage pollution and contamination over decades.

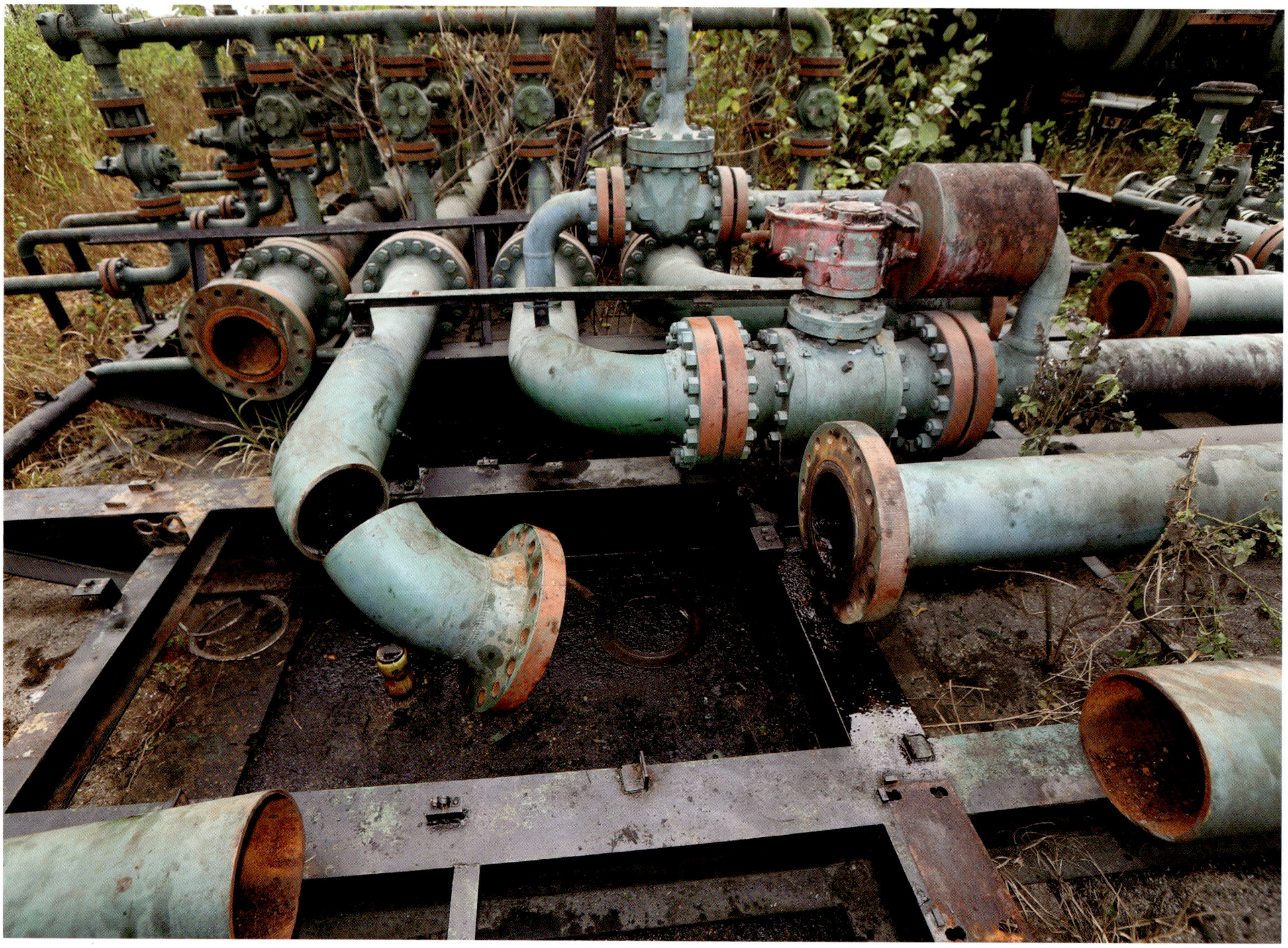

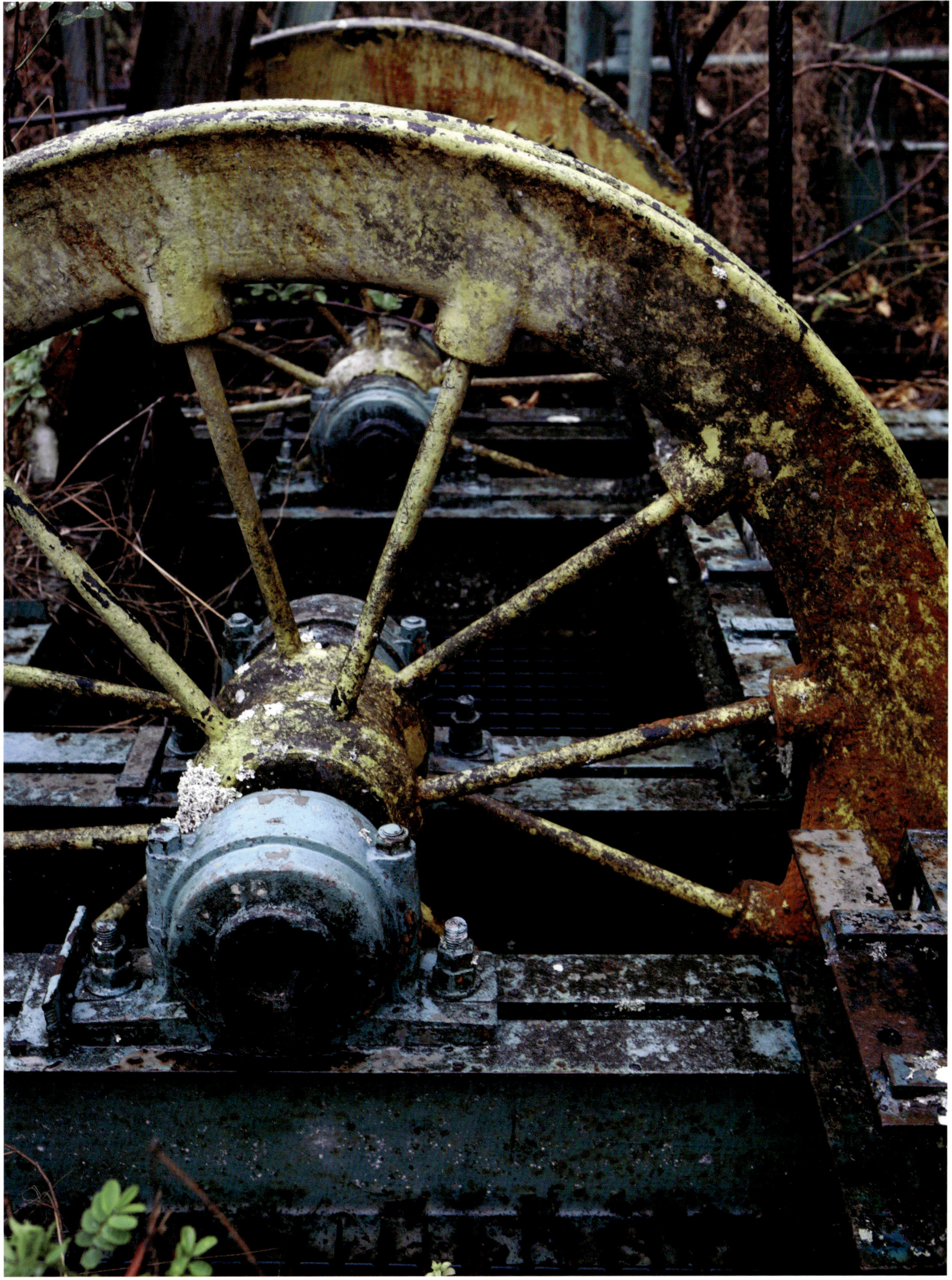

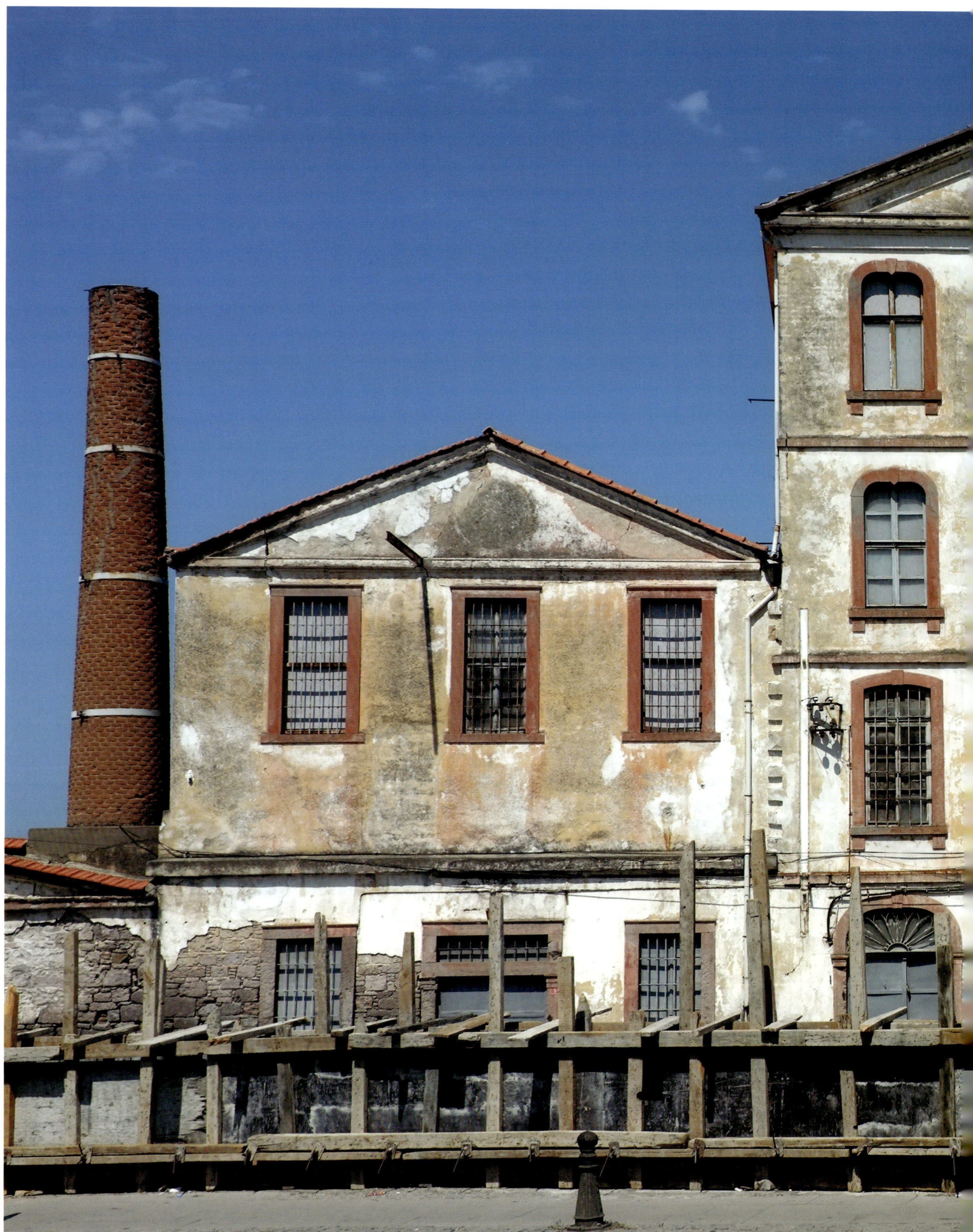

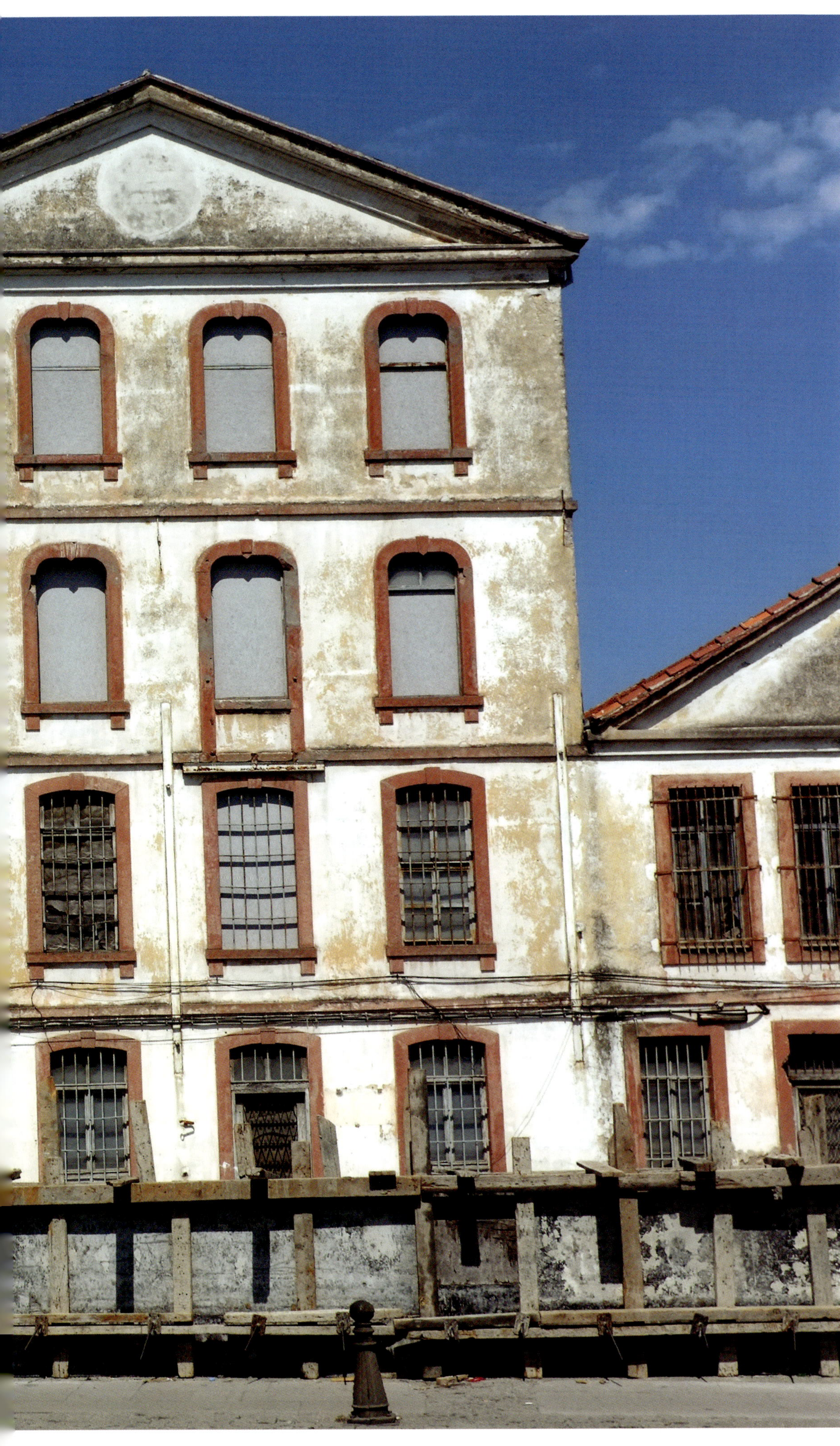

Winding Machinery, Barberton Gold Mine, Mpumalanga, South Africa
Gold mining in South Africa began here, and from the late 1880s there were many gold mines in the area, almost all now closed. Discarded, obsolete or defunct machinery abounds. With four active mines, site exploration is not encouraged.

LEFT:

Olive Oil Factory, Ayvalik, Balikesir Province, Turkey
On Turkey's Aegean coast, the town has been a centre of olive processing for centuries. Olive oil and soap were produced in this works, dating from the 1800s, and which closed in 2001. It is hoped to regenerate the building as a culinary arts centre.

Ngwenya Mine, Swaziland
A truly historic site, perhaps the world's first mine: red ochre was dug here over 40,000 years ago. This terraced pit is modern, a relic of an open-cast mine begun in 1966 and currently not being worked.

Marble Cutting Room, Marmara Island, Turkey
Fine white marble has been quarried here for over 3500 years and many techniques have been used to cut and polish the slabs. The redundant sawing machine was driven from a shaft turned by a steam engine or, later, electric motor.

Oil Pipe Line, Bahrain
Dismantling of an old pipeline seems to have come to a stop here. Judging from the condition of its concrete supports, the pipeline was an early part of the oil installations and has clearly been out of use for a long time.

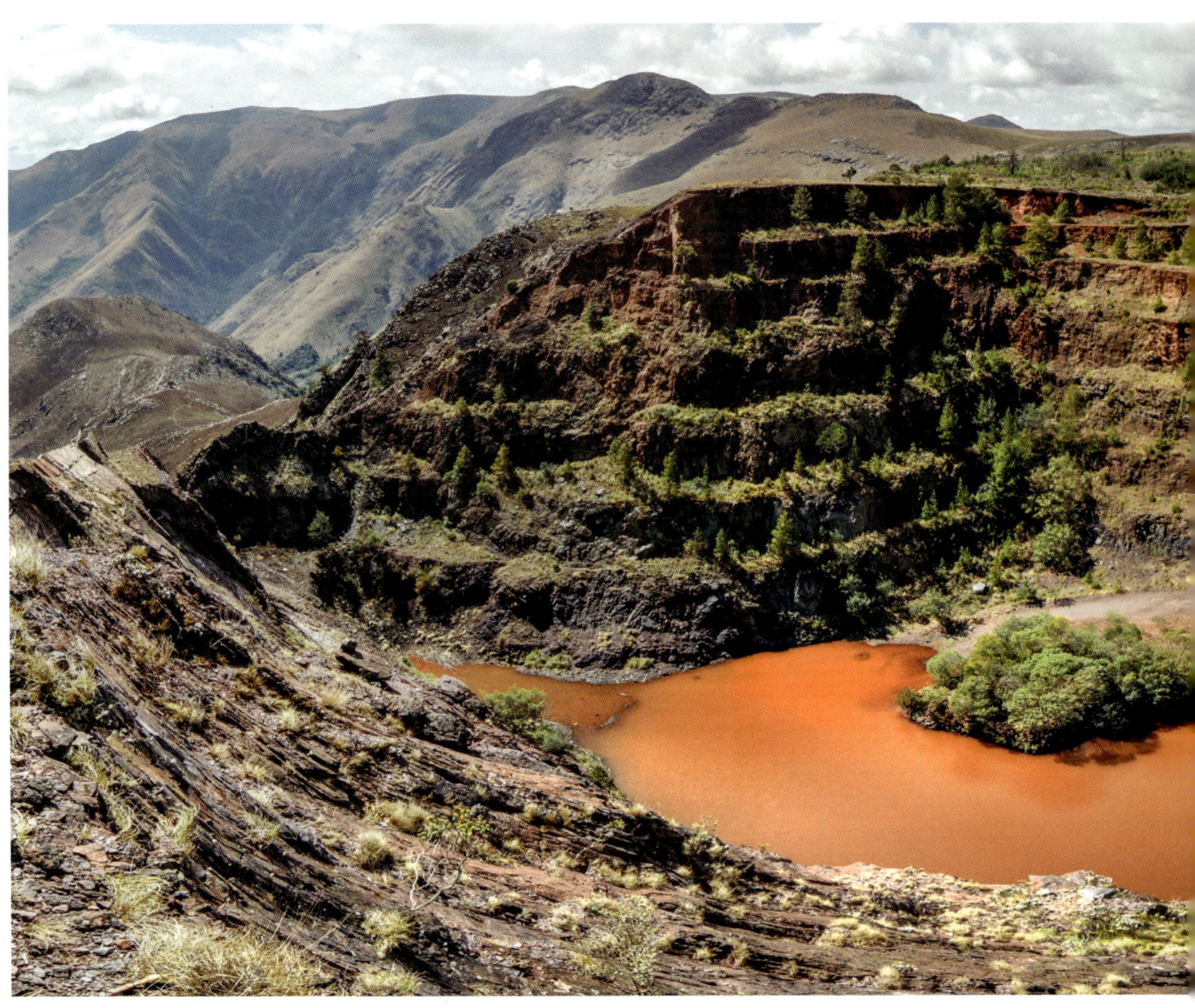

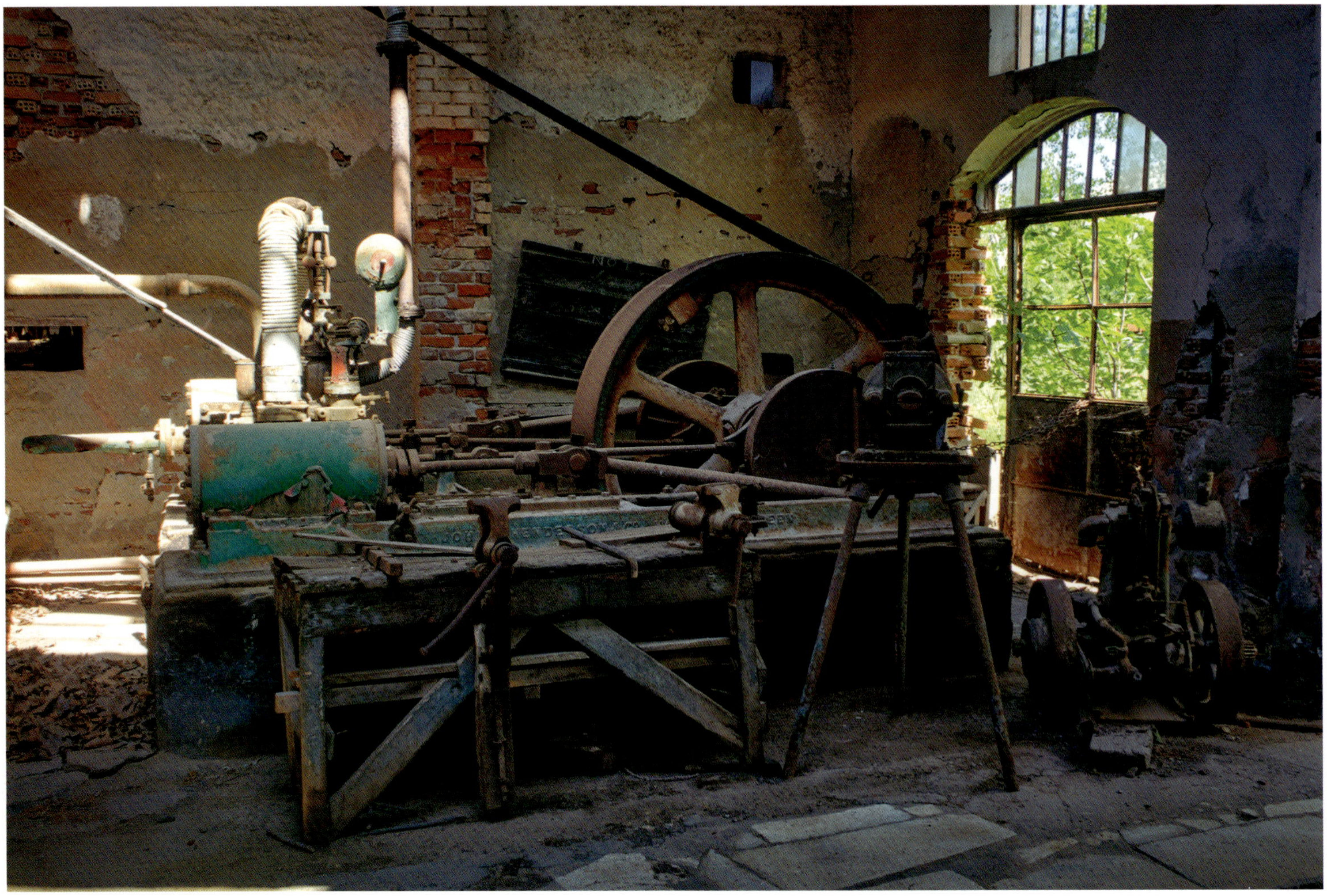

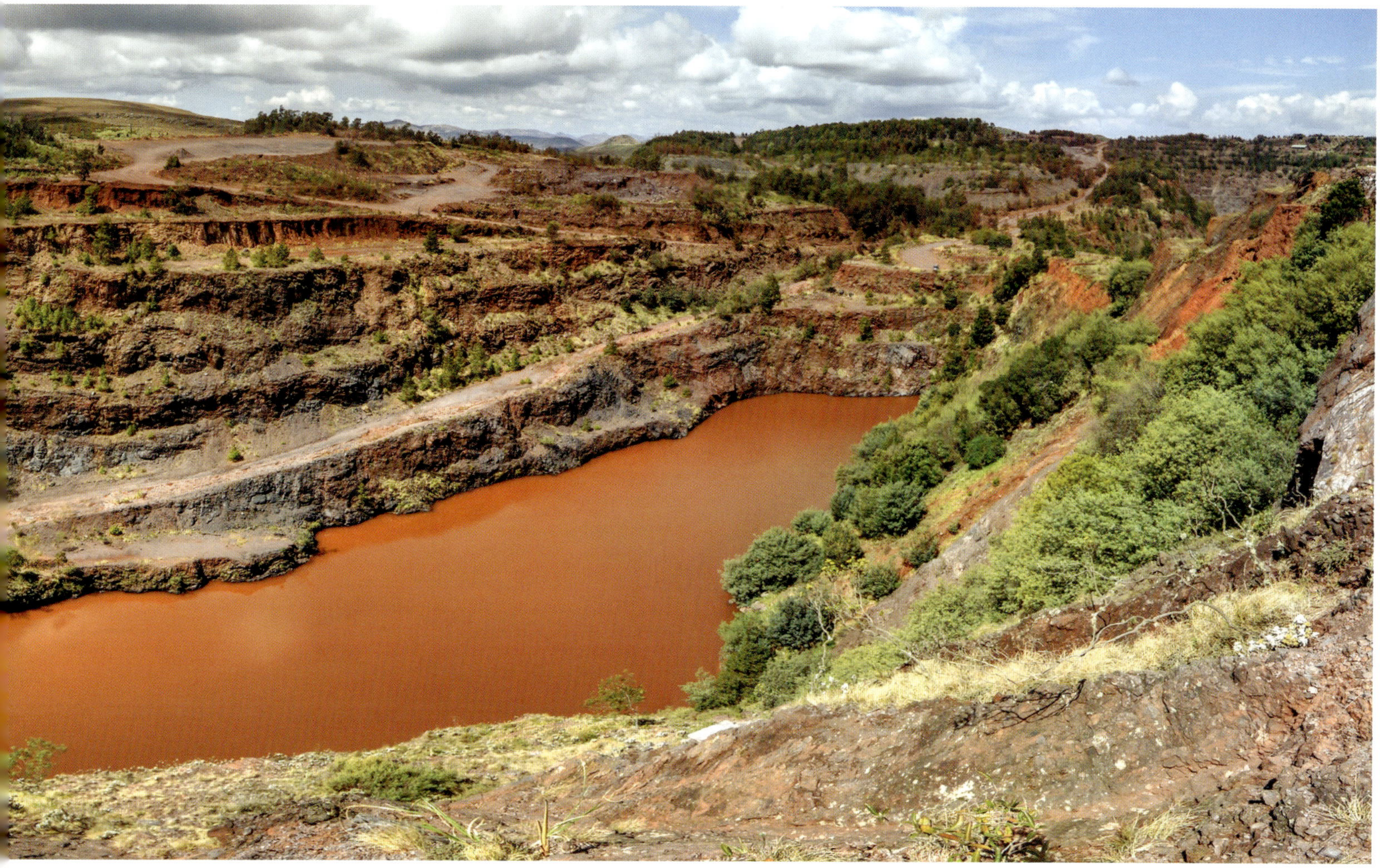

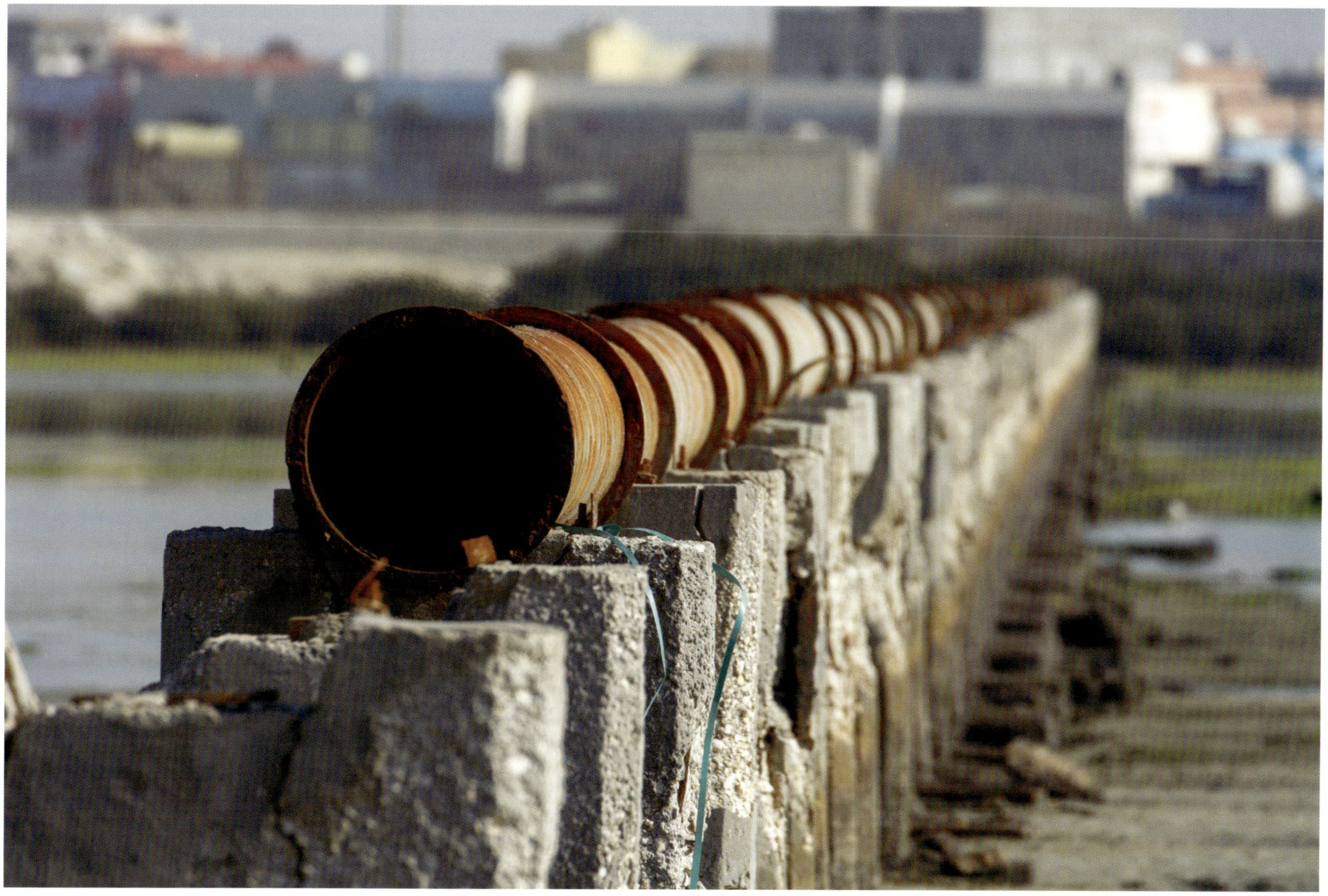

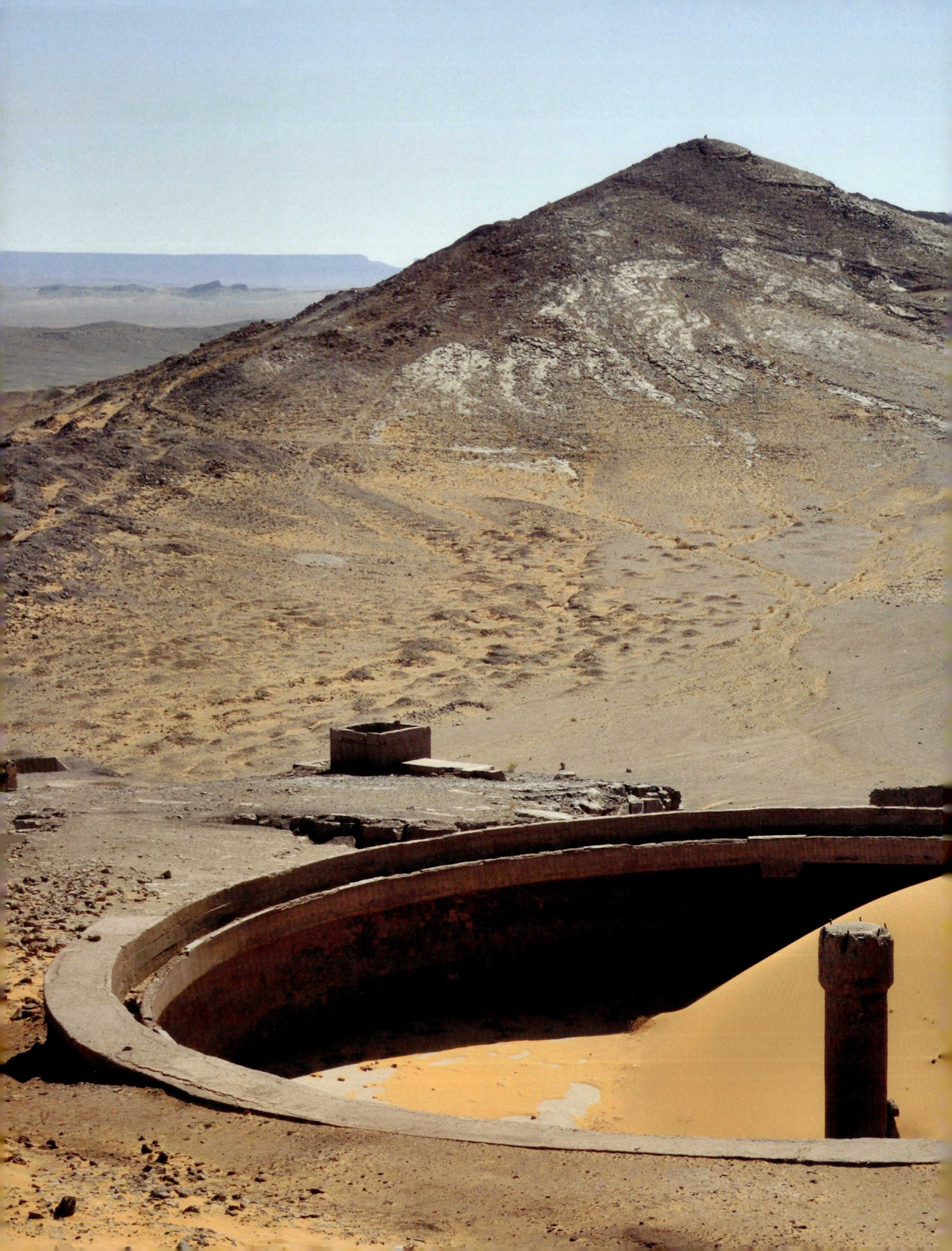

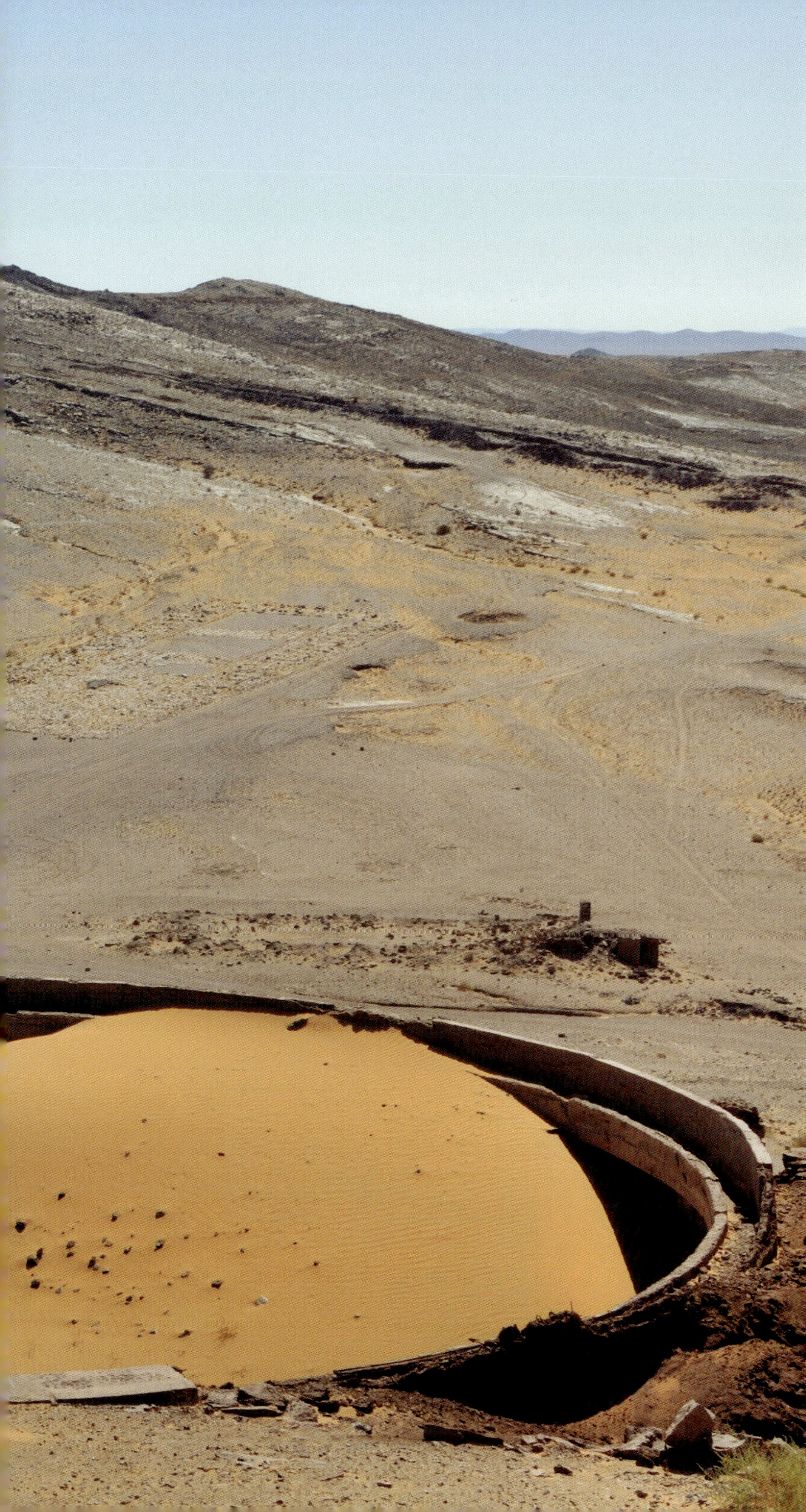

Mine, Erg Chebbi, Morocco
An erg is an area of wind-created sand dunes; Erg Chebbi is also a location of mineral mines, some of them very small-scale, and many now abandoned. The circular remains are of a separator which would have sifted mineral elements from rock and sand.

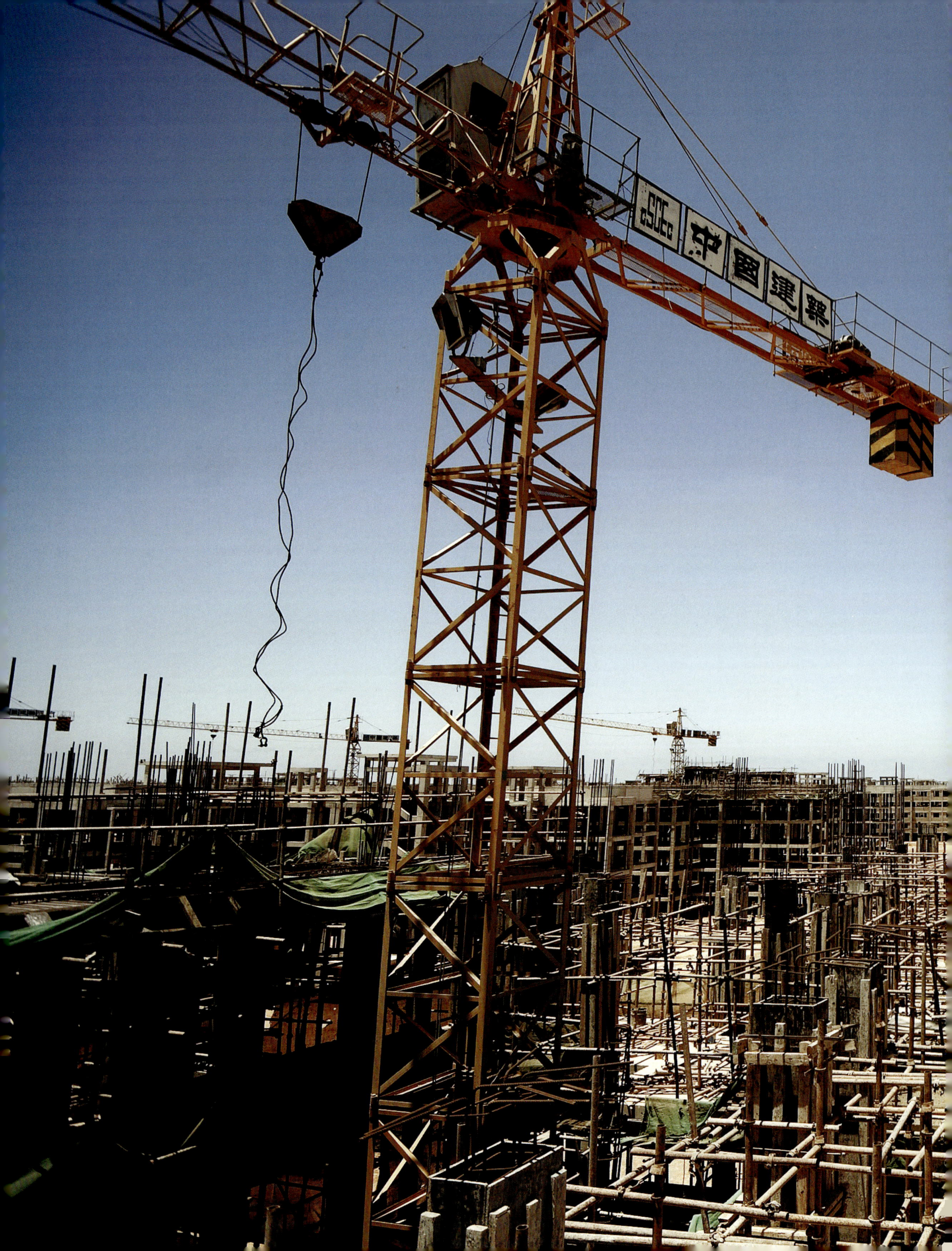
CSCEC
中國建築

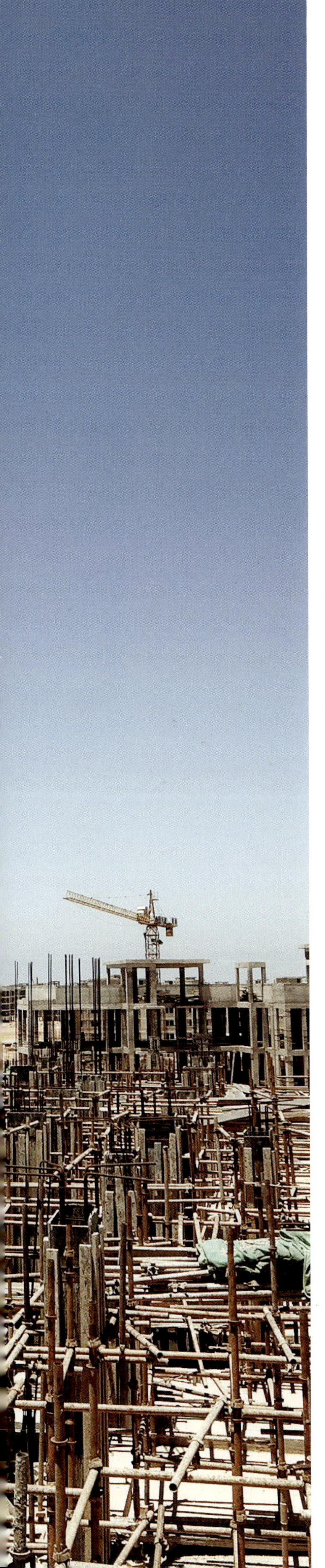

Abandoned 'New Benghazi' Project, Benghazi, Libya
Chinese symbols on the crane indicate China's involvement in the ambitious building project which fell victim to Libya's troubled history in 2011. As many as 11,000 Chinese and other Asian workers were involved. When the civil war began, they were quickly evacuated, leaving the site, intended to house 150,000 people, abandoned.

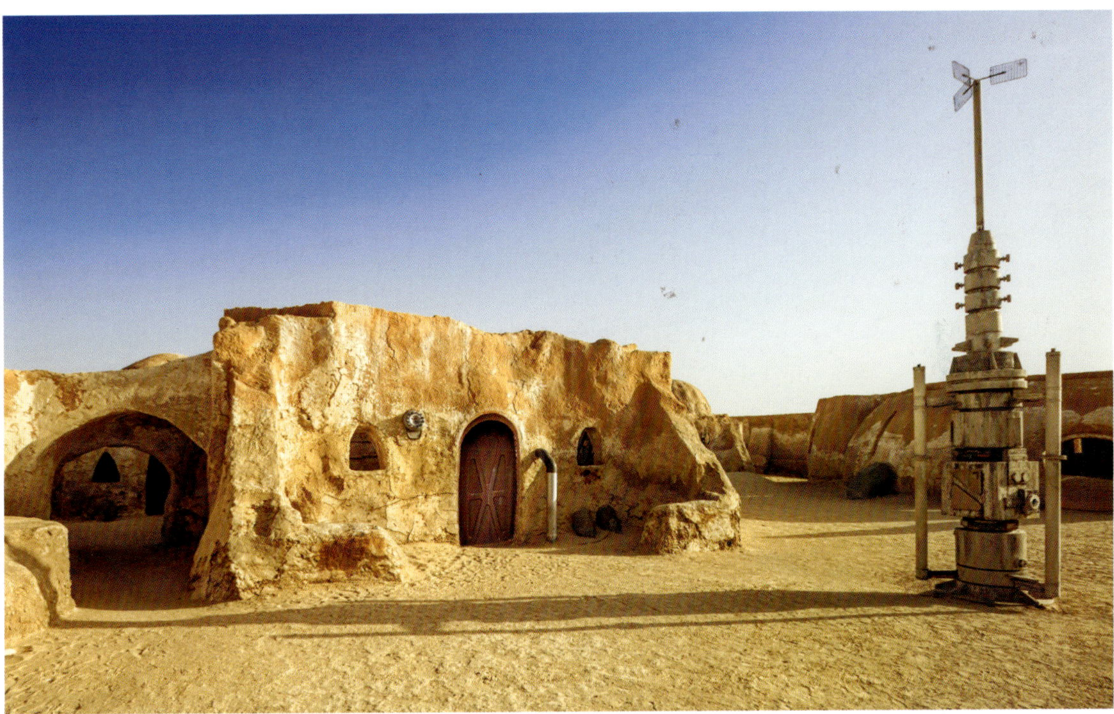

***Star Wars* Film Set, Mos Espa, Tunisia**
The buildings look as if they are formed from the desert landscape but inside, as one observer remarked, 'it's all decaying chicken wire, plaster and nails'. Still, this and other *Star Wars* sites in southern Tunisia are evocative pilgrimage places for fans of the film series.

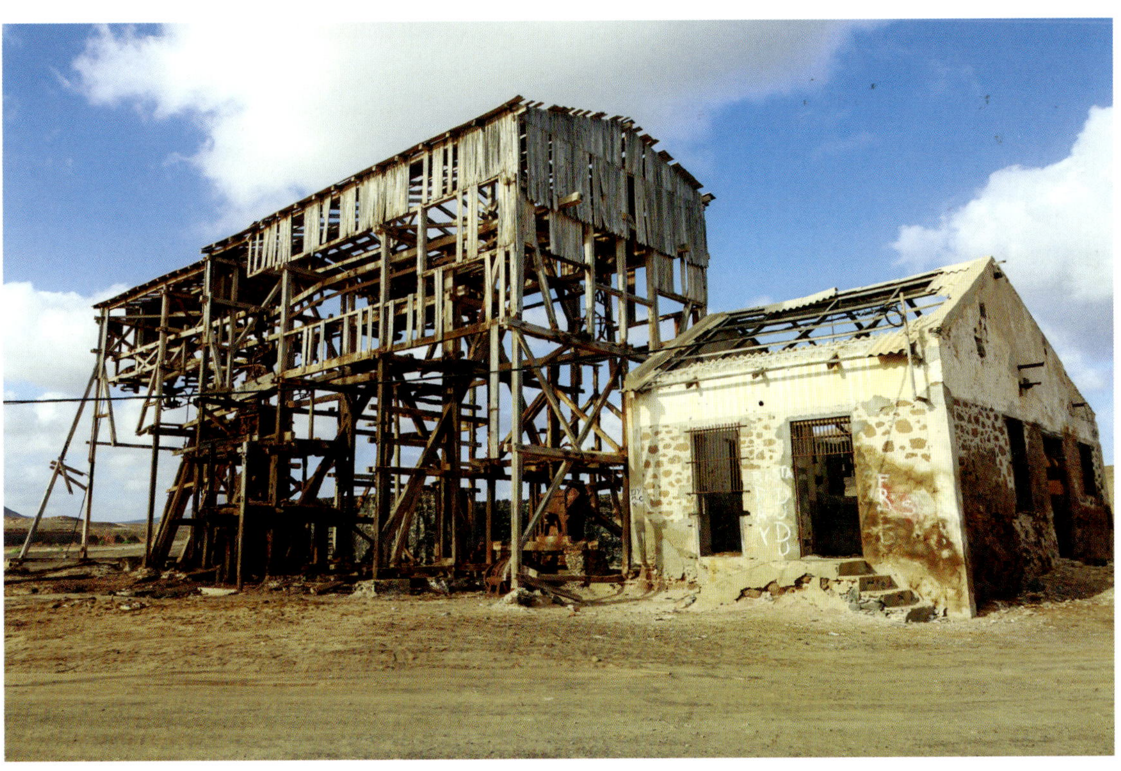

Salt Works, Pedra de Lume, Cape Verde Islands
Set in an extinct volcanic crater, partly below sea level, the salinas set up a cable car system in 1921 to transport salt from the drying pans for packing and shipping. It was later replaced by a tunnel through the crater wall, but the ramshackle remains of the terminal still stand.

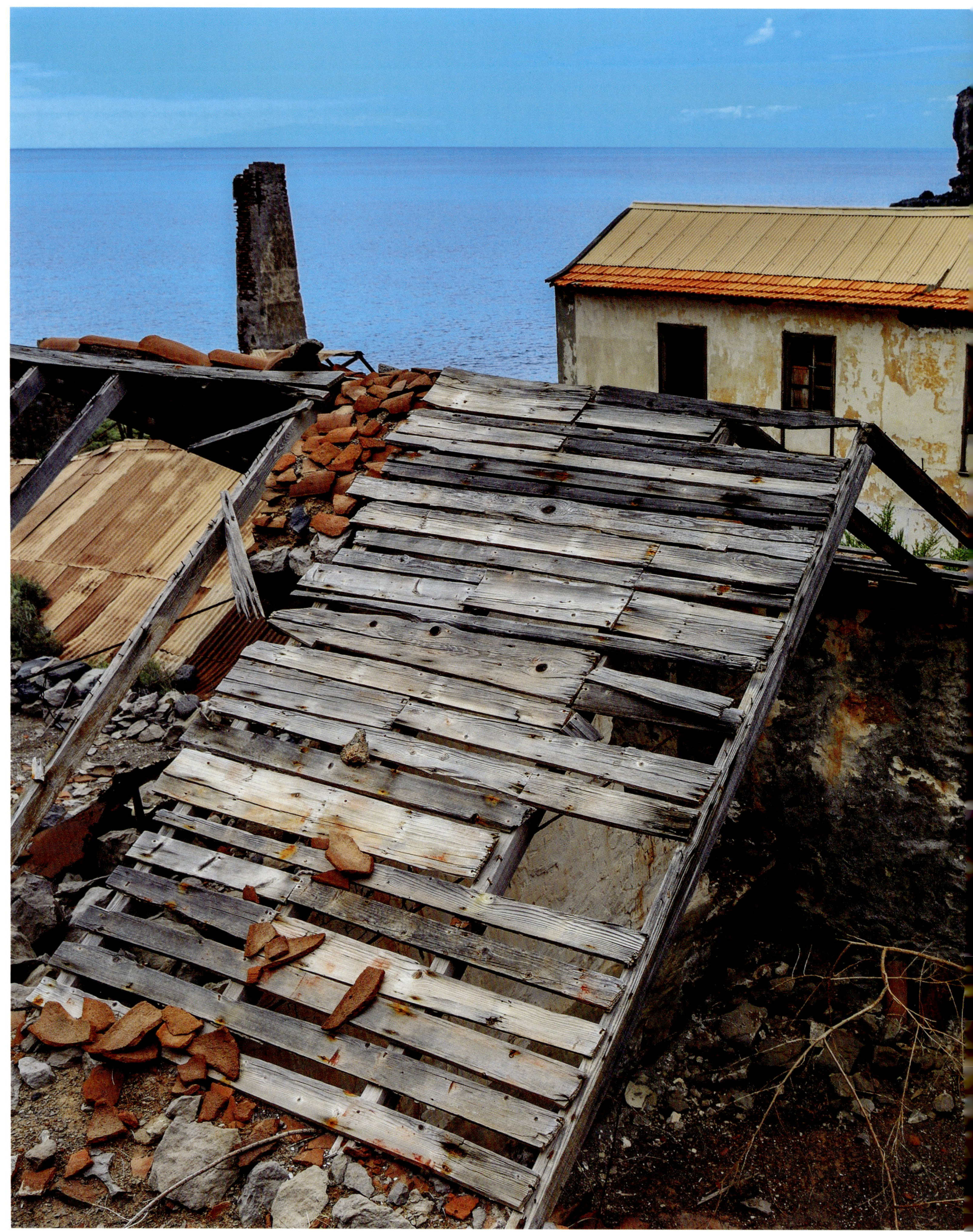

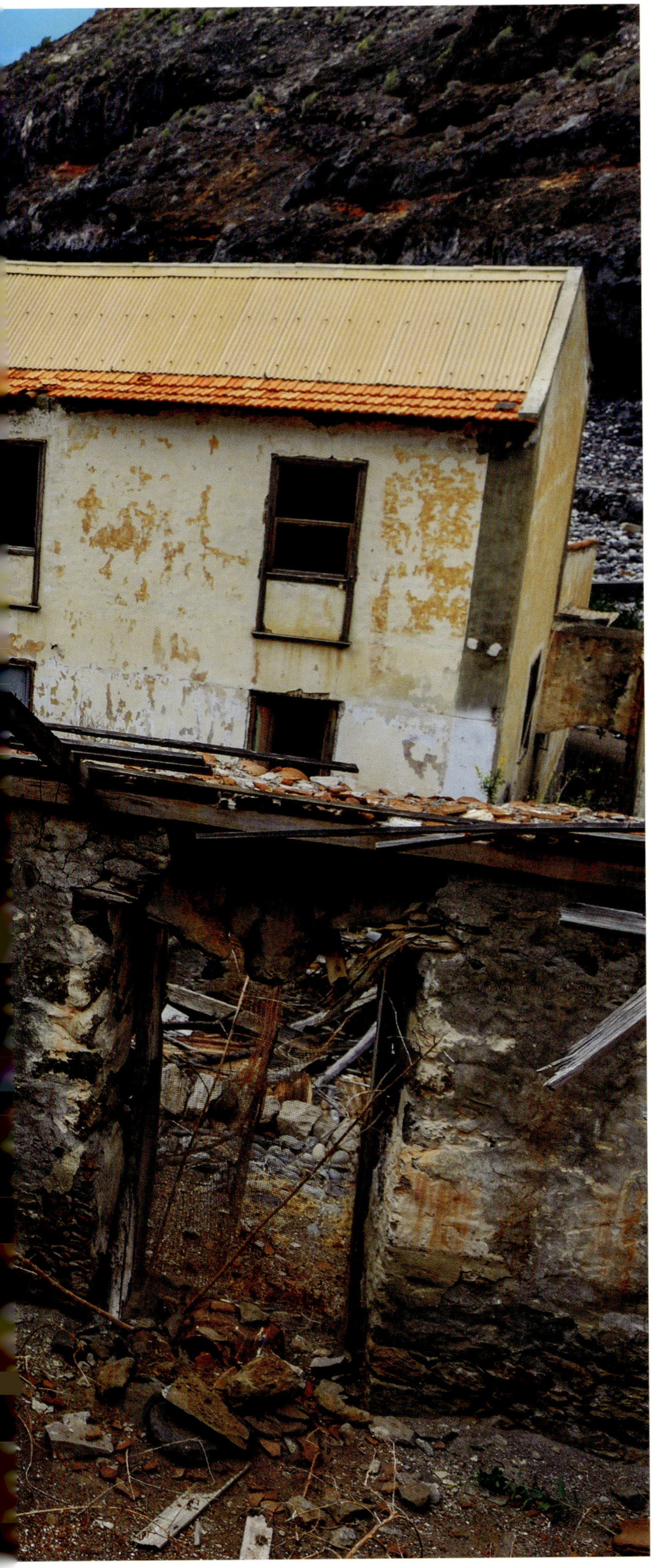

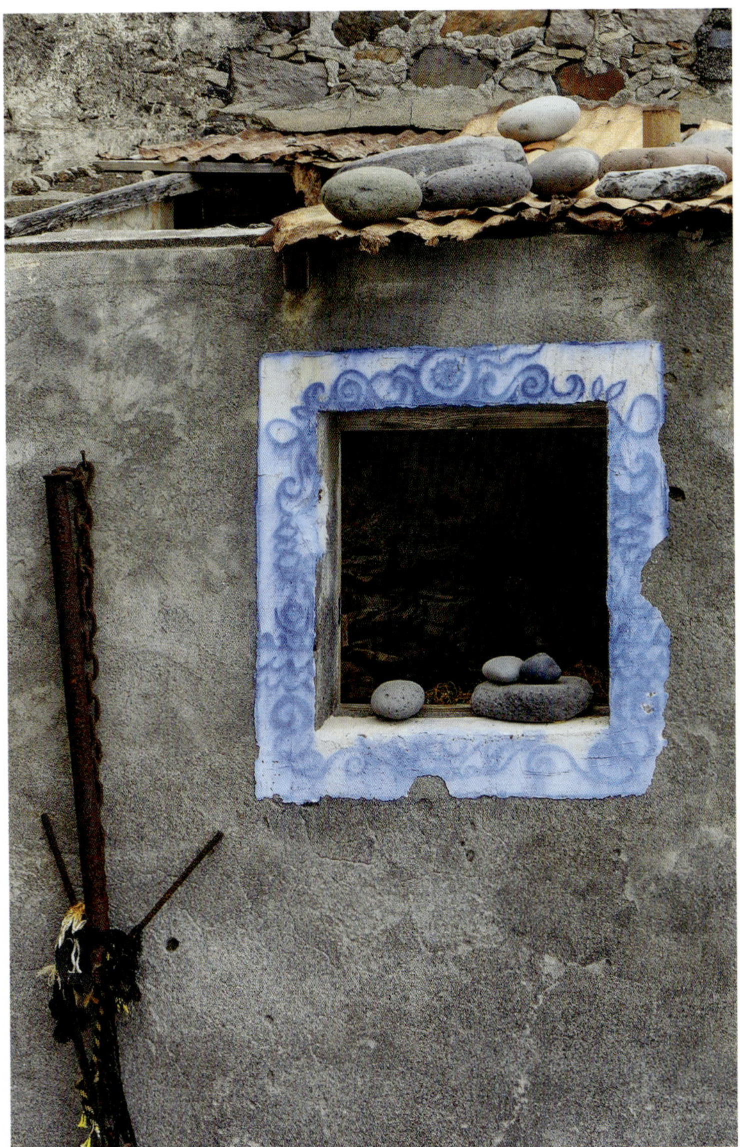

Former Fish Processing Plant, La Cantera, Gomera, Canary Islands
From 1891 until the 1970s this was one of several factories serving the tuna and mackerel fishing industry. Steady diminution of the fish stocks led to their closure, with devastating effect on the local economy. So far, proposals for 'heritage' development have come to nothing and the buildings are gradually disintegrating.

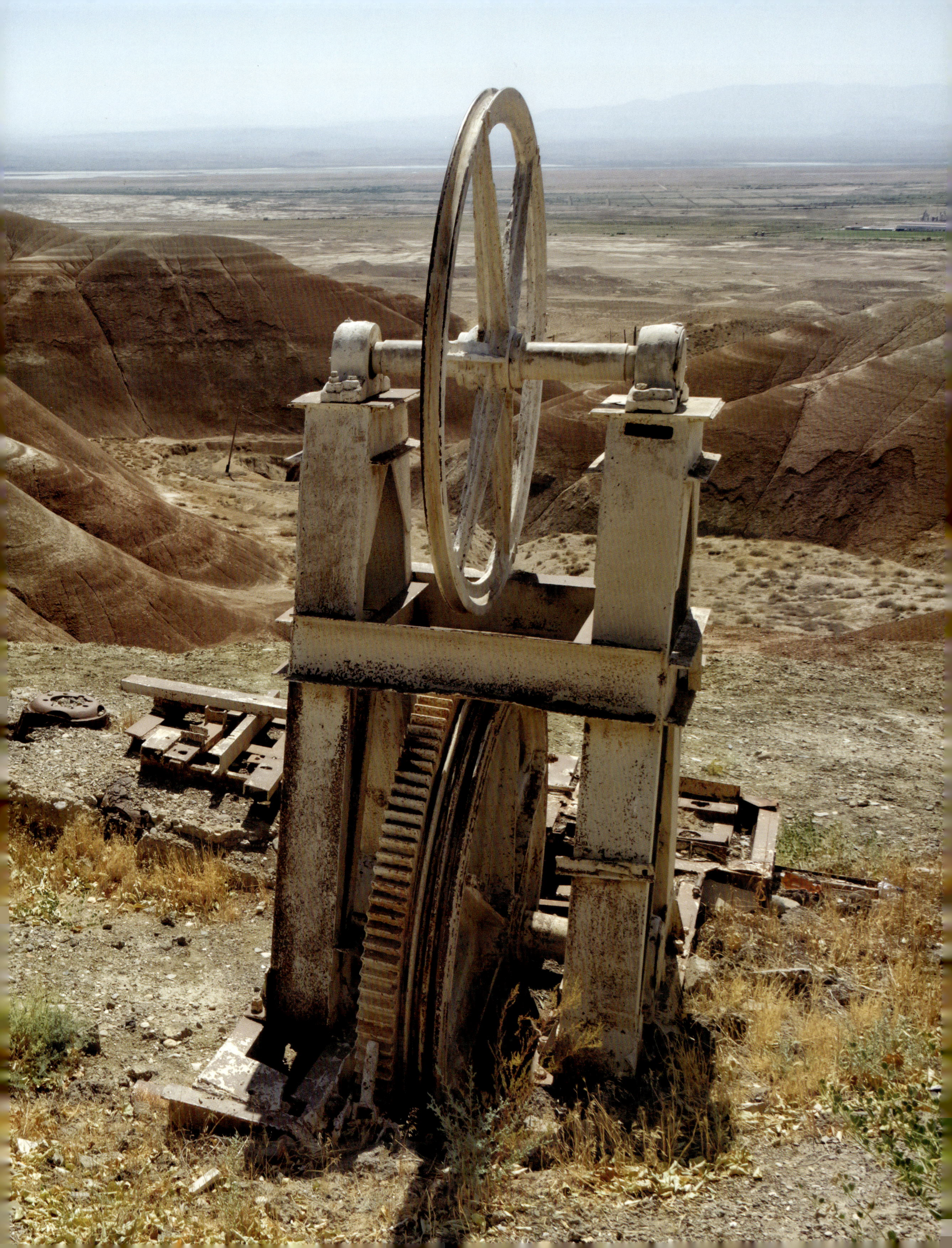

Asia and the Pacific

The lure of industrial ruins is as strong here as in other parts of the world. In Japanese there is a word, *haikyo*, which once simply meant 'ruin' but has now taken on the sense of 'explorable ruin'. Boatloads of visitors make for Japan's derelict offshore islands, once tightly-packed with mining equipment and coal-burning plants. The sheer size of some of these installations is startling, notably in China, where a huge expansion of industry in recent decades has also led to atmospheric pollution on a dangerous scale, resulting in the closure of some very large and historic iron and steel works.

Some of these works, like Chongqing Steelworks, Sydney's historic naval dockyard, and New Zealand's last steam-powered timber mill, have been preserved as visitor ventures to commemorate the human activity that went on, and their place in the national story. At present we can still look backwards, and appreciate the immense work and effort that was put into such places, while acknowledging that two hundred years of global industrialisation have gravely damaged the natural environment and compromised the prospects of future generations. Perhaps our descendants will wonder why it was ever allowed to happen.

OPPOSITE:
Salt Mine, Duzdag Cave, Nakhchivan, Azerbaijan
The oldest known rock salt mine, dating back to the 5th millennium BCE, has also some of the oldest known industrial relics, including tools and ceramic objects. As this piece of winding gear shows, salt was also mined in much more recent times. Nowadays the site is primarily a salt therapy centre.

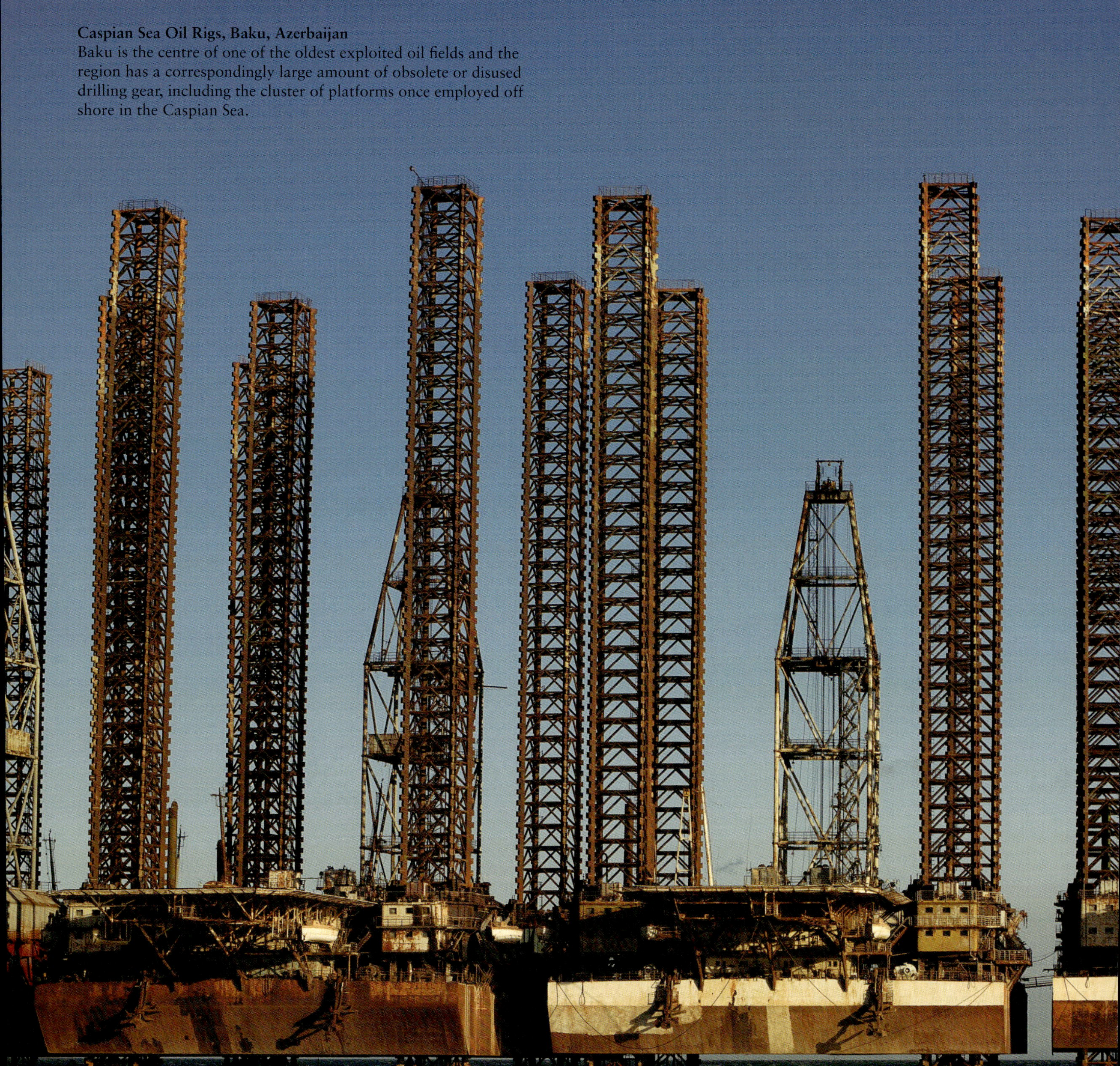

Caspian Sea Oil Rigs, Baku, Azerbaijan
Baku is the centre of one of the oldest exploited oil fields and the region has a correspondingly large amount of obsolete or disused drilling gear, including the cluster of platforms once employed off shore in the Caspian Sea.

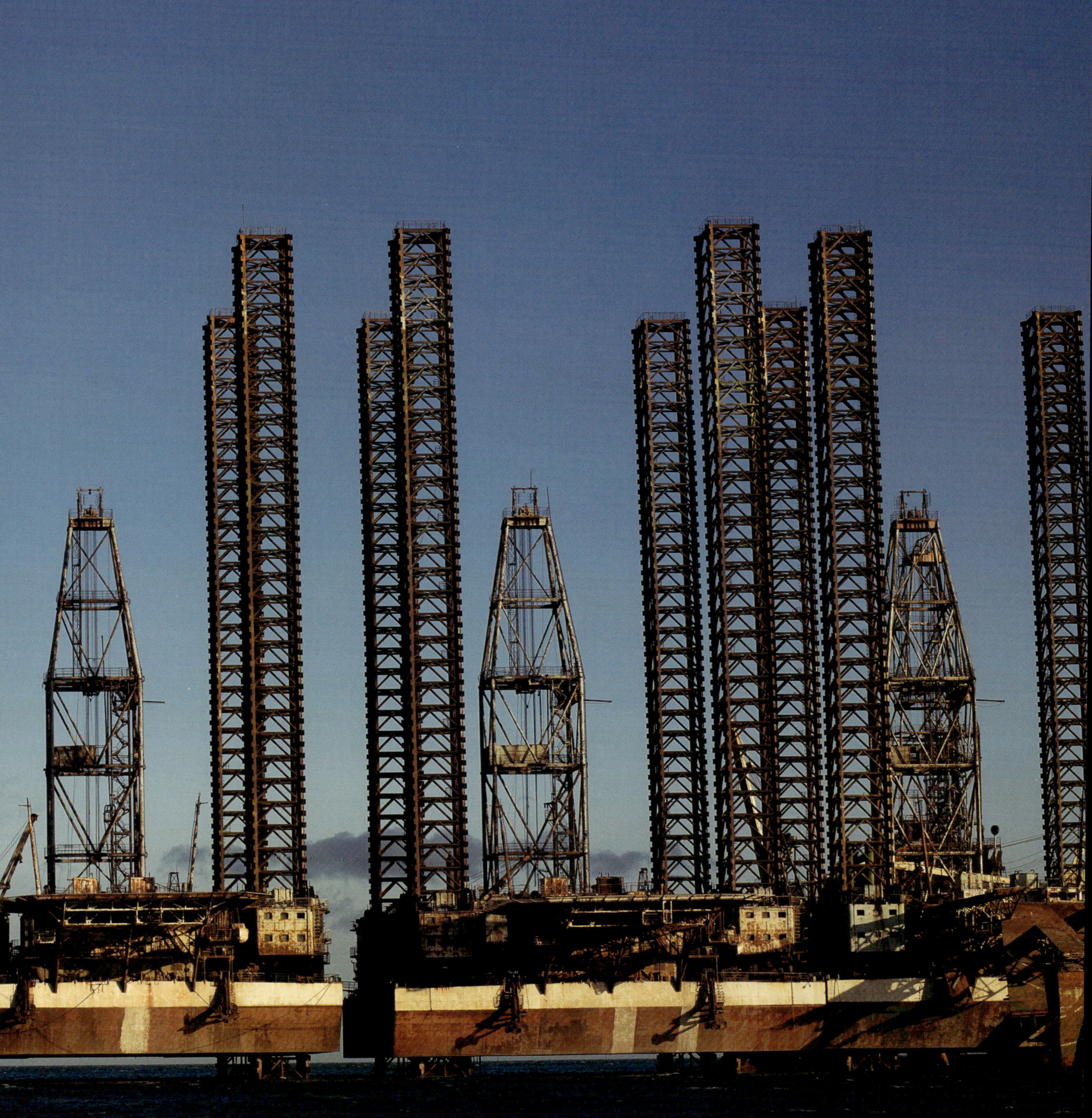

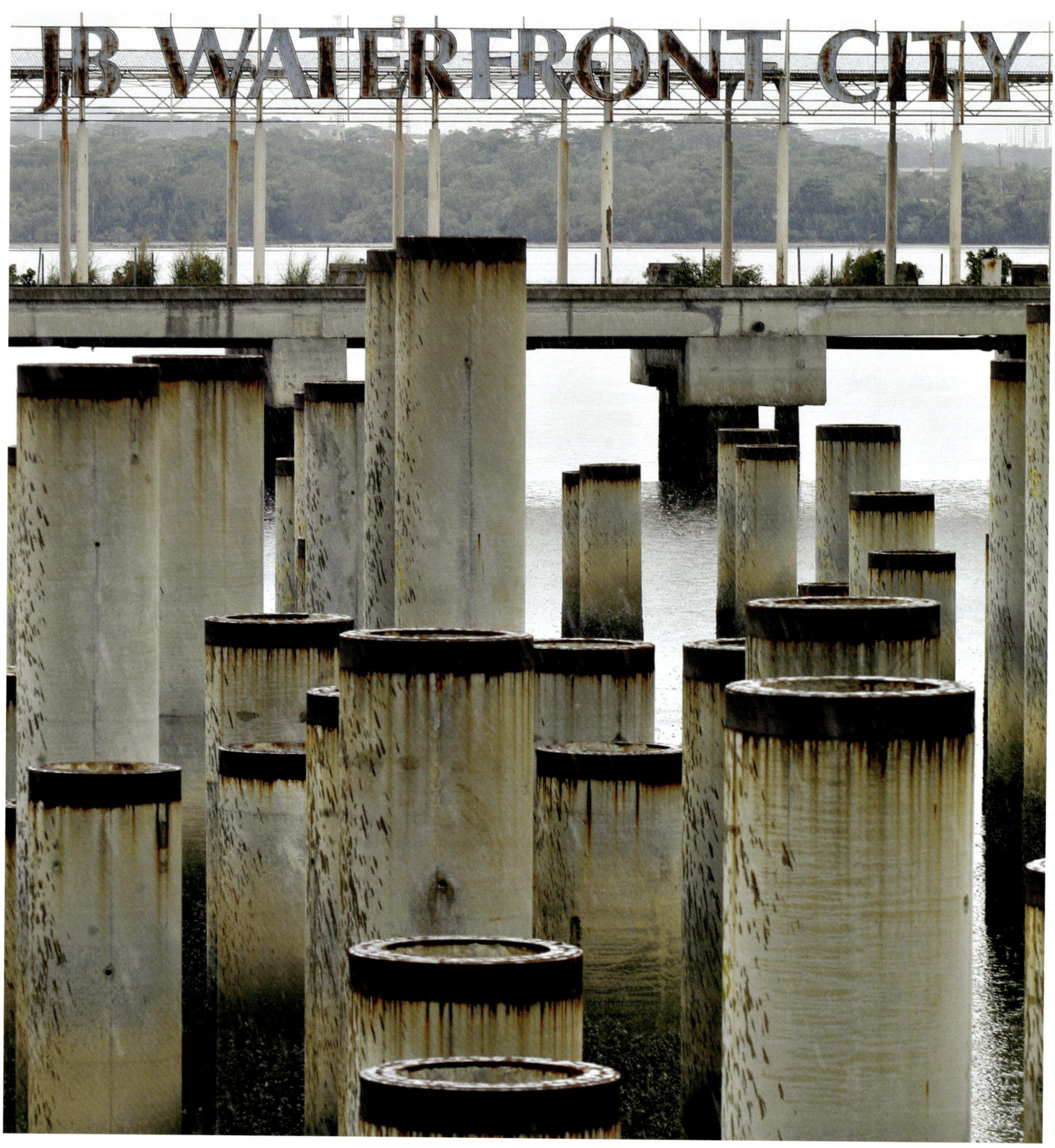

ABOVE:
Waterfront City, Johor Baru, Malaysia
Unused support piles of a huge urban project at Malaysia's southern tip, looking towards Singapore – monuments to a grandiose shopping mall/hotel/residential project of the 1990s, part-constructed in 2000, but shut down in 2003 amid mutual recriminations by financiers and politicians.

OPPOSITE TOP AND BOTTOM:
Electrical Equipment from Abandoned Tin Mining Dredge, Tanjung Tualak, Perak, Malaysia
Now museum pieces within a vaster museum piece (see next spread) this circuit breaker and ampere gauge or ammeter (used to measure the strength of an electric current) were part of the electrical system of a huge floating tin dredger.

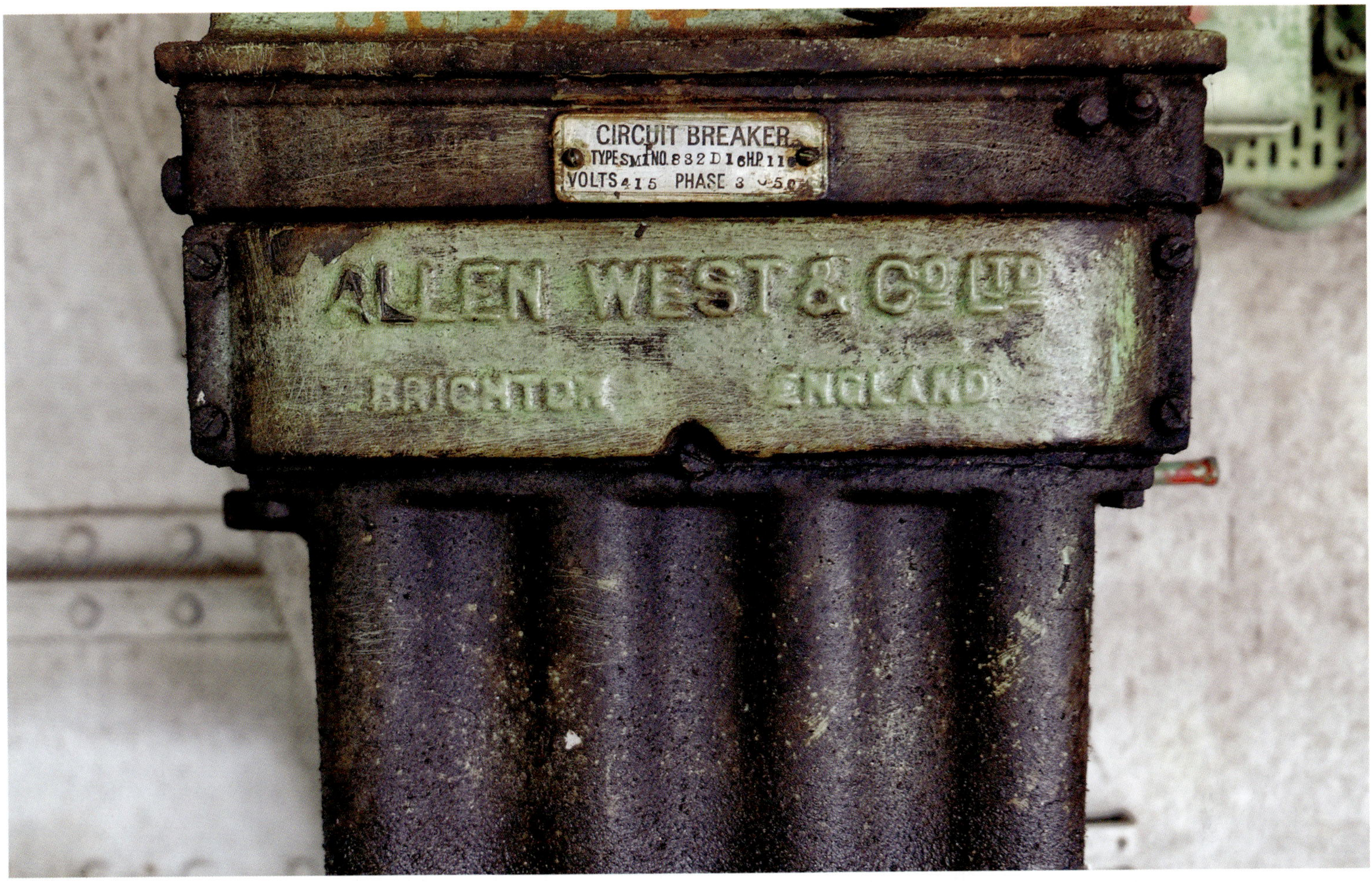

CIRCUIT BREAKER
TYPES MINO.832 D 16HP 11
VOLTS 415 PHASE 3 50
ALLEN WEST & Co LTD
BRIGHTON ENGLAND

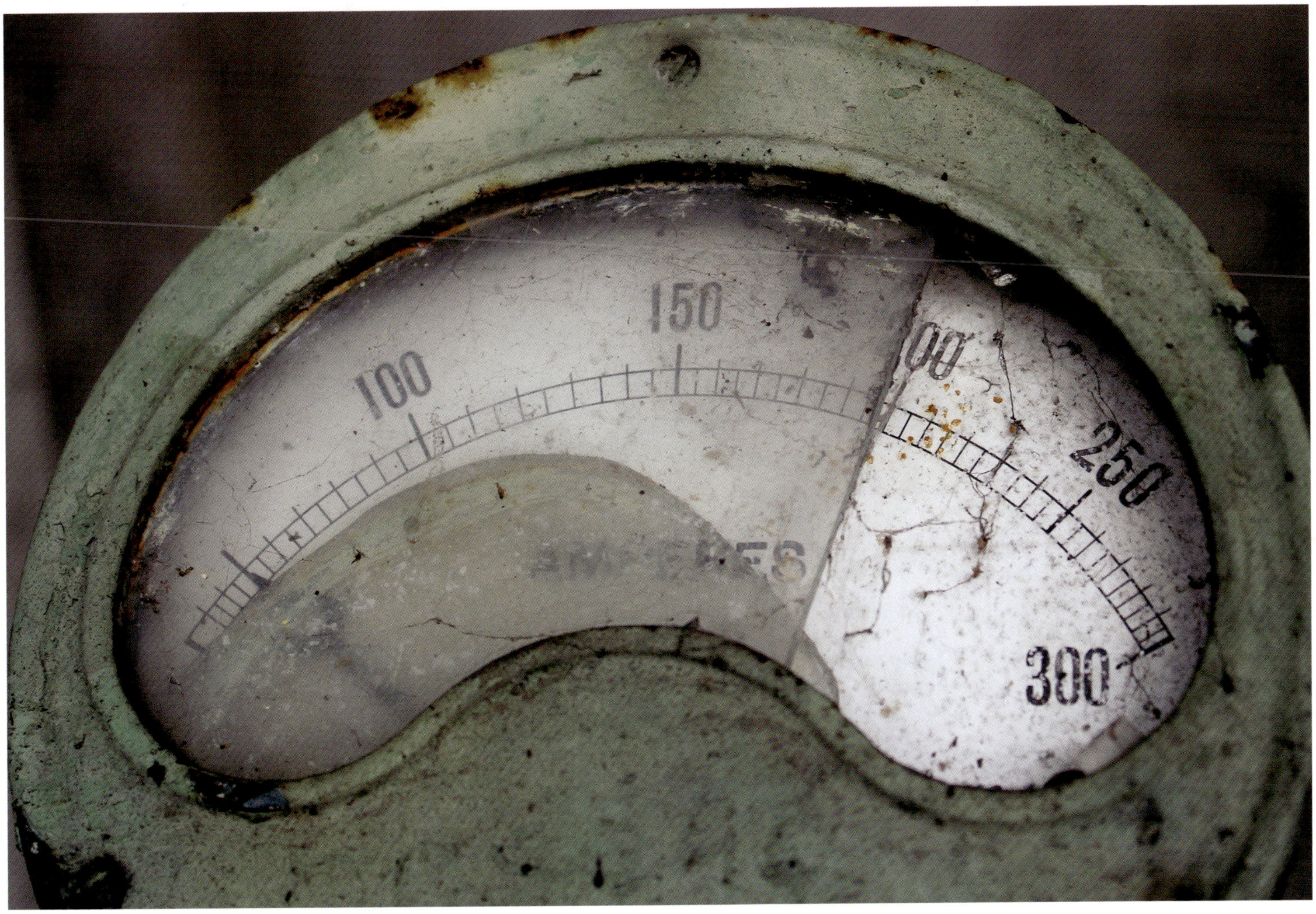

100
150
200
250
300
AMPERES

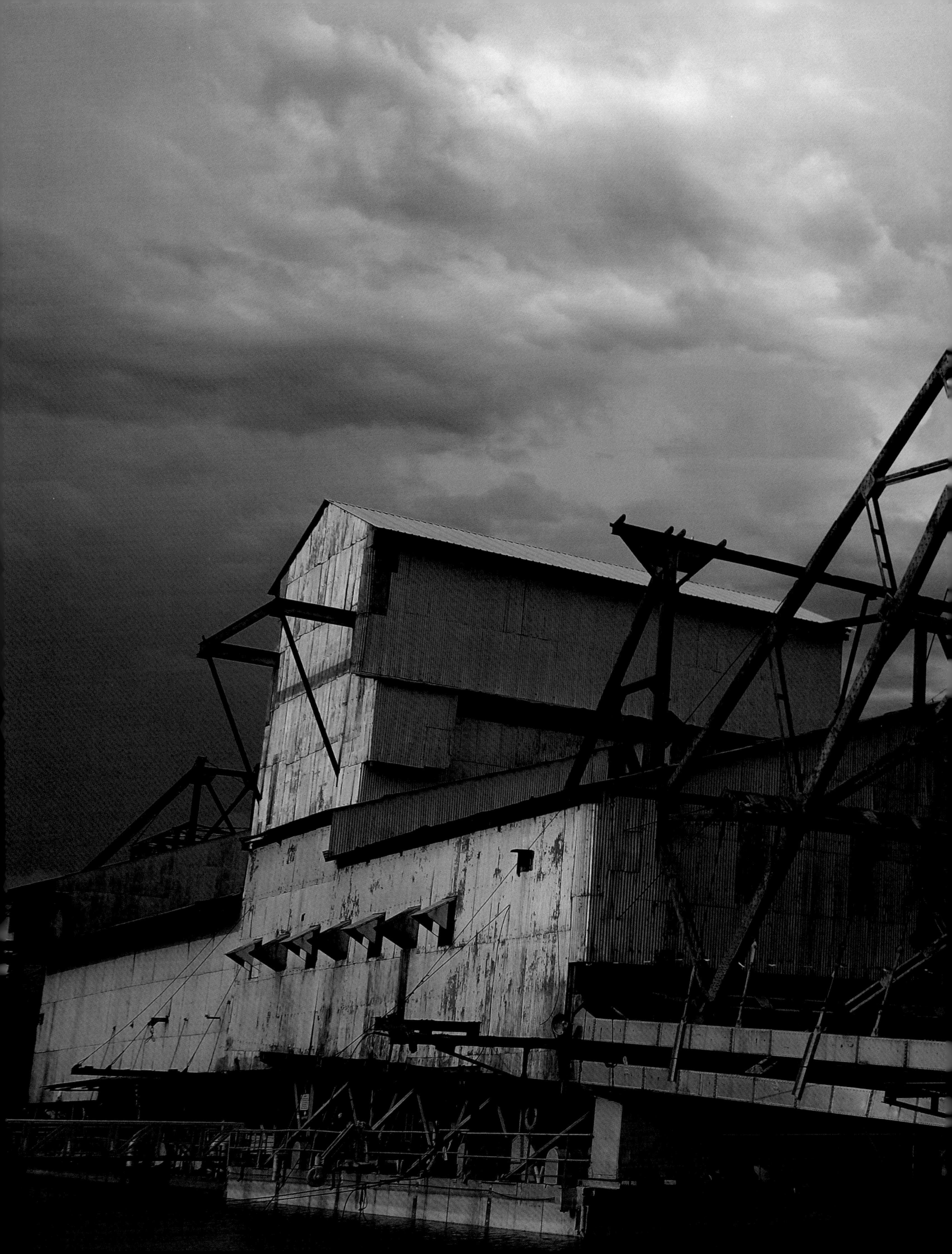

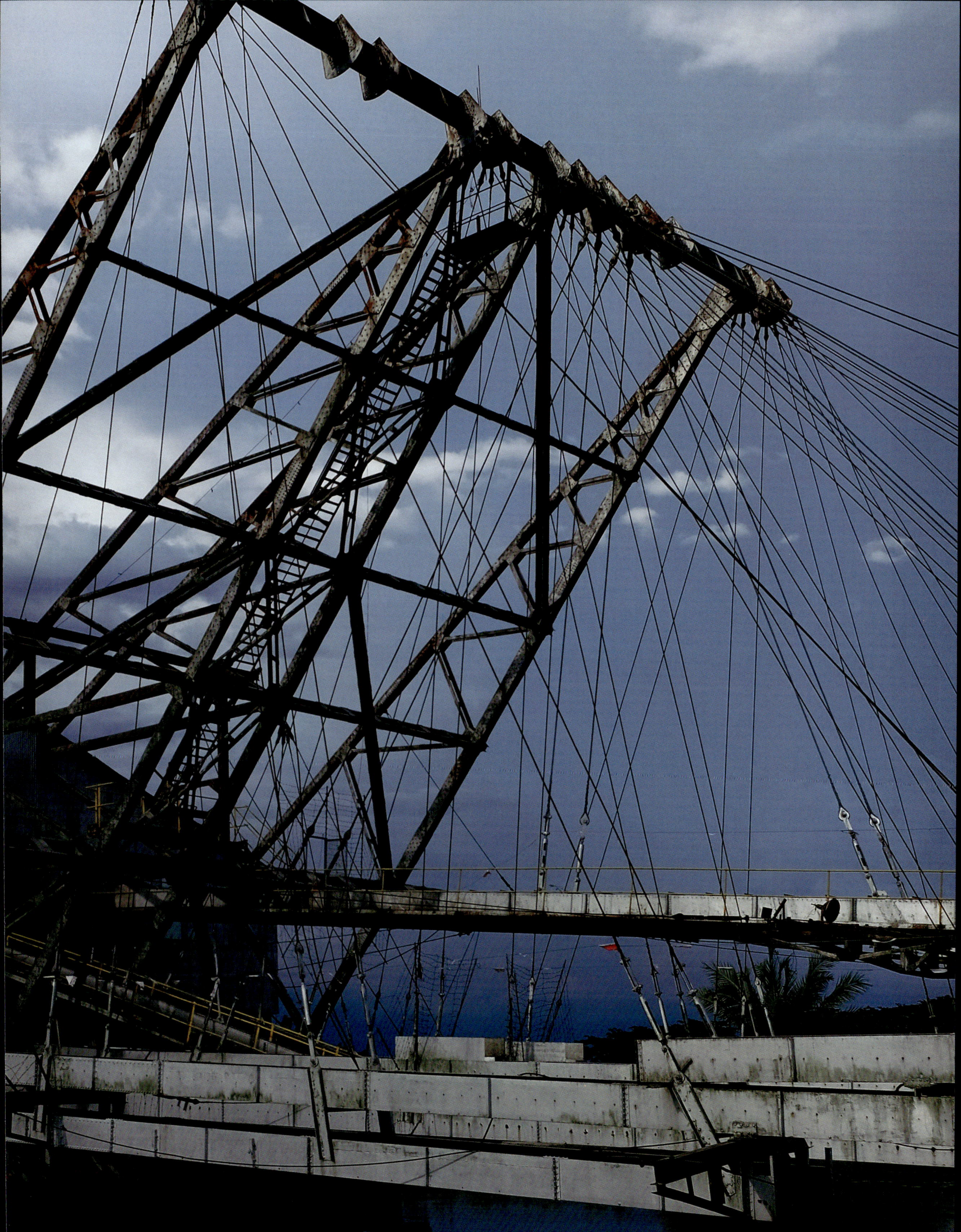

Tin Dredge No. 5, Tanjung Tualak, Perak, Malaysia
Floating on marshland that covered sub-surface tin deposits, this giant machine was mounted on a 75m (246ft) long pontoon. Its total weight was 4572 tonnes (4500 tons) and its 115 digger buckets could reach 15m (49ft) into the ground. It worked between 1938 and 1982. Semi-derelict by 2010, it is now maintained as a memorial to Malaysia's mining heritage.

Abandoned Air Conditioner Factory, Baku, Azerbaijan
Set up in the 1970s with Soviet capital to supply the Russian market, production at this large plant ended in 1991 when the Soviet Union collapsed. The same thing happened in many other places. Much of Soviet-era Baku has been demolished but some pockets remain. This photograph was taken in 2014.

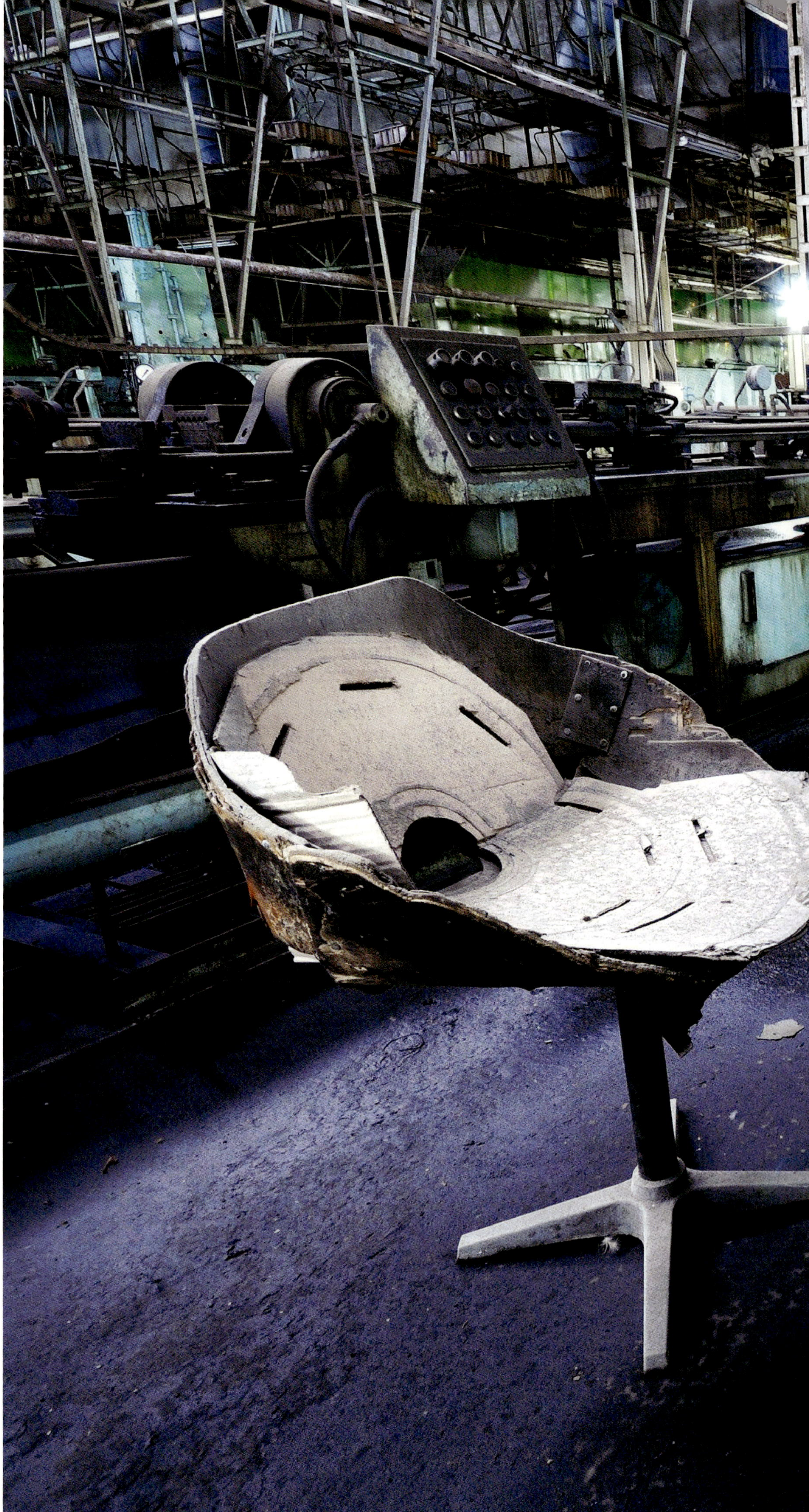

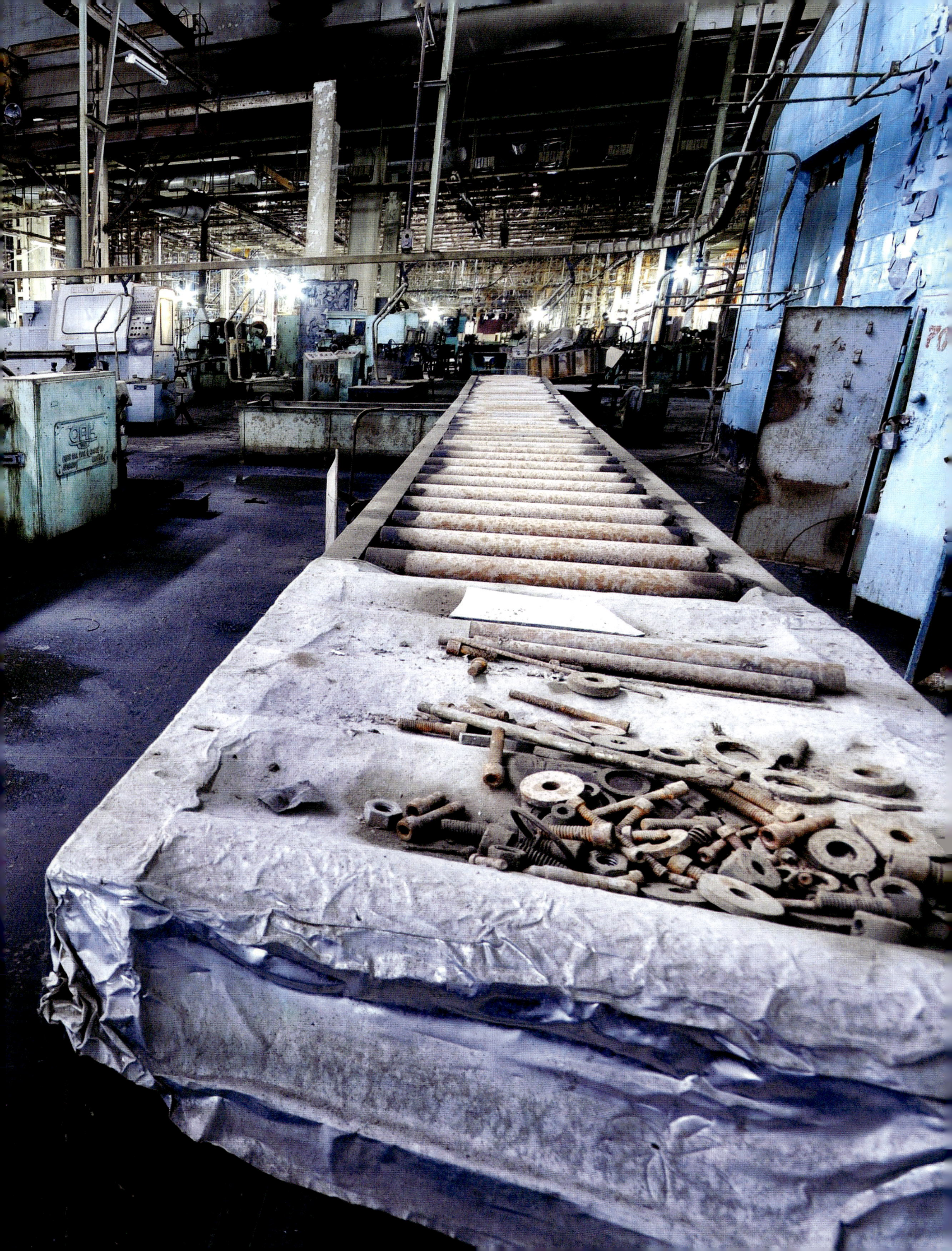

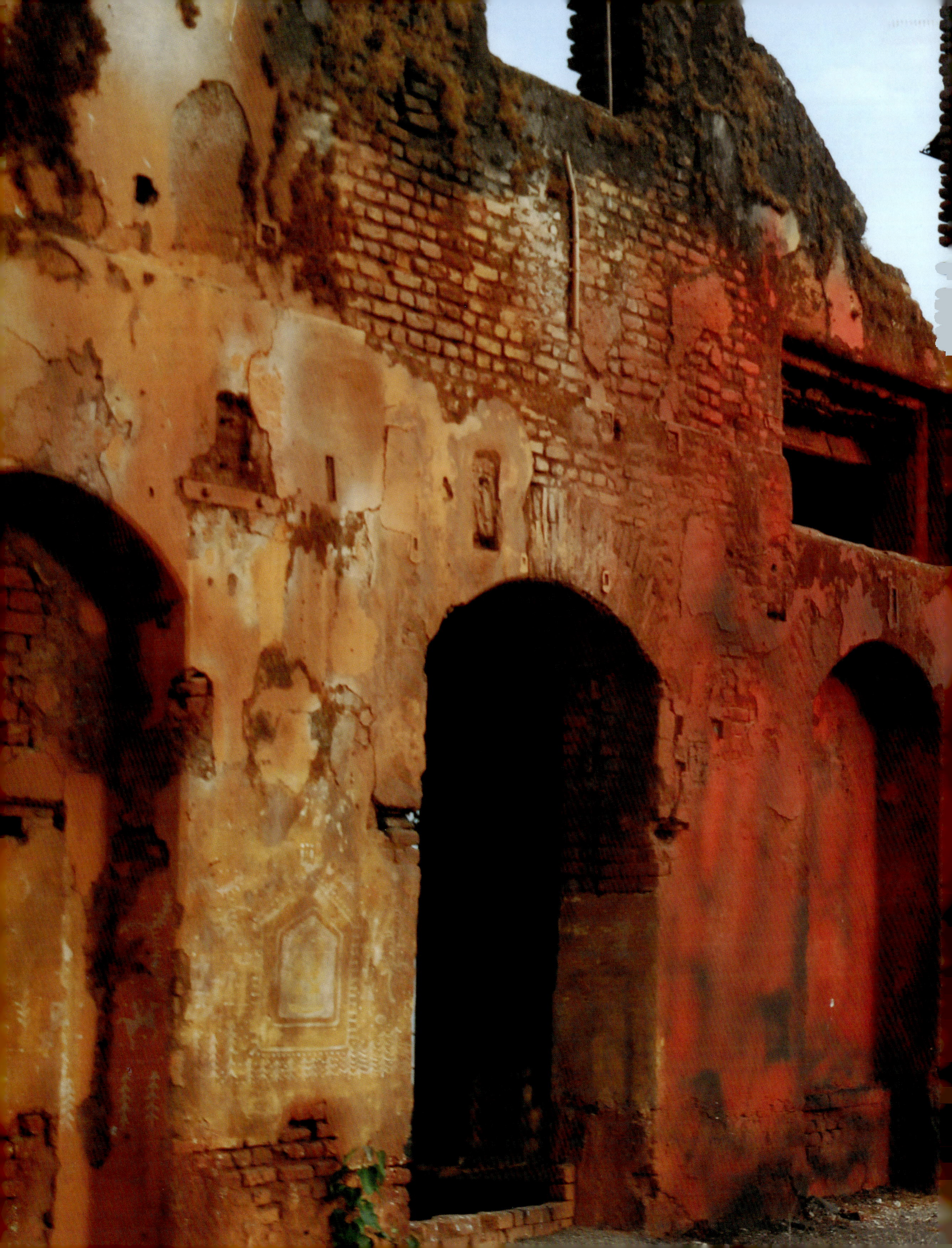

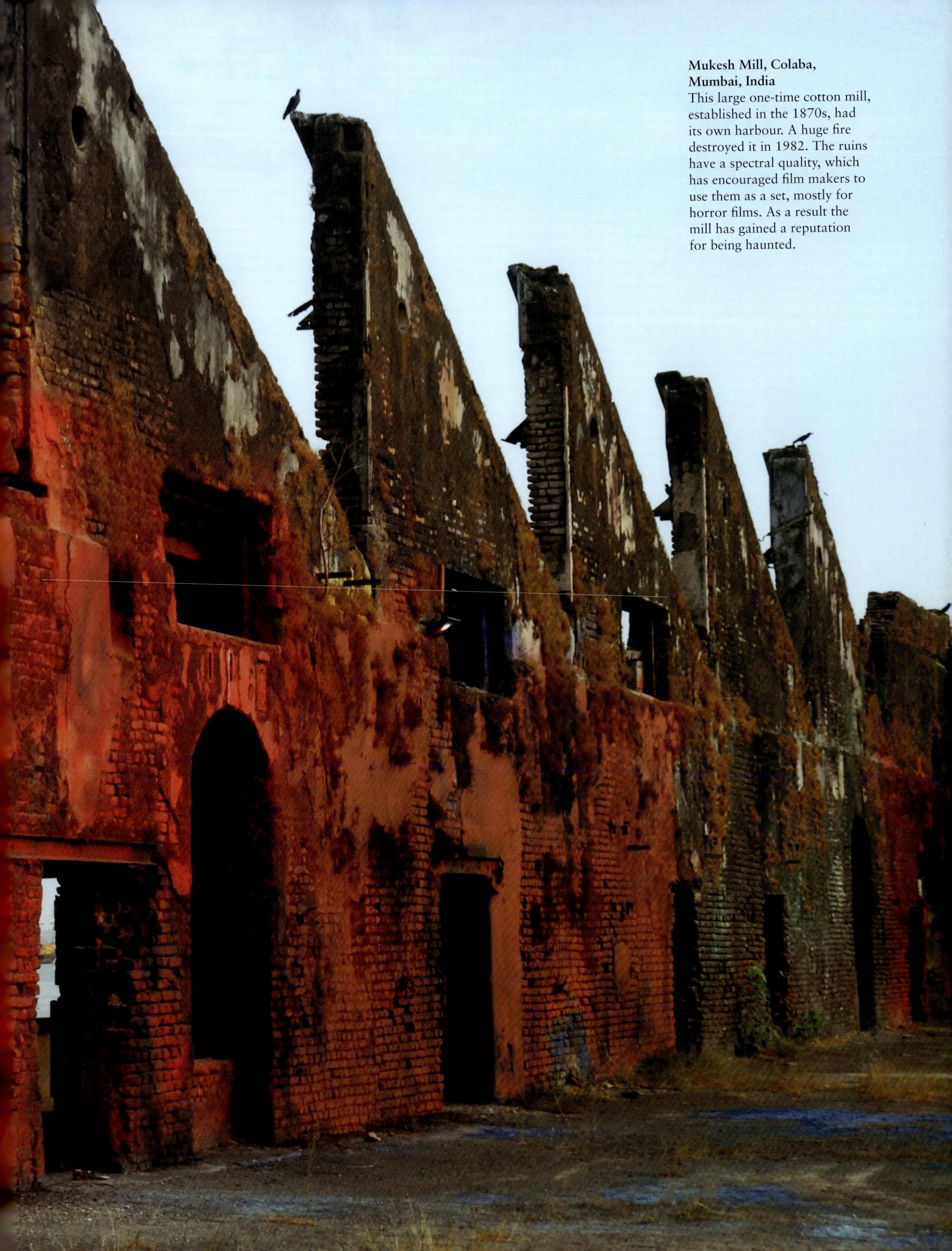

Mukesh Mill, Colaba,
Mumbai, India
This large one-time cotton mill,
established in the 1870s, had
its own harbour. A huge fire
destroyed it in 1982. The ruins
have a spectral quality, which
has encouraged film makers to
use them as a set, mostly for
horror films. As a result the
mill has gained a reputation
for being haunted.

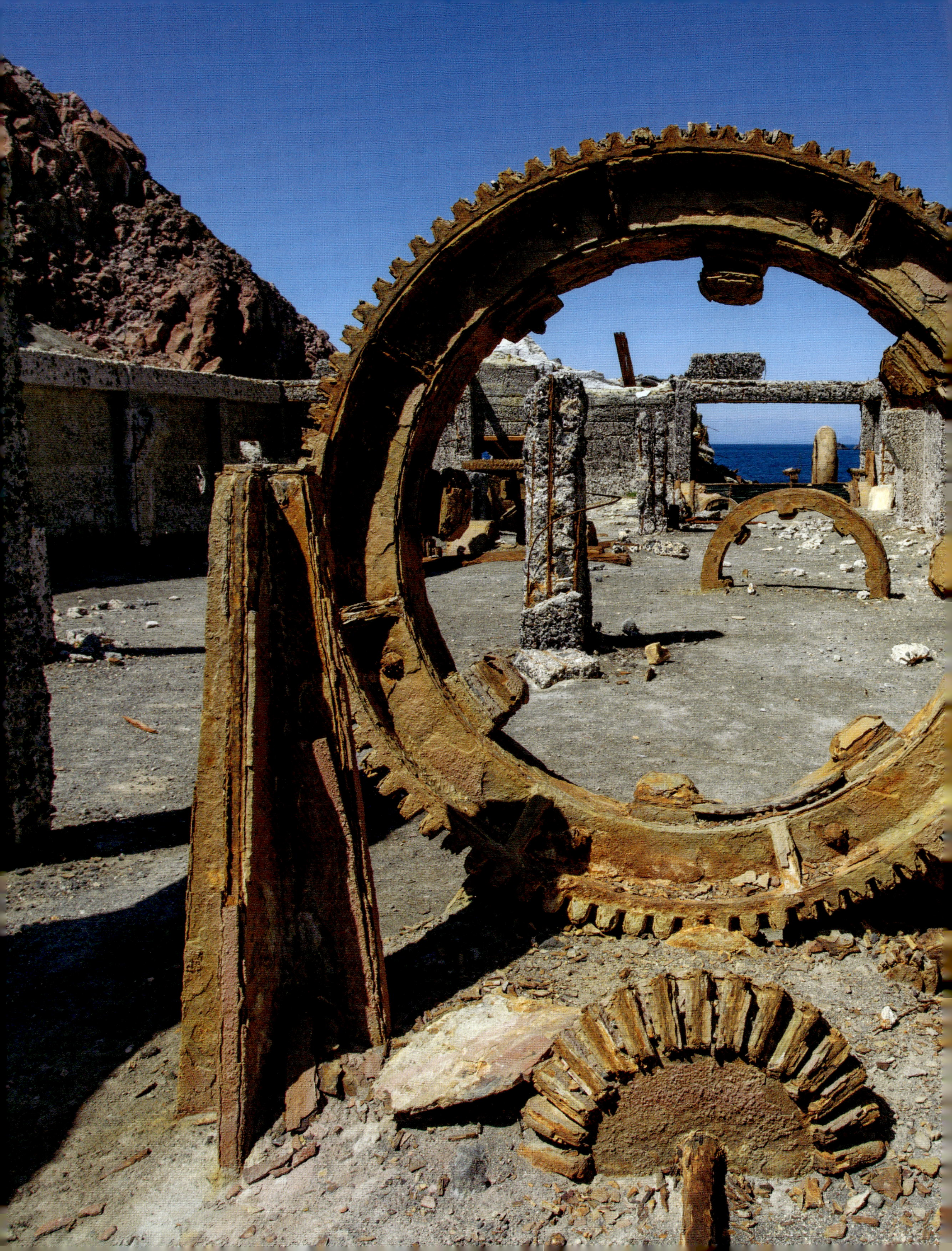

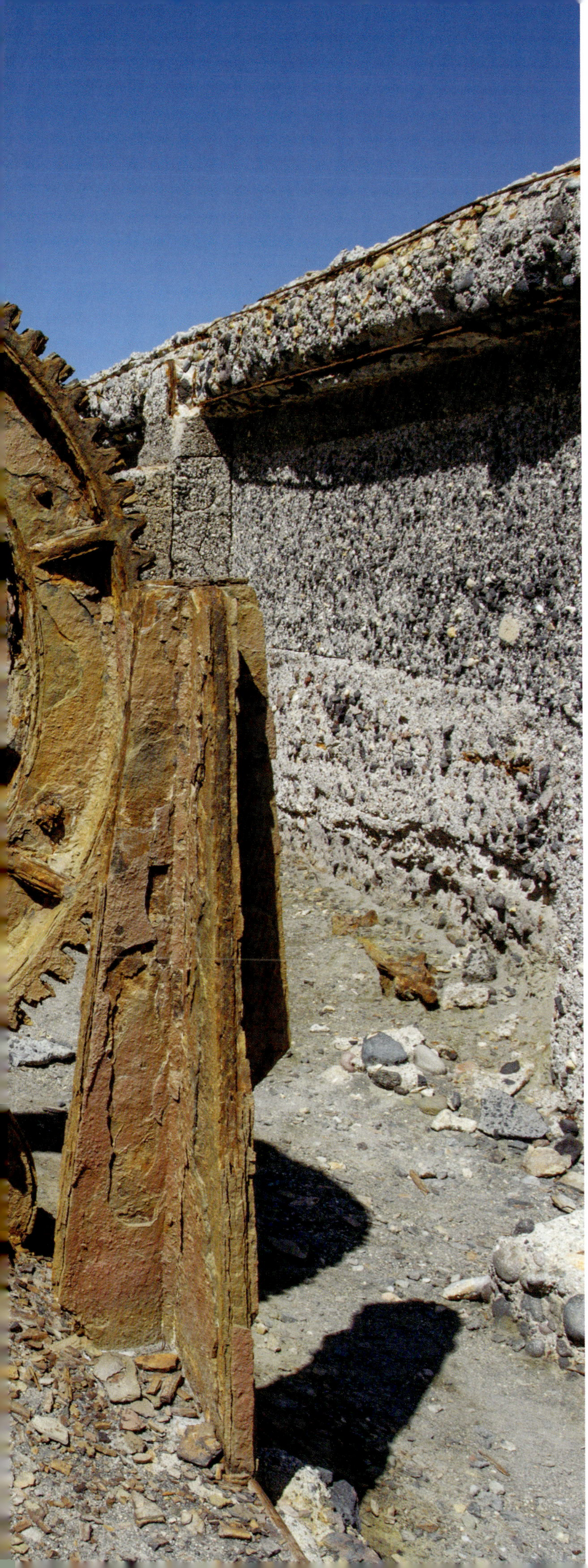

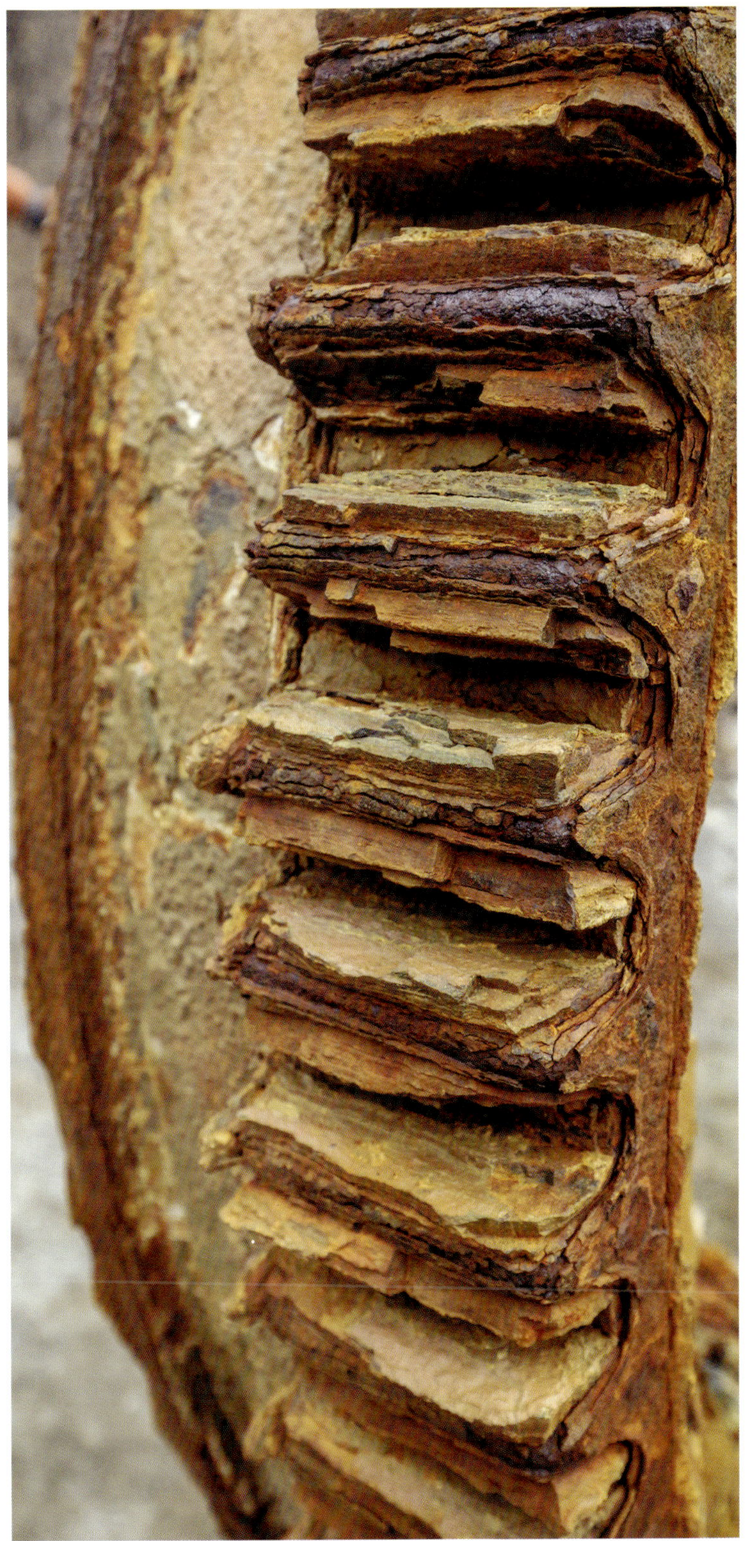

Abandoned Mining Site, White Island/Whakaari, Bay of Plenty, New Zealand
Despite the hazards of mining on an active volcano, sulphur was mined here for almost a century up to 1933. Chemical action has eaten deeply into the abandoned ironwork. The array of relic machinery in the old processing chamber looks almost like an art display. A sudden volcanic eruption in December 2019 resulted in the deaths of at least eight tourists on the island.

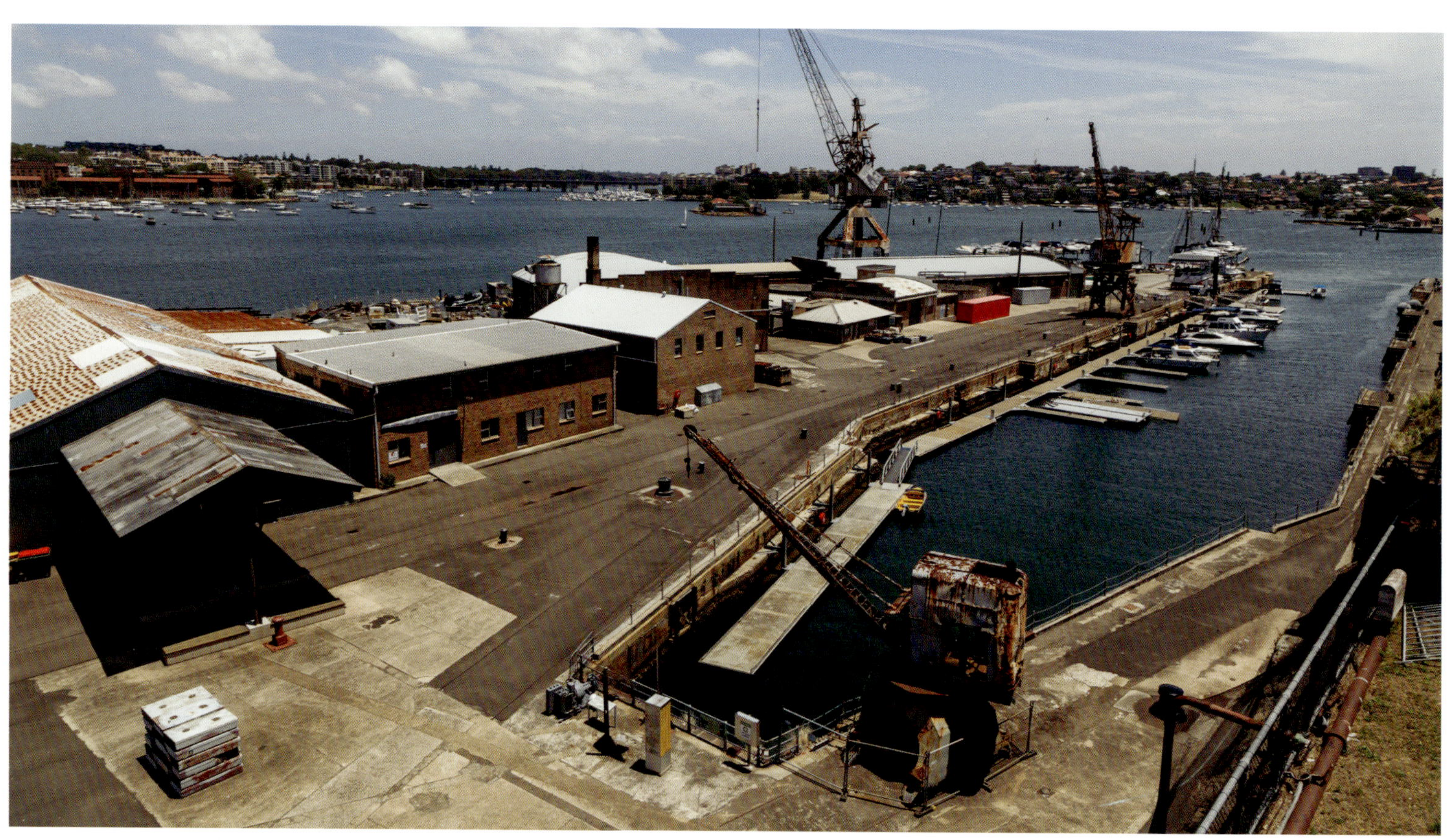

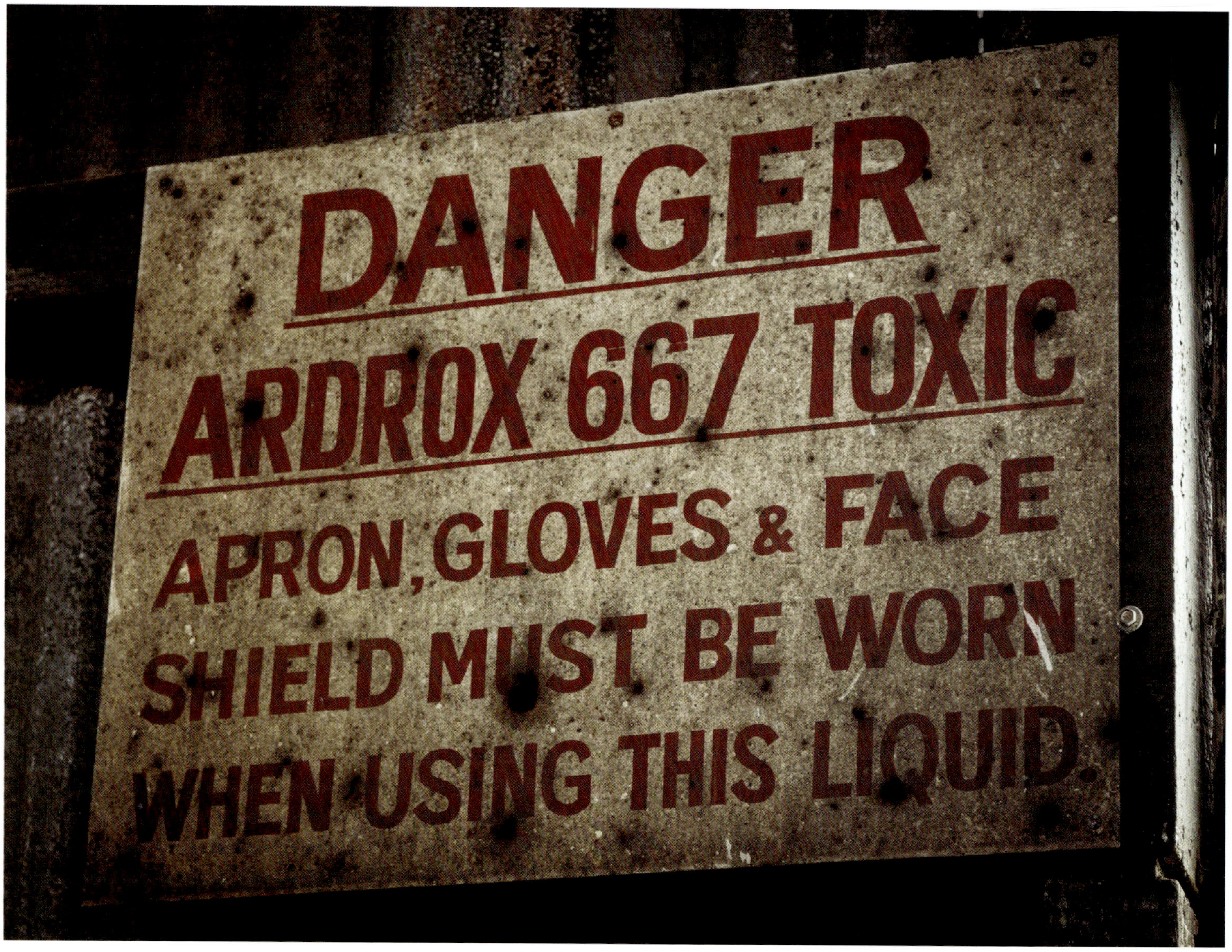

DANGER
ARDROX 667 TOXIC
APRON, GLOVES & FACE
SHIELD MUST BE WORN
WHEN USING THIS LIQUID.

Cockatoo Island Dockyard, Sydney Harbour, Australia
Established in 1857 using convict labour, this was for a long time a naval base and shipyard, extended and adapted over the years. It was decommissioned in 1991 and a campaign begun in 1995 ensured conservation of the site. In 2010 it was added to the UNESCO World Heritage list. Nowadays it is often used as the location for arts and music festivals.

Much of its equipment is of a historic nature, not least its collection of travelling cranes, which date back to the 1890s. Those shown here, including a steam-powered Priestman crane from 1893 (below left), are no longer in working order. The power and pumping house, with its tall brick chimney built in 1918 (below right), still contains the original machinery.

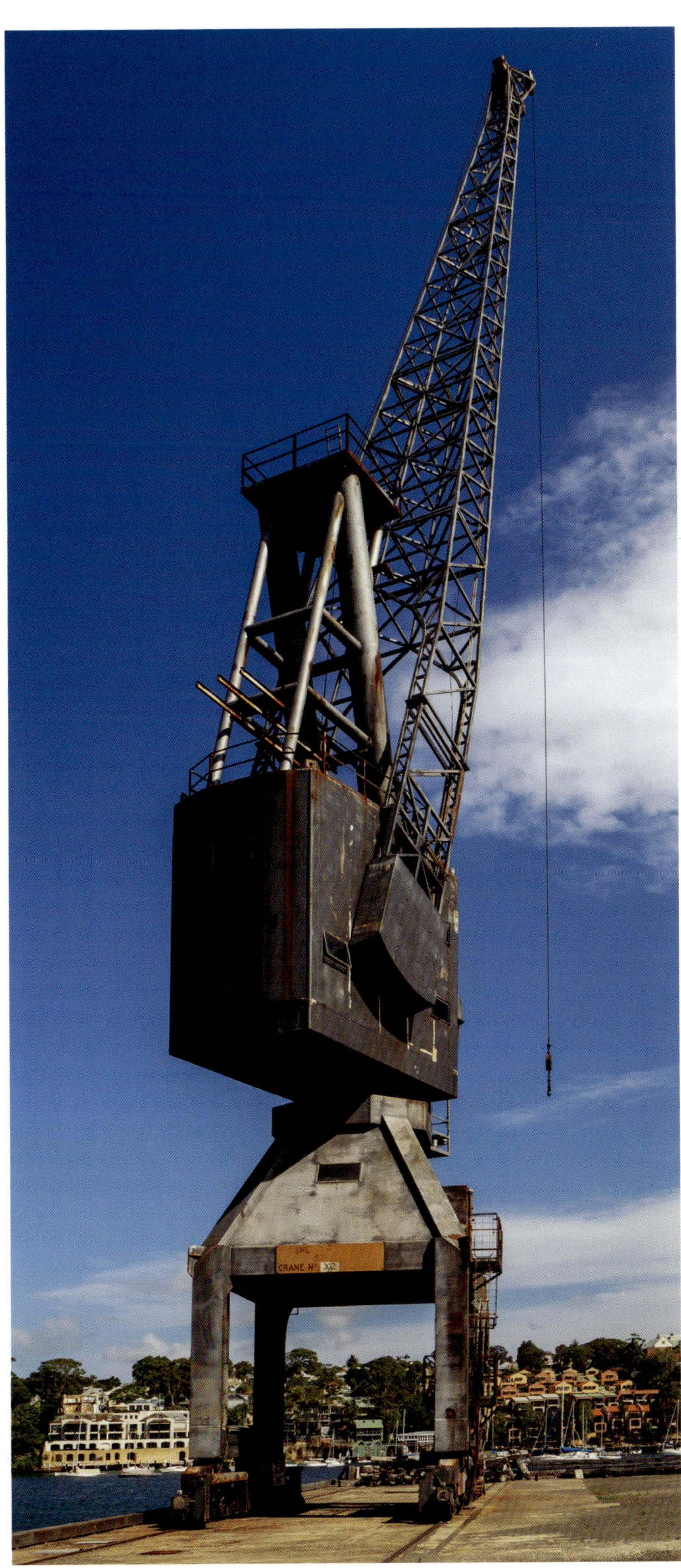

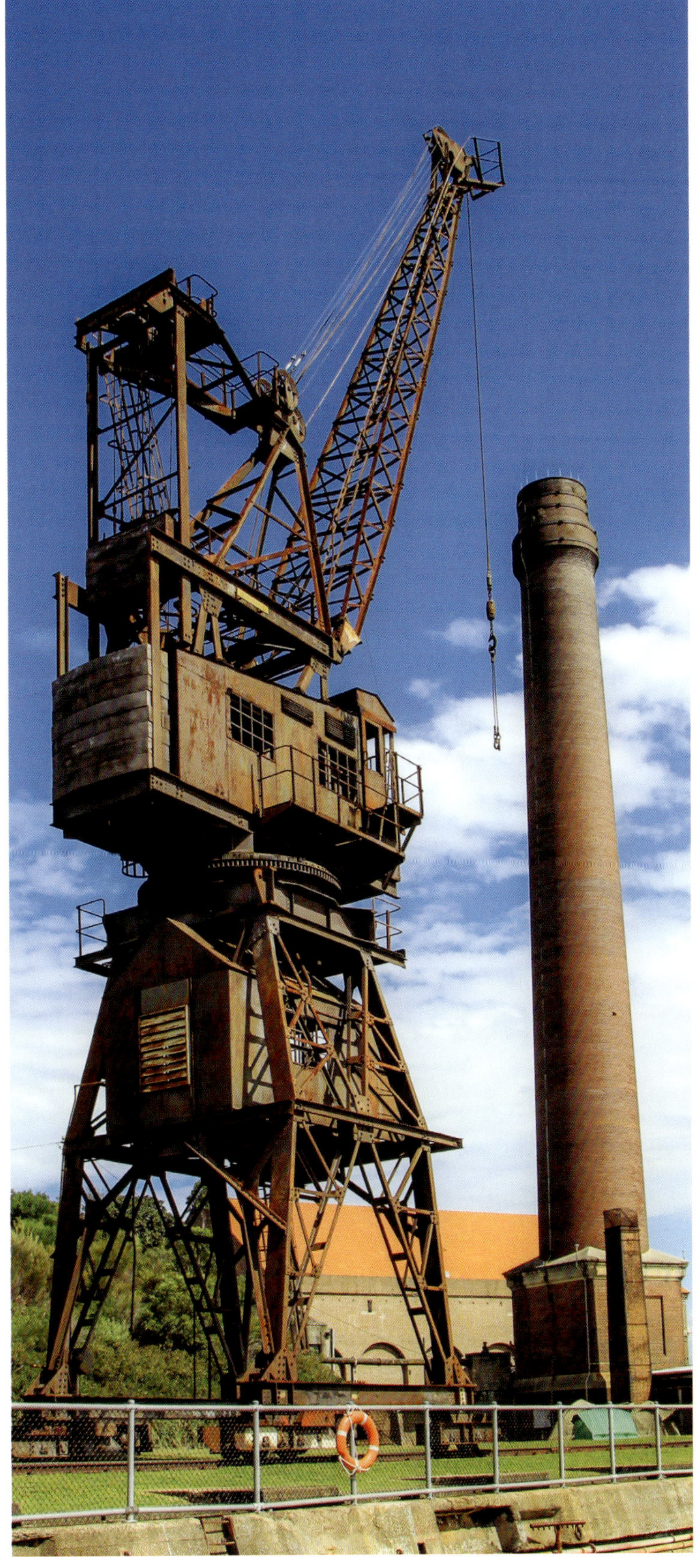

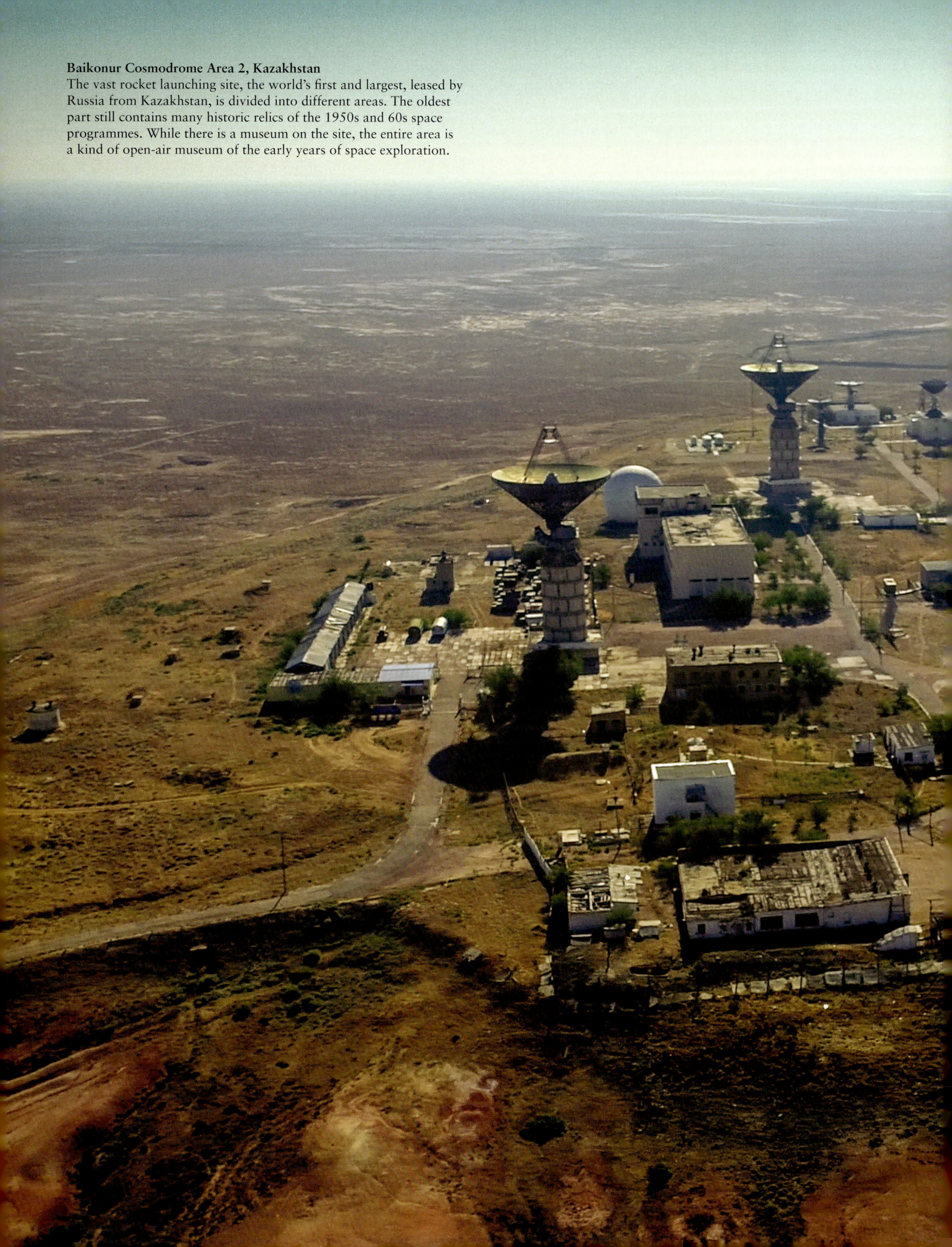

Baikonur Cosmodrome Area 2, Kazakhstan
The vast rocket launching site, the world's first and largest, leased by
Russia from Kazakhstan, is divided into different areas. The oldest
part still contains many historic relics of the 1950s and 60s space
programmes. While there is a museum on the site, the entire area is
a kind of open-air museum of the early years of space exploration.

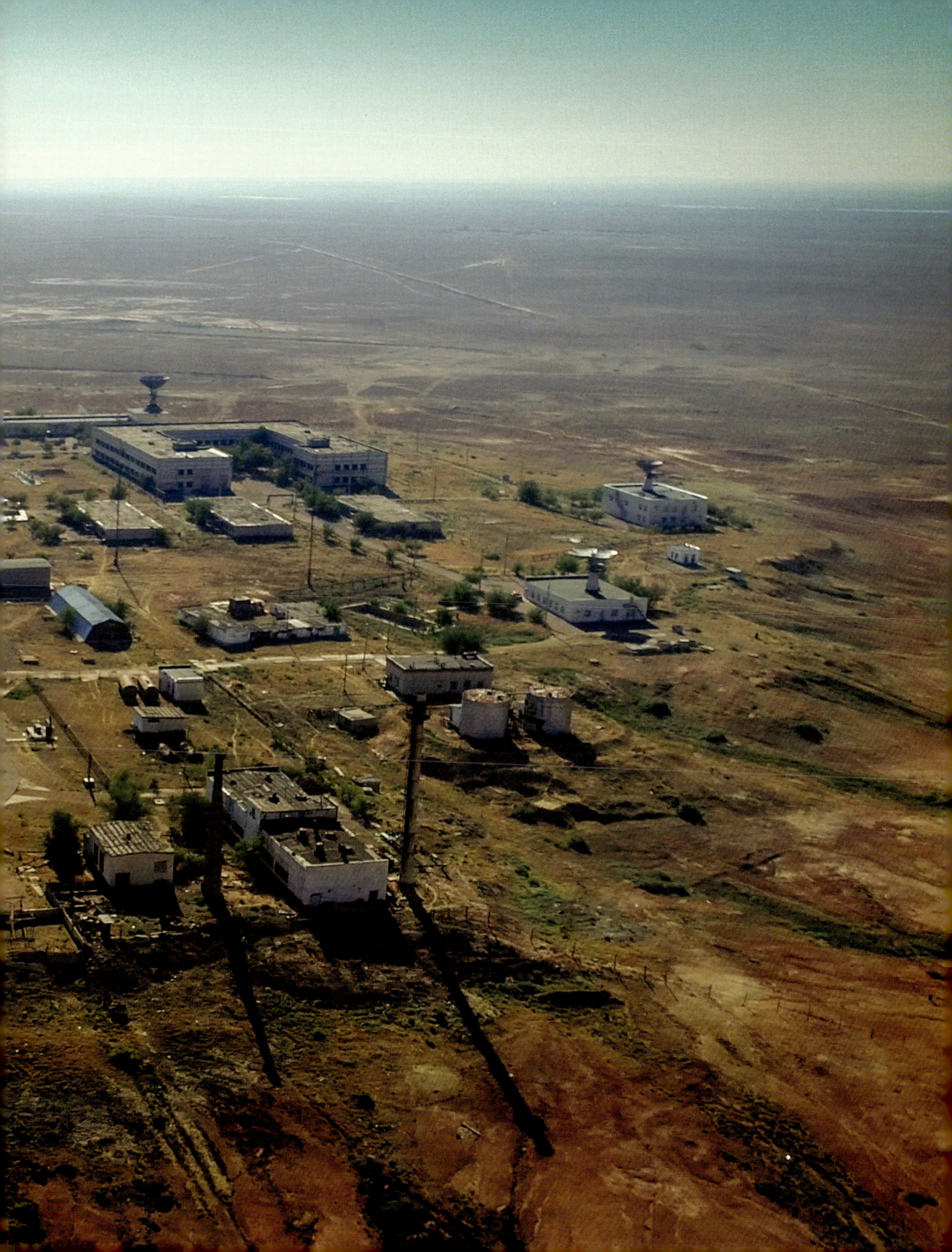

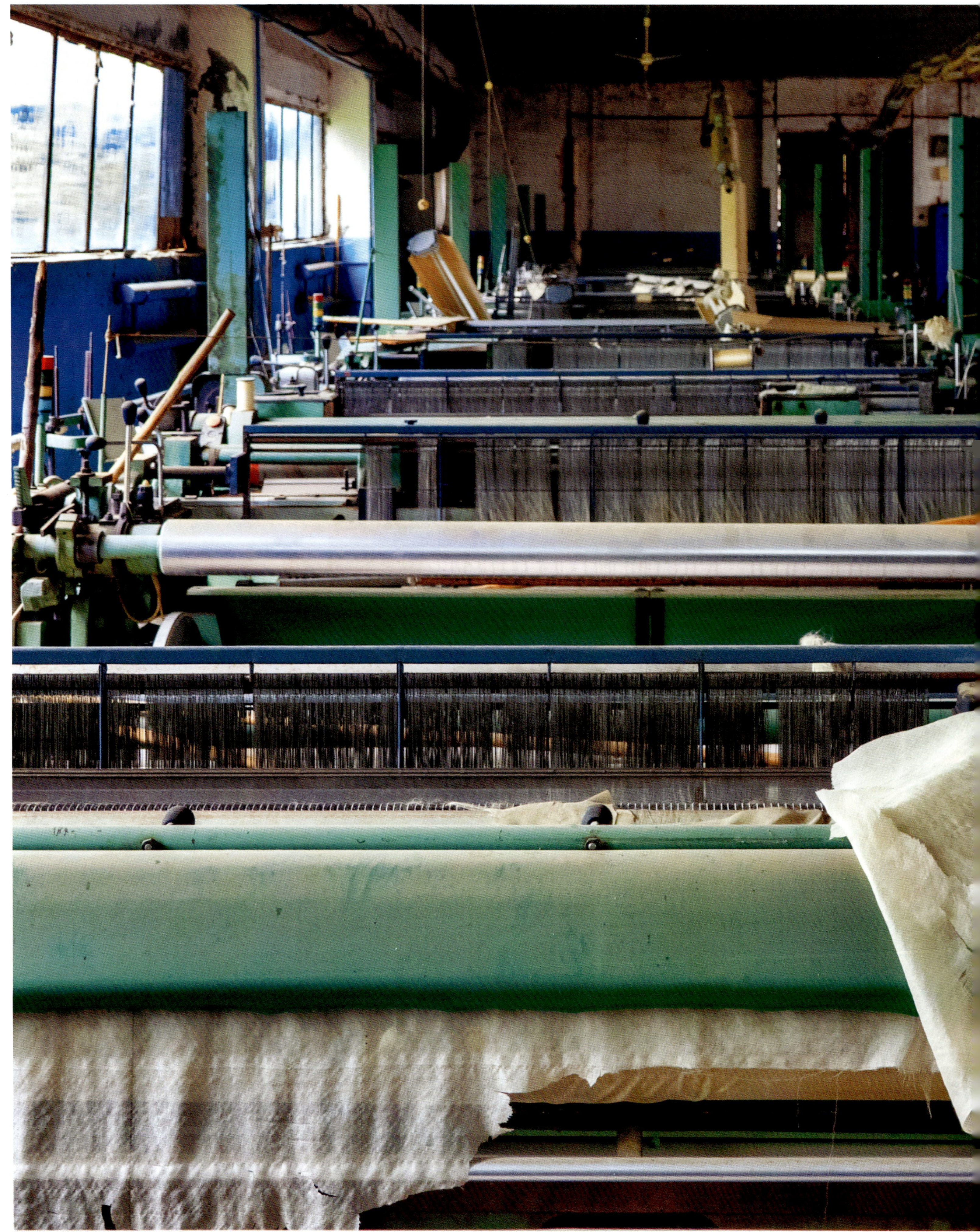

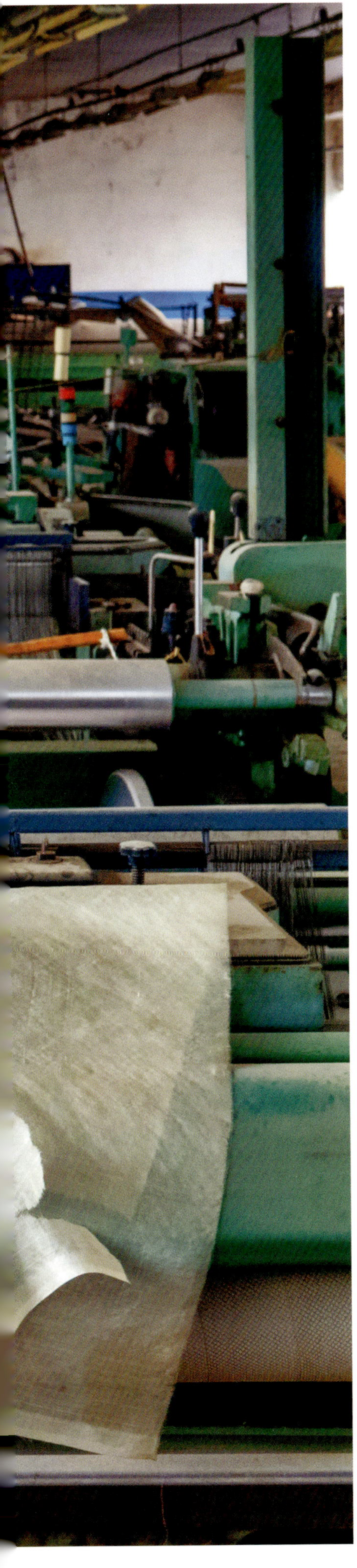

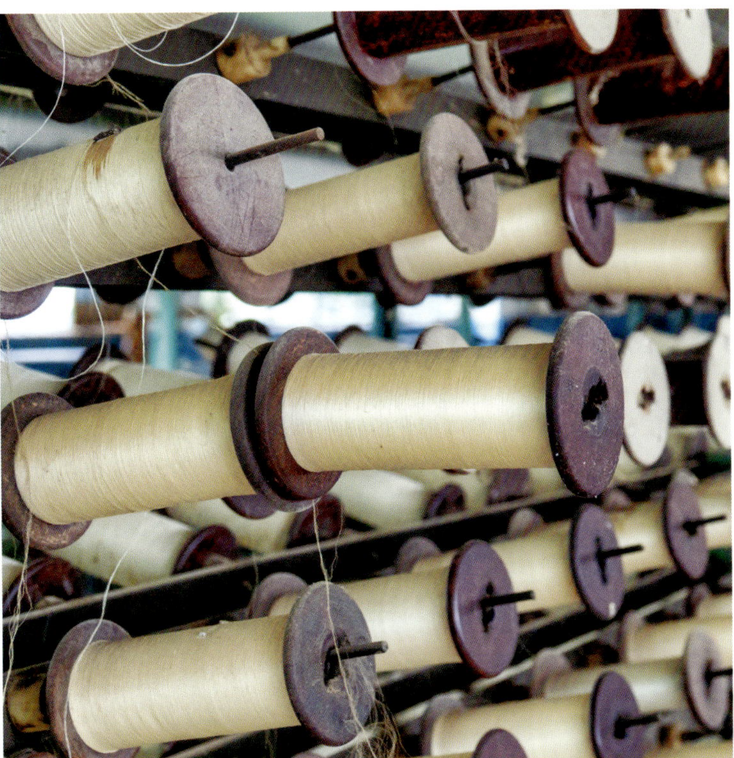

Abandoned Silk Weaving Factory, Basqal, Azerbaijan
Basqal, on the ancient East-West 'Silk Road', has for centuries been a centre of silk weaving. An industrial-scale weaving plant was set up here in the 1960s. It closed in 1997, leaving part-finished silk still on the looms (left and below) and thread still loaded on the bobbins (top right). Its machinery produced a somewhat coarser silk than the fine handmade silk for which Basqal was famous and which is still hand-woven at a small factory nearby.

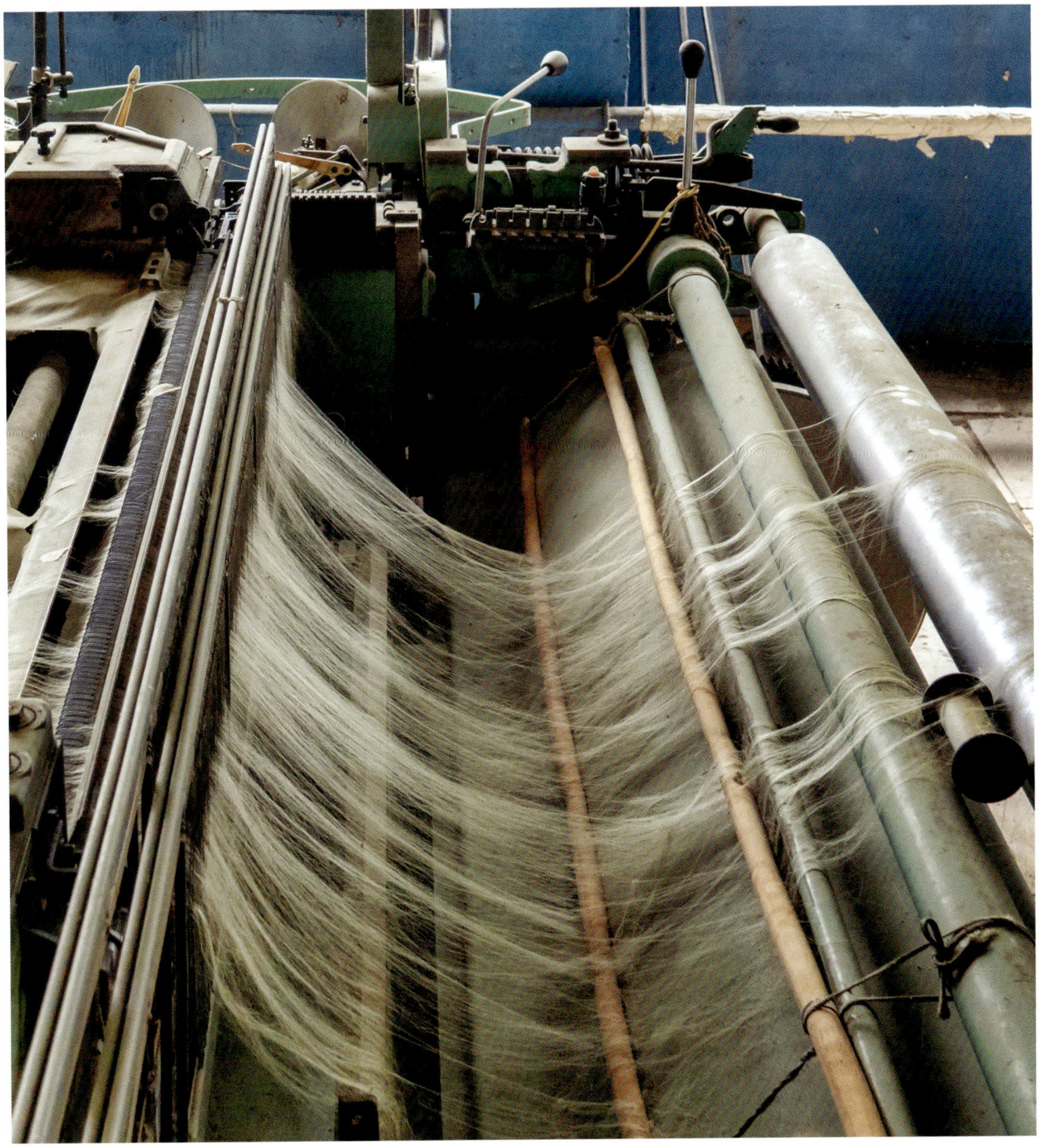

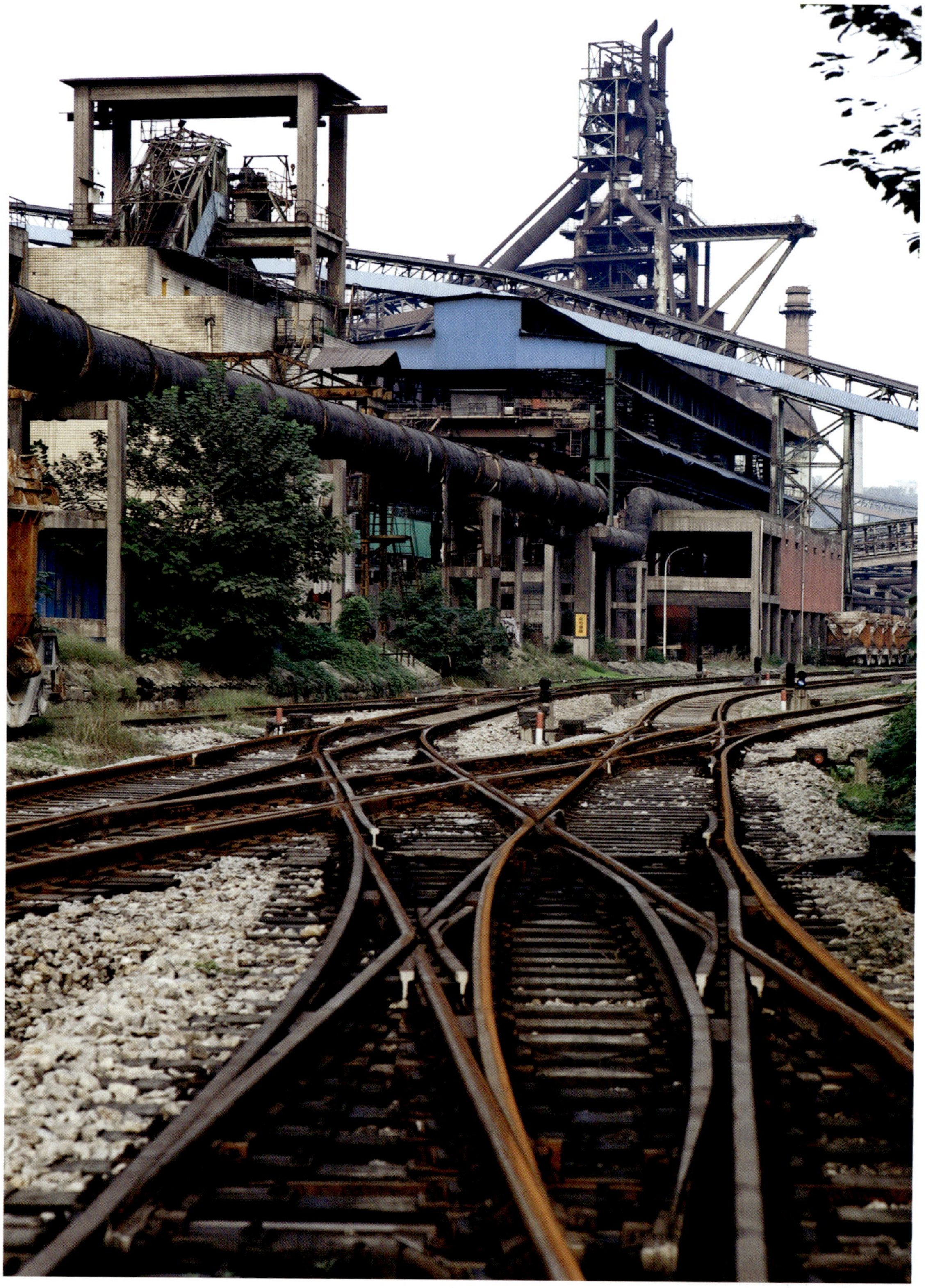

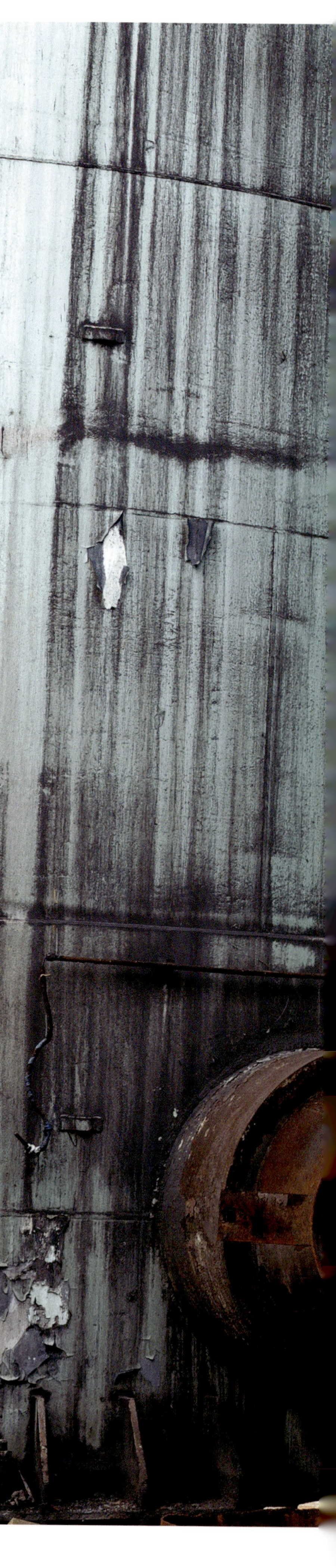

ALL PHOTOGRAPHS ON
THESE PAGES:
**Disused Iron and Steelworks,
Chongqing, China**
Chongqing became China's 'steel city' in 1938 when an entire steelworks was moved here during the Second Japanese-Chinese war. It was in full operation until 1995 when its age and environmental considerations brought closure and transfer of its output to a different site. Part of the works complex has been turned into an industrial museum as part of the Chongqing Industrial Culture Expo Park, opening in 2019.

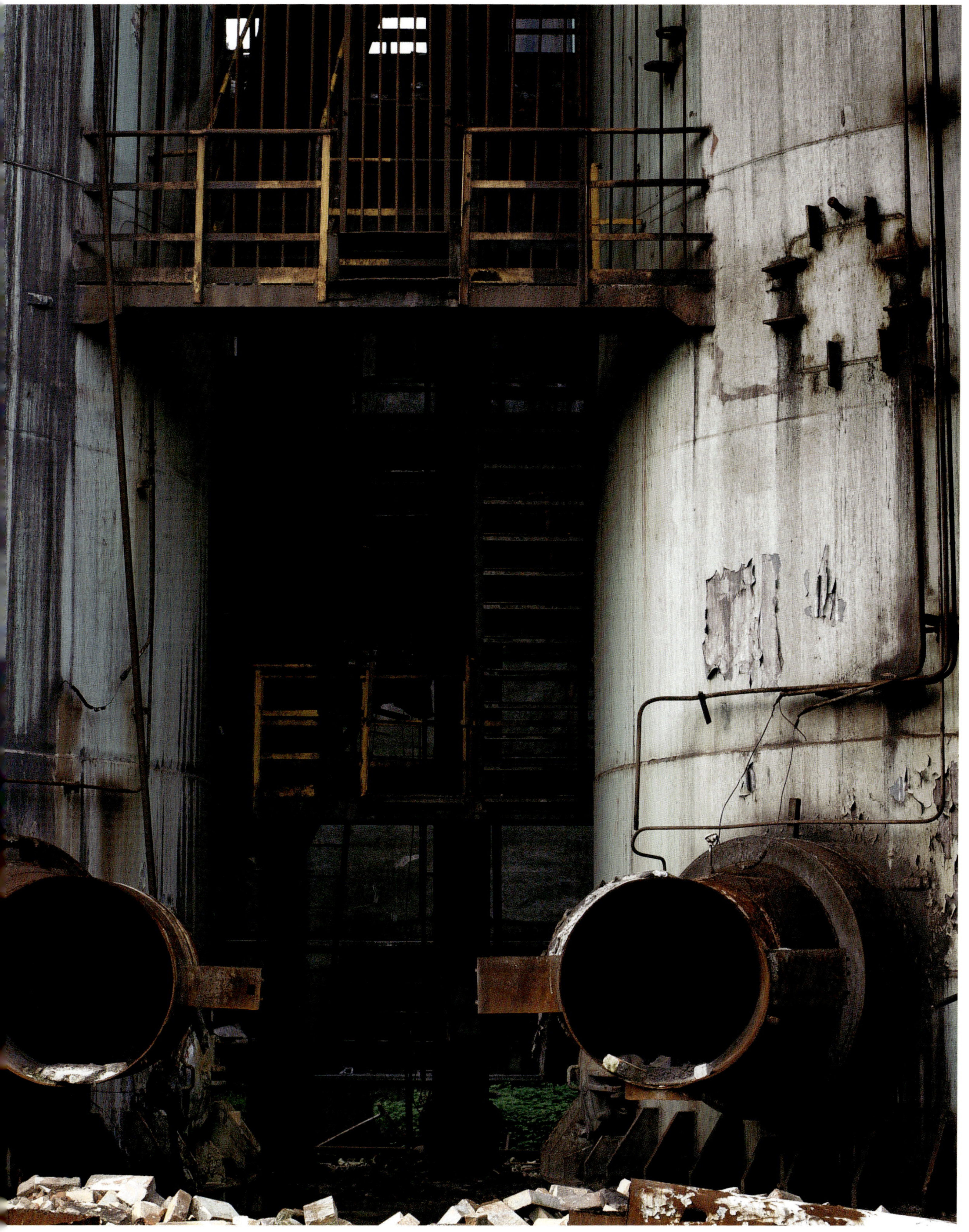

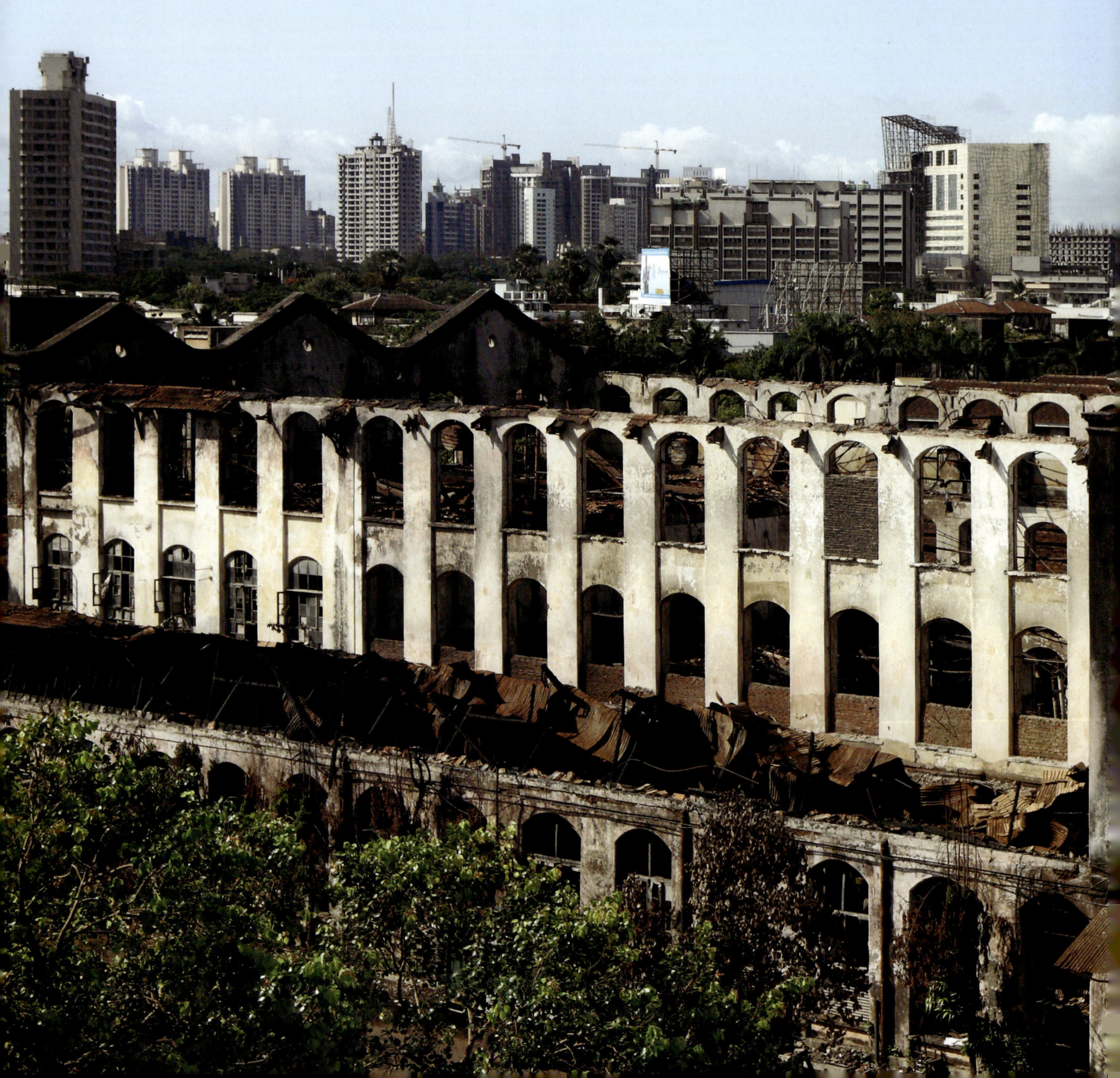

Burnt-out Cotton Mill, Dadar, Mumbai, India
Dadar is a densely-populated area of Mumbai, with industrial and residential buildings packed close together. It was the city's original cotton-milling district and many factories date from the later 19th centuries. The Gold Mohur mill was destroyed by a fire in January 2010, thought to have been caused deliberately.

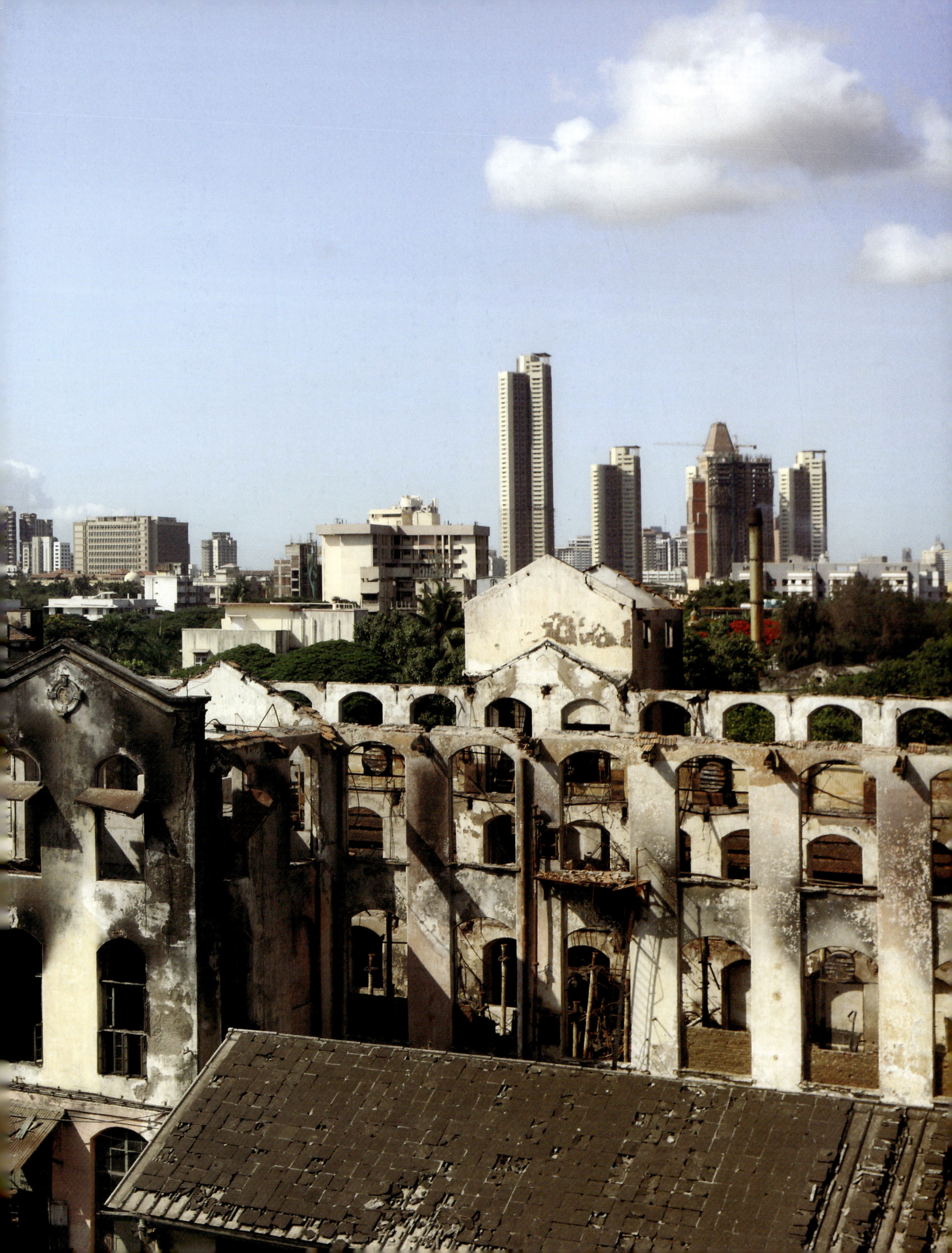

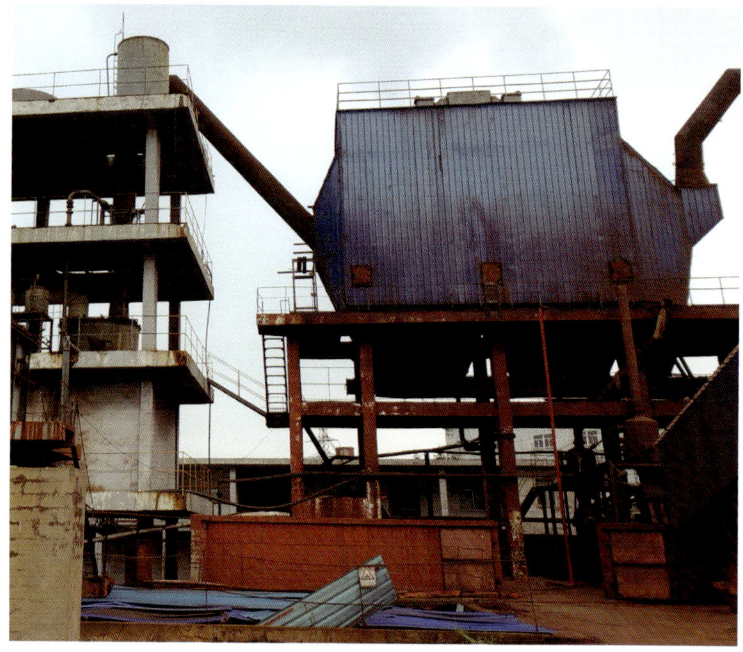

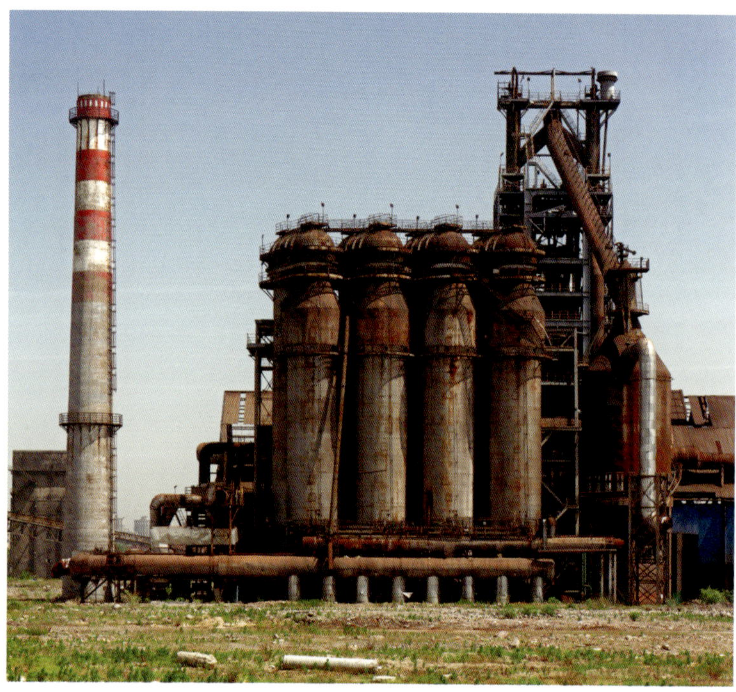

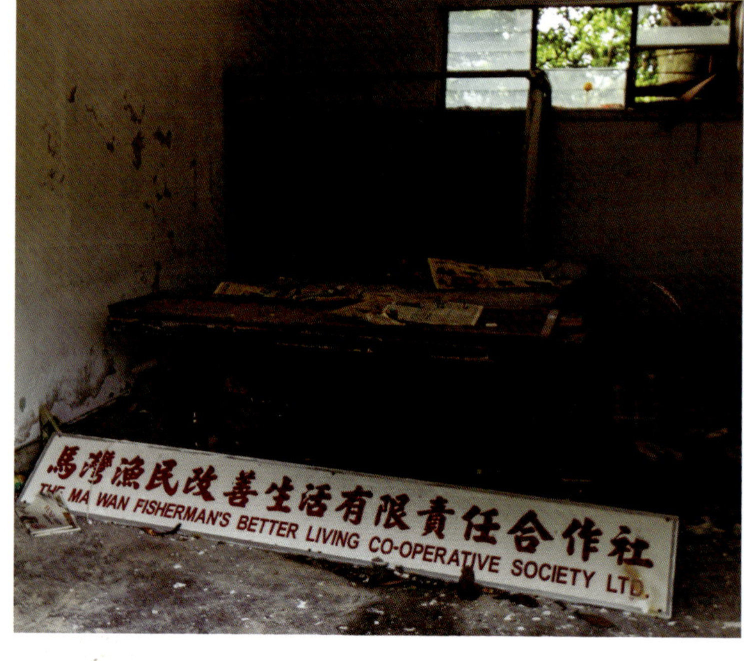
馬灣漁民改善生活有限責任合作社
THE MA WAN FISHERMAN'S BETTER LIVING CO-OPERATIVE SOCIETY LTD.

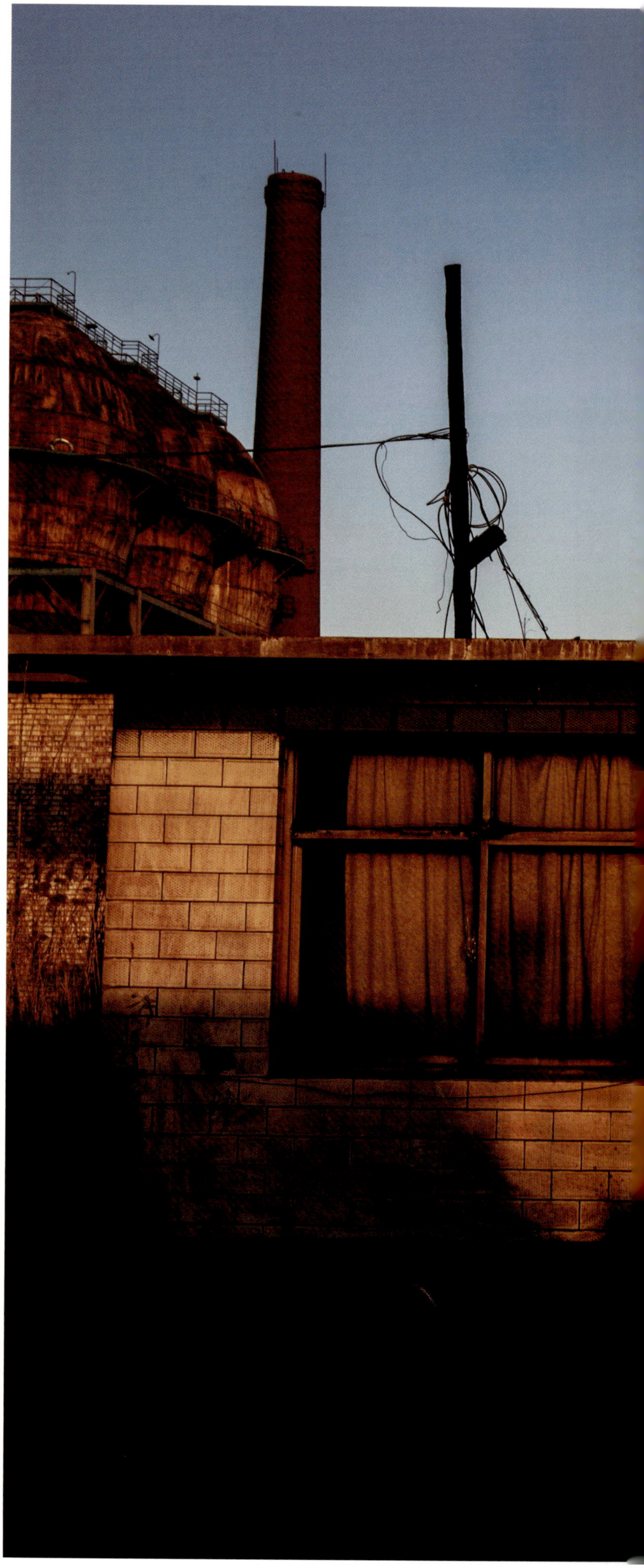

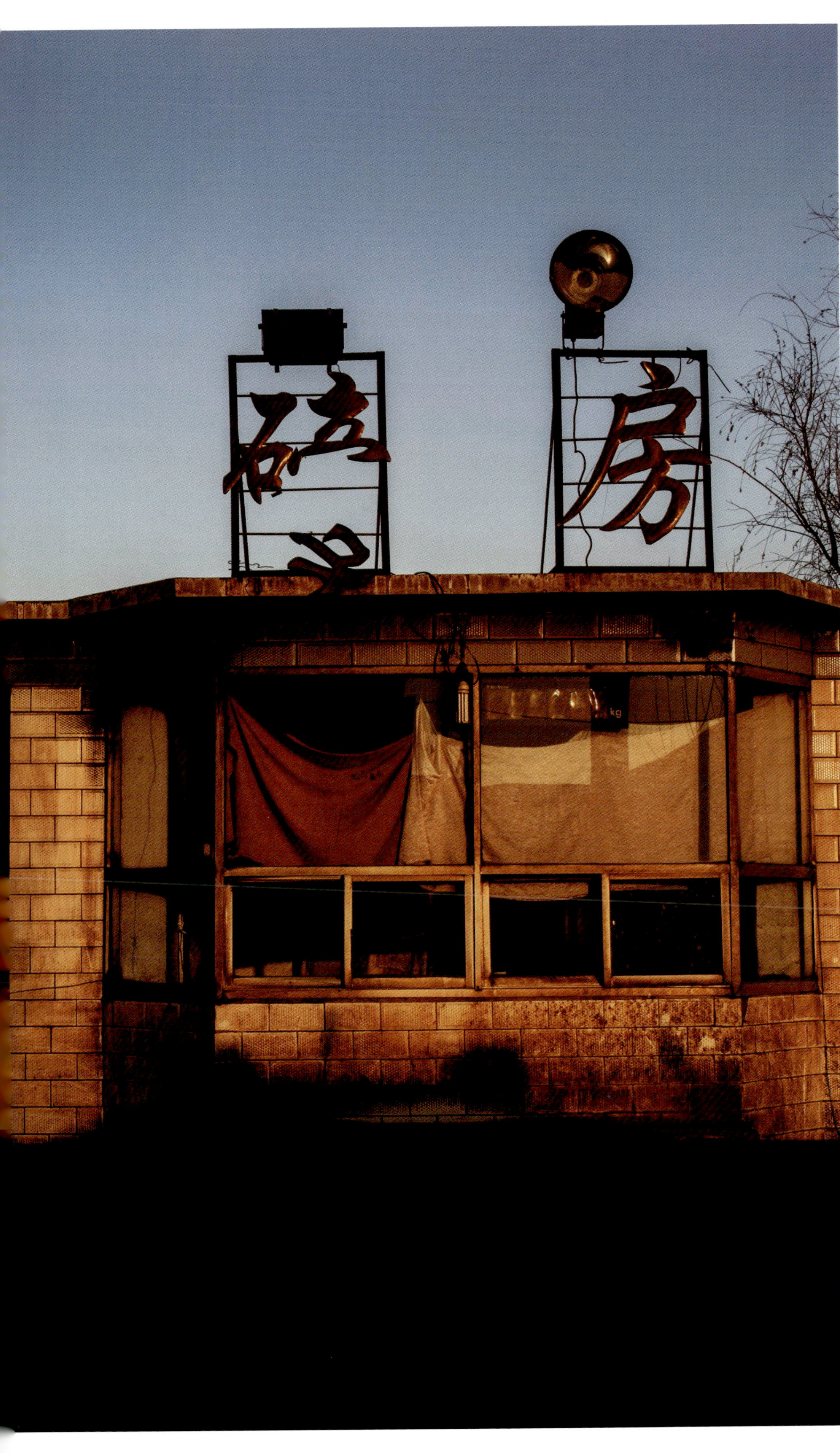

OPPOSITE TOP:

Disused Sulphur Mine, Yuntai Mountain, Henan, China
Yuntai Mountain is a region of spectacular scenery and complex geology on the border of Henan and Shanxi Provinces. It has many attractions for tourists but this abandoned sulphur mine and its processing plant are not on any tour itinerary. Its gate is locked and it appears to be quite abandoned.

OPPOSITE MIDDLE:

Steel Mill, Hangzhou, Zhejiang Province, China
Retorts and furnaces stand unused at this steel plant: another industrial site closed down (and demolished since this pre-2017 photograph was taken) in China's drive to improve the efficiency of its steel industry and cut down atmospheric pollution.

OPPOSITE BOTTOM:

Derelict Office Building, Ma Wan Island, Hong Kong, China
The old village on Ma Wan Island houses a much-reduced fishing industry. Shrimping and shrimp-paste making have almost died out due to a trawling ban. The bravely-named fishermen's co-operative appears to be a victim of the situation.

LEFT:

Weigh House, Qingquang Steelworks, Tangshan, China
There has been no steel output to weigh at Qingquang since 2014. Over-production and concern about air pollution have led to the closure of numerous older and less efficient steelworks in China.

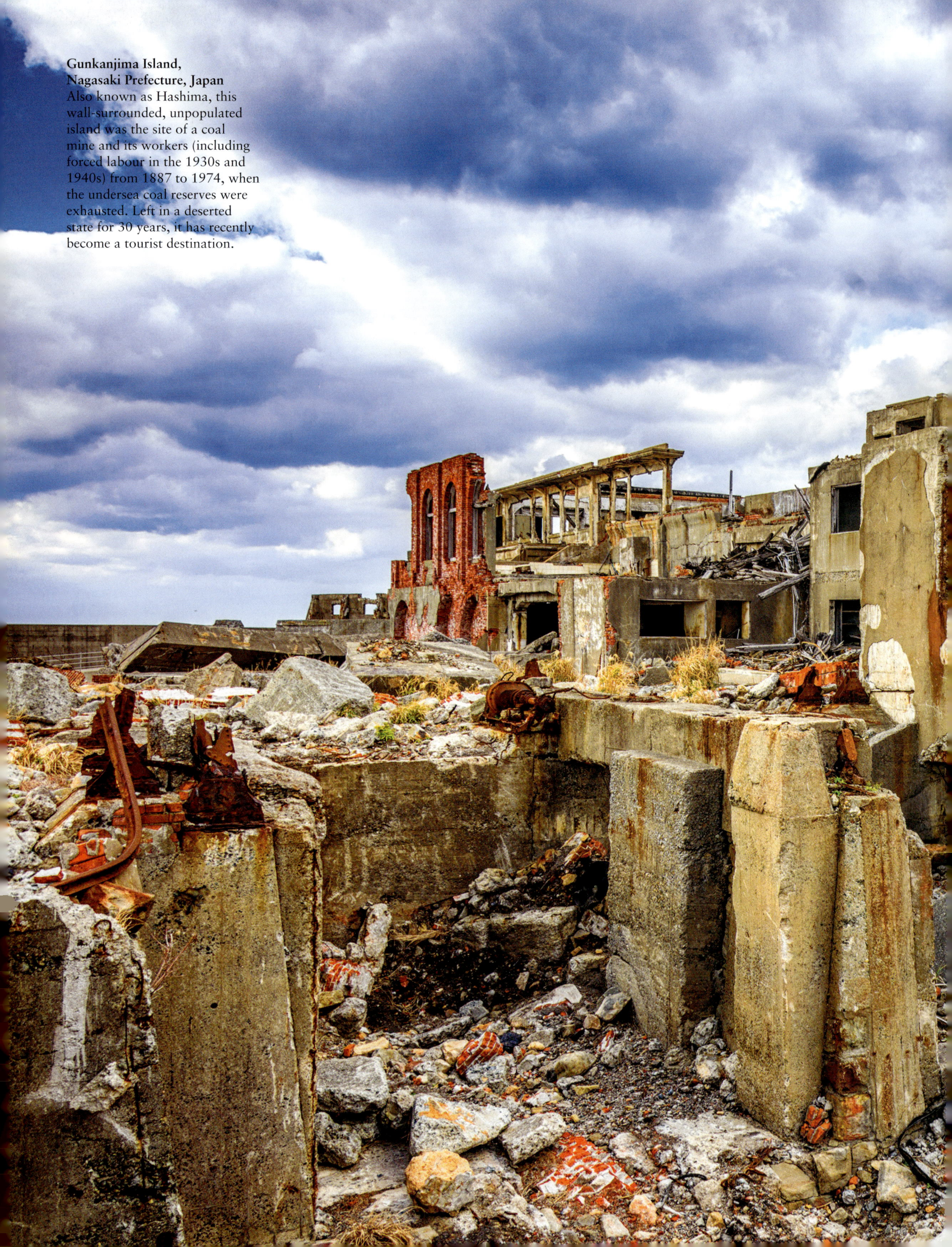

**Gunkanjima Island,
Nagasaki Prefecture, Japan**
Also known as Hashima, this
wall-surrounded, unpopulated
island was the site of a coal
mine and its workers (including
forced labour in the 1930s and
1940s) from 1887 to 1974, when
the undersea coal reserves were
exhausted. Left in a deserted
state for 30 years, it has recently
become a tourist destination.

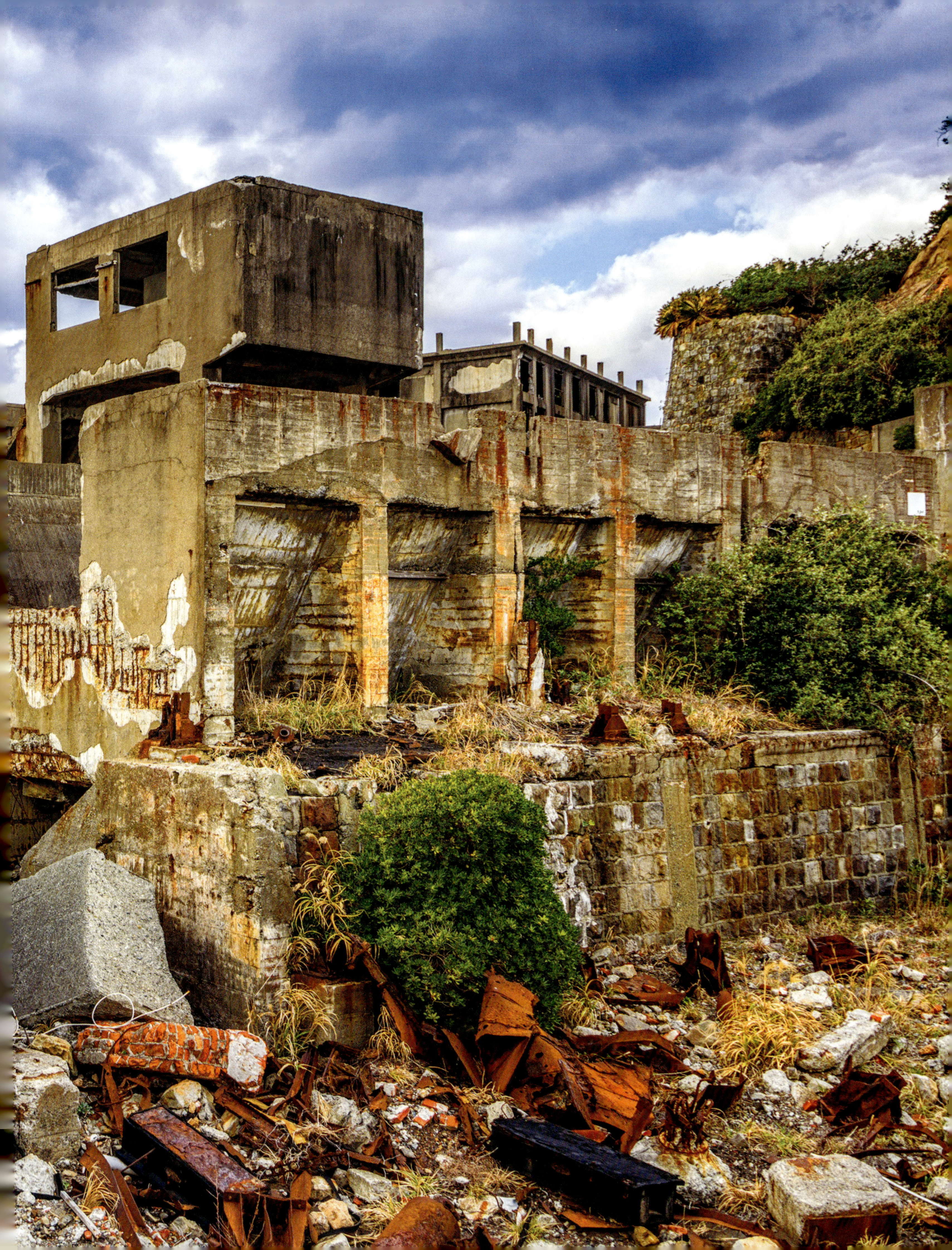

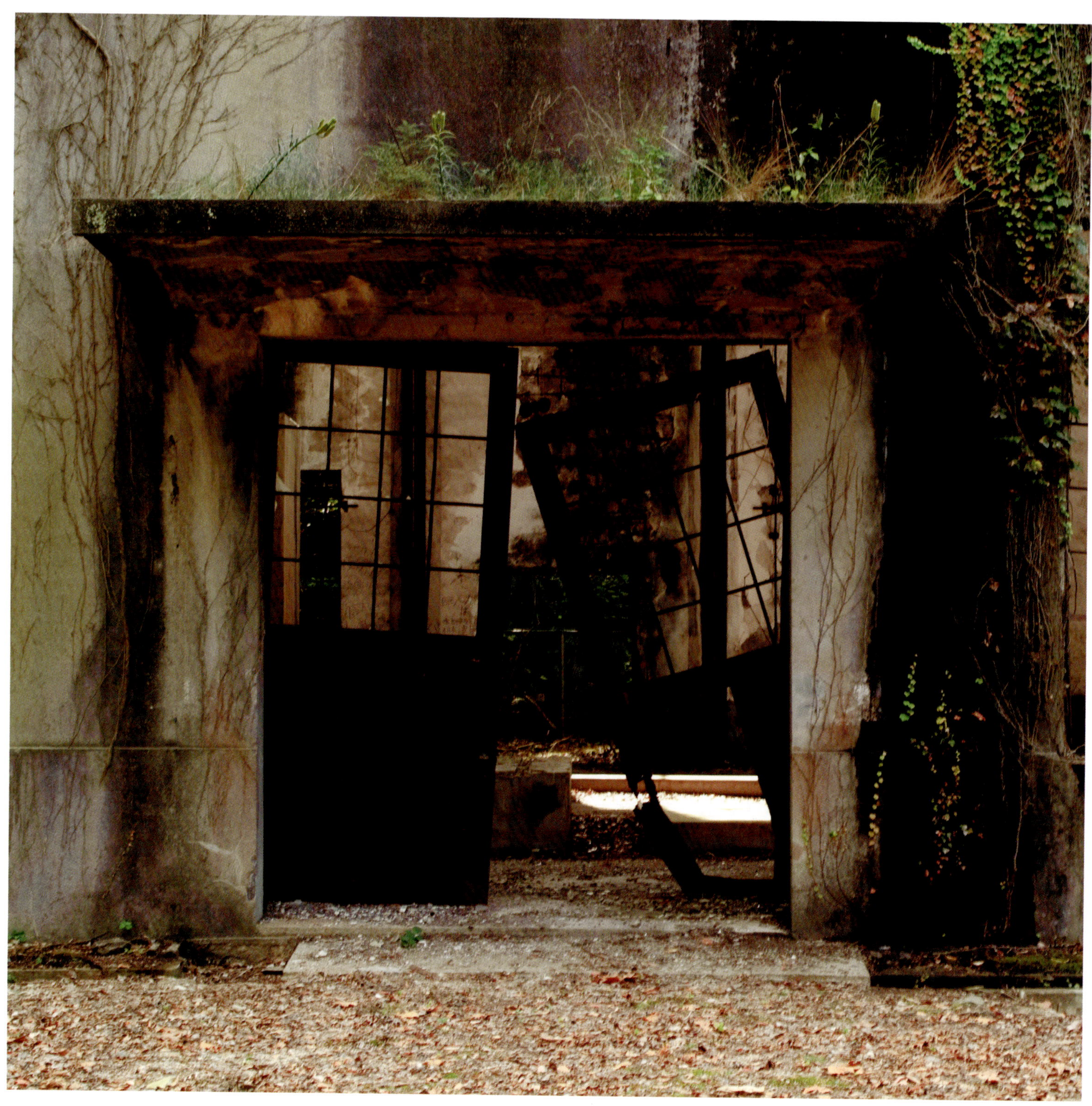

Abandoned Military Factory, Okunoshima Island, Seto Inland Sea, Japan
Now known as 'Rabbit Island' because of its large rabbit population, Okunoshima became notorious for its secret factories producing poison gas and other chemical weapons before and during World War II. They have long since been stripped and left derelict. A small museum tells their story.

Disconnected Oil Well Head, Gobustan, Azerbaijan
Oil extraction in Azerbaijan has largely moved to the Caspian Sea, and the sites of abandoned wells are common in the Gobustan region. The numerous bolts are necessary to prevent the escape of residual liquid or gases from the well.

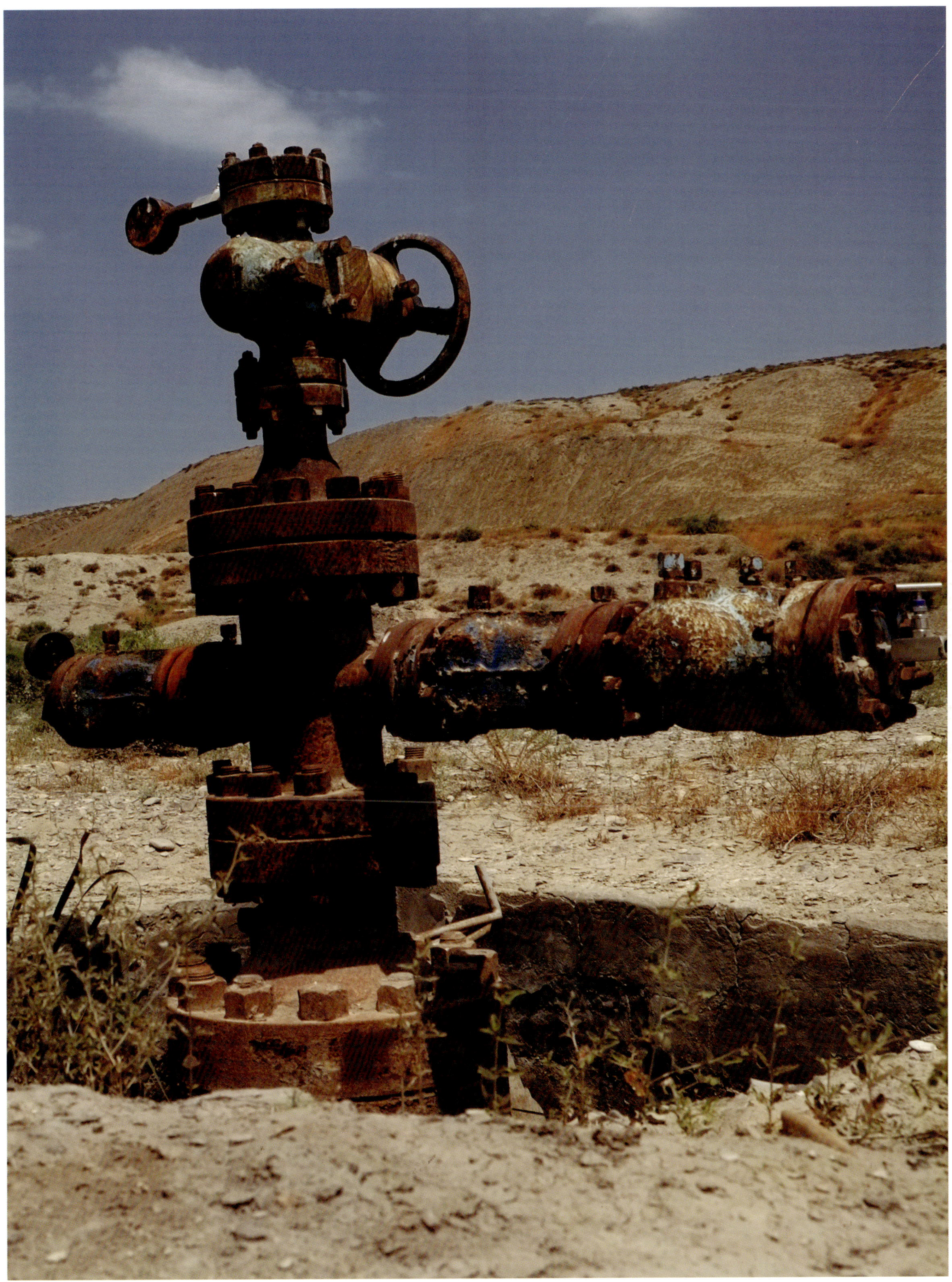

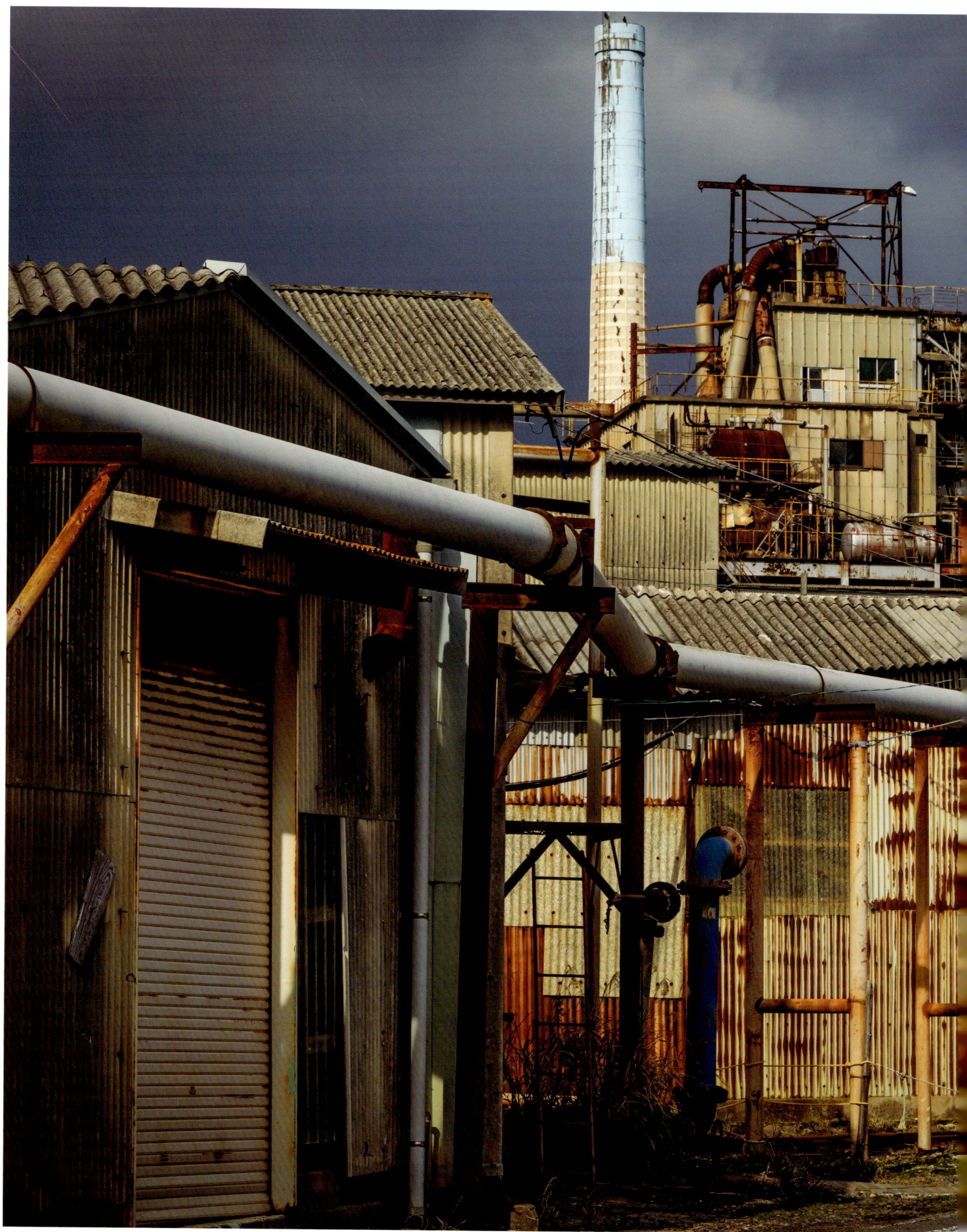

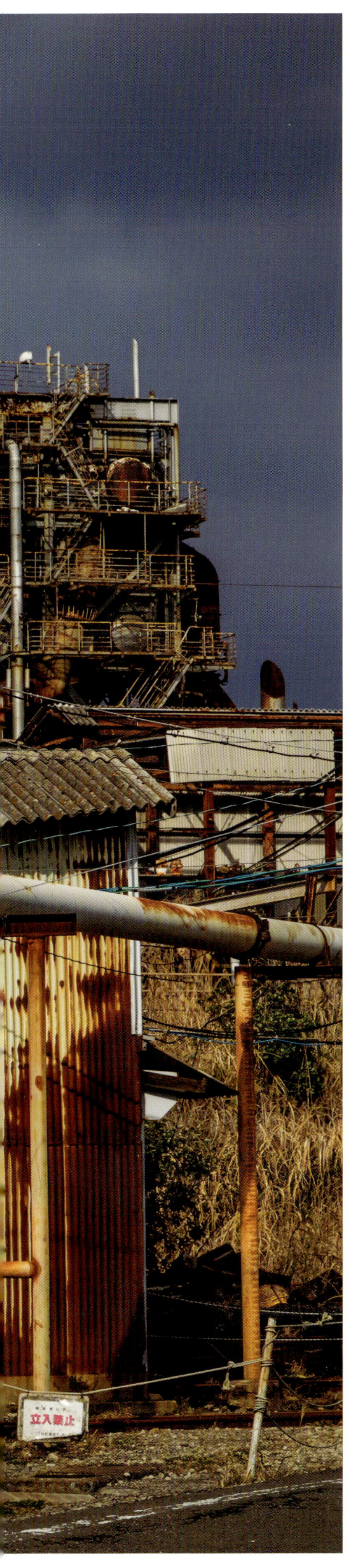

LEFT AND BELOW:
**Ikeshima Island,
Nagasaki Province, Japan**
Situated above the same undersea
coalfield as Gunkanjima,
Ikeshima Island's mine was
worked from 1959 to 2001.
Once packed with 8000
residents, it now has 300 who
guide visitors round the still-
standing complex, which
included a desalination plant
and a power station generating
electricity from coal dust.

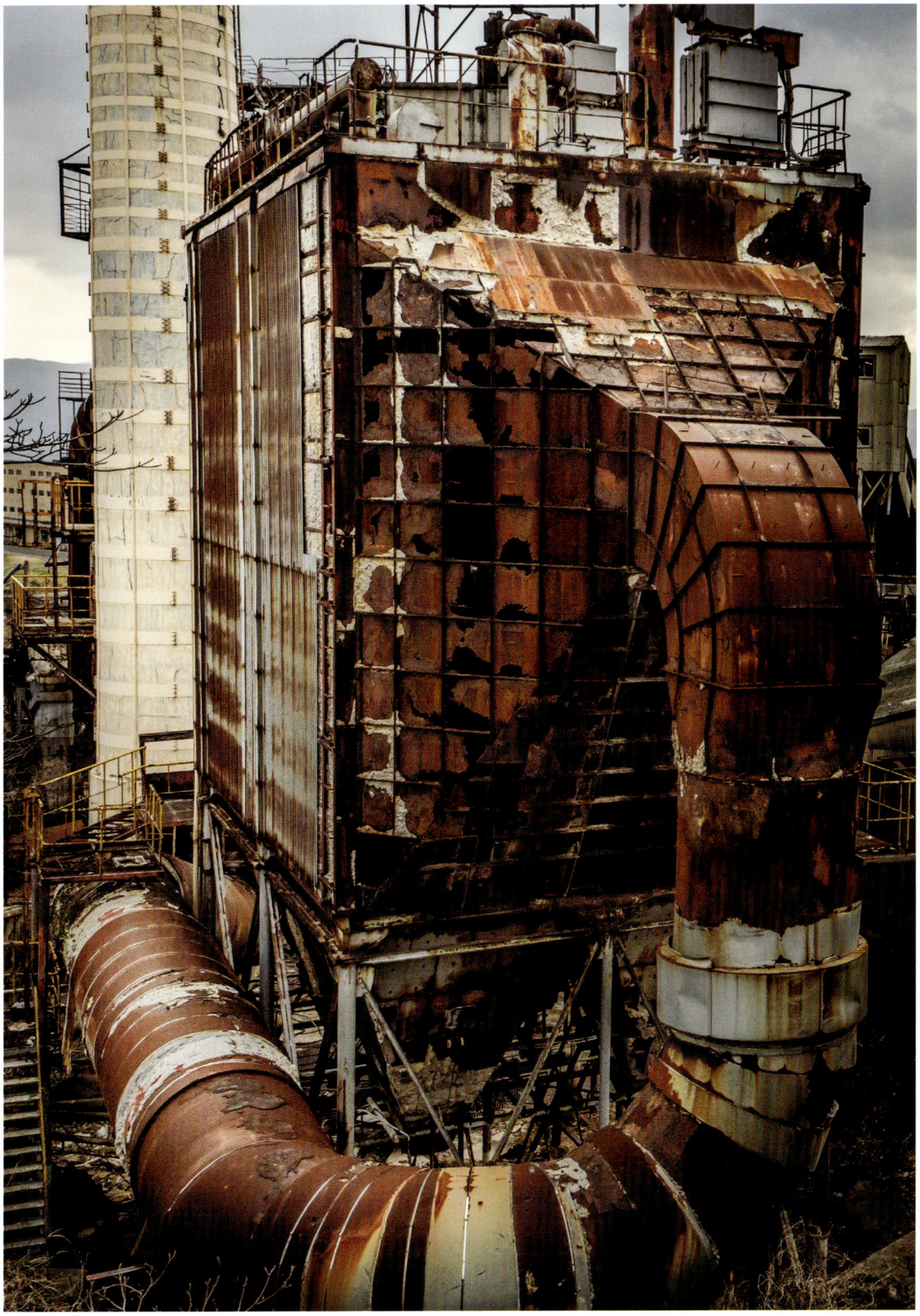

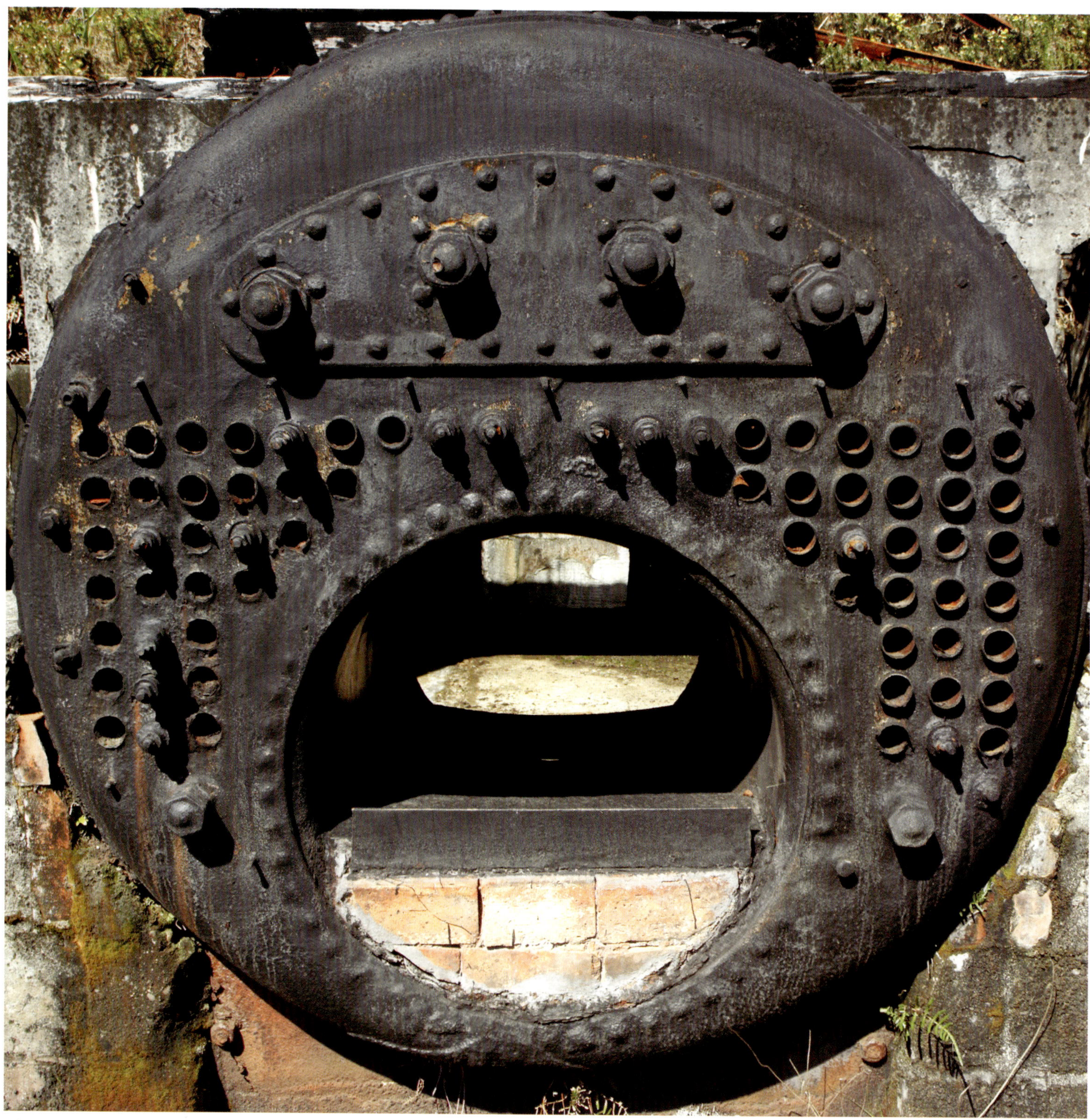

Abandoned Coal Mine, Millerton, South Island, New Zealand
An old boiler shows its firebox hole and the ends of the heating tubes. It is mounted just outside the miners' bath-house. The district is rich in industrial relics, including a rope-worked incline. The mine ceased production in the late 1960s.

OPPOSITE TOP LEFT:

Endeans Mill, Wimiha, Ongarue, North Island, New Zealand
New Zealand's oldest steam timber mill was closed down as a working sawmill in 1996 and is now an industrial museum. The power saws for cutting planks were driven by steam. Alongside, the workers' houses form a ghost town.

OPPOSITE TOP RIGHT:

Derelict Freezing Factory, Patea, North Island, New Zealand
Patea was the meat and cheese processing and export centre for a wide area. The meat canning and freezing works opened in 1883, was shut down in the 1980s, and demolished in 2010.

OPPOSITE BOTTOM:

Former Ice Cream Factory, Coal Creek, Greymouth, South Island, New Zealand
Ice cream making in New Zealand began with small family-run enterprises in the early 20th century. This was the home of Sunshine Ice Cream, taken over and used as a store in the 1930s by the larger Westland Snowflake company.

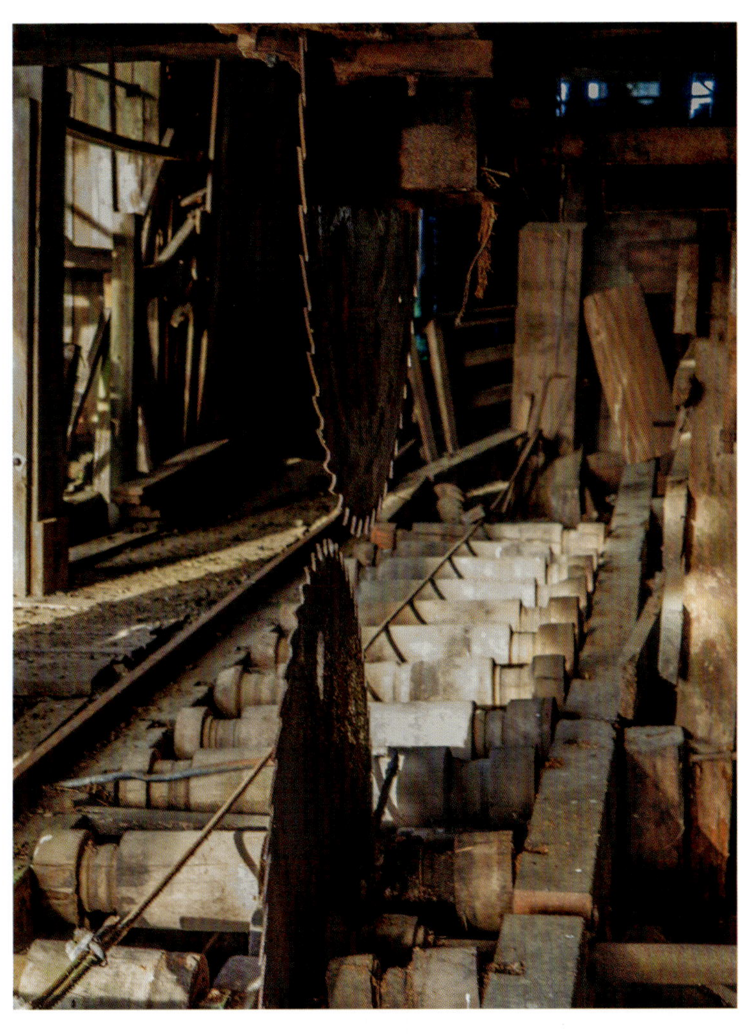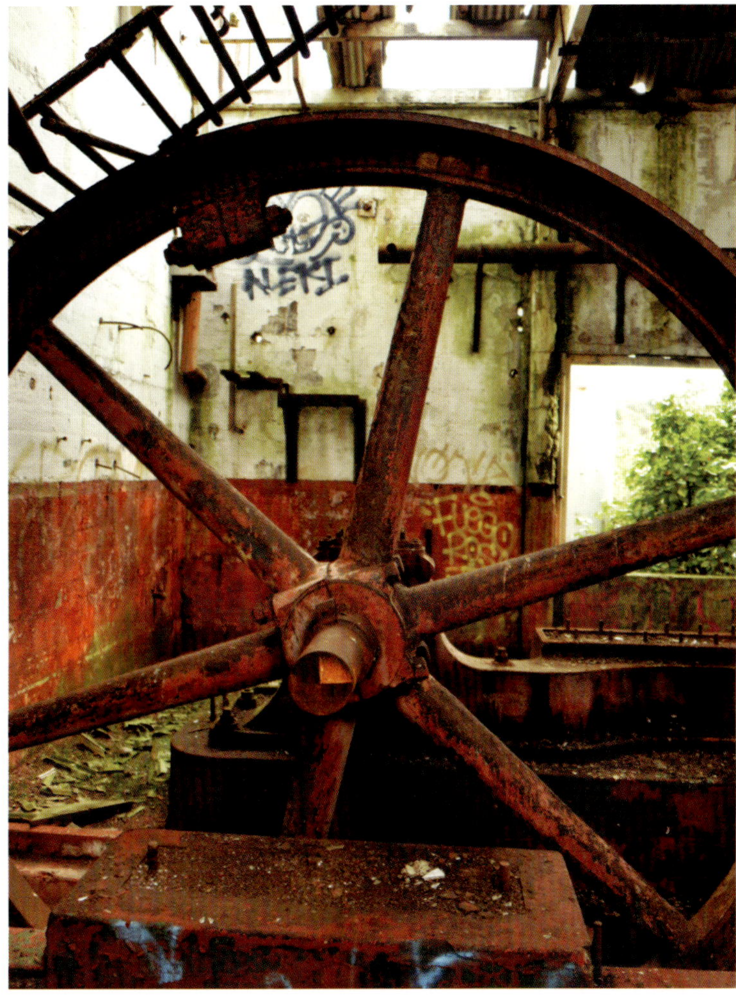

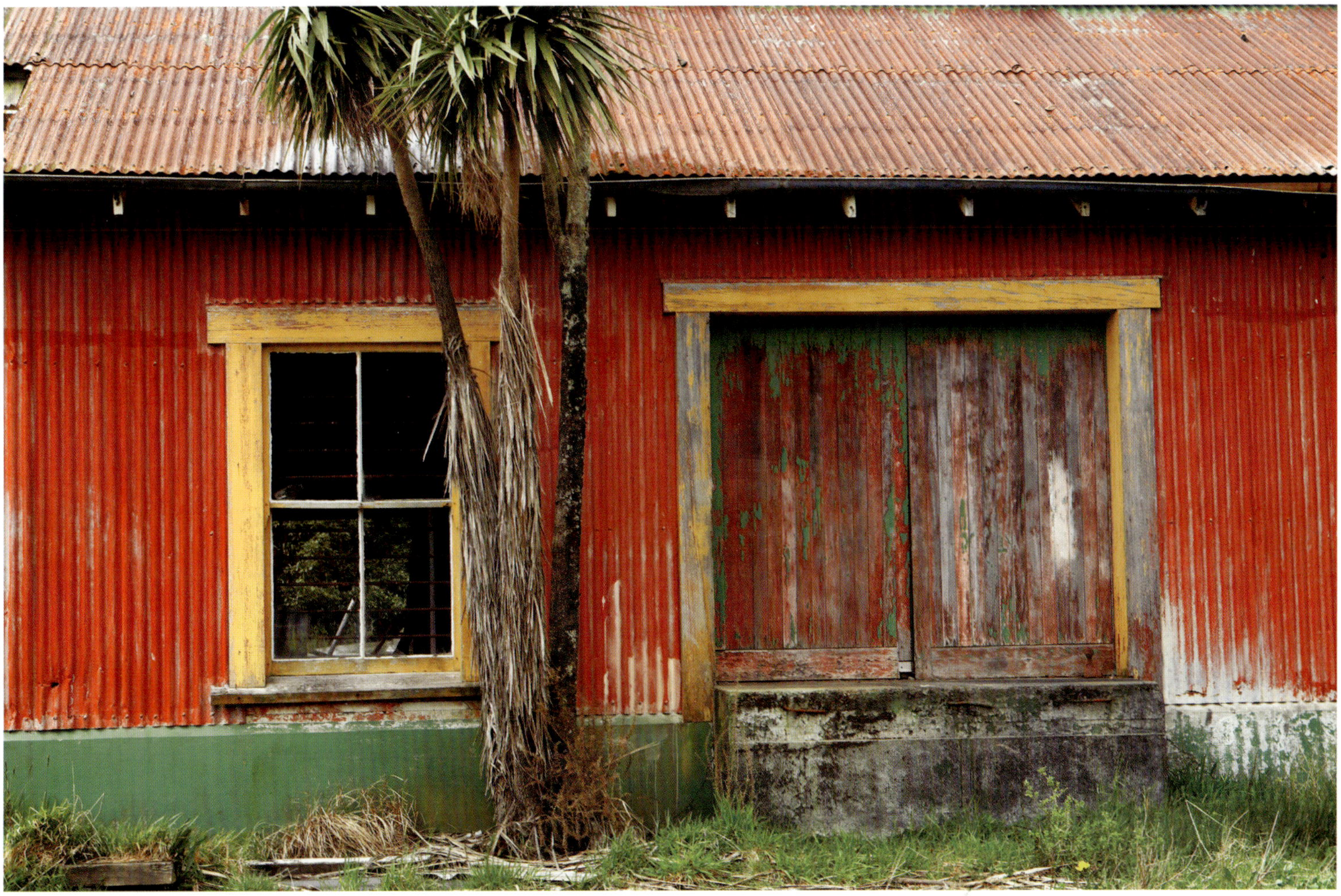

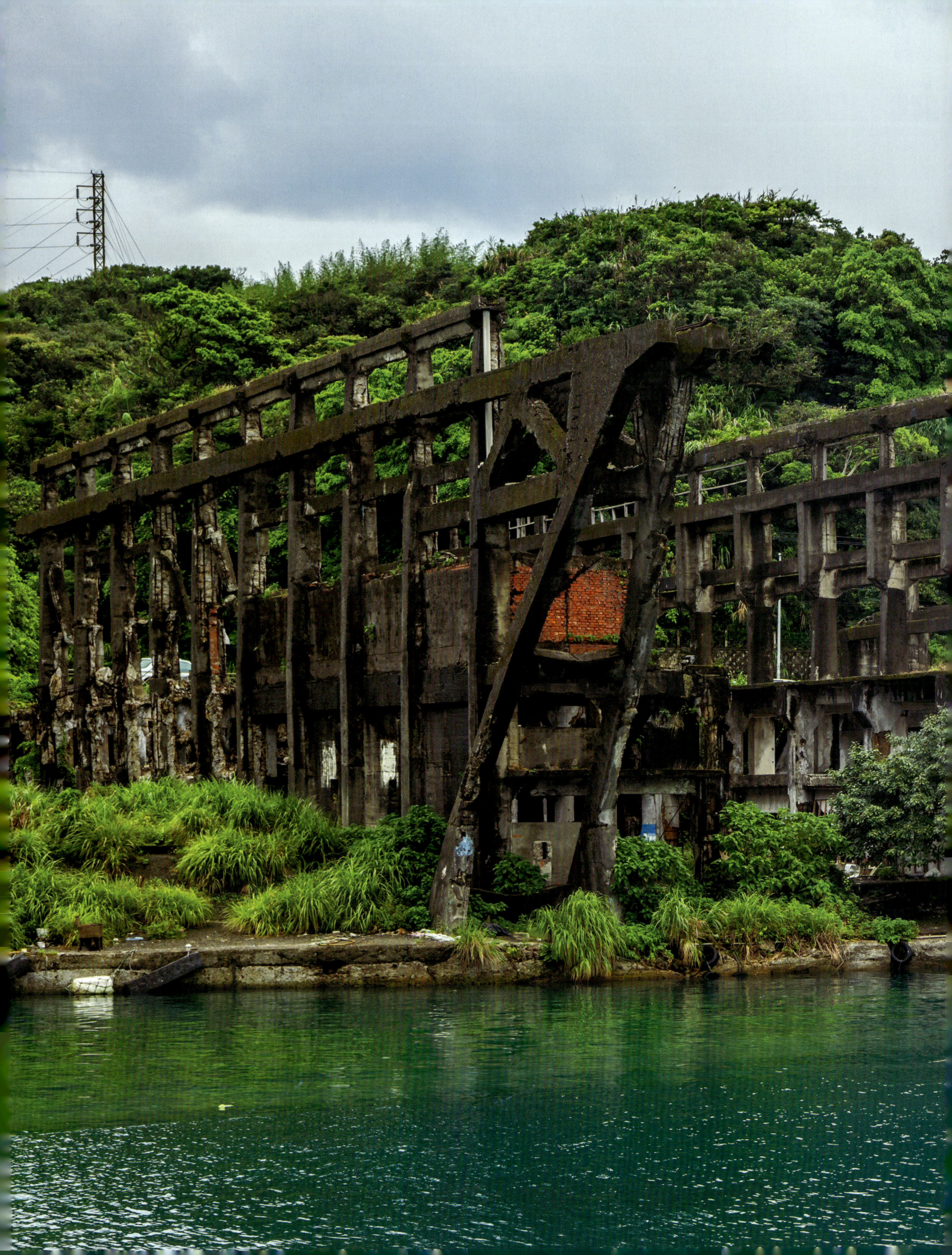

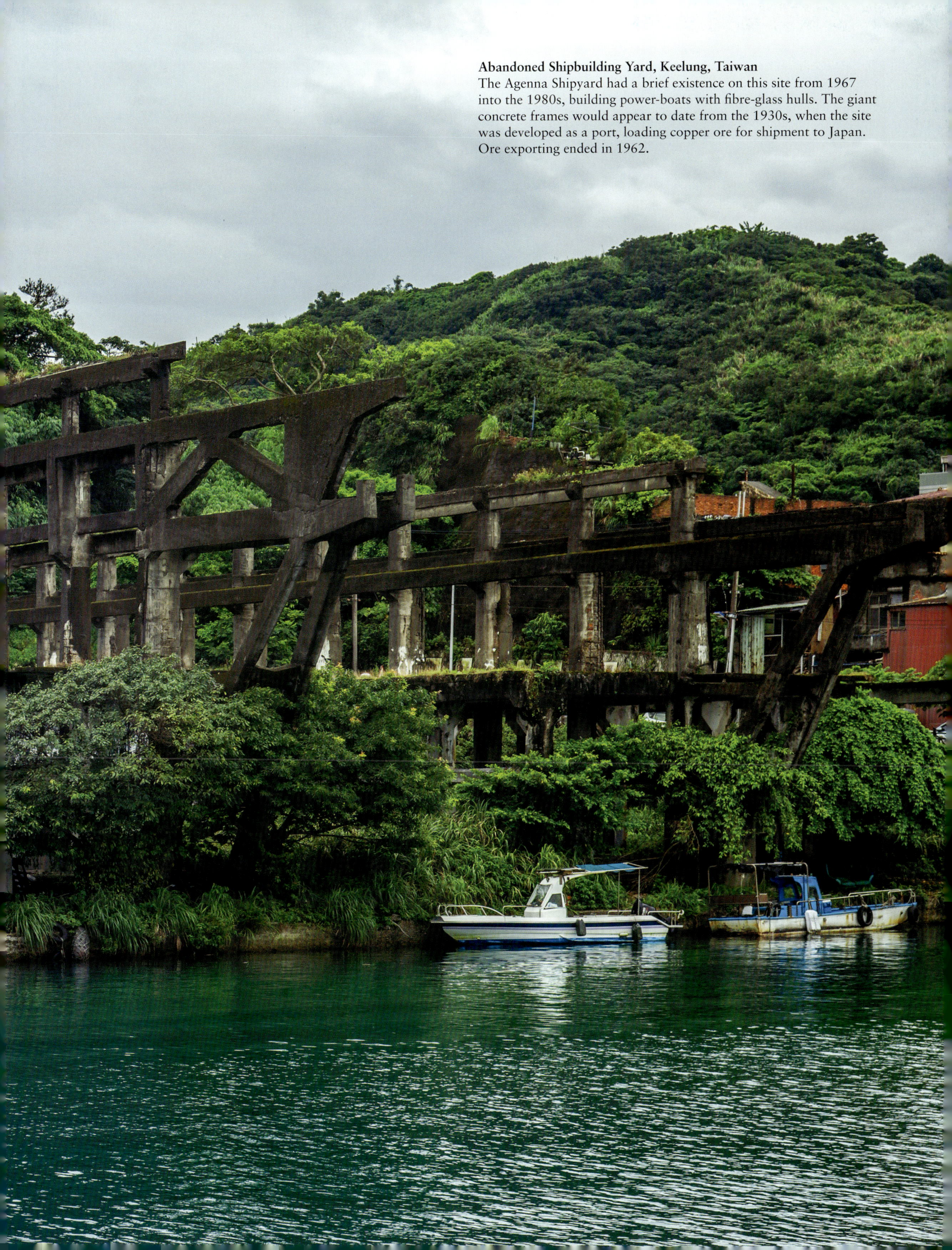

Abandoned Shipbuilding Yard, Keelung, Taiwan
The Agenna Shipyard had a brief existence on this site from 1967
into the 1980s, building power-boats with fibre-glass hulls. The giant
concrete frames would appear to date from the 1930s, when the site
was developed as a port, loading copper ore for shipment to Japan.
Ore exporting ended in 1962.

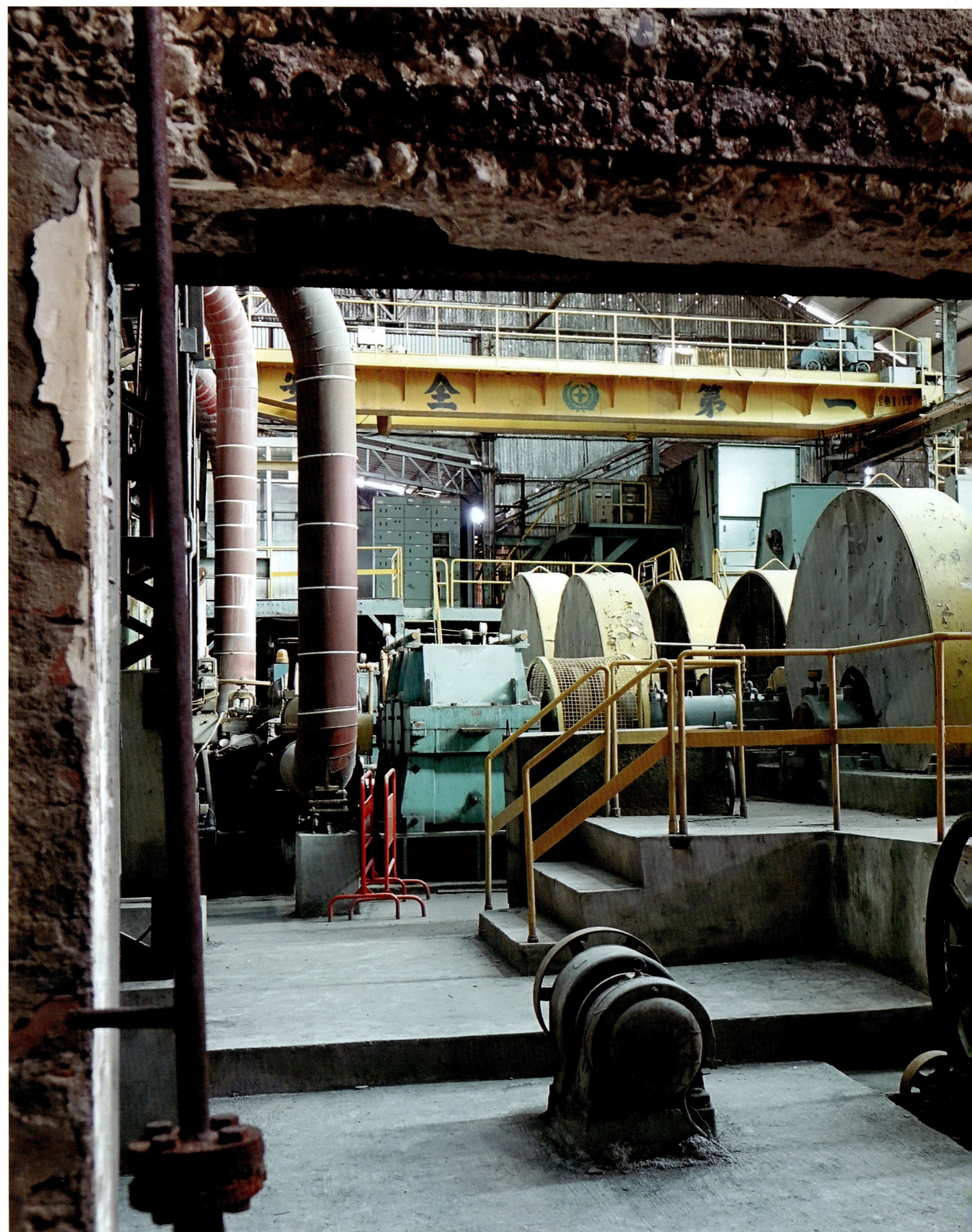
安全第一

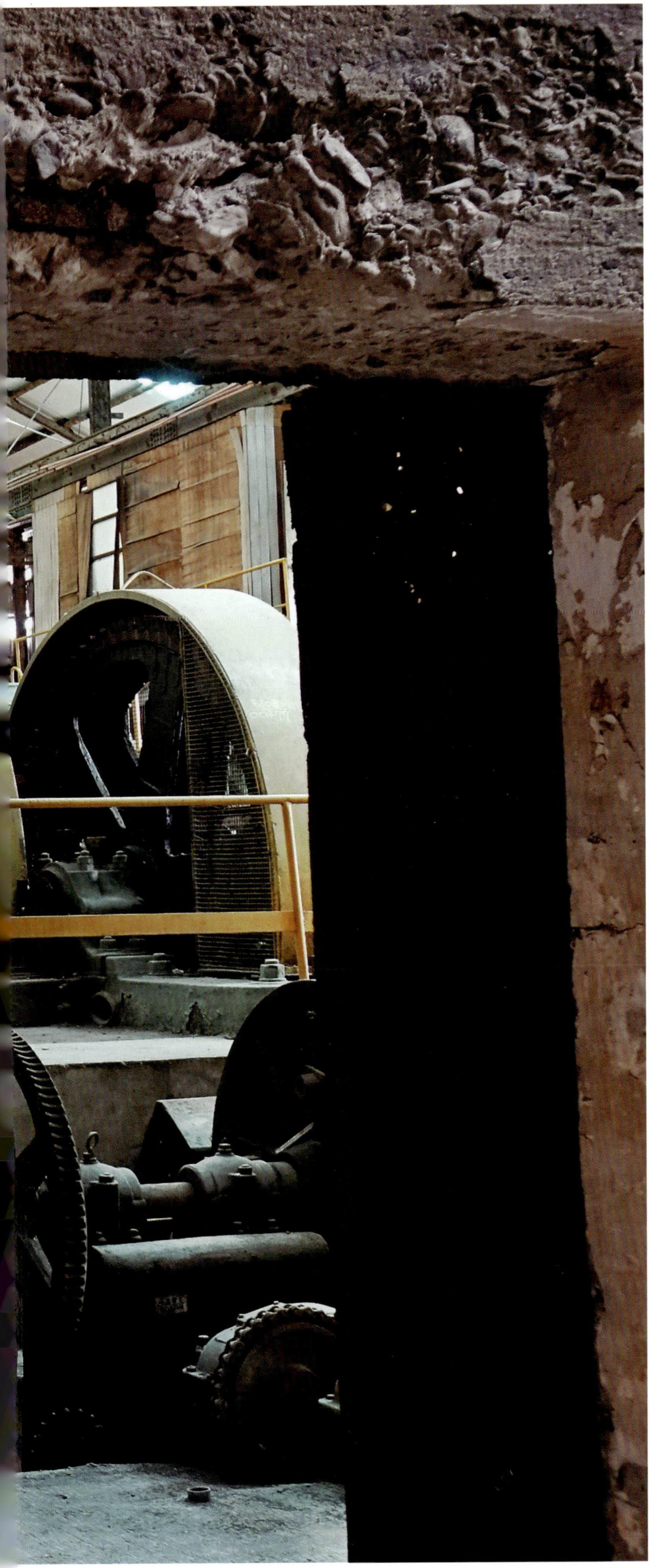

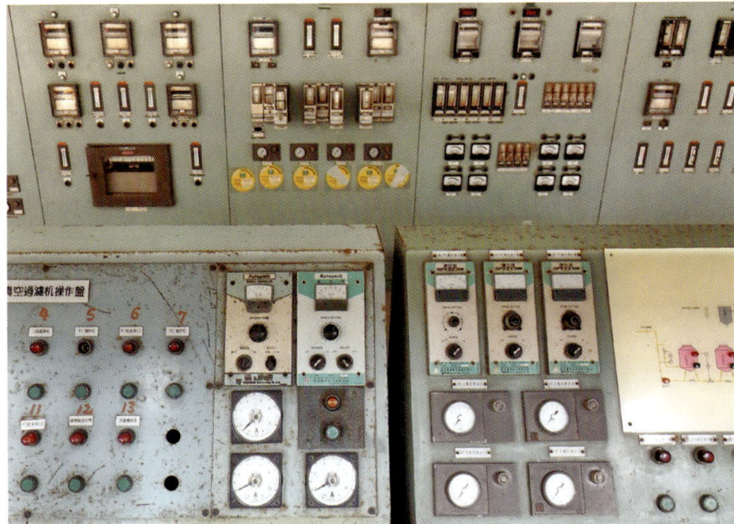

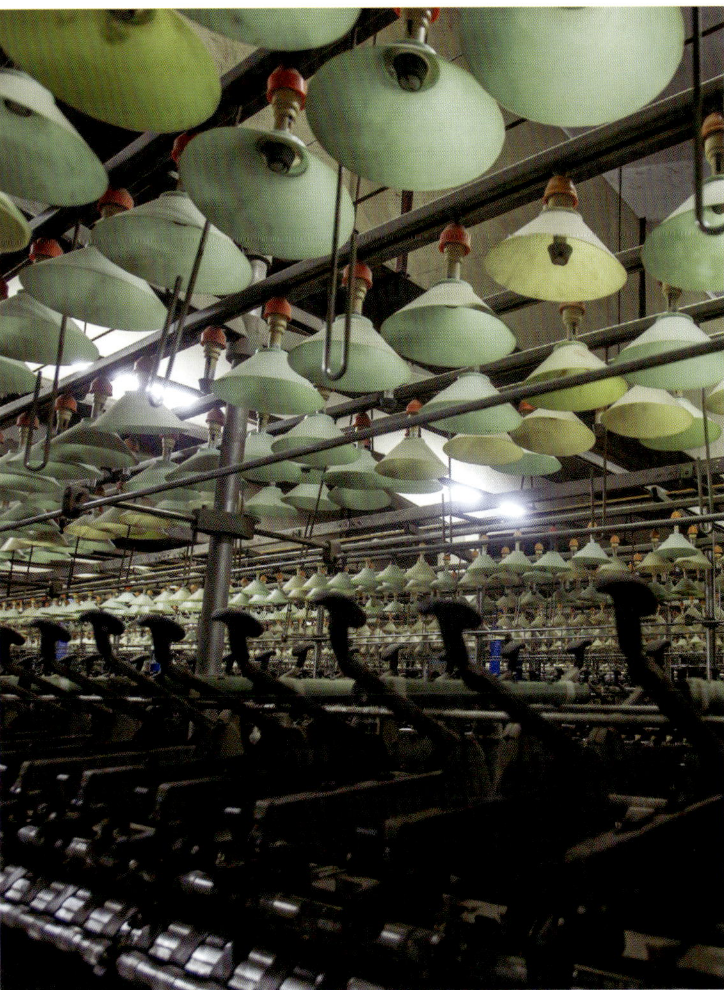

Ciaotou Sugar Refinery, Kaohsiung, Taiwan
Mothballed in 1999 against future use which has not happened, Taiwan's first large sugar refinery was set up here in 1901. Extended and modernised during the 1950s and 1960s, it still contains most of its equipment. Part of it is now a museum, but much is left to rust away.

Abandoned Cotton Mill, Karachi, Pakistan
A spinning shop in full production is a place of furiously rapid and noisy mechanical clicking and clacking. While most abandoned mills in Karachi are burned-out or derelict, this one, though the spinning machines stand silent and threadless, looks ready for renewed action.

Picture Credits

Alamy: 7 (Mick Sharp), 22/23 (Francis Vachon), 28/29 (Performance Image), 30 top (Darby Sawchuck), 30 bottom (Paul Harrison), 34/35 & 36/37 (Tim Fleming), 38/39 (Morten Larsen), 40 (Catnap), 42/43 (Dan Leeth), 45 (Jim West), 47 (Michelle Gilders), 54 (Cottle Run), 55 (BDP), 58 (Mostardi Photography), 63 (Russell Kord), 66 bottom left (Jim West), 66 bottom right (David Litschel), 68 (Minden Pictures/Yva Momatiuk & John Eastcott), 73 top left (James Brunker), 73 bottom (Michele Burgess), 74 & 75 (Michael Honegger), 76/77 (Marina Spironetti), 80/81 (Philip Pound), 82/83 (Ian Fleming), 84 (Don Paulson), 87 bottom (Christian Ouellet), 92/93 (AGB Photo Library), 96/97 (Robert Harding/Simon Montgomery), 100/101 (Jakub Dvorak), 104/105 & 104 (Jason Langley), 108 top (Hercules Milas), 109 top (Simon Webster), 113 top right (David Parker), 116/117 top (Michael Scott), 120 (Mike Twigg, fotocapricorn), 121 top (Simon Webster), 124 top (Age Fotostock/Xavier Subias), 126/127 (Razvan Cosac), 130 top (Adrian Weston), 131 (Incamerastock), 132/133 (JB-2078), 137 (Arcaid), 140/141 (Design Pics Inc), 142/143 (Kpzfoto), 145 (Image Broker/Stanislav Belicka), 154 (Rob Carter), 155 (Loop Images/Chris Herring), 164/165 (Grethe Ulgjell), 166 (Greatstock), 168 top (GFC Collection), 168 bottom (Francesco Ridolfi), 175 (Egg Images), 180/181 (Image broker/Walter G Allgower), 183 bottom (Findlay), 194/195 (Hemis/Julien Garcia), 196/197 (Andrew Sole), 198 (Galaxiid), 200 bottom (Stuart Gray), 204–205 all (Fabrizio Troiani), 208/209 (Dinodia Photos), 218 & 219 bottom (David Wall), 219 top left (John Steele), 219 top right (Jon Davison)

Dreamstime: 6 (Venemama), 12/13 (Mike Clegg), 14 (Diane Picard), 31 both top (Sherman Cahal), 46 (Boreccy), 60/61 (Gerda Beekers), 64/65 (Alexander Oganezov), 67 (Robert Carner), 73 top right (Matyas Rehak), 78/79 (Tupungato), 90/91 (Rainer Lesniewski), 108 bottom (Arkadiusz Weglewski), 125 bottom (Iva Vagnerova), 128 (Vladimir Zapletin), 130 bottom (RIRFStock), 134/135 (Sergey Kohl), 146/147 (Andrea G Ricordi), 159 top right (Rosario Manzo), 201 right (Daniel Dep), 202/203 (Radist), 210 top (Kejoou)

Getty Images: 20/21 (National Geographic Image Collection/Pete Ryan), 26/27 (E+/Ryerson Clark), 31 bottom (Aurora/Dan Shugar), 34/35 (Corbis/Steve Proehl), 41 bottom (Andrew Lichtenstein), 44 (Moment/Busa Photography), 48/49 (Jean-Pierre Lavoie), 52/53 (Moment/Tudor ApMadoc), 59 (Lonely Planet Images/Witold Skrypczak), 62 (Portland Press Herald), 66 top (Photographers Choice/Bryan Mullennix), 72 top (Corbis/Colin McPherson), 72 bottom (Universal Images Group/VW Pics), 85 bottom (Bloomberg), 105 (In Pictures/Barry Lewis), 109 bottom (Moment Open/Rudolf Vicek), 110/111 (Corbis/Atlantide Phototravel), 114 & 115 (Gamma-Rapho/Edwige Lamy), 121 bottom (Heritage Images), 124 bottom (Photographers Choice/Tim E White), 138/139 (Moment/Eve Livesey), 148 (Universal Images Group/Arterra), 149 (Photolibrary/Christian Aslund), 158/159 (Westend61), 169 (Robert Harding/James Kerwin), 170 top (Christopher Furlong), 172/173 (AFP/Marc Jourdier), 174 both (Bloomberg), 182 (AFP/Gianluigi Guercia), 186 (Photodisc/Keren Su), 190 (AFP/Tengku Bahar), 210 middle (Moment/Xin Yuah), 211 (Kevin Frayer), 215 (Moment Open/Eddie Gerald), 223 (Bloomberg)

Shutterstock: 8 (Romiana Lee), 10/11 (James Pintar), 15 (Meunierd), 16/17 (James Gabbert), 18 & 19 top (Roland Shainidze), 19 bottom (Reimar), 24/25 (Marjorie Anctil), 41 top (Rick Beauregard), 50–51 all (Sherman Cahal), 56/57 (Matt Regan), 70/71 (Leon Rafael), 85 top (Daniel Wiedmann), 86 (Simon Dannhauer), 87 top (Framos74), 88/89 (Mark Green), 94 & 95 top (Juan Vilata), 95 bottom (Helissa Grundemann), 98 (Dleeming69), 102–103 all (Andrew J Billington), 106/107 (Posztos), 112 (Peter Turner Photography), 113 top left (Ken Taylor Design), 113 bottom (Marbury), 116/117 bottom (Michalakis Ppalis), 118/119 (Khaled Fazely), 122/123 (Marbury), 125 top (360degreeAerial), 129 (Fotogrin), 136 top (Merlot Levert), 136 bottom (Vladimir Mulder), 144 (Tobias Arhelger), 150/151 (Gerorgeopera.raw), 152/153 (Annaj77), 156/157 (Vladimir Mulder), 158 top (Fausto Riolo), 159 top left (Maudandros), 160/161 (Stano Kovacic), 162/163 (Rolf_52), 170/171 (Grobler du Preez), 171 top left (Khaled El Adawy), 171 top right (Chris Sheppard), 176/177 (Uyanik), 178/179 (Felix Lipov), 178 bottom (Canyalcin), 179 bottom (Manu M Nair), 183 top (Marques), 184 & 185 (Luc Kohnen), 188/189 (Dave Minchin), 191 top (Syahtuah Mohamed), 191 bottom (Lee Meng Poh), 192/193 (Syahtuah Mohamed), 199 (Philip Schubert), 200 top & 201 left (Uwe Aranas), 202/203 (Kaiser-V), 206 & 207 (HelloRF Zcool), 210 bottom (Volodymyr Dvornyk), 212/213 (Sean Pavone), 214 (Glassflowerhead), 216 & 217 (Faer Out), 220/221 (Richie Chan), 222 & 223 top (Shi Yali)